After reading Mode---   ---nyon spent some
time in the So--- --- ---aught at L   ---ef---re returning
to Oxfor--- --- lectures on Russ---   He--- ---enior
Resear--- ---w a--- ---adham College. His --- ---t is crim--- ---ction:
he h--- ---ten a history of the fictional dete---.---, *Murder Will Out*, and
two--- ---llers, *Swan Song* and *Greek Gifts*.

From the reviews:

'Tim Binyon's long-awaited life of Pushkin is by far the most important
to appear in many years. It is a magnificent achievement, a monument
to a life of scholarship . . . a deeply learned book.'

ORLANDO FIGES, *The Times*

'T. J. Binyon's new biography of Pushkin is a masterpiece. It places
Russia's greatest poet in the context of his life and times, and pretty
exciting times they were (1799–1837) in Russia.'

A. N. WILSON, *Daily Telegraph*

'A magnificent life of a great Russian writer and poet. It sits so close
to the man and his times that by the time Pushkin is dead, at 37 after
a stupid duel, you almost feel you have lived his life.'

Books of the Year, *Economist*

'This is a work of great compassion and humanity, as well as careful
scholarship and exacting detail. It is an exceptional biography but, even
more, a compelling and moving narrative, beautifully told. It is clear
that Binyon loves his subject, but his portrait is unsparing, honest and
generous. It is utterly convincing and thoroughly absorbing and deserves
the highest praise.'

JAMES O'BRIEN, *Tablet*

'T. J. Binyon has told his story with all of the verve and wit of the great
masters of Russian prose. Deeply sympathetic to his subject, he provides
a full and balanced portrait of the man and poet . . . An utterly compelling work about one of the finest figures of European literature.'

JUSTIN QUINN, *Irish Times*

'A superb biography . . . grippingly entertaining and magnificently auth-
oritative.'   ALAN MARSHALL, *Daily Telegraph*

'A remarkable achievement ... Binyon's book is poignant, brisk and at times downright funny: the best possible tribute to the changeable and elusively fascinating character of its subject.'

CATRIONA KELLY, *Guardian*

'This is a fine, precise and elegant biography ... it should prod a new readership towards the writings themselves – the output of the first of the 19th-century Russian grand masters, those craftsmen, tormented and cynical, of unparalleled emotional power.'

JOHN LLOYD, *Financial Times*

'A marvellously detailed account of the poet's short and stormy life.'

JOHN BAYLEY, Books of the Year, *TLS*

'Binyon's Life gives a marvellously clear sense of the man Pushkin might have been to meet: alternately belligerent and sweet, physically small. On the matter of Pushkin's politics, Binyon is excellent.'

IAN THOMPSON, *Independent on Sunday*

'This biography, written with great understanding and sympathy, has nevertheless a magisterial tone about it which is based on years of research. It is a joy to read.'   *Contemporary Review*

'Tim Binyon has written a very fine biography indeed, a tour de force. He combines true scholarship with readability.'

IAIN SPROAT, *Scotland on Sunday*

'A full and scrupulous biography of Russia's greatest poet ... No admirer of Pushkin should fail to honour the years of dedication and love that have gone into this book.'

ELAINE FEINSTEIN, *Sunday Times*

'A readable, scholarly work that firmly resists sentimental mystifications ... Binyon captures well the restless energy of Pushkin, and the level of detail of his account is formidable.'

TONY WOOD, *New Left Review*

'A readable, perceptive and witty biography ... a valuable achievement.'

JONATHAN SUMPTION, *Spectator*

'Binyon's documentation is scrupulous ... his penetrating scholarship and calm sympathy serve Pushkin the man very well.'

CAROL RUMENS, *Independent*

PUSHKIN

A Biography

T. J. BINYON

HARPER PERENNIAL

ALSO BY T. J. BINYON

Murder Will Out
Swan Song
Greek Gifts

Harper Perennial
An imprint of HarperCollins*Publishers*
77–85 Fulham Palace Road,
Hammersmith, London w6 8JB

www.harpercollins.co.uk/harperperennial

This paperback edition published by Harper Perennial 2004

First published in Great Britain by
HarperCollins*Publishers* 2002

Copyright © T. J. Binyon 2002

T. J. Binyon asserts the moral right to
be identified as the author of this work

ISBN 978-0-00-637338-4

Set in Postscript Linotype Minion
with Spectrum display by
Rowland Phototypesetting Ltd,
Bury St Edmunds, Suffolk

For Helen
and
In memory of my father
Denis Binyon

CONTENTS

LIST OF ILLUSTRATIONS

PLATE SECTION I

Nadezhda Osipovna Pushkina (*All-Russian Pushkin Museum, St Petersburg (ARPM)/Petrushka, Moscow*)

Sergey Lvovich Pushkin (*ARPM/Petrushka*)

Vasily Lvovich Pushkin (*ARPM/Petrushka*)

Emperor Alexander I (*ARPM/Petrushka*)

Empress Elizaveta Alekseevna (*ARPM/Petrushka*)

Tsarskoe Selo: Sadovaya Street and the Lycée (*Novosti, London*)

Ekaterina Bakunina (*ARPM/Petrushka*)

K.N. Batyushkov (© *State Literary Museum, Moscow (SLM)/Petrushka*)

N.M. Karamzin (*State Pushkin Museum, Moscow (SPM)/Petrushka*)

Mikhailovskoe (*ARPM/Petrushka*)

Panorama of the Nevsky Prospect (ARPM/Petrushka)

Filipp Wiegel (*ARPM/Petrushka*)

Emperor Nicholas I (*ARPM/Petrushka*)

Nicholas I, Empress Alexandra Fedorovna & Grand Duke Alexander (*Hulton Archive*)

Elise Khitrovo (*SPM/Petrushka*)

Dolly Ficquelmont & Ekaterina Tiesenhausen (*SPM/Petrushka*)

Annette Olenina (*SPM/Petrushka*)

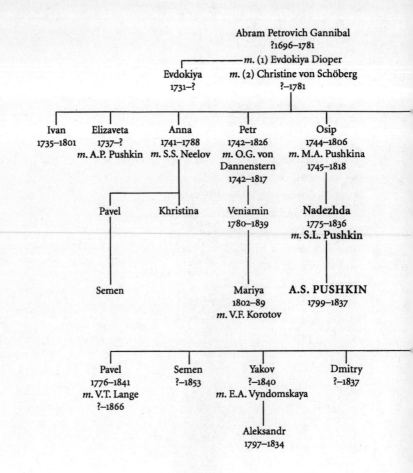

Abram Petrovich Gannibal
?1696–1781

m. (1) Evdokiya Dioper

Evdokiya   *m.* (2) Christine von Schöberg
1731–?   ?–1781

Ivan	Elizaveta	Anna	Petr	Osip
1735–1801	1737–?	1741–1788	1742–1826	1744–1806
	m. A.P. Pushkin	*m.* S.S. Neelov	*m.* O.G. von Dannenstern 1742–1817	*m.* M.A. Pushkina 1745–1818

Pavel   Khristina   Veniamin   **Nadezhda**
                                      1780–1839   1775–1836
                                                          m. **S.L. Pushkin**

Semen   Mariya   **A.S. PUSHKIN**
                                      1802–89   1799–1837
                                      m. V.F. Korotov

Pavel	Semen	Yakov	Dmitry
1776–1841	?–1853	?–1840	?–1837
m. V.T. Lange ?–1866		*m.* E.A. Vyndomskaya	

Aleksandr
1797–1834

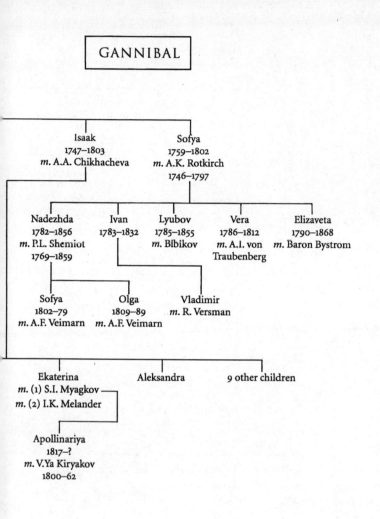

GANNIBAL

Isaak
1747–1803
m. A.A. Chikhacheva

Sofya
1759–1802
m. A.K. Rotkirch
1746–1797

Nadezhda
1782–1856
m. P.L. Shemiot
1769–1859

Ivan
1783–1832

Lyubov
1785–1855
m. Bibikov

Vera
1786–1812
m. A.I. von
Traubenberg

Elizaveta
1790–1868
m. Baron Bystrom

Sofya
1802–79
m. A.F. Veimarn

Olga
1809–89
m. A.F. Veimarn

Vladimir
m. R. Versman

Ekaterina
m. (1) S.I. Myagkov
m. (2) I.K. Melander

Aleksandra

9 other children

Apollinariya
1817–?
m. V.Ya Kiryakov
1800–62

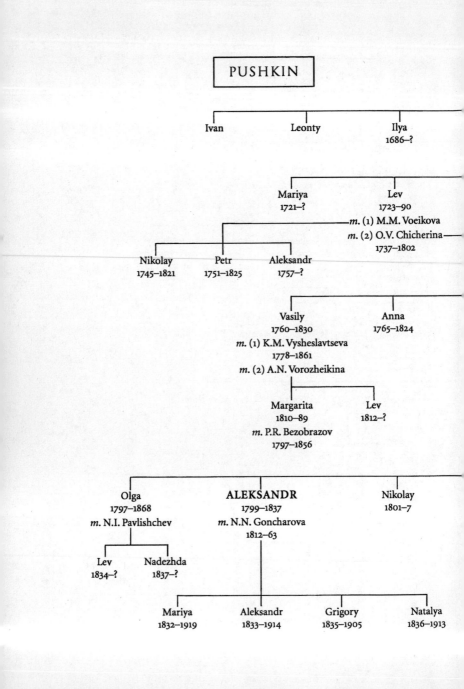

PUSHKIN

Ivan — Leonty — Ilya
1686–?

Mariya — Lev
1721–? 1723–90
m. (1) M.M. Voeikova
m. (2) O.V. Chicherina
1737–1802

Nikolay — Petr — Aleksandr
1745–1821 1751–1825 1757–?

Vasily — Anna
1760–1830 1765–1824
m. (1) K.M. Vysheslavtseva
1778–1861
m. (2) A.N. Vorozheikina

Margarita — Lev
1810–89 1812–?
m. P.R. Bezobrazov
1797–1856

Olga — **ALEKSANDR** — Nikolay
1797–1868 1799–1837 1801–7
m. N.I. Pavlishchev *m.* N.N. Goncharova
1812–63

Lev — Nadezhda
1834–? 1837–?

Mariya — Aleksandr — Grigory — Natalya
1832–1919 1833–1914 1835–1905 1836–1913

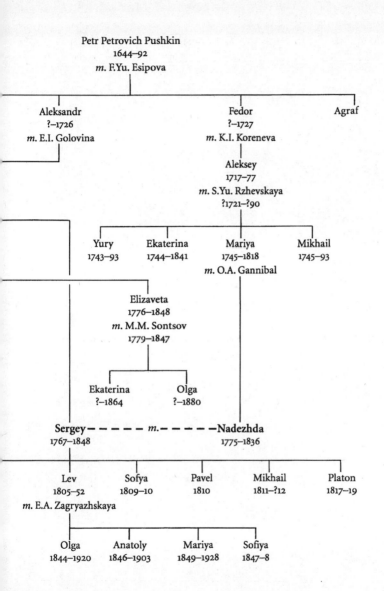

Petr Petrovich Pushkin
1644–92
m. F.Yu. Esipova

Aleksandr
?–1726
m. E.I. Golovina

Fedor
?–1727
m. K.I. Koreneva

Agraf

Aleksey
1717–77
m. S.Yu. Rzhevskaya
?1721–?90

Yury
1743–93

Ekaterina
1744–1841

Mariya
1745–1818
m. O.A. Gannibal

Mikhail
1745–93

Elizaveta
1776–1848
m. M.M. Sontsov
1779–1847

Ekaterina
?–1864

Olga
?–1880

Sergey — — — — *m.* — — — — Nadezhda
1767–1848   1775–1836

Lev
1805–52
m. E.A. Zagryazhskaya

Sofya
1809–10

Pavel
1810

Mikhail
1811–?12

Platon
1817–19

Olga
1844–1920

Anatoly
1846–1903

Mariya
1849–1928

Sofiya
1847–8

What business is it of the critic or reader whether I am handsome or ugly, come from an ancient nobility or am not of gentle birth, whether I am good or wicked, crawl at the feet of the mighty or do not even exchange bows with them, whether I gamble at cards and so on. My future biographer, if God sends me a biographer, will concern himself with this.

PUSHKIN, 1830

A NOTE ON TRANSLATION,
TRANSLITERATION, DATES,
CURRENCY AND RANKS

All the translations in the text, both of Pushkin's prose and his verse, are my own. I chose to retranslate his works, not from a presumptuous belief that my versions would be superior to all others, but in order that they might be uniform: Pushkin would at least speak with a single voice, however flawed this might be. No one could be more conscious of the deficiencies of the verse translations than I, or more aware of how much of the original they ignore. The primary aim, for the sake of which all others were disregarded, was to preserve the literal meaning of the original; at the same time I have endeavoured wherever possible to retain in the English line the content of the corresponding Russian line.

For the sake of readers without Russian a greatly simplified system of transliteration has been adopted, which, to avoid confusion, has been carried over into the notes and bibliography; scholars of Russian will, however, have no difficulty in reconstructing the Cyrillic original.

Since Russia used the Julian calendar, rather than the Gregorian, until 1917, it was eleven days behind Europe in the eighteenth century, twelve in the nineteenth and thirteen in the twentieth. To avoid the complication of giving all dates according to both calendars, the Russian Julian calendar has been used throughout, apart from a few dates referring to events in Europe, which are given according to the Gregorian and are followed by the notation (NS).

The monetary unit in Russia was (and is) the rouble, containing 100 copecks. Two types of rouble were in circulation, the silver and the paper (known as *assignats*). The value of the latter – that most often employed in financial transactions – fluctuated, but was generally about a quarter of that of the silver rouble. In 1835, when calculating the yearly expenditure of Byron's father in an article on the poet, Pushkin uses an exchange rate of 25 paper roubles to the pound sterling (XI, 275).

The Table of Ranks, by which Peter the Great had in 1722 systematized the hierarchies of the civil service, the army, the navy and the court, still remained in force in the nineteenth century. The fourteen civil and military ranks (omitting the naval and court equivalents) were the following:

Class	Civil rank	Military rank
1st	chancellor	field-marshal
2nd	active privy councillor	{ general of cavalry general of infantry general of artillery
3rd	privy councillor	lieutenant-general
4th	active civil councillor	major-general
5th	civil councillor	
6th	collegial councillor	colonel
7th	aulic councillor	lieutenant-colonel
8th	collegial assessor	captain
9th	titular councillor	staff-captain
10th	collegial secretary	lieutenant
11th	ship's secretary	
12th	provincial secretary	{ second lieutenant cornet
13th	{ senatorial registrar synodal registrar cabinet registrar	ensign
14th	collegial registrar	

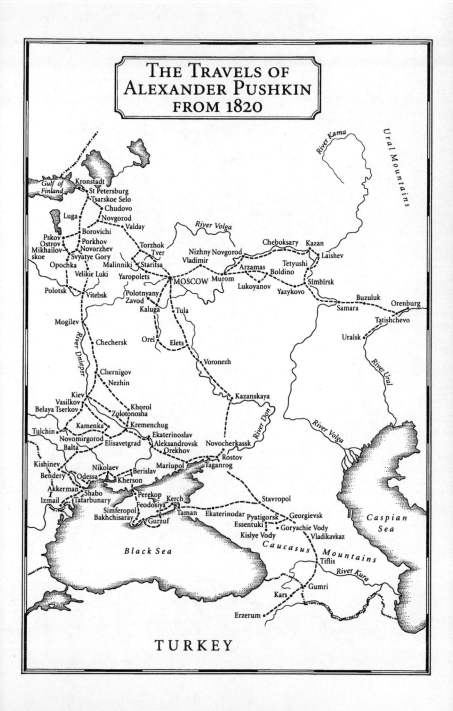

THE TRAVELS OF
ALEXANDER PUSHKIN
FROM 1820

Ural Mountains

River Kama

Gulf of Finland

Kronstadt
St Petersburg
Tsarskoe Selo
Chudovo
Luga
Novgorod
Valday
River Volga

Pskov
Ostrov
Mikhailov-
skoe
Borovichi
Porkhov
Novorzhev
Svyatye Gory
Opochka
Velikie Luki
Malinniki
Yaropolets
Torzhok
Tver
Staritsa
Nizhny Novgorod
Vladimir
Cheboksary
Kazan
Laishev
Tetyushi
Arzamas
Boldino
Simbirsk
MOSCOW
Murom
Lukoyanov
Yazykovo

Polotsk
Vitebsk
Polotnyany
Zavod
Kaluga
Tula
Buzuluk
Orenburg
Samara
Tatishchevo

Mogilev
River Dnieper
Chechersk
Orel
Elets
Uralsk
River Ural

Chernigov
Nezhin
Voronezh

Kiev
Vasilkov
Belaya Tserkov
Khorol
Zolotonosha
Kazanskaya
River Don
River Volga

Tulchin
Kamenka
Novomirgorod
Balta
Elisavetgrad
Kremenchug
Ekaterinoslav
Aleksandrovsk
Orekhov
Novocherkassk
Rostov
Taganrog

Kishinev
Bendery
Nikolaev
Berislav
Mariupol
Odessa
Kherson
Akkerman
Shabo
Perekop
Kerch
Stavropol
*Caspian
Sea*

Izmail
Tatarbunary
Simferopol
Feodosiya
Bakhchisaray
Gurzuf
Taman
Ekaterinodar
Pyatigorsk
Georgievsk
Essentuki
Goryachie Vody
Kislye Vody
Vladikavkaz

Black Sea

Caucasus Mountains
Tiflis
River Kura

Gumri
Kars

Erzerum

TURKEY

Gulf
of
Finland

Novaya Derevnya

Black River

Great
Nevka

Elagin Island

Elagin
Palace

Kamenny Island

Little Nevka

Krestovsky Island

Aptekarsky Island

Kamennoostrovsky Prospect

Petrovsky Island

Little Neva

Peter-Paul
fortress

Goloday Island

Dvortsovaya
Embankment

Winter Palace

Admiralty

11

Vasilevsky Island

Admiralty Square

10

Great Neva

English Embankment

19

Galernaya
Street

15

Dumé's
restaurant

12

Bolshaya Morskaya St.

English Club

Bolshoy Theatre

25

24

22

Voznesensky Prospect

Ekateringofsky Prospect

Fontanka

Izmailovsky
Bridge

Izmailovsky Prospect

Izmailovsky Prospect

Izmailovsky Prospect

Ismailovsky Prospect

Izmailovsky Prospect

Izmailovsky Prospect

Izmailovsky Prospect

Kalinkin
Bridge

Ekaterininsky

Canal

Ekateringof Park

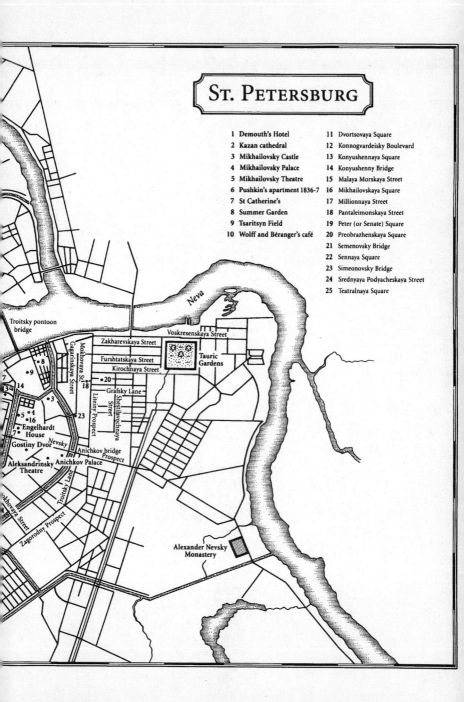

St. Petersburg

1 Demouth's Hotel
2 Kazan cathedral
3 Mikhailovsky Castle
4 Mikhailovsky Palace
5 Mikhailovsky Theatre
6 Pushkin's apartment 1836-7
7 St Catherine's
8 Summer Garden
9 Tsaritsyn Field
10 Wolff and Béranger's café

11 Dvortsovaya Square
12 Konnogvardeisky Boulevard
13 Konyushennaya Square
14 Konyushenny Bridge
15 Malaya Morskaya Street
16 Mikhailovskaya Square
17 Millionnaya Street
18 Pantaleimonskaya Street
19 Peter (or Senate) Square
20 Preobrazhenskaya Square
21 Semenovsky Bridge
22 Sennaya Square
23 Simeonovsky Bridge
24 Srednyaya Podyacheskaya Street
25 Teatralnaya Square

Neva

Troitsky pontoon bridge

Voskresenskaya Street

Zakharevskaya Street

Molhovaya St.

Gagarinskaya Street

Furshtatskaya Street

Tauric Gardens

Kirochnaya Street

Grafsky Lane

Litejny Prospect

Shestilawotchnaya Street

Engelhardt House

Gostiny Dvor

Nevsky

Anichkov bridge Prospect

Aleksandrinsky Theatre

Anichkov Palace

Troitsky Lane

Mokhovaya Street

Zagorodny Prospect

Alexander Nevsky Monastery

PROLOGUE

> By now it is not so much Pushkin, our national poet, as
> our relationship to Pushkin that has become as it were
> our national characteristic.
>
> ANDREY BITOV, 1986

'PUSHKIN IS OUR ALL,' declared the critic and poet Apollon
Grigorev in 1854.[1] His famous remark is perhaps the best
expression of Pushkin's significance, not merely for Russian
literature, or even for Russian culture, but for the Russian ethos generally
and for Russia as a whole. At the time, however, his was a lone voice.
Though Pushkin had been acclaimed as Russia's greatest poet during
his lifetime, his reputation had begun to sink during his last years. The
decline continued after his death in 1837, reaching perhaps its lowest
point in the 1850s. In 1855 a petition, noting that monuments to a
number of other writers – Lomonosov, Derzhavin, Koltsov, Karamzin
and Krylov – had been erected, called for Pushkin to be added to their
number. It met with no response. In 1861 Pushkin's school, the Lycée
– which had moved from Tsarskoe Selo to St Petersburg and been
renamed the Alexandrine Lycée – celebrated its fiftieth anniversary. In
conjunction with this a public subscription was opened to erect a statue
to Pushkin in Tsarskoe Selo. Three years later less than a fifth of the
necessary sum had been subscribed, and interest in the project had
lapsed completely. However, by 1869, when the idea was revived by a
group of former lycéens, Pushkin's reputation was on the rise. This time
the subscription was successful, raising over 100,000 roubles. The suggestion of Admiral Matyushkin, a schoolfellow of Pushkin, that the monument should be placed in Moscow, the poet's native city, was accepted,
and a site on Strastnaya Square, at the end of Tverskoy Boulevard, was

chosen. After three competitions A.M. Opekushin's design for a statue showing a meditating Pushkin emerged as the winner.

Only after eleven years of procrastination and preparation, however, was the project completed. The unveiling ceremony was planned for 26 May 1880, the eighty-first anniversary of Pushkin's birth, but the death of Empress Mariya caused it to be postponed until Friday 6 June. At one o'clock that day, after a service in the Strastnoy monastery opposite the site of the monument, the statue was unveiled in the presence of an immense crowd. Cheers rang out, and many wept. 'Where are the colours, where are the words to convey the intoxication of the triumphal moment?' wrote one reporter. 'Those who didn't see it did not see the populace in one of its best moments of spiritual joyousness.'[2] That evening a banquet, given by the city duma, was followed by a literary-musical evening in the hall of the Noble Assembly. Overtures from operas based on Pushkin's works were performed; congratulatory tele-grams from Tennyson, Victor Hugo and others were read out; Dosto-evsky, Turgenev and others gave readings from Pushkin: Turgenev especially being greeted with tumultuous applause.

The next day, 7 June, at a public meeting of the Society of Amateurs of Russian Literature, Turgenev gave an elegant and civilized speech. Pushkin was, he said, repeating Belinsky, Russia's 'first artist-poet'. 'There is no doubt,' he continued, 'that he created our poetic, our literary language and that we and our descendants can only follow the path laid down by his genius.' But in the end he had reluctantly to deny Pushkin the title of 'a national poet in the sense of a universal poet', as were Shakespeare, Goethe or Homer. Unlike them, he had had to per-form two tasks simultaneously, 'to establish a language and create a literature'. And, unlike them, he had had the misfortune to die young, without fulfilling his true potential. Turgenev ended his speech by apos-trophizing the statue itself. 'Shine forth, like him, thou noble bronze visage, erected in the very heart of our ancient capital, and announce to future generations our right to call ourselves a great nation, because this nation has given birth, among other great men, to *such* a man!', a peroration which was greeted with enthusiasm and loud applause.[3]

Its reception, however, was completely overshadowed by that given to Dostoevsky's long, passionate and emotional address the following morning, the third and last day of the celebrations. He began by quoting

Gogol's remark that Pushkin was 'an extraordinary, and perhaps unique manifestation of the Russian spirit', and added that he was, too, 'a prophetic one'. Whereas Turgenev had been unable to rank Pushkin with poets such as Shakespeare, Dostoevsky proclaimed his superiority to the 'Shakespeares, Cervanteses and Schillers', because of 'something almost even miraculous', his 'universal responsiveness', a characteristic which he shared with the Russian people. Whereas Shakespeare's Italians are disguised Englishmen, Pushkin's Spaniards are Spanish, his Germans German and his Englishmen English. 'I can positively say that there has never been a poet with so universal a responsiveness as Pushkin, and it is not just his responsiveness, but its astounding depth, the reincarnation of his spirit in the spirit of foreign peoples, an almost complete, and hence miraculous reincarnation, because nowhere, in no poet of the entire world has this phenomenon been repeated.' It is this national characteristic which will eventually enable Russia to save Europe and 'to pronounce the final word of great, general harmony, of the final brotherly agreement of all nations in accordance with the law of Christ's Gospel!' If this seems a presumptuous claim for a land as poor as Russia, 'we can already point to Pushkin, to the universality and panhumanity of his genius [. . .] In art at least, in artistic creation, he undeniably manifested this universality of the aspiration of the Russian spirit.' Had Pushkin lived longer his message would perhaps have been clearer. 'But God decreed otherwise. Pushkin died in the full development of his powers, and undoubtedly carried to his grave a certain great mystery,' Dostoevsky concluded. 'And now we must solve this mystery without him.'[4]

Screams and cries were heard from the audience. A number of people fainted; a student burst through the throng and fell in hysterics at Dostoevsky's feet where he lost consciousness. At the end of the session a hundred young women, pushing Turgenev aside, made their way on to the stage bearing a huge laurel wreath, nearly five feet in diameter, and placed it round the author's neck. It bore the inscription 'For the Russian woman, about whom you said so much that was good!' Late that evening Dostoevsky took a cab to Tverskaya Square, placed the wreath at the foot of the granite pedestal on which the statue stood, and, stepping back a pace, bowed to the ground.[5]

Dostoevsky's speech had little to do with the reality of Pushkin's work: he had, rather, unscrupulously made use of the other's reputation to propagate his own belief in Russia's messianic mission. However, it came as a fitting conclusion to what one newspaper referred to as 'days of a magically poetic fairy-tale', and others as 'days of holy ecstasy' and 'the "holy week" of the Russian intelligentsia'. Some witnesses experienced something akin to a religious conversion, one reporter writing, 'It was as if the atmosphere surrounding the celebration caught fire and was lit by an iridescent radiance. One's heart beat faster, more joyfully, one's thoughts became bright and lucid, and one's whole being opened up to impressions and emotions that would have been incomprehensible and strange given other less elevating circumstances. Some kind of moral miracle took place, a moral shock that stirred one's innermost soul.'[6] But it also established a new attitude to Pushkin: from now on he was not merely a poet superior to all others, but also was no longer a man; he had become a symbol, a myth, an icon.

By 1899, the hundredth anniversary of his birth, the state had taken account of the potency of the poet's image, and organized for the occasion an immense celebration throughout the Russian empire. Busts and portraits were mass-produced, and schoolchildren given free copies of his works, together with bars of chocolate stamped with his picture. The Pushkin of 1899 was far removed from the prophetic, miraculously responsive Pushkin of 1880; he was a solid, upright, moral citizen, a firm patriot and a loyal supporter of autocracy. In 1937 the Soviet state launched an even more massive celebration of the hundredth anniversary of Pushkin's death. His works were recruited to assist the drive towards universal literacy in the Soviet Union, while his image was tailored to fit Soviet ideology. 'Pushkin is completely ours, Soviet, for the Soviet state inherited everything that is best in our people, and itself is the embodiment of the best aspirations of our people,' wrote *Pravda*.[7] The myth had now become the basis for a cult – at times uncomfortably close to the Stalin cult – and Pushkin himself a quasi-divine figure, not only 'creator of the Russian literary language, father of new Russian literature, a genius who enriched humanity with his works',[8] but also a proto-Marxist who espoused the cause of liberty and of the common people; a man who gilded everything he touched and was without fault in every aspect of his life. Most recently, the celebrations of 1999 have enlisted Pushkin in the service of capitalism and commercial enterprise.

The Bank of Russia brought out a number of commemorative silver and gold coins; the twenty-five-rouble silver has on its reverse 'a picture of A.S. Pushkin holding a writing book and a goose-quill in his hands, in the background to the right – personages of his works of literature'.[9] His portrait was to be seen in shop windows, on the sides of buses and trams, on billboards, boxes of matches, vodka bottles and T-shirts, while Coca-Cola ran an advertisement featuring lines from his most famous love lyric, 'I recollect a wondrous moment'. And the Foreign Minister, Igor Ivanov, when condemning in language reminiscent of the Cold War western intervention in Yugoslavia, added that NATO had foolishly ignored Pushkin's lessons on the Balkans – thus preserving the poet's reputation, acquired in the Soviet era, for being a genius in every sphere.*

Of course, in one sense the myth is justified: Pushkin is Russia's greatest poet, the composer of a large body of magnificent lyrics, extraordinarily diverse both in theme and treatment; of a number of great narrative poems – *Ruslan and Lyudmila*, *The Gypsies*, *Poltava* and *The Bronze Horseman* – and of a unique novel in verse, *Eugene Onegin*. He reformed Russian poetic language: in his hands it became a powerful, yet flexible instrument, with a diapason stretching from the solemnly archaic to the cadences of everyday speech. The aim of this biography, however, is, in all humility, to free the complex and interesting figure of Pushkin the man from the heroic simplicity of Pushkin the myth. It concerns itself above all with the events of his life: though the appearance of his main works is noted, and the works themselves are commented on briefly, literary analysis has been eschewed, as being the province of the critic, rather than the biographer.

* He is presumably referring to Pushkin's remarks on the Polish revolt of 1830, particularly the poem 'To the Slanderers of Russia'.

ANCESTRY AND CHILDHOOD

1799–1811

> Lack of respect for one's ancestors is the first sign
> of barbarism and immorality.
>
> VIII, 42

ALEKSANDR PUSHKIN was born in Moscow on Thursday 26 May 1799, in a 'half-brick and half-wooden house' on a plot of land situated on the corner of Malaya Pochtovaya Street and Gospitalny Lane.[1] This was in the eastern suburb known as the German Settlement, to which foreigners had been banished in 1652. Though distant from the centre, it was, up to the fire of 1812, a fashionable area, 'the faubourg Saint-Germain of Moscow'.[2] On 8 June he was baptized in the parish church, the Church of the Epiphany on Elokhovskaya Square.* And that autumn his parents, Sergey and Nadezhda, took him and his sister Olga – born in December 1797 – to visit their grandfather Osip Gannibal, Nadezhda's father, on his estate at Mikhailovskoe, in the Pskov region. Most of the next year was spent in St Petersburg. The Emperor Paul, coming across Pushkin and his nurse, reprimanded the latter for not removing the baby's cap in the presence of royalty, and proceeded to do so himself. In the autumn they moved back to Moscow, where they were to remain for the duration of Pushkin's childhood.

Pushkin was proud of both sides of his ancestry: both of his father's family, the Pushkins, and of his mother's, the Gannibals. However, the

---

* Pulled down in 1837; the present church on the same site in what is now Bauman Square was finished in 1845.

Paul I

two were so different from one another, antipodes in almost every respect, that to take equal pride in both required the reconciliation of contradictory values. In Pushkin the contradictions were never completely resolved, and the resulting tension would occasionally manifest itself, both in his behaviour and in his work. The most obvious difference lay in the origins of the two families: whereas the Pushkins could hardly have been more Russian, the Gannibals could hardly have been more exotic and more foreign.

On 15 November 1704 an official at the Foreign Office in Moscow passed on to General-Admiral Golovin, the minister, news of a Serbian trader who was employed by the department. 'Before leaving Constantinople on 21 June,' he wrote, 'Master Savva Raguzinsky informed me that according to the order of your excellency he had acquired with great fear and danger to his life from the Turks *two little blackamoors and a third* for Ambassador Petr Andreevich [Tolstoy], and that he had sent these blackamoors with a man of his for safety by way of land through the Walachian territories.'[3] The boys had just arrived, the writer added; he had dispatched one to the ambassador's home, and the other two, who were brothers, to the Golovin palace. The younger of these was in the course of time to become General Abram Petrovich Gannibal, cavalier of the orders of St Anne and Alexander Nevsky: Pushkin's maternal great-grandfather.*

---

* Abram's origins are obscure. In a petition of 1742 he wrote, 'I . . . am from Africa, of the high nobility there, was born in the town of Logon in the domain of my father, who besides had under him two other towns' (Teletova, 170). And a short biography of Abram, written in German, probably in the late 1780s, by his son-in-law, Adam Rotkirch, asserts that he 'was by birth an African Moor from Abyssinia' (*Rukoyu Pushkina*, 43). Logon has hence traditionally been placed in Ethiopia. Recently, however, it has been identified with Logone, a town in the north-east corner of the present state of Cameroon: a conjecture which is more in agreement with the sparse evidence than the Ethiopian hypothesis (see Gnammankou, 19–26.) Though Pushkin had a translation of the German biography, he never refers to a specific region when writing of his ancestor's origins, but remarks, for instance, that he was 'stolen from the shores of Africa' (VI, 530). However, his friend Aleksey Vulf mentions in his journal that on 15 September 1827 Pushkin showed him the first two chapters of *The Blackamoor of Peter the Great*, 'in which the main character represents his great-grandfather Gannibal, the son of an Abys-sinian Amir, captured by the Turks (Ljubovnyy byt, I, 200).

Golovin had acquired the two boys as a gift for the tsar, to whom they were presented when he came to Moscow in December 1704. Peter had the elder brother baptized in the Preobrazhensky parish in Moscow, when he was given the name Aleksey, and the patronymic Petrov, from the tsar's own name. He was trained as a musician and attached to the Preobrazhensky regiment, where he played the hautboy in the regimental band. Unlike his younger brother Abram, he then vanishes from the pages of history.

Abram was from the beginning a favourite of the tsar. On 18 February 1705 the account-book of the royal household notes: 'to Abram the negro for a coat and trimming were given 15 roubles 45 copecks'.[4] In the spring of 1707 Peter began a campaign against the Swedes. That autumn he celebrated a victory over Charles XII in the Orthodox Pyatnitskaya church in Vilna and simultaneously had his new protégé baptized, acting as his godfather and giving him, like his brother, the patronymic Petrov. And a document of 1709 notes that 'by the tsar's order caftans have been made for Joachim the dwarf and Abram the blackamoor, for the Christmas festival, with camisoles and breeches'.[5]

In 1716 Peter made a second journey to Europe. Abram was one of his retinue, and was left in France together with three other young Russians to study fortification, sapping and mining at a military school. They returned to Russia in 1723, when Abram was commissioned as a lieutenant and posted to Riga. Peter died in February 1725, but his wife, Catherine, who succeeded him, continued his favours to Abram: he was employed to teach the tsar's grandson – the short-lived Peter II (1715–30; tsar 1727–30) – geometry and fortification. About this time he is first referred to as Gannibal. The acquisition of a surname was a step up the social ladder, differentiating him from the serfs and others known only by Christian name and patronymic; while that he should have called himself after the great Carthaginian general implies no lack of confidence in his own abilities.* His fortunes changed after Catherine's death: under a vague suspicion of political intrigue he was posted, first

---

* There is no h in the Russian alphabet; in transliteration g (or kh) is substituted for it. The assertion in Rotkirch's biography that Abram's princely father 'proudly derived his descent in a direct line from the lineage of the renowned Hannibal, the terror of Rome' (*Rukoyu Pushkina*, 43) is plainly ridiculous, though it might have suited Abram for this to be believed.

to Siberia, then to the Baltic coast. It was not until the accession of Elizabeth, Peter the Great's younger daughter, that his situation improved. In December 1741 she promoted him major-general from lieutenant-colonel, and appointed him military commander of Reval. The following year she made him a large grant of land in the province of Pskov: this included Mikhailovskoe, the estate where Pushkin was to spend two years in exile, from 1824 to 1826. In 1752 he was transferred to St Petersburg, promoted general in 1759, and, in charge of military engineering throughout Russia, oversaw the building of the Ladoga canal and the fortification of Kronstadt. That a black slave, without relations, wealth or property, should have risen to this position is in the highest degree extraordinary: so remarkable, indeed, as to argue a character far beyond the common, one that was more than justified in appropriating the name and reputation of the great Carthaginian. Elizabeth's death in 1761 put an end to his career; he was retired without promotion or gratuity, and lived for the rest of his life in his country house at Suida, near St Petersburg, where he died on 20 April 1781.

In 1731 he had married Evdokiya Dioper, the daughter of a Dutch sea captain. When she gave birth to a child, who was plainly not his, he divorced her (though bringing up the daughter as his own), and married the daughter of a Swedish officer in the Russian army, Christine von Schöberg. Of his seven children by Christine (three more died in infancy) the eldest son, Ivan, was a distinguished artillery officer who reached the rank of lieutenant-general. Petr, the second son, in old age lived in Pokrovskoe, some four kilometres from Mikhailovskoe, where he occupied himself with the distillation of home-made vodka. 'He called for vodka,' Pushkin wrote after visiting him there in 1817. 'Vodka was brought. Pouring himself a glass, he ordered it to be offered to me, I did not pull a face – and by this seemed to gratify extraordinarily the old Negro. A quarter of an hour later he called for vodka again – and this happened again five or six times before dinner.'[6] He visited him again in 1825, when he was thinking of composing a biography of Abram, a project which later turned into the fictional *Blackamoor of Peter the Great*. 'I am counting on seeing my old negro of a Great-Uncle who, I suppose, is going to die one of these fine days, and I must get from him some memoirs concerning my great-grandfather,' he wrote on 11 August.' He carried out the intention a week or so later, bringing back with him to Mikhailovskoe not only the manuscript of Abram's biography, written by his son-in-law, Adam Rotkirch, but also a short, unfinished note composed by Petr himself, outlining his and his father's careers.[8]

Osip, Abram's third son and Pushkin's maternal grandfather, was a gunnery officer in the navy, reaching the rank of commander. Careless and dissolute, he ran up large debts, which his father in the end refused to pay and forbade him the house. At the beginning of the 1770s he was posted to Lipetsk, in the Tambov region, where he met and, in November 1773, married Mariya Pushkina.* Mariya was generally held to have thrown herself away; her Moscow cousins made up an epigram on the marriage:

> There was once a great fool,
> Who without Cupid's permission
> Married a Vizapur.

The last line is a hit at Osip's complexion; it is a reference to the 'swarthy Vizapur', Prince Poryus-Vizapursky, an Indian and a well-known eccentric.[9]

Abram forgave the newly-married Osip; he was allowed to return home, and his daughter Nadezhda, Pushkin's mother, was born in Suida on 21 June 1775. However, Osip found his father overbearing and family life excruciatingly boring. Leaving a note to say he would never return, he fled to Pskov, where he met a pretty young widow, Ustinya Tolstaya. Having received – so he said – a mysterious message announcing his wife's death, he married Ustinya in November 1778. Mariya, who was far from dead, lodged a complaint against him; after years of petitions and counter-petitions the marriage to Ustinya was annulled, and the estate of Kobrino outside St Petersburg (which he had now inherited, together with Mikhailovskoe, from his father) made over in trust to Nadezhda. Osip retired in dudgeon to a lonely existence at Mikhailovskoe, where he died in 1806, leaving the estate encumbered with debt.

After the separation Mariya moved to St Petersburg, spending the summers in Kobrino, some thirty miles from the capital. Nadezhda was therefore brought up in far from provincial surroundings. She was well-read, spoke excellent French, and through Mariya's relations in

---

* This marriage would make Osip's daughter, Nadezhda, and her husband, Sergey Pushkin, distant cousins, sharing a common ancestor: Petr Pushkin (1644–92), Nadezhda's maternal great-great-grandfather and Sergey's paternal great-grandfather.

the capital gained entrée into society, where she became known as 'the beautiful creole'.[10] Here she met Sergey Pushkin; the couple – the poet's father and mother – were married on 28 September 1796 in the village church at Voskresenskoe on the Kobrino estate.

Though Pushkin claimed to be able to trace his ancestry on the paternal side back to the times of Alexander Nevsky,* the first to bear the family name was Konstantin Pushkin, born in the early fifteenth century, the younger son of a Grigory Pushka. There is a direct line of descent from him to the poet. From this time to the seventeenth century the Pushkins were a minor boyar family whose members never wielded great influence or occupied high positions in the state. They played, however, a lively part during the Time of Troubles (1584–1613), when one Gavrila Pushkin was a prominent supporter of the Pretender Dmitry. Pushkin put him into his historical drama *Boris Godunov*, remarking, 'Finding in history one of my ancestors, who played an important role in that unhappy epoch, I brought him on the stage, without worrying about the delicacies of propriety, *con amore*, but without aristocratic conceit.'[11] But a decline in importance set in during the reign of Peter the Great. By the Table of Ranks, promulgated in 1722, an hierarchical system of rank, consisting of fourteen grades, was imposed on the military, civil and court services. Those in the first eight grades automatically became gentry: henceforth, therefore, social position was to be determined not by birth, but by rank. The more powerful aristocratic families were little affected, but the less important, such as the Pushkins, were submerged in the influx of the newly ennobled. During the eighteenth century no member of the family achieved distinction in any field, though family tradition erroneously maintained that Aleksey Fedorovich Pushkin, Mariya's father, had been *voevoda* (governor) of Tambov.

Lev Pushkin, the poet's paternal grandfather, served in the artillery, reaching the rank of major, before retiring in 1763. He settled in Moscow, in a large house on the Bozhedomka (now Delegatsky Street), in the northern suburbs. The grounds covered nearly fifteen acres, running down to an orangery and large fish-pond, formed by damming up the

* Alexander Nevsky (c.1220–63), canonized in 1547, was prince of Novgorod (1236–52), of Kiev (1746–52) and grand prince of 1.1 limsir (1111) (1)

Neglinnaya River. By his first wife he had three children, and his second, Olga Vasilevna (née Chicherina), was to give him four more: Anna, Vasily, Sergey, and Elizaveta. As was the custom, Vasily and Sergey were entered for the army at a very early age: Vasily was seven and Sergey six when their names first appeared in the list. Actual service with the regiment – the Izmailovsky Life Guards – began much later: for Sergey at the end of the 1780s. He was promoted to ensign in 1794, to lieutenant in 1796, and in 1797 transferred to the chasseur battalion with the rank of captain-lieutenant. Both brothers left the army in the autumn of 1797. Neither was cut out for military service, but it is likely that their retirement was brought about by the changes introduced by the Emperor Paul, who had come to the throne the previous year. A military tyrant and pedant, he forced a tight Prussian uniform on the army; would arbitrarily consign officers to Siberia for a minor fault on parade; and repeatedly threatened to banish fashionable regiments such as the Izmailovsky from St Petersburg to the provinces. The brothers, together with their young wives, both metropolitan beauties, all of whom adored the social whirl, would have viewed with horror the prospect of exile to some dull provincial backwater.

In 1834 Pushkin, looking back with nostalgia on the Moscow of his childhood, before the fire of 1812, wrote:

At one time there really was a rivalry between Moscow and Petersburg. Then in Moscow there were rich nobles who did not work, grandees who had given up the court, and independent, carefree individuals, passionately devoted to harmless slander and inexpensive hospitality; then Moscow was the gathering place for all Russia's aristocracy, which streamed to it in winter from every province. Brilliant young guardsmen flew thither from Petersburg. Every corner of the ancient capital was loud with music, there were crowds everywhere. Five thousand people filled the hall of the Noble Assembly twice a week. There the young met; marriages were made. Moscow was as famous for its brides as Vyazma for its gingerbread; Moscow dinners became a proverb. The innocent eccentricities of the Muscovites were a sign of their independence. They lived their own lives,

amusing themselves as they liked, caring little for the opinion
of others. One rich eccentric might build himself on one of the
main streets a Chinese house with green dragons and with
wooden mandarins under gilded parasols. Another might drive
to Marina Roshcha in a carriage covered with pure silver plate.
A third might mount five or so blackamoors, footmen and
attendants on the rumble of a four-seat sleigh and drive it
tandem along the summer street. Alamode belles appropriated
Petersburg fashions, putting their indelible imprint on them.
From afar haughty Petersburg mocked, but did not interfere
with old mother Moscow's escapades. But where has this noisy,
idle, carefree life gone? Where are the balls, the feasts, the eccen-
trics, the practical jokers? All have vanished.[12]

He could have mentioned, too, the classically laid-out Yusupov garden,
open to the 'respectable public', with its alleys and round pond, marble
statues and grotto, where he played as a child; the private theatres with
troupes of serf actors; or the 'magic castle', the Pashkov mansion on
Mokhovaya Street, whose garden, full of exotic birds at large or in gilded
cages, was known as 'Eden': at night it was lit by lanterns, and a private
orchestra played there on feast-days.[13]

For Pushkin's parents social life was infinitely preferable to the ted-
ium of domesticity. Nadezhda was the dominant partner. Beautiful,
charming, frivolous and – outwardly at least – always good-humoured,
she was strong-willed and could be despotic, both to her husband and
her children. She was cool towards Pushkin, preferring first Olga, then
his younger brother Lev. When angry, she sometimes would not speak
to him for weeks, or even months. Once, annoyed by his habit of
rubbing his hands together, she tied them behind his back and starved
him for a day; since he was always losing his handkerchiefs, she sewed
one to the shoulder of his jacket like an epaulette, and forced him to
wear the garment in public.

She was incurably restless: never satisfied with her surroundings, she
drove the family from lodging to lodging, or, if a move was impossible,
continually moved the furniture and changed the wallpapers, turning
a bedroom into a dining-room, a study into a drawing-room. On
returning to Moscow they lodged in I.M. Volkov's house on the same

of Chistoprudny Boulevard and Bolshoy Khari-
tonevsky Lane: here Pushkin's brother Nikolay
was born on 27 March 1801. A year later they
moved up the lane into a wooden house on
Prince N.B. Yusupov's property, where they
stayed for a year and a half; then, forfeiting six
months' rent, in the summer of 1803, they
moved down the lane again into accommodation belonging to Count A.L. Santi. 'It is difficult
to understand,' one historian writes, 'how the
Pushkins managed to fit into the cramped con-

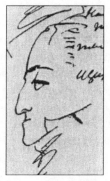

Nadezhda Pushkina

fines of Santi's court; Santi had up to sixteen house serfs, Sergey Lvovich
from four to thirteen; besides them in the court lived the civil servant
Petrov and the district surveyor Fedotov, while another of Santi's serfs,
the women's dressmaker Berezinsky, squeezed in somewhere.'[14] Nevertheless, the Pushkins remained there over two years; here Lev was born
on 9 April 1805. But, before Pushkin left for boarding-school in 1811,
they would move eight more times, criss-crossing Moscow from east to
west and back again.

Sergey, Pushkin's father, was short and stout,
with a nose like a parrot's beak. He was a weak
character, easily dominated by his more forceful
wife, and inclined to lachrymose emotional outbursts. At the same time he was hot-tempered
and irritable, and would fly into rages at the
slightest provocation, with the result that his children feared, rather than loved him. He had a poor
head for finances, knew nothing of his estates –
he visited Boldino, his property in Nizhny Novgorod province, twice in his lifetime – and refused
to have anything to do with their management:

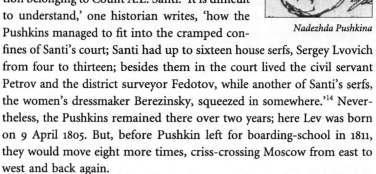

Sergey Pushkin

everything was left in the hands of inefficient or dishonest stewards. His
income was consequently insecure and continually decreased. Though,
like his father, he was hospitable to his friends, he showed a remarkable
lack of generosity towards his children and took little interest in them. He
was fond of French literature, and an inveterate theatre-goer, but his
main preoccupation was his social life. He was at his best in some salon,

elaborately polite and delicately witty, throwing off a stream of French puns, or inscribing elegant sentiments in French verse or prose in ladies' albums.

In January 1802, after the death of the Emperor Paul, he had returned to government service, taking up a post in the Moscow military commissariat. In 1812, when Napoleon approached Moscow, he was transferred to Orel, and given the task of organizing supplies for a reserve army under the command of General Lobanov-Rostovsky. The latter, a hot-tempered and ruthless disciplinarian, soon found fault with him, and in February 1813 requested the head of the commissariat, 'for neglect of duty and disobedience of my instructions, to remove Pushkin from his present position as incompetent and incapable and to reprimand him severely'.[15] At this time the Russian armies had begun to move rapidly westwards, and it was not until the following year, when they stood outside Warsaw, that Sergey was relieved of his command: his successor found him reading a French novel in his office. He retired with the rank of civil councillor in January 1817.

The gap left in the children's lives by the parents' lack of attention was filled by their grandmother, Mariya Gannibal. At the beginning of 1801 she moved to Moscow and settled close to the Pushkins. She spent most of each day with her grandchildren and from 1805 lived with the family. She took over the running of the house and saw to the education of the children, teaching them their letters, and engaging governesses and tutors for them. In 1800 Nadezhda had sold Kobrino, no longer useful as a summer residence after the move to Moscow. One of the women on the estate, Arina Rodionovna, though freed from serfdom, had preferred to come to Moscow and become Olga's nurse. She introduced the children to the world of Russian legends and fairy-tales, while Mariya related family history to them:

> From my Moscow grandmother I love
> To hear stories of ancestors,
> And of the distant past.[16]

In early childhood Pushkin was an excessively plump, silent infant, clumsy and awkward, who hated taking exercise, and, if forced to go for a walk, would often sit down in the middle of the street in protest. His character and physique changed markedly around the age of seven.

In November 1804 Mariya Gannibal bought Zakharovo, an estate of nearly two and a half thousand acres with sixty male serfs, situated some thirty miles to the east of Moscow. From 1805 to 1809 the family spent the summers there. Instead of the continual displacement from one rented apartment to another, Zakharovo provided relative permanency; instead of the cramped surroundings of a Moscow lodging, the children had separate quarters, where they lived with the current governess or tutor. And most of all, of course, instead of the Moscow streets or the confined expanse of the Yusupov gardens, there was the countryside, the large park with its lake, its alleys and groves of birches. In these new surroundings Pushkin became an active and mischievous child, at times difficult to control. Here, in the summer of 1807, the six-year-old Nikolay fell severely ill – though he was still able to put his tongue out at Pushkin when the latter visited his sickbed. However, his condition worsened, and he died on 30 July. Pushkin was much affected by the loss: 'Nikolay's death' is one of the few notes relating to this period in a sketchy autobiographical plan he drew up in 1830.[17]

As was usual at the time, the education of Olga and Aleksandr was entrusted to a series of foreign émigrés, who had in most cases little to recommend them as teachers other than their nationality and whom, for the most part, the children disliked. Their first tutor was the Comte de Montfort, a man of some culture, a musician and artist; he was followed by M. Rousselot, who wrote French verse, and then by a M. Chédel, of whom little is known other than that he was sacked for playing cards with the servants. Miss Bailey, one of Olga's governesses, was supposed to teach them English, but failed to do so, while a German governess refused to speak any language except Russian. They went to dancing classes at their cousins, the Buturlins, on Malaya Pochtovaya Street, at the Trubetskoys, also cousins, on the Pokrovka, and at the Sushkovs, on the Bolshaya Molchanovka – their daughter, Sonya, a year younger than Pushkin, is supposed to have been the object of his first love. On Thursdays they went to the children's dances arranged by the celebrated Moscow dancing master Iogel.*

From early years Pushkin had a passion for reading; by ten, according to his sister, he had read Plutarch, the *Iliad* and the *Odyssey* in French,

* Tolstoy describes one of Iogel's dances in *War and Peace*, book 2, part 1, chapter 12.

and would rummage among his father's books – mainly consisting of French eighteenth-century authors – in search of interesting volumes. The atmosphere in their house was a cultured, literary one. Sergey read Molière to the children and wrote French verse; his brother, Vasily, was an established poet, published in periodicals, and acquainted with many of the authors of the day, including Karamzin, Zhukovsky and Batyushkov; a more distant relative, Major-General Aleksey Mikhailovich Pushkin, who had translated Molière, was a frequent guest. Among the regular visitors to Nadezhda's salon were Ivan Dmitriev, the poet and fabulist, Minister of Justice from 1810 to 1814, an unsuccessful suitor for the hand of Sergey's sister Anna; the 'pretty, clever and talented' French pianist Adélaïde Percheron de Mouchy, later wife of the émigré Irish composer John Field;[18] and the French novelist Count Xavier de Maistre, born in Savoy, who had followed Suvorov back to Russia after the Italian campaign of 1800 and had joined the Russian army.* An amateur artist, he painted a miniature of Nadezhda on ivory.

Perhaps one should not take too literally Sergey's story that the six-year-old Pushkin abandoned his toys to sit listening to his father's conversation with Karamzin, not taking his eyes from the visitor's face, all the more so since Karamzin did not frequent the Pushkins; nor can one accept without reservation the remark of an earlier biographer, that the child 'listened attentively to their judgements and conversation, knew the coryphaei of our literature not only through their works, but through their living speech, which expressed the character of each, and often involuntarily but indelibly impressed itself on the young mind'.[19] But at the very least the atmosphere could not have been more favourable to the formation of the desire to write poetry: Pushkin would never have to struggle with the incomprehension of his family, or the view that the occupation of poet was not one to be taken seriously.

At seven he was found awake in bed late at night; when asked why he was not asleep, he replied that he was making up poems. At ten he improvised little comedies in French and performed them in front of his sister; one was hissed off the stage by the audience, and the author composed a self-critical epigram on the event:

---

* Author of *A Journey round My Room* (1794), and younger brother of the more famous Joseph de Maistre, Sardinian ambassador in St Petersburg 1802–17, best known for his *St Petersburg Dialogues* [*Les soirées de Saint Pétersbourg*] (1821).

'Tell me, why was *The Filcher*
Hissed by the pit?'
'Alas! it's because the poor author
Filched it from Molière.'[20]

A little later, having discovered Voltaire, and read *La Henriade*, he composed a parodic emulation: *La Tolyade*, a comic-heroic poem in six cantos, depicting a battle between male and female dwarfs, the hero of which is King Dagobert's dwarf Toly. Olga's governess impounded the notebook containing the poem and showed it to the tutor, M. Chédel, who read the first few lines and laughed heartily. Pushkin burst into tears and in a rage threw the manuscript into the stove.

'I've no idea what will become of my eldest grandson: he's a clever boy and loves books, but he's a bad student and rarely prepares his lessons properly,' Mariya Gannibal told her friends.[21] His dislike for his tutors was not conducive to diligence in any subject, but he found arithmetic particularly incomprehensible and, his sister recollected, 'would weep bitter tears over the first four rules, especially that of division'.[22] As the calculations scribbled here and there on his manuscripts demonstrate, the rules always remained something of a puzzle to him. Foreign tutors were, it was clear, not the answer to the problem of his education, and it was decided to send him to school. A private Jesuit boarding-school in St Petersburg was chosen, and in February 1811 Sergey and Nadezhda travelled to the capital to enter Pushkin as a pupil there. However, a family friend, Aleksandr Turgenev, suggested that the new Imperial Lycée at Tsarskoe Selo, which was to open in the autumn, might be a more suitable establishment, all the more so as its director was to be Vasily Malinovsky: he and his brothers, Aleksey and Pavel, were well known to the Pushkins; indeed Pavel had been one of the witnesses at their marriage in 1796. These considerations were supported by a more practical one: while education at the Jesuit boarding-school would put a strain on the family's finances, that at the Lycée would be free. On 1 March Sergey sent a petition to the Minister of Education, Count A.K. Razumovsky, requesting that A.S. Pushkin should be admitted to the Lycée, and stating that 'he had been educated in his parents' house, where he had acquired initial knowledge of the grammar of the Russian and French languages, of arithmetic, geography, history and drawing'.[23]

2

THE LYCÉE

1811–17

In those days, when in the Lycée gardens
I serenely flourished,
Read Apuleius eagerly
But did not read Cicero,
In those days, in mysterious vales,
In spring, to the cry of swans,
Near waters gleaming in stillness,
The Muse began to visit me.

Eugene Onegin, VIII, i

IN 1710 PETER THE GREAT GRANTED to his consort Catherine an estate some fifteen miles to the south of Petersburg, a locality which later acquired the name Tsarskoe Selo – Tsar's Village. Catherine replaced the old wooden mansion with a small stone palace, laid out a park and a vegetable garden, and constructed greenhouses, an orangery and a menagerie. On her death in 1727 the estate passed to her daughter Elizabeth, whose favourite residence it soon became. To begin with she lacked the means to improve it, but after her accession in 1741 she called on her architects to turn it into a Russian Versailles. In 1752–6 the palace was completely rebuilt by the Italian architect Rastrelli, who later designed the Winter Palace in St Petersburg. Rastrelli's Catherine or Great Palace is a magnificent three-storey Baroque edifice with a façade of colossal length – 306 metres – and an immense cour d'honneur formed by a low, single-storeyed semi-circle of service buildings pierced by three fine wrought-iron gates. The park was laid out in the formal Dutch style, with 'fish canals, avenues, neat bowers, alleys, espaliers, and "close boskets with mossy seats"', and ornamented with pavilions and follies.[1]

Elizabeth was succeeded by Peter III, Peter the Great's grandson, who ruled for only six months before being deposed and assassinated. His wife, the German princess Sophia of Anhalt-Zerbst, who had changed her name on her conversion to Orthodoxy, then came to the throne as Catherine II. Her passion for Tsarskoe Selo was even greater than that of Elizabeth, and, like her predecessor, she completely changed the nature of the palace and its grounds. The Dutch style was swept away and the park recast in the English fashion. 'I love to distraction these gardens in the English style – their curving lines, the gentle slopes, the ponds like lakes. My Anglomania predominates over my plutomania,' she wrote to Voltaire in 1772.[2] She employed as landscape gardener an Englishman, John Bush, head of a noted nursery garden at Hackney, who came out to Russia in the late 1770s. New dams and ponds were created, and the park wall replaced by a canal. 'At the moment I have taken possession of mister Cameron, a Scot by nationality, a Jacobite by profession, a great designer nurtured by antiquities; together we are fashioning a terraced garden with baths beneath, a gallery above; that will be so beautiful, beautiful.'[3] Cameron remodelled much of the interior of the Catherine Palace, built the famous Cameron Gallery: a large, covered Ionic terrace which juts out at right angles from the south-east corner of the palace, on the garden side, and added to the constructions in the park several examples of *chinoiserie*: a theatre, a bridge on whose balustrade sit four stone Chinamen with parasols, and a village – nineteen little houses surrounding a pagoda. His summer-house in the form of a granite pyramid was a memorial to Catherine's favourite dogs, three English whippets: Sir Tom Anderson, Zemira and Duchesse, who are buried behind it, on the bank of a small stream. Catherine's anglomania was catered for by the Marble Bridge, a copy of the Palladian bridge in the grounds at Wilton, and the red-brick Admiralty on the bank of the lake, built in the English Gothic style. The most prominent addition to Tsarskoe Selo in these years, however, was the severely classical Alexander Palace, built in 1792–6 to the designs of the Italian architect Quarenghi for Catherine's grandson, the future Alexander I. Earlier, in 1789, she had employed a Russian architect,

Neelov, to add a wing to the Great Palace for the accommodation of her grandchildren: this stands across the street from the north end of the main building, to which it is connected by a triple-bay arch. In 1811, after a complete renovation, it became the building of the Lycée. The ground floor was occupied by the domestic offices and staff apartments; the dining-room, sickbay, school office and teachers' common-room were on the first floor; classrooms, reading-room, science laboratory and the school hall on the second; the third was divided into fifty small study-bedrooms with a central corridor, and the gallery over the arch became the library. Games were to be played on the Champ des Roses, so called because it had in Elizabeth's time been bounded by wild rose bushes, in the south-western corner of the Catherine park. The palace swimming-pool, constructed for the empress's grandsons in a grove near the Great Pond, with its two bright yellow wooden pavilions in the style of Louis XVI, was taken over by the school a little later. One of the houses built for court functionaries in the time of Elizabeth, on the corner of Sadovaya Street and Pevchesky Lane, just opposite the Lycée, was allotted to the school's director, Malinovsky. A single-storey wing of this house became the school's kitchen and bath-house.

Education reform in Russia had begun in 1803, and had had considerable success, both at secondary and university level. Alexander, influenced by Speransky, his principal adviser on internal administration and reform, now wished to establish a school to provide a cadre for the highest ranks of the civil service. His proposal, drawn up originally in 1808 by Speransky, was issued as an imperial decree on 12 August 1810, later ratified by the Senate. The school's purpose was to be 'the education of youth especially predestined for important parts of government service'. Among the subjects taught special stress was laid on 'the moral sciences, under which is to be understood all that knowledge relating to the moral position of man in society and, consequently, the concepts of the system of Civic societies, and of the rights and duties arising therefrom'. 'Beginning with the most simple concepts of law', the pupils should be brought to 'a deep and firm understanding of differing rights and be instructed in the systems of public, private and Russian law'. Teachers were 'never to allow [pupils] to use words without clear ideas', and in all subjects were to encourage the 'exercise of reason'.[4] Corporal punishment was forbidden, which made the Lycée probably unique in its time. There were to be two courses, junior and senior, each lasting for three years.* The first intake would consist of not less than twenty, and not more than fifty children of the nobility between the ages of ten and twelve; on graduation the students would be appointed, depending on achievement, to a civil service rank between the fourteenth class – the lowest – that of collegial registrar, and the ninth, that of titular councillor.

The *St Petersburg Gazette* of 11 July 1811 announced that children wishing to enter the Imperial Tsarskoe Selo Lycée should present themselves to the Minister of Education, A.K. Razumovsky, on 1 August together with a birth certificate, attestation of nobility, and testimonial of excellent behaviour. They would be medically examined, and there would be an examination conducted by the minister himself and the director of the Lycée. They would be expected to have: 'a) some grammatical knowledge of the Russian and either the French or the German language, b) a knowledge of arithmetic, at least up to the rule of three, c) an understanding of the general properties of solids, d) some knowledge of the basic fundamentals of geography and e) be able to divide ancient history into its chief epochs and periods and have some knowledge of the most important peoples of antiquity'.[5]

Sergey Lvovich applied to the commissariat for a month's leave to take his son to the examination. Permission was slow in coming and, realizing he might be detained in St Petersburg for more than a month, he entrusted Pushkin to his brother, Vasily, who was himself travelling to the capital at that time. Together with Vasily's mistress, Anna Vorozheikina, they set off in the third week of July. Pushkin's sister, Olga, gave him as a parting present a copy of La Fontaine's *Fables*, which he left behind on the table. His great-aunt, Varvara Chicherina, and his aunt, Anna Pushkina, together gave him a hundred roubles 'to buy nuts'.[6] Vasily immediately borrowed the money and never returned it: behaviour that long rankled with Pushkin; he mentions it, albeit jokingly, in a letter of 1825.

Vasily had published his first verses in 1793, but since then he had produced little: only twenty poems over one five-year period, causing Batyushkov to remark that he had 'a sluggish Muse'.[7] She was, however,

---

* In January 1814 a preparatory school was set up, also in Tsarskoe Selo, whose pupils replaced the junior course on the latter's graduation to the senior level.

eventually stirred into action by the heated contemporary debate on literary language and style, and inspired a number of poems in which Vasily enthusiastically ridiculed the conservative faction. Indeed, he was now journeying to St Petersburg to publish two epistles in reply to a veiled personal attack on him by the leader of the conservatives, Admiral

Vasily Pushkin

A.S. Shishkov, who had recently written of his opponents that they had 'learnt their piety from *Candide* and their morality and erudition in the back streets of Paris'.*[8] Though in childhood Pushkin had some respect for his uncle as a poet, his attitude towards him would soon settle into one of amused, if affectionate irony. Indeed, Vasily's verse scarcely reaches mediocrity, with the exception of *A Dangerous Neighbour*, a racy little epic only 154 lines in length, written in lively and colourful colloquial Russian. Though too risqué to be published – it did not appear in Russia until 1901 – it circulated widely in manuscript. Pushkin gave the poem a nod of acknowledgement in *Eugene Onegin*; among the guests at Tatyana's name-day party is Vasily's hero,

> My first cousin, Buyanov
> Covered in fluff, in a peaked cap
> (As, of course, he is known to you).
>
> (V, xxvi)

The second line is a quotation from Vasily's poem; Buyanov, his progeny, would of course be Pushkin's cousin.

On arrival in St Petersburg the party put up at the Hotel Bordeaux, but Vasily complained that he was being 'mercilessly fleeced', and they moved to an apartment 'in the house of the merchant Kuvshinnikov' on the bank of the Moika canal, near the Konyushenny Bridge.[9] Taking his nephew with him, Vasily made a round of visits to literary acquaintances. At I.I. Dmitriev's, before reciting *A Dangerous Neighbour*,

---

* After being sued for divorce by his wife on grounds of adultery, Vasily had spent two years in France with his mistress, returning 'dressed in Parisian finery from head to toe' (Veresaev (1937), I, 17)

composed earlier that year, he told Pushkin to leave the room, only to receive the embarrassing retort: 'Why send me out? I know it all. I've heard it all already.'[10]

The medical took place on 1 August; the examination, conducted by Count Razumovsky, the Minister of Education, I.I. Martynov, the director of the department of education, and Malinovsky, the head-master of the Lycée, was held a week later in Razumovsky's house on the Fontanka. While waiting to be called in, Pushkin met another candidate, Ivan Pushchin. 'My first friend, friend without price!' he wrote of him in 1825.[11] Both soon learnt that they had been accepted, though Malinovsky's private note on Pushkin read: 'Empty-headed and thought-less. Excellent at French and drawing, lazy and backward at arithmetic.'[12] The two met frequently while waiting for the beginning of term. Vasily occasionally took them boating; more often, however, they would go to the Summer Gardens – a short walk from the apartment on the Moika – with Anna Vorozheikina and play there, sometimes in the company of two other future lycéens, Konstantin Gurev and Sergey Lomonosov. They were measured for the school uniform, which was supplied free to the pupils: for ordinary wear blue frock-coats with red collars and red trousers; for Sundays, walking out, and ceremonial occasions a blue uniform coat with a red collar and silver (for the junior course) or gold (for the senior) tabs, white trousers, tie and waistcoat, high polished boots and a three-cornered hat. Later the boots were abandoned, the white waistcoat and trousers replaced by blue, and the hat by a peaked cap.

On 9 October Pushkin and four other pupils with their relatives travelled to Tsarskoe Selo and had lunch with Malinovsky. In the evening they parted from their families and went across to the Lycée where they were allocated rooms. Pushkin's was number fourteen, on the palace side. Next to him, in thirteen, was Pushchin. In his room he had an iron bedstead with brass knobs, a mattress stuffed with horse-hair and covered in leather, a chest of drawers, a mirror, a wash-stand, a chair and a desk with inkwell, candlestick and snuffer. In the next few days the other pupils – thirty in all – joined them.†

*   *   *

† The thirty who formed the first course at the Lycée were Aleksandr Bakunin, Count Silvery Broglio, Konstantin Danzas, Baron Anton Delvig, Semen Esakov, Prince Aleksandr Gorchakov, Baron Pavel Grevenits, Konstantin Gurev, Aleksey Illichevsky, Sergey Komovsky,

The ceremonial opening of the new school took place on 19 October 1811. It began with a service in the palace church, to whose choir access could be gained over the arch, through the school library. The priest then proceeded to the Lycée, where he sprinkled the pupils and the establishment with holy water. Between two columns in the school hall had been placed a table covered with a red cloth with a gold fringe. On it lay the imperial charter of the Lycée. The boys lined up in three ranks on one side of the table with their teachers facing them on the other. The guests – senior officials from St Petersburg and their wives – occupied chairs in the body of the hall. When all were present the emperor, the empress, the dowager empress, Grand Duke Constantine and Grand Duchess Anna (Alexander's brother and sister) were invited in by Razumovsky and took their places in the front row.

The school charter was now read by Martynov. This was followed by a speech from the director, Malinovsky, whose indistinct utterance soon lost the audience's attention. It was regained, however, by Aleksandr Kunitsyn, the young teacher of moral and political science, although he purported to address the boys, rather than the audience. 'Leaving the embraces of your parents, you step beneath the roof of this sacred temple of learning,' he began, and went on, in a rhetoric full of fervent patriotism, to inspire them with the duties of the citizen and soldier. 'In these deserted forests, which once resounded to victorious Russian arms, you will learn of the glorious deeds of heroes, overcoming enemy armies. On these rolling plains you will be shown the blazing footsteps of your ancestors, who strove to defend the tsar and the Fatherland – surrounded by examples of virtue, will you not burn with an ardent love for it, will you not prepare yourselves to serve the Fatherland?'[13] Alexander was so pleased with this speech that he decorated Kunitsyn with the Vladimir Cross. The pupils were now called up one by one and introduced to the emperor, who, after a short speech in return, invited the empresses to inspect the Lycée. They returned to watch the

---

Baron Modest Korff, Aleksandr Kornilov, Nikolay Korsakov, Konstantin Kostensky, Wilhelm Küchelbecker, Sergey Lomonosov, Ivan Malinovsky, Arkady Martynov, Dmitry Maslov, Fedor Matyushkin, Pavel Myasoedov, Ivan Pushchin, Aleksandr Pushkin, Nikolay Rzhevsky, Petr Savrasov, Fedor Steven, Aleksandr Tyrkov, Vladimir Volkhovsky, Mikhail Yakovlev and Pavel Yudin. Gurev was expelled in September 1813 for 'Greek tastes', i.e. homosexuality.

lycéens eating their dinner. The dowager empress approached little Kornilov, one of the youngest boys, and, putting her hand on his shoulder, asked him whether the soup was good. 'Oui, monsieur,' he replied, earning himself a smile from royalty and a nickname from his fellows.[14] In the evening, by the light of the lampions placed round the building and of the illuminated shield bearing the imperial arms which flickered on the balcony, the boys had a snowball fight: winter had come early that year. The next day Malinovsky made known a number of regulations he had received from the Minister of Education.* The most significant, as far as the boys were concerned, and which caused several to break into tears, was that they would not be permitted to leave the Lycée throughout the six years of their education. Even their vacation – the month of July – would have to be spent at the school. Parents and relatives would be allowed to visit them only on Sundays or other holidays.

The school day began at six, when a bell awoke the pupils. After prayers there were lessons from seven to nine. Breakfast – tea and white rolls – was followed by a walk, lessons from ten to twelve, another walk, and dinner at one: three courses – four on special occasions – accompanied, to begin with, by half a glass of porter, but, as Pushchin remarks, 'this English system was later done away with. We contented ourselves with native kvas or water.'[15] From two to three there was drawing or calligraphy, lessons from three to five, tea, a third walk, and preparation or extra tuition until the bell rang for supper – two courses – at half past eight. After supper the boys were free for recreation until evening prayers at ten, followed by bed. On Wednesdays and Saturdays there were fencing or dancing lessons in the evening, from six until supper-time.

Several servants, each responsible for a number of boys, looked after the domestic side of school life. Prokofev was a retired sergeant, who had served in the army under Catherine. The Pole Leonty Kemersky, though dishonest, was a favourite, since he had set up a tuck-shop, where the boys could buy sweets, drink coffee or chocolate, or even – strictly against the school rules – a glass of liqueur. Young Konstantin Sazonov looked after Pushkin. Much to the astonishment of the school,

---

* Until 1816 the school was under the direct supervision of the minister, Razumovsky, who controlled its activities down to the most trivial detail.

on 18 March 1816 the police turned up and arrested him on suspicion of half a dozen murders committed in or around Tsarskoe Selo, to which he promptly confessed. A few weeks later, when in the Lycée sickbay under the care of the genial Dr Peschl, Pushkin composed an epigram:

> On the morrow, with a penny candle,
> I will appear before the holy icon:
> My friend! I am still alive,
> Though was once beneath death's sickle:
> Sazonov was my servant
> And Peschl – my physician.[16]

Vasily Malinovsky was forty-six when he became director of the Lycée. He was an odd choice, since he had no previous experience in education. He had been a diplomat, but had held no post since 1801. While with the embassy in London, he had published *A Discourse on Peace and War*, which anticipated Woodrow Wilson in suggesting that peace could be maintained by the establishment of a league of nations. And in 1802, like others at this time, he had put forward a project for the emancipation of the serfs – a reform which was only put into effect in 1861. He carried his liberal idealism into his new post, being responsible for the ban on corporal punishment. But his tenure was short-lived: he died, after a sudden illness, in March 1814. His death was followed by the period called by Pushkin 'anarchy', and by Pushchin 'the interregnum',[17] when the school had no director. It was governed sometimes by a committee of the teachers, sometimes by a succession of individual teachers, each abruptly appointed as temporary director by Razumovsky and as abruptly dismissed after some disagreement or minor scandal.

Anarchy came to an end in March 1816, when the forty-year-old Egor Antonovich Engelhardt became the school's director. Born in Riga and of German-Italian parentage, Engelhardt enjoyed the patronage of Alexander, and on occasion was to make use of this to the school's advantage. Unlike Malinovsky, he had some qualifications for the post, having been the director of the St Petersburg Pedagogic Institute. But whereas Malinovsky's aim had been to form virtuous individuals, imbued with high civic ideals, 'Engelhardt was chiefly concerned with turning his charges into "*des cavaliers galants et des chevaliers servants*".'[18]
Indeed, the social life of the pupils outside the walls of the Lycée –

absent before – was one of Engelhardt's main concerns. He entertained them at his house in the evenings, took them for walks and drives in the neighbourhood, organized picnics and skating parties, providing, on all these occasions, feminine company from his own family or from those of friends and acquaintances in Tsarskoe Selo: 'In a word, our director understood that forbidden fruit can be a dangerous attraction, and that freedom, guided by an experienced hand, can preserve youth from many mistakes,' wrote Pushchin sagely.[19]

Engelhardt

Above all he was concerned to establish 'amical relations' between himself and the lycéens, guiding himself by the maxim that 'only through a heartfelt sympathy with the joys and sorrows of one's pupils can one win their love'.[20] Many succumbed to his wooing; for some he became a surrogate father, and the correspondence between himself and a number of former pupils, lasting in some cases until his death in 1862, testifies to the sincere affection in which he was held. Others, however, held themselves aloof. Among these was Pushkin. 'Why Pushkin rejected all the attentions of the director and his wife remains an unsolved mystery for me,' wrote Pushchin forty years later.[21]

The lycéens, thrown intimately together, isolated from outside influence, never leaving the Lycée from one year's end to the next, formed a close-knit society: indeed, they referred to themselves as 'a nation', emphasizing their independence and unity. An extraordinarily strong *esprit de corps* bound the group together, persisting long after they had quitted the Lycée. For most, 19 October remained a significant anniversary throughout their lives. Pushkin had known little parental affection, and was now, in addition, cut off from his family: though his mother visited him in January 1812, he next saw her in April 1814, after the family had moved to St Petersburg. For him, more than for most of his companions, the Lycée nation became a replacement for the family. The bond was too strong for him to accept, as others did, Engelhardt as a surrogate parent.

Of his tutors only Aleksandr Kunitsyn, the young teacher of moral and political science whose speech had so impressed Alexander, had a lasting influence: his teachings on natural law, on the rights and obligations of the citizen, the relationship between the individual and society are reflected in Pushkin's work. 'He created us, nourished our flame/He placed the cornerstone,/He lit the pure lamp,'[22] Pushkin wrote of him in 1825; and, sending him in January 1835 a copy of his *History of the Pugachev Rebellion*, inscribed it 'To Aleksandr Petrovich Kunitsyn from the Author as a token of deep respect and gratitude'.[23]

Other than as a poet, he had an undistinguished school career. In November 1812 the academic and moral supervisor, Martyn Piletsky, wrote of him:

> His talents are more brilliant than fundamental, his mind more ardent and subtle than deep. His application to study is moderate, as diligence has not yet become a virtue with him. Having read a great number of French books, often inappropriate to his age, he has filled his memory with many successful passages of famous authors; he is also reasonably well-read in Russian literature, and knows many fables and light verses. His knowledge is generally superficial, though he is gradually accustoming himself to a more thorough mode of thought. Pride and vanity, which can make him shy, a sensibility of heart, ardent outbursts of temper, frivolity and an especial volubility combined with wit are his chief qualities. At the same time his good-nature is evident; recognizing his weaknesses, he is willing, with some success, to accept advice [...] In his character generally there is neither constancy nor firmness.[24]

The comments of the different subject teachers echo Piletsky's assessment: 'His reasonable achievement is due more to talent than to diligence'; 'very lazy, inattentive and badly-behaved in the class'; 'empty-headed, frivolous, and inclined to temper'.[25] In the list of pupils, ordered according to their deportment, which was drawn up at regular intervals, Pushkin's place was invariably towards the bottom: twenty-third in 1812; twenty-fourth, twenty-eighth and twenty-sixth in the three following years. His best subjects at school were Russian literature, French literature and fencing. In the final examinations, taken in May 1817, he was judged 'excellent' in those three subjects; 'very good' in Latin literature and state economics and finances; and 'good' in scripture and Biblical studies, in logic and moral philosophy, in natural, private and public law, and in Russian civil and criminal law. He had also studied, his graduation certificate noted, history, geography, statistics, mathematics and the German language.

Of the lycéens he was closest to Pushchin, Delvig, Küchelbecker, and Yakovlev. Pushchin was upright, honest, honourable; a hard-working, intelligent student; liked by all, yet, perhaps, a little imperceptive. His nickname was 'tall Jeannot'; Pushkin was known as 'the Frenchman', for his proficiency in the language and encyclopaedic knowledge of the country's literature.* They are linked in a verse of one of the songs the lycéens composed about each other:

> Tall *Jeannot*
> Without knowing how
> Makes a million bons mots,
> While our *Frenchman*
> Lauds his own taste
> With a string of four-letter words.[26]

Anton Delvig was plump, clumsy and phenomenally lazy. He was a very poor student, continually rebuked for his behaviour: 'He is rude in his manner, insolent in his speech, and so disobedient and obstinate as to ignore all admonitions and even to laugh when he is reprimanded.'[27] His only interest was Russian literature; he knew a mass of verse by heart. As with Pushkin, his talent for poetry blossomed at the Lycée. He was the first to appear in print, when a poem on the capture of Paris appeared in the *Herald of Europe* in June 1814. In one Lycée poem – one of the best he ever wrote – dedicated to Pushkin, he prophesies literary immortality for his friend:

> Pushkin! Even in the forests he cannot hide himself,
> His lyre will betray him with loud singing,
> And from the mortals Apollo will carry away
> The immortal to rejoicing Olympus.†[28]

---

* Possibly also because of his use of coarse, smutty language and his obsession with sex, France being commonly associated with sexual immorality.
† 'A boy of sixteen, prophesying in exact detail literary immortality to a boy of fifteen, and doing it in a poem that is itself immortal – this is a combination of intuitive genius and actual destiny to which I can find no parallel in the history of world poetry' (Nabokov, III, 23).

The third of the Lycée's poets was Wilhelm Küchelbecker, in some ways the strangest of all the pupils. Tall and very thin, he had had an attack of St Vitus's Dance (Sydenham's chorea) in childhood, which had left him with a facial tic and deaf in one ear. Engelhardt wrote of him: 'He has read all the books in the world about all the subjects in the world; has much talent, much diligence, much good will, much heart and much feeling, but, alas, with all this he has no taste, tact, grace, moderation or clear aim. However, he is an honest, innocent soul, and the obstinacy he sometimes displays is only the result of a Quixotic honour and virtue with a considerable admixture of vanity.'[29] No other pupil was referred to so often in the lycéens' songs, or had so many epigrams written about him. In general Küchelbecker bore the attacks stoically, but when Malinovsky threw a plate of soup over his head at dinner he had to be taken to the sickbay with a fever, escaped, and tried to drown himself in the lake. A cartoon in one of the magazines produced by the lycéens shows a boat-load of teachers fishing for him with a boat-hook. His passionate, impractical idealism manifested itself even in his views on literature, in which he preached the virtues of the eighteenth-century ode, of archaic language, and of the hexameter.

'Coarse, passionate, but appreciative, zealous, clean and very diligent': so reads a report on Mikhail Yakovlev.[30] A talented musician, who sang to the guitar, he set a number of Delvig's and Pushkin's works to music, both at the Lycée and later. At the Lycée, however, where his nickname was 'the clown', he was best known for his imitations. He had a huge repertoire of two hundred roles. They include, besides all the teachers and most of the pupils, Italian bears (no. 93), their attendants (no. 94), a samovar (no. 98), Russian bear attendants (no. 109), Alexander I (no. 129), a ship (no. 170) and a mad sergeant of hussars (no. 179).[31] Later, when Pushkin was living in Moscow, he asked a friend from St Petersburg what the subject of Yakovlev's latest imitation was. 'The St Petersburg flood' was the reply. 'And how's that?' 'Very lifelike.'[32]

The first three months of the Lycée's existence passed quietly; Alexander I's birthday was celebrated on 12 December; Volkhovsky was adjudged the best student of the term: his name, and that of Gorchakov (first in deportment), were inscribed in gold letters on a board which was put up in the school hall. Razumovsky ordered it to be taken down and

informed Malinovsky that innovations of this kind were not to be introduced without his permission. The last week of the year was a holiday.
By the beginning of 1812 war with France seemed imminent. In February
and March the lycéens turned out to cheer the guards and army regiments passing through Tsarskoe Selo on their way south to join the
Russian First Army in Vilna. Commander-in-chief of this army, and
Minister of War, was Mikhail Barclay de Tolly, who was distantly related
to Küchelbecker, and had been instrumental in securing a place for him
at the Lycée.

In May Pushkin spent five days in the sickbay with a feverish cold;
he was thirteen on the twenty-sixth of that month; on 9 June the Lycée
was visited by the Metropolitan of Moldavia, Gabriel Banulescu-Bodoni;
and on 12 June Napoleon's army of half a million men crossed the
Neman. The news was received in Tsarskoe Selo five days later. From
that time on the lycéens followed, with growing anxiety and dismay,
the progress of the invasion in the Russian and foreign newspapers in
the reading-room, and in the bulletins which Nikolay Koshansky, who
taught Latin and Russian literature, made it his business to compose and
to read on Sundays in the school hall. Delvig earned instant popularity by
his vivid account of the events he had witnessed as a nine-year-old
during the campaign of 1807: a complete fantasy which, nevertheless,
deceived the lycéens and even Malinovsky.

As the Grande Armée advanced, Barclay retreated before it. Napoleon was in Vilna on 16 June, Vitebsk on 16 July. After fierce fighting,
Smolensk fell on 6 August, destroyed by fire. 'The spectacle Smolensk
offered the French was like the spectacle an eruption of Mount Vesuvius
offered the inhabitants of Naples,' wrote Napoleon.[33] Having given battle
at Lubino, the Russian army then retreated again, towards Moscow,
whose inhabitants had already begun to leave the city. Nadezhda Pushkina, taking her children and mother, Mariya Gannibal, left for Nizhny
Novgorod.

The commander of a retreating, apparently beaten army, Barclay
had lost Alexander's confidence and become widely unpopular. He had
often urged on the emperor the necessity for a single commander-in-
chief of all the Russian armies. Alexander belatedly took his advice and
appointed Kutuzov. Barclay remained as commander of the First Army,
but had to give up his post as Minister of War. Küchelbecker, in dismay

at the taunts, even accusations of treason, that were being levelled at his relative, turned to his mother for consolation. He was not wholly comforted by the reassurances offered in her letters, and in October she had to dissuade the fourteen-year-old from joining the army as a volunteer in order to redeem the family honour. She mentioned the immorality of the young men in the volunteer army, protested against 'the slaughter of children', and pointed out that it would interrupt his education. Küchelbecker abandoned the idea.[34]

Even under Kutuzov the Russian army continued to retreat. Abandoning a favourable position at Tsarevo-Zaimishche, he moved east to Gzhatsk and, fighting off the French under Murat with his rearguard, arrived near the village of Borodino on the Kolocha river, seventy-two miles from Moscow, on 22 August. Here he drew up his armies and waited for the French. On the twenty-fourth the French captured the Shevardino redoubt; on the twenty-sixth, after a day's lull, the battle of Borodino took place, lasting from six in the morning until dusk. Napoleon's withdrawal across the Kolocha at the end of the day convinced Kutuzov that, despite the enormous Russian losses, the French had been beaten. He sent a short dispatch claiming victory to Alexander, and retreated to Mozhaisk. Meanwhile a letter from Napoleon was on its way to the Empress Marie-Louise in Paris: 'I write to you from the battlefield of Borodino. Yesterday I beat the Russians [...] The battle was a hot one: victory was ours at two in the afternoon. I took several thousand prisoners and sixty cannons. Their losses can be estimated at 30,000 men. I lost many killed and wounded [...] My health is good, the weather a little fresh'.[35]

Five days later the lycéens read Kutuzov's dispatch from Borodino in the *Northern Post*. As they were cheering the news, the victorious Russian army was passing through Moscow and retreating to the southeast, towards Ryazan. Alexander learnt of this on 7 September. Rumour of the retreat quickly spread through St Petersburg, causing an abrupt change of mood. Napoleon now stood between the capital and the main Russian army. Only Wittgenstein's weak First Corps protected the city; if Napoleon turned north, an evacuation would be necessary. Government archives and the pictures in the Hermitage were packed up; plans were made for removing the statues of Peter the Great and Suvorov; many of the books of the imperial public library were crated and sent up the

Neva.* And Razumovsky wrote to Malinovsky, telling him that the Lycée, like the court, would be evacuated to Åbo (Turku) in Finland, and asking him to supply a list of necessities for the move. When Malinovsky did so, the minister objected that tin plates and cups for travelling were not essential and that trunks for the pupils' clothes could be replaced by wooden crates. He added that the items should be bought only on the condition that a refund would be made, should they not be required.

Napoleon entered Moscow on 2 September. Fires broke out that night and the night after, apparently lit on the orders of the Governor-General of Moscow, Count Fedor Rostopchin. The city burned for four days. Pushkin's uncle lost his house, his library and all his possessions, and – one of the last to leave – arrived in Nizhny Novgorod with no money and only the clothes he stood up in. The Grande Armée left Moscow on 7 October, and after a bloody battle at Maloyaroslavets, which both sides again claimed as a victory, was forced back on its old line of march, losing stragglers to cold, hunger, illness and Davydov's partisans each day. News of Maloyaroslavets and of General Wintzinger-ode's entry into Moscow reached the Lycée simultaneously. The fear of evacuation was past, and with the French on the retreat normal life could be resumed. Pushkin called Gorchakov a 'promiscuous Polish madam'; insulted Myasoedov with some unrepeatable verses about the Fourth Department, in which the latter's father worked (since the Fourth Department of the Imperial Chancery administered the charitable foundations and girls' schools of the dowager empress, a guess can be made at the nature of the insult); and pushed Pushchin and Myasoedov, saying that if they complained they would get the blame, because he always managed to wriggle out of it.[36]

On 4 January 1813 the *Northern Post* reported the reading in St Petersburg's Kazan Cathedral of the imperial manifesto announcing the end of the Fatherland War: the last of Napoleon's troops had recrossed the Neman. Napoleon, however, was not yet beaten. Fighting continued throughout that year, with Austria, Prussia and Russia in alliance. Alexander was determined to avenge the fall of Moscow with

---

* The brig carrying them wintered on the Svir River, between Lakes Ladoga and Onega: on its return most of the books were found to be spoilt by water.

the surrender of Paris, but it was not until 31 March 1814 (NS) that he entered the city and was received by Talleyrand. The news reached St Petersburg three weeks later, and Koshansky immediately gave his pupils 'The Capitulation of Paris' as a theme for prose and poetic composition.

If Pushkin produced a composition on this occasion, it has not survived. However, when in November 1815 Alexander returned from the peace negotiations in Paris that followed Waterloo, Pushkin was asked by I.I. Martynov, the director of the department of education, to compose a piece commemorating the occasion. He completed the poem by 28 November, and sent it to Martynov, writing, 'If the feelings of love and gratitude towards our great monarch, which I have described, are not too unworthy of my exalted subject, how happy I would be, if his excellency Count Aleksey Kirilovich [Razumovsky] were to deign to put before his majesty this feeble composition of an inexperienced poet!'[37] The poem, written in the high, solemn style that befits the subject, begins with an account of the French invasion and ensuing battles – in which, Pushkin laments, he was unable to participate, 'grasping a sword in my childish hand' – before describing the liberation of Europe and celebrating Alexander's return to Russia. It ends with a vision of the idyllic future, when

> a golden age of tranquillity will come,
> Rust will cover the helms, and the tempered arrows,
> Hidden in quivers, will forget their flight,
> The happy villager, untroubled by stormy disaster,
> Will drag across the field a plough sharpened by peace;
> Flying vessels, winged by trade,
> Will cut the free ocean with their keels;

and, occasionally, before 'the young sons of the martial Slavs', an old man will trace plans of battle in the dust with his crutch, and

> With simple, free words of truth will bring to life
> In his tales the glory of past years
> And will, in tears, bless the good tsar.[38]

The Pushkins had decided not to return to Moscow, four-fifths of which had been destroyed by the fire of 1812, but to move to St Petersburg.

Nadezhda, with her surviving children, Olga and Lev (Mikhail, born in October 1811, had died the following year), arrived in the capital in the spring of 1814, and rented lodgings on the Fontanka, by the Kalinkin Bridge, in the house of Vice-Admiral Klokachev. When she and the children drove out to visit Pushkin at the beginning of April, it was the first time for more than two years that he had seen his mother, and nearly three years since he had last seen his brother and sister. Lev became a boarder at the Lycée preparatory school, and from now on Nadezhda, usually accompanied by Olga, came to Tsarskoe Selo almost every Sunday. In the autumn the family circle was completed by the arrival of Sergey, after a leisurely journey from Warsaw. His first visit to his sons was on 11 October. In the final school year Engelhardt relaxed the regulations and allowed lycéens whose families lived nearby to visit them at Christmas 1816 and at Easter 1817. Pushkin spent both holidays with his family.

'I began to write from the age of thirteen,' Pushkin once wrote.[39] The first known Lycée poem was written in the summer of 1813. From then on the school years were, in Goethe's words, a time *'Da sich ein Quell gedrängter Lieder/Ununterbrochen neu gebar'.** Impromptu verse sprang into being almost without conscious thought: Pushchin, recuperating in the sickbay, woke to find a quatrain scrawled on the board above his head:

> Here lies a sick student –
> His fate is inexorable!
> Away with the medicine:
> Love's disease is incurable![40]

Semen Esakov, walking one winter's day in the park with Pushkin, was suddenly addressed:

> We're left with the question
> On the frozen waters' bank:
> 'Will red-nosed Mademoiselle Schräder
> Bring the sweet Velho girls here?'[41]

* 'When a fountain of pent-up songs/Would ceaselessly replenish itself each day', *Faust*, 154–5.

Sophie Velho

Like other lycéens, the two were ardent admirers of Sophie and Josephine, the banker Joseph Velho's two beautiful daughters, whom they often met at the house of Velho's brother-in-law, Ludwig-Wilhelm Tepper de Ferguson, the Lycée's music teacher. Sophie was unattainable, however: she was Alexander I's mistress, and would meet him in the little, castle-like Babolovsky Palace, hidden in the depths of the park.

> Beauty! Though ecstasy be enjoyed
> In your arms by the Russian demi-god,
> What comparison to your lot?
> The whole world at his feet – here he at yours.[42]

Not wishing to be outdone by Delvig, Pushkin sent one of his poems – 'To My Friend the Poet', addressed to Küchelbecker – anonymously to the *Herald of Europe* in March 1814. The next number of the journal contained a note from the editor, V.V. Izmailov, asking for the author's name, but promising not to reveal it. Pushkin complied with the request, and the poem, his first published piece, appeared in the journal in July over the signature Aleksandr N.k.sh.p.: 'Pushkin' written backwards with the vowels omitted. While at the Lycée he was to publish four other poems in the *Herald of Europe*, five in the *Northern Observer*, one in the *Son of the Fatherland*, and eighteen in a new journal, the *Russian Musaeum, or Journal of European News*. The only poem published during the Lycée years without a pseudonym was 'Recollections in Tsarskoe Selo', which appeared in the *Russian Musaeum* in April 1815 accompanied by an editorial note: 'For the conveyance of this gift we sincerely thank the relatives of this young poet, whose talent promises so much.'[43]

Pushkin wrote this poem at the end of 1814, on a theme given to him by the classics teacher, Aleksandr Galich, for recital at the examination at the end of the junior course. Listing the memorials to Catherine's victories in the Tsarskoe Selo park, he apostrophizes the glories of her age, hymned by Derzhavin, before describing the 1812 campaign and capitulation of Paris and paying a graceful tribute to Alexander the peace-maker, 'worthy grandson of Catherine'. In the final stanza he turns to Zhukovsky, whose famous patriotic poem, 'A Bard in the Camp of Russian Warriors', had been written immediately after the battle of Borodino, and calls upon him to follow this work with a paean to the recent victory:

> Strike the gold harp!
> So that again the harmonious voice may honour the Hero,
> And the vibrant strings suffuse our hearts with fire,
> And the young Warrior be impassioned and thrilled
> By the verse of the martial Bard.[44]

The examinations took place on Monday 4 and Friday 8 January 1815, before an audience of high state officials and relatives and friends of the lycéens. The seventy-one-year-old Derzhavin, the greatest poet of the preceding age, was invited to the second examination.

When we learnt that Derzhavin would be coming – Pushkin wrote – we all were excited. Delvig went out to the stairs to wait for him and to kiss his hand, the hand that had written 'The Waterfall'. Derzhavin arrived. He came into the vestibule and Delvig heard him asking the porter: 'Where, fellow, is the privy here?'. This prosaic inquiry disenchanted Delvig, who changed his intention and returned to the hall. Delvig told me of this with surprising simplicity and gaiety. Derzhavin was very old. He was wearing a uniform coat and velveteen boots. Our examination greatly fatigued him. He sat, resting his head on his hand. His expression was senseless; his eyes were dull; his lip hung; his portrait (in which he is pictured in a nightcap and dressing-gown) is very lifelike. He dozed until the Russian literature examination began. Then he came to life, his eyes sparkled; he was completely transformed. Of course, his verses were being read, his verses were being analysed, his verses were being constantly praised. He listened with extraordinary animation. At last I was called out. I read my 'Recollections in Tsarskoe Selo', standing two paces away from Derzhavin. I cannot describe the condition of my spirit: when I reached the line where I mention Derzhavin's name, my adolescent voice broke, and my heart beat with intoxicating rapture . . .

I do not remember how I finished the recitation, do not remember whither I fled. Derzhavin was delighted; he called for me, wanted to embrace me ... There was a search for me, but I could not be found.[45]

'Recollections in Tsarskoe Selo' made, for the first time, Pushkin known as a poet beyond the walls of the Lycée; the promise it gave for the future was immediately recognized. 'Soon,' Derzhavin told the young Sergey Aksakov, 'a second Derzhavin will appear in the world: he is Pushkin, who in the Lycée has already outshone all writers.'[46] Pushkin sent a copy of the poem to his uncle; Vasily passed it on to Zhukovsky, who was soon reading it, with understandable enthusiasm, to his friends. Prince Petr Vyazemsky, a friend of Pushkin's family, wrote to the poet Batyushkov: 'What can you say about Sergey Lvovich's son? It's all a miracle. His "Recollections" have set my and Zhukovsky's head in a whirl. What power, accuracy of expression, what a firm, masterly brush in description. May God give him health and learning and be of profit to him and sadness to us. The rascal will crush us all! Vasily Lvovich, however, is not giving up, and after his nephew's verse, which he always reads in tears, never forgets to read his own, not realizing that in verse compared to the other it is now he who is the nephew.'[47] Vasily, unlike his fellow poets, was not totally convinced of Pushkin's staying-power, remarking to a friend: '*Mon cher*, you know that I love Aleksandr; he is a poet, a poet in his soul; *mais je ne sais pas, il est encore trop jeune, trop libre*, and, really, I don't know when he will settle down, *entre nous soit dit, comme nous autres.*'[48]

Recognition led to a widening of Pushkin's poetic acquaintance. Batyushkov had called on him in February; in September Zhukovsky – after Derzhavin, the best-known poet in Russia – wrote to Vyazemsky: 'I have made another pleasant acquaintanceship! With our young miracle-worker Pushkin. I called on him for a minute in Tsarskoe Selo. A pleasant, lively creature! He was very glad to see me and firmly pressed my hand to his heart. He is the hope of our literature. I fear only lest he, imagining himself mature, should prevent himself from becoming so. We must unite to assist this future giant, who will outgrow us all, to grow up [...] He has written an epistle to me, which he gave into my hands, – splendid! His best work!'[49]

In March 1816 Vasily Lvovich, who was travelling back to Moscow from St Petersburg with Zhukovsky, Vyazemsky and Karamzin, persuaded them to stop off at the Lycée; they stayed for about half an hour: Pushkin spoke to his uncle and Vyazemsky, whom he had known as a child in Moscow, but did not meet Karamzin. Two days later he sent Vyazemsky a witty letter, complaining of his isolated life at the Lycée: 'seclusion is, in fact, a very stupid affair, despite all those philosophers and poets, who pretend that they live in the country and are in love with silence and tranquillity', and breaking into verse to envy Vyazemsky's life in Moscow:

> Blessed is he, who noisy Moscow
> Does not leave for a country hut . . .
> And who not in dream, but in reality
> Can caress his mistress! . . .

Only a year of schooling remains, 'But a whole year of pluses and minuses, laws, taxes, the sublime and the beautiful! . . . a whole year of dozing before the master's desk . . . what horror.'[50]

In April he received a letter from Vasily Lvovich, telling him that Karamzin would be spending the summer in Tsarskoe Selo: 'Love him, honour and obey. The advice of such a man will be to your good and may be of use to our literature. We expect much from you.'[51] Nikolay Karamzin, who at this time had just turned fifty, was Russia's most influential eighteenth-century writer, and the acknowledged leader of the modernist school in literature. Though best-known

Karamzin

as author of the extraordinarily popular sentimental tale *Poor Liza* (1792), his real achievement was to have turned the heavy and cumbersome prose of his predecessors into a flexible, supple instrument, capable of any mode of discourse. He arrived in Tsarskoe Selo on 24 May with his wife and three small children, and settled in one of Cameron's little Chinese houses in the park to complete work on his monumental eight-volume *History of the Russian State*. He remained there throughout the summer, returning to St Petersburg on 20 September. During this time Pushkin visited him frequently, often in the company of another lycéen, Sergey Lomonosov. The acquaintance ripened rapidly: on 2 June

Karamzin informs Vyazemsky that he is being visited by 'the poet Push-kin, the historian Lomonosov', who 'are amusing in their pleasant art-lessness. Pushkin is witty.'[52] And when Prince Yury Neledinsky-Meletsky, an ageing privy councillor and minor poet, turned to Karamzin for help because he found himself unable to compose the verses he had promised for the wedding of the Grand Duchess Anna with Prince William of Orange, Karamzin recommended Pushkin for the task. Pushkin pro-duced the required lines in an hour or two, and they were sung at the wedding supper in Pavlovsk on 6 June. The dowager empress sent him a gold watch and chain.

Pushkin's work – like that of Voltaire, much admired, and much imitated by him at this time – is inclined to licentiousness, but any coarseness is always – even in the Lycée verse – moderated by wit. Once Pushchin, watching from the library window as the congregation dispersed after evening service in the church opposite, noticed two women – one young and pretty, the other older – who were quarrelling with one another. He pointed them out to Pushkin, wondering what the subject of the dispute could be. The next day Pushkin brought him sixteen lines of verse which gave the answer: Antipevna, the elder, is angrily taking Marfushka to task for allowing Vanyusha to take liberties with her, a married woman. 'He's still a child,' Marfushka replies; 'What about old Trofim, who is with you day and night? You're as sinful as I am,'

> In another's cunt you see a straw,
> But don't notice the beam in your own.[53]

'Pushkin was so attracted to women,' wrote a fellow lycéen, 'that, even at the age of fifteen or sixteen, merely touching the hand of the person he was dancing with, at the Lycée balls, caused his eye to blaze, and he snorted and puffed, like an ardent stallion in a young herd.'[54] The first known Lycée poem is 'To Natalya', written in 1813, and dedicated to a young actress in the serf theatre of Count V.V. Tolstoy. He imagines himself an actor, playing opposite her: Philemon making love to Anyuta in Ablesimov's opera, *The Miller, Sorcerer, Cheat and Matchmaker*, or Dr Bartolo endeavouring to seduce Rosina in *The Barber of Seville*. Two summers later he made her the subject of another poem. You are a terrible actress, he writes; were another to perform as badly as you do, she would be hissed off the stage, but we applaud wildly, because you are so beautiful.

> Blessed is he, who can forget his role
> On the stage with this sweet actress,
> Can press her hand, hoping to be
> Still more blessed behind the scenes![55]

When Elena Cantacuzen, the married sister of his fellow-lycéen Prince Gorchakov, visited the Lycée in 1814, he composed 'To a Beauty Who Took Snuff':

> Ah! If, turned into powder,
> And in a snuff-box, in confinement,
> I could be pinched between your tender fingers
> Then with heartfelt delight
> I'd strew myself on the bosom beneath the silk kerchief
> And even . . . perhaps . . . But no! An empty dream.
> In no way can this be.
> Envious, malicious fate!
> Ah, why am I not snuff![56]

There is far more of Pushkin in the witty, humorous light verse of this kind, when he can allow himself the expression of carnal desire, than in his love poems of the Lycée years – such as those dedicated to Ekaterina Bakunina, the sister of a fellow-lycéen. She was four years older than he and obviously attractive, for both Pushchin and the young Malinovsky were his rivals. In a fragment of a Lycée diary he wrote, on Monday 29 November 1815:

> I was happy! . . . No, yesterday I was not happy: in the morning I was tortured by the ordeal of waiting, standing under the window with indescribable emotion, I looked at the snowy path – she was not to be seen! – finally I lost hope, then suddenly and unexpectedly I met her on the stairs, a delicious moment! [. . .] How charming she was! How becoming was the black dress to the charming Bakunina! But I have not seen her for eighteen hours – ah! what a situation, what torture – But I was happy for five minutes.[57]

There is, however, no trace of this artless sincerity in any of the twenty-three poems he devoted to his love between the summer of 1815 and that of 1817, which are, almost without exception, expressions of blighted love. No doubt Pushkin's grief was real; no doubt he experienced all the torments of adolescent love. But the agony is couched in such conventional terms, is often so exaggerated, that the emotion comes to seem as artificial as the means of its expression. The cycle begins with the sadness he experiences at her absence; she returns, only for him to discover he has a successful rival; having lost her love, he can only wish for death. 'The early flower of hope has faded:/Life's flower will wither from the torments!' he laments[58] – an image with which, in *Eugene Onegin*, he would mock Lensky's adolescent despair: 'He sang of life's wilted flower/At not quite eighteen years of age' (II, x).

Far less ethereal were his feelings for Natasha, Princess Varvara Volkonskaya's pretty maid, well-known to the lycéens and much admired by them. One dark evening in 1816, Pushkin, running along one of the palace corridors, came upon someone he thought to be Natasha, and began to 'pester her with rash words and even, so the malicious say, with indiscreet caresses'.[59] Unfortunately the woman was not Natasha, but her mistress, who recognized Pushkin and through her brother complained to the emperor. The following day Alexander came to see Engelhardt about the affair. 'Your pupils not only climb over the fence to steal my ripe apples, and beat gardener Lyamin's watchmen,' he complained, 'but now will not let my wife's ladies-in-waiting pass in the corridor.' Engelhardt assured him that Pushkin was in despair, and had asked the director for permission to write to the princess, 'asking her magnanimously to forgive him for this unintended insult'. 'Let him write – and there will be an end of it. I will be Pushkin's advocate; but tell him that it is for the last time,' said Alexander, adding in a whisper, 'Between ourselves, the old woman is probably enchanted at the young man's mistake.'[60] Pushkin made up for the letter of apology with a malicious French epigram:

> One could easily, miss,
> Take you for a brothel madam,
> Or for an old hag;
> But for a trollop, – oh, my God, no.[61]

Another object of desire was the young Marie Smith, 'very pretty, amiable and witty',[62] who came to stay with her relations the Engelhardts towards the end of 1816. Pushkin was soon addressing his verse to her, not a whit discomposed by the facts that she had very recently lost her husband and was three months' pregnant. At first the tone is light and humorous, no word of love is breathed; but early in 1817 he sent her 'To a Young Widow':

> Lida, my devoted friend,
> Why do I, through my light sleep,
> Exhausted with pleasure,
> Often hear your quiet sigh?

'Will you eternally shed tears,/Eternally your dead husband/Call from the grave?' If so, she will call in vain, 'the furious, jealous husband/Will not arise from eternal darkness.'[63] In a sense the poem is harmless. Pushkin is not serious in imagining himself to be in bed with Mrs Smith, urging her to forget her husband: these are mere poetic conceits, no different, in a way, from those of an earlier poem, when he calls her 'the confidante of Venus/[. . .] whose throne Cupid/And the playful children of Cytheraea/Have decorated with flowers.'[64] But it is understandable that literary considerations of this kind did not present themselves to Mrs Smith's mind when she received the poem. She saw only the literal, highly indecent meaning, was insulted by it, and took the poem to Engelhardt, who was obliged to give Pushkin another severe dressing-down.

In the spring of 1817 the Karamzins returned to Tsarskoe Selo. Karamzin's second wife, the severely beautiful Ekaterina Andreevna, was then thirty-six. Of her Filipp Wiegel, whom Pushkin later knew well, wrote in his memoirs, 'What can I say of her? If the pagan Phidias could have been inspired by a Christian ideal, and have wished to sculpt a Madonna, he would of course have given her the features of Karamzina in her youth.'[65] Pushkin, always susceptible to beauty, and who was, in addition, beginning to be attracted chiefly to older women, sent her a love-letter. Ekaterina, unaffected by his devotion, was amused, and showed it to her husband; they laughed heartily over it. Nevertheless, Karamzin felt it necessary to read Pushkin a stern lecture, affecting the latter so much that he burst into tears. In later years Karamzin took pleasure in showing friends the spot in his study which had been sprinkled with Pushkin's sobs.

As the course of the first intake at the Lycée neared its end, the thoughts of its members turned towards the future, and Pushkin startled his father with a letter requesting permission to join the Life Guards Hussars. It was an odd request, for he had not attended any of the classes on military subjects which had been held for those intending to enter the army. Sergey Lvovich wrote back to say that while he could not afford to support Pushkin in a cavalry regiment, he would have no objection were his son to join an infantry guards regiment. But it was the glamour of the hussars which had attracted Pushkin:

> I'll put on narrow breeches,
> Curl the proud moustache in rings,
> A pair of epaulettes will gleam,
> And I – a child of the severe Muses –
> Will be among the martial cornets![66]

The regiment's barracks were just outside the park, facing the south bank of the Great Lake, in Sofiya, the new settlement built by Catherine II. The lycéens were frequent visitors, Pushkin becoming acquainted 'with a number of hussars, living then in Tsarskoe Selo (such as Kaverin, Molostvov, Solomirsky, Saburov and others*). Together with these he loved, in secret from the school authorities, to make an occasional sacrifice to Bacchus and to Venus,' a fellow-lycéen later wrote, with metonymical delicacy.[67] Kaverin was a well-known rake, and in his company Pushkin would certainly have made considerable sacrifices to both gods. But in the end his military career went no further, and he resigned himself to entering the civil service. Looking back on the episode in the winter of 1824, he wrote:

> Saburov, you poured scorn
> On my hussar dreams,
> When I roistered with Kaverin,
> Abused Russia with Molostvov,

---

* Their society is adequately characterized by Molostvov's *mot*, 'The best woman is a boy, and the best wine vodka' (Modzalevsky (1999), 480).

> Read with my Chedaev,
> When, casting aside all cares,
> I spent a whole year among them,
> But Zubov did not tempt me
> With his swarthy arse.[68]

The final examinations at the Lycée lasted a fortnight, from 15 to 31 May 1817. The graduation ceremony took place on 9 June in the presence of the emperor. Engelhardt gave a short speech; Kunitsyn a factual report on the achievements of the Lycée; Prince Aleksandr Golitsyn, who had succeeded Razumovsky as Minister of Education in 1816, introduced the pupils to Alexander, who presented their medals and graduation certificates, gave a 'short, fatherly exhortation', and thanked the director and the staff for their work.[69] The ceremony ended with the lycéens singing a farewell hymn, composed by Delvig and put to music by Tepper de Ferguson. Pushkin had been asked by Engelhardt to write a poem for the occasion, but had evaded the task. In the evening at the director's house Lomonosov, Gorchakov, Korsakov, Yakovlev, Malinovsky and Engelhardt's children performed a French play written by Marie Smith. Korsakov and Yakovlev read poems. Finally, Engelhardt gave each of his pupils a cast-iron ring on which was engraved a phrase of Delvig's hymn.

On 11 June Pushkin, in the company of six other lycéens, left Tsarskoe Selo for St Petersburg. He had been appointed to the Ministry of Foreign Affairs as a collegial secretary – the tenth rank – with a salary of 700 roubles a year.

ST PETERSBURG

1817–20

I: Literature and Politics

> A weak and cunning ruler,
> A balding fop, an enemy of labour,
> Fortuitously favoured by Fame,
> Reigned over us then.
>
> *Eugene Onegin*, X, i

WHEN PUSHKIN ARRIVED in St Petersburg, he had just turned eighteen. This 'ugly descendant of negroes', as he called himself, was small in stature – just under five foot six.[1] He had pale blue eyes, curly black hair, usually dishevelled, and extraordinarily long, claw-like fingernails – often dirty – of which he was inordinately proud. When the actress Aleksandra Kolosova – just sixteen when Pushkin met her in 1818 – tried to hold his hands so that her mother could punish him for some prank by 'clipping his claws', 'he screamed loud enough to bring the house down, feigned sobs, groans, complained that we were insulting him, and reduced us to tears of laughter'.[2] He promenaded the streets in a long black frock-coat 'in the American style' and silk top-hat 'à la Bolivar': funnel-shaped, with a wide, upturned brim, and carrying a heavy cane.*[3] In a pencil sketch

---

* A reference to contemporary portraits of Simon Bolivar (1783–1830), the hero of South American independence.

he made as a guide to the illustrator of the first chapter of *Eugene Onegin*, he depicts himself and Eugene leaning on the granite parapet of the Neva Embankment, gazing across at the Peter-Paul fortress. He is seen from behind: a shortish man in the Bolivar top-hat, with thick curly hair down to his shoulders, wearing tapering pantaloons and a frock-coat nipped at the waist, with two buttons in the small of the back and long, bell-shaped skirts. A note underneath instructs the illustrator that Pushkin should be made 'good-looking'.*⁴ Though often morose and silent in large gatherings, or among those he did not know well, in the company of his friends and intimates he displayed an extraordinary, superabundant liveliness and gaiety, combined with a continual restlessness. 'He could never sit still for a minute,' Kolosova wrote; 'he would wriggle, jump up, sit somewhere else, rummage in my mother's work-basket, tangle the balls of yarn in my embroidery, scatter my mother's patience cards . . .'⁵

When Pushkin's mother had moved to the capital in 1814 she had taken a seven-room apartment on the upper floor of a large house on the right, or north embankment of the Fontanka canal, near the Kalinkin Bridge. Now Pushkin moved into the apartment, joining his parents and the nineteen-year-old Olga. Lev had left the Lycée and moved to a St Petersburg boarding-school. The lodgings were in the Kolomna quarter, an unfashionable district, 'neither metropolitan nor provincial [. . .] here all is tranquillity and retirement, all the sediment of the capital's traffic has settled here'.⁶ Pushkin came to feel some affection for the area, lodging the hero of *The Bronze Horseman* here, and making it the setting for his comic narrative poem *The Little House in Kolomna*. The apartment below the Pushkins was occupied by the Korffs, whose

---

* The artist, Aleksandr Notbek, ignored Pushkin's instructions; his ill-executed engraving, printed in the *Neva Almanac* in January 1829, shows the poet facing the spectator with arms crossed on his chest. Pushkin greeted the travesty with an amusing, if scatological epigram:

> Here, having crossed Kokushkin Bridge,
> Supporting his arse on the granite,
> Aleksandr Sergeich Pushkin himself
> Stands with Monsieur Onegin.
> Scorning to glance
> At the citadel of fateful power,
> He has proudly turned his posterior to the fortress:
> Don't spit in the well, dear chap. (III, 165)

son, Modest, had been a fellow lycéen. According to him the Pushkins' 'lodging was always topsy turvy; valuable antique furniture in one room, in another nothing but empty walls or a rush-bottomed chair; numerous, but ragged and drunken servants, fabulously unclean; decrepit coaches with emaciated nags, and a continual shortage of everything, from money to glasses. Whenever two or three extra people dined with them they always sent down to us, as neighbours, for cutlery and china.'[7] Ashamed of the shabbiness of the apartment, Pushkin concealed his address from most of his acquaintance. Those given the entrée might find him in dishabille, as did Vasily Ertel, who was taken there by Delvig in February 1819. 'We went up the stairs, the servant opened the door, and we entered the room. By the door stood a bed on which lay a young man in a striped Bokhara dressing-gown with a skull-cap on his head. Near the bed, on a table, lay papers and books. The room united the characteristics of the abode of a fashionable young man with the poetic disorder of a scholar.'[8]

On 13 June 1817, two days after arriving in St Petersburg, Pushkin, together with the other lycéens who had joined the Foreign Ministry, was presented to the Foreign Minister, Count Nesselrode. Two days later, at the ministry on the English Embankment, he took and signed an oath of allegiance, and was given the decrees of Peter the Great and Catherine II relating to the foreign service to read. From the beginning the sole attraction of the ministry was that it provided him with a rank in the civil service and a minimal income. There are no references to his work there in his correspondence; his attendance soon became desultory and his diligence non-existent: 'I know nothing about [Pushkin],' Engelhardt wrote in January 1818, 'other than that he does nothing at the Ministry.'[9] On 3 July he applied for leave until 15 September, to travel with his family to his mother's estate at Mikhailovskoe. The journey of some 288 miles took three days, passing through Tsarskoe Selo, Luga, Porkhov, Bezhanitsa and Novorzhev, and producing an epigram:

> There is in Russia the town of Luga
> In the Petersburg region;
> One could not imagine
> A worse dump than this,

If there didn't exist
My Novorzhev.[10]

In 1742 the Empress Elizabeth had made a large grant of land in the Pskov province to Abram Gannibal. This estate, some five thousand desyatins in extent, included forty-one villages, populated by – according to the census of 1744 – 806 serfs.* Through it ran a small river, the Sorot, fed by a chain of lakes. A few miles to the south, on the Sinichi hills, lay the small settlement of Svyatye Gory, crowned by the white walls and silver spire of the Svyatogorsky monastery. Although Abram, first occupied with his military duties and later preferring to retire to his estate at Suida, spent little time here, he arranged for the construction of a manor house at Petrovskoe, on the north-east bank of Lake Kuchane. On his death in 1781 the lands in the Pskov province were divided between his three younger sons, Petr, Osip and Isaak. Petr took Petrovskoe, Osip Mikhailovskoe and Isaak Voskresenskoe.

At Petrovskoe Petr knocked down the old house and built another, much larger, further from the lake, and laid out a small park, with an alley of lime trees leading from the lawn behind the house to the lake shore. In 1817 he was seventy-five, and was living here by himself, having seen little or nothing of his wife and children since he had packed them off, with a meagre allowance, to his estate near St Petersburg in the 1780s.

Voskresenskoe, Isaak's patrimony, was some eight miles to the east of Petrovskoe, on the road to Novorzhev. Here, on a hill overlooking Lake Belogul – twice the size of Lake Kuchane – he built an unassuming, but capacious one-storey manor to house his large family: eight sons and seven daughters. On the slope of the hill descending to the lake was a large park with alleys, ponds and summer-houses. On the other side of the house a drive flanked with birch trees, concealing numerous outbuildings and servants' quarters, led to the road. Isaak had died in 1804, heavily in debt, and having had to mortgage and then sell the greater part of his estate. His wife, Anna Andreevna, remained at the manor house, visited each summer by some of her numerous brood, together with their wives, husbands and children.

* A desyatin is approximately 2.7 acres: only adult male serfs were numbered in the census.

Mikhailovskoe lay between the two other estates, just over two miles from Petrovskoe, and nearly six from Voskresenskoe. The manor house was built on the high wooded south bank of the Sorot, between Lake Kuchane and the much smaller Lake Malenets. It was a small – fifty-six feet by forty-five – single-storey wooden house on a stone foundation with an open porch before the front door. On either side, shaded by limes and maples, stood smaller buildings in the same style, on the left the bath-house, on the right the kitchen and servants' quarters. Two long, low buildings at right angles to the kitchen contained the estate office and lodgings for the bailiff and his family with a coach-house beyond; behind these lay the orchard. In front of the house was a circular lawn, surrounded by a path bordered with lilac and jasmine, the whole being enclosed by a fence with wicket gates. Behind the bath-house a steep path led to the Sorot. In front of the house, beyond the fence, lay the well-wooded park, divided in two by a wide linden alley down which ran the entrance drive. In the middle of the portion to the left stood a small summer-house from which radiated alleys of limes, birches and maples. Flower-beds, little artificial mounds topped with benches and ponds, small and large, were scattered here and there, and the boundary was marked by an avenue of birches.

By contemporary standards Mikhailovskoe was a small to modest estate: according to the census of 1816, some five thousand acres (1,863 desyatins) with 164 male serfs on the land and 23 attached to the household. In 1806, on Osip's death, the estate had passed to Nadezhda. But the Pushkins' financial circumstances were hardly improved, since for several years thereafter the income of the estate had to be used to extinguish the large debts Osip had accumulated. Since Nadezhda had little taste for provincial life, her mother, Mariya Gannibal, having sold Zakharovo, had moved to Mikhailovskoe, taking with her the family's old nurse, Arina Rodionovna.

These two and a crowd of servants now greeted the Pushkins on their arrival: it was the first time that Pushkin had seen his grandmother since parting from her six years before to go to the Lycée. The district, very different from the countryside around Moscow or St Petersburg, was completely new to him. He wandered round the park, with its 'pond in the shadow of thick willows,/Playground for ducklings',[11] and stood on the heights above the Sorot, looking over

the azure levels of two lakes,
Where sometimes gleams the fisherman's white sail,
Behind them a ridge of hills and striped cornfields,
Scattered huts in the distance,
On the moist banks wandering herds,
Smoking drying-barns and winged windmills . . .[12]

'I remember how happy I was with village life, Russian baths, strawberries and so on, but all this did not please me for long. I loved and still love noise and crowds.'[13] The district certainly lacked metropolitan bustle; Voskresenskoe, inhabited by his great-aunt and a swarm of cousins, was a poor substitute. Dancing there one evening, Pushkin fell into a quarrel with his cousin Semen when the latter cut him out in a figure of the cotillion with a Miss Loshakova, 'with whom, despite her ugliness and false teeth, Aleksandr Sergeevich had fallen head over heels in love'.[14]

The most congenial local society was to be found at Trigorskoe, an estate some two miles from Mikhailovskoe, reached by a path along the bank of the Sorot. Here lived Praskovya Osipova, an attractive thirty-six year-old, together with the five children from her first marriage to Nikolay Vulf: the eighteen-year-old Annette, Aleksey, Mikhail, Evpraksiya (known as Zizi) and Valerian, respectively twelve, nine, eight and five; and Aleksandra, the nine-year-old daughter of her second husband, Ivan Osipov. The Osipovs were not provincial philistines, but a cultured family. Praskovya's father, Aleksandr Vyndomsky, had collected a large library, had corresponded with Novikov, imprisoned for his writings by Catherine II, and had subscribed to Moscow and St Petersburg literary journals, one of which had even printed his poem 'The Prayer of a Repentant Sinner'. Pushkin's acquaintance with the family was the most significant event of the visit: on 17 August, just before leaving, he wrote, in the only lyric produced during his stay,

Farewell, Trigorskoe, where joy
So often was encountered!
Did I discover your sweetness
Only in order to leave you for ever?
From you I take memories,
To you I leave my heart.[15]

When Vasily Pushkin had brought his nephew to St Petersburg in 1811, he was engaged in a polemic with Admiral Shishkov, leader of the conservative, or Archaist group of Russian writers. Opposed to this were the more liberal modernists, whose centre was Karamzin. In March 1811 Shishkov had founded the *Symposium of Amateurs of the Russian Word*, a society whose purpose was to defend 'classical' forms of Russian against foreign infection. The writers of both factions directed at each other a continual cross-fire of articles and reviews, enlivened by satirical jibes. If the dramatist Prince Shakhovskoy poked fun at Karamzin's sentimentalism in the one-act comedy *A New Sterne* (1805), in Vasily's *A Dangerous Neighbour* admirers of the prince's dramatic talents were discovered among the strumpets in a brothel.

Zhukovsky

On 23 September 1815 several of the younger group – Dmitry Bludov, Dmitry Dashkov, Stepan Zhikharev, Filipp Wiegel, Aleksandr Turgenev and Zhukovsky – attended the première of Shakhovskoy's new comedy, *The Lipetsk Waters; or, A Lesson for Coquettes* at the Bolshoy Theatre. Zhukovsky's companions were soon embarrassed to discover that Shakhovskoy 'in the poet Fialkin, a miserable swain, whom all scorned, and who bent himself double before all, intended to represent the noble modesty of Zhukovsky; [. . .] One can imagine the situation of poor Zhukovsky, on whom numerous immodest glances were turned! One can imagine the astonishment and indignation of his friends, seated around him! A gauntlet had been thrown down; Bludov and Dashkov, still ebullient with youth, hastened to pick it up.'[16] Bludov's reply was a wretchedly unfunny lampoon directed at Shakhovskoy, *A Vision in some Tavern, published by the Society of Learned People.** This purported to have taken place in the little provincial town of Arzamas. The idea that a learned society, dedicated to literature, could exist in such a sleepy backwater famous only for its geese amused Bludov's friends, and led in October to the foundation of the *Arzamas Society of Unknown People*.

---

* Modelled on 'The Vision of Charles Palissot' (1760), an attack by Abbé André Morellet on Palissot's play *Les Philosophes*, itself a satire directed at the *Encyclopédistes*.

From the beginning *Arzamas* was an elaborate joke, a parody of the solemn proceedings of the *Symposium of Amateurs of the Russian Word*. These took place in the huge hall of Derzhavin's house on the Fontanka, when 'the members sat at tables in the centre, around them were arm-chairs for the most honoured guests, and round the walls in three tiers was well-arranged seating for other visitors, admitted by ticket. To add greater lustre to these gatherings, the fair sex appeared in ball-gowns, ladies-in-waiting wore their royal miniatures,* grandees and generals their ribbons and stars, and all their full-dress uniform.'[17] The lively facetiousness of *Arzamas* could hardly have been more different. The meetings took place on Thursday evenings, usually at the home of one of the two married members – Bludov's on the Nevsky Prospect or Sergey Uvarov's in Malaya Morskaya Street. Each member had been given a name taken from one of Zhukovsky's ballads. The president for the evening wore a Jacobin red cap; the proceedings were conducted in a parodic imitation of the high style employed at the *Symposium* and invariably ended with the consumption of an Arzamas goose. Vyazemsky and Batyushkov soon joined; and when Vasily Pushkin – at fifty-one, the oldest of the group – was elected in March 1816, advantage was taken of his good-natured credulity to stage a parody of Masonic initiation rites, an immensely long mummery which concluded with Vasily shooting an arrow into the heart of a dummy representing the bad taste of the Shishkovites.† This set the tone for his position in *Arzamas*: he became the internal butt for its members' jokes, as members of the *Symposium* were the external. Having dallied at a cake-shop, he arrived late at the next meeting, to be greeted with a flood of facetious speeches and resolutions; but, forgiven, he was made the society's elder with various privileges, including that of having 'at *Arzamas* suppers a special goose roasted for him alone, which, at his choice, he may either consume entirely, or, having consumed a portion, may take the rest home'.[18]

---

* In the reign of Peter the Great the custom had been established of presenting to ladies attached to the court a miniature portrait of the monarch which was worn on state occasions.
† Other members included Dmitry Kavelin, Aleksandr Voeikov, Aleksandr Pleshcheev, Petr Poletika, Dmitry Severin; and, later, Nikita Muravev, General Mikhail Orlov and Nikolay Turgenev.

While still at the Lycée Pushkin had taken an eager interest in the literary debate, naturally ranging himself on the side of his friends against Shishkov and the *Symposium*. He learnt of the foundation of *Arzamas*, and was soon addressing Vyazemsky as 'dear Arzamasite',[19] and calling his uncle 'the Nestor of *Arzamas*'.[20] He already felt himself spiritually to be a member: in 'To Zhukovsky' (1816), calling on the 'singers, educated/In the happy heresy of Taste and Learning', to 'strike down the brazen friends of Ignorance' – the Shishkov circle – he signs himself 'An Arzamasite'.[21] Shortly after he arrived in St Petersburg he was elected to the society, and given the name of the Cricket. The reality he encountered was rather different from the ideal of 'To Zhukovsky': though the Arzamasites were a congenial, convivial set, they were hardly that band of brothers devoted to the cause of art envisaged in the epistle. He arrived, too, at a time when the society was beginning to lose its point. Derzhavin had died in July 1816; the *Symposium* ceased its existence not long afterwards, and *Arzamas*, whose whole essence was parody, could, like a reflection in a mirror, hardly remain once the original had disappeared. The last formal meeting of the society was held in the spring of 1818; though some of the members continued to come together informally thereafter, *Arzamas* had come to an end.

Long after it had ceased to exist it still remained a pleasant memory for Pushkin: 'Is your swan-princess with you? Give her the respects of an *Arzamas* goose,' he wrote to Vyazemsky in 1825.[22] He felt for it, too, something akin to that loyalty inspired by the Lycée – though the feeling was, naturally, far less deep. As a literary group, it was, paradoxically, more important to him before he became a member than subsequently. While he was at the Lycée it represented for him the forces of enlightenment, ranged against those of darkness and ignorance; after his election it became merely a circle of acquaintances, some of whom – Zhukovsky, Vyazemsky, Batyushkov, Aleksandr Turgenev – were already close friends, while others – Bludov, Dashkov, Wiegel, Poletika, and, to a lesser extent, Zhikharev – were to become so.* Indeed, this gathering of diplomats and civil servants, of literary practitioners and dilettantes,

---

* On 7 January 1834 after a visit from Wiegel Pushkin noted in his diary, 'I like his conversation – he is entertaining and sensible, but always ends up by talking of sodomy' (Wiegel was homosexual), and in June, after an evening at the Karamzins, wrote, 'I am very fond of Poletika' (XII, 318, 330).

represented such a heterogeneous collection of views – ranging from Kavelin's dogmatic conservatism to Nikolay Turgenev's radical republicanism – that it could in no way have had an influence, as a whole, on one who was a part of it. But among its members were some of the liveliest minds in Russia at the time, and Pushkin undoubtedly absorbed much from his intercourse with them: particularly, perhaps, from Nikolay Turgenev.

The Turgenev brothers shared an apartment on the Fontanka Embankment, on the top floor of the official residence of Prince A.N. Golitsyn, the Minister of Spiritual Affairs and Education. Aleksandr Turgenev was indolent, easy-going, an intellectual *flâneur*; Nikolay energetic, single-minded, with far more radical political views. Pushkin visited them often, to be berated by Aleksandr for his laziness, and urged by Nikolay to abandon the Anacreontic muse of the Lycée and turn to more serious themes. A third, younger brother, Sergey, was at this time with the diplomatic mission attached to the Russian forces of occupation in France. At the beginning of December 1817 he noted in his diary: '[My brothers] write again about Pushkin, as a developing talent. Ah, let them hasten to breathe liberalism into him, and instead of self-lamentation let his first song be: Freedom.'[23] He showed remarkable prescience, for towards the end of the month Pushkin produced 'Liberty. An Ode'.[24]

Nikolay Turgenev

The Turgenevs' apartment looked out across the canal at the gloomy Mikhailovsky Castle, the scene of the Emperor Paul's assassination in 1801. According to Wiegel, one of the 'high-minded young free-thinkers' gathered in the apartment, gazing out at the castle, jokingly suggested it to Pushkin as the subject for a poem. 'With sudden agility he leapt on the large, long table before the window, stretched out, seized pen and paper and, laughing, began to write.'[25] The poem opens with the dismissal of the poet's former muse, Aphrodite, 'the weak queen of Cythera'. In her stead Pushkin invokes 'the proud songstress of Freedom' to indict the present age: 'Everywhere iniquitous Power/In the inspissated gloom of prejudice/Reigns.' The proper society is the state in which 'with sacred

Liberty/Powerful Laws are firmly bound'. The rule of law applies to tyrant and mob alike: the French revolution, an infraction of law by the people, led to the despotism of Napoleon, 'the world's horror, nature's shame,/A reproach on earth to God'. Three brilliant stanzas – a vivid contrast to the abstract rhetoric that has gone before – follow. The 'pensive poet', gazing at midnight on the Mikhailovsky Castle, imagines the assassination of Paul on the night of 11 March 1801:

> in ribbons and in stars,
> Drunk with wine and hate
> The secret assassins come,
> Boldness on their face, fear in their heart.

A final stanza, added later, reverts to the preceding style and draws a general conclusion.

Yakov Saburov, one of the hussar officers whom Pushkin frequented in Tsarskoe Selo, later told Pushkin's biographer, Annenkov, that the poem was known to the emperor, 'but [he] did not find in it cause for punishment'.[26] Indeed, the ideas of the poem are those of Kunitsyn, who had told the lycéens, 'Preparing to be protectors of the laws, you must learn yourselves first to respect them; for a law, broken by its guardians, loses its sanctity in the eyes of the people,' adding a quotation from the Abbé Raynal, one of the French *Encyclopédistes*, 'Law is nothing if it is not a sword, which moves indiscriminately above all heads and strikes everything which rises above the level of the horizontal plane in which it moves.'[27] Pushkin echoes this almost verbatim,

> grasped by trusty hands
> Above the equal heads of citizens
> Their sword sweeps without preference.

'Liberty. An Ode' is Pushkin's first great mature poem, but is far from being a revolutionary one; it expresses, rather, a conservative liberalism, defending the monarchy, provided that the monarch respects the law that binds him as well as his subjects. Opinion, however, seizing on the poem's title and ignoring its content, held it to be subversive, and it came to have talismanic significance for the younger generation. Manuscript copies were widely circulated. D.N. Sverbeev, a coeval of Pushkin, then a junior civil servant, read to his colleagues 'this new production of Pushkin's then desperately liberal muse'.[28] A copy was confiscated on the arrest of a certain Angel Galera in 1824; another was among the 'disloyal writings possessed by officers of the Kiev Grenadier Regiment' in 1829. Herzen published the ode in London in 1856, but it did not appear in its entirety in Russia until 1906.[29]

Pushkin's other great poem of this period, 'The Country', was written during a second visit to Mikhailovskoe in the summer of 1819. An idyllic description of the countryside and its ability to inspire the poet is followed by an eloquent denunciation of serfdom:

> Savage *Lordship* here, feelingless, lawless,
> With violent rod has appropriated
> The peasant's labour, property and time.
> Bowed over another's plough, to whips obedient,
> Here emaciated Servitude drags itself along the furrows
> Of its pitiless Master.[30]

The serf's obligations to his landlord took one of two forms: either that of the *barshchina*, the *corvée*: forced labour on the landlord's fields (as in the poem); or the *obrok*, the quit-rent, a sum paid to the landlord in lieu of service. The latter was for the serf much less of a burden, and was the form of service preferred by progressive landlords. So Eugene Onegin, on inheriting his uncle's estate, demonstrates his liberal credentials by replacing 'ancient corvée's yoke/With a moderate quit-rent' (II, iv). Naturally, harsh treatment led to retaliation. Landlords were often killed, and minor uprisings occurred. In 1783 the arbitrary and tyrannical regime of Aleksandr Vyndomsky's estate manager at Trigorskoe led to a revolt eventually put down, after an engagement which left forty dead or wounded, by a squadron of dragoons and a detachment of infantry under the command of the governor of Pskov. The seven ring-leaders were publicly knouted, branded, their nostrils slit, and were exiled to hard labour for life.

Since the time of Catherine II various projects had been put forward for reforming the system, or emancipating the serfs, but with no result. The accession of the liberal-minded Alexander in 1801 gave hope to the abolitionists; but, following the Napoleonic wars, a period of reaction set in, marked, in external affairs, by Alexander's creation of the Holy Alliance and internally by his appointment in 1815 of Count Arakcheev, a narrow-minded, brutal martinet, as deputy president of the Committee of Ministers: for the next ten years Arakcheev's house on the corner of the Liteiny Prospect and Kirochnaya Street was the effective centre of government.

> Oppressor of all Russia,
> Persecutor of governors
> And tutor to the Council,
> To the tsar he is – a friend and brother.
> Full of malice, full of vengeance,
> Without wit, without feeling, without honour,
> Who is he? *Loyal without flattery*,
> The penny soldier of a whore.*[31]

Opinions differed on how the abolition of serfdom was to be brought about. In the view of the more conservative, it had to be preceded by constitutional reform. More radical opponents of the institution believed that constitutional reform would merely strengthen the hand of the landowners and worsen the condition of the serfs. Paradoxically, therefore, they saw the solution to lie in the exercise of autocratic power, through an arbitrary fiat of the emperor. It is this view which Pushkin, echoing the ideas of Nikolay Turgenev, expresses in the concluding stanza of 'The Country':

> Will I see, o friends! a people unoppressed
> And Servitude banished by the will of the tsar,
> And over the fatherland will there finally arise
> The sublime Dawn of enlightened Freedom?

Towards the end of 1819 Alexander expressed the wish to see some of Pushkin's work. The request was made to General Illarion Vasilchikov, commander of the Independent Guards Brigade, who handed it on to his aide-de-camp, Petr Chaadaev, possibly knowing that he and Pushkin were acquainted. Pushkin gave Chaadaev 'The Country'; it was presented to Alexander, who, reading it with interest, is reported to have said to

---

* 'Loyal without flattery' was the motto adopted by Arakcheev for his coat-of-arms; the last line is a reference to his mistress, Anastasiya Minkina, in 1825 murdered by the serfs for her intolerable cruelty.

Vasilchikov: 'Thank Pushkin for the noble sentiments which his verse inspires.'[32]

He would have been less gracious had he
seen Pushkin's more overtly political verse,
much of which was directed at him: such as
the playful satire 'Fairy Tales', in which the tsar
promises to dismiss the director of police, put
the censorship secretary in the madhouse, and
'give to the people the rights of the people' –
all of which promises are, of course, fairy tales.[33]
The scatological is also pressed into the service
of lese-majesty: in 'You and I' Pushkin draws a
series of comparisons between himself and the tsar, ending:

Alexander I

> Your plump posterior you
> Cleanse with calico;
> I do not pamper
> My sinful hole in this childish manner,
> But with one of Khvostov's harsh odes,
> Wipe it though I wince.*[34]

Equally unacceptable are the witty, occasionally obscene, epigrams dedicated to prominent members of the government: Arakcheev, Golitsyn,
and others such as Aleksandr Sturdza, a high official in the Ministry of
Education, known for his extreme obscurantist views.

> Slave of a crowned soldier,
> You deserve the fame of Herostratus
> Or the death of Kotzebue the Hun,†
> And, incidentally, fuck you.[35]

Nikolay Turgenev took Pushkin to task on several occasions, scolding
him for 'his epigrams and other verses against the government' and

---

* Count Dmitry Ivanovich Khvostov, the Alfred Austin of Alexandrine Russia, an extraordinarily prolific, but talentless poet, the constant butt of Pushkin's jokes.
† Herostratus set fire to the temple of Artemis in Ephesus in order, he confessed, to gain
everlasting fame; the German dramatist Kotzebue, employed by the Russian foreign service
as a political informant, was assassinated in 1819 by the student Karl Ludwig Sand.

appealing to his conscience, saying it was 'wrong to take a salary for doing nothing and to abuse the giver of it'.[36]

If late eighteenth-century opponents of serfdom had attacked it chiefly as a morally repugnant system, by now it was also seen as a brake on economic progress. But it was not wholly responsible for the post-war crisis which Russia experienced after 1815. In 1825 the Decembrist Kakhovsky wrote to Nicholas I from his cell in the Peter-Paul fortress: 'We need not be afraid of foreign enemies, but we have domestic enemies which harass the country: the absence of laws, of justice, the decline of commerce, heavy taxation and widespread poverty.'[37] This sense among the younger generation of indignant dissatisfaction with the state of the nation was exacerbated – for those who had fought through Germany and France – by the vivid contrast between Russia and the West. But the absence in Russia of freedom of speech, freedom of the press, and freedom of assembly forced those who wished for reform to turn to secret political activity. Freemasonry – often connected, if as often unjustifiably, with secret revolutionary activity and for that reason suppressed by conservative governments – provided a means of association. In Russia the number of lodges grew rapidly after the war, and many of the future Decembrists were, or had been – like Pierre Bezukhov in *War and Peace* – Masons.

On 9 February 1816 six young officers – Aleksandr Muravev and Nikita Muravev, Prince Sergey Trubetskoy, Ivan Yakushkin, and the brothers Matvey and Sergey Muravev-Apostol, the eldest twenty-six, the youngest twenty-one – met in a room of the officers' quarters of the Semenovsky Life Guards on Zagorodny Prospect. All had served abroad, and all – with the exception of Yakushkin – were Masons. They agreed to organize a secret political society to be called the *Union of Salvation or Society of True and Faithful Sons of the Fatherland*: from this beginning came the Decembrist revolt of 1825. According to Aleksandr Muravev, the society's primary aims were the emancipation of the serfs, the establishment of equality before the law and of public trial, the abolition of the state monopoly on alcohol, the abolition of military colonies,* and

* By an order of 5 August 1816 certain districts in the Novgorod province and, later, in the south, had been turned into military colonies. Every village was transformed into an army camp; all peasants under fifty had to shave their beards and crop their hair, while

the reduction of the term of military service. More members were soon enrolled, including the twenty-three-year-old Pavel Pestel, an officer in the Chevalier Guards. 'Spent the morning with Pestel, a wise man in every sense of the word,' Pushkin noted in his diary in April 1821. 'We had a conversation on metaphysics, politics, morality, etc. He is one of the most original minds I know.'[38] Charismatic, erudite, with an iron will and a clear vision, Pestel became the moving spirit in the conspiracy. Under his influence a constitution was drawn up, entitled the *Green Book*, at the same time the Union of Salvation was dissolved and its members joined the new Union of Welfare. And in 1818 Pestel set up a southern branch of the society at Tulchin in the Ukraine.

Much ink has been spilt in debating the question of the extent of Pushkin's knowledge of the conspiracy, and of his involvement in it. The simplest answer seems the most correct. A number of the future Decembrists were his close friends, and he was acquainted with many others. He frequented houses in which they held meetings; he shared many of the political views of their programme. Nevertheless, he was never, as far as we know, involved in the conspiracy, never invited to become a member of it, never – consciously – present at a gathering of the conspirators, and, though he had a vague suspicion that something was afoot, never knew what this was.

The clearest evidence of his lack of involvement comes from his closest friend at the Lycée, Pushchin. In the summer of 1817 the latter, then an ensign in the Life Guards Horse Artillery, was recruited into the Union of Salvation. 'My first thought,' he writes, 'was to confide in Pushkin: we always thought alike about the *res publica*.' But Pushkin was then in Mikhailovskoe. 'Later, when I thought of carrying out this idea, I could not bring myself to entrust a secret to him, which was not mine alone, where the slightest carelessness could be fatal to the whole affair. The liveliness of his ardent character, his association with untrustworthy persons, frightened me [. . .] Then, involuntarily, a question occurred to me: why, besides myself, had none of the older members who knew him well considered him? They must have been held back

---

those under forty-five had to wear uniform. Children received military training, and girls were married by order of the military authorities. Arakcheev was particularly hated for his merciless enforcement of the rules governing these colonies.

by that which frightened me: his mode of thought was well known, but he was not fully trusted.'*[39]

Pushkin was still ignorant of the society's existence in November 1820, when a guest on Ekaterina Davydova's estate at Kamenka, in the Ukraine. A number of the conspirators were present: Yakushkin, Major-General Mikhail Orlov, his aide-de-camp, Konstantin Okhotnikov, and Vasily Davydov, Ekaterina's son. Among the other guests were Vasily's elder brother Aleksandr and General Raevsky, half-brother to the Davydovs and soon to become Orlov's father-in-law. According to Yakushkin, the behaviour of the conspirators aroused Raevsky's suspicions; becoming aware of this, they resolved to dissipate them by means of a hoax. During the customary discussion after dinner, the arguments for and against the establishment of such a society were rehearsed. Orlov put both sides of the case, Pushkin 'heatedly demonstrated all the advantages that a Secret society could bring Russia'. When Raevsky too seemed in favour, Yakushkin said to him: 'It's easy for me to prove that you are joking; I'll put a question to you: if a Secret society now already existed, you certainly wouldn't join it, would you?'

'On the contrary, I certainly would join it,' he replied. 'Then give me your hand,' I said. He stretched out his hand to me, and I burst out laughing, saying to him: 'Of course, all this was only a joke.' Everyone else laughed, except for A.L. Davydov, the majestic cuckold,† who was asleep, and Pushkin, who was very agitated; before this he had convinced himself that a Secret society already existed, or would immediately begin to exist, and he would be a member; but when he realized that the result was only a joke, he got up, flushed, and said with tears in his

* The Decembrist Ivan Gorbachevsky, a member of the Society of United Slavs (which amalgamated with the southern society in 1825), who knew Pushchin well, having shared a cell with him in the Peter-Paul fortress, after reading this passage in the latter's memoirs, remarked in a letter to M.A. Bestuzhev dated 12 June 1861: 'Poor Pushchin, – he did not know that the Supreme Duma [of the society] had even forbidden us to make the acquaintance of the poet Aleksandr Sergeevich Pushkin, when he lived in the south; – and for what reason? It was openly said that because of his character and pusillanimity, because of his debauched life, he would immediately inform the government of the existence of a secret society [. . .] Muravev-Apostol and Bestuzhev-Ryumin told me about such antics of Pushkin in the south that even now turn one's ears red.' Shchegolev (1931), 294–5.
† A quotation from Eugene Onegin, I, xii; Davydov's wife, Aglaë (née de Grammont) was generous with her favours

eyes: 'I have never been so unhappy as now; I already saw my life ennobled and a sublime goal before me, and all this was only a malicious joke.'[40]

Considered objectively, it is difficult to imagine that any serious conspirator belonging to a secret society which had the aim of overthrowing an absolute monarchy would wish to enlist a crackbrained, giddy, intemperate and dissolute young rake, whose heart and sentiments – as his poetry demonstrated – might have been in the right place, but whose reason all too often seemed absent. How could any conspiracy remain secret which had as one of its members someone who, in a theatre swarming with police spies, paid and amateur, was capable of parading round the stalls carrying a portrait of the French saddler, Louvel, who assassinated Charles, duc de Berry, in 1820, inscribed with the words 'A Lesson to Tsars'?[41]

Chaadaev

Or who, again in the theatre, could shout out 'Now is the safest time – the ice is coming down the Neva'?[42] – meaning that, since the pontoon bridges across the river, removed when it froze, could not yet be re-established, a revolt would not have to contend with the troops of the fortress.

> In Rome he would have been Brutus, in Athens Pericles,
> But here he is – a hussar officer,[43]

Pushkin wrote of Petr Chaadaev, whom he first met at the Karamzins in Tsarskoe Selo in 1816. '*Le beau* Tchadaef', as his fellow officers called him,[44] had a pale complexion, grey-blue eyes and a noble forehead. He was always dressed with modish elegance: Eugene Onegin is dubbed 'a second Chaadaev', for being in his dress 'a pedant/And what we used to call a dandy' (I, xxv). Yet at the same time he was curiously asexual: no trace of a relationship is to be discovered in his life. Wiegel, who disliked him intensely, attributes this to narcissism: 'No one ever noticed in him tender feelings towards the fair sex: his heart was too overflowing with adoration for the idol which he had created from himself.'[45] In December 1817 he moved to St Petersburg on his appointment as aide-de-camp to General Vasilchikov. Extremely learned, and with a brilliant mind – he was described by General Orlov's wife as 'the most striking and most brilliant young man in St Petersburg'[16] – he seemed on the threshold of a dazzling military career, and was widely expected to become aide-de-camp to Alexander himself. But in February 1821 he suddenly and inexplicably resigned from the army and, after undergoing a spiritual crisis so severe as to affect his health, went abroad in 1823, intending to live in Europe for the rest of his life. He was a Mason, and a member of the Society of Welfare, but played no active part in the Decembrist conspiracy, and later severely condemned the revolt of 1825. However, there is no doubt that, while at Tsarskoe Selo and St Petersburg, he was 'deeply and essentially linked with Russian liberalism and radicalism',[47] sharing the ideals of the future Decembrists.

In St Petersburg Chaadaev lived in Demouth's Hotel, one of the most fashionable in the capital, on the Moika, but a stone's throw from the Nevsky. Here, according to Wiegel, he received visitors, 'sitting on a dais, beneath two laurel bushes in tubs; to the right was a portrait of Napoleon, to the left of Byron, and his own, on which he was depicted as a genius in chains, opposite'.[48] Pushkin was a constant visitor, abandoning in Chaadaev's presence his adolescent antics and behaving with sober seriousness. Chaadaev's 'influence on Pushkin was astonishing', Saburov – who knew both well – remarked. 'He forced him to think. Pushkin's French education was counteracted by Chaadaev, who already knew Locke and substituted analysis for frivolity [. . .] He thought about that which Pushkin had never thought about.'[49] He not only introduced logic into Pushkin's thought, he also widened his literary horizons. Pushkin was to be deeply grateful for Chaadaev's sympathy and support in the first months of 1820, when he was both the victim of malicious slander, and being threatened by exile to the Solovetsky monastery on the White Sea for his writings. 'O devoted friend,' he wrote in 1821, 'Penetrating to the depths of my soul with your severe gaze,/You invigorated it with counsel or reproof.'[50] To express his gratitude, he gave Chaadaev a ring: engraved on the inner surface was the inscription 'Sub rosa 1820'.*

In 1818 he had addressed a poem to him which concludes with the stirring lines,

* I.e. in secret, in strict confidence.

While we yet with freedom burn,
While our hearts yet live for honour,
My friend, let us devote to our country
The sublime impulses of our soul!
Comrade, believe: it will arise,
The star of captivating joy,
Russia will start from her sleep,
And on the ruins of autocracy
Our names will be inscribed![51]

The epistle, which has been called 'the most optimistic verse in Pushkin's entire poetry',[52] circulated widely in manuscript, together with 'Fairy Tales', 'The Country' and the epigrams on Arakcheev; according to Yakushkin 'there was scarcely a more or less literate ensign in the army who did not know them by heart'.[53]

4

ST PETERSBURG

1817–20

II: Onegin's Day

I love thee, Peter's creation,
Love thy stern, harmonious air,
The Neva's majestic flow,
The granite of her embankments,
Thy railings' iron pattern,
Thy pensive nights'
Translucent twilight, moonless glimmer,
When in my room
I write and read without a lamp,
And distinct are the sleeping piles
Of the empty streets, and bright
The Admiralty's spire,
And, not admitting nocturnal dark
To the golden heavens,
Dawn to replace dusk
Hastens, giving to night but half an hour.
I love your cruel winter's
Still air and frost,
The flight of sleighs along the broad Neva,
Maidens' faces brighter than roses,
The brilliance, hubbub and chatter of balls,
And at the bachelor banquet
The hiss of foaming beakers
And the blue flame of punch.

The Bronze Horseman, 43–66

THE PETERSBURG THROUGH WHICH the hero of *Eugene Onegin* moves in the first chapter of the poem is not fictional: it is the Petersburg of Pushkin. Eugene's friends and acquaintances, his amusements and diversions, his interests and infatuations are also Pushkin's. This 'description of the fashionable life of a St Petersburg young man at the end of 1819, reminiscent of *Beppo*, sombre Byron's comic work',[1] thus provides a skeleton on which to drape a description of Pushkin's own social life at St Petersburg: his friends and associates, literary salons, the theatre, balls, gambling, liaisons, romances and flirtations.

Rising late, Eugene dons his 'wide *Bolivar*' to saunter up and down 'the boulevard' – the shaded walk, lined by two rows of lime trees, which ran down the middle of the Nevsky from the Fontanka canal to the Moika. Warned by his watch that it is around four in the afternoon, he hurries to Talon's French restaurant on the Nevsky, where Petr Kaverin, the hard-drinking hussar officer who considers cold champagne the best cure for the clap, is waiting. On 27 May 1819 Kaverin noted in his diary: 'Shcherbinin, Olsufev, Pushkin – supped with me in Petersburg – champagne had been put on ice the day before – by chance my beauty at that time (for the satisfaction of carnal desires) passed by – we called her in – the heat was insupportable – we asked Pushkin to prolong the memory of the evening in verse – here is the result:

> A joyful evening in our life
> Let us remember, youthful friends;
> In the glass goblet champagne's
> Cold stream hissed.
> We drank – and Venus with us
> Sat sweating at the table.
> When shall we four sit again
> With whores, wine and pipes?'[2]

Pushkin had not lost his taste for military company, though now he was as apt to mingle with generals as with subalterns, much to Pushchin's disapproval. 'Though liberal in his views, Pushkin had a kind of pathetic habit of betraying his noble character and often angered me and all of us by, for example, loving to consort in the orchestra-pit with Orlov, Chernyshev, Kiselev and others: with patronizing smiles they listened to his jokes and witticisms. If you made him a sign from the stalls, he would run over immediately. You would say to him: "Why do you want, dear chap, to spend your time with that lot; not one of them is sympathetic to you, and so on." He would listen patiently, begin to tickle you, embrace you, which he usually did when he was slightly flustered. A moment later you would see Pushkin again with the lions of that time!'[3] However, something was to be gained from their company. When in 1819 he resurrected the idea of joining the hussars – 'I'm sorry for poor Pushkin!' Batyushkov wrote from Naples. 'He won't be

Evdokiya Istomina

a good officer, and there will be one good poet less. A terrible loss for poetry! Perchè? Tell me, for God's sake.'[4] – General Kiselev promised him a commission. However, Major-General Aleksey Orlov – brother of Mikhail, he had 'the face of Eros, the figure of the Apollo Belvedere and Herculean muscles'[5] – dissuaded him from the idea, a service for which Pushkin, on second thoughts, was grateful: 'Orlov, you are right: I forgo/My hussar dreams/And with Solomon exclaim:/Uniform and sabre – all is vanity!'[6] Orlov was either extraordinarily magnanimous, or had no knowledge of the epigram Pushkin had devoted to him and his mistress, the ballet-dancer Istomina, in 1817:

> Orlov in bed with Istomina
> Lay in squalid nudity.
> In the heated affair the inconstant general
> Had not distinguished himself.
> Not intending to insult her dear one,
> Laïs took a microscope
> And says: 'Let me see,
> My sweet, what you fucked me with.'[7]

Among other new acquaintances a colleague at the Foreign Ministry, Nikolay Krivtsov, was a congenial companion. An officer in the Life Guards Jägers, Krivtsov had lost a leg at the battle of Kulm in 1813, but in England had acquired a cork replacement, so well fashioned as to allow him to dance. Pushkin saw much of him before he was posted to London in March 1818. Bidding him farewell, he gave him a copy of

Voltaire's *La Pucelle d'Orléans* – one of his own favourite works – inscribed 'To a friend from a friend',[8] accompanied by a poem:

> When wilt thou press again the hand
> Which bestows on thee
> For the dull journey and on parting
> The Holy Bible of the Charites?*[9]

The two shared anti-religious, humanist views: 'Krivtsov continues to corrupt Pushkin even from London,' Turgenev told Vyazemsky, who had been posted to Warsaw, 'and has sent him atheistic verses from pious England.'[10]

At this time he got to know two of Lev's friends: Pavel Nashchokin and Sergey Sobolevsky, the illegitimate son of a well-to-do landowner. Nashchokin was extremely rich, and was an inveterate gambler. His addiction later reduced him to poverty. Though he lived with his mother, he also kept a bachelor apartment in a house on the Fontanka, where his friends, either alone or with a companion, could spend the night. Sobolevsky, tall, and inclined to portliness due to a fondness for good food and drink, was a cynical and witty companion with a flair for turning epigrams. They were to be Pushkin's closest non-literary friends; perhaps, indeed, his most intimate and trusted friends during the last decade of his life.

Of his fellows at the Lycée Delvig had taken lodgings in Troitsky Lane, which he shared with Yakovlev and the latter's brother Pavel. Pushkin called here almost daily; together they frequented common eating-houses, or, like the London Mohocks, assaulted the capital's policemen. Küchelbecker, like Pushkin, had joined the Foreign Ministry, eking out the meagre stipend by teaching at the school for sons of the nobility where Lev and Sobolevsky were pupils. He religiously attended Zhukovsky's Saturday literary soirées in the latter's apartment on Ekateringofsky Prospect – Pushkin and Delvig were less regular – and often called at other times to read Zhukovsky his verse. Zhukovsky proffered an original excuse for not attending one social function: 'My stomach had been upset since the previous evening; in addition Küchelbecker

---

* I.e. *La Pucelle*: the Charites were the daughters of Zeus, goddesses personifying charm, grace and beauty.

came, so I remained at home,' he explained.[11] Vastly amused by this combination of accidents, Pushkin composed a short verse:

> I over-ate at supper,
> And Yakov mistakenly locked the door, –
> So, my friends, I felt
> Both *küchelbeckerish* and sick![12]

Insulted, Küchelbecker issued a challenge. They met in the Volkovo cemetery, to the south-east of the city. Delvig, as Küchelbecker's second, stood to the left of his principal. Küchelbecker was to have the first shot. When he began to aim, Pushkin shouted: 'Delvig! Stand where I am, it's safer here.' Incensed, Küchelbecker made a half-turn, his pistol went off and blew a hole in Delvig's hat. Pushkin refused to fire, and the quarrel was made up.[13]

He seemed determined to acquire a reputation for belligerence equal to that of his acquaintance Rufin Dorokhov – the model for Dolokhov in *War and Peace* – an ensign in a carabinier regiment noted for his uncontrolled temper and violent behaviour. At a performance of the opera *The Swiss Family* at the Bolshoy Theatre on 20 December 1818 he began to hiss one of the actresses. His neighbour, who admired her performance, objected; words were spoken, with Pushkin using 'indecent language'. Ivan Gorgoli, the head of the St Petersburg police, who was present, intervened. 'You're quarrelling, Pushkin! Shouting!' he said. 'I would have slapped his face,' Pushkin replied, 'and only refrained, lest the actors should take it for applause!'[14]

Almost exactly a year later the incident was repeated when Pushkin, bored by a play, interrupted it with hisses and cat-calls. After the performance a Major Denisevich, who had been sitting next to him, took him to task in the corridor, waving his finger at him. Outraged by the gesture, Pushkin demanded Denisevich's address, and appointed to meet him at eight the following morning. Denisevich was sharing the quarters of Ivan Lazhechnikov, then aide-de-camp to General Count Ostermann-Tolstoy, in the general's house between the English Embankment and Galernaya Street. At a quarter to eight Pushkin, accompanied by two cavalry officers, appeared and was met by Lazhechnikov. The latter, who was to be acclaimed as 'the Russian Walter Scott' for his historical novels *The Last Page* (1831–3) and *The Ice Palace* (1835), takes up the story in a letter to Pushkin written eleven years later: 'Do you remember a morning in Count Ostermann's house on the Galernaya, with you were two fine young guardsmen, giants in size and spirit, the miserable figure of the Little Russian [Denisevich], who to your question: had you come *in time?* answered, puffing himself up like a turkey-cock, that he had summoned you not for a chivalrous affair of honour, but to give you a lesson on how to conduct yourself in the theatre and that it was unseemly for a major to fight with a civilian; do you remember the tiny aide-de-camp, laughing heartily at the scene and advising you not to waste honest powder on such vermin and the spur of irony on the skin of an ass. That baby aide-de-camp was your most humble servant.'[15] No wonder that Karamzin's wife Ekaterina should write to her half-brother, Vyazemsky, in March 1820: 'Mr Pushkin has duels every day; thank God, not fatal, since the opponents always remain unharmed',[16] or that Pushkin, in preparation for an occasion when cold steel might be preferred to honest powder, should have attended the school set up in St Petersburg by the famous French fencing master Augustin Grisier.*

In St Petersburg Pushkin had been reunited with Nikita Kozlov, a serf from Sergey Lvovich's estate at Boldino, who had looked after him as a child. Nikita became his body-servant, and remained with him until his death. Tall, good-looking, with reddish side-whiskers, he married Nadezhda, Arina Rodionovna's daughter. Like his master, he was fond of drink. Once, when in liquor, he quarrelled with one of Korff's servants. Hearing the row, Korff came out and set about Nikita with a stick.

---

* Grisier was a friend of Alexandre Dumas, who mentions him in *The Count of Monte Cristo*, and based a novel, *Le Maître d'armes* (3 vols, Paris, 1840–1), on his experiences in St Petersburg.

Duelling had been banned in France from 1566, in England from 1615, and in Russia from 1702. The relevant ukase of Peter the Great runs: 'Inhabitants of Russia and foreigners residing there shall not engage in duels with any weapon whatsoever, and for this purpose shall not call out anyone nor go out: whosoever having issued a challenge inflicts a wound shall be executed' (*Duel Pushkina s Dantesom-Gekkerenom*, 104). However, in all three countries there always had been a very wide gap between ban and enforcement. This was especially true of Russia, where the authorities would usually turn a blind eye to *rencontres* which did not have a fatal result; in the case of those which ended with the death of one combatant, the fate of the survivor often depended on the arbitrary whim of the tsar. Ivan Annenkov, a lieutenant in the Chevalier Guards, who killed an officer of the Life Guards Hussars in a duel, was, on Alexander's orders, given the extraordinarily light sentence of three months in the guard-house. And when, in June 1823, General Kiselev, the chief of staff of the Second Army, killed Major-General Mordvinov, Alexander took no action at all: Kiselev remained in his post and underwent no punishment.

Pushkin, feeling that he had been insulted in the person of his servant, called Korff out. Korff refused the challenge with a note: 'I do not accept your challenge, not because you are Pushkin, but because I am not Küchelbecker.'[17] Pushkin's way of life aroused a puritanical disgust in Korff:

> Beginning while still at the Lycée, he later, in society, abandoned himself to every kind of debauchery and spent days and nights in an uninterrupted succession of bacchanals and orgies, with the most noted and inveterate rakes of the time. It is astonishing how his health and his very talent could withstand such a way of life, with which were naturally associated frequent venereal sicknesses, bringing him at times to the brink of the grave [. . .] Eternally without a copeck, eternally in debt, sometimes even without a decent frock-coat, with endless scandals, frequent duels, closely acquainted with every tavern-keeper, whore and trollop, Pushkin represented a type of the filthiest depravity.[18]

The passage, though savagely caricatural, is a recognizable portrait. 'The Cricket hops around the boulevard and the bordellos,' Aleksandr Turgenev told Vyazemsky, later referring to his 'two bouts of a sickness with a non-Russian name', caught as a result. Once, however, the illness was not that which might have been expected. 'The poet Pushkin is very ill,' Turgenev wrote. 'He caught cold, waiting at the door of a whore, who would not let him in despite the rain, so as not to infect him with her illness. What a battle between generosity and love and licentiousness.'[19] The girl in question might have been the charming Pole, Angelica, who lived with her stout and ugly aunt and a disagreeable little dog on the Moika near Pushchin, also one of her clients.

Intercourse of a different kind was to be had in one of the capital's salons – that, for instance, of Ekaterina Muraveva, the widow of Mikhail Muravev, a poet and the curator of Moscow University. Nikita, her elder son, was a member of *Arzamas* and one of the founders of the Union of Salvation; the younger, Aleksandr, a cavalry cornet, joined the conspiracy in 1820. She entertained in a large house on the Fontanka near the Anichkov Bridge, 'one of the most luxurious and pleasant in the capital'.[20] The Karamzins usually stayed here when in St Petersburg, as did Batyushkov, to whom Ekaterina Fedorovna was related by marriage: her husband's sister had been the poet's grandmother.

When Batyushkov set out to join the Russian diplomatic mission in Naples on 19 November 1818, she gave a farewell party for him. 'Yesterday we saw off Batyushkov,' Turgenev wrote to Vyazemsky. 'Between one and two, before dinner, K.F. Muraveva with her son and niece, Zhukovsky, Pushkin, Gnedich, Lunin, Baron Schilling and I drove to Tsarskoe Selo, where a good dinner and a battery of champagne awaited us. We grieved, drank, laughed, argued, grew heated, were ready to weep and drank again. Pushkin wrote an impromptu, which it is impossible to send, and at nine in the evening we sat our dear voyager in his carriage and, sensing a protracted separation, embraced him and took a long farewell of him.'[21] The first signs of Batyushkov's mental illness showed themselves in Italy. When he returned to Russia in 1822 he was suffering from persecution mania, which grew ever more severe, and was accompanied by attempts at suicide.

The best-known literary salon in St Petersburg was that of the Olenins. Aleksey Olenin was one of the highest government officials, having replaced Speransky as Imperial Secretary in 1812; he was also president of the Academy of Arts, director of the Public Library, an archaeologist and historian. He was charming and extremely hospitable, as was his wife, Elizaveta Markovna – though she was a chronic invalid who often received her guests lying on a sofa.* She had inherited a house on the Fontanka near the Semenovsky Bridge: a three-storey building whose entrance columns supported a first-floor balcony; inside the rooms were ornamented with Aleksey Nikolaevich's collection of antique statues and Etruscan vases. Pushkin was a frequent visitor, both to the St Petersburg house and to Priyutino, the Olenins' small estate some twelve miles to the north of the capital, and enthusiastically took part in their amateur theatricals. He played Alnaskarov in Khmelnitsky's one-act comedy *Castles in the Air*, and, on 2 May 1819, composed together with Zhukovsky

A.N. Olenin

* Elizaveta Markovna was related to Praskovya Osipova, the owner of Trigorskoe: her brother, Petr Poltoratsky, had married Ekaterina Vulf, the sister of Praskovya's first husband, Nikolay Vulf.

a ballad for a charade devised by Ivan Krylov, in honour of Elizaveta Markovna's birthday. At a party at the Olenins earlier that year, as a forfeit in some game, Krylov – whose satirical fables rival those of La Fontaine – declaimed one of his latest compositions, 'The Donkey and the Peasant', before an audience which included Pushkin and an innocent-looking nineteen-year-old beauty, Anna Kern – the daughter of Petr Poltoratsky and hence the niece, both of her hostess and of Praskovya Osipova.

Anna had been married at sixteen – 'too early and too undiscriminatingly'[22] – to Lieutenant-General Ermolay Kern, thirty-five years her senior. Kern, who had lost his command through injudicious behaviour towards a superior officer, had come to St Petersburg in order to petition the emperor for reinstatement. Aware that Alexander was not unsusceptible to Anna's beauty – which he had compared to that of Princess Charlotte of Prussia, wife of his brother Nicholas – he sent her out to the Fontanka each day in the hope of meeting the emperor, whose habits were well-known: 'At one in the afternoon he came out of the Winter Palace, walked up the Dvortsovaya Embankment, at Pracheshny Bridge turned down the Fontanka to the Anichkov Bridge [. . .] then returned home by the Nevsky Prospect. The walk was repeated each day, and was called le tour impérial.'[23] 'This was very disagreeable to me and I froze and walked along annoyed both with myself and with Kern's insistence,' Anna wrote.[24] Kern's intelligence sources were at fault, for Anna and the emperor never met.

Enchanted by Krylov's recital, she noticed no one else. But Pushkin soon forced himself on her attention:

> During a further game to my part fell the role of *Cleopatra* and, as I was holding a basket of flowers, Pushkin, together with my cousin Aleksandr Poltoratsky, came up to me, looked at the basket, and, pointing at my cousin, said: 'And this gentleman will no doubt play the asp?' I found that insolent, did not answer and moved away [. . .] At supper Pushkin seated himself behind me, with my cousin, and attempted to gain my attention with flattering exclamations, such as, for example, 'Can one be allowed to be so pretty!' There then began a jocular conversation between them on the subject of who was a sinner and who not,

who would go to hell and who to heaven. Pushkin said to my cousin: 'In any case, there will be a lot of pretty women in hell, one will be able to play charades. Ask Mme Kern whether she would like to go to hell.' I answered very seriously and somewhat drily that I did not wish to go to hell. 'Well, what do you think now, Pushkin?' asked my cousin. 'I have changed my mind,' the poet replied. 'I do not want to go to hell, even though there will be pretty women there . . .'[25]

Eugene has enjoyed his dinner with Kaverin –

> . . . the cork hit the ceiling,
> A stream of the comet year's wine spurted out,
> Before him is bloody *roast-beef*
> And truffles – the luxury of our young years,
> The finest flower of French cuisine,
> And Strasbourg's imperishable pie
> Between a live Limburg cheese
> And a golden pineapple –
>
> (I, xvi)

but it is now half past six, and he hurries to the Bolshoy Theatre, where the performance of a new ballet is beginning.

When Pushkin came to St Petersburg in 1817 the capital's chief theatre was the Maly (or Kazassi Theatre), a wooden building situated on the south side of the Nevsky near the Anichkov Bridge, in what is now Ostrovsky Square, approximately where the Aleksandrinsky Theatre (designed by Rossi, and built in 1832) stands. On 3 February 1818, however, the Bolshoy (or Kamenny) Theatre, burnt down in 1811, was reopened in Teatralnaya Square in Kolomna, on the site of the present Conservatoire. There was also the German (or Novy) Theatre on Dvorts-ovaya Square, where a troupe of German actors performed, which existed until the early 1820s. When the Maly Theatre was pulled down at the end of the 1820s, its actors moved for some time to the building of the former circus, near Simeonovsky Bridge on the Fontanka, but this was closed when the Aleksandrinsky Theatre and, a year later, the Mikhailov-sky Theatre on Mikhailovskaya Square were opened. In 1827 the wooden Kamennoostrovsky Theatre was built on Kamenny Island, a popular resort for the nobility in the summer months. There was also a theatre, seating four hundred, in the Winter Palace, built by Quarenghi between 1783 and 1787, where performances were given for the royal family and the court, while a number of the richer nobles had small, domestic theatres in their palaces.

The Bolshoy Theatre was huge. Behind the immense colonnade of its portico was a double ramp, enabling carriages to be driven up to the theatre entrance. Immediately inside were a succession of foyers: these, however, were only used when a ball was held at the theatre; they remained empty during the intervals, the audience preferring to circulate in the theatre itself. This consisted of a parterre, above which rose five tiers of boxes and galleries. The vast stage could accommodate several hundred performers at once, and was equipped with the most modern machinery for the production of spectacular effects, which were particularly appreciated by the audience. Performances took place every evening, with the exception of Saturday,* each performance usually comprising two works: a ballet and a comedy, for example, or an opera and a tragedy.

'Beneath the shade of the coulisses/My youthful days were spent,' Pushkin writes in *Eugene Onegin* (I, xviii). Only unforeseen circumstances could keep him away. When, at the end of October 1819, he arrived late for a performance of the 'magical ballet' *Hen-Zi and Tao* staged by the French ballet master Charles Didelot, it was with the excuse that an exciting event in Tsarskoe Selo had delayed his return. A bear had broken its chain and escaped into the palace gardens where it could have attacked the emperor, had he chanced to be passing. He ended the anecdote with the regretful quip: 'When a good fellow does turn up, he's only a bear!'[26]

In August 1817, during an interval at the Bolshoy, Pushkin was introduced to Pavel Katenin, an officer in the Preobrazhensky Life Guards. Katenin's regiment left for Moscow shortly afterwards, but when he returned the following summer, Pushkin came to see him: 'I have come to you as Diogenes came to Antisthenes,' he said. 'Beat me, but teach me.'[27] 'Round-faced, with full, red cheeks, like a toy cherub from

---

* The theatres were also closed from the Monday of the first week of Lent to the Sunday after Easter.

a Palm Sunday fair',[28] Katenin was a poet, playwright, critic and literary theorist, closer in his views to the Archaic school than that of Karamzin; influential in the theatre, his chief service was to introduce Pushkin into theatrical circles. In early December 1818 he took him to see Prince Shakhovskoy, who lived with his mistress, the comic actress Ekaterina Ezhova, on the upper floor – known as 'the garret' – of a house in Srednyaya Podyacheskaya Street. Extraordinarily ugly – he was immensely stout, with a huge, beak-like nose – Shakhovskoy was not only a playwright, but also the repertoire director of the St Petersburg theatres, instructing the performers in acting and declamation. His methods, however, were not to the taste of all. 'His comic pronunciation with its lisp, his squeaky voice, his sobs, his recitatives, his wails, were all intolerable,' one actress commented. 'At the same time he showed one at which line one had to put one's weight on one's right foot, with one's left in the rear, and when one should sway on to one's left, stretching out the right, which to his mind had a majestic effect. One line had to be said in a whisper, and, after a "pause", making an "indication" with both hands in the direction of the actor facing one, the last line of the monologue had to be cried out in a rapid gabble.'[29] He was, however, extremely charming, and Pushkin, walking back with Katenin after the first meeting, exclaimed: 'Do you know that at bottom he's a very good fellow?', and expressed the hope that he did not know of 'those schoolboy's scribblings': an epigram on him Pushkin had written at the Lycée.[30]

Shakhovskoy entertained most evenings after the theatre, and Pushkin became a constant visitor to these Bohemian revels, remembering one occasion as 'one of the best evenings of my life'.[31] Vasily Pushkin was saddened when he heard of the visits; he remained true to the hostile view of Shakhovskoy taken by *Arzamas*. 'Shakhovskoy is still in Moscow,' he wrote to Vyazemsky in April 1819. 'He told me that my nephew visited him practically every day. I said nothing, but only sighed quietly.'[32] The main attraction of the garret lay perhaps not so much in the personality of the host, as in the presence of young actresses, in whose careers Shakhovskoy took a paternal interest, assisting them

Shakhovskoy (with ass's ears)

not only by instruction in elocution, but also by bringing them together with rich young officers. 'He is really a good chap, a tolerable author and an excellent pander,' Pushkin commented to Vyazemsky.[33] In 1825 the playwright Griboedov, another of Pushkin's colleagues at the Foreign Office, wrote to a friend: 'For a long time I lived in seclusion from all, then suddenly had an urge to go out into the world, and where should I go, if not to Shakhovskoy's? There at least one's bold hand can rove over the swan's down of sweet bosoms etc.'[34]

At the garret Pushkin met the nineteen-year-old actress Elena Sosnit-skaya, to whose album he contributed a quatrain:

> With coldness of heart you have contrived to unite
> The wondrous heat of captivating eyes.
> He who loves you is, of course, a fool;
> But he who loves you not is a hundred times more foolish.[35]

'In my youth, when she really was the beautiful Helen,' he later remarked, 'I nearly fell into her net, but came to my senses and got off with a poem.'[36] He was also seduced by the more mature charms of the singer Nimfodora Semenova, then thirty-one, more renowned for her appearance than her voice: 'I would wish to be, Semenova, your cover-let,/Or the dog that sleeps upon your bed,' he sighed.[37] More serious was his infatuation – despite the fact that she was thirteen years his senior – with Nimfodora's elder sister, the tragic actress Ekaterina Semenova. The essay 'My Remarks on the Russian Theatre', composed in 1820, though purporting to be a general survey of the state of the theatre, is merely an excuse for praising Semenova. 'Speaking of Russian tragedy, one speaks of Semenova and, perhaps, only of her. Gifted with talent, beauty, and a lively and true feeling, she formed herself [. . .] Semenova has no rival [. . .] she remains the autocratic queen of the tragic stage.'[38] He bestowed the manuscript on her. Somewhat unfeelingly she immediately handed it on to her dramatic mentor, Gnedich, who noted on it 'This piece was written by A. Push-

Ekaterina Semenova (left)

kin, when he was pursuing, unsuccessfully, Semenova, who gave it to me then.'[39]

Semenova had, however, a stage rival: the seventeen-year-old Aleksandra Kolosova, who made her debut at the Bolshoy on 16 December 1818 as Antigone in Ozerov's tragedy *Oedipus in Athens*. The following Easter Pushkin, who had admired her demure beauty at the Good Friday service in a church near the Bolshoy, made her acquaintance. But he naturally took Semenova's side in the rivalry, all the more as he fancied Kolosova had slighted his attentions: she should 'occupy herself less with aide-de-camps of his imperial majesty and more with her roles'. 'All fell asleep,' he added, at a performance of Racine's *Esther* (translated by Katenin), on 8 December, in which she took the title role.[40] 'Everything in Esther captivates us' begins an epigram; her speech, her gait, her hair, voice, hand, brows, and 'her enormous feet!'[41]

When Eugene enters the theatre Evdokiya Istomina, the great beauty among the ballet-dancers, is on the stage:

> Brilliant, half-ethereal,
> Obedient to the violin's magic bow,
> Surrounded by a crowd of nymphs,
> Stands Istomina; she
> Touching the floor with one foot,
> Slowly gyrates the other,
> And suddenly jumps, and suddenly flies,
> Flies, like fluff from Aeolus's lips;
> Now bends, now straightens,
> And with one quick foot the other beats.
>
> (I, xx)

Pushkin pursued her too, but with less zeal than Semenova: he was only one of a crowd of admirers. An amusing sketch, executed by Olenin's son, Aleksey, shows a scene at Priyutino: a dog, with the head and neck of the dark-haired Istomina, is surrounded by a host of dog admirers with the heads of Pushkin, Gnedich, Krylov and others.[42]

Another visitor to Shakhovskoy's garret was Nikita Vsevolozhsky, Pushkin's coeval, a passionate theatre-goer, 'the best of the momentary friends of my momentary youth'.*[43] He was the son of Vsevolod Vsevolozhsky, known, for his wealth, as 'the Croesus of St Petersburg', who, after the death of his wife in 1810, had caused a long-lasting scandal in society by taking to live with him a married woman, Princess Ekaterina Khovanskaya. The injured husband, Petr Khovansky, complained publicly of the insult done to him, and went so far as to petition the emperor for the return of his wife, but without success. In the end, financially ruined, he was forced to accept Vsevolozhsky's charity, and lived with the family until his death. To complicate the situation further, Nikita Vsevolozhsky later married Khovansky's daughter, Princess Varvara. Pushkin, intrigued by the family history, in 1834–5 planned to incorporate it in a projected novel entitled *A Russian Pelham*. Vsevolozhsky, who received a large income from his father, had an apartment near the Bolshoy and a mistress, the ballet-dancer Evdokiya Ovoshnikova. 'You remember Pushkin,' runs a letter of 1824, 'Pushkin, who sobered you up on Good Friday and led you by the hand to the church of the theatre management so that you could pray to the Lord God and gaze to your heart's content at Mme Ovoshnikova.'[44]

In March 1819 Vsevolozhsky set up a small theatrical-literary society among his friends. It met fortnightly, in a room at his apartment, and became known as the *Green Lamp* after the colour of the lamp-shade. Besides Pushkin and Vsevolozhsky the members included Delvig, Nikolay Gnedich, Nikita's elder brother, Aleksandr, Fedor Glinka, Arkady Rodzyanko, a lieutenant in the Life Guards Jägers, and a poet whose work is an odd mixture of high-minded poems on civic themes and pornographic verse: Pushkin later dubbed him 'the Piron of the Ukraine'[45] (a reference to the seventeenth-century French poet Alexis Piron, author of the licentious *Ode to Priapus*); and another 'momentary friend' of this period, Pavel Mansurov, an ensign in the Life Guards Jäger Horse, who, after his marriage to Princess Ekaterina Khovanskaya, became Vsevolozhsky's brother-in-law.†

The tone of Pushkin's relationship with Mansurov – and hence with

---

* The phrase is an adaptation of a line in a poem of 1820, 'Extinguished is the orb of day . . .' ['Pogaslo dnevnoe svetilo . . .'], II, 146.

† The known other members are Sergey Trubetskoy, Fedor Yurev, Dmitry Barkov, Yakov Tolstoy, Aleksandr Tokarev, Ivan Zhadovsky, Aleksandr Ulybyshev, and Prince Dmitry Dolgorukov.

most of the Green Lamp's members – is conveyed by a verse epistle in which Pushkin urges his 'bosom friend' to persevere in his pursuit of the young ballerina Mariya Krylova, then still a pupil at the Theatre Academy, for

> soon with happy hand
> She will throw off the school uniform,
> Will lie down before you on the velvet
> And will spread her legs;[46]

and by a letter written to Mansurov after the latter had been posted to Novgorod province:

> Are you well, my joy; are you enjoying yourself, my delight – do you remember us, your friends (of the male sex) . . .We have not forgotten you and at 1/2 past seven every day in the theatre we remember you with applause and sighs – and say: our darling Pavel! What is he doing now in great Novgorod? Envying us – and weeping about Krylova (with the lower orifice, naturally). Each morning the winged maiden* flies to rehearsal past our Nikita's windows, as before telescopes rise to her and pricks too – but alas . . . you cannot see her, she cannot see you. Let's abandon elegies, my friend. I'll tell you about us in historical fashion. Everything is as before; the champagne, thank God, is healthy – the actresses too – the one is drunk, the others are fucked – amen, amen. That's how it ought to be. Yurev's clap is cured, thank God – I'm developing a small case [. . .] Tolstoy is ill – I won't say with what – as it is I already have too much clap in my letter. The *Green Lamp's* wick needs trimming – it might go out – and that would be a pity – there is oil (i.e. our friend's champagne).[47]

The note struck here suggests that the Green Lamp was a Russian version of the Hell-fire Club. This was certainly the view taken by earlier biographers of Pushkin, Annenkov, for example, writing: 'Researches and investigations into this group revealed that it . . . consisted of nothing more than an *orgiastic* society.'[48] Unfortunately, the reality was somewhat less than orgiastic. Though no doubt a good deal of champagne and

* I.e. Krylova: the Russian for wing is *krylo*.

other wines was consumed during and after the meetings – Küchelbecker puritanically refused to join, 'on account of the intemperance in the use of drink, which apparently prevailed there'[49] – and the younger members were in constant pursuit of actresses and ballerinas, the actual proceedings of the society were of a more serious nature.

One of the policies of the Supreme Council of the Union of Welfare was to 'set up *private societies*. These, directed by one or two members of the Union, whose existence was not revealed to the societies, did not form part of the Union. No political aim was intended for them, and the only benefit that was hoped for was that, guided by their founders or heads, they could, especially through their activity in literature, art and the like, further the achievement of the aim of the Supreme Council.'[50] Besides Trubetskoy, three other members of the society were Decembrists: Tolstoy, the usual president at its meetings, Glinka and Tokarev; and there is no doubt that under their direction the Green Lamp became a society of this type. Its name, fortuitously chosen, came to have emblematic significance; Tolstoy, in his deposition to the Committee of Investigation in 1826, remarked that it 'concealed an ambiguous meaning and the motto of the society consisted of the words: *Light* and *Hope*; moreover rings were also made on which a lamp was engraved; each member was obliged to wear one of these rings.'[51] Pushkin used his to seal his letter to Mansurov. Rodzyanko later remarked that at each meeting 'were read verses against the emperor and against the government',[52] and Tolstoy speaks of 'some republican verses and other fragments'.[53] But it was never a political society with a definite programme and specific aims. It was, however, a secret society, in that its existence had not been officially sanctioned, and its members were hence to some extent at risk, given the climate of the time: a fact which brought about its dissolution at the end of 1820.

The meetings usually opened with a review, hastily written by Barkov, of the theatre production its members had witnessed that evening. Then followed contributions from those present. On 17 April 1819, for example, Delvig read his poems 'Fanny' – addressed to a prostitute he and Pushkin frequented – and 'To a Child'; Ulybyshev followed with a political article; a fable by Zhadovsky, two poems by Dolgorukov, and one by Tolstoy ended the proceedings. Only two contributions by Pushkin are listed in the – incomplete – records of the society. Of these the more interesting – and the better poem – is the verse epistle to Vsevolozhsky on the latter's departure for Moscow, read on 27 November 1819. Urging his friend to avoid high society there, he imagines a far more congenial scene:

> In the foaming goblet froths
> *Ay*'s cold stream;
> In the thick smoke of lazy pipes,
> In dressing-gowns, your new friends
> Shout and drink![54]

Like *Arzamas*, the Green Lamp provided Pushkin with a ready-made circle of friends, though in the majority of cases his intimacy with them was confined to this period of his life. They were, however, closer to him in age than the Arzamasites, and shared the tastes and predilections which governed his life in these years. Whereas his elder friends sighed over his behaviour and saw him as wasting his talent – Aleksandr Turgenev told Zhukovsky that he daily scolded Pushkin for 'his laziness and neglect of his own education', to which 'he had added a taste for vulgar philandering and equally vulgar eighteenth-century freethinking'[55] – the members of the Green Lamp were companions in his amusements: drinking, whoring and gambling. As with *Arzamas*, his loyalty to the group persisted in exile; in 1821 he looked back nostalgically at its meetings:

> Do you still burn, our lamp,
> Friend of vigils and of feasts?
> Do you still foam, golden cup,
> In the hands of merry wits?
> Are you still the same, friends of mirth,
> Friends of Cypris and of verse?
> Do the hours of love, the hours of drunkenness
> Still fly to the call
> Of Freedom, indolence and idleness?[56]

Pushkin's tastes were not wholly identical with those of Eugene: 'I am always glad to note the difference/Between Onegin and myself', he remarks, in case some 'sarcastic reader' should imagine that, like Byron, he is painting his own portrait (I, lvi). One vice Eugene did not share was Pushkin's addiction to gambling.

> *Passion for bank!* neither the love of liberty,
> Nor Phoebus, nor friendship, nor feasts
> Could have distracted me in past years
> From cards.[57]

So he described, in a cancelled stanza of the second chapter of *Eugene Onegin*, himself during the years in St Petersburg. It was an addiction, moreover, not confined to this period, as he here implies, but which lasted throughout his life. The game to which he was addicted – which was also Casanova's passion – was bank, also known as faro (or pharo, originally *le pharaon*) or shtoss, a descendant of lansquenet, the game played by d'Artagnan and the musketeers on the bastion at La Rochelle while under Huguenot fire, and of basset, the favourite card-game at the court of Charles II. Each player chose a card from his pack, placed it either face-up or face-down – in the latter case it was known as a 'dark' card – in front of him on the table and set his stake upon it. The banker, taking a fresh pack, turned the cards up from the top, dealing them alternately to his right and left, stopping momentarily if a player called out *attendez*, in order to make or reconsider a bet. If a card which fell to the right was of the same denomination as one on which a stake had been placed the banker won; he lost, and paid out the amount of the stake, when such a card fell to the left. If both cards exposed in one turn were the same, a player wagering on that denomination lost either half, or the whole of his stake, depending on the rules in force at the game. Having won once, the player could then cock his card – turn up one corner – to wager both his original stake and his gains: this was known as a *parolet*; or bend the card, to bet only his gains. This was a *paix*, or *parolet-paix*, if he had just won a *parolet*. After winning a *parolet*, he could cock another corner, to double his winnings again (*sept-et-le-va*), followed by a third (*quinze-et-le-va*) and a fourth (*trente-et-le-va*).[58]

Pushkin gambled constantly, and as constantly lost, as a result having to resort to money-lenders. He played frequently with Nikita Vsevolozhsky, whose deep pockets enabled him to bear his losses. Pushkin, less fortunate, was compelled to stake his manuscripts, and in 1820 lost to

Vsevolozhsky a collection of poems which he valued at 1,000 roubles. When, four years later, he was preparing to publish his verse, he employed his brother Lev to buy the manuscript back. Vsevolozhsky generously asked for only 500 roubles in exchange, but Pushkin insisted that the full amount should be paid. 'The second chapter of "Onegin"/ Modestly slid down [i.e., was lost] upon an ace,' Ivan Velikopolsky, an old St Petersburg acquaintance, recorded in 1826, adding elsewhere: 'the long nails of the poet/Are no defence against the misfortunes of play.'[59] And in December of the same year, when Pushkin was staying at a Pskov inn to recover after having been overturned in a carriage on the road from Mikhailovskoe, he told Vyazemsky that 'instead of writing the 7th chapter of Onegin, I am losing the fourth at shtoss: it's not funny'.[60] Another favourite opponent at the card-table was Vasily Engel-hardt, described by Vyazemsky as 'an extravagant rich man, who did not neglect the pleasures of life, a deep gambler, who, however, during his life seems to have lost more than he won'. 'Pushkin was very fond of Engelhardt,' he adds, 'because he was always ready to play cards, and very felicitously played on words.'[61] In July 1819, having recovered from a serious illness – 'I have escaped from Aesculapius/Thin and shaven – but alive' – Pushkin, who was leaving for Mikhailovskoe to convalesce, in a verse epistle begged Engelhardt, 'Venus's pious worshipper', to visit him before his departure.[62]

The cold he had caught while, as Turgenev reported, standing out-side a prostitute's door, had turned into a more serious illness – it seems likely to have been typhus. On 25 June his uncle wrote from Moscow to Vyazemsky in Warsaw: 'Pity our poet Pushkin. He is ill with a severe fever. My brother is in despair, and I am extremely concerned by such sad news.'[63] James Leighton, the emperor's personal physician, was called in. He prescribed baths of ice and had Pushkin's head shaved. After six weeks' illness Pushkin recovered, but had to wear a wig while his own hair grew again. This was not Pushkin's only illness, though it was the most severe, during these years in the unhealthy – both in climate and amusements – atmosphere of St Petersburg. Besides a series of venereal infections, he was also seriously ill in January 1818: 'Our poet Aleksandr was desperately ill, but, thank God, is now better,' Vasily Pushkin informed Vyazemsky.[64] During this illness Elizaveta Schott-Schedel, a St Petersburg *demi-mondaine*, had visited him dressed as an hussar officer, which apparently contributed to his recovery. 'Was it you, tender maiden, who stood over me/In warrior garb with pleasing gaucherie?' he wonders, pleading with her to return now he is convalescent:

> Appear, enchantress! Let me again glimpse
> Beneath the stern shako your heavenly eyes,
> And the greatcoat, and the belt of battle,
> And the legs adorned with martial boots.[65]

'Pushkin has taken to his bed,' Aleksandr Turgenev wrote the following February;[66] a year later, in February 1820, he was laid up yet again. Unpleasant though the recurrent maladies were, the periods of convalescence that followed afforded him the leisure to read and compose: he can have had little time for either in the frenetic pursuit of pleasure that was his life when healthy. The first eight volumes of Karamzin's *History of the Russian State* had come out at the beginning of February 1818. 'I read them in bed with avidity and attention,' Pushkin wrote. 'The appearance of this work (as was fitting) was a great sensation and produced a strong impression. 3,000 copies were sold in a month (Karamzin himself in no way expected this) – a unique happening in our country. Everyone, even society women, rushed to read the History of their Fatherland, previously unknown to them. It was a new revelation for them. Ancient Russia seemed to have been discovered by Karamzin, as America by Columbus.'[67]

The friendship between Pushkin and the Karamzins, begun at Tsarskoe Selo, had continued in St Petersburg. During the winter of 1817–18 he was a frequent visitor to the apartment they had taken in the capital on Zakharevskaya Street; at the end of June 1818 he stayed with them for three days at Peterhof, sketched a portrait of Karamzin, and, with him, Zhukovsky and Aleksandr Turgenev went for a sail on the Gulf of Finland. He was in Peterhof again in the middle of July, and, when the Karamzins moved back to their lodging in Tsarskoe Selo, visited them three times in September. At the beginning of October they took up residence in St Petersburg for the winter, staying this time with Ekaterina Muraveva on the Fontanka. Pushkin visited them soon after their arrival, but then the intimacy suddenly ceased: apart from two short meetings at Tsarskoe Selo in August 1819 there is no trace of any lengthy encounter until the spring of 1820. During this period Pushkin composed a biting epigram on Karamzin's work:

> In his 'History' elegance and simplicity
> Disinterestedly demonstrate to us
> The necessity for autocracy
> And the charm of the knout.[68]

Shortly after Karamzin's death on 22 May 1826 Vyazemsky wrote to Pushkin in Mikhailovskoe: 'You know the sad cause of my journey to Petersburg. Although you are a knave and have occasionally sinned with epigrams against Karamzin, in order to extract a smile from rascals and cads, without doubt you mourn his death with your heart and mind.'* 'Your short letter distresses me for many reasons,' Pushkin replied on 10 July. 'Firstly, what do you mean by my epigrams against Karamzin? There was only one, written at a time when Karamzin had put me from himself, deeply wounding both my self-esteem and my heartfelt attachment to him. Even now I cannot think of this without emotion. My epigram was witty and in no way insulting, but the others, as far as I know, were stupid and violent: surely you don't ascribe them to me? Secondly. Who are you calling rascals and cads? Oh, my dear chap ... you hear an accusation and make up your mind without hearing the justification: that's Jeddart justice. If even Vyazemsky already etc., what about the rest? It's sad, old man, so sad, one might as well straightaway put one's head in a noose.'[69]

The 'rascals and cads' of Vyazemsky's letter are the Decembrists. Their trial had opened a month earlier, on 3 June: no wonder he should sadly reproach Vyazemsky for prematurely passing sentence on them. However, as his letter makes clear, though the epigram is a political attack, his rejection by Karamzin was on personal, not political grounds. In April 1820 Karamzin wrote to Dmitriev, 'Having exhausted all means of knocking sense into his dissolute head, I already long ago abandoned the unfortunate fellow to Fate and to Nemesis.'[70] What wounded

---

* Vyazemsky had almost filial feelings for Karamzin: after his father's death in 1807 (his mother, an O'Reilly, had died in 1802) Karamzin, whose second wife was Vyazemsky's illegitimate half-sister, had come to live on the family estate at Ostafevo, near Moscow, and had acted as the young prince's guardian.

Pushkin so deeply was an unsparing castigation of his follies, followed by banishment into outer darkness.

The performance at the Bolshoy has ended, and Eugene hurries home to change into 'pantaloons, dress-coat, waistcoat' (I, xxvi) – probably a brass-buttoned, blue coat with velvet collar and long tails, white waist-coat and blue nankeen pantaloons or tights, buttoning at the ankle – before speeding in a hackney carriage to a ball. This has already begun; the first dance, the polonaise, and the second, the waltz, have taken place; the mazurka, the central event of the ball, is in full swing and will be followed by the final dance, a cotillion.

> The ballroom's full;
> The music's already tired of blaring;
> The crowd is busy with the mazurka;
> Around it's noisy and a squash;
> The spurs of a Chevalier guardsman jingle;*
> The little feet of darling ladies fly;
> After their captivating tracks
> Fly fiery glances,
> And by the roar of violins are drowned
> The jealous whispers of modish wives.
>
> (I, xxviii)

'In the days of gaieties and desires/I was crazy about balls' (I, xxix), wrote Pushkin: for the furtherance of amorous intrigue they were supreme. He was simultaneously both highly idealistic and deeply cynical in his view of and attitude towards women. In a letter to his brother, written from Moldavia in 1822, full of sage and prudent injunctions on how Lev should conduct his life – none of which Pushkin himself observed – he remarked: 'What I have to say to you with regard to women would be perfectly useless. I will only point out to you that the less one loves a woman, the surer one is of possessing her. But this pleasure is worthy of an old 18th-century monkey.'[71] Though he fell violently in love, repeatedly, and at the least excuse, he never forgot that the objects of

---

* Pushkin later added a manuscript note to this line: 'An inaccuracy. Chevalier Guards officers, like other guests, appeared at balls in undress and low shoes. A just remark, but there is something poetic about the spurs' (VI, 528).

his passion belonged to a sex of which he held no very high opinion. 'Women are everywhere the same. Nature, which has given them a subtle mind and the most delicate sensibility, has all but denied them a sense of the beautiful. Poetry glides past their hearing without reaching their soul; they are insensitive to its harmonies; remark how they sing fashionable romances, how they distort the most natural verses, deranging the metre and destroying the rhyme. Listen to their literary opinions, and you will be amazed by the falsity, even coarseness of their understanding ... Exceptions are rare.'[72] The hero of the unfinished *A Novel in Letters* echoes these views. 'I have been often astonished by the obtuseness in understanding and the impurity of imagination of ladies who in other respects are extremely amiable. Often they take the most subtle of witticisms, the most poetic of greetings, either as an impudent epigram or a vulgar indecency. In such a case the cold aspect they assume is so appallingly repulsive that the most ardent love cannot withstand it.'[73]

Pushkin's first St Petersburg passion was Princess Evdokiya Golitsyna, whom he met at the Karamzins in the autumn of 1817. This thirty-seven-year-old beauty, known, from her habit of never appearing during the day, as the *princesse nocturne*, had been married in 1799, at the behest of the Emperor Paul and against her wishes, to Prince Sergey Golitsyn. After Paul's death, however, she was able to leave her husband and lead an independent, if somewhat eccentric life at her house on Bolshaya Millionnaya Street. 'Black, expressive eyes, thick, dark hair, falling in curling locks on the shoulders, a matte, southern complexion, a kind and gracious smile; add to these an unusually soft and melodious voice and pronunciation – and you will have an approximate understanding of her appearance,' writes Vyazemsky, one of her admirers. At midnight 'a small, but select company gathered in this salon: one is inclined to say in this temple, all the more as its hostess could have been taken for the priestess of some pure and elevated cult'.[74] Here the conversation would continue until three or four in the morning. In later life her eccentricities became more pronounced; in the 1840s she mounted a campaign against the introduction of the potato to Russia, on the grounds that this was an infringement of Russian nationality.

'The poet Pushkin in our house fell mortally in love with the Pythia Golitsyna and now spends his evenings with her,' Karamzin wrote to

Vyazemsky in December 1817. 'He lies from love, quarrels from love, but as yet does not write from love. I must admit, I would not have fallen in love with the Pythia: from her tripod spurts not fire, but cold.'*[75] For some months he was deeply in love with her. Sending her a copy of 'Liberty. An Ode', he accompanied the manuscript with a short verse:

> I used to sing of
> The splendid dream of Freedom
> And breathed it sweetly.
> But then I see you, hear you,
> And so? . . . man is weak!
> Losing freedom for ever,
> I adore captivity with my heart.[76]

But her attractions were purely spiritual; this was an ethereal love devoid of any taint of physicality. Other desires had to be satisfied elsewhere. 'In the mornings Pushkin tells Zhukovsky where he spent the night without sleep; he spends the entire time paying visits to whores, to me, and to Princess Golitsyna, and in the evenings sometimes plays bank,' Turgenev noted.[77] After meeting the princess in Moscow in June 1818, Vasily Pushkin wrote to Vyazemsky: 'I spent the entire evening with her and we talked much about you. She loves you and respects you. My nephew Aleksandr called on her every day. She gladdened me by saying that he was a very good, very clever young fellow.'[78] By this time Pushkin's emotions had begun to cool, and by December the episode was over.

'Pushkin is possessed,' Turgenev wrote to Vyazemsky on 12 November 1819. 'I catch a glimpse of him only in the theatre, he looks in there in his free time from the animals. In general his life is spent at the office where one obtains admission tickets to look at the animals that have been brought here, among which the tiger is the most tame. He has fallen in love with the ticket-girl and has become her *cavalier servant*;

---

* Pythia was the priestess of Apollo at Delphi, who 'delivered the answer of the god to such as came to consult the oracle, and was supposed to be suddenly inspired by the sulphureous vapours which issued from the hole of a subterranean cavity within the temple, over which she sat bare on a three-legged stool, called a tripod' (*Lemprière's Classical Dictionary*, 3rd ed. (London, 1984, 554).

meanwhile he is observing the nature of animals and noticing the difference from the swine he sees gratis.' Vyazemsky's reply is somewhat cryptic but undoubtedly indecent: 'Pushkin's love is surely my friend, who tortured me for a whole night . . . at a masked ball. Do me a favour and ask him to convey my respects to them; there should be two of them. One lion was in love with her, and when she caressed him, he displayed a leonine sceptre. Does Pushkin know about his rival? However, it's more difficult getting a man away from a woman than having a tug-of-war with a donkey.'[79] The girl – she seems to have been called Nastasya – sold tickets for one of the travelling menageries which visited St Petersburg at Easter, Shrove-tide and other times, setting up their booth, alongside others occupied by fortune-tellers, trained canaries, dancing dogs, jugglers, magicians, tight-rope walkers and the like, on Admiralty Square, Theatre Square in front of the Bolshoy, or on Tsaritsyn Field.

He also knew, and admired – but was never in love with – the eighteen-year-old Pole Sofya Potocka, whom he met in 1819. Her family history was an intriguing one. Her mother, Sofya Clavona, was a Greek from Constantinople, who had, it was said, been bought from her mother for 1,500 piastres by the Polish ambassador. As she was journeying to Poland with her protector, at Kamenets-Podolsk in the Ukraine she met Major Joseph Witt, who fell in love with her, married her secretly and took her to Paris. The portraitist Elisabeth Vigée-Lebrun saw her here in the early 1780s, noting that she 'was then extremely young and as pretty as it is possible to be, but tolerably vain of her charming face'.[80] Later Sofya attracted the attention of Potemkin, Catherine's favourite, who, besotted with her, made her husband a general and a count, took her as his mistress and bestowed on her an estate in the Crimea. In 1788 she became the mistress of General Stanislaw-Felix Potocki, a claimant to the throne of Poland with huge estates in the Ukraine. He paid Witt two million zlotys to divorce her, and married her in 1798, after the death of his wife. He hardly received full value for his money, since she soon began an affair with his son, later living openly with him in Tulchin. Her husband died in 1805, and his son soon afterwards. Her two daughters, Sofya and Olga, rivalled their mother in beauty: Sofya married Pushkin's friend General Kiselev in 1821, but separated from him in 1829, supposedly on learning that he had had an affair with her sister (who had married General Lev Naryshkin).

Vyazemsky met the Potocki family in Warsaw in October 1819, and immediately succumbed to Sofya's attractions. 'With us for a few days longer are Potocka and Sofya, who is as beautiful as Minerva in the hour of lust,' he informed Turgenev, and a fortnight later wrote: 'Give my respects to all our acquaintance; and, if you see her and get to know her, – to the sovereign of my imagination, Minerva in the hour of lust, in whom everything is not earthly, apart from the gaze, in which there glows the spark of earthly desire. Happy is he who will fan the spark: in it the fire of poetry glows.'[81] In December Turgenev told Vyazemsky of Pushkin's new verses; he had written 'an epistle to a masturbator, and, really, it can be read even by the most bashful ... How Sofya's roses fade, because she allows no one to pick them.' In January he sent Vyazemsky the poem in question, together with a request for enough striped black velvet to make a waistcoat, since it was unobtainable in St Petersburg. 'Pushkin's verses are charming!' Vyazemsky replied. 'Did he not write them to my lustful Minerva? They say she deals in that business.'[82] Vyazemsky was right; the poem, ironically enitled 'Platonic Love', was addressed to Sofya Potocka. In 1825, when preparing his verse for publication, Pushkin wrote on the margin of the poem's manuscript: 'Not to be included – since I want to be a moral person.'[83]

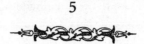

ST PETERSBURG

1817–20

III: Triumph and Disaster

Thus, an unconcerned dweller in the world,
On the lap of idle quiet,
I celebrated with obedient lyre
The legends of dark antiquity.
I sang – and forgot the insults
Of blind fate and of my enemies,
Flighty Dorida's treacheries,
And the loud slanders of fools.
Borne on the wings of invention,
My spirit soared beyond the earth's confine;
But meanwhile an invisible thunder-storm's
Cloud gathered over me! . . .

Ruslan and Lyudmila, Epilogue

AT THE LYCÉE Pushkin had begun his first long poem, the mock-heroic epic *Ruslan and Lyudmila*. He continued to work on it – slowly and spasmodically, most productively when confined to his bed – in St Petersburg, reading excerpts to his friends as he progressed. 'Pushkin is writing a charming poem and is maturing,' Batyushkov told Vyazemsky in May 1818;[1] and in autumn wrote to Bludov in London: 'The Cricket is beginning the third canto of his poem. What a marvellous, rare talent! Taste, wit, invention and gaiety. Ariosto at nineteen could not have done better. I see with grief that he is letting himself be distracted, harming himself and us, lovers of beautiful verse.'[2] In December Vyazemsky heard of further progress from Turgenev: '[Pushkin], despite his whole dissolute way of life, is finishing the fourth canto of his poem. If he were to have three or four more doses of clap, it would be in the bag. His first dose of venereal disease was also the first wet-nurse of his poem.'[3] The fifth canto was written in the summer of 1819 at Mikhailovskoe; in August Fedor Glinka, the fellow-member of the *Green Lamp*, read the first two in manuscript. 'O Pushkin, Pushkin! Who/Taught you to captivate with miraculous verse?' he exclaimed.[4] In February 1820 Pushkin, ill again, revised the fifth and worked on the sixth and final canto while convalescing. He completed this a month later, and immediately read it to Zhukovsky, who in admiration presented his young rival with his portrait, bearing the inscription: 'To the pupil-conqueror from the conquered teacher on that most solemn day when he completed *Ruslan and Lyudmila*. Good Friday, 26 March 1820.'[5] It was a generous gesture, acknowledging Pushkin's graceful and affectionate parody of Zhukovsky's own work, 'The Twelve Sleeping Maidens', within the poem. Pushkin later regretted the imitation: 'It was unforgivable (especially at my age) to parody, for the amusement of the mob, a virginal, poetic creation,' he wrote.[6]

Ruslan and Lyudmila opens in Kiev, at the feast given by Prince Vladimir to celebrate the marriage of his daughter, Lyudmila, to Ruslan. The couple repair to the bridal chamber, but, before their union can be consummated, Lyudmila is carried away by the wizard Chernomor, a hunchbacked dwarf with a magic nightcap. After many adventures Ruslan vanquishes Chernomor and brings his bride back to Kiev, routing an army of Pechenegs that is besieging the city.

Portions of the first and third cantos of the poem appeared in periodicals – the *Neva Spectator* and *Son of the Fatherland* – in 1820, and the whole poem was published as a separate edition at the end of July, after Pushkin's departure for the south: a paperback of 142 pages, selling for ten roubles (fifteen if printed on vellum). It was Pushkin's first published book. Earlier, in 1818 and 1819, he had tried to raise interest in a subscription edition of his poems, employing his brother Lev and Sergey Sobolevsky to sell tickets. Some had been sold (Zhukovsky had taken a hundred), but the enterprise had collapsed after the loss of the manuscript at cards to Vsevolozhsky. Before leaving St Petersburg he entrusted the manuscript of *Ruslan and Lyudmila* to Zhukovsky, Lev and Sobolevsky, who prepared it for publication: a difficult task in the case of canto six, since Pushkin had not had time to produce a fair copy. Gnedich took charge of the book's production: he was experienced in these matters, having already acted as publisher for a number of authors. He was, however, a sharp operator. In 1817 he agreed to publish a work by Batyushkov, but insisted that the poet be responsible for any loss the book might make, and, when it proved surprisingly popular, passed on to him only two thousand roubles out of the fifteen thousand the book made. He was to be similarly sharp in dealing with Pushkin and, even by publishers' standards, dilatory: Pushkin first saw a copy of *Ruslan and Lyudmila* on 20 March 1821, some eight months after its publication. The entire print-run of the work was bought by Ivan Slenin, one of the largest book-sellers in St Petersburg. Gnedich's production costs were therefore immediately covered; it has been calculated that his profit was in the region of six thousand roubles, of which Pushkin received only fifteen hundred. The poem proved extraordinarily popular; the edition soon sold out, after which copies changed hands for the unheard-of price of twenty-five roubles. And in December 1821 the imperial theatre in Moscow put on *Ruslan and Lyudmila, or the Downfall of Chernomor, the evil magician,* a 'heroico-magical pantomine ballet' in five acts, adapted by A. Glushkovsky, with music by F. Scholz: in order to help the audience in the comprehension of the plot, placards were exhibited on stage with inscriptions such as: 'Tremble, Chernomor! Ruslan approaches.'[7]

In July 1820, in the south, Pushkin wrote an epilogue to the poem, and for the second edition in 1828 added the famous and extraordinary prologue (written at Mikhailovskoe in 1824), one of his finest poems, the first line of which – 'On the sea-shore stands a green oak'[8] – haunts Masha Prozorova in Chekhov's *Three Sisters*. For this edition he also, perhaps mistakenly – but no doubt sensibly, in view of his situation at the time – toned down some of

Gnedich

the more risqué passages of the first version. The loss of Chernomor's attempted seduction of Lyudmila at the end of the fourth canto is particularly to be regretted: a scene which has been claimed to represent Pushkin's view of the marital relations between an ill-matched St Petersburg couple – the seventy-one-year-old Count Stroinovsky and his eighteen-year-old wife, Ekaterina Butkevich.

In October 1820 A.A. Bestuzhev, a lieutenant in the Life Guards Dragoons, later an extremely popular short-story writer under the pseudonym Marlinsky, another habitué of Shakhovskoy's garret, wrote to his sister Elena: 'On account of Pushkin's poem *Ruslan and Lyudmila* a terrible ink war has started up here – idiocy upon idiocy – but the poem itself is good.'[9] The war had begun in June with an article in the *Herald of Europe*, directed chiefly against Zhukovsky, but deploring *en passant* the intrusion into literature of such coarse material as the published extracts from Pushkin's poem. 'Let me ask you: what if somehow [...] a guest with a beard, in a peasant coat and bast shoes were to worm his way into the Moscow Noble Assembly, and were to cry in a loud voice: *Greetings, folk!* Would one admire such a rascal?'[10] In August and September Voeikov, a member of *Arzamas*, who hence might have been expected to be on Pushkin's side, devoted four long and tedious articles to the poem in *Son of the Fatherland*, in the last of which he accused Pushkin of using 'peasant' rhymes, and 'low' language, and of one expression remarked 'here the young poet pays tribute to the Germanicized taste of our times', a dig at romanticism and Zhukovsky.[11] The *Neva Spectator* now chimed in, complaining of the 'insignificant subject', taking particular exception to the intrusion of a contemporary narrator into the narrative, and deploring the presence of 'scenes, before which it is impossible not to blush and lower one's gaze'; these possibly encouraged revolution, and were certainly unsuited to poetry.[12] In September an article signed N.N. – thought then to be by Pushkin's friend Katenin, but now known to have been written, under Katenin's influence, by a fellow-officer in the Preobrazhensky Life Guards, Dmitry Zykov – in *Son of the Fatherland* concentrated on what the author saw as the implausibilities of the poem: 'Why does Ruslan *whistle* when he sets off? Does this indicate a man in despair? [...] Why does Chernomor, having got the magic sword, hide it on the steppe, under his brother's head? Would it not be better to take it home with him?' In October Aleksey Perovsky came to the poem's defence with two witty articles in *Son of the Fatherland*, in which he took issue both with

Voeikov and Zykov: 'Unfortunate poet! Hardly had he time to recover from the severe attacks of Mr V., when Mr N.N. appeared with a pack full of questions, each more subtle than the other! [...] Anyone would think that at issue was not a Poem, but a criminal offence.'[13]

Most of these critical remarks, though annoying, were too ludicrous to be taken seriously; and the success of the work was wonderfully consoling. However, Pushkin was hurt when Dmitriev, whom he had known since childhood, commented to Vyazemsky – who passed the remark on – of the poem: 'I find in it much brilliant poetry, lightness in the narrative: but it is a pity that he should so often lapse into *burlesque*, and a still greater pity that he did not use as an epigraph the well-known line, slightly amended: "A mother will forbid her daughter to read it".* Without this caution the poem will fall from a good mother's hand on the fourth page.'[14]

Pushkin hardly conceals his multiple borrowings in the poem: from Zhukovsky, from Ossian, from the Russian folk epic, and, above all, from Ariosto and Voltaire. The first two are the least important: Zhukovsky's influence is limited to the parody of 'The Twelve Sleeping Maidens', where Pushkin's lively irreverence, his delight in the physical, his attention to detail are an invigorating contrast to Zhukovsky's somewhat plodding gothic narrative with its lack of specificity. From Ossian Pushkin borrows a line from the poem 'Carthon', 'A tale of the times of old! The deeds of days of other years', which, translated, forms the first and last two lines of his poem.[15] He seems, too, to have adapted some names from this poem for his characters: Moina, the mother of Carthon, becoming Naina, and Reuthamir, her father, Ratmir. His debt to the Russian folk epic, the *bylina*, is somewhat greater. The poem employs the traditional setting of the Kievan *bylina* cycle: the court of Prince Vladimir in Kiev, and follows the folk epic in referring to the prince as 'Vladimir the Sun', a legendary figure who is seen as an amalgam of the Kievan rulers Vladimir I (d. 1015) and Vladimir II Monomakh (d. 1125). Pushkin, however, no doubt as a result of his reading of Karamzin, is more historically correct than his model: the nomadic army, one of a succession of invaders from the East, which besieges Kiev in *Ruslan and*

---

* An adaptation of a line from Alexis Piron's comedy, *Le Métromanie* (1738), where the author, striving to expunge the memory of his earlier *Ode to Priapus*, wrote, '[in my works] I wish that virtue more than wit should shine/A mother will prescribe them to her daughter.'

Lyudmila, is that of the Pechenegs, against whom Vladimir I fought; in the *byliny* such enemies are usually generalized as Tatars.

But Pushkin had no intention of creating a modern *bylina*: he makes no use of the mythology of the genre, nor of its traditional heroes. Instead, he invents his own characters, who, on leaving Vladimir's court, leave the world of the *bylina* and abruptly find themselves confronting the crenellated battlements of a Western European castle. Neither was he inclined to write a Russian heroic epic, as many wished him to do: the tone of *Ruslan and Lyudmila* is determinedly mock-heroic throughout, as Pushkin's comic treatment of the most obviously heroic episodes demonstrates, such as Ruslan's defeat of the Pecheneg army:

> Wherever the dread sword whistles,
> Wherever the furious steed prances,
> Everywhere heads fly from shoulders
> And with a wail rank on rank collapses;
> In one moment the field of battle
> Is covered with heaps of bloody bodies,
> Living, squashed, decapitated,
> With piles of spears, arrows, armour.
>
> (VI, 299–306)

The models to which *Ruslan and Lyudmila* owes most are Ariosto's *Orlando Furioso* (1532) – which Pushkin would have read in a French prose version – and Voltaire's *La Pucelle* (1755), itself modelled on Ariosto, though Pushkin's work is on a much smaller scale than its predecessors.* Like them, he will begin a canto with general remarks, often addressed to his readers, and tantalizingly break off the narration at a crucial moment to turn to the adventures of another character. His narrator, like those of Ariosto and Voltaire, is not contemporary with the events, but of the present day, intrusive, digressive, and constantly ironizing at the expense of the characters, the plot and its devices. Both Ariosto and Voltaire claim that their works are based upon actual chronicles; composed, in Ariosto's case, by Tripten, Archbishop of Reims, a legendary figure; and, in Voltaire's, by l'abbé Tritême, a real figure, but innocent of the authorship foisted upon him. Pushkin follows

---

* In its final form *Ruslan and Lyudmila* has 2,761 lines; *Orlando Furioso* 38,736 and *La Pucelle* 8,234.

suit with another ecclesiastic, a 'monk, who preserved/For posterity the true legend/Of my glorious knight' (V, 225–7).

It is here, however, that Pushkin parts company with his predecessors. Fantastic as the events in both Ariosto and Voltaire are, the narratives rest on some slight residue of fact, and the backgrounds against which the action unfolds have, for the most part, some semblance of geographical plausibility. With the exception of the Kievan court, however, *Ruslan and Lyudmila* is pure fantasy, set in a land of pure romance. If Ariosto's aim is to please his patrons by extolling the glorious, if legendary past of the House of Este, and Voltaire's to satirize – powerfully, if often crudely – religion, superstition and monarchical rule, Pushkin's is far more intimate, as his poem is on a far more intimate scale: to entertain his friends and social acquaintances. In his asides, foreshadowing *Eugene Onegin*, he brings himself and St Petersburg society into the poem. When he compares Lyudmila with 'severe Delfira', who 'beneath her petticoat is a hussar,/Give her only spurs and whiskers!' (V, 15–16), he is referring to Countess Ekaterina Ivelich, a distant relation of the Pushkins, who lived near them on the Fontanka, and was described by Delvig's wife as 'more like a grenadier officer of the worst kind than a lady'.[16] He begins, too, at first timidly, to experiment with a literary device that was to become a favourite, both in verse and in prose: he plays with his readers, teasing them and subverting their expectations.

When, in the third stanza of *Eugene Onegin*, he calls on the 'friends of Lyudmila and Ruslan' to meet his new hero, he is not merely attempting to capitalize on the popularity of the earlier poem, but hinting that those who had enjoyed it would also enjoy his latest work: despite the obvious dissimilarities – one a mock epic, set in a fabulous past, the other a contemporary novel in verse – the two share a common tone. Batyushkov was right when he spoke of the poem's 'taste, wit, invention and gaiety'; to these he could have added youthful exuberance, charm, and the effortless brilliance of the verse: characteristics which are also those of *Eugene Onegin*. The poem improves as it continues, and is at its best when Pushkin's fantasy is least constrained by the demands of the plot or a traditional setting: Prince Ratmir in the hands of his female bath attendants, and Lyudmila in Chernomor's castle and garden are episodes which outshine the rest.

*   *   *

One of the most colourful characters of this time – an age when they were not in short supply – was Count Fedor Tolstoy (his first cousin, Nikolay, was the father of Leo Tolstoy*). Born in 1782, he joined the Preobrazhensky Life Guards, where he soon made a reputation for himself as a fire-eater, duellist – he was said to have killed eleven men in duels in the course of his life – and card-sharp. In 1803 he was a member of an embassy to Japan, taken there by Admiral Krusenstiern on his circumnavigation of the world. Tolstoy made himself so obnoxious on board that Krusenstiern abandoned him on one of the Aleutian Islands – together with a pet female ape, which he may later have eaten. Crossing the Bering Straits, he wandered slowly back through Siberia, arriving in St Petersburg at the end of 1805: hence his nickname 'the American'.

Tolstoy the American

Coincidentally, Wiegel, who, as a member of Count Golovkin's embassy to China, was travelling in the opposite direction in the summer of that year, met him at a post-station in Siberia. 'What stories were not told about him! As a youth he was supposed to have had a passion for catching rats and frogs, opening their bellies with a pen-knife, and amusing himself by watching their mortal agonies for hours on end [...] in a word, there was no wild animal comparable in its fearlessness and bloodthirstiness with his propensities. In fact, he surprised us with his appearance. Nature had tightly curled the thick black hair on his head; his eyes, probably reddened with heat and dust, seemed to us injected with blood, his almost melancholy gaze and extremely quiet speech seemed to my terrified companions to conceal something devilish.'[17] Settling in Moscow – where in 1821 he married a beautiful gypsy singer, Avdotya Tugaeva – he spent his time gambling at the English Club, usually winning large sums through his skill in manipulating the deck. He was a close friend of Shakhovskoy – the two had been fellow-officers in the Preobrazhensky Guards – and of Vyazemsky.

---

* Tolstoy described his relative as 'an unusual, criminal and attractive man' (Chereisky, 138)

'Count Tolstoy the American is here,' Turgenev wrote to Vyazemsky from St Petersburg in October 1819. 'He is staying with Prince Shakhovskoy, and therefore we will probably see each other rarely.'[18] Pushkin, however, as a regular visitor to Shakhovskoy's garret, soon met Tolstoy, and was soon, unwisely, playing cards with him. Noticing that Tolstoy had slipped a card from the bottom of the pack, he commented on this. 'Yes, I'm aware of that myself,' Tolstoy replied, 'but I don't care to have it pointed out to me.'[19] Whether because of this, or whether out of sheer malice, Tolstoy, on returning to Moscow, wrote a letter to Shakhovskoy in which he asserted that, on the direct orders of the tsar, Count Miloradovich, the military governor-general of St Petersburg, had had Pushkin flogged in the secret chancellery of the Ministry of the Interior. Shakhovskoy made the libel known to the frequenters of his garret. Though other friends, such as Katenin, energetically refuted it, it spread quickly through literary and social circles. Pushkin eventually learnt of it – though not of its author – from Katenin. Humiliated and infuriated, he oscillated between thoughts of suicide and of reckless defiance of authority.

Though, with Chaadaev's help, he overcame his initial despair – 'The voice of slander could no longer wound me,/Able to hate, I was able to despise'[20] – he burnt with the desire to avenge himself. In the draft of a letter to the emperor (which was never sent), composed in 1825 in Mikhailovskoe, he wrote, 'the rumour spread that I had been brought before the secret chancellery and whipped. I was the last to hear this rumour, which had become widespread, I saw myself as branded by opinion, I became disheartened – I fought, I was 20 in 1820.'[21] There is no direct evidence that Pushkin fought a duel early in 1820 over this matter. However, in June 1822 the seventeen-year-old ensign Fedor Luginin recorded in his diary a conversation with Pushkin in Kishinev: 'There were rumours that he was whipped in the Secret chancellery, but that is rubbish. In Petersburg he fought a duel because of that.'[22] If he did fight a duel, it has been suggested that his opponent was the poet and Decembrist Kondraty Ryleev.[23] The conjecture is based on a letter of March 1825 from Pushkin to Ryleev's friend Bestuzhev. 'I know very well that I am his teacher in verse diction – but he goes his own way. He is a poet in his soul. I am afraid of him in earnest and very much regret that I did not shoot him dead when I had the chance, but how the devil could I have known?'[24] He certainly met Ryleev a number of times between September 1819 and February 1820 (when Ryleev returned to his wife's parents' estate near Voronezh) and preserved a sufficiently vivid memory of him to sketch, in January 1826, his profile, with ski-jump nose, protruding lower lip and lank hair next to a portrait of Küchelbecker on a page of the manuscript of the fifth chapter of *Eugene Onegin*.[25] But whether a duel did take place, and, if it did, whether Ryleev was his opponent are questions which cannot be answered without more evidence.

Ryleev

Pushkin did not learn that Tolstoy had been responsible for the rumours until the autumn of 1820. Then he took partial revenge with an epigram, an adaptation of which he inserted into an epistle to Chaadaev in April 1821. Tolstoy is called a 'philosopher, who in former years/With debauchery amazed the world's four corners,/ But, growing civilized, effaced his shame/Abandoned drink and became a card-sharp.'[26] The poem appeared in *Son of the Fatherland* in August. Tolstoy had no difficulty in recognizing his portrait, and composed his own epigram in reply. 'The sharp sting of moral satire/ Bears no resemblance to a scurrilous lampoon,' he wrote, advising Pushkin to 'Smite sins with your example, not your verse,/And remember, dear friend, that you have cheeks.'[27] He too submitted his lines to the *Son of the Fatherland*, which, however, declined the honour of printing them.

Pushkin had no intention of avenging himself with the pen, rather than the pistol. 'He wants to go to Moscow this winter,' Luginin wrote in his diary, 'to have a duel with one Count Tolstoy the American, who is the chief in putting about these rumours. Since he has no friends in Moscow, I offered to be his second, if I am in Moscow this winter, which overjoyed him.'[28] But Pushkin's exile did not end, as he had hoped, in the winter of 1821, and the following September he wrote to Vyazemsky, 'Forgive me if I speak to you about Tolstoy, your opinion is valuable to me. You say that my lines are no good. I know, but my intention was not to start a witty literary war, but with a sharp insult to repay for his hidden insults a man from whom I parted as a friend, and whom I defended with ardour whenever the occasion presented itself. It seemed amusing to him to make an enemy of me and to give Prince Shakhovskoy's garret a laugh at my expense with his letters, I found out about all this when already exiled, and, considering revenge one of the first Christian virtues – in the impotence of my rage showered Tolstoy from afar with journalistic mud. [. . .] You reproach me for printing, from Kishinev, under the aegis of exile, abuse of a man who lives in Moscow. But then I did not doubt in my return. My intention was to go to Moscow, where only I could completely clear myself. Such an open attack on Count Tolstoy is not pusillanimity.'[29] The burning feeling of insult, exacerbated by the impossibility of redeeming it in the only honourable way, remained with Pushkin throughout exile: his first action, on the day he reached Moscow in 1826, was to send Sobolevsky round to Tolstoy with a challenge. Luckily, the count was away from Moscow.

In November 1819 V.N. Karazin, a forty-six-year-old Ukrainian landowner, joined the *Private Society of Amateurs of Russian Literature*,* established three years earlier in St Petersburg. The society's president was Count Sergey Saltykov, but Glinka, the vice-president, was effectively in control. Obedient to the orders of the Union of Welfare's Supreme Council, he set about turning the society, like the *Green Lamp*, into one of those which would further the aims of the Union through its activities and discussions.†

Karazin was an idealistic, romantic conservative who had come to Alexander I's attention in 1801, when 'he left on the emperor's study-table an anonymous letter, greeting his accession in exalted terms and appealing to him to lead Russia to a glorious new age'.[30] Alexander discovered his identity, embraced his admirer and showed him great favour for a time, appointing him to the new Ministry of Education. In 1804 Karazin resigned to found a university at Kharkov, which opened in January 1805. For some time thereafter he lived on his estate, opened a tanning factory, made efforts to found a meteorological observatory, forwarded

---

* Not to be confused with the similarly named *Private Society of Amateurs of Literature, Sciences and the Arts*.

† The society was, of course, much larger than the unofficial *Green Lamp*: in 1824 it had 82 full, 24 associate, 34 corresponding and 96 honorary members.

to the Ministry of War his method of preparing food concentrates, and wrote articles on a variety of subjects, such as 'The description of an apparatus for distilling spirit', 'On the possibility of adapting the electric forces of the upper layers of the atmosphere to the needs of man' and 'On baking a tasty and healthy bread from acorns'.

Now, on his return to St Petersburg, Karazin was appalled by the political atmosphere of the city, the lack of respect for authority in the discussions, the conversations and jokes he heard, and the poems and epigrams recited at meetings of the society. 'Some young brat, Pushkin, a pupil of the Lycée, *in gratitude*, has written a despicable ode, in which the names of the Romanovs are insulted, and the Emperor Alexander called a wandering despot [. . .] Whither are we going?'*[31] he commented in his diary on 18 November 1819. He went to see Prince Kochubey, the Minister of the Interior, whom he had known when at the Ministry of Education, and offered to inform him of the proceedings of the society and of what he might hear elsewhere, promising to keep 'an unsleeping eye' on 'suspicious persons' such as Prince Sergey Volkonsky, Küchelbecker, Ryleev, Glinka, who was 'all the more dangerous because through the especial trust of the governor-general he was employed to collect in secret rumours going about the town for the information of the emperor', and, finally, Pushkin.[32]

By the end of March he had collected a good deal of what he considered to be subversive literature – including Pushkin's epigram on Sturdza – which he incorporated into a report sent to Kochubey on 2 April. Though this consisted largely of a disquisition on the present state of Russia, combined with proposals for a number of reforms, it included an attack on the Lycée, where, he wrote, 'the emperor is educating pupils who are ill-disposed both to him and to the fatherland [. . .] as is demonstrated by practically all those who graduate from it. It is said that one of them, Pushkin, was secretly punished by imperial command. But among the pupils more or less each one is almost a Pushkin, and they are all bound together by some kind of suspicious union, similar to Masonry, some indeed have joined actual lodges.' To this remark he appended a note: 'Who are the composers of the caricatures or epigrams, such as, for example, on the *two-headed eagle*, on *Sturdza*

* Karazin is confusing 'Liberty. An Ode' and 'Fairy Tales'.

in which the person of the emperor is referred to very indecently and so on? The pupils of the Lycée! Who make themselves known to the public with suggestive songs at an age when honesty and modesty are most decorous? They do.'[33]

Having submitted this report to the emperor, Kochubey invited Karazin to call on him on the evening of 12 April. After their conversation Karazin made an emotional note of its content on the back of the invitation. He was extremely disconcerted to discover that the emperor was not at all interested in the substance of his paper, neither in his analysis of the situation nor his proposals for reform. Its sole result, he wrote, 'was the desire of his majesty to assure himself that the epigram mentioned in my note was actually written [. . .] that it was not my invention! [. . .] My God! [. . .] It's almost unbelievable! [. . .] What a sad but true picture of the position of the state is produced!'[34] He washed his hands of the whole affair, refusing Kochubey's request to obtain manuscript copies of the epigram.

Following this conversation Miloradovich, the military governor-general of St Petersburg, was ordered to impound Pushkin's writings. He sent a police spy, Fogel, round to Pushkin's apartment when the latter was out. Fogel offered Nikita fifty roubles for the loan of his master's poems, promising to bring them back in a short time. Nikita refused and, on Pushkin's return, told him of the visitor. Pushkin immediately burnt his manuscripts. The following day he was summoned to see Miloradovich. Before going, he went to see Glinka – who had been the general's adjutant during the war and was now attached to his office – to ask his advice. 'Go straight to Miloradovich, don't show confusion and don't be afraid. He is not a poet; but in his soul and in his chivalrous impulses there is much that is romantic and poetic: he is misunderstood. Go and rely unconditionally on the nobility of his spirit: he will not abuse your trust.' Heartened, Pushkin set off for Miloradovich's house on the Nevsky. A few days later Miloradovich told Glinka of the meeting:

Do you know, my dear fellow, *Pushkin* was with me the other day! You see, I'd been ordered to arrest him and impound all his papers; but I thought it more *delicate* to invite him to my house and ask him himself for his papers. Well, he turned up, very calm, with a bright face, and, when I asked about the papers, answered: 'Count! all my poems are burnt! you will find nothing of mine in my apartment, but if you please, everything is *here* (he pointed to his forehead with his finger). Order a quire of paper to be brought, I'll write everything that *I've* ever written (of course, except that which has been printed), with a *note*: what is mine and what has been circulated *under my name.*' Paper was brought. Pushkin sat down and wrote, wrote ... and filled *a whole note-book* ... Here *it* is, look at that! Tomorrow I'll take it to the emperor. And do you know? Pushkin charmed me with his noble tone and *manner* of behaviour.[35]

Miloradovich had read the verses, laughed, and said to Pushkin: 'If you've really decided to attack the government, why don't you write something about the Senate, which is nothing but a menagerie or pig-sty.' He had concluded by pardoning Pushkin in the name of the emperor.[36]

Alexander, however, extremely displeased with the idea that the Lycée was a hot-bed of revolutionary fervour, and outraged by Pushkin's verse, was disinclined to ratify Miloradovich's generous gesture. Meeting the director of the Lycée, Engelhardt, he expressed his feelings to him as they strolled through the palace garden at Tsarskoe Selo. 'Engelhardt!' he said. 'Pushkin must be exiled to Siberia: he has flooded Russia with seditious verses; the entire youth knows them by heart. His frank conduct with Miloradovich pleases me, but that does not amend matters.' Engelhardt endeavoured to soften the tsar's attitude, referring to Pushkin's literary reputation, and adding: 'Exile could have a baneful effect on the ardent temper of this young man. I think that magnanimity, your majesty, would be more likely to make him sensible.'[37]

Alarmed by the danger – it was rumoured that Pushkin would be sent, if not to Siberia, then to the Solovetsky monastery on the White Sea – his friends hurried to his aid. Chaadaev asked his superior, General Vasilchikov, to intercede with Alexander; and, going to Karamzin, persuaded him to speak with the dowager empress, Mariya Fedorovna, on Pushkin's behalf. Zhukovsky and Aleksandr Turgenev used their influence at the court, and Gnedich visited Olenin, who promised to mention the matter to Alexander. Pushkin himself, somewhat cowed by events, swallowed his pride and called on Karamzin. After exacting a pledge that he should refrain from writing verse against the government for two years, Karamzin undertook to help him, and, going to the empress, asked her to intercede. The emperor relented. Pushkin was not to be banished, but was to be attached to the chancellery of General Ivan Inzov, the Chief Trustee of the Interests of Foreign Colonists in the Southern Territory of Russia, then stationed in Ekaterinoslav. '[Pushkin's] liberal mouth has been closed for two years,' Aleksandr Turgenev wrote to Vyazemsky on 21 April. 'He has been saved from the misfortune into which he fell by my good genius and his good friends,' and, on 5 May, 'He has become quieter and more modest and, in order not to compromise himself, even avoids me in public.'[38] A few days later Vyazemsky heard from Karamzin: 'Pushkin, having been for a few days completely in unpoetical fear because of his verses on freedom and some epigrams, gave me his word to cease [. . .] He was, I think, moved by the emperor's magnanimity, which was genuinely touching. It would take too long to describe the details, but if Pushkin does not reform now, he will be a devil long before he gets to hell.'[39]

On 4 May 1820, Count Capo d'Istrias, the head of the Foreign Office, an honorary member of *Arzamas*, who, according to Wiegel, had 'dared to point out' to Alexander the cruelty of exiling Pushkin to Siberia, and had suggested that he should be transferred to Inzov's chancellery,[40] composed a letter to Inzov which was signed the following day by the Foreign Minister, Count Nesselrode. 'At the Lycée,' Capo d'Istrias wrote, 'his progress was rapid, his wit was admired, but his character appears to have escaped the vigilance of the tutors.' He continued:

There is no excess in which this unfortunate young man has not indulged – as there is no perfection he cannot attain through the transcendent superiority of his talents [. . .] Some pieces of verse and above all an ode to liberty directed the attention of the government towards Mr Pushkin. Amid the greatest beauties of conception and style this latter piece gives evidence of dangerous principles drawn from the ideas of the age, or, more accurately, that system of anarchy dishonestly called the system of the rights of man, of liberty and of independence of nations.

However Messrs Karamzin and Zhukovsky, realizing the dangers to which the young poet was exposing himself, hastened to offer him their advice, made him recognize the error of his ways and brought him to give a solemn promise that he would abjure it for ever. Mr Pushkin appears to be cured – if, that is, his tears and protestations are to be believed. However, his guardians think his repentance to be sincere, and that, by banishing him for a time from St Petersburg, by putting him to work, and by surrounding him with good examples, he can be turned into an excellent servant of the state, or at least a man of letters of the first distinction. In response to their wishes the Emperor has authorized me to give the young Pushkin leave and recommend him to you. He will be attached to your person, General, and will work as a supernumerary in your chancellery. His fate will depend on your good advice.[41]

Alexander approved the letter, writing 'So be it' at the foot. On 4 May the accounts department at the Foreign Office handed out a thousand roubles in *assignats* to Pushkin for travel expenses; on the fifth he received a *podorozhnaya*, an official pass entitling him to use post-horses on state business. On 6 or 7 May, accompanied by his servant Nikita Kozlov, he left St Petersburg. Delvig and Pavel Yakovlev travelled with him as far as Tsarskoe Selo. On 9 May he set out for the south.[42]

THE CAUCASUS
AND CRIMEA
1820

> Forgotten by society and by gossip,
> Far from the Neva's banks,
> I see before me now
> The proud Caucasian peaks.
>
> *Ruslan and Lyudmila*, Epilogue

PUSHKIN'S ROUTE TO EKATERINOSLAV took him initially along the well-known road towards Mikhailovskoe. At Porkhov, however, he turned off and, entering lands unknown to him, hurried on south through Velikie Luki, Vitebsk, Orsha, Mogilev and Chernigov towards Kiev. The monotonous scenery of the White Russian post-road offered no temptation to linger; in any case he could not, for the Foreign Ministry, under whose aegis Inzov's command lay, seizing an opportunity to avoid expense, had made him an official courier. Besides the letter from Capo d'Istrias to Inzov concerning himself, he bore other documents for the general, including the latter's appointment as plenipotentiary governor of Bessarabia.

At a post-house somewhere between Chernigov and Mogilev his Lycée companion Pushchin, who was returning to St Petersburg after four months in Bessarabia with his sister, and thus knew nothing of recent events in the capital, scanning the list of travellers, noticed the name of Pushkin among them. 'I asked the postmaster who this Pushkin was. I had no idea that it could be Aleksandr. The postmaster answered that it was the poet Aleksandr Sergeevich, apparently travelling on official business, in a post-chaise, wearing a red Russian shirt with a belt and a felt hat.'[1]

Just over a week after leaving St Petersburg, on 14 or 15 May, Pushkin arrived in Kiev. Here he found a friend, Nikolay Raevsky, an officer in

General N. N. Raevsky

the Life Guards Hussars. On leave, he was staying with his father, General Raevsky. The latter had had a distinguished military career: he had served under Suvorov in the Turkish war of 1787–90, becoming a major at eighteen; had been wounded when commanding Bagration's avant-garde in 1805; and in 1812, in the battle for Smolensk, had held off with ten thousand troops a much larger French force under Marshal Davout. It was said that during this encounter he had taken his sons, Aleksandr and Nikolay, by the hand and led the advance, calling out, 'Forward, men, for the tsar and the fatherland! I and my sons will show you the way!'[2] The episode was commemorated in popular prints, and earned him a mention in Zhukovsky's 'A Bard in the Camp of Russian Warriors'. It was, however, apocryphal. 'It is true that I was

Nikolay Raevsky

in front,' Raevsky later told Batyushkov. 'But my sons were not there at that time. My youngest child was gathering berries in a wood (he was then a mere child, and a bullet made a hole in his breeches); that was all, the entire anecdote was made up in St Petersburg.'[3] Nikolay – long grown out of his perforated breeches, he was now a Herculean giant who could bend an iron poker in his hands – like Chaadaev had supported and consoled Pushkin when, distressed by Tolstoy's insinuations, he had harboured

thoughts of suicide. Writing to his brother, Pushkin mentions Nikolay's 'important services, eternally unforgettable for me';[4] he would later dedicate *The Prisoner of the Caucasus* to him.

The meeting in Kiev had been arranged before Pushkin left St Petersburg. General Raevsky was planning to travel with Nikolay and his two younger daughters, Mariya and Sofya, to the Caucasus, where his elder son, Aleksandr, was taking the waters. They would then go on to the Crimea and join the general's wife, Sofya Alekseevna, and the two elder daughters, Ekaterina and Elena. The party's route to the Caucasus would pass through Ekaterinoslav; here General Raevsky would seek to persuade Inzov to give Pushkin permission to accompany them. Pushkin dined with the Raevskys and Lev Davydov,* stayed the night, and set out for Ekaterinoslav the following morning. His route took him down the bank of the Dnieper, passing through Zolotonosha and Kremenchug; three days later he arrived in Ekaterinoslav (now Dnepropetrovsk), presented himself to General Inzov, and handed over the letters he was carrying.

Ekaterinoslav had been founded in 1778 by Potemkin, then Viceroy of New Russia – the steppe area north of the Black Sea and the Sea of Azov. The city, named after the empress, was intended as the capital of New Russia, and was planned on a grandiose scale, with a circumference of thirty-three miles, main streets seventy yards wide and a cathedral – the first stone of which was laid by Catherine – which was to compete with St Peter's in Rome in splendour and size. However, after Potemkin's death a decline set in; the city lost its administrative status; its magnificent buildings were never completed or fell into decay. Pushkin took lodgings in the suburb of Mandrykovka, renting a wretched little shack from a Jewish merchant, Krakonini. Behind ran the Dnieper, and he spent much of his time bathing, or watching the traffic on the river, where he witnessed the most exciting event of his stay in Ekaterinoslav: two convicts, who had escaped from the prison nearby, though shackled together and pursued by guards, swam across the river to freedom – an incident incorporated in his unfinished narrative poem *The Robber Brothers* (1821–2).

He made a favourable impression on Inzov, who wrote to Capo d'Istrias: 'I have not yet got to know Pushkin well; but I see, however, that the cause of his sins is not depravity of heart, but youthful ardour of spirit, unrestrained by morality.'[5] Inzov had, however, been thrown into great agitation by his appointment as governor of Bessarabia, being particularly perturbed by the thought of the expenses he would have to

---

* Brother of the poet, Denis Davydov, and tenuously related to General Raevsky: his uncle was the second husband of Raevsky's mother.

incur in the post. Consumed by these worries, and preoccupied by the administrative problems of transferring his chancellery to Kishinev, he had little or no time for Pushkin, who, during the weeks he spent in Ekaterinoslav, found himself very much at a loose end. Local society offered none of the attractions which had been so numerous in St Petersburg, and he made no effort to form new acquaintances. Indeed, he went out of his way to gratuitously offend or shock those whom he met. Learning that the poet was in Ekaterinoslav, two young enthusiastic amateurs of literature, Andrey Ponyatovsky, a teacher at the seminary, and Sergey Klevtsov, a local landowner, hurried round to see him. He met them in the door of his hut, chewing a roll spread with caviare and holding a glass of red wine. 'What do you want?' he asked. The honour of seeing him, the famous poet, they replied. 'Well, have you seen him now? Then good-bye!'[6] He displayed an equal disregard for propriety at a dinner given by the town's civil governor, Vikenty Shemiot.* Andrey Fadeev, who later knew Pushkin well in Kishinev, describes the occasion:

[The dinner] took place in the summer, at the hottest time of the year. The guests gathered, Pushkin too appeared, and from the first moment of his appearance threw the whole company into extreme embarrassment by the unusual eccentricity of his attire: he was wearing muslin trousers, transparent, without any underwear. The governor's wife, Mrs Shemiot, née Princess Gedroits, an old friend of my wife's mother, being very short-sighted, was the only person not to notice this peculiarity. Her three daughters, young girls, were also present at this time. My wife quietly advised her to take the girls out of the drawing-room, explaining the necessity for their removal. Mrs Shemiot, disbelieving her, and not crediting the possibility of such indecency, maintained that Pushkin was simply wearing flesh or skin coloured summer trousers; finally, arming herself with her lorgnette, she assured herself of the bitter truth and immediately escorted her daughters out of the room. This was the only result of the exhibition. Although all were highly indignant and

* Though Pushkin's invitation was no doubt due to his reputation as a poet, he was also distantly related to Shemiot: the latter's brother, Pavel, had married Nadezhda Rotkirch, Pushkin's mother's cousin.

embarrassed, they tried to pretend that they had noticed nothing; the host and hostess were silent, and Pushkin's prank had no consequences.[7]

Meanwhile General Raevsky had set off from Kiev. His party consisted of the eighteen-year-old Nikolay, the latter's sisters, Mariya and Sofya, fourteen and thirteen respectively; Miss Matten, the girls' English governess, and M. Fournier, their French tutor; Anna Ivanovna, a Tatar *dame de compagnie*; Evstafy Rudykovsky, an army doctor, and a Russian nurse. They travelled in two immense berlins and a light calash, and, after calling at Kamenka to allow the girls to see their grandmother, arrived in Ekaterinoslav late in the evening on 26 May, Pushkin's twenty-first birthday. Despite the advanced hour Nikolay, his father, and Rudykovsky set off to see him. They found him, pale and unshaven, lying on a wooden settle in his lodging: he had caught a chill after bathing. Rudykovsky examined him, found that he had a slight fever, and advised him to drink something hot.

The next day Pushkin called on the Raevskys, and, overjoyed at finding himself once more in congenial company, chatted volubly with Nikolay in French over dinner, until overtaken again by fever, whereupon Rudykovsky gave him a dose of quinine. During that day General Raevsky had seen Inzov, and had had no difficulty in extracting from him permission for Pushkin to accompany the party to the Caucasus and the

Mariya Raevskaya

Crimea; he would take up his duties with Inzov in Kishinev in the autumn. 'His disturbed health at so young an age, and the unpleasant position in which he finds himself through youth, demanded on the one hand help, and on the other harmless diversion, and therefore I allowed him to depart with General Raevsky, who, when passing through Ekaterinoslav, was willing to take him with him,' Inzov wrote. 'I hope I will not be reproved for this and thought to have been over-indulgent.'[8]

On the morning of 28 May Pushkin seated himself in the calash with Nikolay, and the caravan rolled off to the east, towards the Caucasus. But he was still troubled with the ague, and, on the insistence of General Raevsky, soon moved into the covered berlin with him. They crossed the Dnieper, and 'plunged into the level and monotonous steppes, always the same, without a single object which might arrest the gaze of the traveller'.[9] On the twenty-ninth they passed through Mariupol, and, early the following day, between Sambek and Taganrog, stopped to admire the Sea of Azov. They arrived in Taganrog later that day, dining and staying the night with the town governor, P.A. Papkov, in the house in which Alexander I was to die in 1825. Passing through Rostov, on 1 June they were entertained in Novocherkassk by General Denisov, the ataman of the Don Cossacks. Ignoring Rudykovsky's advice, Pushkin injudiciously consumed a large portion of blancmange, and was again ill. After crossing the Don, their route took them through Stavropol, and, having been held up by a violent storm, which forced them to spend the night in a post-station, they arrived in Pyatigorsk on 6 June. Here they were met by Aleksandr, General Raevsky's twenty-five-year-old elder son, and took up residence in a house which the general had rented.

The Caucasus region consists of the great mountain range which stretches from the Taman peninsula on the Black Sea to the Apsheron peninsula on the Caspian, the territory immediately to the north, and the southern hinterland, Transcaucasia. It has had a turbulent history since ancient times, and in the eighteenth century Russia, Turkey and Persia contended for domination here. However, in 1801 Alexander I annexed Georgia – which had been under Russian protection since 1783 – and in the following years Russia acquired most of present-day Azerbaijan from Persia. Turkey and Persia gradually withdrew, and Russia set about extending its rule over the remaining nationalities – a task which was not completed until the 1870s. As a first step in the region's pacification, under the supervision of General Ermolov, who commanded the Russian armies in the Caucasus from 1816 to 1827, the Georgian military highway was driven south, from Ekaterinograd to the north of the mountain range, through its central pass and down the Daryal gorge to Tiflis, the capital of Georgia. In the mountains it passed through the territory of the Ossetians, a Christian nation friendly to the Russians. To the west, however, were the Circassians, to the east the Chechens and Ingush, and, beyond them, the Lezgins and Avars who inhabited Dagestan. All were Moslems, who bitterly resisted Russian imperialism. Pyatigorsk lies on the southern slopes of Mount Mashuk, on the outskirts of the Caucasus, some way to the north of the main mountain chain, from which it is separated by the lands of the Kabardians. These, though Sunni Moslems, had earlier professed Orthodoxy, and had long ties with Russia; in 1557 they had petitioned Ivan IV for protection against the Tatars, and he had strengthened the alliance by marrying a Kabardian princess. The settlement was thus isolated from the areas of conflict.

Mineral springs are plentiful in the district, and Pyatigorsk had gained a reputation as a spa in the late eighteenth century. Development was slow, however, and the earliest visitors had to reside at Fort Constantine, a few miles distant, or put up in temporary shacks, tents or covered carts: even by 1829 there were only forty-seven permanent buildings. Nine years after his first visit Pushkin passed through Pyatigorsk again, on his way to Tiflis. 'I found a great change. In my time the baths were in hastily constructed shacks. The springs, for the most part in their original form, spouted up, steamed, and flowed down the mountain-side in various directions, leaving white and reddish traces behind. We scooped up the boiling water with bark ladles or the bottom of a broken bottle. Now [...] everywhere there is order, neatness, prettiness ... I must confess: the Caucasian waters present more comforts now; but I regret their earlier, wild condition; I regret the steep stony paths, the shrubs and the unfenced precipices where I once clambered...'[10]

For a Russian writer the Caucasus, with its mountains and valleys, its fierce, independent, warring tribes, had the same exotic, romantic allure which the Levant had for Byron, or the American wilderness for Fenimore Cooper. Like his predecessors and his successors, Pushkin found the new, unfamiliar scenery exhilaratingly beautiful. 'I regret, my friend,' he wrote to his brother, 'that you could not gaze with me on the splendid chain of these mountains; on their icy summits, which from afar, on a clear dawn, seem like strange clouds, many-coloured and motionless; that you could not climb with me to the sharp peak of Beshtu with its five hills, of Mashuk, of the Zhelezny, Kamenny and Zmeiny mountains.'[11] But the purpose of the visit was to take the waters. General Raevsky observed a strict regimen: 'I rise at five, go to the baths, return an hour later for coffee, read, go for a walk, dine at one, read again, take another walk, go to the baths, we drink tea at seven, take another walk and go to bed.' His walk occasionally took him back to the baths, where from the gallery he would admire the mountains and amuse himself with 'the comic sight of the settlement, its inhabitants, their caricatures of carriages, and their colourful attire; a mixture of Kalmyks, Circassians, Tatars, local Cossacks, local residents and visitors'. He used the hot sulphurous springs, where the temperature was over 38°C; the two girls, 'just for amusement', would bathe once or twice a day in the warm baths.[12] Pushkin drank the waters. 'They have done me a great deal of good, especially the hot sulphurous ones,' he wrote. 'In addition I bathed in the warm sulphur-acidulous springs, and in the cold ferruginous and acidulous ones.'[13]

The party also visited the other spas at Zheleznovodsk, Kislovodsk and Konstantinogorsk. In the last Pushkin, sitting on a pile of logs, compiled a list of the general's suite for the local commandant's book of arrivals, in which he described Rudykovsky as 'physician-in-ordinary' and himself as 'Pushkin, a minor'. The general berated him soundly for his facetiousness.[14] In the evenings the company would play boston, a form of whist; once a lottery was organized: it was won by Mariya; and, in Pyatigorsk on 29 June, they watched a small firework display celebrating the Orthodox feast of SS Peter and Paul. Among the other visitors Pushkin discovered two former acquaintances: Grigory Rzhevsky, the father of a former lycéen, Nikolay, who had died in 1817, and Apollon Marin, an amateur poet and former guards officer, who had been stationed in Tsarskoe Selo in 1816. Marin introduced Pushkin to his brother, Nikolay, and also to another visitor to the region, Gavriil Gerakov, tutor to young Prince Kurakin, whom he was accompanying on a tour of Russia. 'Pushkin, Marin and I wagged our tongues together for an hour and then parted,' Gerakov noted in his diary, adding: '[Pushkin] is ready to attract general attention of a laudatory kind; as he may with his gifts; I wish him all the best from the bottom of my heart.'[15]

In Pyatigorsk Pushkin also met an English officer, Captain George Willock, who was attached to the British mission in Persia – his brother, Henry, was the British Resident in Teheran – and had been granted permission to travel in the Caucasus. However, General Velyaminov, Ermolov's second-in-command, suspecting the visit to be a pretext for 'spying on our military affairs in Chechnya and Dagestan', had given orders to 'observe all his activities and watch with whom he consorts and how often'.[16] Willock, accompanied by an interpreter, arrived in

Pyatigorsk on 20 June at two in the afternoon, Velyaminov's agents informed him. 'Here,' their report continued, 'he put up in the house of the provincial secretary's widow Anna Petrova Makeeva, paying for this three roubles in copper a day. On the same date he was in the old baths, [. . .] listened to the band playing outside the guard-room of the main guard, and afterwards visited His Excellency, General of Cavalry and Chevalier Raevsky, drank tea and stayed some time with him, whence he returned to his lodgings at night and slept.' The following day he was visited in his lodgings by 'Lieutenant of the Life Guard Grenadiers Prince Sergey Ivanovich Meshchersky the first, Captain of the Life Guards Nikolay Nikolaevich Raevsky, and a minor, a member of the suite of His Excellency Raevsky, Aleksandr Sergeev Pushkin'.[17] Pushkin's little joke had rebounded on him: the military authorities had taken his facetious self-description at face value. They were less gullible with respect to Willock. A month after he had left Pyatigorsk he was caught trying to persuade soldiers of the 4th Jäger Regiment to desert to Persia; his interpreter turned out to be an Armenian employed by the Persian army. Griboedov, now secretary to the Russian diplomatic mission in Persia, wrote two sharp notes to the British Resident about his brother's activities.

For Pushkin by far the most significant experience of the sojourn in the Caucasus was his acquaintance with Aleksandr Raevsky. '[General Raevsky's] elder son will be more than well-known,' he wrote to his brother.[18] During the next few years Raevsky was to exert an influence on Pushkin perhaps greater – and certainly less beneficial – than that of his earlier mentor, Chaadaev. Born in 1795, Raevsky had entered the army at fifteen, fought in the Russo–Turkish war of 1810, and took part in the war of 1812 and the following campaigns. Promotion was rapid: at twenty-three he was a colonel commanding the Rzhevsk infantry regiment. In 1819 he was attached to Ermolov's forces in the Caucasus, but, taking leave, had come to Pyatigorsk in an attempt to cure a long-standing affliction of his legs – possibly the result of a war-wound, or possibly, in Ermolov's words, 'the bitter fruits of the sweetest of memories'.[19] Tall, but emaciated – 'physical and mental ailments had desiccated him and lined his brow'[20] – he had a wide mouth whose thin lips were usually curled in a sarcastic smile, and, behind his spectacles, small brown eyes with whites of a jaundiced yellow; his voice, however, was exceedingly charming. In character he was very different from the open-hearted, generous and straightforward Nikolay. His father, not long after their reunion, wrote despondently to his eldest daughter: 'I live at peace with Aleksandr, but how cold he is! I seek in him manifestations of love, of tenderness and do not find them. He does not reason, but argues, and the wronger he is, the more unpleasant his tone becomes, even coarse. We have agreed not to enter into any arguments, or abstract discussions. It is not that I am dissatisfied with him, but I see no cordial relationship on his side. What can one do? Such is his character, and one cannot hold it against him. His mind is turned inside out: he philosophizes about things which he does not understand, and subtilizes in such a way that any sense evaporates. It is the same with his feelings [. . .] I think that he does not believe in love, since he himself neither experiences it, nor tries to inspire it.'[21] 'His character was a mixture of excessive self-esteem, indolence, cunning and envy,' commented Wiegel, adding, 'like a cat, he loved to soil only all that was pure, all that was elevated.'[22]

Aleksandr Raevsky

Pushkin and he spent long hours together, reading and discussing Byron: they had to hand the first four volumes of Pichot's and de Salle's translation of the poet into French prose, which had appeared in 1819.* These contained, among other works, *The Corsair, Manfred* and the first two cantos of *Childe Harold's Pilgrimage*. Or they would sit at night on the bank of the Podkumok River, listening to the sound of its waters, while Raevsky expounded his philosophy of life to an eager listener. Clever, mocking, sceptical, cynical and manipulative, Raevsky played Mephistopheles to an innocent Faust. Later, in October or November 1823, when Pushkin was beginning to escape Raevsky's influence, he described him in 'The Demon':

---

* 'The French translation of us!!! *Oime! Oime!*' was Byron's reaction to this version. Later he added: 'Only think of being *traduced* into a foreign language in such an abominable travesty!' Leslie A. Marchand, *Byron, A Biography*. New York & London, 1957, II, 881–2.

His smile, his wondrous gaze,
His caustic speech
Poured cold poison into my soul.
With inexhaustible slander
He tempted providence;
He called the beautiful an illusion;
He despised inspiration;
He did not believe in love, in freedom:
Looked mockingly at life –
And nothing in all of nature
Did he wish to bless.[23]

For Pushkin these few weeks had an influence disproportionate to their length. They coincidentally brought together three elements – the wild, exotic scenery of the Caucasus with its fierce native tribes, the poetry of Byron, and the demonic teachings of Aleksandr Raevsky – which were to determine the next stage in his development as a poet. He was all the more receptive in that he felt himself, like some Byronic hero, to be a doomed outcast: had he not, during his last months in St Petersburg, experienced the treachery of friends, the deceit of women and the perfidy of society?

In the first week of August, leaving Aleksandr behind in Pyatigorsk, General Raevsky and his party set out for the Crimea. They retraced their route to Stavropol, but then turned west. Since the region they were to traverse could be dangerous for travellers, a military escort accompanied the party. 'I travelled in sight of the hostile lands of the free mountain peoples,' Pushkin wrote. 'Around us rode sixty cossacks, behind us was drawn a loaded cannon, its match lit. Although the Circassians nowadays are relatively peaceful, one cannot rely on them; in the hope of a large ransom they are ready to fall upon a well-known Russian general. And there, where a poor officer safely gallops along in a post-chaise, his excellency may easily fall prey to some Circassian's lasso. You will understand how pleasing this shadow of danger is to the fanciful imagination.'[24]

They passed through Temizhbek on 8 August, and spent the night at a neighbouring fort, where they dined with the commandant. The heat was oppressive throughout the journey, and all the party suffered from it. On the eleventh they were in Ekaterinodar, and two days later arrived in Taman on the Black Sea coast – 'the foulest little town of all Russia's coastal towns', Lermontov calls it in *A Hero of Our Time*. In 1820 it was 'a miserable collection of wooden shacks with two hundred inhabitants, half of whom were beggars, the other half bandits'.[25] However, they did not have to test its hospitality, since both the party and escort were accommodated at the fortress in nearby Fanagoriya. Meanwhile the weather had changed: though the Crimea could be seen in the distance on the far side of the Kerch Strait, the crossing could not be attempted for a day or two.

On the morning of 15 August they were able to embark, though weather conditions were still unfavourable: the crossing took nine hours, instead of the usual two and a half. They arrived in Kerch – the ancient Panticapaeum, founded by Greeks in the seventh century BC, and later the capital of Mithridates the Great's territory in southern Russia – towards evening. 'The view of Kertch, and the large bay in which it is situated, was very beautiful,' noted Laurence Oliphant, who visited the town in 1852; 'the broken outline of the opposite hills projected far across the straits; while the houses of the town rose one above another up the steep side of the hill of Mithridates; – the whole reminding me of Naples, to which it certainly bears a humble resemblance.'[26] Pushkin, eager to glimpse the classical remains, rushed up the hill at sunset, as soon as they had disembarked. 'Here I will see the ruins of the tomb of Mithridates, here I will see the remains of Panticapaeum, I thought – on the nearest hill amidst a cemetery I saw a heap of stones, of boulders, rudely chiselled – noticed a few steps, the work of human hands. Whether this was the tomb, the ancient fundament of a tower – I do not know.'*[27] He 'plucked a flower for remembrance, but lost it the next day – without regret'.[28] On the following morning the party left for Feodosiya, halting, as all visitors did, to view the Golden Barrow, a huge Cimmerian funeral mound, and the ruins of Panticapaeum. The latter proved as disappointing as the tomb: 'Rows of stones, a ditch,

---

* Pushkin, like most visitors, did not know that, though Mithridates committed suicide here in 63 BC, his body was handed over by his son Pharnaces – who had revolted against his father – to the Roman general Pompey, who allowed its burial in Sinope, Mithridates's native city

almost level with the ground – that is all that remains of the city of *Panticapaeum*. There is no doubt that much that is valuable is concealed beneath the earth, accumulated through the ages; a certain Frenchman has been sent from St Petersburg for excavations, but he lacks money and knowledge, as usually is the case with us.'*[29]

In Feodosiya (or Kefa, as it was then known) they stayed two nights with the former town governor, Semen Bronevsky, and at dawn on 18 August boarded a navy brig, the *Mingreliya*, for the passage to Gurzuf. During the journey Pushkin composed the elegy 'Extinguished is the orb of day', which in manuscript bore the heading 'An Imitation of Byron', and had the epigraph 'Good night my native land' – a misquotation of Byron's line 'My native Land – Good Night!' from 'Childe Harold's Good Night'. They arrived before dawn on 19 August:

> Splendid are you, shores of the Tauris;
> When one sees you from the ship
> By the light of morning Cypris,†
> As I for the first time saw you;
> You appeared before me in nuptial brilliance:
> Against the blue, transparent sky
> Shone the masses of your mountains,
> The pattern of your valleys, trees and villages
> Was spread before me.
> And there, among the Tatar huts . . .
> What ardour woke within me!
> What magical yearnings
> Compressed my fiery breast!
> But, Muse! forget the past.[30]

The ardour which turned his breast to fire was inspired by the Raevskys' eldest daughter, the twenty-three-year-old Ekaterina. He had known her well in St Petersburg, but she did not possess the mature charms which he had then admired; here, however, she was without rivals, and Pushkin's all too susceptible heart was soon hers. 'Mikhailo Orlov is to marry

---

* The Frenchman, Paul Dubrux, an amateur, self-taught archaeologist, who was employed as administrator of the local salt-pans, had not been sent from St Petersburg, nor was he without knowledge.
† I.e. the planet Venus.

General Raevsky's daughter, after whom the poet Pushkin languished,' Aleksandr Turgenev wrote to Vyazemsky the following year.[31] She was a splendid, tall, goddess-like creature, with a strong will and forceful personality; the very 'ideal of a proud maid' seen against a background of sea and cliffs.[32] Several years later, when engaged on his historical drama *Boris Godunov*, in a letter to Vyazemsky he remarked of his heroine, the haughty and ambitious Marina Mniszek, 'My Marina is a

fine wench: a real Katerina Orlova! Do you know her? However, don't tell anyone this.'[33]

Nothing could come of the infatuation: Ekaterina was two years older than he, did not return his feelings, and was already informally engaged to General Orlov. Moreover, in a few weeks he would have to leave for Kishinev. A few months later, in perhaps the finest lyric of this period, he returned in spirit to Gurzuf and memories of Katerina:

Ekaterina Raevskaya

Sparser grows the flying range of clouds:
Melancholy star, evening star,
Your ray has silvered the faded levels,
The dreaming gulf, the dark crags' summits;
I love your weak light in the heavenly height:
It awakened thoughts, which slumbered in me.
I remember your rising, familiar orb,
Above that peaceful land, where all is dear to the heart,
Where graceful poplars in the valleys rise,
Where dream the tender myrtle and the dark cypress,
And sweetly sound the southern waves.
There once on the hills, full of thoughts of love,
Above the sea in brooding idleness I wandered,
While on the huts the shade of night descended –
And a young maiden sought you in the darkness
And to her friends named you by her name.*[34]

---

* A case of poetic licence: Venus would not have been visible to the naked eye as an evening star while Pushkin was at Gurzuf.

Ekaterina, in beauty herself a very Venus, is seeking the planet Venus in the evening dusk and, it has been suggested, humorously confusing 'Cytherean' – a title given to Aphrodite from the legend that she landed at Cythera after her birth in the sea – with her own name, Katerina.[35] She certainly identified herself with the star; in 1823 her husband wrote to her: 'I feel myself near to you or imagine you near each time I see that memorable star which you pointed out to me. You may be sure that the moment it rises above the horizon I will catch its appearance from my balcony.'[36] When Pushkin speaks of first seeing Gurzuf 'By the light of morning Cypris', using another of Aphrodite's titles, he is making a coded reference to Ekaterina.

'If there exists on earth a spot which may be described as a terrestrial paradise, it is that which intervenes between Kütchückoy and Sudack on the south coast of the Crimea,' wrote Edward Clarke, an English traveller.[37] It is here that Gurzuf is situated – a small Tatar village of clay huts, clinging to the steep, craggy, pine-covered slopes which rise from the sea-cliff to the stone brow of the plateau above. On the edge of the cliff are the remains of a fortress, built by the orders of Justinian in the sixth century, and refortified by the Genoese, who had a settlement here, in the fourteenth. They were followed by the Turks, who controlled the Khanate of the Crimea until 1774, when it became independent, only to be annexed by Catherine in 1783. The village and surrounding district had belonged to Potemkin, but its ownership had passed to Armand Emmanuel du Plessis, duc de Richelieu, governor-general of Odessa and New Russia from 1803 to 1814. He had built a small palazzo, which he only visited once for a few weeks in 1811, and which otherwise stood empty. A three-storeyed edifice, built into the mountain slope, it had a profusion of windows and huge, light galleries on the first floor, which enabled its inhabitants to enjoy the splendid views, but did little for their comfort. It was here that the Raevskys stayed.

My friend, – Pushkin wrote to his brother from Kishinev – I spent the happiest moments of my life amidst the family of the estimable General Raevsky. I did not see in him the hero, the glory of the Russian army, I loved in him a man with a lucid mind, with a simple, beautiful soul; an indulgent, solicitous friend, always a dear, affectionate host [...] All his daughters are charming, the eldest is an extraordinary woman. Judge, whether I was happy. a free, carefree life surrounded by a dear family; a life which I love so much and with which I can never become satiated – the gay, southern sky; charming surroundings; nature, satisfying my imagination – hills, gardens, sea; my friend, my dearest wish is to see again the southern shore and the Raevsky family.'[38]

'In Gurzuf I did not stir from the spot, bathed in the sea and stuffed myself with grapes; I immediately took to southern nature and enjoyed it with all the indifference and carelessness of a Neapolitan Lazzarono. I loved, waking at night, to listen to the sound of the sea – and would listen spellbound for hours on end. Two steps from the house grew a young cypress; I visited it each morning, and became attached to it with a feeling not unlike friendship.'[39] He spent much of the time reading: he had discovered some Voltaire in the palazzo library and Nikolay lent him a volume of André Chénier, but he mainly devoted himself to Byron. He also wrote, composing several lyrics and the initial draft of his first 'southern' narrative poem, *The Prisoner of the Caucasus*, eventually completed at the beginning of the following year.

On 5 September he, General Raevsky and Nikolay left Gurzuf on horseback for a short sight-seeing tour before leaving the Crimea. Passing through the Ay-Danil woods, they took the track along the coast to Yalta – then a tiny coastal village – and went on through Oreanda to Alupka, where they spent the night in a Tatar homestead. The next day they continued down the coast to Simeis before turning inland. Ascending the gorge known as the Devil's Stairs – 'we clambered up on foot, holding the tails of our Tatar horses. This amused me exceedingly, seeming to be some mysterious, eastern ritual'[40] – and crossing the pass, they descended into the Valley of Baidar. Their route then took them through Balaclava, and at evening they reached the St George monastery where they put up for the night. The monastery stood on a cliff overlooking the sea; the site was spectacular. 'The St George monastery and its steep staircase to the sea left a strong impression on me. There I saw the fabulous ruins of the temple of Diana.'[41] These were on nearby Cape Fiolente, and were popularly supposed to be the remains of that temple of Artemis* to

* The Romans identified Artemis with Diana, as they did Aphrodite with Venus.

which the goddess had carried Iphigenia, after rescuing her from sacrifice in Aulis. 'Why these cold doubts?/I believe: here was the dread temple/ Where to the gods, thirsty for blood,/Smoked sacrifices.'*[42]

The following morning they rode north along a narrow track, past several hamlets, before striking the high road from Sebastopol to Bakhchisaray. Pushkin was again suffering from an ague, and was too ill for much sight-seeing when they arrived in Bakhchisaray, 'the Garden Pavilion', the former seat of the Crimean khans. The palace, restored by Potemkin in 1787 for the visit of Catherine, made little impression on him at the time, though he was to use it as the setting for *The Fountain of Bakhchisaray*. 'Entering the palace, I saw a ruined fountain; from a rusty iron pipe dripped water. I went round the palace, greatly annoyed at the neglect in which it was decaying, and the half-European refurbishment of some of the rooms. NN [Nikolay Raevsky] almost by force led me up a decrepit stair to the ruins of the harem and to the burial-place of the khans, "but not with this/At that time my heart was full:† I was tormented by fever." '[43]

The next day, 8 September, they rode on to Simferopol. A few days later Pushkin left the Crimea. Passing through Perekop, Berislav, Kherson and Nikolaev, he arrived in Odessa on 17 September. Here he stayed for three days. On the twentieth he set out for Kishinev and the following day entered the town where he was to live for the next three years.

---

* The 'cold doubts' are those of I.M. Muravev-Apostol, who devoted a chapter of his *Journey through Tauris in 1820* (1823) to a confutation of the popular view of the site.
† *The Fountain of Bakhchisaray*, 531–2.

KISHINEV

1820–23

Cursed town of Kishinev!
My tongue will tire itself in abuse of you.
Some day of course the sinful roofs
Of your dirty houses
Will be struck by heavenly thunder,
And – I will not find a trace of you!
There will fall and perish in flames,
Both Varfolomey's motley house
And the filthy Jewish booths:
So, if Moses is to be believed,
Perished unhappy Sodom.
But with that charming little town
I dare not compare Kishinev,
I know the Bible too well,
And am wholly unused to flattery.
Sodom, you know, was distinguished
Not only by civilized sin,
But also by culture, banquets,
Hospitable houses
And by the beauty of its far from strict maidens!
How sad, that by the untimely thunder
Of Jehovah's wrath it was struck!

From a letter to Wiegel, October 1823

KISHINEV WAS THE CAPITAL OF BESSARABIA, which lies
between the rivers Dniester and Prut, the Danube delta and the
Black Sea. It had been colonized successively by the Greeks,
Romans and Genoese, had been annexed by the principality of Moldavia
in 1367, became part of the Ottoman empire in 1513, and had been ceded

to Russia in 1812 by the Treaty of Bucharest. When Pushkin arrived on 21 September 1820, he found a bustling, lively, colourful town, very different from the decaying imperial pomp of Ekaterinoslav. At that time it had some twenty thousand inhabitants. The majority were Moldavians, but there were also large Bulgarian and Jewish colonies, numbers of Greeks, Turks, Ukrainians, Germans, and Albanians, and even French and Italian communities; the relatively small Russian population consisted mainly of military personnel and civil servants. The old town, 'with its narrow, crooked streets, dirty bazaars, low shops and small houses with tiled roofs, but also with many gardens planted with Lombardy poplars and white acacias',[1] was spread out along the flat and muddy banks of a little river, the Byk. On the hills above was the new town, with the municipal garden, the theatre and the casino, administrative offices, and a number of stone houses in which the governor, the military commander, the metropolitan and other notables lived.

Initially Pushkin put up in a small inn in the old town. At the beginning of October, however, he moved into a house rented by Inzov: a large, stone building in an isolated position near the old town, on a hill above the Byk. Inzov and several officials lived on the upper floors; Pushkin and his servant Nikita inhabited two rooms on the ground floor, through whose barred windows he looked out over an orchard and vineyard to the open country and mountains beyond. The walls were painted

Inzov

blue; one was soon disfigured with blobs of wax: Pushkin, sitting naked on his bed, would practise his marksmanship by – like Sherlock Holmes at 221B Baker Street – picking out initials on the wall with wax bullets from his pistols. Another of Inzov's officials, Andrey Fadeev, was obliged to share this room on his visits to Kishinev. 'This was extremely inconvenient, for I had come on business, had work to do, got up and went to bed early; but some nights he did not sleep at all, wrote, moved about noisily, declaimed, and recited his verse in a loud voice. In summer he would disrobe completely and perform in the room all his nocturnal evolutions in the full nudity of his natural form.'[2] On 14 July and 5 November 1821 earthquakes struck Kishinev. The second, more severe, damaged the house. Inzov and the civil servants moved out immediately, but Pushkin, either through indolence or affection for his quarters – the first independent lodging he had had – stayed put, living there by himself for several months.

The day after his arrival Pushkin presented himself to Inzov, who introduced him to some members of his staff: Major Sergey Malevinsky, the illegitimate son of General Ermolov, then commanding the Russian armies in the Caucasus; and Nikolay Alekseev, who was to become a close friend. Ten years older than Pushkin, he knew many of the latter's friends in St Petersburg, and, with a taste for literature, 'was the only one among the civil servants in whose person Pushkin could see in Kishinev a likeness to that cultured society of the capital to which he was used'.[3] That evening Malevinsky took him to the casino in the municipal gardens, which also served as a club for officers, civil servants and local gentry. A rudimentary restaurant was attached to the club, run by Joseph, the former *maître d'hôtel* of General Bakhmetev, Inzov's predecessor. It became a regular port of call for Pushkin, who heard from a waitress, Mariola, the Moldavian song on which he based his poem 'The Black Shawl'.*

The following day Pushkin dined with his old friend and fellow-member of *Arzamas*, General Mikhail Orlov, recently appointed to the command of the 16th Infantry Division, whose headquarters were in Kishinev. Here he met Orlov's younger brother, Fedor, a colonel in the Life Guards Uhlans, who had lost a leg at the battle of Bautzen, together with several of Orlov's officers: Major-General Pushchin, who commanded a brigade in the division; Captain Okhotnikov, Orlov's aide-de-camp; and Ivan Liprandi, a lieutenant-colonel in the Kamchatka regiment, and one of Orlov's staff officers. Liprandi was an interesting, somewhat mysterious character, who soon became another of Pushkin's intimates.

Born in 1790, the son of an Italian émigré and a Russian baroness, he had made a name for himself in military intelligence during the Napoleonic wars. He was promoted lieutenant-colonel at twenty-four, and seemed on the verge of a brilliant career, but after a duel – one of

---

* Written in November 1820 and published the following year, 'The Black Shawl', in which a jealous lover kills his Greek mistress and her Armenian paramour, became, though an indifferent work, one of Pushkin's most popular poems. It was set to music by the composer Aleksey Verstovsky in 1824, and often performed.

several – which resulted in the death of his opponent, was transferred from the guards to an army regiment and posted to Kishinev. Pushkin, who would describe him as 'uniting genuine scholarship with the excellent qualities of a military man',[4] was immediately attracted to him, pestered him with questions about his duels, and borrowed books from his library. The day after meeting Pushkin, Liprandi dined with Prince George Cantacuzen and his wife Elena, the addressee of Pushkin's Lycée poem, 'To a Beauty Who Took Snuff'. They asked Liprandi to bring Pushkin round to see them; though protesting that his acquaintance with the poet was very short, the next day he, Fedor Orlov, and Pushkin called on the Cantacuzens, stayed for dinner, and remained drinking until well after midnight.

Pushkin soon had a wide circle of acquaintances and friends among the civilians and officers in the town. Some he had known, or heard of, earlier: a Lycée friend, Konstantin Danzas, now an officer in the engineers, was stationed here, as were the cousins Mikhail and Aleksey Poltoratsky, both cousins of Anna Kern, whose beauty had so impressed Pushkin

George and Elena Cantacuzen

at the Olenins in St Petersburg. They were attached to a unit of the general staff which was carrying out a military topographical survey of Bessarabia. Another member was Aleksandr Veltman. Later a well-known novelist, at this time he dabbled in poetry, and, cherishing a profound admiration for Pushkin's work, initially held himself timidly aloof from him, fearing a comparison between their achievements. Chance, however, brought them together; Pushkin learnt of his verse and, calling at Veltman's lodgings, asked him to read the work on which he was then engaged: an imitation Moldavian folk-tale in verse, entitled 'Yanko the Shepherd', some episodes of which caused him to laugh uproariously.

Among the local inhabitants he frequently visited the civil governor, Konstantin Katakazi: 'Having yawned my way through mass,/I go to Katakazi's,/What Greek rubbish!/What Greek bedlam!' he wrote.[5] Most evenings a company gathered to play cards at the home of the vice-governor, Matvey Krupensky; here Pushkin could satisfy his addiction to faro. Krupensky's large mansion housed not only the province's revenue department, but also, in a columned hall decorated with a frieze emblematic of Russian military achievement, the town's small theatre. At the beginning of November, a twenty-year-old ensign, Vladimir Gorchakov, who had just arrived in Kishinev and was attached to Orlov's staff, attended a performance given by a travelling troupe of German actors. 'My attention was particularly caught,' he wrote in his diary, 'by the entrance of a young man of small stature, but quite strong and broad-shouldered, with a quick and observant gaze, extraordinarily lively in his movements, often laughing in a surfeit of unconstrained gaiety and then suddenly turning meditative, which awoke one's sympathy. His features were irregular and ugly, but the expression of thought was so fascinating that involuntarily one wanted to ask: what is the matter? What grief darkens your soul? The unknown's clothing consisted of a closely buttoned black frock-coat and wide trousers of the same colour.'[6] This was Pushkin; during the interval Alekseev introduced Gorchakov to him, and the two were soon deep in reminiscences of the St Petersburg theatre and of their favourite actresses, Semenova and Kolosova.

Another prominent member of Kishinev society was Egor Varfolomey, a wealthy tax-farmer and member of the supreme council of Bessarabia. He was extremely hospitable: it was very difficult to visit him and not stay to dinner; but for the young officers and civil servants the main attractions of the house were the informal dances in his ballroom and his eighteen-year-old daughter, Pulkheriya. She was a pretty, plump, healthy, empty-headed girl, with few powers of conversation, whose invariable reply to advances, compliments or witticisms was 'Who do you think you are! What are you about!' – Veltman, in a flight of fancy, surmised that she might be an automaton.[7] Nevertheless, Pushkin, for want of a better object for his affections, fell in love with her during his stay in Kishinev. It was hardly a passionate affair, and did not prevent him from languishing, during the next three years, after many others: Mariya Schreiber, the shy seventeen-year-old daughter of the president of the medical board, for example; or Viktoriya Vakar, a colonel's wife with whom he often danced; or the playful, dark-complexioned Anika Sandulaki. He sighed from afar after pretty Elena Solovkina, who was married to the commander of the Okhotsk infantry regiment and occasionally visited Kishinev, and made a determined assault on the virtue of Ekaterina Stamo, whose husband Apostol, a counsellor of the Bessarabian civil court, was some thirty years older than her. 'Pushkin was a great rake, and in addition I, unfortunately, was considered a beauty in my youth,' Ekaterina remarked in her recollections. 'I had great difficulty in restraining a young man of his age. I always had the most strict principles, – such was the upbringing we all had been given, – but, you know, Aleksandr Sergeevich's views on women were somewhat lax, and then one must take into account that our society was strange to him, as a Russian. Thanks to my personal tact [. . .] I managed finally to arrange things with Aleksandr Sergeevich in such a way that he did not repeat the declaration which he had made to me, a married woman.'[8] She was one of the seven children of Zamfir Ralli, a rich Moldavian landowner with estates to the west of Kishinev. Pushkin got to know the family very well during his stay in Kishinev: they were his closest friends among the Moldavian nobility, and he was especially intimate with Ivan, Ekaterina's brother, a year younger than himself, who shared his literary tastes. Another Kishinev beauty was Mariya Eichfeldt, 'whose pretty little face became famous for its attractiveness from Bessarabia to the Caucasus'.[9] She had a much older husband: Pushkin christened the couple 'Zémire and Azor', after the French *opéra comique* with that name on the theme of Beauty and the Beast. He flirted with her in society, but refrained from pressing his advances further, as she was Alekseev's mistress: 'My dear chap, how unjust/Are your jealous dreams,' he wrote.[10]

At the beginning of November General Raevsky's two half-brothers, Aleksandr and Vasily Davydov, came to stay with Orlov. 'Aleksandr Lvovich,' Gorchakov noted, 'was distinguished by the refinement of a marquis, Vasily flaunted a kind of manner peculiar to the common man [. . .] They were both very friendly towards Pushkin, but Aleksandr Lvovich's friendliness was inclined to condescension, which, it seemed to me, was very much disliked by Pushkin.'[11] Orlov was about to visit the Davydov estate at Kamenka – some 160 miles to the south-east of Kiev, not far from the Dnieper – and the brothers also extended an invitation to Pushkin. He accepted with alacrity; Inzov gave his permission; and in the middle of November he left with the Davydovs. Passing through Dubossary, Balta, Olviopol and Novomirgorod, they arrived in Kamenka three days later. General Raevsky and his son Aleksandr were already there, having travelled down from Kiev; Mikhail Orlov and his aide-de-camp Okhotnikov soon followed, bringing with them Ivan Yakushkin, who 'was pleasantly surprised when A.S. Pushkin [. . .] ran out towards me with outstretched arms': they had been introduced to one another in St Petersburg by Chaadaev.[12]

Kamenka was one of the centres of the Decembrist movement in the south; the other, more important, was Tulchin, the headquarters of the Second Army, where Pestel was stationed. The gathering here, ostensibly to celebrate the name-day, on 24 November, of Ekaterina Nikolaevna, the mother of General Raevsky and of the Davydov brothers, was in effect a meeting of a number of the conspirators: Orlov, Okhotnikov, Yakushkin and Vasily Davydov. The party dined luxuriously each evening with Ekaterina Nikolaevna, and then retired to Vasily's quarters for political discussions.

Orlov and Okhotnikov left at the beginning of December. Pushkin had intended to accompany them, but was prevented by illness. Aleksandr Davydov made his excuses to Inzov, writing that 'having caught a severe cold, he is not yet in a condition to undertake the return journey [. . .] but if he feels soon some relief in his illness, will not delay in setting out for Kishinev'.[13] Inzov replied sympathetically, thanking Davydov for allaying his anxiety, since, he wrote, 'Up to now I was in fear for Mr Pushkin, lest he, regardless of the harsh frosts there have been with wind and snow, should have set out and somewhere, given the inconvenience of the steppe highways, should have met with an accident [but am] reassured and hope that your excellency will not allow him to undertake the journey until he has recovered his strength.'[14] He enclosed with his letter a copy of a demand for the repayment of 2,000 roubles, which Pushkin had borrowed from a money-lender in November 1819 to pay a debt at cards.

A few days later Pushkin wrote to Gnedich: 'I am now in the Kiev province, in the village of the Davydovs, charming and intelligent recluses, brothers of General Raevsky. My time slips away between aristocratic dinners and demagogic arguments. Our company, now dispersed, was recently a varied and jolly mixture of original minds, people well-known in our Russia, interesting to an unfamiliar observer. Women are few, there is much champagne, many witty words, many books, a few verses.'[15] Though there may have been few women in Kamenka, Pushkin made the best of the situation and enjoyed an affair with Aglaë Davydova, Aleksandr Lvovich's thirty-three-year-old wife. It was a short-lived liaison. The difference in age and social position between the two led Aglaë to treat him with a patronizing condescension that was as distasteful to Pushkin in his mistress as it had been in her husband. When Liprandi dined with Davydov and his wife in St Petersburg in March 1822 he noted that she 'was not very favourably disposed towards Aleksandr Sergeevich, and it was obviously unwelcome to her, when her husband asked after him with great interest', and added: 'I had already heard a number of times of the kindness shown to Pushkin at Kamenka, and heard from him enthusiastic praise of the family society there, and Aglaë too had been mentioned. Then I learnt that there had been some kind of quarrel between her and Pushkin, and that the latter had rewarded her with some verses!'[16] The affair had indeed broken off acrimoniously, and Pushkin, hurt and insulted, gave vent to his feelings with four extraordinarily spiteful epigrams. One, commenting on her promiscuity, wonders what impelled her to marry Davydov; another, coarse and excessively indecent even by Pushkin's standards, portrays her as sexually insatiable; the least offensive, and the wittiest, is in French:

> To her lover without resistance Aglaë
> Had ceded – he, pale and petrified,
> Was making a great effort – at last, incapable of more,
> Completely breathless, withdrew ... with a bow, –
> 'Monsieur', says Aglaë in an arrogant tone,
> 'Speak, monsieur: why does my appearance
> Intimidate you? Will you tell me the cause?
> Is it disgust?' 'Good heavens, it's not that.'
> 'Excess of love?' 'No, of respect.'[17]

Pushkin did not leave Kamenka until the end of January 1821, then travelling, in the company of the Davydov brothers, not to Kishinev but to Kiev, where he put up with General Raevsky, and met the 'hussar-poet' Denis Davydov, cousin both of the Davydovs and of General Raevsky, famous for his partisan activities during the French army's retreat in 1812 – the model for Denisov in *War and Peace*. 'Hussar-poet, you've sung of bivouacs/Of the licence of devil-may-care carousals/Of the fearful charm of battle/And of the curls of your moustache,' he wrote.[18] In the second week of February he and the Davydovs set off for Tulchin, some 180 miles to the west. His St Petersburg acquaintance General Kiselev was now chief of staff of the Second Army here: he was to marry Sofya Potocka later that year. 'I had the occasion to see [Pushkin] in Tulchin at Kiselev's,' wrote Nikolay Basargin, a young ensign in the 31st Jägers. 'I was not acquainted with him, but met him two or three times in company. I disliked him as a person. There was something of the bully about him, an element of vanity, and the desire to mock and wound others.'[19] After a week in Tulchin Pushkin, still avoiding his official duties, returned to Kamenka with the Davydovs, arriving on or about 18 February.

Denis Davydov

During his first stay on the estate he had begun a new notebook, copying into it fair versions of his Crimean poems 'A Nereid' and 'Sparser grows the flying range of clouds', and continuing to work on *The Prisoner of the Caucasus*. Now, lying on the Davydovs' billiard table surrounded by scraps of manuscript, so engrossed in composition as to ignore everything about him, he produced the first fair copy of the poem, adding at the end of the text the notation '23 February 1821, Kamenka'.[20] Despite this achievement, he was often in a bleak mood. 'Beneath the storms of harsh fate/My flowering wreath has faded,' he had written the previous day.[21] He was isolated from his family and his closest friends, from the literary and social life of the capital; the best years of his poetic and personal life were being wasted in a provincial slough. Melancholy was to recur ever more frequently during his years of exile: 'I am told he is fading away from depression, boredom and poverty,' Vyazemsky wrote to Turgenev in 1822.[22] Constantly deluding himself with hopes of an end to his exile, or at least of being granted leave to visit St Petersburg 'I shall try to be with you myself for a few days,' he wrote to his brother in January 1822[23] – he was as constantly brought to face the reality of his situation. When, a year later, he made a formal application to Nesselrode for permission to come to St Petersburg, 'whither,' he wrote, 'I am called by the affairs of a family whom I have not seen for three years',[24] he found that Alexander had not forgotten his misdemeanours: Nesselrode's report was endorsed by the emperor with a single word: 'Refused'.[25] He could not but compare himself to Ovid: their fates were strangely alike. Because of their verse (and, in Ovid's case, also for some other, mysterious crime) both had been exiled by an emperor – Ovid by Augustus, the former Octavian, in AD 8 – to the region of the Black Sea. In Ovid's works written in exile – *Tristia* and *Black Sea Letters* – Pushkin found reflections of an experience analogous to his own, and contrasted his emotions as an exile from St Petersburg with those of Ovid as an exile from Rome. 'Like you, submitting to an inimical fate,/ I was your equal in destiny, if not in fame,' he wrote in 'To Ovid', completed on 26 December 1821.[26]

Financial worries – 'He hasn't a copeck', Vyazemsky noted[27] – added to his depression. He had been paid no salary since leaving St Petersburg. In April 1821 Inzov pointed this out to Capo d'Istrias, adding: 'since he receives no allowance from his parent, despite all my assistance he sometimes, however, suffers from a deficiency in decent clothing. In this respect I consider it my most humble duty to ask, my dear sir, that you should instruct the appointment to him of that salary which he received in St Petersburg.'[28] As a result he received a year's salary – less hospital charges and postal insurance it came to 685 roubles 30 copecks – in July, and was thereafter paid at four-monthly intervals. But this, though welcome, could not resolve his financial problems. On 5 May, in reply to the demand for 2,000 roubles forwarded by Inzov, he wrote, 'not being yet of age and possessing neither movable nor immovable property, I am not capable of paying the above-mentioned promissory note.'[29] The 'deficiency in decent clothing' was noted by others: 'He leads a dissipated life, roams the inns, and is always in shirt-sleeves,' wrote Liprandi.[30] His attire in Kishinev tended towards the bizarre: sometimes he dressed as a Turk, sometimes as a Moldavian, sometimes as a Jew, usually topping the ensemble with a fez – costumes which were adopted, not primarily from eccentricity, but because of the absence from his wardrobe of more formal wear. 'My father had the brilliant idea of sending me some clothes,' he wrote to his brother. 'Tell him that I asked you to remind him of it.'[31]

He had eventually left Kamenka towards the end of February, and, taking a long way round through Odessa, where he spent two days, arrived in Kishinev early in March.* He found a town much stirred by events which had taken place during his absence. In 1814 three Greek merchants in Odessa, one of the most important Greek communities outside the Ottoman empire, had founded the *Philike Hetaireia* (Society of Friends), whose aim was the liberation of Greece from Turkish rule. The society was soon actively engaged in conspiracy: intriguing with potential rebels, it persuaded its Greek supporters that the tsar, as the head of the greatest Orthodox state, would be unable to ignore any bid for Greek independence. In 1819–20 the time seemed ripe for an uprising: there were intimations or outbreaks of revolt in Germany, Spain, Piedmont and Naples. The society offered its leadership to Capo d'Istrias; he refused, and it turned in his stead to Alexander Ypsilanti, a Phanariot Greek,† the son of the former *hospodar* of Moldavia and Wallachia. An officer in the Russian army, Ypsilanti had distinguished himself in the campaigns of 1812 and 1813, losing an arm at the battle of Dresden. He had attended Alexander I, as one of the emperor's adjutants, at the congress of Vienna, and in 1817 had been promoted major-general and given command of a cavalry brigade. On his election to the leadership of the society he moved to Kishinev.

On the night of 21 February 1821, at Galaţa – the principal port of Moldavia, on the left bank of the Danube – the small Turkish garrison and a number of Turkish merchants were massacred by Greeks; the following day Alexander Ypsilanti, accompanied by his brothers, George and Nicholas, Prince Cantacuzen, and several other Greek officers in Russian service, crossed the Prut. At Iaşi on the twenty-third, in proclamations addressed to the Greeks and Moldavians, he called on them to

---

* It is thought that Pushkin might have paid a second visit to Kamenka, Kiev, and possibly Tulchin in November-December 1822, but there is no direct evidence as to his whereabouts at this time. The arguments supporting the hypothesis are summarized in *Letopis*, I, 504–5.
† From the Phanari, or lighthouse quarter of Constantinople, which became the Greek quarter after the Turkish conquest: and hence the appellation of the Greek official class under the Turks, through whom the affairs of the Christian population in the Ottoman empire were largely administered.

rise against the Turks, declaring that his enterprise had the support of a 'great power'. Though Michael Souzzo, the *hospodar*, threw in his lot with the uprising, it enjoyed no popular support, and Ypsilanti condemned it to failure by his irresolute leadership, condoning, in addition, the massacre at Galața and a subsequent similar incident at Iași. A final blow to the revolt was a letter from Alexander I, signed by Capo d'Istrias, which denounced Ypsilanti's actions as 'shameful and criminal', upbraided him for misusing the tsar's name, struck him from the Russian army list, and called upon him to lay down his arms immediately.[32] Though Ypsilanti endeavoured to brave matters out, he was abandoned by many of the revolutionary leaders, and, retreating slowly northwards towards the Austrian frontier, underwent a series of humiliating defeats, culminating in that of Dragashan on 7 June, after which he escaped into Austria. Here he was kept in close confinement for over seven years, and, when eventually released at the instance of Nicholas I, died in Vienna in extreme poverty in 1828. A simultaneous revolt in Greece itself, led, among others, by Ypsilanti's brother Demetrios, proved more successful: in 1833, after the intervention of the Great Powers, it eventually resulted in the establishment of an independent Greece.

Ypsilanti's insurrection had been in progress for just over a week when Pushkin returned to Kishinev. The boldness of this exploit in the cause of Greek independence could not fail to arouse his enthusiasm. He dashed off a letter to Vasily Davydov, telling him of the progress of the revolt, speculating on Russia's policy – 'Will we occupy Moldavia and Wallachia in the guise of peace-loving mediators; will we cross the Danube as the allies of the Greeks and the

Alexander Ypsilanti

enemies of their enemies?' – and quoting from an insurgent's letter on events at Iași: 'He describes with ardour the ceremony of consecrating the banners and Prince Ypsilanti's sword – the rapture of the clergy and laity – and the sublime moments of Hope and Freedom.' Ypsilanti, whom Pushkin had met the previous year, is mentioned with admiration: 'Alexander Ypsilanti's first step is splendid and brilliant. He has begun luckily – from now on, whether dead or a victor he belongs to history – 28 years old, one arm missing, a magnanimous goal! – an enviable lot.'[33] 'We spoke about A. Ypsilanti,' he records in his diary of an evening at the house of a 'charming Greek lady'. 'Among five Greeks I alone spoke like a Greek – they all despair of the success of the *Hetaireia* enterprise. I am firmly convinced that Greece will triumph, and that 25,000,000* Turks will leave the flowering land of Hellas to the rightful heirs of Homer and Themistocles.'[34] Indeed, his enthusiasm was such that it became rumoured that he – as Byron was to do two years later – had joined the revolt. 'I have heard from trustworthy people that he has slipped away to the Greeks,' the journalist and historian Pogodin wrote to a friend from Moscow.[35] But his participation was only vicarious.

The question of Russia's attitude to the insurrection, which Pushkin raises in his letter to Davydov, was one which preoccupied both the government and the Decembrists. Both were not averse to striking a blow against Russia's old enemy, Turkey. 'If the 16th division,' Orlov remarked of his command, 'were to be sent to the liberation [of Greece], that would not be at all bad. I have sixteen thousand men under arms, thirty-six cannon, and six Cossack regiments. With that one can have some fun. The regiments are splendid, all Siberian flints. They would blunt the Turkish swords.'[36] Alexander, however, did not wish to back revolutionary activity in Greece, while the Decembrists, though supporters of Greek independence, were not eager to have an illiberal tsar gain kudos by posing as a liberator abroad. And, curiously, they had the opportunity of influencing events. At the beginning of April Kiselev was requested by the government to send an officer to Kishinev to report on the insurrection. His choice fell on Pestel, whose report may have been instrumental in persuading the government not to support the revolt: Pushkin certainly believed this to be the case. In November 1833, at a rout at the Austrian ambassador's in St Petersburg, he met Michael Souzzo, the former *hospodar* of Moldavia. 'He reminded me,' Pushkin wrote in his diary, 'that in 1821 I called on him in Kishinev together with Pestel. I told him how Pestel had deceived him, and betrayed the *Hetaireia* – by representing it to the Emperor Alexander as a branch of Carbonarism. Souzzo could conceal neither his astonish-

A slip of the pen: there were approximately 25,000 Turks in the Morea.

ment nor his vexation – the subtlety of a Phanariot had been conquered by the cunning of a Russian officer! This wounded his vanity.'[37]

Pushkin's confidence in the success of the revolt soon proved unjustified – at least as far as Moldavia was concerned, where the uprising was quickly suppressed by the Turks. After a final, bloody engagement at Sculeni, on the west bank of the Prut, in June, the few survivors escaped by swimming the river. Gorchakov, who had been sent to observe events from the Russian side, gave Pushkin an account of this incident, which he later made use of in the short story 'Kirdzhali'. Though he remained constant in his support for Greek independence, he was disappointed by this 'crowd of cowardly beggars, thieves and vagabonds who could not even withstand the first fire of the worthless Turkish musketry'. 'As for the officers, they are worse than the soldiers. We have seen these new Leonidases in the streets of Odessa and Kishinev – we are personally acquainted with a number of them, we can attest to their complete uselessness – they have discovered the art of being boring, even at the moment when their conversation ought to interest every European – no idea of the military art, no concept of honour, no enthusiasm – the French and Russians who are here show them a contempt of which they are only too worthy, they put up with anything, even blows of a cane, with a sangfroid worthy of Themistocles. I am neither a barbarian nor an apostle of the Koran, the cause of Greece interests me keenly, that is just why I become indignant when I see these wretches invested with the sacred office of defenders of liberty.'[38]

As the failure of the insurrection became apparent, refugees began to flood into Bessarabia: Moldavian nobles, Phanariot Greeks from the Turkish territories and Constantinople, Albanians and others. Their presence certainly made Kishinev a more lively place, and Pushkin's circle of acquaintances was widened by a number of the new arrivals. Among these was Todoraki Balsch, a Moldavian *hatman* – military commander – who had fled from Iaşi with his wife Mariya – 'a woman in her late twenties, reasonably comely, extremely witty and loquacious'[39] – and daughter Anika. For some time Mariya was the sole object of Pushkin's attentions; they held long, uninhibited conversations in French together, and she became convinced that he was in love with her. However, he suddenly transferred his allegiance to another refugee from Iaşi, Ekaterina Albrecht, 'two years older than Balsch, but more attractive, with unconstrained European manners; she had read much, experienced much, and in civility consigned Balsch to the background'.[40] Ekaterina came from an old Moldavian noble family, the Başotăs, and was separated from her third husband, the commander of the Life Guards Uhlans: qualities which attracted Pushkin — he remarked that she was 'historical and of ardent passions'.[41] As a result, Mariya's feelings turned to virulent dislike, which the following year was to give rise to a notable scandal.

Calypso Polichroni

Another refugee was Calypso Polichroni, a Greek girl who had fled from Constantinople with her mother and taken a humble two-room lodging in Kishinev. She went little into society; indeed, would hardly have been welcomed there, for her morals were not above suspicion. 'There was not the slightest strictness about her conversation or her behaviour,' Wiegel noted, adding euphemistically: 'if she had lived at the time of Pericles, history, no doubt, would have recorded her name together with those of Phryne and Laïs'[42] – famous courtesans of the past. 'Extremely small, with a scarcely noticeable bosom,' Calypso 'had a long, dry face, always rouged in the Turkish manner; a huge nose as it were divided her face from top to bottom; she had thick, long hair and huge fiery eyes made even more voluptuous by the use of kohl';[43] and 'a tender, attractive voice, not only when she spoke, but also when she sang to the guitar terrible, gloomy Turkish songs'.[44] But what excited Pushkin's imagination 'was the thought that at about fifteen she was supposed to have first known passion in the arms of Lord Byron, who was then travelling in Greece'.[45] If Vyazemsky came to Kishinev, Pushkin wrote, he would introduce him to 'a Greek girl, who has exchanged kisses with Lord Byron'.[46] 'You were born to set on fire/The imagination of poets,' he told her.[47] A juxtaposition of Byron's life with what is known of Calypso's shows they can never have met. But in inventing the story, Calypso revealed an acute perception of psychology: in dalliance with her there was an extra titillation to be derived from the feeling that one was following, metaphorically, in Byron's footsteps. Bulwer-Lytton is supposed to have gained a peculiar satisfaction from an affair with a woman whom Byron had loved, while the Marquis de Boissy, who married Teresa Guiccioli, would, it was reported, introduce her as 'My wife, the Marquise de Boissy, Byron's former mistress'.[48] Pushkin was not immune to this thrill.*

Meanwhile Inzov had put him to work. Peter Manega, a Rumanian Greek who had studied law in Paris, had produced for Inzov a code of Moldavian law, written in French, and Pushkin was given the task of turning it into Russian. In his spare time he began to study Moldavian, taking lessons from one of Inzov's servants. He learnt enough to be able to teach Inzov's parrot to swear in Moldavian. Chuckling heartily, it repeated an indecency to the archbishop of Kishinev and Khotin when the latter was lunching at Inzov's on Easter Sunday. Inzov did not hold the prank against Pushkin; indeed, when Capo d'Istrias wrote a few weeks later to enquire 'whether [Pushkin] was now obeying the suggestions of a naturally good heart or the impulses of an unbridled and harmful imagination', he replied: 'Inspired, as are all residents of Parnassus, by a spirit of jealous emulation of certain writers, in his conversations with me he sometimes reveals poetic thoughts. But I am convinced that age and time will render him sensible in this respect and with experience he will come to recognize the unfoundedness of conclusions, inspired by the reading of harmful works and by the conventions accepted by the present age.'[49] Had he known what Pushkin was writing he might not have been so generous.

At this period in his life Pushkin was a professed, indeed a militant atheist, modelling himself on the eighteenth-century French rationalists he admired. Whether or not he was the author, while at St Petersburg, of the quatrain 'We will amuse the good citizens/And in the pillory/With the guts of the last priest/Will strangle the last tsar',†[50] an adaptation of a famous remark by Diderot, his view of religion emerges clearly from

---

* Pushkin could later, when in Moscow in 1826–7, have met a woman who had indubitably been Byron's mistress: Claire Clairmont, the mother of Byron's daughter Allegra, was employed as a governess in Moscow from 1825 to 1827, first by the Posnikov, and later by the Kaisarov family. She met Pushkin's uncle, Vasily, and his close friend, Sobolevsky, but Pushkin himself was apparently unaware of her existence.

† The quatrain is listed under *Dubia* in the Academy edition; its ascription to Pushkin is based on an army report of the interrogation of Private (demoted from captain) D. Brandt, who, on 18 July 1827, deposed that his fellow-inmate in the Moscow lunatic asylum, Cadet V.Ya. Zubov, had declaimed this fragment of Pushkin to him (II, 1199–200).

much of his Kishinev work. When Inzov, a pious man, made it clear that he expected his staff to attend church, Pushkin, in a humorous epistle to Davydov, explained that his compliance was due to hypocrisy, not piety, and complained about the communion fare:

> my impious stomach
> 'For pity's sake, old chap,' remarks,
> 'If only Christ's blood
> Were, let's say, Lafite . . .
> Or Clos de Vougeot, then not a word,
> But this – it's just ridiculous –
> Is Moldavian wine and water.'[51]

He greeted Easter with the irreverent poem 'Christ is risen', addressed to the daughter of a Kishinev inn-keeper. Today he would exchange kisses with her in the Christian manner, but tomorrow, for another kiss, would be willing to adhere to 'the faith of Moses', and even put into her hand 'That by which one can distinguish/A genuine Hebrew from the Orthodox'.[52]

At the beginning of May, in a letter to Aleksandr Turgenev, he jokingly suggested that the latter might use his influence to obtain a few days' leave for his exiled friend, adding: 'I would bring you in reward a composition in the taste of the Apocalypse, and would dedicate it to you, Christ-loving pastor of our poetic flock.'*[53] The description of Turgenev alluded to the fact that he was the head of the Department of Foreign Creeds; the work Pushkin was proposing to dedicate to him was, however, hardly appropriate: it was *The Gabrieliad*, a blasphemous parody of the Annunciation.[54]

Far from Jerusalem lives the beautiful Mary, whose 'secret flower' 'Her lazy husband with his old spout/In the mornings fails to water'. God sees her, and, falling in love, sends the archangel Gabriel down to announce this to her. Before Gabriel arrives, Satan appears in the guise of a snake; then, turning into a handsome young man, seduces her. Gabriel interrupts them; the two fight; Satan, vanquished by a bite 'in that fatal spot/(Superfluous in almost every fight)/That haughty

---

* Pushkin is comparing himself to St John; earlier in the letter he refers to Kishinev as Patmos, the island to which the apostle was exiled by the Emperor Domitian, and where he is supposed to have written the Book of Revelation, the Apocalypse.

member, with which the devil sinned' (421–2), limps off, and his place
and occupation are assumed by Gabriel. After his departure, as Mary
is lying contemplatively on her bed, a white dove – God, in disguise –
flies in at the window, and, despite her resistance, has its way with her.

> Tired Mary
> Thought: 'What goings-on!
> One, two, three! – how can they keep it up?
> I must say, it's been a busy time:
> I've been had in one and the same day
> By Satan, an Archangel and by God.'
>
> (509–14)

It is slightly surprising to find the poem in Pushkin's work at this time:
the wit is not that of his current passion, Byron, but that of his former
heroes, Voltaire and Parny; the blend of the blasphemous and the erotic
is characteristic of the eighteenth, rather than the nineteenth century.
Obviously it could not be published, but, like Pushkin's political verses,
was soon in circulation in manuscript.* Seven years later this light-
hearted Voltairean anti-religious squib was to cause him almost as much
trouble as his political verse had earlier.

Fasting seemed to stimulate Pushkin's comic vein; during the following Lent, in 1822, he produced the short comic narrative poem 'Tsar
Nikita and His Forty Daughters'.[55] There is nothing blasphemous or
anti-religious about this work; though it might be considered risqué or
indecent, it is certainly not, as it has been called, 'out-and-out pornogra-
phy'.[56] Written in the manner of a Russian fairy-tale, the poem tells us
that Tsar Nikita's forty daughters, though uniformly captivating from
head to toe, were all deficient in the same respect:

> One thing was missing.
> What was this?
> Nothing in particular, a trifle, bagatelle,
> Nothing or very little,
> But it was missing, all the same.
> How might one explain this,

---

* It was first printed in London in 1861; the first Russian edition – with some omissions
– appeared in 1907.

So as not to anger
That devout pompous ninny,
The over-prim censor?
How is it to be done? . . . Aid me, Lord!
The tsarevnas have between their legs . . .
No, that's far too precise
And dangerous to modesty, –
Let's try another tack:
I love in Venus her breast,
Her lips, her ankle particularly,
But the steel that strikes love's spark,
The goal of my desire . . .
Is what? . . . Nothing!
Nothing or very little . . .
And this wasn't present
In the young princesses,
Mischievous and lively.

Tsar Nikita is simpler, more of a *jeu d'esprit* than *The Gabrieliad*: it consists essentially of a number of variations on the same joke. But it is charmingly written, witty and highly amusing.

Pushkin's readiness to take offence and his profligate way with a challenge were as evident in Kishinev as in St Petersburg. At the beginning of June 1821, having quarrelled with a former French officer, M. Déguilly, for some reason possibly connected with the latter's wife, he called him out, but was incensed to discover the following day that his opponent had managed to weasel his way out of a duel. He dashed off an offensive letter in French, and unable to draw blood with his sabre, consoled himself by doing so with his pen, sketching a cartoon showing Déguilly, clad only in a shirt, exclaiming: 'My wife! . . . my breeches! . . . and my duel too! . . . ah, well, let her get out of it how she will, since it is she who wears the breeches . . .'[57]

Other opponents were more worthy. One evening in January 1822, at a dance in the casino, Pushkin's request that the orchestra should play a mazurka was countermanded by a young officer of the 33rd Jägers, who demanded a Russian quadrille. Shouts of 'Mazurka!', 'Quadrille!'

alternated for some time; eventually the orchestra, though composed of army musicians, obeyed the civilian. Lieutenant-Colonel Starov, the commander of the Jäger regiment, told his officer that he should demand an apology. When the officer hesitated, Starov marched over to Pushkin, and, failing to receive satisfaction, arranged a meeting for the following morning. The duel took place a mile or two outside Kishinev, during a snowstorm: the driving snow and the cold made both aiming and loading difficult. They fired first at sixteen paces and both missed; then at twelve and missed again. Both contestants wished to continue, but their seconds insisted that the affair be postponed. On his return to Kishinev, Pushkin called on Aleksey Poltoratsky and, not finding him at home, dropped off a brief jingle: 'I'm alive/Starov's/Well./The duel's not over.'[58] In fact, it was: Poltoratsky and Nikolay Alekseev, who had acted as Pushkin's second, arranged a meeting at Nikoleti's restaurant, where Pushkin often played billiards, and a reconciliation took place. Pushkin swelled with pride when Starov, who had fought in the campaign of 1812 and was known for his bravery, complimented him on his behaviour: 'You have increased my respect for you,' he said, 'and I must truthfully say that you stand up to bullets as well as you write.'[59] According to Gorchakov, Pushkin displayed even more sangfroid at a duel fought in May or June 1823. This was with Zubov, an officer of the topographical survey, whom he had accused of cheating at cards. Pushkin, like his character the Count, in the short story 'The Shot', one of the Tales of Belkin, arrived with a hatful of cherries, which he ate while Zubov took the first shot. He missed. 'Are you satisfied?' Pushkin asked. Zubov threw himself on him and embraced him. 'That is going too far,' said Pushkin, and walked off without taking his shot.[60]

The Starov affair had, however, unpleasant repercussions. Though the quarrel had been public, the duel and reconciliation were not; and it was rumoured, especially in Moldavian society, that both Starov and Pushkin had acted dishonourably. At an evening party some weeks later Pushkin light-heartedly referred to a remark made by Liprandi to the effect that Moldavians did not fight duels, but hired a couple of ruffians to thrash their enemy. Mariya Balsch, still smarting with jealousy, said acidly, 'You have an odd way of defending yourself, too,' adding that his duel with Starov had ended in a very peculiar manner. Pushkin, enraged, rushed off to Balsch, who was playing cards, and demanded satisfaction for the insult. Mariya complained of his behaviour to her husband, who, somewhat the worse for wine, himself flew into a rage, calling Pushkin a coward, a convict and worse. 'The scene [. . .] could not have been more terrible, Balsch was shouting and screaming, the old lady Bogdan fell down in a swoon, the vice-governor's pregnant wife had hysterics.'[61] The affair was reported to Inzov, who ordered that the two should be reconciled. Two days later they both appeared before the vice-governor, Krupensky; Major-General Pushchin was also present. When they met, Balsch said, 'I have been forced to apologize to you. What kind of apology do you require?' Pushkin, without a word, slapped his face and drew out a pistol, before being led from the room by Pushchin.[62] In a letter to Inzov Balsch demanded, firstly a safeguard against any further attempt which Pushkin might make on him, and, secondly, that the other should be proceeded against with the utmost rigour of the law.[63] Whatever the rights of the situation, there was only one choice Inzov could make between an extremely junior civil servant and a Moldavian magnate: sending Pushkin to his quarters, he placed him under house arrest for three weeks.

Arguments were frequent at Inzov's dinner table. A few months later, on 20 July 1822, when discussing politics with Smirnov, a translator, Pushkin 'became heated, enraged and lost his temper. Abuse of all classes flew about. Civil councillors were villains and thieves, generals for the most part swine, only peasant farmers were honourable. Pushkin particularly attacked the nobility. They all ought to be hanged, and if this were to happen, he would have pleasure in tying the noose.'[64] When both parties were heated with wine a possible explosion was never too far away. One occurred the following day, when the conversation at dinner touched upon the subject of hailstorms; whereupon a retired army captain named Rudkovsky claimed to have once witnessed a remarkable storm, during which hailstones weighing no less than three pounds apiece had fallen. Pushkin howled with laughter, Rudkovsky became indignant, and, after they had risen from table and Inzov had left, an exchange of insults led to an agreement to exchange shots. Both, accompanied by Smirnov, who had suffered Pushkin's abuse the previous day, then went to Pushkin's quarters, where some kind of fracas took place. Rudkovsky asserted that Pushkin attacked him with a knife, and Smirnov, agreeing, claimed to have managed to ward off the blow. Luckily no one was injured; however, Inzov, learning of the incident, put Pushkin under house arrest again.

General Orlov, 'Hymen's shaven-headed recruit',[65] had married Ekaterina Raevskaya in Kiev on 15 May 1821. Pushkin welcomed her arrival in Kishinev, and would visit the couple almost every day, lounging on their divan in wide Turkish velvet trousers, and conversing with them animatedly. He went riding with Orlov and fell off. 'He can only ride Pegasus or a nag from the Don,' the general commented to his wife. 'Pushkin no longer pretends to be

Mikhail Orlov

cruel,' she wrote to her brother Aleksandr in November, 'he often calls on us to smoke his pipe and discourses or chats very pleasantly. He has only just completed an ode on Napoleon, which, in my humble opinion, is very good, as far as I can judge, having heard only part of it once.'[66] Napoleon had died on 5 May 1821 (NS); the news of his death reached Kishinev in July.

> The miraculous destiny has been accomplished;
> The great man is no more.
> In gloomy captivity has set
> The terrible age of Napoleon,

Pushkin wrote.[67] His earlier hatred of the emperor had been replaced, if not by the hero-worship of Romanticism, at least by awe and admiration.

Orlov was a humane and enlightened commander, who was particularly anxious to reduce the incidence of corporal punishment in the units under his command. He had surrounded himself by a number of like-minded officers: Pushchin, his second-in-command, was a Decembrist, as was Okhotnikov, his aide-de-camp. So too was Vladimir Raevsky, 'a man of extraordinary energy, capabilities, very well-educated and no stranger to literature':[68] a distant relative of Pushkin's friends. Born in 1795, Raevsky had entered the army at sixteen; in 1812, as an ensign in an artillery brigade, he had been awarded a gold sword for bravery at Borodino. Now a major in the 32nd Jägers, he was the division's chief education officer, responsible for all its Lancaster schools.* This position gave him great influence on the rank-and-file of the division, and he employed it to inculcate what were considered to be dangerously subversive ideas. A later report on his activities singled out the fact that in handwriting exercises he used for examples words such as 'freedom', 'equality', and 'constitution' and alleged that he told officer cadets that constitutional government was better than any other form of government, and especially than Russian monarchic government, which, although called monarchic, was really despotic.[69] A pedagogue by nature, he exposed the gaps in Pushkin's knowledge, and was a severe critic of his verse.

In December 1821 Liprandi was ordered by Orlov to report on the condition of the 31st and 32nd Jäger regiments, stationed in Izmail and Akkerman at the mouth of the Dniester. He invited Pushkin to accompany him; Inzov, who had just been reprimanded for not keeping a strict watch over his protégé, at first refused his permission, but was persuaded by Orlov to change his mind.

Pushkin was full of historical enthusiasm when the two set off on 13 December. He was eager to stop in Bendery and visit the camp at Varnitsa, where Charles XII of Sweden had lived from 1709 to 1713, having taken refuge on Turkish territory after his defeat by Peter at Poltava – the battle which was to be the climax of, and provide the title for Pushkin's long narrative poem of 1828–9. Liprandi, however, hurried him on. The next post-station, Kaushany, aroused his excitement again: this had been the seat, from the sixteenth century until 1806, of the khans who had ruled Budzhak, the southern region of Moldavia. But according to Liprandi there was nothing to see and, stopping only to change horses, they drove on.

They arrived in Akkerman early in the evening of the fourteenth, and went straight to dinner with Colonel Nepenin, the commander of

Liprandi

---

* A system for mass education devised by the Englishman Joseph Lancaster (1778–1838), by which the advanced pupils taught the beginners

the 32nd Jägers. Among the guests was an old St Petersburg acquaintance, Lieutenant-Colonel Pierre Courteau, now commandant of the fortress. He and Pushkin were both members of Kishinev's short-lived Masonic lodge, Ovid, opened in the spring and closed – together with all other lodges in Bessarabia – in December by Inzov on the emperor's orders. While Pushkin and Courteau were talking, Nepenin asked Liprandi in an undertone, audible to Pushkin, whether his friend was the author of *A Dangerous Neighbour* – the indecent little epic composed by Pushkin's uncle, Vasily. Liprandi, embarrassed, and wishing to avoid further queries, replied that he was, but did not like to have it talked about. His ruse succeeded, the poem was not mentioned further; later that evening, however, Pushkin took him to task for his subterfuge, and called Nepenin an uneducated ignoramus for imagining that he, a twenty-two-year-old, could be the author of a poem which had been well-known ever since its composition ten years earlier, in 1811.

The following day, while Liprandi was inspecting the regiment, Pushkin was shown round the fortress by Courteau; they dined with him, and returned to their quarters in the early hours of the morning, after an evening spent at the card-table and in flirtation with the commandant's 'five robust daughters, no longer in the bloom of youth'.[70] They left for Izmail early the following evening, arriving at ten at night and putting up with a Slovenian merchant, Slavič.

In 1791, during the Russo–Turkish war, Izmail had been stormed and captured by a Russian army commanded by Suvorov – an event celebrated by Byron in the seventh and eighth cantos of *Don Juan*. Pushkin was naturally impatient to inspect the scenes of the fighting: when Liprandi returned to their lodging the next evening he found that his companion had already been round the fortress with Slavič; he was amazed that the besiegers had managed to scale the fortifications facing the Danube. He had also taken down a Slovenian song from the dictation of their host's sister-in-law, Irena. The following morning Liprandi, before leaving to inspect the 31st Jägers, introduced Pushkin to a naval lieutenant in the Danube flotilla, Ivan Gamaley; together they visited the town, the fortress and the quarantine station; were taken to the casino by Slavič, and then had supper at his house with another naval lieutenant, Vasily Shcherbachev. Returning at midnight, Liprandi found Pushkin sitting cross-legged on a divan, surrounded by a large number of little pieces of paper. When asked whether he had got hold of Irena's curling papers, Pushkin laughed, shuffled them together and hid them under a cushion; the two emptied a decanter of local wine and went to bed. In the morning Liprandi awoke to find Pushkin, unclothed, sitting in the same posture as the previous night, again surrounded by his pieces of paper, but holding a pen in his hand with which he was beating time as he recited, nodding his head in unison. Noticing that Liprandi was awake, he stopped and gathered up his papers; he had been caught in the act of composition. That morning Liprandi, after writing his report, called on Major-General Tuchkov, who expressed the wish to meet Pushkin. He came to dinner at their lodgings and afterwards bore off Pushkin, who returned at ten in the evening, somewhat out of sorts; he wished he could stay here a month to examine properly everything the general had shown him. 'He has all the classics and extracts from them,' he told Liprandi, who jokingly suggested that he was more interested in Irena's classical forms.[71]

The next morning they set out for Kishinev. Late that evening, as Pushkin was dozing in his corner of the carriage, Liprandi remarked that it was a pity it was so dark, as otherwise they could have seen to the left the site of the battle of Kagul: here in August 1770 General Rumyantsev with 17,000 men engaged the main Turkish army, winning a hard-fought battle with the bayonet and capturing the Turkish camp. Pushkin immediately started to life, animatedly discussed the battle, and quoted a few lines of verse – perhaps those from his Lycée poem, 'Recollections in Tsarskoe Selo', in which he mentions the monument to the battle in the palace park:

> In the thick shade of gloomy pines
> Rises a simple monument.
> O, how shameful for thee, Kagulian shore!
> And glorious for our dear native land![72]

Arriving in Leovo before midday, they called on Lieutenant-Colonel Katasanov, the commander of the Cossack regiment stationed here. He was away, but his adjutant insisted that they should stay for lunch: caviare, smoked sturgeon – of which Pushkin was inordinately fond – and vodka appeared, succeeded by partridge soup and roast chicken. Half an hour after their departure Pushkin, who had been in a brown study, suddenly burst into such raucous and prolonged laughter that Liprandi thought he was having a fit. 'I love cossacks because they are so individual and don't keep to the normal rules of taste,' he said. 'We – indeed everyone else – would have made soup from the chicken and would have roasted the partridge, but they did the opposite!'[73] He was so struck by this that after his return to Kishinev – they arrived at nine that evening, 23 December – he sought out the French chef Tardif – 'inexhaustible in ideas/For entremets, or for pies'[74] – then living on Gorchakov's charity,* to tell him about it, and two years later, in Odessa, reminded Liprandi of the meal.

During the winter the training battalion of the 16th division had been employed in constructing, at Orlov's expense, a manège, or riding-school. Its ceremonial opening took place on New Year's Day 1822. Liprandi and Okhotnikov had decorated the interior: the walls were hung with bayonets, swords, muskets; on that opposite the entrance was a large shield, with a cannon and heap of cannon-balls to each side; in the centre was the monogram of Alexander, done in pistols, surrounded by a sunburst of ramrods, and flanked by the colours of the Kamchatka and Okhotsk regiments. Before this was a table, laid for forty guests, while eight other tables, four down each side of the hall, were to accommodate the training battalion. Inzov and his officials – including Pushkin – and the town notables were invited. The building was blessed by Archbishop Dimitry and after the ceremony all sat down to a breakfast. 'There was no lack of champagne or vodka. Some felt a buzzing in their heads, but all departed decorously.'[75] A week later Orlov and Ekaterina left for Kiev, where they were to stay for some time. As it turned out, the absence of the division's commander at this moment was unfortunate.

The 16th division was part of the 6th Corps, commanded by Lieutenant-General Sabaneev, whose headquarters were at Tiraspol, halfway between Kishinev and Odessa. Over the previous six months General Kiselev, the chief of staff of the Second Army, had stepped up surveillance of the army's units: he was particularly concerned about the 16th

---

* Formerly proprietor of the Hotel de l'Europe, a luxurious establishment situated at the bottom of the Nevsky Prospect, he took to drink, got into financial difficulty and was ruined when his wife absconded with his cash-box and a colonel of cuirassiers. He fled to Odessa and, after various vicissitudes, ended up in Kishinev.

division, commanded as it was by such a noted liberal. Despite his friendship with Orlov, he had cautiously insinuated to Wittgenstein, the commander of the army, that the latter was unsuited to the command of the division. Raevsky, too, had come to his attention. 'I have long had under observation a certain Raevsky, a major of the 32nd Jäger regiment, who is known to me by his completely unrestrained freethinking. At the present moment in agreement with Sabaneev an overt and covert investigation of all his actions is taking place, and he will, it seems, not escape trial and exile.'[76]

In Orlov's absence General Sabaneev – a short, choleric fifty-two-year-old with a red nose, ginger hair and side-whiskers – began to pay frequent visits to Kishinev. He dined with Inzov on 15 January. Pushkin was present, but was uncharacteristically silent during the meal. Sabaneev was in Kishinev again on the twentieth, when he wrote to Kiselev: 'There is no one in the Kishinev gang besides those whom you know about, but what aim this gang has I do not as yet know. That well-known puppy Pushkin cries me up all over town as one of the Carbonari, and proclaims me guilty of every disorder. Of course, it is not unintentional, and I suspect him of being an organ of the gang.'[77]

On 5 February, at nine in the evening, Raevsky was reclining on his divan and smoking a pipe when there was a knock on the door; his Albanian servant let in Pushkin. He had, he told Raevsky, just eavesdropped on a conversation between Inzov and Sabaneev. Raevsky was to be arrested in the morning. 'To arrest a staff officer on suspicion alone has the whiff of a Turkish punishment. However, what will be, will be,' Raevsky remarked. Lost in admiration at his coolness, Pushkin attempted to embrace him. 'You're no Greek girl,' said Raevsky, pushing him away. The two went round to Liprandi, who was entertaining a number of guests, including his younger brother, Pavel, Sabaneev's adjutant. When Raevsky and Pushkin entered, they were assailed with questions as to what was going on. 'Ask Pavel Petrovich,' Raevsky replied, 'he is Sabaneev's trusted plenipotentiary minister.' 'True,' said the younger Liprandi, 'but if Sabaneev trusted you as he trusts me, you too would not wish to break the codes of trust and honour.'[78] At noon the next day he was summoned to Sabaneev, and confronted with three officer cadets, members of his Lancaster school, whose testimony as to his teaching was the ostensible reason for his arrest. His books and papers were confiscated and a guard put on his quarters. A week later he was taken to Tiraspol and lodged in a cell in the fortress. The investigation into his case and his trial dragged on for years. Only in 1827 was he finally sentenced to exile in Siberia. In March Major-General Pushchin was relieved of his command of a brigade in Orlov's division, and the following April Kiselev succeeded in bringing about Orlov's removal from his command.

In July 1822 Liprandi, passing through Tiraspol on his way from Odessa to Kishinev, managed, with the connivance of the commandant of the fortress, to have half an hour's conversation with Raevsky as they strolled backwards and forwards over the glacis. Raevsky gave him a poem, 'The Bard in the Dungeon', to pass on to Pushkin, who was particularly impressed by one stanza:

> Like an automaton, the dumb nation
> Sleeps in secret fear beneath the yoke:
> Over it a bloody clan of scourges
> Both thoughts and looks executes on the block.

Reading it aloud to Liprandi, he repeated the last line, and added with a sigh: 'After such verses we will not see this Spartan again soon.'[79]

Although the authorities knew that Raevsky was a member of some kind of conspiracy, he remained resolutely silent in prison, and no other arrest followed his. Pushkin was surprised and shocked by the incident, which in addition appeared to him deeply mysterious: the severity of Raevsky's treatment seemed wholly out of proportion to his crime. It was only in January 1825, when his old Lycée friend Pushchin visited him in Mikhailovskoe, that he gained some inkling of what had been going on. 'Imperceptibly we again came to touch on his suspicions concerning the society,' writes Pushchin. 'When I told him that I was far from alone in joining this new service to the fatherland, he leapt from his chair and shouted: "This must all be connected with Major Raevsky, who has been sitting in the fort at Tiraspol for four years and whom they cannot get anything out of."'[80]

In December 1820 Pushkin had written from Kamenka to Gnedich, the publisher of *Ruslan and Lyudmila*, to tell him that his next narrative poem, *The Prisoner of the Caucasus*, was nearly completed. He was unduly optimistic; it was not until the following March that he wrote again. 'The setting of my poem should have been the banks of the noisy Terek, on the frontier of Georgia, in the remote valleys of the Caucasus – I placed my hero in the monotonous plains where I myself spent two months – where far distant from one another four mountains rise, the last spur of the Caucasus; – there are no more than 700 lines in the whole poem – I will send it you soon – so that you might do with it what you like.'[81] Before long, however, he was having second thoughts; he was in need of money and, compared to Gnedich, had made little out of *Ruslan*. In September he wrote to Grech, editor of *Son of the Fatherland*. 'I wanted to send you an extract from my Caucasian Prisoner, but am too lazy to copy it out; would you like to buy the poem from me in one piece? It is 800 lines long; each line is four feet wide; it is chopped into two cantos. I am letting it go cheaply, so that the goods do not get stale.'[82] Unfortunately, Gnedich got wind of the offer. 'You tell me that Gnedich is angry with me,' he wrote to his brother in January 1822, 'he is right – I should have gone to him with my new narrative poem – but my head was spinning – I had not heard from him for a long time; I had to write to Grech – and using this dependable occasion* I offered him the Captive . . . Besides, Gnedich will not haggle with me, nor I with Gnedich, each of us over-concerned with his own advantage, whereas I would have haggled as shamelessly with Grech as with any other bearded connoisseur of the literary imagination.'[83] He also made an attempt to sell the poem directly to book-sellers in St Petersburg, but, offered a derisory sum, had to fall back on Gnedich. On 29 April he sent him the manuscript, accompanying it with a letter which began '*Parve (nec invideo) sine me, liber, ibis in urbem,/Heu mihi! quo domino non licet ire*' – the opening lines of Ovid's *Tristia*,† – and continued: 'Exalted poet, enlightened connoisseur of poets, I hand over to you my Caucasian prisoner [. . .] Call this work a fable, a story, a

---

* Pushkin often uses the word 'occasion' (Russian *okaziya*, borrowed from the French *occasion*) to mean the opportunity to have a letter conveyed privately, by a friend or acquaintance, instead of entrusting it to the post, when it might be opened and read. Here the 'dependable occasion' is a trip by Liprandi to St Petersburg.

† 'Little book (I don't begrudge it), you will go to the city without me,/Alas for me, your master, who is not allowed to go'

poem or call it nothing at all, publish it in two cantos or in only one, with a preface or without; I put it completely at your disposal.'[84]

Pushkin's friends knew that he had been at work on a successor to *Ruslan*: 'Pushkin has written another long poem, *The Prisoner of the Caucasus*,' Turgenev had told Dmitriev the previous May; 'but he has not mended his behaviour: he is determined to resemble Byron not in talent alone.'[85] When the manuscript arrived in St Petersburg, it was bitterly fought over. 'I have not set eyes on the Caucasian captive,' Zhukovsky complained to Gnedich at the end of May; 'Turgenev, who has no interest in reading himself, but only in taking other people's verse around on visits, has decided not to send me the poem, since he is afraid of letting it out of his claws, lest I (and not he) should show it to someone. I beg you to let me have it as soon as possible; I will not keep it for more than a day and will return it immediately.'[86] Turgenev eventually did take the poem out to Zhukovsky in Pavlovsk, but Vyazemsky, who had been clamouring for it – '*The Captive*, for God's sake, just for one post,' he implored Turgenev[87] – had to wait until publication.

The Prisoner of the Caucasus came out on 14 August – a small book of fifty-three pages, costing five roubles, or seven if on vellum. A note at the end of the poem read: 'The editors have added a portrait of the author, drawn from him in youth. They believe that it is pleasing to preserve the youthful features of a poet whose first works are marked by so unusual a talent.'[88] The portrait, engraved by Geitman, depicts Pushkin 'at fifteen, as a Lycéen, in a shirt, as Byron was then drawn, with his chin on his hand, in meditation'.[89] Gnedich, more expeditious than before, sent him a single copy of the poem in September, together with a copy of Zhukovsky's translation of Byron's *The Prisoner of Chillon*. Pushkin wrote to him on 27 September: 'The Prisoners have arrived – and I thank you cordially, dear Nikolay Ivanovich [. . .] Aleksandr Pushkin is lithographed in masterly fashion, but I do not know whether it is like him, the editors' note is very flattering, but I do not know whether it is just.'[90] The edition – probably of 1,200 copies – sold out with remarkable speed: in 1825 Pletnev, searching for a copy to send to Pushkin in Mikhailovskoe, could not find one. Of the profit Gnedich sent Pushkin 500 roubles, keeping, it has been calculated, 5,000 for himself.[91] This time he had been too sharp. The following August

Pushkin wrote to Vyazemsky; 'Gnedich wants to buy a second edition of Ruslan and The Prisoner of the Caucasus from me but *timeo danaos*,* i.e., I am afraid lest he should treat me as before.'[92] Gnedich did not get the rights: *The Prisoner* was the last of Pushkin's works he published.

Its plot is not difficult to recapitulate: a Russian journeying in the Caucasus is captured by a Circassian tribe; a young girl falls in love with the captive, but he cannot return her feeling. Nevertheless, she aids him to escape: he swims the river and reaches the Russian lines; she drowns herself. In a letter to Lev describing his journey through the Caucasus Pushkin had toyed with the fancy of a Russian general falling prey to a Circassian's lasso. The fancy becomes real in the poem's opening lines; but the plot might also owe something to Chateaubriand's *Atala* (1801), in which an American Indian, made prisoner by another tribe and about to be burnt at the stake, is freed by a native girl, with whom he flees; she later commits suicide. The poem's hero is a Byronic figure, and the poem itself resembles Byron's eastern poems, *The Bride of Abydos*, *The Giaour* and particularly *The Corsair*. Pushkin, however, undercuts Romantic ideology with an ironic paradox: fleeing the corruption and deceit of society to search for freedom in a wild and exotic region peopled by man in his natural state, the hero becomes a prisoner of the mountain tribesmen who incarnate his ideal. There is, too, a peculiar ideological discrepancy between the poem and its epilogue, written in Odessa in May 1821. This preaches an imperial message, celebrating the pacification of the Caucasus, and praising the Russian generals who forcibly subdued the tribes. Vyazemsky was shocked. 'It is a pity that Pushkin should have bloodied the final lines of his story,' he wrote to Turgenev. 'What kind of heroes are Kotlyarevsky and Ermolov? What is good in the fact that he "like a black plague,/Destroyed, annihilated the tribes"? Such fame causes one's blood to freeze in one's veins, and one's hair to stand on end. If we had educated the tribes, then there would be something to sing. Poetry is not the ally of executioners; they may be necessary in politics, and then it is for the judgement of history to decide whether it was justified or not; but the

---

* 'I fear the Greeks [though they bear gifts]'. Virgil, *Aeneid*, II, 49. The quotation had especial relevance to Gnedich: he was 'Greek' because he was in the process of translating the *Iliad*.

hymns of a poet should never be eulogies of butchery. I am annoyed with Pushkin, such enthusiasm is a real anachronism.'[93]

Anachronistic or not, these were definitely Pushkin's views. 'The Caucasian region, the sultry frontier of Asia, is curious in every respect,' he had written in 1820. 'Ermolov has filled it with his name and beneficent genius. The savage Circassians have become frightened; their ancient audacity is disappearing. The roads are becoming safer by the hour, and the numerous convoys are superfluous. One must hope that this conquered region, which up to now has brought no real good to Russia, will soon through safe trading bring us close to the Persians, and in future wars will not be an obstacle to us – and, perhaps, Napoleon's chimerical plan for the conquest of India will come true for us.'[94] He obviously could see no contradiction between his fiery support of Greek independence and his equally fiery desire to eradicate Caucasian independence; nor between his whole-hearted support of the government here and his equally whole-hearted denunciation of the government everywhere else. In fact, some of the Decembrists shared his view that the Caucasus could not be independent: Pestel, in his *Russian Justice*, writes that some neighbouring lands 'must be united to Russia for the firm establishment of state security', and names among them: 'those lands of the Caucasian mountain peoples, not subject to Russia, which lie to the north of the Persian and Turkish frontiers, including the western littoral of the Caucasus, presently belonging to Turkey'.[95] They did not, however, share his chimerical Indian plan, nor the pleasure – the real stumbling-block for Vyazemsky – which he apparently took in genocide.

'Tell me, my dear, is my Prisoner making a sensation?' he asked his brother in October 1822. '*Has it produced a scandal*, Orlov writes, *that is the essential*. I hope the critics will not leave the Prisoner's character in peace, he was created for them, my dear fellow.'[96] He was to be disappointed: there was no critical polemic over the poem, as there had been over *Ruslan and Lyudmila*. The Byronic poem had ceased to be a novelty; Pushkin's reputation was now more firmly established, and, above all, *The Prisoner* did not have that awkward contrast between present-day narrator and past narrative which had worried some critics, nor that equally awkward comic intent, which had worried others. Praise was almost unanimous. In September Pushkin's uncle wrote to Vyazemsky: 'Here is what our La Fontaine [Dmitriev] writes to our Livy

[Karamzin]: "Yesterday I read in one breath *The Prisoner of the Caucasus* and from the bottom of my heart wished the young poet a long life! What a prospect! Right at the beginning two proper narrative poems, and what sweetness in the verse! Everything is picturesque, full of feeling and wit!" I confess, that reading this letter, I shed a tear of joy.'[97] Karamzin was slightly less enthusiastic. 'In the poem of that liberal Pushkin *The Prisoner of the Caucasus* the style is picturesque: I am dissatisfied only with the *love intrigue*. He really has a splendid talent: what a pity that there is no order and peace in his soul and not the slightest sense in his head.'[98] Of the critics only Mikhail Pogodin, in the *Herald of Europe*, descended to the kind of pedantic quibbling that had characterized reviews of *Ruslan*. Of the lines 'Neath his wet *burka*, in the smoky hut/The traveller enjoys peaceful sleep' (I, 321–2), he remarks: 'He would be better advised to throw off his wet *burka* [a felt cloak, worn in the Caucasus], and dry himself.'[99] Pushkin's comment, when meditating corrections for a second edition, was: 'A *burka* is waterproof and gets wet only on the surface, therefore one can sleep under it when one has nothing better to cover oneself with.'[100]

Where dissatisfaction was felt, it was, as in Karamzin's case, with the love intrigue: the character of the hero, and the fate of the heroine. In the second edition of 1828 Pushkin inserted a note: 'The author also agrees with the general opinion of the critics, who justifiably condemned the character of the prisoner';[101] and in 1830 wrote: '*The Prisoner of the Caucasus* is the first, unsuccessful attempt at character, which I had difficulty in managing; it was received better than anything I had written, thanks to some elegiac and descriptive verses. But on the other hand Nikolay and Aleksandr Raevsky and I had a good laugh over it.'[102] 'The character of the Prisoner is not a success; this proves that I am not cut out to be the hero of a Romantic poem. In him I wanted to portray that indifference to life and its pleasures, that premature senility of soul, which have become characteristic traits of nineteenth-century youth,' he wrote to Gorchakov.[103] Criticism of the fate of the Circassian maiden, however, he met with some irony: to Vyazemsky, after thanking him for his review* – 'You cannot imagine how pleasant it is to read the

---

* Vyazemsky's enthusiastic article on the poem had appeared in *Son of the Fatherland* in 1822.

opinion of an intelligent person about oneself' – he wrote: '[Chaadaev] gave me a dressing-down for the prisoner, he finds him insufficiently *blasé*; unfortunately Chaadaev is a connoisseur in that respect [...] Others are annoyed that the *Prisoner* did not throw himself into the water to pull out my Circassian girl – yes, you try; I have swum in Caucasian rivers, – you'll drown yourself before you find anything; my prisoner is an intelligent man, sensible, not in love with the Circassian girl – he is right not to drown himself.'[104]

'In general I am very dissatisfied with my poem and consider it far inferior to Ruslan,' he told Gorchakov.[105] He was right: *The Prisoner* has none of the wit, the gaiety and the grace of the earlier poem; he was not 'cut out to be the hero of a Romantic poem'. But a combination of circumstances – his reading of Byron, his acquaintance with Aleksandr Raevsky, his exile – had led him down a blind alley: it was still to take him some time to retrace his steps fully. A significant move in this direction took place when, on 9 May 1823, he began *Eugene Onegin*. At the head of the first stanza in the manuscript this date is noted with a large, portentously shaped and heavily inked numeral. It was a significant, indeed fatidic date in Pushkin's life: on 9 May 1820, according to his calendar, his exile from St Petersburg had begun. He usually worked on the poem in the early morning, before getting up. Visitors found him, as Liprandi had glimpsed him in Izmail, sitting cross-legged on his bed, surrounded by scraps of papers, 'now meditative, now bursting with laughter over a stanza'.[106] 'At my leisure I am writing a new poem, *Eugene Onegin*, in which I am transported by bile,' he told Turgenev some months later.[107]

Meanwhile changes in the region's administration were taking place. On 7 May 1823 Alexander signed an order freeing Inzov from his duties and appointing Count Mikhail Vorontsov governor-general of New Russia and of Bessarabia. Informing Vyazemsky of this, Turgenev wrote: 'I do not yet know whether the *Arabian devil** will be transferred to him. He was, it seems, appointed to Inzov personally.' 'Have you spoken to Vorontsov about Pushkin?' Vyazemsky asked. 'It is absolutely

---

* The nickname often given to Pushkin in the correspondence between Turgenev and Vyazemsky: a pun on *bes arabsky*, 'Arabian devil', and *bessarabsky*, 'Bessarabian'.

necessary that he should take him on. Petition him, good people! All the more as Pushkin really does want to settle down, and boredom and vexation are bad counsellors.' Turgenev's agitation was successful. 'This is what happened about Pushkin. Knowing politics and fearing the powerful of this world, consequently Vorontsov as well, I did not want to speak to him, but said to Nesselrode under the guise of doubt, whom should he be with: Vorontsov or Inzov. Count Nesselrode affirmed the former, and I advised him to tell Vorontsov of this. No sooner said than done. Afterwards I myself spoke twice with Vorontsov, explained Pushkin to him and what was necessary for his salvation. All, it seems, should go well. A Maecenas, the climate, the sea, historical reminiscences – there is everything; there is no lack of talent, as long as he does not choke to death.'[108]

Unaware of these machinations, Pushkin had successfully requested permission to spend some time in Odessa: the excuse being that he needed to take sea baths for his health. He arrived at the beginning of July and put up at the Hotel du Nord on Italyanskaya Street. 'I left my Moldavia and appeared in Europe – the restaurants and Italian opera reminded me of old times and by God refreshed my soul.' Vorontsov and his suite arrived on the evening of 21 July. The following day Vorontsov summoned him to his presence. 'He receives me very affably, declares to me that I am being transferred to his command, that I will remain in Odessa – this seems fine to me – but a new sadness wrung my bosom – I began to regret my abandoned chains.'* On the twenty-fourth a large ball was given in honour of Vorontsov by the Odessa Chamber of Commerce; on the twenty-sixth Vorontsov and his suite, now including Pushkin, left for Kishinev, where, two days later, Inzov handed over his post to his successor. Pushkin had time to collect his salary before accompanying the new governor-general back to Odessa at the beginning of August. 'I travelled to Kishinev for a few days, spent them in indescribably elegiac fashion – and, having left there for good, sighed after Kishinev.'[109]

---

* The last two sentences are a quotation from Zhukovsky's translation of *The Prisoner of Chillon*. The original reads: 'And I felt troubled – and would fain/I had not left my recent chain.' (357–8).

ODESSA

1823–24

> I lived then in dusty Odessa . . .
> There the skies long remain clear,
> There abundant trade
> Busily hoists its sails;
> There everything breathes, diffuses Europe,
> Glitters of the South and is gay
> With lively variety.
> The language of golden Italy
> Resounds along the merry street,
> Where walk the proud Slav,
> The Frenchman, the Spaniard, the Armenian,
> And the Greek, and the heavy Moldavian,
> And that son of the Egyptian soil,
> The retired corsair, Morali.
>
> Fragments from *Onegin's Journey*

IN 1791 THE TREATY OF JASSY, which brought the Russo–Turkish war to an end, gave Russia what its rulers had sought since the late seventeenth century: a firm footing on the Black Sea littoral. To exploit this a harbour was needed; those in the Sea of Azov and on the river deltas were too shallow for large vessels, and attention was turned to the site of the Turkish settlement of Khadzhibei, between the Bug and Dniester, where the water was deep close inshore, and which, with the construction of a mole and breakwater, would be safe in any weather. Here, where the steppe abruptly terminated in a promontory, some 200 feet above the coastal plain, the construction of a new city began on 22 August 1794. Its name, Odessa, came from that of a former Greek settlement some miles to the east, but was, apparently on the orders of the Empress Catherine herself, given a feminine form. The city's architect and first governor was Don Joseph de Ribas, a soldier of fortune in Russian service, born in Naples of Spanish and Irish parentage. With the assistance of a Dutch engineer, he laid out a gridiron plan of wide streets and began construction of a mole.

Under Richelieu, governor from 1803 to 1815 – whose little palazzo in Gurzuf had sheltered Pushkin and the Raevskys – the city prospered and gained in amenities: a wide boulevard was constructed along the cliff edge, overlooking the sea; and 'an elegant stone theatre, [...] the front of which is ornamented by a peristyle supported by columns',[1] was built. It was usually occupied by an Italian opera company: Pushkin became addicted to 'the ravishing Rossini,/Darling of Europe'.[2] However, the town 'was still in the course of construction, there were everywhere vacant lots and shacks. Stone houses were scattered along the Rishelevskaya, Khersonskaya and Tiraspolskaya streets, the cathedral and theatre squares; but for the most part all these houses stood in isolation with wooden single-storey houses and fences between them.'[3] Very few streets were paved: all travellers mention the insupportable dust in the summer, and the indescribable mud in the spring and autumn.

In 1819 Odessa had become a free port: the population increased – there were some 30,000 inhabitants in 1823 – as did the number of foreign merchants and shipping firms. The *lingua franca* of business was Italian, and many of the streets bore signs in this language or in French, until Vorontsov, in a fit of patriotism, had them replaced by Russian ones. But this could not conceal the fact that the city was very different in its population and its manners from the typical Russian provincial town: 'Two customs of social life gave Odessa the air of a foreign town: in the theatre during the entr'actes the men in the parterre audience would don their hats, and the smoking of cigars on the street was allowed.'[4]

Odessa, with its opera and its restaurants, might seem a far more attractive place for exile than Kishinev. Nevertheless, Pushkin was to be considerably less happy here. He had lost the company of his close friends: Gorchakov's regiment was still stationed in Kishinev; Alekseev, not wishing to part from his mistress Mariya Eichfeldt, had turned down a post he had been offered with Vorontsov in Odessa, while Liprandi, who had left the army and was attached to Vorontsov's office, was rarely in Odessa, being continually employed on missions elsewhere. And though Aleksandr Raevsky was now living in the town, the relationship between the two was to become very strained over the following months. Pushkin did make a number of new acquaintances, but they remained acquaintances, rather than friends. He was closest, perhaps, to Vasily Tumansky, a year younger than himself, an official in Vorontsov's bureau and a fellow-poet – 'Odessa in sonorous verses/Our friend Tumansky has described.'[5] But he had no great opinion of his talent: 'Tumansky is a famous fellow, but I do not like him as a poet. May God give him wisdom,' he told Bestuzhev.[6] He found, too, Tumansky's hyperbolic praise – calling him 'the Jesus Christ of our poetry'[7] – and servile imitation of his work distasteful. However, they dined together most evenings in Dimitraki's Greek restaurant, sitting with others over wine until the early hours. An acquaintance of a different kind was 'the retired corsair Morali',[8] a Moor from Tunis, and the skipper of a trading vessel – 'a very merry character, about thirty-five years old, of medium height, thick-set, with a bronzed, somewhat pock-marked, but very pleasant physiognomy'.[9] He spoke fluent Italian, some French, and was very fond of Pushkin, whom he accompanied about the town. Some believed that he was a Turkish spy. Pushkin struck up an acquaintance, too, with the Vorontsovs' family doctor, the thirty-year-old William Hutchinson, whom they had engaged in London in the autumn of 1821. Tall, thin and balding, Hutchinson proved to be an interesting companion, despite his deafness, taciturnity and bad French. The vicissitudes of his emotional life, however, contributed most to his unhappiness. In Kishinev he may have believed himself several times to be in love, but these light and airy flirtations bore no resemblance to the serious and deep involvements he was now to experience. And whereas Inzov had shown a paternal affection towards him, indulgently pardoning Pushkin's misdemeanours, or, if this was impossible, treating him like an erring adolescent, his relationship with Vorontsov, far more of a grandee than his predecessor, was of a very different kind.

In 1823 Count Mikhail Vorontsov was forty-one. He was the son of the former Russian ambassador in London, who had married into the Sidney family and settled in England permanently after his retirement. Vorontsov had received an English education, had studied at Cambridge, and was, like his father, a convinced Anglophile. His sister, Ekaterina, had married Lord Pembroke in 1808, and English relatives would occasionally visit Odessa. A professional soldier, Vorontsov had fought throughout the Napoleonic wars, being wounded at Borodino, and at Craonne in March 1814 had led the Russian corps that took on Napoleon himself in one of the bloodiest battles of the war. After Waterloo he commanded the Russian Army of Occupation in France, when Aleksandr Raevsky was one of his aides-de-camp. He was extremely wealthy, and had added to his fortune by marrying, in 1819, Elizaveta Branicka, who brought with her an enormous dowry: her mother, Countess Branicka, whose estate was at Belaya Tserkov, just south of Kiev, was one of the richest landowners in Russia. Before taking up his new appointment, he had invested massively in land in New Russia, buying immense estates near Odessa and Taganrog, and in the Crimea. He was 'tall and thin, with remarkably noble features, as though they had been carved with a chisel, his gaze was unusually calm, and about his thin long lips there eternally played an affectionate and crafty smile'.[10] 'Perhaps only Alexander could be more charming, when he wanted to please,' remarked Wiegel. 'He had a certain exquisite gaucheness, the result of

Vorontsov

his English upbringing, a manly reserve and a voice which, while never losing its firmness, was remarkably tender.'[11] As a commander he had, like Orlov, discouraged brutality and cruelty in enforcing discipline and had set up regimental schools to educate the troops. He was close to a number of the future Decembrists, and had even, together with Nikolay Turgenev, Pushkin's St Petersburg friend and fellow-Arzamasite, attempted to set up a society of noblemen with the aim of gradually emancipating the serfs. He had thus acquired the reputation of a liberal; a reputation which he was now strenuously attempting to live down, given the current climate in government circles: a mixture of mysticism and reaction, combined with – since the mutiny of the Semenovsky Life Guards in 1820 – paranoid suspicion of anything remotely radical.

*　　*　　*

When, at the beginning of August, Pushkin returned to Odessa in Vorontsov's suite, he took a room in the Hotel Rainaud, where he lived throughout his stay. The hotel was on the corner of Deribasovskaya and Rishelevskaya Streets (named after the first two governors, de Ribas and Richelieu); behind it an annexe, which fronted on Theatre Square, housed the Casino de Commerce, or assembly-rooms: 'The great oval hall, which is surrounded by a gallery, supported on numerous columns, is used for the double purpose of ballroom, and an *Exchange*, where the merchants sometimes transact their affairs,' wrote Robert Lyall, who visited Odessa in May 1822.[12] Baron Rainaud, the owner of the hotel and casino, was a French émigré; he also possessed a charming villa on the coast three miles to the east of the city, with wonderful views over the Black Sea. Vorontsov rented it for his wife, who was in the final stages of pregnancy when she arrived from Belaya Tserkov on 6 September: she gave birth to a son two months later.

Pushkin had a corner room on the first floor with a balcony, which gave a view of the sea. The theatre and casino were two minutes away; five minutes' walk down Deribasovskaya and Khersonskaya Streets took him to César Automne's restaurant, the best in town –

> What of the oysters? they're here! O joy!
> Gluttonous youth flies
> To swallow from their sea shells
> The plump, living hermitesses,
> With a slight squeeze of lemon.
> Noise, arguments – light wine
> From the cellars is borne
> To the table by obliging Automne;
> The hours fly, and the dread bill
> Meanwhile invisibly mounts.[13]

Wiegel, who had been recruited by Vorontsov to join his staff, soon moved into the room next to Pushkin. Before leaving St Petersburg he had been enjoined by Zhukovsky and Bludov to gain Pushkin's confidence in order, if possible, to prevent him from behaving injudiciously. Unfortunately, Pushkin did not enjoy his company for long: Vorontsov sacked the vice-governor of Kishinev for dishonesty and appointed Wiegel in his place. 'Tell me, my dear atheist, how did you manage to

live for several years in Kishinev?' he wrote to Pushkin on 8 October.
'Although you should indeed have been punished by God for your lack
of faith, surely not to such an extent. As far as I am concerned, I can
say too: although my sins or, more accurately, my sin is great, it is not
so great that fate should have destined this cesspit to be my abode.'[14]
The sin Wiegel is referring to is his homosexuality. In a verse reply,
Pushkin promised to visit him: 'I'll be glad to serve you/With my crazy
conversation –/With verses, prose or with my soul,/But, Wiegel, – spare
my arse!' Continuing in prose, he answers a query raised by Wiegel
about the Ralli brothers. 'I think the smallest is best suited to your use;
NB he sleeps in the same room as his brother Mikhail and they tumble
about unmercifully – from this you can draw important conclusions, I
leave them to your experience and good sense – the eldest brother, as
you have already noticed, is as stupid as a bishop's crozier – Vanka
jerks off – so the devil with them – embrace them in friendly fashion
from me.'[15]

Two and a half years earlier, on 2 February 1821, in the governor of
Kiev's drawing-room, Pushkin had been struck by the beauty of a woman
wearing a poppy-red toque with a drooping ostrich feather, 'which set
off extraordinarily well her tall stature, luxuriant shoulders and fiery
eyes'.[16] This was Karolina Sobańska, the twenty-seven-year-old daughter
of Count Adam Rzewuski, one of several attractive and brilliantly clever
brothers and sisters: her sister Ewa Hanska was Balzac's *Étrangère*, who,
after a long correspondence and liaison with the novelist, married him
in 1850, a few months before his death. Karolina had been married at
seventeen to Hieronim Sobański, a wealthy landowner and owner of
one of the largest trading houses in Odessa. He was, however, thirty-
three years older than her; she left him in 1816, and in 1819 met and
began a long liaison with Colonel-General Count Jan Witt.* Since 1817
Witt had been in command of all the military colonies in the south of
Russia; in addition he controlled a wide and efficient network of spies
and secret police agents. He and Sobańska lived openly together; the
liaison was recognized by society, and though its more straitlaced
members might have frowned at the irregularity of the relationship,

* Witt's mother was '*la belle Phanariote*', the beautiful Greek from Constantinople who
had married Major Joseph Witt, been Potemkin's mistress, and, after divorcing her husband,
become General Potocki's third wife.

there were few who wished to incur his enmity by cutting Sobańska in public.

When Pushkin met her again, his interest was immediately rekindled: she was, indeed, almost irresistible – not only beautiful, but also lively, charming and provocative, and a talented musician: 'What grace, what a voice, and what manners!'[17] Few, if any, knew at the time that, as well as being Witt's mistress, she also worked for him, and was an extremely valuable Russian intelligence agent. Only Wiegel appears to have had an inkling of the truth. 'When a few years

Karolina Sobańska

later I learnt [. . .] that for financial gain she joined the ranks of the gendarme agents, I felt an invincible aversion to her. I will not mention the unproved crimes of which she was suspected. What vilenesses were concealed beneath her elegant appearance!'*[18] Witt, eager to obtain evidence of subversive activity, encouraged her friendship with Pushkin, as in 1825 he would encourage her liaison with the Polish poet Mickiewicz. She and Pushkin made an excursion by boat together; he accompanied her to the Roman Catholic church, where she dipped her fingers into the stoup and crossed his forehead with holy water; and there were 'burning readings' of Constant's *Adolphe*,[19] a book so appropriate to their circumstances it might have been written with them in mind: the hero, Adolphe, falls in love with Ellénore, a Polish countess, celebrated for her beauty, who is older than he and is being kept by a M. de P***. But Sobańska did not appear to feel more than friendship for him; piqued, he concocted, together with Aleksandr Raevsky, a scheme to arouse her interest. Before it could be put into practice she left the city, and Pushkin consoled himself for her absence by falling in love with Amaliya Riznich, the daughter of an Austrian-Jewish banker, married to an Odessa shipping merchant.

'Mrs Riznich was young, tall, graceful, and extraordinarily beautiful.

---

* Wiegel's remarks were usually ascribed to malicious spite, all the more so as Sobańska appeared to be a fervent Polish patriot. However, their accuracy was incontrovertibly established in 1935 with the publication of a letter from her to Count Benckendorff, the head of the gendarmerie, detailing her services to the Russian government. See *Rukoyu Pushkina*, 188–93.

Particularly attractive were her fiery eyes, a neck of amazing form and whiteness, and a plait of black hair, nearly five feet long. But her feet were too large; in order to conceal this deficiency, she always wore a long dress, to the ground. She went about wearing a man's hat and dressed in a semi-riding habit. All this gave her originality and attracted both young and not so young heads and hearts.'[20] She distinguished herself by going about much in society – 'Our married ladies (with the exception of the beautiful and charming Mrs Riznich) avoid company, concealing under the guise of modesty either their simplicity or their ignorance,' Tumansky wrote to his cousin[21] – and entertained frequently at home. These were lively gatherings, at which much whist was played: a game of which she was passionately fond. Pushkin was soon obsessed

with her. Profiles of 'Madame Riznich, with her Roman nose'[22] crept out of his pen to ornament the manuscript of the first chapter of *Eugene Onegin*. His emotions reached their zenith in the last weeks of October and the first of November with a sudden burst of poems. The passionate love, the burning jealousy they express are far deeper, far more powerful, far more agonizing than anything he had previously experienced. Though intense, the feelings were short-lived. In January or early February 1824, he bade her farewell with a final

Amaliya Riznich

lyric. She had been pregnant when they first met; early in 1824 she gave birth to a son. Meanwhile her health had deteriorated; the Odessa climate had exacerbated a tendency towards consumption. At the beginning of May she left Odessa; a year later she died in Italy.

> Beneath the blue sky of her native land
>> She languished, faded . . .
> Faded finally, and above me surely
>> The young shade already hovered;
> But there is an unapproachable line between us.
>> In vain I tried to awaken emotion:
> From indifferent lips I heard the news of death,
>> And received it with indifference

> So this is whom my fiery soul loved
>> With such painful intensity,
> With such tender, agonizing heartache,
>> With such madness and such torment!
> Where now the tortures, where the love? Alas!
>> For the poor, gullible shade,
> For the sweet memory of irretrievable days
>> In my soul I find neither tears nor reproaches.[23]

Riznich did not long remain a widower. In March 1827 Tumansky wrote to Pushkin: 'One piece of our news, which might interest you, is Riznich's marriage to the sister of Sobańska, Witt's mistress [. . .] The new Mme Riznich will probably not deserve either your or my verse on her death; she is a child with a wide mouth and Polish manners.'[24]

The social scene in Odessa in the autumn and winter of 1823 was a lively one. Pushkin, in a black frock-coat, wearing a peaked cap or black hat over his cropped hair, and carrying an iron cane, hastened through the mud from one gathering to another. General Raevsky, his wife, and his two younger daughters, Mariya and Sofya, paid a lengthy visit to the town. 'The Raevskys are here,' Tumansky told his cousin, 'Mariya is the ideal of Pushkin's Circassian maid (the poet's own expression), ugly, but very attractive in the sharpness of her conversation and tenderness of her manner.'[25] A sketch of the sixteen-year-old girl with her short nose, heavy jaw and unruly hair escaping from an elaborate bonnet appears in the left-hand margin of a draft of several stanzas from *Eugene Onegin*.[26] Pushkin had finished the first chapter on 22 October and embarked immediately on the second: 'I am writing with a rapture which I have not had for a long time,' he told Vyazemsky.[27] Several other St Petersburg acquaintances were in Odessa. Aleksandr Sturdza, the subject, in 1819, of two hostile epigrams, turned out to be not such a pillar of reaction after all. 'Monarchical Sturdza is here; we are not only friends, but also think the same about one or two things, without being sly to one another.'[28] However, he quarrelled with the Arzamasite Severin, relieving his anger with an epigram ridiculing Severin's pretensions to nobility.

He saw, too, General Kiselev and his wife Sofya, who frequently travelled over from the headquarters of the Second Army at Tulchin. Earlier that year, after the officers of the Odessa regiment had revolted against their colonel, Kiselev had sacked the brigade commander, General Mordvinov. The latter had challenged him to a duel. Kiselev accepted the challenge, the two met, and Mordvinov was killed. Kiselev immediately sent the emperor an account of the affair, saying that the manner of the challenge left him 'no choice between the strict application of the law and the most sacred obligations of honour'.[29] Alexander pardoned him and retained him as chief of staff of the Second Army. The incident caused much stir at the time, and particularly fascinated Pushkin, who, 'for many days talked of nothing else, asking others for their opinion as to whose side was more honourable, who had been the more self-sacrificial and so on'.[30] Though he inclined towards Mordvinov, he could not but admire Kiselev's sangfroid. Also in Odessa were Sofya's twenty-two-year-old sister, Olga, and her recently acquired husband, General Lev Naryshkin, who was Vorontsov's cousin. Olga was as beautiful as her sister, but 'in her beauty there was nothing maidenly or touching [...] in the very flower of youth she seemed already armoured with great experience. Everything was calculated, and she preserved the arrows of coquetry for the conquest of the mighty.'[31] Wiegel's last sentence is a hidden reference to a relationship which was well-known in Odessa: soon after her arrival Olga became Vorontsov's mistress. Naryshkin, seventeen years older than his wife, lacked the character and energy to complain – 'always sleepy, always good-natured' was his brother-in-law's description of him[32] – and, in addition, his affection for his wife was lukewarm: he had long been hopelessly in love with his aunt, Mariya Naryshkina, for many years the mistress of Alexander I.

During the winter there were dances twice a week at the Vorontsovs; Pushkin was assiduous in attending. On 12 December they gave a large ball, at which his impromptu verses on a number of the ladies present caused some offence. On Christmas Day Vorontsov entertained the members of his staff to dinner; Wiegel arrived from Kishinev while they were at table, and Pushkin, learning this, slipped back to the hotel to see him. On New Year's Eve, Tumansky wrote, 'we had a good frolic at the masquerade, which the countess [Elizaveta Vorontsova] put on for us, and at which she herself played the fool very cleverly and smartly.

that is, she had a charmingly satirical costume and intrigued with every-one in it'.[33]

Liprandi had not forgotten Pushkin's disappointment at not being able to visit Charles XII's camp at Varnitsa during their trip in the winter of 1821. Planning another visit to the district, he invited Pushkin to accompany him. The latter accepted with alacrity. He had just been reading a manuscript copy of Ryleev's narrative poem *Voinarovsky*. 'Ryleev's *Voinarovsky* is incomparably better than all his *Dumy*,* his style has matured and is becoming a truly narrative one, which we still almost completely lack,' he wrote to Bestuzhev.[34] The hero of Ryleev's poem is the nephew of Mazepa, the hetman of the Dnieper Cossacks who joined with Charles against Peter the Great and died at Varnitsa in 1709. Pushkin was attracted by the figure of Mazepa himself; three lines of Ryleev's poem describing Mazepa's nightmares, 'He often saw, at dead of night;/The wife of the martyr Kochubey/And their ravished daughter,'[35] planted the germ which grew into his own poem, *Poltava*. Byron, too, had devoted a poem to the hetman: his *Mazeppa* is an account of an early episode of the hero's life, when, according to Voltaire, the poet's source, 'an affair he had with the wife of a Polish nobleman having been discovered, the husband had him bound naked to the back of a wild horse and sent him forth in this state'.[36]

On 17 January 1824 they left Odessa for Tiraspol, where they put up with Liprandi's brother. That evening they had supper with General Sabaneev. Pushkin was cheerful and very talkative: the general's wife, Pulkheriya Yakovlevna, was much taken with him. The following day, accompanied by Liprandi's brother, they set out early for Bendery. Forewarned of their coming, the police chief, A.I. Barozzi, had provided a guide: Nikola Iskra, a Little Russian, who 'appeared to be about sixty, was tall, with an upright figure, rather lean, with thick yellowish-grey hair on his head and chest and good teeth'.[37] He claimed that as a young man he had been sent by his mother to the Swedish camp to sell milk, butter and eggs: which, Liprandi calculated, would make him now about

* A *duma* (meditation; plural *dumy*) is a Ukrainian lyric-epic song of the sixteenth or seventeenth century; Ryleev used the term as a generic title for a collection of short historical poems, glorifying figures from the past, which have little or nothing in common with the original.

135 years old. However, it was certainly true that his description of Charles XII's appearance bore a remarkable resemblance to the illustrations in the historical works Liprandi had brought with him, and he showed an equally remarkable ability, when they arrived at the site of the camp, to describe its plan and fortifications and to interpret the irregularities of the terrain. Much to Pushkin's annoyance, however, he was not only unable to show them Mazepa's grave, but even disclaimed any knowledge of the hetman. They returned to Bendery with Pushkin in a very disgruntled mood. He cheered up, however, after dinner with Barozzi, and in the afternoon set out in a carriage, accompanied by a policeman, to view, as he hoped, the ruined palaces and fountains at Kaushany, the seat of the khans of Budzhak. Later in the evening he returned as disgruntled as before: there were – as Liprandi had warned him two years earlier – no ruins to admire in Kaushany. He was back in Odessa on the nineteenth. Liprandi did not return until the beginning of February. On the evening of his arrival he dined with the Vorontsovs, where a sulky Pushkin was making desultory conversation with the countess and Olga Naryshkina. He vanished after the company rose from table. Calling at his hotel room later, Liprandi found him in the most cheerful frame of mind imaginable: with his coat off, he was sitting on Morali's knee and tickling the retired corsair until he roared. This was the only pleasure he had in Odessa, he told Liprandi.

Pushkin had completed his second southern poem, *The Fountain of Bakhchisaray*, the previous autumn, and had begun to think about publication. Gnedich, though eager, had ruled himself out through excessive sharpness; he therefore turned to Vyazemsky, who agreed to see the work through the press. However, there was a complication. The work was suffused with memories of the Crimea and, in particular, of his love for Ekaterina Raevskaya. Now, three years later, he was not anxious to call attention to this, all the more so as Ekaterina was now Orlov's wife. He hit on a simple solution in a letter to his brother: 'I will send Vyazemsky *The Fountain* – omitting the love ravings – but it's a pity!'[38] Sending the manuscript to Vyazemsky on 4 November, he wrote, 'I have thrown out that which the censor would have thrown out if I had not, and that which I did not want to exhibit before the public. If these disconnected fragments seem to you worthy of type, then print them,

and do me a favour, don't give in to that bitch the censorship, bite back
in defence of every line, and bite it to death if you can, in memory of
me [. . .] another request: add a foreword or afterword to Bakhchisaray,
if not for my sake, then for the sake of your lustful Minerva, Sofya
Kiseleva; I enclose a police report as material; draw on it for information
(without, of course, mentioning the source).'*[39] With the letter he sent
a copy of 'Platonic Love', the immodest poem he had addressed to Sofya
in 1819. 'Print it quickly; I ask this not for the sake of fame, but for the
sake of Mammon,' he urged in December.[40]

But his hopes of concealing his former feelings for Ekaterina were
soon sadly dented. In St Petersburg Bestuzhev and Ryleev had been
preparing a second number of their literary almanac, *Pole Star*. They
obtained Pushkin's permission to include some of his verses which had
been circulating in manuscript in St Petersburg, and others which they
had obtained from Tumansky. When the almanac came out in
December, Pushkin was horrified to discover that the final three lines
of 'Sparser grows the flying range of clouds', the coded reference to
Ekaterina which he had specifically asked Bestuzhev not to include, had
in fact been printed. 'It makes me sad to see that I am treated like a
dead person, with no respect for my wishes or my miserable possessions,'
he wrote reproachfully to Bestuzhev. Worse was to follow. In February,
just before the publication of the poem, he wrote to Bestuzhev again:
'I am glad that my Fountain is making a stir. The absence of plan is
not my fault. I reverentially put into verse a young woman's tale, *Aux
douces loix des vers je pliais les accents/De sa bouche aimable et naïve.*†
By the way, I wrote it only for myself, but am publishing it because I
need money.'[41] As with previous letters to Bestuzhev, he addressed this
care of Nikolay Grech. Unfortunately, it fell into the hands of Faddey
Bulgarin – a close associate of Grech, and from 1825 co-editor, with
him, of *Son of the Fatherland* – who shamelessly printed an extract from
it in his paper, *Literary Leaves*, adding that it was taken from a letter
of the author to one of his St Petersburg friends. Anyone who knew of
Pushkin's visit to the Crimea could make an intelligent guess at the
possessor of the 'lovable and naïve mouth'; even worse, however, were

---

* Pushkin is referring to the fact that the heroine of his poem is, like Sofya, a Potocka.
† 'To the sweet laws of verse I bent the accents/Of her lovable and naïve mouth', a quotation
from André Chénier's ode *La jeune captive*.

the conclusions Ekaterina herself might draw. 'I once fell head over heels in love,' he wrote to Bestuzhev later that year. 'In such cases I usually write elegies, as another has wet dreams. But is it a friendly act to hang out my soiled sheets for show? God forgive you, but you shamed me in the current Star – printing the last 3 lines of my elegy; what the devil possessed me apropos of the Bakhchisaray fountain also to write some sentimental lines and mention my elegiac beauty there. Picture my despair, when I saw them printed – the journal could fall into her hands. What would she think of me, seeing with what eagerness I chat about her with *one of my Petersburg friends*. How can she know that she is not named by me, that the letter was unsealed and printed by Bulgarin – that the devil knows who delivered the damned Elegy to you – and that no one is to blame. I confess that I value just one thought of this woman more than the opinions of all the journals in the world and of all our public.'[42]

As with *The Prisoner*, Pushkin's new narrative poem was eagerly anticipated in literary circles: before publication it was being read everywhere, and even manuscript copies were circulating in St Petersburg – much to Pushkin's annoyance, since he feared this would affect sales. 'Pletnev tells me The Fountain of Bakhchisaray is in everyone's hands. Thank you, my friends, for your gracious care for my fame!' he wrote sarcastically to Lev, whom he deemed responsible.[43] His fears proved unjustified. Having seen the poem through the censorship, Vyazemsky had it printed in Moscow at a cost of 500 roubles, and then began negotiations to sell the entire print-run jointly to two booksellers, Shiryaev in Moscow and Smirdin in St Petersburg. 'How I have sold the *Fountain*!' he exulted to Bestuzhev in March. 'Three thousand roubles for 1,200 copies for a year, and I'm paid for all printing costs. This is in the European style and deserves to be known.'[44] He saw to it that it was by contributing an article about the sale to the April number of *News of Literature*: 'For a line of The Fountain of Bakhchisaray more has been paid than has ever been paid previously for any Russian verse.' The book-seller had gained 'the grateful respect of the friends of culture by valuing a work of the mind not according to its size or weight'.[45] Shalikov, in the *Ladies' Journal*, did the calculation and came out with the figure of eight roubles a line. Bulgarin, too, commented on the transaction in *Literary Leaves*, while the *Russian Invalid* remarked patriotically that it was a 'proof that not in England alone and not the English alone pay with a generous hand for elegant works of poetry'.[46]

Vyazemsky sent a first instalment of the advance in March. Pushkin immediately paid Inzov a debt of 360 roubles which he was 'embarrassed and humiliated' not to have settled earlier,[47] and dashed off a grateful letter to Vyazemsky: 'One thing troubles me, you sold the entire edition for 3000r., but how much did it cost you to print it? You are still making me a gift, you shameless fellow! For Christ's sake take what is due to you out of the remainder, and send it here. There's no point in letting it grow. It won't lie around with me for long, although I am really not extravagant. I'll pay my old debts and sit down to a new poem. Since I'm not one of our 18th century writers: I write for myself, and publish for money, certainly not for the smiles of the fair sex.'*[48]

The Fountain of Bakhchisaray was published on 10 March. Vyazemsky had responded to Pushkin's plea and had contributed an unsigned introductory article which bore the strange title 'Instead of a foreword. A conversation between the publisher and a classicist from the Vyborg Side or Vasilevsky Island'.† This had little to do with the poem, but was a provocative attack, from the standpoint of romanticism, on the literary old guard and classicism. An immediate reply appeared in the *Herald of Europe*; Pushkin came to Vyazemsky's defence with a short letter to *Son of the Fatherland*; and, much to Vyazemsky's delight, a controversy developed which rumbled on in the literary pages for months. Turgenev disapproved: 'Stop squabbling,' he advised his friend. 'It is unworthy of you and I do not recognize you in all this polemical rubbish.'[49] Onlookers took a similar view: 'There has been a shower of lampoons, epigrams, arguments, gibes, personalities, each more nasty and more stupid than the last,' Yakov Saburov wrote to his brother.[50]

Shorter than *The Prisoner of the Caucasus*, *The Fountain of Bakhchisaray* has an equally simple plot. Girey, khan of the Crimea, falls in love

---

* Aleksandr Kornilovich (1800–34) had contributed an article entitled 'On the amusements of the Russian court in the time of Peter I' to *Pole Star*; in the form of a letter, dedicated to the baroness A.E.A., it ended, 'Your indulgent glance will be the author's best reward, the smile of your approbation will give him new force and encourage him to new labours' (*Pisma*, I, 301). Pushkin was much amused by this and refers to it often in his letters of this period.

† The pseudonyms, 'An Inhabitant of Vasilevsky Island' and 'An Inhabitant of the Vyborg Side', had earlier been used by conservative critics to sign articles in the *Well-Intentioned*.

with the latest captive added to his harem, the Polish princess Mariya. She dies, either of illness or at the hand of Girey's previous favourite, Zarema, who is drowned by the khan. He builds a marble fountain in memory of Mariya. For the subject of the poem Pushkin adapted a Crimean legend which he had heard from the Raevskys at Gurzuf, and which Muravev-Apostol recounts in his *Journey through Tauris in 1820*. An extract from this work, describing the palace at Bakhchisaray, was appended to the poem when it was published. *The Fountain* was greeted with a general chorus of praise: there was no pedantic carping at detail and little criticism. Pushkin's own opinion was less favourable. 'Between ourselves,' he had written to Vyazemsky, 'the Fountain of Bakhchisaray is rubbish, but its epigraph is charming.'[51] This, attributed to the thirteenth-century Persian poet Sadi, runs: 'Many, similarly to myself, visited this fountain; but some are no more, others are journeying far.' The second half of the saying came to have a political significance: when the critic Polevoy quoted it in an article in the *Moscow Telegraph* in 1827, he was clearly alluding to the fate of the Decembrists, some of whom had been executed, others exiled to Siberia. Pushkin had not taken the quotation directly from the Persian poet, but from the French translation of a prose passage in Thomas Moore's 'oriental romance' *Lalla Rookh* (1817), which refers to 'a fountain, on which some hand had rudely traced those well-known words from the Garden of Sadi, – "Many, like me, have viewed this fountain, but they are gone, and their eyes are closed forever!"'[52] Despite this borrowing, he was no admirer of Moore. 'The whole of *Lalla Rookh* is not worth ten lines of Tristram Shandy,' he exclaimed; and, commenting on the *Fountain*, told Vyazemsky: 'The eastern style was a model for me, inasmuch as is possible for us rational, cold Europeans. By the by, do you know why I do not like Moore? – because he is excessively eastern. He imitates in a childish and ugly manner the childishness and ugliness of Sadi, Hafiz and Mahomet. – A European, even when in ecstasy over eastern splendour, should retain the taste and eye of a European. That is why Byron is so charming in The Giaour, The Bride of Abydos and so on.'[53] This was the effect at which he aimed, and Byron was undoubtedly his inspiration: in 1830 he remarked: '*The Fountain of Bakhchisaray* is weaker than *The Prisoner* and, like it, reflects my reading of Byron, about whom I then raved.'[54] Pushkin was right. *The Fountain of Bakhchisaray* is weaker than *The*

Prisoner, is indeed the weakest of all his narrative poems, though the portrayal of the languid, surfeited life of the harem breathes an indolent sensuality, while the scene between Mariya and Zarema has, as he remarked, 'dramatic merit'.[55]

But the real significance of the poem for Pushkin – and, indeed, for Russian literature – lay not in its aesthetic, but rather in its commercial value. At the beginning of his stay in Odessa and, as usual, hard-pressed for money, Pushkin had written despairingly to his brother: 'Explain to my father that I cannot live without his money. To live by my pen is impossible with the present censorship; I have not studied the carpenter's trade; I cannot become a teacher; although I know scripture and the four elementary rules – but I am a civil servant against my will – and cannot take retirement. – Everything and everyone deceives me – on whom should I depend, if not on my nearest and dearest. I will not live on Vorontsov's bounty – I will not and that is all – extremes can lead to extremes – I am pained by my father's indifference to my state – although his letters are very amiable.'[56] The successful sale of *The Fountain* changed his views in an instant. 'I begin to respect our booksellers and to think that our trade is really no worse than any other,' he wrote to Vyazemsky.[57] For the first time financial independence seemed possible; the career of a professional writer beckoned. This new-found self-sufficiency strengthened his belief in his talent, his sense of himself as an artist: it was to affect materially his behaviour during the remaining months in Odessa.

Another chance to exploit his work commercially soon arrived; in June he was offered 2,000 roubles for the right to bring out a second edition of *The Prisoner of the Caucasus*. But before Lev in St Petersburg could close the deal, he was forestalled. The previous year a German translation of *The Prisoner* had come out. August Oldekop, the publisher of the *St Petersburg Gazette* and the *Sankt-Peterburgische Zeitung*, now brought out this translation again, printing the original Russian text opposite the German. This was a great success and killed Pushkin's hopes of selling a second edition of the poem. 'I will have to petition for redress under the law,' he told Vyazemsky.[58] But the law respecting authors' rights was unclear and, though the Censorship Committee put a temporary ban on the sale of the edition, this was soon lifted. In addition, Oldekop muddied the waters by insisting that he had bought the right to publish the edition from Pushkin's father. When Vyazemsky anxiously enquired whether this was true, and asked Pushkin to send him, if it was not, a power of attorney, giving him the right to act on his friend's part against Oldekop, Pushkin – who was by this time in Mikhailovskoe – replied: 'Oldekop stole and lied; my father made no kind of bargain with him. I would send you a power of attorney; but you must wait; stamped paper is only to be had in town; some kind of witnessing has to be done in town – and I am in the depths of the country.'[59] The indictment of Oldekop's villainy is certainly positive; but is the disinclination to ride into Pskov for a power of attorney prompted by indolence, by a healthy scepticism about the process of law, or by the suspicion that his father – with whom he was on extremely bad terms – had not been wholly honest with him? Six months later, when he was afraid that *The Fountain* was also being pirated, and was therefore having to turn down offers for it, he wrote to Lev, 'Selivanovsky is offering me 12,000 roubles, and I have to turn it down – this way I'll die of hunger – what with my father and Oldekop. Farewell, I'm in a rage.'[60]

Outside Russia the heady days of the revolution in Spain and of Ypsilanti's Greek revolt, both of which had so aroused Pushkin's enthusiasm, had passed, and a tide of reaction, encouraged by Alexander I, was sweeping over Europe. At the Congress of Verona France asked to be allowed to march into Spain – as Austria had marched into Naples in 1821 – to restore order in the Peninsula; despite British protests, this was agreed, and in April 1823 the duke of Angoulême, at the head of a powerful army, crossed the Bidassoa. Ferdinand, a prisoner since 1820, was restored to the throne, and, in an orgy of revenge, Colonel Rafael Riego, the leader of the revolution, and many other insurgents were executed. Pushkin, disgusted by this, and disillusioned with the Greeks – 'The Jesuits have stuffed our heads with Themistocles and Pericles, and we have come to imagine that this dirty people, consisting of bandits and shopkeepers, is their legitimate descendant, the heir to their fame in school'[61] – came to the conclusion, like Dostoevsky's Grand Inquisitor some sixty years later, that man did not deserve freedom. In 'Of freedom the solitary sower', 'an imitation of a parable by that moderate democrat Jesus Christ (A sower went out to sow his seed)'* he expressed this new cynicism:

* St Luke viii, 5.

Graze, placid peoples!
What good to herds the gift of freedom?
They must be slaughtered or be shorn.
Their inheritance from generation to generation
Is the yoke with bells and the whip.[62]

The two-year moratorium on political verse, agreed with Karamzin, had reached its term long ago, and Pushkin relapsed into his former ways with 'The motionless sentinel slumbered on the royal threshold . . .', a satirical portrait of Alexander after his return from the Congress of Verona.[63]

Though poems such as these were not intended for publication, they were known to Pushkin's friends – 'Of freedom the solitary sower' was included in a letter to Turgenev – and circulated in manuscript: by writing them he was flirting with danger. He was flirting with danger, too, given the pietistic fervour then in vogue, when he wrote to Küchelbecker: 'You want to know what I am doing – I am writing motley stanzas of a romantic poem – and am taking lessons in pure atheism. There is an Englishman here, a deaf philosopher, the only intelligent atheist I have yet met. He has written over 1,000 pages to prove that no intelligent being, Creator and governor can exist, in passing destroying the weak proofs of the immortality of the soul. His system is not so consoling as is usually thought, but unfortunately is the most plausible.'[64] The deaf English philosopher was William Hutchinson, the Vorontsovs' personal physician, a proponent of the new, scientific atheism, which Pushkin – hitherto acquainted only with the rational atheism of the eighteenth century – found excitingly original. This letter, like his verse, circulated in manuscript. Learning of this, Vyazemsky wrote to Pushkin in some agitation, sending his letter by a traveller to Odessa and marking it 'Secret'. 'Please be cautious both with your tongue and your pen,' he urged. 'Do not risk your future. Your present exile is better than anywhere else.'[65] It was too late. 'Thanks to the not wholly sensible publicity given to it by Pushkin's friends and especially by the late Aleksandr Ivanovich Turgenev, who, as we have heard, rushed round his acquaintances with it, the letter came to the knowledge of the administration.'[66] It was to have a decisive influence on his future.

*   *   *

Pushkin's flirtation with danger extended into his emotional life. From the turn of the year a new face appears among those idly scribbled by his pen while waiting for inspiration. It is that of the governor's wife, Elizaveta – or, as he called her, Elise – Vorontsova, with whom he was now violently in love. There are more portraits of her in his manuscripts than of anyone else: indeed, one page of the second chapter of *Eugene Onegin* has no fewer than six sketches of her. She is represented constantly in profile, with and without a bonnet; Pushkin returns over and over again to her graceful shoulders and neck, sometimes encircled by her famous necklace: 'Potocki gave balls and evening parties,' Aleksandra Smirnova-Rosset wrote. 'At his house I saw Elizaveta Vorontsova for the first time, in a pink satin dress. Then people wore *cordelière* necklaces. Hers was made of the largest of diamonds.'[67]

At thirty-one, Elise was seven years older than Pushkin. She was not conventionally beautiful, like her friend Olga Naryshkina, but had a vivacity and charm which were enchanting. 'With her innate Polish frivolity and coquetry she desired to please,' commented Wiegel, 'and no one succeeded better than her in this. [. . .] She did not have that which is called beauty; but the swift, tender gaze of her sweet small eyes penetrated one completely; I have never seen anything comparable to the smile on her lips, which seemed to demand a kiss.'[68] Count Sollogub, who met her years later, devotes a passage to her in his memoirs: 'Small and plump, with somewhat coarse and irregular features, Elizaveta Ksaverevna was, nonetheless, one of the most attractive women of her time. Her whole being was suffused with such soft, enchanting, feminine grace, such cordiality, such irreproachable elegance, that it was easy to understand why such people as Pushkin [. . .] Raevsky and many, many others fell head over heels in love with Vorontsova.'[69]

Pushkin had known her since the previous autumn; in the new year her attractions began to supplant those of Amaliya Riznich; a turning-point in their relationship occurred in February, when Vorontsov was absent in Kishinev. On his manuscripts Pushkin only notes events he considers significant: on 8 February 1824, opposite the first stanza of the third chapter of *Eugene Onegin*, he jotted down 'soupé chez C.E.W' – 'had supper with Countess Elise Woronzof'.[70] The relationship was to be short, and much interrupted. Pushkin himself was in Kishinev for two weeks in March. When he returned to Odessa

he found that Elise had left on a visit to her
mother in Belaya Tserkov; she remained there
until 20 April. As the weather grew warmer
they began to meet at Baron Rainaud's villa.
'Rainaud has successfully made use of the cliffs
which surround his domain,' wrote a visitor.
'In the midst of the cliffs a bathing-place has
been constructed. It is shaped like a large shell,
attached to the cliffs.'[71] This was the site of their
assignations:

Elise Vorontsova

> The shelter of love, it is eternally full
> With dark, damp cool,
> There the constrained waves'
> Prolonged roar is never silent.[72]

The affair brought Pushkin two enemies. Aleksandr Raevsky, who was
himself in love with Elise, and who enjoyed her favours during her visits
to Belaya Tserkov, had originally encouraged her not to reject his friend's
advances in order to divert attention from their own relationship. But
when his cunning overreached itself and pretence became reality, his
attitude towards Pushkin changed: the latter was no longer a naive
young pupil, but a serious rival in love, and Raevsky, while maintaining
a pretence of friendship, lost no opportunity to undermine his position.
The second enemy was Vorontsov himself, who, though the injured
husband, did not in principle disapprove of his wife's infidelity. 'Countess Vorontsova is a fashionable lady, very pleasant, who likes to take
lovers, to which her husband has no objection whatsoever; on the contrary he patronizes them, because this gives him freedom to take mistresses without constraint,' a contemporary observed.[73] Nevertheless, it
went somewhat against the grain to be cuckolded by this self-opinionated
young upstart, without a penny to his name and no profession to speak
of. 'You're fond of Pushkin, I think,' he once said to Wiegel; 'can't you
persuade him to occupy himself with something sensible; under your
guidance?'[74] Matters were made worse when Pushkin succumbed to that
common human trait which leads us to dislike those we have injured.
He had no notion of preserving the decencies and allowing himself to
be patronized by Vorontsov as one of his wife's gigolos; on the contrary,

he was determined to assert that he was the equal of anyone, even if the other were nearly twice his age, the possessor of immense wealth, and governor-general of New Russia to boot. As usual, he voiced his hostility in an epigram:

> Half an English lord, half a merchant
> Half a sage, half an ignoramus,
> Half a scoundrel, but there is the hope,
> That he'll be a whole one in the end[75]

– a verse hardly calculated to endear him to Vorontsov; more likely, indeed, to strengthen the latter's opinion formed earlier that year that, from the point of view of his own career, he had acted unwisely in taking over responsibility for Pushkin from Inzov. 'Should there be foul weather, Vorontsov will not stand up for you and will not defend you, if it is true that he himself is suspected of suspiciousness,' Vyazemsky warned. 'In addition I openly confess: I put no firm trust in Vorontsov's chivalry. He is a pleasant, well-meaning man, but will not take a quixotic line against the government in respect of *a person* or *an idea*, no matter who or what these are, if the government forces him to declare either for them or for it.'[76]

Vorontsov was indeed beginning to feel that he was 'suspected of suspiciousness' and had fallen into disfavour in St Petersburg. The tsar had ignored him during a visit to Tulchin to inspect the Second Army in October 1823, and had passed him over in the annual round of promotions at the end of that year; furthermore, he had recently been reprimanded for recommending as governor of Ekaterinoslav a general who had been involved in 'intrigues and disturbances' in the army.[77] Was he not, he thought, perhaps suspicious because of his association with Pushkin, whose name was anathema in conservative circles? Here the poet was automatically assumed to be the author of any new seditious verses: in January 1824, for example, Major-General Skobelev, provost-marshal of the First Army, in a report to the army's commander, attributed to Pushkin a poem entitled 'Thoughts on Freedom' – of whose composition the poet was wholly innocent – and wrote, 'would it not be better to forbid this Pushkin, who has employed his reasonable talents for obvious evil, to publish his perverted verse? [. . .] It would be better if the author of those harmful libels were to be, as a reward, immediately deprived of a few strips of skin. Why should there be leniency towards a man on whom the general voice of well-thinking citizens has pronounced a strict sentence?'[78] Vorontsov therefore took pains to distance himself from the poet, at the same time keeping him under close surveillance. 'As for Pushkin, I have exchanged only four words with him in the last fortnight,' he wrote to Kiselev in March; 'he is afraid of me because he is well aware that at the first rumour I hear of him I will dismiss him and that then no one will wish to take him on, and I am sure that he is now behaving much better and is more reserved in his conversations than he was with the good General Inzov [. . .] From everything that I learn of him through Gurev [the mayor of Odessa], through Kaznacheev [the head of his chancellery] and through the police, he is being very sensible and restrained at the moment, if he were the contrary I would dismiss him, and personally would be enchanted to do so for I do not love his manners and am no enthusiast of his talent – one cannot be a real poet without study and he has undertaken none.'[79] A few days later Kaznacheev wrote to the Kishinev police chief: 'Our young poet Pushkin with the permission of Count Mikhail Semenovich [Vorontsov] has been given several days leave in Kishinev. He is a fine noble young fellow; but often harms himself by saying too much, loves consorting with Ultra-liberals and is sometimes incautious. The count writes to me from the Crimea to instruct you to keep a surreptitious eye on this ardent youth: note where he makes dangerous remarks, with whom he consorts, and how he occupies himself or spends his time. If you find out anything, give him a tactful hint to be careful and write to me about it in detail.'[80]

Just before his departure for Kishinev Pushkin had received the first instalment of the proceeds from the sale of *The Fountain of Bakhchisaray*. Experiencing an unaccustomed, exhilarating feeling of independence, and cock-a-hoop with his success, he became even more outrageous in his behaviour. Unfortunately for Vorontsov, Pushkin had been attached to his bureau by imperial fiat, and the governor-general could not, therefore, sack him or transfer him – as he could his other civil servants – without the express permission of the emperor. He now resolved to take this step: at the end of March he told Kiselev that he had decided to ask the Foreign Minister, Nesselrode, to transfer Pushkin elsewhere. 'Here there are too many people and especially ones who flatter his conceit,' he wrote.[81] He made the same point to Nesselrode: 'There are many flatterers who praise his work; this arouses in him a harmful delusion and turns his head with the belief that he is a remarkable writer, whereas he is only the weak imitator of a writer on whose behalf very little can be said (Lord Byron) [. . .] If Pushkin were to live in another province he would find more encouragement to work and would avoid the dangerous company here.' He had only Pushkin's best interests in mind in making this request for his transfer, which he begged Nesselrode to bring to the emperor's attention.[82] A month later, having had no reply, he concluded a letter to Nesselrode about the Greek refugees in Moldavia with the words: 'By the by I repeat my prayer – deliver me from Pushkin; he may be an excellent fellow and a good poet, but I don't want to have him any longer, either in Odessa or Kishinev.'[83] On 16 May he finally received a reply, but one which was unsatisfactorily inconclusive: 'I have put your letter on Pushkin before the emperor,' Nesselrode wrote. 'He is completely satisfied with your judgement of this young man, and orders me to inform you of this officially. He has reserved his instructions on what should be finally undertaken with regard to him until a later date.'[84] Vorontsov's patience was running out. He had intended to leave Odessa for the Crimea in the middle of May, to spend the summer there with his family and a large number of guests. However, his daughter fell ill, and the departure had to be postponed. Constrained to remain in Odessa, and waiting vainly for the emperor's permission to transfer Pushkin, he found that circumstances had provided an opportunity to rid himself for some time at least of the poet's presence.

'The neighbourhood of Odessa is very bleak and much infested by locusts, which come in immense bodies and in an hour after they have alighted, every vestige of verdure is effaced,' an English visitor wrote.[85] In fact, the whole of New Russia, including the Crimea, was subject to these plagues. At the end of 1823 the Ministry of Internal Affairs had allocated 100,000 roubles to Vorontsov for a campaign against the infestations expected the following year. From the beginning of May 1824 reports that the insects had begun to hatch flooded in to Odessa. In July the swarms took wing, with catastrophic results, especially in Kherson province and in the Crimea. 'Locusts have spread in terrible quantities,' ran an official report. 'The river Salgir was arrested in its flow by a swarm of these harmful insects, which had fallen into it, and 150 men worked for several days and nights to clear the stream. [. . .] Some houses near Simferopol were so filled with the insects that the inhabitants had to abandon them.'[86] The insects were most vulnerable in the period immediately after hatching, before their wings had formed. During May, therefore, a frenzy of activity took place. Vorontsov sent his civil servants, sometimes with specially designed nets and at the head of companies of infantry, out into the countryside to report on the situation and take measures against the swarms: among them was Tumansky, who was dispatched to the Olviopol and Tiraspol districts at the beginning of the month. On 22 May Pushkin received an official letter from the governor-general which charged him 'to proceed to the Kherson, Elisavetgrad and Aleksandriya districts', where he was to ascertain 'in what localities the locusts have hatched, in what quantities, what instructions have been given for their eradication and what means have been employed for this'. He was then 'to determine with what success the means for their eradication have functioned and whether the measures instituted by the District Offices have been adequate', and to submit a report on his findings.[87]

Horror-struck, Pushkin composed a letter to Kaznacheev, writing and rewriting it with as much care as if it was a poem. Since his appointment to the Foreign Office seven years previously, he had 'not written a single paper, not had dealings with a single departmental head'. He had chosen a different career: 'For God's sake do not think that I regard poetry with the childish vanity of a rhymester or as the recreation of a man of sensibility: it is simply my trade, a branch of honest industry, which provides me with a livelihood and domestic independence.' He then turned to the delicate question of how he could reconcile taking a salary with doing nothing to earn it. The book trade could only be conducted in Moscow or St Petersburg. 'I am continually forced to refuse the most advantageous offers solely for the reason that I am 2,000 versts from the capitals, [. . .] and I accept the 700 roubles not as the salary of a civil servant, but as the ration of an exiled prisoner. I am ready to give it up if I cannot control my own time and occupations.' If he were a civil servant, he 'would choose no other superior than His Excellency', but he had 'already renounced all the advantages of the service and all hope of further success in it'. He concluded on a pathetic note: 'Perhaps you do not know that I have an aneurysm. For the last eight years I have been carrying death with me. I can produce the certificate of any doctor you please. Is it not possible to leave me in peace for the remainder of my life which will surely not be long?'[88]

While the flattery of Vorontsov is comprehensible and, in the circumstances, pardonable, other elements in the letter seem scarcely honest. Pushkin did not have an aneurysm – a morbid dilation of an artery – but a varicose vein in his leg, which was hardly likely to bring about his premature demise. Nor do his remarks on the literary market correspond with reality. Until recently he had not believed it possible to make a living from writing; had only changed his mind after the commercial success of *The Fountain of Bakhchisaray*, which had been achieved while he was 2,000 versts from the capitals; and he had not continually had to refuse advantageous offers for his work. The letter does, however, explain why – disinclined as he was to leave Odessa and concern himself with serious official business – he felt justified in objecting to the instructions. He took the view that, since he had not come to the south of his own free will, he was absolved from the usual duties of his position. It could be said that he had been encouraged in this view by his superiors: Inzov, and, up to now, Vorontsov had only given him inconsequential tasks and had not seen strictly to their fulfilment – but the same could also have been said of his superiors in St Petersburg. From a formal point of view, however, he was a civil servant attached to Vorontsov's bureau, who could be given any task which could be given to his colleagues, though – a consideration which had no doubt influenced Inzov's and Vorontsov's attitude – such a task was hardly likely to be carried out speedily, efficiently or indeed at all.

The letter did not succeed in changing Vorontsov's order. The following day, 23 May, Pushkin drew 400 roubles in travelling expenses and set off for Kherson, Elisavetgrad (now Kirovograd) and Aleksandriya. It was a round trip of 828 versts – 552 miles – which, had he contented himself with merely visiting the towns, would have taken just over a week; had he followed his instructions and made detailed observations of the locust campaign, he would have been nearer a month on the road. Strangely, the travelling allowance he had received was over three times larger than it should have been. The usual rate was eight copecks per horse per verst: the receipt Pushkin signed is for two horses, and he should therefore have received 132 roubles 48 copecks.[89]

On 24 May he arrived in Kherson and left the following day in the direction of Elisavetgrad. Elise Vorontsova had given him a charming little book, printed in Paris, entitled 'A Ladies' Almanac for 1824'. This contained calendar notes, engravings of some famous paintings, a little anthology of French verse, and a number of blank pages, each headed with the name of a month and an engraving – each one different – of a playful Cupid. On the page for May Pushkin has written '26 journey, Hungarian wine':[90] he had celebrated his twenty-fifth birthday that day with a bottle of Tokay in an inn in Nikolaev, on the road to Elisavetgrad. However, he got little further: two days later, on 28 May, he was back in Odessa. 'Pushkin was sent against the locusts,' Orlov wrote to his wife. 'He battled against them and after a very difficult campaign returned yesterday, having retreated before an innumerable enemy.'[91]

During his trip Pushkin had brooded over Vorontsov's orders, eventually convincing himself that they represented a gross affront to his dignity. On the face of it, his feeling is hardly justified: many civil servants, including a number senior to him, had been given similar tasks; the mission he had been sent on was a serious one, and he had been given expenses (the balance of which he seems not to have returned) at three times the going rate for it. His anger arose, rather, from the inescapably comic association of poetry and locusts, leading to the conviction that, both in undertaking the mission and in returning from it having achieved nothing, he had cut a patently ludicrous figure. His only recourse was to stand on his dignity, and so – with the malicious encouragement of Aleksandr Raevsky – he sent in his resignation. 'I have quarrelled with Vorontsov and conducted a polemic correspondence with him, which concluded on my side with a request for discharge. What the authorities will do in the end is yet unknown. Tiberius [Alexander I] will be glad to make use of it; and European talk about the European mode of thought of Count Sejanus [Vorontsov] will make me responsible for everything,' he told Vyazemsky.[92] Vorontsov, given Pushkin's peculiar status, was puzzled as to how to deal with the request. 'Pushkin has presented a petition for discharge,' he wrote to Nesselrode on 9 June. 'In truth, not knowing how to deal with this request and whether an attestation of illness was necessary, I am sending it to you privately and urgently request you either to forward it or to return it to me, as you decide.'[93] Relations became even more strained when Pushkin fancied that Vorontsov had insulted him by his attentions to a young Englishman. 'I am sick of being treated in my native land with less regard than the first English scamp who comes to parade his platitudes and his gibberish among us,' he raged in a letter to Kaznacheev,*[94] and to Turgenev wrote: 'Vorontsov is a Vandal, a court boor and a petty egoist. He saw in me a collegial secretary, but I, I must admit, think something other of myself.'[95]

Pushkin was never slow to take umbrage at a slight, real or fancied, but the morbid sensitivity revealed by his remarks is something new. Its cause, paradoxically, was the success of The Fountain of Bakhchisaray. Something in Vorontsov's behaviour had borne in upon him that a professional writer might be considered not to be a gentleman, and he was fanatically determined that this should not be the case with him. In this respect, he would argue, Russian literature differed from other literatures. 'Patronage,' he wrote in 1833, 'has been preserved up to now in the usages of English literature. The venerable Crabbe, who died last year, presented his fine poems to his grace the Duke etc.† In his humble dedications he respectfully mentions the favours and the noble patronage which he has been vouchsafed. In Russia you will find nothing similar. Here, as Mme de Staël noted, literature is for the most part the occupation of noblemen. [. . .] This has given our literature a particular aspect; our writers cannot seek favours and patronage from those they consider their equals, or present their works to a grandee or a magnate, in the hope of receiving 500 roubles or a ring set with valuable jewels.'[96] He

---

* The identity of the young Englishman whose preference over Pushkin aroused the latter's ire is not known. The suggestion that it was a Mr Sloan, the companion of the young Count Buturlin (see Chereisky, 402; LN, 91, 582–3) is unlikely, given that Buturlin and Sloan did not arrive in Odessa until Vorontsov had left for the Crimea and that, when they did meet, according to Buturlin, 'my guardian scarcely enjoyed the particular favour of Count Vorontsov, although a member of the count's favourite nation' (RA, 1897, II, 30). There were, however, many other young Englishmen working for trading houses in Odessa: Buturlin mentions the three James brothers, Landers, Moberly, Carruthers, Pearson and Gifford. It seems most probable that the young man in question was one of Vorontsov's English relations. The insult, whatever it was, continued to rankle; in his 'Imaginary Conversation with Alexander I', written some six months later, Pushkin writes that, unlike Vorontsov, Inzov did not 'prefer the first English good-for-nothing to all his known and unknown compatriots' (XI, 23).

† In a draft Pushkin refers to 'the Duke of Rutland' (XI, 488).

put the same idea into the mouth of a character in the unfinished prose work, *Egyptian Nights*: 'Our poets do not have gentlemen-patrons; our poets are gentlemen themselves, and if our Maecenases (devil take them!) do not know this, then so much the worse for them.'[97] The Maecenas of whom he is thinking is Vorontsov; in May or June 1825 he wrote to Bestuzhev: 'Our writers come from the highest class of society – in them aristocratic pride is merged with authorial self-esteem. We do not want the patronage of our equals. This is what that blackguard Vorontsov doesn't understand. He imagines that a Russian poet will come to his antechamber with a dedication or an ode – but instead he comes with a demand for respect, as a nobleman of six hundred years standing – a devil of a difference!'[98] Pushkin's friends found this insistence on the length of his lineage faintly ridiculous.* Ryleev, to whom Bestuzhev had shown the letter, wrote in June: 'You have become an aristocrat; that made me laugh. Is it for you to boast of your five-hundred-year-old nobility? I see a slight imitation of Byron here. Be Pushkin, for God's sake. You're a fine enough fellow in your own right.'[99] For Pushkin, however, it was as important to assert his membership of the old nobility, as opposed to the new, service aristocracy – whose families went back only to 'the times of Peter and Elizabeth', and whose ancestors were 'Officers' Servants, Choristers and Ukrainian peasants'[100] – as it was to affirm that he was both a poet and a gentleman: indeed the one depended on the other.

On 7 June Princess Vera Vyazemskaya arrived in Odessa with two convalescent children – the six-year-old Nikolay and the two-year-old Nadinka (Nadezhda) – for whom sea-bathing had been recommended in the hope of improving their health.† She was then thirty-three, and, 'though not a beauty, was more pleasing than one [. . .] Her small stature, little nose, fiery, penetrating gaze, facial expression – which the pen cannot express – and the gracious naturalness of her movements made her seem younger [. . .] In another her pure loud laughter would have been

---

* 'I am proud that Mikhail Fedorovich [Romanov]'s deed of election has the signatures of five Pushkins,' he once exclaimed. 'That is really something to boast of,' said Nikolay Raevsky, reducing Pushkin to silence (*PVVS*, II, 109, 485).
† A forlorn hope: Nikolay died the following January; Nadezhda in 1840, at the age of eighteen.

indecent, but in her was entrancing, for it was made harmless and flavoursome by the wit with which her conversation constantly sparkled.'[101] Though her husband was one of Pushkin's closest friends, Vera herself had never met him: she had not accompanied Vyazemsky on his visits to St Petersburg, but had remained in Moscow or on the family estate at Ostafevo, not far south of the city. 'I have nothing good to say to you about Vasily Lvovich's nephew,' she wrote to Vyazemsky on 13 June, after first meeting Pushkin. 'He is a complete hare-brain, and no one can control him; he has just played some new pranks after which he asked for his discharge; all the fault is on his side. I know on good authority that he will not get it. I do everything I can to calm him; I scold him on your behalf saying that you would be the first to condemn him, for his latest misdemeanours are those of a giddy fool. He attempted to make someone important to him look ridiculous, and succeeded; this became known, and, as might be expected, he is no longer looked on favourably. I am really sorry for him, but I have never met so much thoughtlessness and so great a propensity for scurrility as in him; at the same time I believe he has a good heart and much misanthropy; it is not that he flees society, but he fears men; perhaps his misfortunes and the faults of his parents have made him thus.'[102]

Vera Vyazemskaya

Over the next weeks, however, her view changed. Pushkin visited her daily, even after her move to a farmhouse at the top of a steep hill outside the town – owned by a Greek merchant, it was near the villa taken by the Vorontsovs. During these visits she saw a side of him usually hidden from the outside world: with her he was neither aggressively belligerent nor morbidly sensitive, but simple, trusting and childlike. He and little Nikolay became great friends, and, when they were sitting spitting at each other, Pushkin himself seemed a six-year-old. 'I am beginning to think him not as bad as he seems,' she wrote to Vyazemsky, and, a few days later: 'What a head and what confusion in his poor head! He often gives me pain, but makes me laugh even more often.' By the beginning of July she was writing: 'I am trying to adopt him as a son, but he is as disobedient as a page; if he were less ugly, I would call him a cherub: he really does nothing but childishnesses, but even these will break his neck some day.' As their intimacy progressed, she became the one person in Odessa to whom he could unburden himself: 'I am beginning to love him in friendship. Don't be alarmed,' she told Vyazemsky. 'I think he is good, but his spirit has been embittered by misfortune [. . .] He speaks to me in confidence about his problems and about his loves.' 'I am very fond of him, and he lets me scold him like a mother.'[103]

Byron had died in Missolonghi on 19 April 1824 (NS); the news, repeated from the French press, appeared in the St Petersburg newspapers on 23 May. Pushkin learnt of the event some days later, from a report in the *Odessa Journal*, and made a note inside the back cover of the notebook he was using: '1824 19/7 April death of Byron'.[104] Vyazemsky heard the news in the English Club in Moscow. 'What a poetic death is Byron's death!' he exclaimed in a letter to Turgenev. 'He foresaw that his ashes would rest in a land being reborn to freedom, and fled the dungeon of Europe. I envy those poets who are worthy to sing of his end. What an opportunity for Zhukovsky. If he does not make use of it, the game is up: it means his torch has gone out. Ancient Greece, the Greece of our time and the dead Byron – there's an ocean of poetry there! My hopes are on Pushkin.'[105] A fortnight later, as his wife was approaching Odessa, he wrote to her: 'Give my respects to Pushkin and force him immediately to write on Byron's death, or else I will not send his money.'[106] 'Pushkin absolutely does not want to write on Byron's death,' Vera replied. 'I think he is too busy and above all too in love to work on anything except his Onegin, who to my mind is a second Childe Harold [. . .] it is supposed to be a very licentious poem; it is full of epigrams against women, but in some descriptions is to be found the grace of his early verse.'[107] Vyazemsky had to satisfy himself with his friend's thoughts on Byron's work. 'You mourn Byron, but I am glad of his death as a sublime subject for verse,' Pushkin wrote. 'Byron's genius paled with his youth. In his tragedies, not excluding Cain, he is no longer that fiery demon who composed The Giaour and Childe Harold. The first two cantos of Don Juan are better than the others. His poetry changed visibly. He was created all inside-out; there was no gradualness in him, he suddenly grew up and became mature – sang and fell silent; and his first notes did not return to him again – after the 4th canto of Childe Harold we did not hear Byron, some other poet with a high, human talent was writing. Your idea of singing of his death in a 5th canto of his Hero* is charming – but I am not up to it – Greece has undone me.'[108]

Princess Vera had a number of acquaintances in Odessa: she knew the Raevskys well, the Vorontsovs less so; Elise called on her, however, and, one day not long after Vera's arrival, the two ladies, accompanied by Pushkin, went for a walk along the sea-shore. A month later Vera recalled the occasion. '[The pleasure] which I accord myself in full measure at the moment is to stand on the immense rocks which go out into the sea, watch the waves breaking at my feet and sometimes not have the courage to wait for the ninth, when it approaches too swiftly; then I run away even faster than it, only to return the next moment; Pushkin, Countess Vorontsova and I once waited for it and were so copiously splashed by it that we had to change our clothes.'[109] Pushkin devoted some lines of *Eugene Onegin* to the incident:

> I remember the sea before a storm:
> How I envied the waves,
> Running in turbulent succession
> With love to lie at her feet!
> How I wished then with the waves
> To touch those dear feet with my lips.
>
> (I, xxxiii)

On 14 June Count and Countess Vorontsov with their family and a large number of guests embarked on a yacht – belonging to the commandant of the port at Odessa, Captain Egor Zontag – to make their long-delayed voyage to the Crimea. Here Vorontsov was constructing a magnificent palace at Alupka, where Pushkin had stayed the night during his tour of the region. Earlier he had hoped to be one of the party, but the bad blood between himself and Vorontsov had put an invitation out of the question. Vyazemsky, out of touch with events, when sending Vera another instalment of royalties for Pushkin, added, 'If he should somehow need more money before he leaves, give him a couple of hundred roubles, on the security of his future immortality, that is, his

* I.e. of *Childe Harold*.

new poem. Only see that he doesn't use this money for mischief, on gambling; on whores – he may!'[110] After Elise's departure Pushkin spent even more time with Princess Vera. 'Yesterday in the pouring rain I stayed nearly an hour on the sea-shore with Pushkin to watch a ship struck by the storm,' she wrote. 'The main-mast was broken, the crew took to two boats, the ship was so near capsizing that I had to scream; in the end the weather became so bad that we had to go back, since nothing could be seen for the rain.' Less than a week later she wrote again: 'Pushkin is far more bored than I am: the three women he loved have recently left [. . .] Happily, one of them is returning soon.'[111]

Some distraction was provided when young Count Mikhail Buturlin arrived from Florence at the beginning of July. He was a distant relative of Pushkin, and was accompanied by his English governor, a Mr Sloan. 'My masculine society, which was confined to Pushkin, has been augmented by that of little Buturlin, who is as boring as a young man of 17 can be, with little wit but incredible vivacity, and by that of his so-called governor aged 30, a very handsome fellow and as witty as an Englishman can be when speaking French,' Vera wrote.[112] Buturlin spoke Italian to the opera-singers, went to a ball on Witt's yacht where he met Karolina Sobańska, and made Pushkin's acquaintance. 'In the good, old Russian custom from the first days of our acquaintanceship we called each other "mon cousin". Often meeting him in society or in the theatre (the general rendez-vous), I desired to know him better: but since I had not yet finally left the control of my tutor, I could not satisfy this wish completely. Aleksandr Sergeevich had the reputation of a freethinker, almost of an atheist, and I had been warned against him as a dangerous man in Florence. He obviously knew or guessed this, and once, coming up from the street to my open window (we were then living in a single-storey house on, I think, Tiraspol Street), said: "Is it not true, cousin, that your parents have forbidden you to make friends with me?" I confessed that this was so, and thereafter he ceased to visit me.'[113]

Meanwhile Pushkin's fate was being discussed in St Petersburg: Vorontsov's pleas had had their result. 'The emperor has decided Pushkin's affair: he will not remain with you,' Nesselrode wrote to Vorontsov on 27 June.[114] Turgenev got wind of this and on 1 July wrote to Vyazemsky: 'Count Vorontsov has sent a statement about Pushkin's dismissal.

Wishing, at whatever cost, to keep him there, I drove to see Nesselrode, but learnt that this was already impossible; that Count Vorontsov had several times, and long ago, petitioned about this, and justifiably; and that another Maecenas-superior would have to be found. I discussed this for a long time yesterday with Severin, and our thoughts came to rest on Paulucci, all the more as Pushkin is a Pskov landowner.* Pushkin alone is at fault. The countess distinguished him, distinguishes, as his talent merits, but he rushes on his ruin. It is painful and annoying! What is to be done with him?'[115] In fact, the efforts of Pushkin's friends were pointless: he had sealed his own fate several months earlier. The letter to Küchelbecker in which he had described himself as 'taking lessons in pure atheism' had fallen into the hands of the authorities.

On 11 July Nesselrode sent a copy of it to Vorontsov, writing:

Count! I submitted to the emperor's consideration the letters which your excellency sent me concerning the collegial secretary Pushkin. His majesty is in complete agreement with your pro-posal that he be removed from Odessa, after considering those sound arguments on which you base your proposal, which are strengthened at the same time by other evidence received by his majesty about this young man. Unfortunately, everything indicates that he is too imbued with the harmful principles which expressed themselves so perniciously at his first steps in a public profession. The attached letter will convince you of this. His majesty charged me to send it to you; the Moscow police learnt of it because it was going from hand to hand and became widely known. In consequence, his majesty, as a lawful punishment, has ordered me to exclude him from the list of officials of the Foreign Ministry for his bad conduct; moreover, his majesty does not wish to leave him completely without supervision, for the reason that, making use of his independent position, he will, without doubt, disseminate more and more widely those harmful ideas which he holds and will oblige the authorities to employ against him the most severe measures. In order as far as possible to avoid such consequences, the emperor

* The Marchese Paulucci was military governor of Riga, and governor-general of the Baltic provinces, to which that of Pskov had been added in 1819.

believes that in this case it is not possible to limit matters to his discharge alone, but finds it necessary to send him to his parents' estate in the Pskov province, under the supervision of the local authorities.[116]

Sending a copy of this letter to Paulucci, Nesselrode wrote that, in sending Pushkin to Pskov province, Alexander was 'confiding him to your vigilant care and the custody of the local authorities'. Paulucci in his turn copied Nesselrode's letter to Boris von Aderkas, the civil governor of Pskov, writing: 'I charge you to communicate with the Marshal of Nobility in order that he might choose one of the reliable Noblemen to observe Pushkin's actions and behaviour, so that, on his arrival in Pskov province, and after signing for Your Excellency a pledge that he will conduct himself in well-behaved fashion, not occupying himself with any indecent compositions or opinions, he should be under vigilant surveillance; moreover the Nobleman chosen for the surveillance should be instructed that, should reprehensible actions on the part of Pushkin be observed, they should immediately be reported to me through Your Excellency.'[117]

Nesselrode's letter arrived in Simferopol on 24 July, and Vorontsov, overjoyed, hastened to put it into effect. He wrote to Gurev, the mayor of Odessa, telling him to communicate the tsar's decision to Pushkin and to dispatch him immediately to Pskov, giving him travelling expenses for the journey. If Pushkin agreed to go directly to Pskov, he could travel alone; otherwise a reliable official should be sent with him. On 25 July, before this letter could reach Odessa, Elise returned, accompanied by Olga Naryshkina; the two – close friends, despite Olga's relationship with Elise's husband – took up residence in the Rainaud villa. Though Elise did not know of the decision to send Pushkin to Pskov, she did know that he would not be permitted to remain in Odessa. In despair at learning that he would have to leave the town – and her – for some other Kishinev, Pushkin concocted a harebrained scheme to escape from Russia by sea. He had entertained similar ideas earlier, writing to Lev in February that he thought of 'taking my hat and stick and going to have a look at Constantinople. I can't stand Holy Russia much longer.'[118] Vera entered eagerly into his plans, trying to find him money and a suitable boat. Vorontsov later learnt of this and wrote sarcastically to a friend in Moscow: 'As for Princess Vyazemskaya, I will say to you (but between ourselves) that here our country is not yet civilized enough to appreciate her brilliant and noisy type of wit, we are still flabbergasted by it, and then her actions to assist the attempts to flee planned by that mad good-for-nothing Pushkin seemed to us at the least improper. You are more worthy than us to enjoy her society and we abandon it to you with pleasure. Happily the doctors here have said that the climate of Odessa is only good for her children. I am quite of their opinion.'[119]

On 29 July Gurev summoned Pushkin and told him that he was being sent to Mikhailovskoe. Pushkin signed a document, promising to proceed straight to Pskov, and received, for the journey of 1,621 versts with three horses, travelling expenses of 389 roubles 4 copecks: this time the amount was not padded. The following day he borrowed 600 roubles from Vera, and in the evening saw Rossini's *Il turco in Italia* at the theatre. Elise left for her mother's estate at Belaya Tserkov on 31 July, and on 1 August Pushkin and Nikita Kozlov set out for Mikhailovskoe. On the first finger of his left hand Pushkin wore an old seal-ring, set with a cornelian which was engraved with an inscription in Hebrew – it had belonged to a rabbi – which Elise had given him: he wore it for the rest of his life. 'I accompanied him to the summit of my huge hill and tenderly kissed him,' Vera wrote to Vyazemsky. 'I was the only confidant of his sorrows and witness of his weakness, since he was in despair from having to quit Odessa, especially because of a particular feeling, which had grown in him during the final days, as often happens.'[120] When the news of his dismissal reached Moscow, his uncle, Vasily Lvovich, burst into tears; yet, even as they ran down his cheeks, he could not resist the opportunity for a witticism. '*La sauterelle l'a fait sauter!*' he punned.*[121]

" 'The locusts have got him sacked!'

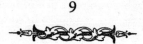

MIKHAILOVSKOE
1824–26

Walks, reading, deep sleep,
The forest shade, the babble of brooks,
At times a white-skinned, dark-eyed girl's
Fresh young kiss,
A spirited horse, obedient to the bit,
A reasonably choice dinner,
A bottle of bright wine,
Seclusion, quiet:
This was Onegin's saintly life
And insensibly he
Surrendered to it, the fair summer days
In carefree languor not counting,
Forgetting the town and his friends
And the boredom of festive events.

Eugene Onegin, IV, xxxviii–xxxix

When I imagine London, railroads, steam-ships, English journals
or Parisian theatres and whorehouses – then my back-of-beyond
Mikhailovskoe inspires boredom and rage in me.

Letter to Vyazemsky, 27 May 1826

FROM ODESSA Pushkin followed the route taken on his locust
campaign as far as Nikolaev, and then drove on through the towns
he should have visited – Elisavetgrad and Aleksandriya. Crossing
the Dnieper to Kremenchug, he turned north up the left bank of the
river: the itinerary he had been given was circuitous, avoiding Kiev, full
of his friends and sympathizers. Near Lubny he left his carriage at the
post-station, and, 'riding a post-horse in a horse-collar, without a

saddle',[1] called on his friend and fellow-poet Arkady Rodzyanko, whom he had known in St Petersburg, when both had been members of the *Green Lamp*. He had a high opinion of Rodzyanko as a satirist. 'That Ukrainian has a malicious pen,' he had remarked. 'I would not like to tangle with him.'[2]

After several hours with his friend Pushkin pressed on north – he had given his word not to delay during the journey – through Priluki and Nezhin to Chernigov, where he joined the main post-road from Kiev to St Petersburg. Here, at the post-station, on the morning of 6 August, the eighteen-year-old Andrey Podolinsky, a pupil at the St Petersburg University boarding-school for the nobility, who was travelling home to Kiev, came down to breakfast and saw beside the counter in the buffet a young man in 'negligently worn wide yellow nankeen trousers and a coloured, creased Russian shirt, belted with a black neckerchief; his curly, rather long thick hair waved in disorder'. He took him for a waiter, and was surprised when the unknown introduced himself with the words: 'I am Pushkin; my brother Lev was at your boarding-school.'[3] The two fell into conversation. Pushkin, laughing, showed Podolinsky his travel warrant, which listed, in order, the towns through which he had to pass, and asked him to deliver a letter to General Raevsky in Kiev.

On the evening of the following day in Mogilev – the town was the headquarters of the First Army – Aleksandr Raspopov, a young hussar officer and the nephew of the headmaster of the Lycée, Engelhardt, was, like many others, strolling up and down the main street, listening to the music of a military band, when he noticed a carriage coming slowly towards him. Before it walked a man wearing an officer's cap and a Russian red silk shirt, with an overcoat thrown over his shoulders. It turned into the post-station; Raspopov followed and, learning the traveller's identity, introduced himself; he was overjoyed when Pushkin remembered meeting him at Tsarskoe Selo. He hurried off to collect his friends and fellow-lovers of literature. Later the party moved to Raspopov's quarters where, as day broke, Prince Obolensky, with the panache to be expected from a hussar, proposed celebrating the occasion by giving Pushkin a bath in champagne. Pushkin, perhaps more sober than the others, was sensible of the honour, but declined. Soon afterwards his carriage rattled out of the town. At Vitebsk he turned left off the St Petersburg road to Polotsk, and then drove on, through Sebezh and Opochka, to Mikhailovskoe, where he arrived on the evening of 9 August 1824. He was met by his parents, his brother and sister, Lev and Olga, and by twenty-nine household servants.

Though, before leaving Odessa, Pushkin had promised in writing that he would on arrival report to the governor in Pskov, he failed to do so, and Aderkas had to summon him to his presence in October. Following Paulucci's instructions, the governor arranged for him to sign a pledge that he would 'live permanently on his parents' estate, conduct himself in well-behaved fashion, not occupy himself with any indecent compositions or reprehensible opinions harmful to public life, and not disseminate such anywhere'.[4] Aderkas had also carried out the order to ask the Marshal of Nobility to recommend 'one of the reliable Noblemen to observe Pushkin's actions and behaviour'. Peshchurov, the Marshal for the Opochka district, had recommended Ivan Rokotov, whose estate of Stekhnovo was some twenty-five miles from Mikhailovskoe. Rokotov had sensibly cried off on the plea of ill-health, and Aderkas suggested in his place Pushkin's father, Sergey Lvovich, 'known in the province both for his good behaviour and his honesty, and who with great sorrow pleaded ignorance of the crime committed by his son'. Paulucci agreed, provided that Sergey pledged himself 'to keep an unremitting watch on the actions and behaviour of his son'; the solution was even to be preferred, for 'parental authority is less restricted than that of a stranger'.[5]

Opinion was divided as to whether Pushkin's exile to Mikhailovskoe was merited. Though Delvig took his friend's side, writing: 'Public opinion is for you and is avenging you well. I have not met a single decent person who did not abuse Vorontsov on your behalf',[6] others, such as Turgenev and Vyazemsky, were inclined to blame Pushkin's behaviour for Alexander's decision. Karamzin was in no doubt that he had brought his fate on himself. 'The poet Pushkin has been ordered to live on his father's estate – until his recovery, of course, from fever and delirium. He did not keep the promise which he gave me when the thought of a fortress cell terrified his imagination: did not cease ranting, both by word of mouth and on paper, could not even get on with Count Vorontsov, who is by no means a despot!'[7] And Aleksandr Gorchakov, Pushkin's companion at the Lycée, now at the Russian embassy in Paris, wrote to his uncle, Peshchurov, the Opochka Marshal of Nobility, 'I have read with lively interest all the details you communicated to me about Pushkin [...] Despite the difference in our opinions, I cannot but feel great sympathy for Pushkin, founded on the memories of youth and the admiration which his poetic talent always aroused within me. His behaviour was, however, always grotesque, and it must be admitted that only the angelic kindness of our sovereign could not tire of treating him with a leniency which he did not always deserve.'[8]

Pushkin's parents, too, were convinced that their son was at fault; in addition, they were concerned at the damage this latest affair might have done to the family's reputation. 'My presence in the midst of my family has only doubled my afflictions, already real enough,' Pushkin wrote to Princess Vera. 'I have been reproached for my exile; they believe they have been also caught up in my misfortune, I am supposed to be preaching Atheism to my sister, who is a heavenly creature, and to my brother who is very funny and very young.'[9] Sergey Lvovich had never been close to his son; and relations between the two had always been tense. If Sergey had often been rendered distraught by his son's behaviour, Pushkin had as often been incensed by his father's meanness to him in money matters. Both felt aggrieved with the other; both were excessively short-tempered; both prone to hysterical exaggeration: the scene was set for an explosion, which took place at the end of October. Pushkin rushed off to take refuge with Praskovya Osipova at Trigorskoe, where, still in a white heat of rage, he composed a letter to Zhukovsky:

> Dear fellow, I resort to you. Judge my situation. On arriving here, I was met by everyone as well as could be, but soon everything changed: my father, frightened by my exile, constantly repeated that the same fate awaited him. Peshchurov, appointed to watch over me, had the shamelessness to offer my father the office of unsealing my correspondence, in short, of being my spy; my father's irascibility and irritable touchiness did not allow me to explain myself to him; I decided to remain silent. My father began to accuse my brother of being taught godlessness by me. I was still silent. They received a document about me. Finally wishing to extract myself from this painful

position, I go to my father and ask his permission to give him
a frank explanation ... My father flew into a temper. I bowed,
got on a horse and left. My father summons my brother and
orders him to have nothing to do with this monster, this unnatural son ... (Zhukovsky, think of my situation and judge). My
head began to boil. I go to my father, find him with my mother
and bring out everything that has lain on my heart for the past
three months. I end by saying that I am speaking to him for
the last time. My father, making use of the absence of witnesses,
runs out and declares to the whole household that *I beat him,
wanted to beat him, raised my hand to him, could have given
him a beating* ... I am not justifying myself to you. But what
does he want for me with this accusation of criminality? the
Siberian mines and the deprivation of honour? Save me, either
with a cell in a fortress or the Solovetsky Monastery. I say
nothing of what my brother and sister are suffering on my
behalf – again, save me. A.P.

31 Oct.

Hurry: my father's accusation is known to the whole house.
No one believes it, but everyone repeats it. The neighbours
know. I do not wish to explain myself to them – should it reach
the government, judge what would happen. To prove in court
my father's slander would be horrible for me, and there is no
court for me. I am an outlaw.[10]

At the same time he sent off a hasty and ill-considered note – laced
with an irony which could only be misunderstood – to the governor,
Aderkas: 'The Sovereign Emperor has imperially deigned to send me to
my parents' estate, thinking thus to lighten their sorrow and the fate of
their son. The government's trivial accusations have powerfully affected
my father's heart and exacerbated a mistrustfulness pardonable to old
age and tender love for his other children. I have decided, for his and
my own peace of mind, to ask His Imperial Majesty to deign to transfer
me to one of his fortresses.'[11] Luckily there had been some days of
torrential rain, the roads had been washed out, and the messenger,
unable to deliver the letter, returned it to Pushkin.

A day or two later, at the beginning of November, Lev left for

St Petersburg, taking with him the letter to Zhukovsky, who hastened to reply:

> Both your letter and Lev's account convince me that you are just as wrong as your father. To everything that has happened to you, and that you have brought upon yourself, I have but one answer: POETRY. You have not a gift, but genius. You are rich, you have an inalienable means of *rising above* undeserved misfortune, and of *turning it into the good* you deserve; you can and must, more than anyone else, preserve your moral dignity. You were born to be a great poet; be worthy of this. [. . .] By the authority conferred on me I offer you the *first* place in the Russian Parnassus. And what a place it will be, if you unite *sublimity of aim* with *sublimity of genius*! Dear brother in Apollo! you can do this! And with it you will be inaccessible to everything that will be in commotion about you in life.[12]

The next week Olga followed Lev to St Petersburg, taking with her a letter for him. 'Tell Zhukovsky from me to keep silent about the happenings he knows about. I absolutely do not want to wash our dirty Mikhailovskoe linen in public – and you, dear fellow, keep a rein on your tongue.'[13] But it was impossible to keep the quarrel a secret, and Pushkin's friends began to worry about the effect it might have. 'We live in an epoch when everything becomes known,' Vyazemsky wrote to Olga. 'Your brother has enemies, – they will not fail to portray him in the eyes of the emperor as a man who has revolted against all laws of God and man, who cannot bear the slightest restriction, and who will be a bad citizen, since he is a bad son.'[14] Zhukovsky promised to preach Sergey a sermon on his arrival in St Petersburg; this had some effect. Sergey informed Aderkas that he could not remain constantly with his son, since affairs summoned him to St Petersburg and Moscow: he therefore withdrew from the duty he had taken on.

Pushkin did not easily forgive his father. In October 1826, by which time the poet had already left Mikhailovskoe and was in Moscow, Sergey Lvovich wrote to his brother Vasily: 'No, dear friend, do not think that Aleksandr Sergeevich will ever be conscious of the wrongs he has done me [. . .] Do not forget that for two years he has nourished his hatred, which neither my silence, nor my endeavour to ease his lot as an exile, was able to soften. He is completely convinced that it is I who should ask for forgiveness, but adds that, if I decided to do this, he would rather hurl himself from a window than forgive me.'[15] There is no doubt that Pushkin's hostility was very real. Both he and Lev felt an unsurmountable physical revulsion – of the kind that can only be provoked by a close relation – for their father. 'After each of our meetings I get nausea and indigestion just from the smell of him,' Lev wrote.[16] Vyazemsky and Turgenev called Sergey 'the Fountain', from his unpleasant habit of showering the person to whom he was speaking with saliva. A partial reconciliation occurred in the spring of 1827, when Pushkin came to St Petersburg: thereafter their relations, though civil, were hardly intimate.

After Odessa with its social bustle, its freedom, and its southern warmth, the thought of being cooped up in a small manor house in northern Russia throughout a gloomy autumn and bleak winter struck despair into Pushkin. He began to ponder schemes of escape. 'Fuck fame, it's money I need,' he exclaimed, urging his brother to get the first chapters of *Eugene Onegin* through the censor as soon as possible: what could he need money for in Mikhailovskoe, other than to finance an escape? After requesting 'some wine, some cheese, and do not forget (speaking in the manner of Delille*) the spiral steel which pierces the bottle's tarred head – i.e. a corkscrew', and denying, for the benefit of those who might read the letter, any thought of flight – 'Why should I flee? It's so wonderful here!' – he went on to refer cryptically to that which he had just denied: 'When you are here we will speak of *a banker, our correspondence, the place where Chaadaev resides*. These are points on which you can already inform yourself.'[17] At the time Chaadaev was living in Switzerland: the message was clear. Praskovya's son, Aleksey Vulf, became involved: 'I suggested the following scheme to him: I would obtain a foreign passport and would take Pushkin, as my serf servant, abroad with me.'[18] Pushkin did not keep his intentions secret, and Praskovya Osipova sent an anxious letter to Zhukovsky, who, she felt, could persuade Pushkin that such a course would not be in his

---

* Jacques Delille (1738–1813), French abbé and mediocre poet, who translated Virgil and Milton: Pushkin is poking fun at his periphrastic style.

best interests. 'I fear to be indiscreet, but hope that you, dear Mr Vasily Andreevich, will guess my meaning,' she wrote: she had to resort to hints, in case her letter should be opened and read. 'If Aleksandr has to remain here for long, then for us Russians farewell to his talent, his poetic genius and one will not be able to blame him. Our Pskov is worse than Siberia, and no ardent head can remain here. He is now so concerned with his position, that without further consideration he will jump out of the frying-pan into the fire – and then it will be too late to think of the consequences. [...] If you think that the air and sun of France or of the neighbouring lands, over the Alps, are beneficial for Russian eagles, – and will not be harmful to ours, then let what I have now written remain an eternal secret. If you are of another opinion, then think how to clip its wings.'[19] However, there proved to be no need for Zhukovsky's intervention: Pushkin's frustration, temporarily at least, gave way to a grudging acceptance of the situation. It could not be denied that life at Mikhailovskoe, whatever its disadvantages, provided the poet with far more leisure and time to compose than he had previously enjoyed.

He soon settled into a regular routine. After – according to season – a cold bath or a dip in the Sorot, he would spend the morning writing, often lying in bed with his notebook propped on his knees, his favourite posture for composition. His room was at the front of the house, close to the entrance, and served as bedroom, study and dining-room. He let his hair and his fingernails grow, and cultivated huge, curly side-whiskers. For recreation he rode or took long walks in the surrounding countryside, taking with him an iron cane, which he would throw in the air and catch, or throw in front of him, pick up, and throw again. When riding he wore a hat with a white peak; when walking one of plaited pith, which he had acquired in Odessa, usually taken to be a straw hat by those who saw him. At the end of May the following year a local tradesman, Ivan Lapin, after visiting the fair at Svyatye Gory, a few miles from Mikhailovskoe, noted: 'I had the pleasure of seeing Mr Aleksandr Sergeevich Pushkin, who in a way surprised me by his strange attire, to wit: he had a straw hat on his head – was wearing a red calico peasant shirt, with a sky-blue ribbon as a sash, carried an iron cane in his hand, had extremely long black side-whiskers, which were more like a beard, and also very long fingernails with which he peeled the rind from oranges and ate them with great appetite, I think about half a dozen.'[20] As in Kishinev, he continually practised with his pistols, firing more than a hundred rounds a morning in a cellar behind the bath-house, or shooting at a target in competition with Vulf. In the evenings he would play billiards by himself, or listen to Arina Rodionovna's folk-songs and fairy-tales – 'How charming these tales are! Each is a poem!'[21] – and call on her to

> Sing me a song of how the bluebird
> Peacefully lived beyond the sea;
> Sing me a song of how the maiden
> Went down for water in the morning.[22]

'As my sole resource I often visit a good old neighbour-woman – and listen to her patriarchal conversations,' he wrote to Princess Vera. 'Her daughters, unattractive enough in all respects, play for me some Rossini which I sent for.'[23] This disparaging description of the household at Trigorskoe was manifestly unfair. In 1824 Praskovya was forty-three. She was small and plump, with a face that would have been, according to her niece, beautiful, had it not been for a protruding lower lip. Pushkin was always adept in evoking – perhaps unconsciously – a quasi-maternal love in women older than himself. Like Princess Vera, Praskovya soon succumbed to his childlike charm. Her feelings for him were obviously more than merely maternal; but there is no evidence that Pushkin ever returned them, or that their relationship was ever a physical one – though both her daughter, Annette, and her son, Aleksey, hint at something of the kind.

Most afternoons, accompanied by a couple of wolfhounds, he would go over to Trigorskoe: sometimes on foot, sometimes on horseback, and once riding a peasant's pony so small that his feet touched the ground. In summer he would climb in through any open window. 'We would all be sitting at our work: one reading, one working, one at the piano [. . .] Well, then Pushkin arrived, – and everything was turned topsy-turvy; laughter, jokes, conversation – there was such a hubbub in the rooms [. . .] And how lively he was, could never sit still, was always walking or running about!'[24] 'There is something very amusing going on between me and the Trigorskoe lot,' Pushkin told his brother. 'I don't have time to tell you about it, but it's killingly funny'; and, asking him to send a copy of Bulgarin's almanac *Thaliu*, 'Apropos of Thalia;* the other day Evpraksiya and I measured ourselves with a belt and our waists turned out to be identical. One of two things follows: either I have the waist of a fifteen-year-old girl, or she the waist of a twenty-five-year-old man. Evpraksiya pouts and is very sweet, I quarrel with Annette; I am fed up with her!'[25] In a stanza of *Eugene Onegin* he compares Evpraksiya's – Zizi's – waist to a champagne flute: 'an array of glasses, narrow, long,/Like your waist,/Zizi, crystal of my soul' (V, xxxii).

Aleksey Vulf was a student at the University of Dorpat (now Tartu, in Estonia). He had been spending the summer vacation at Trigorskoe when Pushkin arrived from the south; they soon became intimate, and when Aleksey returned to university he was followed by a verse epistle addressed to him and his friend and fellow-student, the poet Nikolay Yazykov. Pushkin's relationship with Aleksey echoed his own with Aleksandr Raevsky; this time, however, he was the mentor, not the pupil, the Mephistopheles to Vulf's Faust – as they were indeed called by Vulf's female cousins in Tver province.† And the subject of Pushkin's teaching was not Byronism and a corrosively cynical view of life, but women and how to seduce them. Writing to Vulf from Malinniki in 1828, he begins his letter: 'The Tver Lovelace wishes the St Petersburg Valmont health and successes' – referring to the seducers of Richardson's *Clarissa* and Laclos' *Les Liaisons dangereuses*.[26] According to Vulf Pushkin had worked out a strategy for assaulting feminine virtue which in his hands was irresistible. He was still preaching the same gospel in the late 1830s to Vyazemsky's teenage son, Pavel. 'Pushkin taught me,' he wrote, 'that the whole aim of life consists in this: everything on earth is done to attract the attention of women; not contenting himself with this poetic thought, he taught me that in this matter one must not stop at the first step, but go forward, insolently, without hesitation, in order to force the woman to respect one [. . .] He constantly gave me instructions

* A pun; the Russian for waist is *taliya*.
† The several estates belonging to members of the Vulf family were in close proximity to one another, near Staritsa in the Tver province: Praskovya Osipova had inherited Malinniki from her husband, Nikolay Vulf; his elder brother Petr owned Sokolovo, and of his two younger brothers Pavel lived at Pavlovskoe and Ivan at Bernovo.

on how to treat women, seasoning his moral admonitions with cynical quotations from Chamfort.'*[27]

Initiated into this secret of infallible success with women, Vulf hurried off to put it into practice in the society of Dorpat. Pushkin's options were more limited. Both Zizi – plump, pretty and blonde – and the ardent and passionate Sashenka might have been thought to be too young, but he flirted outrageously with them, and dedicated poems to both. He did eventually succeed in conquering Zizi in the autumn of 1828. The following January Vulf, who had not seen her for a year, noted in his diary: 'In all her movements was noticeable that limpness which her admirers would have called a charming languor, – this seemed to me similar to Liza's† state, to the suffering produced by a not too happy love-affair, in which I was, it seems, not mistaken.' 'Judging by various signs,' he added later, 'her young imagination has too been captured by the irresistible Mephistopheles.'[28] However, at Trigorskoe during Pushkin's exile, there was for most of the time only one possible candidate for dalliance – Annette, a round-faced, sentimental girl, with sad, languid eyes, extremely pretty feet, and a prominent bust. And, in the autumn of 1825, he was to turn his attention to her. But for the time being he had other distractions.

'Tell me, my dear chap,' he wrote to Rodzyanko, 'what is this A.P. Kern, who has written a lot of kind things about me to her cousin?‡ They say she is an extremely sweet piece.' He knew very well who she was: she was the girl whose beauty had so impressed him when he had met her at the Olenins in 1819. Her marriage to General Ermolay Kern, thirty-five years older than her, had broken down and she had gone to live on her parents' estate at Lubny in the Ukraine, where the nearest neighbour was Rodzyanko. Pushkin was sure the two were having an affair: 'Knowing your amorousness and *unusual talents* in all respects, I suppose your business to be done or half-done,' he wrote. 'I congratulate you, my dear fellow: write an elegy or at least an epigram on it all.'

---

* Nicolas-Sébastien de Chamfort (1741–94), whose bitterness and disillusionment, caused by ill-success and disease, are expressed with penetration and succinct irony in his posthumous *Maximes, caractères et anecdotes*.
† Liza Poltoratskaya, Anna Kern's sister, and Vulf's mistress.
‡ Annette; Anna's mother, Ekaterina Poltoratskaya, *née* Vulf, was Praskovya Osipova's sister-in-law.

He ended the letter by remarking that he had written a poem about a gypsy girl and Baratynsky one about a Finnish girl: 'I imagine Apollo, looking at them, will shout: why bring me the wrong one? But which one do you want, damned Phoebus? a Greek girl? an Italian? in what way is a Finn or a gypsy worse than them? Cunt is all the same – fuck it! that is, enliven it with a ray of inspiration and fame. If Anna Petrovna is as sweet as they say, she will surely be of my opinion: ask her about it.'[29] 'Despite your good opinion of my various capabilities, I am at a loss in some things,' Rodzyanko replied – but the tone of the letter, jointly written with Anna Kern, suggests a very close intimacy between the two.[30]

Pushkin's poem was *The Gypsies*. 'I don't know what to say of it,' he wrote to Vyazemsky on the day he completed it. 'At the moment I am sick of it, I have only just finished and have not had time to wash off my sweaty balls.'[31] He often employed ejaculation – or defecation – as a metaphor for composition. His last 'southern' poem, it is set in Moldavia. Aleko, the hero, having fled society, is taken in by the gypsy Zemfira, and is soon performing with a tame bear, singing as it dances, while Zemfira's father plays a tambourine and Zemfira herself collects money from the audience. They have a child, but Zemfira betrays Aleko with a young gypsy. One night he surprises the lovers and murders both. The tribe moves off, leaving him alone on the steppe.

'I know nothing more perfect in style than your Gypsies,' Zhukovsky wrote. 'But, dear friend, what is the aim?' 'You ask what is the aim of the Gypsies?' Pushkin replied. 'Here it is! The aim of poetry is poetry, as Delvig says (if he did not steal it).'[32] Lev got the poem by heart before leaving for St Petersburg, where he garnered considerable popularity by reciting it in his friends' drawing-rooms. 'Yesterday young Pushkin recited to us his brother's *gypsy* poem and something from Onegin; lively, witty, but not wholly mature,' Karamzin told Vyazemsky in December;[33] and in February Turgenev, having heard that his friend had been ill, wrote: 'I have already heard Pushkin's *Gypsies* twice and was enthralled by it twice. I am not alone in thinking it to be his best work. The author made his brother, who recites it, give his word of honour that he would not copy it for anyone; otherwise I would have indulged you and sent you his *Gypsies* instead of strong bouillon for an empty, if no longer sick stomach.'[34] As with *The Fountain of Bakhchisa-*

ray, Pushkin was annoyed by Lev's indiscretion. 'Scold my brother for not keeping his word – I did not want this poem to become known prematurely – now nothing is to be done,' he wrote to Bestuzhev, and, to Lev himself, 'I shall not quarrel with you (although I want to) for 18 reasons: 1) because it would be pointless ... There is nothing for it, I will copy The Gypsies and send it to you and you can print it.'[35] Though much admired on its publication in 1827, some doubts were expressed about its iconoclastic attitude to Romanticism. 'One lady remarked of *The Gypsies*,' Pushkin wrote in 1830, 'that in the whole poem there was only one honest person and that was the bear. The late Ryleev was indignant because Aleko leads a bear and in addition collects money from the gawking public. Vyazemsky repeated the same observation. (Ryleev asked me to make at least a blacksmith out of Aleko, which would be far more noble). It would have been best to make him a civil servant of the 8th rank or a squire, and not a gypsy. In that case, it is true, the whole poem would not have existed, but so much the better.'[36]

Just before eight in the morning on Sunday, 11 January 1825, Pushkin was surprised by the sound of sleigh bells. Although the temperature was well below zero, he ran out into the porch in his nightshirt and with bare feet to see his closest friend at the Lycée, Ivan Pushchin, dismounting from a sleigh. The two embraced. Thirty-three years after the event, Pushchin still found that writing of it brought tears to his eyes.

Soon they were sitting in Pushkin's room, where 'everything was in poetic confusion, sheets of manuscript lay about everywhere, together with bitten and burnt quill-ends'. Over coffee and tobacco they spoke of their lives since they had last met. When Pushchin, who had left the army in order to become a magistrate, explained the reasons for the change, Pushkin's suspicions that he was involved in secret political activity again arose. 'I will not force you to speak, dear Pushchin,' he said. 'Perhaps you are right not to trust me. My many stupidities probably make me unworthy of your trust.' Pushchin, instead of denying his membership of a secret society, said nothing, but warmly embraced his friend.[37]

Pushchin

They looked into Arina Rodionovna's room – the only other in the house to be heated – where a number of household serf girls were sewing or making lace under the supervision of the nurse. 'I immediately noticed among them one figure sharply distinguished from the others, without, however, communicating my conclusion to Pushkin,' Pushchin remarks. 'I involuntarily had come to regard him with a new feeling, born of his exceptional position: it placed him high in my eyes – and I feared to insult him with some inapposite remark. But he immediately guessed my indelicate thought – and smiled meaningfully. Nothing more was necessary – in my turn I winked at him, and everything was understood without further words.'[38]

In passing through Ostrov Pushchin had acquired three bottles of Veuve Clicquot. One was opened at dinner, swiftly followed by another. They drank to Russia, to the Lycée, to absent friends, and to *her*. Pushchin had also brought with him a manuscript copy of Griboedov's new play, completed the previous summer, *Woe from Wit*. Pushkin had begun to read this aloud, commenting as he went, when someone else drove up to the house. He looked out of the window, seemed embarrassed, and hurriedly opened a miscellany of religious texts which lay on the table. A moment later a short, red-haired monk with a flowing beard came in. This was Iona, the prior of the monastery at Svyatye Gory, who had been charged with the invigilation of Pushkin's religious conduct, and to whom Pushchin's arrival had been reported. A desultory conversation followed. Iona drank two glasses of tea, generously qualified with rum, and left. It was after midnight before they supped, drinking the third bottle of champagne. At three in the morning Pushchin left. They were never to meet again.

The girl Pushchin had noticed was Olga, the nineteen-year-old daughter of the Mikhailovskoe bailiff, Mikhail Kalashnikov. In January 1825 Kalashnikov had been sent to manage Sergey Lvovich's estate of Boldino, in Nizhny Novgorod province. His family, however, remained behind at Mikhailovskoe. Though in 'The Country' Pushkin had taken a high moral line against country squires who debauched their serf girls – 'Here young maidens bloom/For the libertine's unfeeling whim' – he had now succumbed to the temptation himself, though his feelings for Olga were perhaps more than just those of the libertine. The affair, begun at the end of 1824, lasted until the spring of 1826. That April

Olga's father returned to Mikhailovskoe in order to take his family to their new home: this could not have been more apropos for Pushkin. He gave Olga a letter for Vyazemsky in Moscow, through which the Kalashnikovs would pass on their way to Boldino. 'This letter will be handed to you by a very sweet and good girl whom one of your friends has carelessly got with child,' he wrote. 'I rely on your humaneness and friendship. Put her up in Moscow and give her money, as much as she needs – and then send her to Boldino [...] At the same time with paternal tenderness I ask you to look after the future infant, if it is a boy. I don't want to send him to a foundling home – would it be possible for the time being to send him to some village or other, – perhaps Ostafevo.* My dear chap, I'm truly ashamed . . . but it's a little late for that now.'[39]

Vyazemsky was loth to get involved. 'I have just received your letter,' he replied on 10 May, 'but did not see your live pregnant missive, since it was given to me by your servant. Your missive is travelling tomorrow to Boldino with its family and father, whom your father has appointed there as bailiff. How can one keep the daughter here and to what purpose? It can't be done without her father knowing, and if he does know it is better for her to be with her family. Here is my advice: you should write a half-affectionate, half-repentant, half-landownerish letter to your future father-in-law, confess all to him, entrust the fate of his daughter and the future being to him, but entrust them to his responsibility, reminding him that some day, God willing, you will be his master and will then call him to account for the good or bad execution of your trust. I see no other way of settling this according to conscience, sense and for the general advantage.' 'Thou art right, favourite of the Muses,'† Pushkin replied. 'I shall use the rights of a prodigal son-in-law and future master and settle the whole affair with a letter.'[40] On 1 July Olga gave birth to a son, Pavel, who died two and a half months later, on 15 September 1826.

Soon after Pushchin's visit, at the beginning of February 1825, Trigorskoe society was augmented by the arrival of another of Praskovya Osipova's nieces, Anna Vulf – always called Netty to distinguish her

---

* Vyazemsky's estate, about twenty-five miles south of Moscow.
† The first words of Batyushkov's poem, 'An Epistle to I.M. Muravev-Apostol' (1814–15).

from her cousin Annette (the two were the same age, as well as having
the same name) – 'a very clever, well-educated, attractive girl – and a
beauty as well'.[41] Pushkin immediately struck up a flirtation which lasted
until she left on 1 April. 'Anna Nikolaevna [Annette] sends you her
respects,' he told Lev, 'and very much regrets that you are not here;
because I have fallen in love and am Myrtilizing.* Do you know her
cousin, Anna Ivanovna Vulf [Netty]? there's a woman!'[42] Some months
later he noted that he had written 'a very tender, very humble letter' to
'the Netty of the North whom I shall always regret having seen, and
even more not having possessed'.[43]

A week after Netty's departure he was overjoyed by the arrival of
Delvig – after Pushchin the closest to him of his Lycée friends. Tall,
corpulent, and bespectacled, incurably indolent and eternally indigent,
Delvig had moved from one civil service department to another after
leaving school, and had finally taken a post as Krylov's assistant in the

Delvig

Public Library at St Petersburg. His sloth
and inefficiency soon brought this also to
an end. When he returned to St Petersburg,
after a fortnight at Mikhailovskoe, he was
invited to submit his resignation or be
sacked. In the mornings the two poets read
one another their latest works, and argued
over literature; in the afternoons played
billiards, and after dinner walked over to
spend the evening at Trigorskoe. 'How glad
I was at the Baron's arrival,' Pushkin wrote
to his brother. 'He is very nice. All our
young ladies have fallen in love with him –
but he is as indifferent as a block of wood, he likes to lie on his bed,
captivated by the Chigrinsk Bailiff.'†[44]

One evening in the middle of June Pushkin walked over to Trigorskoe and found the company at dinner, laughing over the bad French

---

* A nonce-word, coined by Pushkin from the name Myrtilus, traditionally used in eighteenth-century French pastorals for a love-sick shepherd.
† 'The Death of the Chigrinsk bailiff', an episode from Ryleev's unfinished narrative poem
Nalivaiko, had just appeared in the 1825 number of Ryleev's and Bestuzhev's almanac, *Pole
star*

of Ivan Rokotov, a neighbouring landowner. He was astonished to see among them Anna Kern, who had just arrived from the Ukraine. Praskovya Osipova introduced him to her niece: he made a low bow, but said nothing. As on their previous meeting, he was disconcerted by her beauty, which immediately and completely subjugated him. In his eyes she could do nothing that was not perfect. 'Tell Kozlov from me,' he wrote to Pletnev, 'that recently our region has been visited by a charming person, who sings in heavenly fashion his Venetian night to the air of a gondolier's recitative – I promised to inform the dear, inspired blind man of this. What a pity that he will not see her – but let him imagine beauty and spirituality – may God grant at least that he should hear her!'*[45] But she was no longer the inexperienced young girl she had been six years ago. Since then she had separated from her husband, and had an affair with Rodzyanko. Pushkin was determined to make a conquest of her, and threw himself into a hectic courtship which lasted throughout her stay at Trigorskoe. His efforts were not successful: he was too infatuated, regressing at times into the behaviour of an insecure, love-sick adolescent.

Praskovya Osipova had determined to reconcile her niece with her husband, who was then stationed in Riga; she, Anna, and Annette were to travel there on 19 July. On the evening before their departure, the party drove over to Mikhailovskoe in two carriages: Aleksey and his mother in the first; Anna, Annette and Pushkin in the second. During the ride he showered Anna with fatuous compliments: 'I love the moon when it shines on a beautiful face,' he sighed. 'My dear Pushkin, do the honours of your garden to Madame,' said Praskovya when they arrived. 'He swiftly gave me his arm and ran off quickly, quickly, like a school-boy who has unexpectedly been given permission to go for a walk. I do not remember the details of our conversation: he reminisced about our first meeting at the Olenins, spoke about it with fascination and delight and at the end of the

Anna Kern

---

* Anna had sung 'Venetian Night. A Fantasy' by the poet and translator I.I. Kozlov, who began to write verse after going blind in 1821. Published in *Pole Star* for 1825, the poem, in memory of Byron, describes Teresa Guiccioli mourning over him.

conversation said: "You had such a virginal air; were you not wearing then something like a cross?" [46]

The next morning he turned up to bid them farewell and gave Anna a copy of the recently published first chapter of *Eugene Onegin*. As she leafed through its uncut pages a sheet of note-paper, folded in four, fell out. She picked it up and opened it to discover one of Pushkin's best-known and most anthologized love lyrics:

> I recollect a wondrous moment:
> Before me you appeared,
> Like a fleeting vision,
> Like a genius of pure beauty. [47]

The reconciliation with Kern did take place, and Anna remained in Riga, besieged with a succession of half-flirtatious, half-passionate letters from Pushkin. Before him on the table as he wrote were a faded bloom of heliotrope from her bosom, and a stone, over which she had tripped in the garden. 'I had the weakness to ask you for permission to write to you, and you the foolishness or the coquetry to permit me. A correspondence leads to nothing, I know; but I cannot resist the desire to have a word from your pretty hand. Your visit to Trigorskoe has left a stronger and more painful impression than that produced earlier by our meeting at the Olenins.' And, on receiving her reply, 'I am rereading your letter up and down and from side to side and say: dear one! charming one! divine! ... and then: oh, you disgusting person! ... Pardon, my beautiful sweet one; but that is how it is. There is no doubt that you are divine, but sometimes you do not have any common sense.' 'Adieu,' he ends his next letter, 'it is night and your image appears before me, all sad and voluptuous – I fancy I see your glance, your half-open lips. Adieu – I fancy myself at your feet, I press them, I feel your knees – I would give all my life's blood for a minute of reality. Adieu and believe in my delirium; it is ridiculous but true.' 'Come at least to Pskov,' he pleads. 'That would be easy for you. – My heart pounds, my sight blurs, I languish just at the idea of it.' [48]

Praskovya disapproved of the correspondence, thinking it might lead to another rift between Anna and her husband. Unable to persuade her niece to give it up, she left Riga in a huff. Pushkin cared nothing for Praskovya's disapproval, he was, however, worried by an ever-growing

ABOVE LEFT Nadezhda Osipovna Pushkina, Pushkin's mother, by Xavier de Maistre, 1802-5

ABOVE Sergey Lvovich Pushkin, Pushkin's father by Karl von Hampeln, 1824

LEFT Vasily Lvovich Pushkin, Pushkin's uncle by J. Vivien, 1823

Emperor Alexander I by Henri Benner, 1821

Empress Elizaveta Alekseevna
by Henri Benner, 1821

Tsarskoe Selo: Sadovaya Street and the Lycée, lithograph by A.E. Martynov, 1821-2

Ekaterina Bakunina, Pushkin's first love,
self-portrait, 1816

ABOVE K.N. Batyushkov by
O. Kiprensky, 1819

LEFT N.M. Karamzin by
G.B. Damon-Ortolani, 1805

The manor house at Mikhailovskoe, Pushkin's mother's estate; lithograph by
P.A. Aleksandrov from a drawing by I.S. Ivanov, 1837

Part of a panorama of the Nevsky Prospect. Wolff and Béranger's café is on the
extreme left; Bellizard's bookshop on the right, with the Moika canal between.
Lithograph by P. Ivanov from an original by V. Sadovnikov, 1835

Filipp Wiegel; lithograph from
a portrait by K.S. Osokin, 1836

RIGHT Emperor Nicholas I
by P.F. Sokolov, 1820s

ABOVE Nicholas I,
Empress Alexandra
Fedorovna and
Grand Duke
Alexander by
P.F. Sokolov

RIGHT Elise
Khitrovo by
P.F. Sokolov, 1838

Dolly Ficquelmont and her sister Countess Ekaterina Tiesenhausen
(daughters of Elise Khitrovo) by A.P. Bryullov, 1825

Annette Olenina by G.G. Gagarin, 1833

Countess Agrafena Zakrevskaya
by an unknown artist, 1820s

A.S. Griboedov, by V.I. Moshkov, 1827

jealousy. Aleksey Vulf had left Trigorskoe to return to university at Dorpat, but had gone by way of Riga, where, thought Pushkin, he was staying far too long. 'What are you doing with your cousin?' he asked. 'Inform me, frankly. Send him quickly to his university, I don't know why, but I don't like these students any more than Mr Kern does. He is a very worthy man is Mr Kern, a wise, prudent man, etc.; he has only one fault – that of being your husband.' On 21 August he sent another enquiry: 'I would very much like to know why your cousin only left Riga on the 15th of this month and why his name turns up on the end of your pen three times in your letter to me? would it be indiscreet to inquire why?' Learning in September that the two were exchanging letters, he wrote: 'Jealousy aside, as a friend who is really devoted to you, plainly and without affectation, I advise you to break off this correspondence. I cannot conceive what your aim is in playing the coquette with a young student (who is not a poet) at such a respectable distance.'[49]

At the beginning of October the Kerns came to Trigorskoe for a short visit to make up Anna's quarrel with her aunt: 'Her husband is a nice chap,' Pushkin commented. 'We met and became friends.'[50] And in December Anna sent him a book he had been longing for, the recently published volume VII of the fourth edition of Pichot's prose translation of Byron, containing cantos six to sixteen of *Don Juan* – 'What a marvel *Don Juan* is! I know only the first five cantos,' he had told Vyazemsky the previous month.[51] 'I scarcely expected, enchantress, to hear from you, and it is from the bottom of my soul that I thank you,' he wrote, sending her 125 roubles in payment. 'Byron has acquired for me a new charm – all his heroines will assume in my imagination features which cannot be forgotten. [. . .] I take up my pen again to tell you that I am at your knees, that I love you still, that I detest you sometimes, that the day before yesterday I said horrid things about you, that I kiss your beautiful hands, that I kiss them again pending something better, that I can't go on, that you are divine etc.'[52]

Anna did, as Pushkin had feared, become Vulf's mistress: Mephistopheles had been hoist with his own petard. 'What is the Whore of Babylon Anna Petrovna doing?' he asked Vulf in disgust the following May.[53] She had left her husband and moved to St Petersburg; her liaison with Vulf lasted until the early 1830s, despite his frequent infidelities –

he had a long affair with her sister, Liza Poltoratskaya. When Pushkin came to St Petersburg after his exile, he met Anna again. This time he was more successful: in a letter of February 1828 he mentions 'Mme Kern, whom with God's help I managed to fuck the other day'.[54] For a short time he shared her with Vulf: a sordid conclusion to a relationship which had begun with so pure and ethereal an emotion.

Having failed with Anna, in the winter of 1825 he turned his attentions to Annette. He met no resistance, for she was already half in love with him. It had been painful and galling for her to hear him complimenting Anna, and to receive, while in Riga, a letter which, after recommending her to 'wear short dresses because you have very pretty feet, and do not fluff up your hair even if it is the fashion, because you have the misfortune to have a round face', went on to dilate on Anna's beauty and his love for her. 'I would rather have no letters from you than have ones like those you sent to me in Riga,' she wrote later.[55] But he was never in love with her. His conquest of her was completely cynical. 'The less one loves a woman, the surer one is of possessing her. But this pleasure is worthy of an old eighteenth-century monkey,' he had written sententiously to Lev in 1822.[56] It was, however, a pleasure which he now did not deny himself, though even an old eighteenth-century monkey might have felt a twinge of remorse at the manner in which Annette was treated.

Annette Vulf

He was unkind – and sometimes crude – in conversation with her: 'What shall I regale you with?' he asked Vyazemsky. 'Here are my bon mots (to add savour, imagine them said to a sentimental girl of twenty-six): What is sentiment? – A supplement to temperament. What do you like best? the scent of roses or of mignonette? – The scent of herring.'[57] The verses he wrote to her are heavily ironic, with a barely concealed patronizing contempt; for her name-day, punning on the meaning of the Hebrew original of her name (He [=God] has favoured me) he wrote: 'I'll be cursed/If I know, why/You were christened *a favour!*'[58] and, in another short piece, lapsed into obscenity. When he copied this effusion into her album, he replaced the offensive lines with dots, and refused to tell Annette what these concealed. Something of the nature of the three cornered relationship between Pushkin, Annette and Anna Kern can be apprehended from the fact that he revealed the obscenity to Anna.

On 9 February 1826 Praskovya, Annette and Netty – who had arrived for a short visit some weeks earlier – set out for Malinniki. Pushkin accompanied them as far as Pskov, and stayed there with them until they resumed their journey, on 12 February. The fortnight-long annual fair in Pskov began on the tenth; for Annette the two days that she and Pushkin spent together here were the happiest of the relationship. For once he was affectionate; he took a tender farewell of her, and seemed sad at their parting. She had bought a cup which she gave him as a present to remember her by. He remained in Pskov for a few days, dining with the governor and playing cards with acquaintances before leaving for Mikhailovskoe. At the beginning of April Praskovya returned to Trigorskoe, but without Annette. She had horrified her daughter by telling her that she must remain at Malinniki: the two had had a violent quarrel, but the mother's will had prevailed. 'Like Anna Kern, I really believe that she wants to be the only one to make your conquest, and that she is leaving me here from jealousy,' Annette wrote.[59] Over the next few months she sent him a series of letters in bad French, heartrending in their pathos and naiveté, which left him completely unmoved. He treated them with careless contempt, flinging them aside with the exclamation, 'Oh Lord, what a letter, just like a woman's!', and – despite her injunction that he should destroy them – leaving them lying about at Trigorskoe.[60]

Meanwhile, an intrigue of a different kind had been in progress: together with Aleksey Vulf Pushkin had concocted another scheme for escape. This hinged upon the fact that a well-known and much-respected professor of surgery at Dorpat University, Ivan Moyer, was the husband of Zhukovsky's niece, Mariya Protasova – or rather the relict, for Mariya had died in March 1823. Pushkin's 'aneurysm', which had first made its appearance in Odessa, in a letter to Kaznacheev, was to be brought into play again: Zhukovsky was to be persuaded of its danger; he would enlist Moyer's aid; and Pushkin would be allowed to go to Riga or Dorpat so that Moyer could operate on it. Once in either of these towns, both staging-posts for travellers to Europe, Pushkin might be able to flee abroad with Vulf's assistance. However, they envisaged a much more satisfactory solution: Moyer would be persuaded to testify that the condition was so complex and life-threatening that it could only be treated in, say, Paris. In order to convey information from Dorpat to Mikhailovskoe they concocted an elaborate code in which the movements of Pushkin's coach and – based on the fiction that his works were to be published in Dorpat – the behaviour of the censor and of the first, second and third compositors stood for various possible eventualities. The best that can be said of this scheme is that it was slightly less reminiscent of the exploits of the Scarlet Pimpernel than the proposal that Pushkin should dress up as Vulf's servant. But at least that involved only one other participant. This new idea, dependent on the reactions and interactions of so many different characters, was like some vast mechanical contrivance drawn by Heath Robinson. Among its more obvious flaws was the fact that its success depended on suborning Moyer, a man known for his honesty and probity, with whom neither was acquainted, to commit perjury. Everything went wrong, and in a manner which is irresistibly comic.

Lev, who was privy to the plan, started the ball rolling in April 1825 by putting about rumours on the state of Pushkin's veins. This produced an anxious letter from Zhukovsky: 'My dear friend, I ask you to reply as soon as possible to this letter, and reply in human fashion, not extravagantly. I have heard from your brother and mother that you are ill: is this true? Is it true that you have something like an aneurysm in your leg and that you have entertained this lodger for some ten years without telling anyone?' He thought it would be possible to get Pushkin sent to Riga to be cured. Pushkin immediately replied, manfully making light of the fact that he had been condemned to an early grave, indeed almost betraying the real purpose of the exercise: 'I have had my aneurysm for ten years and with God's help can bear it another three. Consequently there is no hurry, but Mikhailovskoe is stifling for me.' He enclosed with the letter a petition, which Zhukovsky was to submit to Alexander, asking for permission to go abroad for his health and his aneurysm.[61]

So far the plan had succeeded; now, however, things took a different turn. When the petition arrived in St Petersburg, his friends thought it far too restrained and not nearly sufficiently humble. They replaced it, therefore, with a letter from Pushkin's mother, sent to the tsar on 6 May:

Sire!

It is with all the solicitude of a Mother's wounded heart that I dare to implore at Your Imperial Majesty's feet a boon for my son! my maternal tenderness, anguished by his unhappy situation, alone gives me the hope that Your Majesty will deign to pardon me for soliciting His beneficence. Sire, it is a question of his life. My son has suffered for more than ten years from an aneurysm of the leg; my son, having neglected this ill generally, finds his days menaced by it at any moment, above all since he is situated in the province of Pskov a region lacking all assistance. Sire, do not deprive a mother of the object of all her tenderness! Deign to allow my son to travel to Riga or to some other Town which Your Majesty might deign to designate to undergo an Operation which alone gives me the hope of being able to preserve him. I venture to assure Your Majesty that his conduct there will be irreproachable. The Clemency of Your Majesty is the surest guarantee that I can offer of this.

I remain with deep respect Your Imperial Majesty's most humble, most devoted, and most thankful subject Nadezhda Pushkina, née Gannibal.[62]

Puzzled, Field-Marshal Diebitsch, the Chief of the General Staff, through whom such correspondence passed, on 11 June ordered an aide, Colonel Bibikov, to find out 'who this Pushkina, née Gannibal, is, and whether she is the mother of that Pushkin who writes verse'.[63] Discovering that she was, he wrote on 26 June: 'His Majesty the Emperor, having acquainted himself with the letter addressed to His Majesty on 6 May, has charged me, Madam, to inform you that His Majesty permits your elder son to travel for treatment to Pskov, where he can find all the necessary help, without the necessity of travelling to Riga.' At the same time an order was sent to the governor, Aderkas, informing him of the emperor's decision, and requiring him to keep a close watch on Pushkin's conduct and conversation.[64]

When this news reached Pushkin at the beginning of July, it sent him into a paroxysm of rage and annoyance, feelings which simmered on within him for several months. There was no hope of escaping to Europe from Pskov; he would be no better off there than in

Mikhailovskoe. He dashed off a bitterly sarcastic letter to Zhukovsky: 'His Majesty's unexpected favour has touched me indescribably, all the more so as the governor here had already offered me residence in Pskov, but I strictly observed the injunctions of higher authority. I have enquired about the surgeons at Pskov; there I was directed towards a certain Vsevolozhsky, very skilful in veterinary work and known in learned circles for his book on the treatment of horses. Notwithstanding all that, I have resolved to stay at Mikhailovskoe, sensible nevertheless of His Majesty's paternal condescension.'[65]

Over the next weeks the fundamental contradiction – easily foresee-able – of Pushkin's scheme emerged. He was absolutely opposed to an operation, which would reveal the far from life-endangering nature of the complaint. But he had succeeded only too well in convincing his friends that his death was imminent: anguished, they begged him to submit himself to the surgeon's knife. Zhukovsky kept urging him to go to Pskov; obstinately, he kept refusing. At the end of July Zhukovsky wrote to Moyer – who had declared that 'he was ready to sacrifice anything to save the premier poet of Russia'[66] – asking him to travel to Pskov to perform the operation. Learning this, Pushkin sent a desperate letter to Moyer: 'For God's sake do not come and do not worry about me. The operation demanded by the aneurysm is too unimportant to divert a famous man from his occupation and his place of residence. Your good deed would be agonizing for my conscience.'[67] Moyer could hardly operate on an unwilling patient, and stayed away, but the narrow escape brought Pushkin's annoyance to a head, and in August he poured out his bile in a letter to his sister, then in Reval with his mother and the Vyazemskys.

My friends [. . .] have expressly done that which I begged them not to do. What madness is this to take me for a fool and push me into a misfortune which I had foreseen, which I had pointed out? They annoy His Majesty, prolong my exile, make fun of my existence, and when they are astonished at all these blunders they compliment my fine verses and go out to dinner. [. . .] All this is inconceivably frivolous and cruel. One word more: my health demands a different climate, nothing of this was said to His Majesty. Is it his fault he knows nothing? I am told that

the public is indignant; I am too, but because of the insouciance
and frivolity of those who meddle in my affairs. O, God, deliver
me from my friends!⁶⁸

A little later he wrote to Vulf, telling him, by reference to their code,
that the plan had failed: 'I did not manage to thank you for your friendly
efforts on behalf of my damned works, the devil take them and the
Censor, and the compositor and everything else – they are not the point
now. My friends and parents keep on constantly making mischief for
me.'⁶⁹ His envy of his friends' situation is understandable, but his comments on their behaviour were grossly unfair: refusing to see that he
himself was the architect of the fiasco, he preferred to blame them for
their interference.

At the end of August Vyazemsky, scolding him for writing as he
had to Olga, pointed out how his mysterious and incomprehensible
intransigence might be interpreted: 'By refusing to go [to Pskov], you
bring on your mother the suspicion that she wished to delude the trust
of the tsar and forcibly extract your freedom with a fictitious aneurysm'
– a suspicion uncomfortably close to the truth. His counsel was that
Pushkin – for once – should stop being awkward, should let himself go
with the current, put up with the conditions of his exile – for which he
was himself partially to blame – and should have the operation in
Pskov. 'I cherished my aneurysm for five years, as the final pretext for
deliverance, *ultima ratio libertatis* – and suddenly my hope is destroyed
by the accursed permission to have treatment in exile!' Pushkin replied.
'My dear fellow, my head spins willy-nilly. They care about my life; I'm
grateful – but what the devil is such a life. It would be far better to die
in Mikhailovskoe from lack of treatment. At least then my grave would
be a living reproach, and you could write a pleasing and edifying epitaph
on it. No, friendship enters into conspiracy with tyranny, tries itself to
justify it, to avert indignation; they send me Moyer, who, of course,
could carry out the operation in a Siberian mine; deprive me of the right
to complain (not in verse, but in prose, there's a devilish difference!), and
order me not to be enraged [. . .] I am not sufficiently wealthy to
send for famous doctors and pay them for my treatment – Moyer is
Zhukovsky's friend – but I am not Zhukovsky. I wish for no charity
from him. That is all [. . .] You find that allowing me to go to Pskov

is a step forward, I think it is a step back – but enough of the aneurysm – I am sick of it, as I am of our journals.'[70]

A little earlier he had still been hoping to extract something from the complaint. Anna Kern, who had met Alexander several times – attracted by her beauty, he had once danced a polonaise with her – had advised Pushkin to write directly to the emperor. He took her advice. After explaining his behaviour in 1820 to despair caused by Count Tolstoy's slanders, thanking the tsar for his magnanimity, and assuring him that while in the south he had 'always respected, both in writing and speech, the Person of Your Majesty' – he had conveniently forgotten about the satirical poem on Alexander composed in Odessa – he concluded: 'My health was greatly impaired in my youth – an aneurysm of the heart demands an immediate operation or prolonged treatment. Residence at Pskov, the town assigned to me, can afford me no help, I beseech Your Majesty to permit me residence in one of our capitals or to indicate a locality in Europe where I can take care of my life.'[71] How the aneurysm has travelled from his leg to his heart is left unexplained. On consideration he did not send the letter off. 'Your advice to write to His Majesty touched me as a proof that you have thought of me – on my knees I thank you for it, but I can not follow it,' he told Anna on 22 September. 'Fate must decide my existence; I will not interfere.'[72]

A fortnight later he wrote to Zhukovsky. 'The other day, seeing autumn through my window, I got in my carriage and galloped to Pskov. The governor received me very nicely, I chatted with him about my vein, consulted a very kind doctor, and drove back to my Mikhailovskoe. Now, having detailed information about my aneurysm, I will speak of it sensibly. P.A. Osipova, being in Riga, with all the solicitude of friendship spoke of me to the surgeon Ruehland; the operation is not a problem, he said, but the consequences could be grave: the patient must lie motionless for several weeks etc. No matter what you wish, dear fellow – I will not agree to this either in Pskov or Mikhailovskoe; it doesn't matter whether one dies of boredom or an aneurysm, but the first is surer than the second – I can't stand bed, no matter what. Secondly, the Pskov doctor says: it is possible to do without an operation, but strict precautions are necessary: don't walk a lot, don't ride, don't make violent movements etc., etc. I appeal to everyone: what can I do in the country of Pskov if all physical movement is forbidden? The governor promised to report that it is impossible for me to be treated in Pskov – so let's wait, perhaps the tsar will decide something in my favour.'[73] Here the aneurysm saga comes at last to an end: Pushkin is driven to confess that an operation is not necessary after all. Nor, of course, did he follow the strict regime laid down by the Pskov physician. A footnote followed on 27 November, when Pushkin's mother, no doubt at the instance of those still credulous friends who feared for his health, wrote to the tsar again: 'Deign, Your Majesty, to allow him to travel to another locality, where he can find a more experienced surgeon, and pardon a mother, trembling for the life of her son, for daring to appeal a second time to your mercy. Only on the breast of the father of his subjects may a mother weep out her grief, only from her sovereign, from his unbounded goodness does she dare to expect deliverance from her fears and anxieties.'[74] Alexander, however, made no reply to this pathetic petition: unsurprisingly, since a week earlier, on 19 November 1825, he had died – probably of typhoid – in the governor's house in Taganrog.

The news of Alexander's death reached St Petersburg on 27 November. On that day the Guards and officers of state institutions took an oath of allegiance to the next in succession to the throne, Alexander's brother, Grand Duke Constantine, the viceroy of Poland. Moscow followed suit three days later. Pushkin was overjoyed at the news: he had conceived a deep hatred for the tsar. 'My dear! I'm a prophet, really a prophet!' he exulted. 'I will order André Chénier to be printed in Church Slavonic letters in the name of the Father the Son etc.'[75] – he was referring to the lines 'And the hour will come ... it is already near/You will fall, tyrant!' from his elegy 'André Chénier': the French poet, on the eve of his execution, is addressing Robespierre, who fell two days later.[76] He was rather more diplomatic when addressing Katenin. 'Perhaps the present change will bring me together with my friends,' he wrote. 'As a faithful subject, I must of course mourn the death of the emperor; but, as a poet, I rejoice at the accession to the throne of Constantine I. There is much romanticism in him; his stormy youth, campaigns with Suvorov, enmity to the German Barclay remind one of Henry V.'[77]

Constantine had, however, married a Polish countess, who was Catholic: this would have been an obstacle to his accession. He was settled in Warsaw and had no desire to come to St Petersburg: in 1823 he had formally renounced the throne in favour of his younger brother, Nicholas. This renunciation had been embodied in a secret manifesto, copies of which had been deposited in the Uspensky Cathedral in Moscow, and with the Senate and State Council in St Petersburg. Though Nicholas knew of this, he was reluctant to make use of it, and indeed had taken the oath of allegiance to Constantine. For the next three weeks correspondence passed between Warsaw and St Petersburg in an attempt to end this interregnum; during this time Russia, as the London *Times* put it, was 'in the strange predicament of having two self-denying Emperors, and no active ruler'.[78] Finally Nicholas, realizing that Constantine was determined in his renunciation and learning, too, of the existence of conspiracies directed against the government, resolved to have himself proclaimed emperor and the oath of allegiance administered on 14 December.

The conspiracies were those of the Decembrists. The northern society had made little progress since the early 1820s. Pestel, the leader of the southern society, who believed that a successful revolution could begin only in St Petersburg, sent a succession of delegates to the north, and in March 1824 travelled there himself, but had little success in influencing the society's policies. It became more active from the beginning of 1825, when Ryleev became its *de facto* leader. Stronger on idealism than practicality, however, he was not wholly suited to the planning of an uprising. He did recruit two volunteer regicides: Aleksandr Yakubovich and Petr Kakhovsky. Yakubovich had fought in the Caucasus with great dash and bravery, sustaining a dangerous head wound in 1823, which, though operated on in St Petersburg, never healed completely. Somewhat deranged from the constant pain, and cherishing a personal grudge against Alexander, he was persuaded to postpone his intention of assassinating the emperor until a suitable time occurred. Kakhovsky was an idealist, who had come to the conclusion that the assassination of the tsar was essential for the success of a revolution, and was willing to sacrifice himself for the cause.

Matters were very different in the south. In 1824 the society had formed an alliance with the Polish Secret Patriotic Society, whose aim was an independent Poland; and in 1825 had amalgamated itself with the Society of United Slavs, thus greatly increasing its membership. It had, however, been betrayed to the authorities by two of its members, whose testimony, at first disbelieved, was confirmed by Witt, whose agents had infiltrated the organization. As a result Pestel was arrested on 13 December, and a search made for Sergey Muravev-Apostol.

Pestel

In St Petersburg, after much indecision, the northern society resolved to act before Nicholas was proclaimed emperor; Sergey Trubetskoy was chosen as 'dictator' and given full powers to conduct the uprising. The troops taking part and refusing to take the oath of allegiance were to gather on Senate Square on the morning of 14 December. However, many of the regiments whose support had been relied upon now refused to move: only a battalion of the Moscow Regiment and some detachments of the Grenadier and Marine Guards occupied the square – by midday the uprising consisted of some 3,000 troops, while the government had 9,000 to call upon. Ryleev had planned to wear peasant dress, but with a knapsack on his back and a rifle in his hand: thus symbolizing the union between soldier and peasant. He was persuaded, however, that the symbolism would not be universally comprehended, and joined the conspirators on the square in more normal garb. Yakubovich, after marching there with his hat on the end of his sword, huzzaing for Constantine, complained of a blinding headache and left. Trubetskoy never went to the square at all, but, after enquiring where he might take the oath to Nicholas, took refuge in the Austrian embassy.

Nicholas, who did not wish to begin his reign with bloodshed, made several attempts to end the affair peaceably. But when Miloradovich, the governor-general of St Petersburg, approached the troops in order to persuade them to return to their barracks, he was shot dead by Kakhovsky. Kakhovsky also killed Colonel Stürler, the commander of the Grenadiers, and wounded an officer of Nicholas's suite. The Metropolitan Serafim, wearing his episcopal robes, was now sent, but was told by the insurgents to go back and pray for their souls. Finally the Grand Duke Michael appeared, but was advised by the rebels to return, as he was only putting his own life in danger: indeed, he narrowly escaped being shot by Pushkin's old friend Küchelbecker – who would have been better advised, in view of future events, to have taken the post of professor of Russian and Slavonic languages at Edinburgh which he had been offered that spring. Finally three cannon were brought up, and, after a warning had been given, the square was cleared with canister shot. Towards evening three days later Arseny, the cook at Trigorskoe, who had been sent to St Petersburg for provisions, returned unexpectedly and announced 'that there was a revolt in Petersburg, that he had been frightened out of his life, that patrols and guards were everywhere, and that he had had difficulty in passing the city barrier'.[79] Pushkin paled when he heard the news, and remained uncharacteristically silent during the rest of the evening.

The southern society had been handicapped by the arrest of Pestel. But rumours of events in St Petersburg induced them to revolt to aid their colleagues. On 29 December the police found Sergey Muravev-Apostol and detained him. He was, however, freed by members of the United Slavs and, recruiting several companies of the Chernigov Regiment – some 800 men – marched them for six days around the countryside. He considered – and rejected – the idea of attacking Kiev, and on 3 January 1826 was defeated near Pologi by a force of cavalry and artillery. Muravev-Apostol was severely wounded; his teenage brother, Ippolit, shot himself. The rebels were arrested and put in irons; their leaders were later sent to St Petersburg to be tried with the participants in the northern revolt.

Nicholas himself saw nearly all those who were arrested; after a brief examination, he would dispatch them to the Peter-Paul fortress with a note indicating the treatment they were to receive. By 17 December he had set up a special commission of inquiry to investigate the conspiracy. In the course of the next months it examined about 600 persons, presenting a final report to the emperor at the end of May. Psychologically broken down by constant interrogation, and physically undermined by the conditions of imprisonment, many of the conspirators recanted and pleaded for mercy – as did Trubetskoy, who, on his knees and kissing the emperor's hands, begged that his life might be spared. Some told all that they knew, implicating their friends and relatives, while others gave fantastically exaggerated versions of events. Only Yakushkin – Pushkin's St Petersburg friend, whom he had met again in Kamenka in 1820 – and Pushchin remained firm.

Pushkin himself, fearing that the commission should extend its investigation to him, burnt the autobiographical notes on which he had been working while at Mikhailovskoe. Yet, curiously, while apprehensive of arrest, at the same time he was optimistic that the new emperor might put an end to his exile. 'Cannot Zhukovsky find out whether I can hope for the Sovereign's leniency?' he enquired in January.[80] He would hardly have been optimistic about the future, had he known that witness after witness, testifying before the commission, mentioned the influence of his work. Mikhail Bestuzhev-Ryumin, one of the leaders of the southern society, when interrogated on 27 January, said: 'I heard everywhere Pushkin's verse being read with enthusiasm. This more and more strengthened my liberal opinions.' The deposition of Staff-Captain Paskevich, given on 9 April, read: 'I acquired my first liberal thoughts last year, 1825, partly from books I came across and partly from meeting people with such opinions, but mainly from reading Mr Pushkin's freedom poems.' And Baron Steinheil, a retired lieutenant-colonel, a veteran of 1812, and one of the leaders of the northern society, wrote to Nicholas: 'Who among the youth with anything of an education has not read and been carried away by the works of Pushkin, which breathe freedom!'[81]

In the context of the time, and given the treatment of some of those only peripherally connected with the revolt,* it could be thought that Pushkin was being treated leniently by not being called to account by the commission of inquiry. Besides the evidence concerning the effect of his verse, in February a report on him was submitted by a secret police agent, Stepan Viskovatov, a minor poet and prolific dramatist, obviously a man of vivid imagination. He wrote: 'Some persons worthy of trust, recently arrived from the Pskov province, attest that the titular councillor Aleksandr Pushkin,† known for his freethinking, harmful and depraved poems, [. . .] is now with violent and depraved behaviour openly preaching atheism and disobedience to the authorities and on receiving the news, most grievous for all Russia, of the death of His Majesty the Emperor Alexander Pavlovich he, Pushkin, vomited forth

---

* Daniel Keizer, a priest in Vasilkov, whose only connection with the revolt was to read, with great reluctance, Muravev-Apostol's 'Orthodox Catechism' to the rebellious troops, was unfrocked, court-martialled, disenfranchised, disinherited and sentenced to hard labour; he was amnestied in 1858 and given an annual pension of 57 roubles.

† A mistake: Pushkin still held the tenth rank, that of collegial secretary, in the civil service. He was not promoted to titular councillor (the ninth rank) until 1832.

the following hellish words: "Finally the Tyrant has gone, and the rest of his family will not be alive for long!!"' And, during the trial of the Decembrists another, less imaginative agent reported: 'People are extremely astonished that the celebrated Pushkin, whose manner of thought was always well-known, has not been implicated in the affair of the conspirators.'[82]

In March Pushkin wrote to Zhukovsky again, an official letter, 'in a three-cornered hat and shoes', which Zhukovsky was to pass on. After an exceedingly brief account of the reason for his exile – the aneurysm put in another short appearance – he went on: 'The accession to the throne of His Majesty Nicholas Pavlovich gives me joyful hope. Perhaps His Majesty will see fit to change my lot. Whatever my mode of thought, political and religious, may have been, I keep it to myself and do not intend to contradict insanely the accepted order and necessity.'[83] The letter was certainly not ingratiating. Delvig thought he would have done better to wait until the coronation, while Katenin urged him to write directly to Nicholas. Zhukovsky replied in April. 'What can I say to you about your wish to leave country life? In the present circumstances there is no possibility of doing anything for you. What is most sensible for you is to remain quietly in the country, not to call attention to yourself, and to write, *but write for fame*. Let this unhappy time pass. I cannot understand why you wrote me your last letter. If it is *only to me*, then it is strange. If it is to be *shown*, it is senseless. You are not involved in anything – that is true. But in the papers of each of those who took part are your verses. This is a bad way of making friends with the government. You know how I love your Muse [. . .] But I hate everything you have written subversive of order and morality. Our youths (that is all the maturing generation), with their bad education, which gives them no support in life, got to know your dangerous thoughts, clad in the charm of poetry: you have done many incurable harm. That should force you to tremble. Talent is nothing. The most important is moral greatness. Forgive these lines from the catechism. I love you and your Muse, and want Russia to love you. I end as I began: do not ask to come to Petersburg. It is not yet time. Write Godunov and the like: they will open the doors of freedom.'[84]

Zhukovsky's last sentence refers to Pushkin's play, the historical drama *Boris Godunov*, born of a sudden humour, his admiration for

Shakespeare and for Karamzin's *History of the Russian State*. The view that the work might 'open the doors of freedom' rests, one supposes, on the assumptions that a dramatist is a solider citizen than a poet; and that a play based on an episode taken from the history of Russia's rulers can hardly be politically subversive – indeed, in this case it is rather conservative, since it deals with the tragedy brought about by the interruption of the legitimate succession. Zhukovsky may even have reflected that, since the period known as 'The Time of Troubles' (1598–1613), ushered in by Boris's seizure of the throne, ended with the accession of the first Romanov, the play could be seen as an implicit tribute to that dynasty. Pushkin, as always far more sagacious and sensible in literary matters than in life, was less sanguine. On completing the first draft of the play the previous November he had written to Vyazemsky: 'I congratulate you, my joy, with a romantic tragedy, in it the principal personage is Boris – Gudunov! My tragedy is finished; I read it aloud, alone, and clapped my hands and cried, well done Pushkin, well done you son of a bitch! – My holy fool is a highly comic fellow; Marina will get your prick up – since she's Polish and very beautiful (in the manner of K. Orlova, did I tell you?). The others are also very nice; apart from Captain Margaret, who swears obscenely all the time; the censor will not let him through. Zhukovsky says that the tsar will pardon me because of the tragedy – hardly, my dear fellow. Although it is written in a good spirit, I couldn't hide my ears completely beneath a fool's cap. They stick out!'[85]

Despite Zhukovsky's gloomy prognostications, Pushkin's optimism was incurable: he wrote to the emperor himself. In April Nicholas had issued a rescript to the Minister of the Interior in which, after expressing his anger that Alexander's order against secret societies should have been disobeyed, he ordered that all civil servants, active and retired, and all other noblemen, should take an oath that they would in future belong to no secret societies of any kind. Summoned to Pskov by Aderkas, Pushkin took this oath on 11 May; a fortnight later he was in Pskov again, resurrecting the aneurysm in a letter to Vyazemsky: 'A young doctor who was in liquor told me that without an operation I would not last until 30.'[86] On 19 July Aderkas forwarded to Paulucci in Riga Pushkin's signed statement of the oath; a medical certificate from the Pskov medical board to the effect that Pushkin had 'on his lower extremities, and especially on the right calf, a general dilatation of the veins (Varicositas totius cruri dextri); from which Mr Collegial Secretary Pushkin is generally hindered in walking' – it was hardly a life-threatening aneurysm; and a letter from Pushkin to the tsar:

> Most gracious sovereign!
>
> In 1824, having had the misfortune to merit the wrath of the late emperor by a thoughtless judgement concerning atheism, expressed in a letter, I was expelled from the civil service and exiled to the country where I am still under the surveillance of the provincial authorities.
>
> Now, hoping for the magnanimity of Your Imperial Majesty, with genuine repentance and with the firm intention not to contradict with my opinions the accepted order (to which I am ready to bind myself by my signature and word of honour), I have decided to have recourse to Your Imperial Majesty with my most humble petition.
>
> My health, shattered in my early youth, and a type of aneurysm have long demanded constant treatment, in support of which I present medical testimony; I most humbly presume to request permission to travel for this purpose either to Moscow, or to Petersburg, or to foreign lands.

Sending the documents on to Nesselrode, Paulucci remarked that, according to police reports, Pushkin had behaved himself well, and added that in passing his letter on for consideration by the tsar, he had been influenced by his repentance and undertaking not to contradict the accepted order; nevertheless, he recommended that permission to travel abroad should not be given.[87]

In the middle of June Nikolay Yazykov, Aleksey Vulf's fellow-student at Dorpat, finally – he had been expected since the autumn of 1824 – arrived at Trigorskoe. He remained for a month, living in the family bath-house, where Pushkin would also occasionally stay the night. After dinner Zizi would make hot punch, while Sashenka played the piano, and they would dance on the lawn. 'I spent the summer in the Pskov province with Mrs Osipova, the mother of a student here, my good friend, and spent it very pleasurably,' Yazykov wrote to his mother. 'An abundance of fruits of the earth, a healthful climate, the favourable disposition towards me of our hostess, a clever and kind woman, the attractiveness, moral civility and good education of her daughters, life, or rather a completely carefree and untrammelled existence, then the country charm of nature, and finally artful sweets and sweetmeats, such as: preserves, wines and so on, – all this together makes up something very good, honoured, splendid, delightful, in a word – living!'[88]

Yazykov was nearly four years younger than Pushkin, and had been publishing verse since 1819. Pushkin had a high opinion of him: 'I share your hopes regarding Yazykov,' he had written to Delvig in 1823;[89] in *Eugene Onegin* he refers to him as 'inspired Yazykov' (IV, xxxi); and at the end of the year wrote to Vyazemsky, after reading Yazykov's latest poems: 'You would be astonished at how he has developed, and what will become of him. If one has to envy anyone, then it's he I should envy. Amen, amen, I say unto you. He'll outdo all of us old folk.'[90] When Yazykov left for Dorpat Pushkin accompanied him as far as Pskov. He stayed here for a couple of days, playing cards and visiting the local brothel, where he caught a dose of gonorrhoea from one of the girls: before coming to Mikhailovskoe the following year, forewarned, he jotted down in his notebook a prescription against the malady.

In St Petersburg meanwhile the trial of the Decembrists had been proceeding. On 1 June Nicholas had appointed a Special Supreme Court, which handed down its sentences on 9 July. Of the hundred and twenty-one leaders five – Pestel, Sergey Muravev-Apostol, Ryleev, Kakhovsky and Bestuzhev-Ryumin – were to be quartered, thirty-one decapitated, and the remaining eighty-five exiled to Siberia. These sentences – intended more to express outrage than for execution – were modified by Nicholas: the five leaders were to be hanged; thirty-one exiled for life; and the remainder for various terms. The defendants were assembled in the Peter-Paul fortress to hear their fate: this came as a surprise to them, since they did not know that they had been put on trial, still less that they had been convicted. None had appeared before the court; they had merely been visited in their cells and asked whether they agreed with the testimony they had given to the commission.

Capital punishment had been abolished in Russia by the Empress Elizabeth in 1754. Though reintroduced by Catherine II for certain crimes, it was rarely applied: the general belief, therefore, was that Nicholas would commute the sentences. He did not. The executions took place on 13 July at three in the morning on the Crownwork bastion of the fortress. Ryleev, Kakhovsky and Muravev-Apostol fell down when the stools beneath their feet were pulled away, and had to be hanged again. 'Poor Russia, she cannot even hang decently,' remarked Muravev-Apostol.[91] The bodies were later removed, stripped naked and cast into a common, unmarked grave on Goloday Island. On the same day the first party of convicts left for Siberia.

Pushkin learnt of the executions – he had known all five of the victims – on 24 July. He made a cryptic note recording this. Later, on another manuscript, he drew in ink, in the upper margin of the page, a sketch of a gibbet with five bodies dangling from it, repeating the sketch, with more details, further down. Above the upper sketch is written the beginning of a line of verse, 'And I could have, like a clown on . . .'[92] 'A clown on a string' is how Pushkin would have completed the phrase: he is thinking of a jumping-jack.* Of his closest friends among the Decembrists, Pushchin had been sentenced to hard labour for life, later reduced to twenty years; Küchelbecker – who had fled to Warsaw, where he was arrested – to twenty years, later reduced to fifteen. Nikolay Turgenev was luckier. He was in England at the time of the revolt, and sensibly remained there, being sentenced, *in absentia*, to exile for life. He stoutly resisted all the government's attempts to have him returned to Russia. On 31 July Vyazemsky sent Pushkin his poem 'The Sea', which praises the beauty and purity of the element. Pushkin, hearing rumours – which later proved to be unfounded – that the British government had deported Turgenev by ship to St Petersburg, replied on 14 August with a brilliant epigram:

> So, is it the sea, that ancient cutthroat,
> Which kindles your genius?
> You praise with your golden lyre
> Dread Neptune's trident.
>> Praise him not. In our vile age
> Grey Neptune is the Earth's ally.
> On all elements man
> Is a tyrant, traitor or a prisoner.[93]

---

* R.L. Stevenson uses the same image in *Weir of Hermiston* of the hanging of Duncan Jopp, 'the palm, dangling of the remains like a broken jumping-jack.'

Turgenev, who remained abroad until the general amnesty of 1856, continually and vehemently denied having any connections with the Decembrists.*

The success of *The Fountain of Bakhchisaray* had made Pushkin eager to publish further works. But he could not exploit Vyazemsky's generosity again, and it would have been grotesque to enter into a financial arrangement with a man who was not only one of his closest friends, but also an aristocrat and a wealthy landowner. In addition, living in Mikhailovskoe, he needed a collaborator in St Petersburg, rather than in Moscow. He turned therefore to the poet and critic Petr Pletnev, whom he had known before his exile to the south. Pletnev, a gentle, even timid creature, was born in 1792, the son of a poor village priest. Orphaned at an early age, he was educated at a seminary in Tver, and at the Pedagogical Institute in St Petersburg; in the 1820s he taught literature to young ladies and cadets at various schools in the capital, and from 1826, on Zhukovsky's recommendation, was a tutor at the Imperial Palace. Though only a mediocre poet himself, he had real feeling for literature, and was an unselfish admirer of the talent of others. Given his social position and financial circumstances, there was, too, no potential for embarrassment in the commercial side of the relationship. 'I was everything for him [Pushkin],' he wrote in 1838, 'a relative, and a friend, and a publisher, and a cashier.'[94] Pushkin also relied on his brother Lev, now a junior civil servant in the Department of Foreign Creeds, to assist Pletnev. Lev, however, was far from reliable. Feckless, irresponsible, inefficient, untrustworthy in money matters and irredeemably lazy, he was more interested in gaining popularity by reciting his brother's verse in the St Petersburg salons than in getting it published. By contrast Pletnev accounted in his letters for every copeck received and disbursed.

At the end of October 1824 Pushkin wrote asking him to publish the first chapter of *Eugene Onegin*. This had been written between May and October 1823, in Kishinev and Odessa, and Pushkin had originally

---

* Pushkin knew at least eleven of the other convicted Decembrists: Nikolay Basargin, Aleksandr Bestuzhev, Vasily Davydov, Mikhail Lunin, Petr Mukhanov, Nikita Muravev, Prince Sergey Trubetskoy, Prince Sergey Volkonsky, Aleksandr Yakubovich, Ivan Yakushkin, and Aleksey Yushnevsky.

Pletnev

thought it to be unpublishable. 'As for my doings,' he had told Vyazemsky, 'I am now writing not a novel, but a novel in verse – there's a devilish difference. In the manner of Don Juan – there's no point in even thinking of publication; I am writing without circumspection. Our censorship is so arbitrary that it is impossible to make one's sphere of activity commensurate with it.' After the success of *The Fountain of Bakhchisaray*, however, all his work became sought after – 'Slenin [a St Petersburg book-seller] offers me as much as I want for Onegin' – and the thought of not profiting from the poem was galling.[95] In May 1824 there was a change at the Ministry of Education, which was responsible for censorship: Prince Golitsyn resigned as minister, and was replaced by Admiral Shishkov. Although Shishkov, as leader of the Archaist group of writers, and founder of the *Symposium of Amateurs of the Russian Word*, had been an ideological enemy, he was at least interested in literature. 'I hope for good for literature generally, and send him [Shishkov] a kiss, not as a Judas-Arzamasite, but as a Robber-Romantic.* I will try to push through to the gates of censorship with the first chapter or canto of Onegin.'[96]

It passed the censor without difficulty, and Pletnev saw to its printing. 'Your Onegin will be a pocket mirror of St Petersburg youth,' he commented, rather charmingly.[97] The book was published on 18 February 1825, and was greeted by universally favourable reviews. 'In this poem the charm of joyful, witty and noble satire is combined with authentic and sharp descriptions of society life'; 'The narration is superb: everywhere are spontaneity, gaiety, feeling and picturesque verse'; in the *Moscow Telegraph* Polevoy used the poem to strike a blow for Romanticism. 'The dictators of our Parnassus and stick-in-the-mud critics of our literature' had 'just assured their clients, that by the power of this or that paragraph of a poetics, published in such-and-such year, Pushkin's poem is not a poem and that this can be proved by all the rules of polemics, when their hoarse whispers are drowned by the sound

* I.e., as author of the unfinished narrative poem *The Robber Brothers*.

of applause and the general rapture forces them again to seek proofs on the tattered pages of the afore-mentioned poetics'.[98]

If for Polevoy *Onegin*'s infraction of the classical rules was a proof of its Romantic credentials, for others it was, compared with Pushkin's earlier works, a regression, a move away from Romanticism. Yazykov, whose brother Aleksandr had sent him a copy from St Petersburg immediately after publication, wrote back: 'I very, very much disliked *Onegin* [. . .] the sophisms of the past century are very obvious in *Onegin* when the poet himself speaks.'[99] '*Onegin*, to judge by the first canto, is inferior to *The Fountain of Bakhchisaray* and *The Prisoner of the Caucasus*,' Ryleev told Pushkin in February, repeating this stunningly perverse judgement a few weeks later. Bestuzhev told Pushkin that he had 'caught Petersburg society, but not penetrated it', and advised him to read Byron: 'without knowing our Petersburg, he painted its likeness – in as much as deep understanding of people is concerned. Even his feigned idle talk conceals philosophical remarks, without mentioning his satire. I know no one better, more portrait-like at sketching characters, catching in them new flashes of passions and lusts. And how malicious, how fresh his satire is!' Pushkin replied, keeping his temper admirably, on 24 March: 'Your letter is very clever, but all the same you are mistaken, all the same you are viewing *Onegin* from the wrong point of view, all the same it is my best work. You compare the first chapter with *Don Juan*. – No one respects *Don Juan* more than I do (the first five cantos, I haven't read the others), but it has nothing in common with *Onegin*. You speak of the Englishman Byron's satire and compare it with mine, and demand the same thing from me! No, dear fellow, you want too much. Where is my *satire*? there is not so much as a mention of it in *Eugene Onegin*. The embankment would have cracked, if I had touched satire.'[100]

The book was not the commercial success Pushkin and Pletnev had hoped for. Although 700 copies went in February, only 245 were sold in March, and only 161 over the next four months. In the end – by January 1827 – Pushkin made just over six thousand roubles, but saw rather less: fifteen hundred or so vanished on Lev's amusements. Though the high price – five roubles for a booklet of some eighty pages – might have been partly responsible for the relative failure, Pletnev's contractual arrangements were also to blame. He gave the St Petersburg book-seller

Slenin the exclusive right to sell the book, letting him have copies at a discount of ten per cent. But this meant not only that Pletnev could not supply any other book-seller, but also that Slenin could not do so either, for the discount was too small to allow both a profit. Pletnev had also miscalculated by printing 2,400 copies – double the usual print-run – and in August still had 1,250 on his hands, which the book-sellers refused to take, even at a large discount. 'They think that this book has ceased to sell and forget how it will be snapped up, when you print another canto or two. We will then laugh at the fools,' he wrote, outlining a fantastical plan by which Pushkin was to make fifty thousand roubles by 1 January 1826, if not earlier.[101] He was somewhat over-optimistic on both counts: although another canto of *Onegin* came out in October 1826, in January 1827 750 copies of the first remained unsold; by 1 January 1826 Pushkin had made not a copeck more from his work.

Immediately after the appearance of *Onegin* Pushkin turned to the publication of his collected lyrics. This manuscript, lost at cards to Vsevolozhsky, had been bought back, enlarged by the addition of new poems, and sent off in March 1825 to Lev, who did nothing with it for months. 'You took 2,000 roubles from Pletnev to buy my manuscripts, paid out 500, have you paid up the remaining 500? and is there anything left of the remaining 1,000? [. . .] Have the 600 roubles been paid to Vyazemsky?' Pushkin wrote angrily.* 'I sent you my manuscripts in March – they have not been arranged, not been to the censor. You read them to your friends until they can recite them by heart to the Moscow public. I thank you.'[102] After this Pushkin ceased using Lev as his agent.

Pletnev now took over the manuscript and, enlisting Zhukovsky's help in arranging the poems, sent them off to the censor in September, simultaneously forwarding to Pushkin the proposed table of contents: the book would not be sent to the printers until he had agreed this. It was now Pushkin's turn to procrastinate. When the poems returned from the censor, Pletnev, having heard nothing for some time, wrote

---

* Pushkin had told Lev to take 2,000 roubles from Pletnev – out of the profit on *Onegin* – to buy back the manuscript from Vsevolozhsky. The latter, very honourably, refused to take more than the 500 for which the poems had originally been pledged; the other 500 Pushkin had lost in cash, and insisted that this debt should be paid at the same time. The 600 roubles he owed Vyazemsky were those he had borrowed from Princess Vera before leaving Odessa. Pletnev eventually paid this debt from the profit on the collected poems. Lev seems to have spent about 4,100 roubles on himself.

urging expedition. But circumstances had suddenly changed: Pushkin had just learnt of Alexander I's death, and optimism had returned: the new tsar, Constantine, might be more lenient towards him, and release had a higher priority than publication. 'Dear fellow,' he replied early in December, 'it's not a matter of poems – listen *in both ears*:* if I haven't weaned my friends too successfully from petitioning, they'll probably remember about me ... If one's going to take, then take – why dirty one's conscience else† – for God's sake don't ask the tsar for permission for me to live in Opochka or Riga; what the devil is there there? *but ask either for entry to the capitals, or about foreign lands.*'[103]

But nothing came of the hopes. Pletnev went ahead, and the collection, *Poems of Aleksandr Pushkin*, came out at the end of December: a book of 204 pages, containing just over a hundred poems. 'Here's what the preface should consist of,' Pushkin had written to Lev. 'Many of these poems are rubbish and unworthy of the attention of the Russian public – but since they have often been published by God knows whom, under the devil knows what titles, with corrections by the compositor and mistakes by the publisher – here they are, pray sir, have a taste, sir, although this, sir, is shit, sir (to be said more mildly). 2) We (that is to say the publishers) had to throw out of the complete edition many pieces, which could have seemed obscure, having been written in circumstances unknown to or of little interest to the most worthy (Russian) public or interesting only to certain private personages, or too immature, since Mr Pushkin was pleased to publish his verses in 1814 (i.e. at 14), or as you will. 3) Please, without the slightest praise of me. This is indecent and in *The Fountain of Bakhchisaray* I forgot to remind Vyazemsky of it. 4) All this should be expressed romantically, without buffoonery. On the contrary. For all this I rely on Pletnev.'[104] The 'obscure' pieces are the political and obscene poems. In the event Pletnev contributed a short note entitled 'From the publisher', which made some of the above points, but 'more mildly'.

Pushkin received five copies of the volume in January. He gave one

---

* A quotation from Küchelbecker's play *Shakespearean Spirits*; in a letter to the author – written possibly on the same day as that to Pletnev – Pushkin had pointed out that some 'expressions were not exactly Russian – e.g. listen in both ears' (XIII, 248).
† A paraphrase of two lines from Krylov's fable, 'The Little Raven': 'If one's going to take, then take,/Why dirty one's claws!'

to Annette on her name-day, 3 February, inscribing it 'from her most humble admirer A. Pushkin'.[105] There were very few reviews, possibly because most of the poems had already appeared before in periodicals, though in the *Ladies' Journal* Shalikov 'hastened to inform our lady readers' of the book's appearance. 'We already see,' he continued, 'a joyful smile on fair lips at the name of the poet whose works can by no account of their beauty be made more attractive than by the name of the poet alone! Meanwhile the taste of the lady readers will determine the worth of each piece more truly than a *prose* judgement on poetical works.'[106] He confined his criticism to quoting Pletnev's introductory note in its entirety. In the *Moscow Gazette* the following March Vladimir Izmailov, surveying works published in 1826, wrote rhapsodically, 'with each new hymn garnering new laurels, flying from success to success and in his youthful years ready, it seems, to conquer alone the heights of Parnassus, Pushkin has awakened new astonishment with his *Poems*'.[107]

Warned by the fate of *Onegin*, Pushkin had told Pletnev to print only 1,200 copies, but had insisted on the extraordinarily high price of ten roubles. Pletnev too had learnt by experience: he had not given one bookseller exclusive rights and had, in addition, used a sliding scale of discounts, ranging from nothing to thirty per cent. But these precautions proved almost unnecessary, for the book was an immense success. By 21 January half the edition had been sold, and on 27 February Pletnev told Pushkin triumphantly that he had not a single copy left. Pushkin's profit, less the discount, the printing and binding costs and Pletnev's commission – he seems to have taken nothing for publishing *Onegin*, but a thousand roubles for the *Poems* – came to about 7,000 roubles: ten times the annual salary he had been paid by the Foreign Ministry.

Pletnev was keen to exploit the situation. 'I beg you, print one or at once two chapters of *Onegin*,' he implored. 'There's no getting rid of them: they're all thirsting for it. It will be not so good when this fever cools. There's just one thing I'm afraid of: they frighten me by saying that copies of the second chapter are in town. You can no longer plead that you're waiting for *Pole Star*. It won't come out. Send something along, dear fellow!'[108] Pletnev's fears were justified; in February Delvig told Pushkin that the second canto of *Onegin* was being 'read and copied everywhere'.[109] There is something slightly cold-blooded about Pletnev's mention of *Pole Star*. Pushkin had earlier sold an extract from the third chapter of *Onegin* to *Little Star*, an almanac planned as the successor to *Pole Star*, and therefore could not publish the chapter separately until the almanac had come out. This it certainly would not do: both its editors, Ryleev and Bestuzhev, were sitting in damp cells in the Peter-Paul fortress. In February 1827 Pushkin paid back the money he had received – 600 roubles – to Ryleev's widow.

In February Pletnev wrote again, begging Pushkin to send something – if *Boris Godunov* needed copying, then let him hire some quill-driver from Opochka and put him to work for three days. Haste was necessary, he explained, because sales fell off after Easter. 'Do me a favour, send Onegin,' he concluded. 'Surely you won't refuse my request.'[110] 'There will be no Boris for you until you call me to Petersburg,' Pushkin replied on 3 March. 'And you're a fine one! writing to me: copy and hire Opochka scribes and publish Onegin. I'm not in the mood for Onegin. The devil take Onegin! It's myself I want to publish or release into society.'[111] It is not immediately apparent why Pushkin should have blown hot and cold on the publication of his works, now urging haste, now engineering delay with one insubstantial pretext after another. At this moment he had three more chapters of *Onegin* ready for publication: why did he not send at least one to Pletnev? In autumn 1825 he had a good excuse for losing enthusiasm in the publication of the *Poems*: dispirited after the failure of the aneurysm plot, he no longer needed the money to flee abroad. But the reason he gave Pletnev for his procrastination then is that which he gives him for his procrastination now: release from Mikhailovskoe is far more important than the publication of his work. Naturally he was desperate to leave Mikhailovskoe; but this desire does not seem incompatible with, say, sending Pletnev the second canto of *Onegin*. Indeed, were his exile to be ended, life in one of the capitals – or, *a fortiori*, abroad – would be far more of a drain on his purse than rusticating in Mikhailovskoe. It would therefore seem that the campaign for release and publication should be complementary, rather than, as Pushkin suggests, opposed. But it is possible to see a reason for his seemingly illogical point of view. The failure of the aneurysm plot is the hinge in his change of attitude: before it he is eager for publication, after it lukewarm. As we have seen, he attributed the failure to the mistaken and misdirected efforts of his friends. They were incapable of acting correctly if they were told what to do; perhaps they

would if they were not told. By withholding his works from publication
he was exerting gentle suasion on them, blackmailing them – and the
public – into campaigning for his release, if they wanted to read his
verse. The line in his letter to Pletnev: 'There will be no Boris for you
until you call me to Petersburg' is a joke, but a serious one.

Irksome though confinement at Mikhailovskoe was, it proved
extremely productive. In just over two years Pushkin completed *The
Gypsies*, composed a mass of lyrics, wrote a historical drama in blank
verse, and added nearly a hundred stanzas to *Eugene Onegin*. It was a
period of experimentation, in which he was discovering himself anew
as a poet, and the quality of the work is understandably uneven. In one
sense Pushkin had discovered himself already. In the opening chapter
of *Eugene Onegin* – which, as he had noted in the preface, bore a
resemblance to Byron's *Beppo* – he had brought to perfection that
strain which had first emerged in *Ruslan and Lyudmila*: witty, brilliantly
sparkling verse which could accommodate digressions on any subject
that might come into the wayward author's head, while still maintaining
a narrative drive. In December 1825 he dashed off the short narrative
poem *Count Nulin*, a wonderfully comic piece of work, much more
akin to *Beppo* in fact than is *Onegin*.[112] 'Reading Lucretia,* a rather weak
poem by Shakespeare, I thought: what if Lucretia had had the thought
of slapping Tarquin's face?' he wrote in 1830. 'Would that perhaps have
cooled his enterprise and would he have been obliged to retreat in
shame? – Lucretia would not have committed suicide, Publicola would
not have flown into a rage, Brutus would not have expelled the kings,
and the world and history would not have been the same. So, for the
republic, the consuls, the dictators, Catos, Caesar, we have to thank an
episode of seduction, similar to one which recently occurred in my
neighbourhood, in the Novorzhev *uezd*.† I conceived the idea of parody-

---

* *The Rape of Lucrece.*
† A reference to an incident of January 1829. Pushkin and Aleksey Vulf, who were staying
at Malinniki, paid a visit to the latter's uncle, Pavel Ivanovich, at Pavlovskoe: 'Pushkin and
I' – writes Vulf in his diary – 'each taking a bottle of champagne on ice, and holding it
on our lap, drove to Pavel Ivanovich's. At dinner we plied with Muscat de Lunel, which
Pushkin had brought from Moscow, Fritzinka (a Hamburg beauty, whom my uncle brought
back from the wars and afterwards married), a German woman from Riga, half-governess,
half-servant, the betrothed of his manager, and a young, quite amusing girl, the daughter
of the former priest at Bernovo, who was also under Fritzinka's protection. I mention her
because quite a funny thing happened ... with her. We danced and played the fool a

ing history and Shakespeare, could not resist the double temptation and in two mornings finished writing this tale.'[113]

Returning from Paris, Count Nulin, after overturning his travelling-carriage on a provincial road, is offered hospitality by the local land-owner's wife, Natalya Pavlovna. They dine; Natalya asks him about the theatre, the latest books, the latest fashions: '"Where are waists being worn?" – "Very low,/Almost to the . . . well, to about here."' Attracted to his hostess, Nulin that night makes an attempt on her virtue, and is repulsed with a slap. She is not, however, as virtuous as she seems; the person most amused by her account of the incident is not her husband, but their twenty-three-year-old neighbour.

'His Majesty the Emperor deigned to read *Count Nulin* with great pleasure,' Pushkin was told when the poem was published in 1827.[114] Elsewhere, however, it aroused indignation. '*Count Nulin* caused me much trouble,' Pushkin wrote. 'It was found (if I may be excused for the word) obscene, – in the journals of course, in society it was received favourably – and not one of the journalists would defend it. A young man dares to enter a young woman's bedroom at night and receives a slap in the face from her! What a horror! how dare one write such repulsive filth? The author asks what St Petersburg ladies would have done in Natalya Pavlovna's place: what impertinence!' There was far more eroticism in classical and European literature than in *Count Nulin*, 'which is, I may say in parenthesis, written in the most sober and decorous style [. . .] An immoral work is one whose aim or effect is to undermine those principles on which social happiness or human dignity is based. – Poems, whose aim is to excite the imagination with lascivious descriptions, degrade poetry, turn it from divine nectar into an inflammatory mixture, and the Muse into a repulsive Canidia.* But a joke, inspired by heartfelt gaiety and the momentary play of imagination, can

---

lot with them, and the young village maiden very unambiguously showed that she favoured me. This attracted my attention to her, since previously, when she was surrounded by beauties of the first order, I had not noticed her at all. I imagined that with her I could very easily console myself for my lack of success with others, so a few days later, driving to Pavlovskoe again, I made a visit to her in the manner of Count Nulin, with the sole difference that I did not receive a slap in the face' (*Lyubovny byt*, I, 302–3). Pushkin is sparing Vulf's blushes by transferring the incident from Tver to Pskov province.
* Neapolitan courtesan beloved by Horace, who, when deserted by her, reviled her as a sorceress.

seem immoral only to those who possess a childish or obscure concept of morality, confusing it with moralizing, and who view literature solely as a propaedeutic activity.'[115]

The government's most successful agent in southern Russia – 'a more cunning spy than all the well-known heroes of that type in [Fenimore] Cooper's novels', according to the Polish poet Mickiewicz[116] – was Aleksandr Boshnyak, the son of a small landowner in the Kostroma province. He had been a civil servant in the Moscow archives of the Foreign Ministry, but had retired and, inheriting in 1820 a small estate near Elisavetgrad, moved there, intending to devote himself to botany and literature – in 1830 he published, anonymously, a four-volume novel, a moral satire entitled *Yakup Skupolov or the Reformed Husband*. The move brought him within the ambit of Colonel-General Jan Witt, Karolina Sobańska's lover. By the beginning of 1825 Witt had become convinced that some revolutionary society existed, and that its centre was at Kamenka. Boshnyak was ordered to infiltrate its membership. 'Adopting the guise of the vilest Jacobinism', he was soon deep in the conspirators' confidence, and was reporting to Witt on their activities.[117] After the failure of the revolt he was summoned to St Petersburg, and, in recognition of his services, was restored to the civil service, promoted one rank, and presented with 3,000 roubles by the emperor. Later that year he was awarded the order of St Anne and given an annual salary of 5,000 roubles.

Major-General Pavel Pushchin, whom Pushkin had known in Kishinev – he had commanded a brigade in Orlov's division and had founded the Masonic lodge Ovid – had now retired and was living on his estate not far from Mikhailovskoe. He had been a member of the southern society of Decembrists, but, by order of the emperor, had been exempted from investigation – which suggests that he had changed his views and been of service to the regime before the abortive revolt. Pushkin and he had never been close; indeed, he may have actively disliked the younger man. He had often been the butt of Pushkin's jokes, and had been mercilessly ridiculed after a comic fiasco at the Kishinev lodge involving a Bulgarian archimandrite. He now informed the Third Department that rumours were circulating in the district that Pushkin was responsible for 'the composition and the singing of subversive songs', encouraging the peasants to revolt. The authorities, remembering the earlier reports, ordered Boshnyak to carry out a 'secret and circumstantial investigation of the conduct of the well-known versifier Pushkin, suspected of actions akin to the incitement of peasants to freedom'. He left St Petersburg on 19 July 1826, accompanied by a military courier, Vasily Blinkov, who had been furnished with an open warrant for Pushkin's arrest, should the suspicions prove correct. The two arrived in Porkhov the following morning. Leaving Blinkov at Bezhanitsa, a few post-stations along the road, Boshnyak drove on to Novorzhev, which he reached on the twenty-first. Putting up at the inn under the guise of a travelling botanist, he learnt from the landlord that Pushkin had been seen at the fair at Svyatye Gory wearing a 'shirt belted with a pink ribbon, a wide-brimmed straw hat and carrying on iron cane'; that he was 'modest and cautious and never spoke about the government'; and that 'he had never at all been known to compose or sing subversive songs, still less incite the peasants'. He spoke to another guest at the inn, the district assessor Chikhachev, and, ingratiating himself with the district judge Tolstoy, dined with him and two others, the liquor inspector Troyanovsky and Colonel Lvov, the provincial marshal of nobility. All agreed that Pushkin lived modestly, and that stories of his inciting the peasants had no justification.[118]

The following day Boshnyak called on the Pushchins. Here he represented himself as a travelling botanist bearing greetings from Count Langeron (whom he had never met), the former governor-general of New Russia and Pushchin's brother-in-law. He was received hospitably, and spent the day with the family. They told him that they had sometimes seen Pushkin in a Russian shirt and wide-brimmed straw hat; that he was friendly with the peasants, and often took them by the hand when greeting them; that, when he had ridden somewhere, he often ordered his man to let the horse go, saying that every animal deserved its freedom; that he was so indiscreet that no secret society would wish to have him as a member; finally, that 'he was a person who wished to distinguish himself by eccentricity, but that he was completely incapable of any course of action based on calculation'. Boshnyak completed his investigations at the Svyatogorsky monastery, where he arrived on the evening of the twenty-third and put up in a peasant's hut. Its owner, Ivan Stolyarev, informed him that Pushkin usually came to church on

Sundays, and that he was a very generous gentleman, who gave even his own peasants money for vodka when they performed a service for him. The next morning he interviewed Prior Iona. Pushkin visited no one, apart from Iona and Osipova, he was told; and in answer to Boshnyak's question 'Does he incite the peasants?' Iona replied, 'He meddles in nothing and is as shy as a young girl.' Returning to Bezhanitsa, Boshnyak dispatched the courier Blinkov back to St Petersburg, and, following more slowly in his wake, submitted his report – which declared the rumours wholly unjustified – on 1 August.[119]

Nicholas I read it, making pencil notes in the margin, on the morning of 7 August; at the same time he considered Pushkin's letter and Paulucci's recommendation, which had been received by Nesselrode on 30 July. The emperor was then preoccupied with preparations for his coronation, which took place in Moscow on 22 August. But immediately afterwards he came to a decision. On 28 August General Potapov took down, at Diebitsch's dictation, the tsar's resolution: 'His Majesty orders Pushkin to be summoned here. A military courier is to be assigned to accompany him. Pushkin may travel at liberty in his own carriage, under the surveillance of the courier, not as one under arrest. Pushkin should come straight to me. Write to the Pskov civil governor of this.'[120] Aderkas received Diebitsch's letter on 3 September and immediately dispatched an officer to Mikhailovskoe with a copy. He arrived in the early hours of the fourth. Sending the gardener, Arkhip, to Trigorskoe for his pistols, Pushkin packed hurriedly and left with the officer at five in the morning.

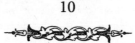

IN SEARCH OF A WIFE

1826–29

Blessed is he, who was youthful in his youth,
Blessed who at the proper time matured,
Who gradually the chill of life
With the years was able to withstand;
Who was not addicted to strange dreams,
Who did not shun the fashionable crowd,
Who at twenty was a fop or rake,
And at thirty advantageously married.

Eugene Onegin, VIII, x

FROM MIKHAILOVSKOE Pushkin travelled to Pskov and, after a short interview with Aderkas, set out for Moscow. The journey, accomplished at a hectic pace, took just over three days instead of the more usual five. On Wednesday 8 September 1826 – a cold, dull and rainy day – Pushkin entered his native city, much changed by the fire of 1812, for the first time since he had left for the Lycée fifteen years earlier. His arrival was reported to the Chief of the General Staff, Field-Marshal Diebitsch, who ordered him to be brought to the Kremlin at 4 p.m. During the coronation ceremonies the tsar had been living in Countess Orlova-Chesmenskaya's palace in Neskuchnoe Park (now the presidium of the Academy of Sciences), but had recently moved to the Chudov palace in the Kremlin. At half past three Nicholas sat down to dinner with his family, and, after the meal, between half past four and five, Pushkin was presented to him.

Nicholas was then thirty, three years older than Pushkin. 'With his height of more than six feet, his head always held high, a slightly aquiline nose, a firm and well-formed mouth under a light moustache, a square chin, an imposing, domineering, set face, noble rather than tender, monumental rather than human, he had something of Apollo and of Jupiter [. . .] Nicholas was unquestionably the most handsome man in Europe,' wrote an American diplomat.[1] There could hardly have been a greater contrast between this figure and the small, swarthy, ape-like poet, still stained with the dirt of travel and marked, as a contemporary noticed, by the years of exile. There was no longer anything youthful about him: he was 'thin, with deep lines on his face, and with extensive side-whiskers which covered the lower part of his cheeks and chin'.[2] 'The emperor received me in the kindest possible way,' Pushkin told Praskovya Osipova.[3] No one else was present during the interview, which lasted for over an hour.

'I first saw Pushkin,' Nicholas related years later, 'after my coronation, when he was brought from his exile to me in Moscow, quite ill and covered with sores (from a *notorious* disease*). "What would you have done if you had been in Petersburg on 14 December," I asked him among other things. "I would have been in the ranks of the rebels," he answered. When I then asked him whether his way of thought had changed and would he give me his word to think and act in a different fashion, if I were to release him, he hesitated for a very long time and only after a lengthy silence stretched out his hand to me with the promise – to become different.'[4] At the end of the meeting the two left the emperor's study together. 'Gentlemen,' said Nicholas, presenting the poet to the courtiers in the antechamber, 'here is my Pushkin!'[5] From the Kremlin Pushkin drove to his uncle Vasily's apartment on Staraya Basmannaya Street.

That evening Nicholas attended a ball given by Marshal Marmont, the French representative at the coronation. This took place in the Kurakin mansion, also on Staraya Basmannaya Street. Noticing Dmitry Bludov, the former Arzamasite, now deputy Minister of Education, the tsar beckoned to him and said: 'Do you know that today I have had a long conversation with the cleverest man in Russia?' When Bludov,

---

* Nicholas is obviously referring to syphilis, which Pushkin possibly had, as the disease often accompanied gonorrhoea. However, Nicholas would have to have had a preternaturally keen eye to diagnose the disease merely from Pushkin's outward appearance at this time; most probably rumour ascribed the disease to him as the natural result of his reputed excesses.

astonished, enquired who this might be, the tsar named Pushkin.[6] The news that the poet was in Moscow spread quickly round the ballroom. Seventeen-year-old Princess Aleksandra Trubetskaya, who was standing up with Dmitry Venevitinov, remarked that she had a better opinion of the emperor, now that he had brought Pushkin back.[7] Sobolevsky also was among the guests. Leaving the ball, he hurried down the street, found Pushkin at supper with his uncle and was immediately dispatched to call on Tolstoy the American and challenge him to a duel: Pushkin had not forgotten the allegation that he had been whipped in the secret chancellery, put about by Tolstoy in 1820. Fortunately the count was not in Moscow; later Sobolevsky succeeded in smoothing the matter over.

Nicholas was never to be so eulogistic about Pushkin again; and it is surprising that he should have chosen to praise him as an intellectual rather than a poet. It seems likely that in their conversation Pushkin put forward the views which he was to express a few months later in the poem 'Stanzas', where the past – the age of Peter the Great – and the future – that of Nicholas – are brought together.[8] Had Pushkin implied during the conversation that Nicholas might accomplish for nineteenth-century Russia that which Peter had accomplished for that of the seventeenth century, the tsar might well have considered him the cleverest man in Russia.*

Another topic touched on was that of censorship, which Pushkin confessed to finding irksome. His hope, when in Odessa, that the appointment of Admiral Shishkov as Minister of Education would improve matters had proved unjustified. He was thus overjoyed when Nicholas declared that henceforth he would be the poet's censor. 'The tsar has freed me from the censorship,' he wrote to Yazykov. 'He himself is my censor. The advantage is, of course, immense.'[9] In fact, the advantage was, as Pushkin soon discovered, illusory. Though Nicholas was perhaps less likely than the official censor to demand minor changes, he was more likely to forbid completely the publication of a work, and there was no appeal against his decision. He could not be approached

---

* The poem aroused some indignation when it was published in 1828; Pushkin was attacked for sycophancy towards the emperor, particularly by his former friend, Katenin. He defended himself with two poems, 'To My Friends', which begins 'No, I am no flatterer ...', and 'A Reply to Katenin' ('Druzyam', 'Otvet Kateninu', III, 89, 135).

directly, but only through an intermediary. One of his first acts as emperor had been to turn His Imperial Majesty's Own Chancery into an important centre of power. In July 1826 the Third Department of this Chancery was established, and made responsible for state security – it was to become infamous as the tsarist secret police organ.* Its first head was Count Aleksandr Benckendorff, who was also head of the gendarmerie – a uniformed and well-armed police force. It was through Benckendorff that Pushkin had to submit his works to Nicholas, and from him heard the emperor's decisions.

It would not be wholly absurd to see Nicholas's decision to pardon Pushkin as a gesture of pure generosity; he was by no means incapable of such an action. Countess Dolly Ficquelmont, the wife of the Austrian ambassador and later a close friend of Pushkin, who saw much of the emperor at close quarters, wrote of him: 'He has an eminently chivalrous character and all his initial impulses will always be noble and beautiful, he understands and is sensible of everything which is sublime, which is really good.'[10] At the same time Nicholas, who had been received solemnly but coolly in Moscow, and whose coronation had not been greeted with great enthusiasm, might have calculated that he could increase his popularity by releasing the poet. And, finally, the decision might have been influenced by a calculation Benckendorff expressed in a letter to the tsar. '[Pushkin] is undoubtedly pretty much of a good-for-nothing, but if one is successful in directing his pen and his words, then this will be advantageous.'[11]

Release from the six-year exile produced an incredible feeling of freedom. It was as if he had been resurrected: new life coursed within him, accompanied by a surge of creative power. Occasionally he would affix to a poem when it was published a date which was not that of the poem's composition: it symbolically linked, rather, the poem with a fatidic date in his life, or with some significant event. In 1828 he published in the *Moscow Herald* 'The Prophet', a poem based on Isaiah vi, 2–9, one of the most extraordinary he ever wrote. To it he added the date '8 September 1826', the day of his meeting with Nicholas.

---

* The First Department of the Chancery was Nicholas's personal secretariat; the Second was occupied with the codification of laws.

Parched with spiritual thirst,
I tarried in a dark desert, –
And a six-winged seraph
At a crossing of the ways appeared to me.
With fingers light as sleep
He touched the pupils of my eyes.
My prophetic pupils opened,
Like those of a startled eagle.
He touched my ears, –
And filled them with noise and sound:
And I heard the heaven's shudder,
And the angels' supernal flight,
And the moving of sea-serpents under the waters,
And the growth of the valley vine.
And he bent to my lips,
And plucked out my tongue, sinful
And idle-talking and cunning,
And the fork of a wise serpent
Between my palsied lips
Set with his bloody right hand.
And he clove my breast with a sword,
And took out my trembling heart
And a coal, burning with fire,
Placed within my open breast.
Like a corpse in the desert I lay,
And the voice of God called unto me:
'Arise, prophet, and see, and hear,
Be filled with my will,
And, going about the seas and lands,
Burn with my word the hearts of men.'[12]

The coronation celebrations had not yet come to an end. 'Moscow, still full of visitors, who had travelled hither for the coronation from the whole of Russia, from Petersburg and from Europe, hummed terribly in the quiet of the dark night which embraced its forty versts of ramparts,' wrote Sergey Aksakov, who arrived in the city a few hours after

Pushkin. 'Thousands of carriages, dashing along the streets, the cries and shouts of its as yet unsleeping four hundred thousand inhabitants produced such a chorus of sounds as cannot be expressed in words.'[13] 'Moscow is noisy and full of celebrations,' Pushkin told Praskovya Osipova. 'Today, 15 September, we are having the grand public celebration,* there will be three versts of tables set up on the Maidens' Field; pasties have been provided by the foot, as if they were timber; since they were cooked some weeks ago, they will be difficult to swallow and digest, but the respectable public will have fountains of wine to wet them with; that is today's news. Tomorrow Countess Orlova is giving a ball; an immense riding-school has been turned into a hall; she has borrowed 40,000 roubles worth of bronze† and a thousand people have been invited.'[14] Pushkin visited the festival on the Maidens' Field, and in the evening dined at the nearby villa of Prince Ivan Trubetskoy and his wife Ekaterina – they were old family friends, and Ivan was a distant relative; as a child Pushkin had gone to dancing lessons in their house on the Petrovka. He thanked their daughter, Aleksandra, for her kind remark at Marshal Marmont's ball, causing her to go as red as a poppy.

He had moved into the Hotel Europe on Tverskaya Street, where he occupied 'a pretty filthy two-roomed apartment'. A visitor found him, 'as one usually found him in the mornings in Moscow and Petersburg, in a silvery Tartar dressing-gown, with a bare chest, without the slightest of comforts around him'.[15] After the isolation of Mikhailovskoe he threw himself with abandon into social life: he was – according to a secret report sent to Benckendorff – an assiduous visitor of Princess Zinaida Volkonskaya's salon in her mansion on Tverskaya Street: she was the sister-in-law of the Decembrist Sergey Volkonsky, who had married Mariya Raevskaya and been sentenced to fifteen years in Siberia. On 26 October Mariya Rimskaya-Korsakova gave a party in Pushkin's honour; the family belonged to the old nobility of Moscow and, following tradition, kept open house. He often availed himself of her hospitality, being not insensible to the attraction of her pretty twenty-three-year-old daughter, Aleksandra.

One of the few things he had brought with him from Mikhailovskoe

---

* This in fact took place on 16–17 September; Pushkin was confused as to the date.
† then cost I think the ball was reputedly illuminated by 7,990 candles

was the manuscript of *Boris Godunov*. He gave readings from it every-where he went: at Sobolevsky's apartment on Sobachya Place on 10 and 12 September; at the Venevitinovs' house on the Myasnitskaya on 25 September and 12 October; and at Baratynsky's apartment on 29 October. 'It is impossible to convey the effect that this reading had on all of us [. . .] The awaited high priest of the sublime art turned out to be a little man of medium, almost low stature, fidgety, with long, slightly curling hair, unpretentious, with lively, darting eyes, a quiet, pleasing voice, in a black frock-coat and tightly buttoned black waistcoat, with a carelessly knotted cravat. Instead of the high-flown language of the gods, we heard simple, clear, ordinary, but at the same time – poetic and captivating speech! We listened to the first scenes quietly and calmly, or rather with a certain perplexity. But the further it advanced, the stronger our emotions grew [. . .] Some were thrown into a sweat, others shivered. Our hair stood on end. It was impossible to restrain oneself. Now someone would suddenly leap to his feet, now another would suddenly cry out. Now there was silence, now a burst of exclamations [. . .] The reading finished. For a long time we looked at one another, and then rushed towards Pushkin. Embraces began, noise arose, laughter resounded, tears and congratulations flowed. *Evan, evoë*, fill your cups! Champagne appeared, and Pushkin became animated, seeing what an effect he had had on the young people gathered there.'[16]

He saw much of his friends from the St Petersburg days: Baratynsky, Vyazemsky – when he was in town and not on his estate at Ostafevo – Sobolevsky, and his chief companion at cards and drink, Nashchokin. And he made, too, a host of new friends and acquaintances. Among these was Vasily Zubkov, whom Pushkin took to because he was a close friend of his Lycée intimate, Pushchin. Like Pushchin, Zubkov was a magistrate, and like him had been involved in the Decembrist revolt. But he had not been on the square in St Petersburg, and, though arrested, was released after two months in the Peter-Paul fortress. On his return to Moscow, he resigned his post – owning some 1,500 serfs, he could afford to do so. Pushkin was a frequent visitor to the family lodgings on Malaya Nikitskaya Street, where Zubkov's sister-in-law, Sofya Push-kina (a distant relation: her father and Pushkin's were fourth cousins), 'tall and shapely, with a splendid Grecian profile and jet-black eyes, a very sweet and clever girl', also lived.[17] Pushkin fell headlong in love with her after seeing her in the theatre. He was not deterred in his courtship by the presence of a recognized suitor for Sofya's hand, Valerian Panin, nor by a powerful attraction to Sofya's sister Anna, Zubkov's wife, a 'small subtle blonde, [. . .] extremely pretty, very lively and gay'.[18] 'S.P. is my good angel,' he wrote to Princess Vyazemskaya, adding in a note 'This is of course not Sergey Pushkin'; 'but *the other* is my demon; this troubles me in my poetic and amorous meditations in the most inopportune way possible'.[19]

In these weeks he met, too, the chief members of Moscow's literary life. Among these was the thirty-year-old Nikolay Polevoy – 'I want to see the sights of Moscow, and begin with Polevoy,' he said on their first meeting.[20] Pale and desiccated, with a hint of fanaticism in his expression, Polevoy was unusual among the literary figures of the day, in that his social background was that of the merchant class, rather than the aristocracy – his father was a vodka distiller in Kursk. In 1825 he had founded the *Moscow Telegraph*, a vehicle for its editor's ardent allegiance to Romanticism. Vyazemsky had supported the journal from its inception, and had persuaded Pushkin, while at Mikhailovskoe, to contribute to it. Though Pushkin had at first been enthusiastic about the journal's qualities, calling it, in a letter to Polevoy, 'the best of all our journals',[21] he had later cooled towards it – partly because of its harsh criticism of Karamzin's *History of the Russian State*, and partly because of what he considered to be a general lack of taste: this coolness was reflected in his relationship with Polevoy.

More congenial was the company of some younger writers, united, in the main, by an interest in German metaphysics and particularly in the philosophy of Schelling. Some worked in the Moscow archives of the Ministry of Foreign Affairs, and hence were nicknamed 'archival youths'. Most had been members of the Society of Wisdom Lovers, a philosophical and literary association which had disbanded itself after the Decembrist revolt. When Pushkin arrived, the group was on the point of setting up a new literary journal, the *Moscow Herald*. Its editor was to be the historian Mikhail Pogodin. Born in 1800, Pogodin was the son of Count Saltykov's steward, a serf who had been freed, together with his family, in 1806. He had studied history at Moscow University, where he later taught, and was tutor to the Trubetskoy children. Shambling, boor-like and ugly, he got on well with Pushkin, who came to have a high opinion of him. A few years later he wrote to Pletnev: 'Pogodin is a very, very sensible and honourable young man, a real German in his pure love for science, in his industry, and in his moderation.'[22] Another leading member of the circle was the poet and critic Venevitinov, a talented and erudite twenty-one year-old. Others – all in their early twenties – were Stepan Shevyrev, Aleksey Khomyakov, and the Kireevsky brothers, Ivan and Petr.

Dissatisfied with contemporary literary journals, Pushkin had long cherished the idea of founding one of his own, through which he could give expression to his views on literature and his tastes. Though the projected *Moscow Herald* would not be his journal, he felt some kinship with the writers involved, and believed that he would be able to influence editorial policy. Indeed, at one point he thought his relationship would be even closer: 'Perhaps not Pogodin, but I – will be the proprietor of a new journal,' he wrote to Vyazemsky.[23] But this was not to be. On 24 October he attended a dinner in Khomyakov's rooms to celebrate its foundation. 'It is impossible to describe how joyful that dinner was,' wrote Pogodin. 'How much noise and laughter there was, how many jokes were told, how many plans and suggestions were made!'[24] Over the next few years Pushkin regularly contributed poems to the journal, and urged friends such as Yazykov to do likewise, although he soon realized that he did not share the ideology of the group. 'You reproach me for the Moscow Herald – and for the German metaphysics,' he wrote to Delvig the following March. 'God knows, how I hate and despise it, but what can be done? ardent, obstinate lads have gathered together.'[25] He had been promised the astonishing amount of 10,000 roubles a year for his contributions. In the event, however, the circulation was less than had been hoped for, and he barely made more than 1,000 roubles in the first year, and insignificant amounts thereafter.

Among those present at the dinner was the Polish poet Adam Mickiewicz. Involved in a society dedicated to the restoration of Polish independence, he had been arrested in Lithuania in 1823 and sent first to St Petersburg, where he had met Ryleev and Bestuzhev, and then to Odessa, where he had a short affair with Karolina Sobańska. After spending the summer of 1825 in the Crimea with Sobańska and Witt at the latter's villa, in November he had been transferred to Moscow. Here he had become intimate with Sobolevsky, who invited him to meet Pushkin

Mickiewicz

soon after the latter's arrival in Moscow. 'Pestilence and famine on you, dear Demon,' Mickiewicz replied. 'May the Lord God afflict you with leanness. I will come, but for the sake of this will have to miss dinner with a fascinating woman.'[26] He was five months older than Pushkin, and outwardly very different. 'His appearance was truly beautiful. Black, expressive eyes, luxuriant black hair, a brightly ruddy complexion,' noted Polevoy's younger brother, Ksenofont.[27] He had, too, a talent which Pushkin lacked: that of improvisation. In Vilna, given a subject, he had improvised on it in Polish, in verse; in Russia he did so in French prose, but the effect was almost as striking. 'Do you remember that extraordinary transformation of his face, that brilliance of his eyes, that penetrating voice, which even induced fear, as though a spirit were speaking through him?' a friend wrote.[28] His performances caused a sensation in Russian society, as he brought his audiences to a state approaching delirium. At a party given in Pushkin's honour in Zinaida Volkonskaya's salon his improvisation so impressed Pushkin that 'he leapt from his seat and, clutching his head in his hands, almost running round the room, exclaimed: "What genius! What sacred fire! What am I compared to him?" and, throwing himself on Adam's neck, embraced him and began to kiss him like a brother.'[29] Mickiewicz was slightly more reserved. 'Pushkin is 28,' he wrote, 'he is very witty and impetuous in conversation; he has a profound knowledge of contemporary literature, and a pure and elevated understanding of poetry. He has just written an historical tragedy *Boris Godunov*. I have read extracts from it; its general idea is powerfully conceived, the extracts are splendid.'[30] Though the two became close, they were never intimate; their characters were too different, and Mickiewicz found in particular – as did many others – Pushkin's careless, often scatological or lubricious bawdiness in conversation distasteful. Some eighteen months later Aksakov, in a letter to Shevyrev, wrote: 'About a week ago I had lunch with Pushkin, Mickiewicz and others at Mikhail Petrovich [Pogodin]'s. The former [Pushkin] conducted himself terribly vilely and disgustingly; the latter [Mickiewicz] – beautifully. You can judge for yourself what the conversations were like; *the latter* was twice obliged to say: "Gentlemen, decent people even when they are alone by them-selves do not speak of such things!" '[31]

On 6 October the court and its attendant officials left Moscow for St Petersburg. On the eve of departure Benckendorff wrote to Pushkin expressing his surprise that he had not been to call on him since the interview with the tsar. He continued: 'His Majesty remains completely confident that you will employ your excellent abilities to transmit to posterity the glory of our Fatherland, while at the same time transmit-ting your name to immortality. In this conviction His Majesty is pleased to wish that you should occupy yourself with the subject of the edu-cation of youth. You may do this at your leisure, you are given complete and absolute freedom as to how and when you might present your thoughts and considerations; and you should represent this subject in its widest aspects, since experience has shown the fatal consequences of a false system of education.' He concluded by reiterating Nicholas's promise to be the sole censor of Pushkin's works, which should be forwarded, either to him, or to the emperor himself'.[32] Benckendorff's 'fatal consequences' are the ideas of Decembrism; one result of the revolt had been to turn attention to the educational system, in the suspicion that it might have been the source of the seditious views held by the conspirators. In April Nicholas had ordered Count Stroganov to inspect Moscow University and look into the loyalty of its members. Witt had submitted a report on education to the tsar, and the curator of Kharkov University, A.A. Perovsky, had composed a memorandum claiming that reform of the school system was essential. At a lower level the journalist Bulgarin had written a paper for the Third Department entitled 'Some-thing on the Tsarskoe Selo Lycée and its spirit'. 'What in society is termed the Lycée spirit,' he wrote, 'is when a young man does not respect his elders, treats his superiors familiarly, his equals haughtily, and his inferiors contemptuously, with the exception of those occasions when it is necessary, as a fanfaronade, to show oneself a lover of equality.'[33]

At the beginning of November Pushkin set out for Mikhailovskoe. He had to settle the affairs his precipitate departure had left undone, and arrange for his books and papers to be brought to Moscow. His route took him through Torzhok, a town noted for its leather goods made of morocco embroidered with gold and silver. He bought a number of belts and dispatched them with a letter to Princess Vyazemskaya. 'Are you mad,' she wrote in reply, 'how can you use your beautiful verse so frivolously and spend your money so gratuitously? The number of belts make me indignant, only their quality can secure your pardon, and they are all charming.'[34] The journey took eight days, since two wheels of his carriage broke on the road – an accident he attributed to Sobolevsky's furious driving in Moscow. In the end he had to abandon the carriage and finish the journey by post-chaise.

'I've somehow taken a liking to the countryside,' he wrote to Vyazemsky on his arrival. 'There is a certain poetic pleasure in returning to an abandoned prison as a free man. You know that I don't go in for sentimentality, but meeting my house-servants, boors and my nurse – more pleasantly tickles the heart, I swear, than fame, the pleasures of egoism, of the social whirl etc. My nurse is killingly funny. Imagine, at the age of 70 she has learned a new prayer "for the softening of the heart of the Sovereign and the taming of the ferocity of his spirit", a prayer probably composed in the reign of Tsar Ivan [the Terrible].'[35]

He had left Moscow 'with death in his heart',[36] for it meant abandoning the field to Panin, his rival for Sofya Pushkina's affection. Having promised her that he would unfailingly be back by 1 December, he began the return journey on 25 or 26 November, in good time to fulfil his promise. But the carriage overturned; his chest and ribs were injured, making breathing difficult, and he was confined to his bed in a Pskov inn for a fortnight. His only solace was gambling: it was now that he lost the fourth chapter of *Onegin* at shtoss. On 1 December, the day he should have been in Moscow, he wrote to Zubkov. 'Since I am here in an inn in Pskov instead of being at Sofya's feet, let us converse, that is, reason.' He was twenty-seven, he continued; it was time for him to marry and settle down. He did have doubts. 'It is not my happiness which worries me, how could I not be the happiest of men beside her – I tremble only in thinking of the fate which, perhaps, awaits her – I tremble that I may not be able to make her as happy as I wish. My life up to now so wandering, so stormy; my character so changeable, jealous, susceptible, violent and weak, all at the same time – that is what gives me moments of painful reflection. Ought I to unite to so sad a lot, to so unhappy a character, the fate of so sweet and beautiful a being?' But he had resolved to offer for her, and, contrasting Panin's sluggishness – he had been courting Sofya for two years – with his own impetuosity – 'I see her the first time in a box at the theatre, the second at a ball, and on the third send my matchmakers!' – begged Zubkov to plead his cause and arrange his marriage.[37] Though apparently serious in the proposal, he cannot have been sanguine about its success; indeed, Sofya married Panin later that month. But the letter does mark an important watershed: for the first time, when speaking of love, he has also spoken of marriage. It is clear that he is more than eager to acquire a wife. Life was passing him by; his former bachelor way of life was no longer appropriate for his years and social position. Yet at the same time he found it impossible to abandon the pleasures of a carefree, single existence. Though Sofya was the first of a number of young women he pursued with a view, not to seduction, but to marriage, these courtships did not exclude liaisons of a less formal nature, nor prevent him from enjoying the pleasures of a bachelor.

While in Pskov he received a second letter from Benckendorff. After referring to his previous remarks on submitting works to the tsar, Benckendorff continued: 'Though I had from you no notification of the receipt of this communication, I was however obliged to conclude that it had reached you; since you informed several persons of its contents. Information has now reached me that you were pleased to read at a number of gatherings your recently composed tragedy. This prompts me humbly to ask you to inform me whether this information is correct or not. I am however convinced that you are too right-minded not to be fully sensible of the extent of His Majesty's magnanimous leniency towards you, and not to strive to make yourself worthy of it.'[38] Benckendorff's elaborately formal courtesy concealed an ominous message. He was making it clear to Pushkin, firstly that he was under constant surveillance by agents of the Third Department; secondly that he had misunderstood the tsar's censorship conditions: all works had to be submitted, before being either read or published; thirdly, and most sinisterly, that his release from exile was not absolute, but that he was on parole.

Pushkin was seriously alarmed. He dashed off a note '*to be forwarded as quickly as possible to Mr Pogodin*', asking him to withdraw the poems he had sent him for the first issue of the *Moscow Herald*,[39] and composed

Benckendorff

a grovellingly contrite – 'no one feels more keenly than I the graciousness and magnanimity of the emperor, as well as the indulgent favour of your excellency' – reply to Benckendorff, enclosing a copy of *Boris Godunov*, 'in the form in which it was read, that you might deign to see the spirit in which it was composed; up to now I have not made bold to present it to the emperor's eyes, intending first to expunge some indelicate expressions'.[40] At the same time he hurriedly put the finishing touches to a short article on education, written in response to Benckendorff's first letter, had a fair copy made in Pskov, and sent this also to St Petersburg. He had no illusions as to why he had been asked to write on education. 'I was in difficulty, when Nicholas asked my opinion of this matter,' he later told Aleksey Vulf. 'I could easily have written what they wanted, but I could not pass up such a chance to do good. However, I said among other things that private education should be suppressed. Despite this I got a dressing-down.'[41] 'His majesty was pleased to remark,' Benckendorff wrote, 'that the rule you adopt, according to which teaching and genius are the exclusive basis of perfection, is a dangerous rule for public order, one which brought you yourself to the edge of an abyss, and precipitated into it so many young people. Morality, diligent service and zeal must be preferred to inexperienced, immoral and useless teaching. On these principles a well-directed education should be based.'[42] The attempt to direct Pushkin's 'pen and words' had failed, and was not made again.

Nicholas's opinion of *Boris* was more favourable, but no less disappointing. Benckendorff had commissioned a report on it from Bulgarin, who concluded that its 'literary merit was considerably lower than expected', that it was not an 'imitation of Shakespeare, Goethe, Schiller', but that it seemed like 'a collection of pages torn out of a novel by Scott'.[43] Nicholas profited from these observations. 'His majesty deigned to read it with great pleasure,' Benckendorff told Pushkin, 'and on a note I presented on this subject wrote with his own hand the following: "I consider that Mr Pushkin's aim would be fulfilled, were he to turn his Comedy, *after purging it as necessary*, into an historical tale or novel in the manner of Walter Scott."'[44] 'I agree that it is closer to an historical

novel than a tragedy, as the Sovereign Emperor deigned to observe,'
Pushkin replied. 'I regret that I am incapable of refashioning that which
I have once written.'[45] The emperor's judgement had, however, made
it impossible to publish the play for the time being.

Pushkin arrived back in Moscow on the evening of 19 December, and
put up with Sobolevsky on Sobachya Place. Here the two, living in
some squalor, led a dissipated existence. 'Our police precinct is in fine
condition – precinct commander Sobolevsky curses and brawls as before,
spies, dragoons, whores and drunkards hang about our place from
morning to evening,' Pushkin told Kaverin.[46] Pogodin visited them
together with a general of gendarmes, Aleksandr Volkov. 'It is vexing,' he
noted in his diary, 'that that swine Sobolevsky should behave swinishly in
front of everyone, and vexing that Pushkin should arrive in a debauched
state when Volkov was there.'[47]

Towards the end of the month Mariya Volkonskaya passed through
Moscow on her way to Siberia to join her husband Sergey in exile. She
was travelling against the wishes of her family – particularly of her
father, General Raevsky – and had, by the tsar's order, been obliged to
leave her eleven-month-old son, little Nikolino, with her parents. She
stayed with her sister-in-law, who, knowing Mariya's love for music,
arranged a small concert for her on the evening of 26 December. Pushkin
was among the guests, as was Aleksey Venevitinov, one of the 'archival
youths' and brother of the poet Dmitry. 'Yesterday I passed an unforgettable evening,' he noted. 'I saw the unhappy Princess Mariya Volkonskaya [. . .] Throughout the whole evening she listened to the singing,
and when one piece was finished asked for another. She did not go into
the drawing-room before midnight, because there were a lot of people
at Princess Zinaida's, but sat behind the door in the other room.' But
when Zinaida herself was singing an aria from Paer's opera Agnese, in
which 'an unfortunate daughter begs an even more unfortunate father
for forgiveness', the 'involuntary similarity between Agnese's and her
father's misfortune and the actual situation of her unseen relative cut
short Princess Zinaida's voice and strength, while her poor sister-in-law
was obliged to leave the room, as she had burst into a flood of tears
and did not want this to be noticed'.[48] A few days later Mariya left for
Siberia, where she remained until the general amnesty granted to the

Decembrists by Alexander II in 1856. Her son died at the age of two; Pushkin, at General Raevsky's request, composed an epitaph for the gravestone. Mariya wrote to her brother Nikolay: 'In my position one can never be sure that one gives pleasure by reminding others of oneself. Nevertheless speak of me to Aleksandr Sergeevich, I charge you to convey to him my gratitude for Nikolino's epitaph. The words he found to console maternal love are the expression of his talent and his capability for sympathy.'[49]

The meeting with Mariya turned Pushkin's thoughts to the exiled Decembrists; he began a poem addressed to them, intending to give it to her, but had not finished it when she left. A week or so later, however, Aleksandra Muraveva passed through Moscow; like Mariya, she was on her way to join her Decembrist husband in Siberia. Pushkin called upon her, found her writing letters, and entrusted the poem – 'Deep in Siberian mines . . .' to her, together with one addressed to Pushchin – 'My first friend, friend without price . . .' – originally written under the impression of their meeting in Mikhailovskoe, and recently revised.[50] On bidding her goodbye, overcome with emotion, he squeezed her hand with such force that for some time thereafter she could not resume her correspondence.

Pushkin's attitude towards Decembrism and the Decembrists after his release from Mikhailovskoe is an ambivalent one. He had not been a member of the conspiracy; had he been in St Petersburg, comradeship and loyalty might have brought him to Senate Square on 14 December – though there is perhaps more than a touch of braggadocio about the manner in which he asserted this to Nicholas. But the Decembrists had consciously excluded him from their ranks. 'I understand very well why those gentlemen did not wish to take me into their society,' he told Aleksandra Muraveva, 'I was not worthy of that honour.'[51] Nor does his work, other than in most general fashion, reveal any deep involvement with Decembrist ideas. Though he had conceived a violent antipathy to Alexander, who had been responsible for his exile to the south and his isolation in Mikhailovskoe, his attitude to Nicholas, who had brought an end to his exile, was very different. 'The author Pushkin is in Moscow and speaks everywhere of Your Majesty with gratitude and with the deepest devotion,' Benckendorff told Nicholas towards the end of 1826.[52] 'The poet Pushkin conducts himself in the political respect excellently well,' Benckendorff's assistant, von Fock, reported in October 1827. 'He unfeignedly loves the emperor, and even says that he owes his life to him, since in exile and eternally in constraints he had become so tired of life he wanted to die. Recently a literary dinner took place, at which champagne and Hungarian wine inclined all to candour. There was much joking and laughter, and astonishingly, at this time, whereas in the past there would have been jokes about the government, today the emperor was praised openly and sincerely. Pushkin said: "I should be called Nikolaev, or Nikolaevich, since without him I would not have lived. He gave me life, and, what is much more, liberty: Vivat!"' Another Third Department report described a dinner given to sixty-two guests by Nikolay Grech on 6 December 1827, St Nicholas's Day, to celebrate his name-day – also, of course, the emperor's name-day – and the completion of his Russian grammar. 'Towards the end of dinner one of those present sang verses (composed by A.E. Izmailov who is known to us) in honour of Grech and his *Grammar*.' The third stanza ended with the lines 'So let us pray,/First, here's a health to the Tsar!' 'It is difficult to imagine the joy these verses produced,' continued von Fock. 'But most pleasant of all was that the lines to the Tsar were repeated loudly by all the guests again and again in rapture. Immediately after dinner many began to copy the verses down. Pushkin was in rapture and, walking up and down, constantly sang: "So let us pray,/First, here's a health to the Tsar!" He copied the lines down and took them to Madame Karamzina (the widow of the historiographer N.M. Karamzin).'[53]

However, Pushkin found it impossible to rid himself of the image he had earlier acquired: those at one end of the political spectrum persisted in regarding him as a pernicious dissident, those at the other as an apostle of liberty. 'All subversive manuscripts are attributed to me, just as all obscene ones are to Barkov,' he had commented in annoyance to Vyazemsky in July 1826, while still at Mikhailovskoe.*[54] A

---

* I.S. Barkov (1732–68), poet, author of a large number of very varied parodies of Russian classical verse, which are noted for their wit, elegance, highly obscene language and porno-graphic content, and which, up to now, have only been published in heavily censored excerpts. Pushkin was a great admirer of his work. 'Barkov is one of the most remarkable figures in Russian literature ... The first books that will be published in Russia without censorship will be a complete collection of Barkov's works,' he told Vyazemsky's son Pavel in 1836 (Veresaev (1936), II, 297).

month later General Skobelev – who had earlier advocated removing a few strips of skin from the poet's back with a knout – triumphantly sent Benckendorff a poem allegedly by Pushkin, which appeared to be an incitement to revolution. In this case Skobelev was correct: the lines were Pushkin's. They were those excised by the censor from the elegy 'André Chénier', and formed part of Chénier's soliloquy on the night before his execution. Some unknown hand had given them the title 'On 14 December', assuming that lines such as: 'Where are freedom and the law? Over us/The axe alone reigns'[55] could not refer to anything but the situation in Russia. The chain by which the poem had reached Skobelev proved to be a long one. He had had it from one of his informers, a Kaluga squire named Konoplev. Konoplev, in his turn, had acquired it from Leopoldov, a lively young man who had just left Moscow University. Leopoldov had taken a copy of the poem, 'more evil and more desperate' than anything he had read before,[56] from a guards cavalry ensign, Molchanov, who had been given it by Aleksandr Alekseev, a staff-captain in the Jäger Horse Guards. When questioned, Alekseev confirmed that he had given Molchanov his copy of the lines, which he believed to be by Pushkin; asserted that they had had no title when he passed them on; and, despite repeated interrogations, maintained that he could not remember how he had obtained them.

For passing on the lines Molchanov, by imperial edict, was transferred out of the guards into the Nizhny Novgorod Dragoons; the more contumacious Alekseev was court-martialled and sentenced to death for concealing and communicating to others subversive verses in violation of his oath of allegiance. In the end he escaped with the same punishment as Molchanov, being transferred out of the guards into a line regiment. The court-martial commission was instructed to question Pushkin as to 'whether he had composed the aforesaid verses; when and how he had become aware of the intentions of the conspirators, expressed in the verses'.[57] On 13 January it ordered the Moscow chief of police, Major-General Shulgin, to put these questions and others about the 'notorious verses' to Pushkin, but, no doubt deeming them sufficiently notorious and too dangerous to circulate, attached no copy of them to its letter. Shulgin summoned Pushkin on 19 January; in answer to his questions Pushkin very reasonably replied that 'he did not know which notorious verses were in question, and asked to see them'.[58] Receiving Shulgin's report, the commission resolved 'to send the Moscow chief of police a copy of the verses in question, in an envelope specially sealed by the commission addressed to A. Pushkin himself to be delivered into his hand'. After opening the envelope and reading the verses Pushkin was to replace them immediately and reseal the envelope with his own seal; Shulgin was to attach his, and return the envelope secretly with his report.[59] Shulgin summoned Pushkin again on 27 January and gave him the envelope. Pushkin opened it, read the verses – with, surely, immense hidden amusement – and, before putting them back in the envelope, could not resist correcting two mistakes made by one of the many copyists and emending one line. In his deposition he acknowledged that he had written the lines; they were those removed by the censor from 'André Chénier'; had been written 'much before the recent disturbances'; were about the French Revolution and contained obvious references to the fall of the Bastille, the oath in the Jeu de Paume, to Mirabeau, and to Robespierre and the Convention. 'All these lines can in no way, without obvious absurdity, refer to 14 December,' he added. He did not know who had added the title, nor to whom he might have given the draft of the poem.[60]

The affair had unpleasant consequences for Pushkin. The court merely reprimanded him 'for careless custody of a work which had not passed censorship and which could have a harmful effect on minds inclined to free-thinking'.[61] The Senate, however, regretting that, because of the coronation amnesty of August 1826, he could not be prosecuted for circulating uncensored works in 1825, resolved that 'he should sign a pledge that henceforth he would undertake not to release to the public his works until they had been scrutinized and passed by the censor on pain of a severe penalty according to law'. The Council of State approved this resolution, adding that 'because of the unfitting expressions in his answers on the events of 14 December 1826 and because of the spirit of the work itself, published in 1825, secret surveillance should kept on him at his dwelling-place'.[62] Nicholas confirmed the resolution on 28 July 1828; but, because of Pushkin's many travels and the inherent inefficiency of the system, it was not communicated to him until 15 January 1831, when he was summoned to the police office in Moscow, had it read to him, and put his signature to it. If taken seriously, this meant that henceforth he could not read his newly composed works, even to his friends, until they had been censored.

Pushkin's disappointment at the failure of his matrimonial plans was short-lived: there were, after all, other marriageable girls in Moscow. His eye, always appreciative of aesthetic values, fell on the twenty-two-year-old Princess Sofya Urusova, 'the queen of the Moscow beauties' – also known as 'the goddess of stupidity'.[63] The Urusovs were a well-known Moscow family; Sofya's father, Prince Aleksandr, was a member of the Council of State and a high official of the imperial court. The Urusov house, on Sadovo-Kudrinskaya Street, 'renowned for its cordiality and hospitality', was full of life and bustle, for they had no fewer than twelve children, eight sons and four daughters.[64] During the spring of 1827 Pushkin was constantly to be found there. His obvious pursuit of Sofya aroused the jealousy of her cousin, Vladimir Solomirsky, a gloomily Byronic young artillery officer, who found an opportunity to call his rival out. Pushkin replied to his challenge with a laconic note: 'Immediately, if you wish, come with a second.'[65] But friends intervened, and amicable relations were re-established at a champagne lunch in Sobolevsky's apartment. Sofya's beauty had, however, attracted an admirer of rather greater social importance than either Pushkin or Solomirsky. 'The empress has invited Sofya Urusova to come and live in the palace, in her own apartment,' Vyazemsky told his wife in October. 'The Moscow old women of both sexes are gossiping about this in a thousand ways.' On the eve of her departure he added: 'She is very sweet, may God grant her happiness in Petersburg. I told you how her move was decided. It was impossible for them to refuse. What kind of excuse can one put forward, all the more since, as a maid-of-honour, she will be in the service of the Court.'[66] Behind Vyazemsky's cryptic comments lies the commonly held view that the duties of a maid-of-honour could include the granting of sexual favours to the tsar. The view proved correct: Sofya soon became Nicholas's mistress, though, for appearance's sake, she later married a complaisant husband, Prince Leon Radziwill.

Balked in his wooing of Sofya, Pushkin turned his attention to her sister, Mariya. At twenty-five, she was the eldest of the Urusov children and could hardly become his bride, since she had been married since the summer of 1822 to Count Ivan Musin-Pushkin, eighteen years her senior. Like her sister, she was a beauty, though piquantly unusual in appearance, with eyes of different colours; she was, too, extraordinarily charming. Pushkin soon succumbed to her attractions, and for several years considered himself in love with her. After her marriage she had spent some years in Florence with her husband. 'In her meditative beauty/She is more enchanting than the pictures', he wrote, imagining her wandering through the city's galleries.[67] His feelings for her, however, did not prevent him from falling in love with another Moscow girl – unlike Mariya, highly marriageable.

During the winter months there were frequent balls at the Moscow Noble Assembly. This was a handsome classical building on the corner of the Bolshaya Dmitrovka and Okhotny Ryad, built by Kazakov in 1784–7, and remodelled after the fire of 1812.* The balls – Tatyana attends onc in the seventh chapter of *Onegin* – took place in the great Hall of Columns, 'all white, all full of columns, so brightly lit that it seemed on fire [. . .] and at the end of the ballroom, on a pedestal, a marble effigy of Catherine smiling on the general gaiety.'[68] At a ball here during the Christmas season in 1826 Pushkin met the sisters Elizaveta and Ekaterina Ushakova. Both were extremely pretty; both were lively, playful young girls. The sixteen-year-old Elizaveta was already spoken for, and in 1830 was to marry her intended, Colonel Sergey Kiselev, a younger brother of General Pavel Kiselev. But Ekaterina, a year older, with blue eyes and long tresses of ash-blonde hair, was unattached: Pushkin was soon infatuated with her. The Ushakovs were a prominent Moscow family; the father, Nikolay Vasilevich, was a highly placed civil servant; he, his wife, and their five children lived in a large two-storey house in the Presnya district – then a very out-of-the-way region of the town. Pushkin was soon visiting them, not merely every day, but two or three times a day. Elena Telepneva, a girl of Ekaterina's age, who, while passing through Moscow in the summer of 1827 on her way to Europe with her parents, made the sisters' acquaintance, wrote in her diary: 'The younger is very, very pretty, but the elder interests me exceedingly because, apparently, our poet, our famous Pushkin intends to trust her with the

---

* Fundamentally remodelled in 1913, its exterior bears only a distant resemblance to the building of Pushkin's time.

Ekaterina Ushakova

fate of his life, since he has already laid his weapons at her feet, that is, to put it simply, has fallen in love with her. That is the general rumour, and the voice of the people is the voice of God. Before meeting them I had heard that during his whole stay in Moscow Pushkin occupied himself with nothing but N**** [Ekaterina]: at balls, on walks he spoke only to her, and when she was absent from a gathering Pushkin sat the whole evening pensively in a corner and no one was able to distract him!'[69]

Despite the attractions of Moscow, Pushkin was eager to visit Petersburg: he had many friends there; the literary scene was livelier in the capital than in Moscow; and he could too, in all decency, hardly postpone any longer a reunion with his parents.

Elizaveta Ushakova

'Family circumstances', he told Benckendorff, demanded his presence in St Petersburg. In Benckendorff's reply the iron fist is again to be detected beneath the velvet glove. 'His Majesty,' he wrote, 'allowing your visit to St Petersburg, deigned to make the imperial comment that he did not doubt that the word of honour given by a Russian nobleman to his sovereign: to conduct himself in a noble and becoming manner, would be kept in the fullest sense.'[70]

Pushkin's brother Lev, after two years as a civil servant in the Department of Foreign Creeds, had resigned and gone into the army: he was now a cadet in the Nizhny Novgorod Dragoon Regiment, which, under the command of the younger Raevsky, was taking part in the Persian campaign – a war which had begun in July 1826, when the Persian army had crossed the frontier in the hope of recovering Azerbaijan and Georgia. He had passed through Moscow in February: 'Lev was here – a nimble young fellow, it's a pity that he drinks,' Pushkin told Delvig. 'He owes your Andrieu [a St Petersburg restaurateur] 400 roubles and has debauched the garrison major's wife. He imagines his estate is ruined and that he has drained the cup of life.

He's going to Georgia to renew his withered soul. Killingly funny'[71] 'Tomorrow I travel to Petersburg to see the dearest parents, as they say, and put my financial affairs in order,' he wrote to Lev on 18 May 1827. 'From Petersburg I will either travel abroad, that is, to Europe, or to my place, that is, Pskov, but most probably to Georgia, not for the sake of your beautiful eyes, but for Raevsky.'[72] The following day Sobolevsky gave a farewell dinner for his friend in a villa in Petrovsky Park, outside the town on the Petersburg *chaussée*: among the guests were Mickiewicz and the Polevoy brothers. Pushkin left that evening. 'He has gone to Petersburg,' Ekaterina wrote to her brother a week later. 'Perhaps he will forget me, but no, no, let us believe, let us hope that he is bound to return.'[73]

Pushkin's closest friend in St Petersburg, Delvig, had married some months after his visit to Mikhailovskoe in 1825. Through him his young wife, Sofya Mikhailovna, became acquainted with the Pushkin family, took a great liking to the scapegrace Lev and was soon the bosom friend of Pushkin's sister, Olga. On 25 May, in a letter to an old school-friend, she wrote: 'Apropos of the Pushkins: I have now met Aleksandr – he arrived yesterday and we spent the day with him at his parents. This evening we expect him to come to us, – he will read his tragedy *Boris Godunov*. I am delighted to have met him at last. [. . .] That he is clever we have known for a long time, but I do not know whether he is polite in company, – yesterday he was quite boring and said nothing special; only read a charming excerpt from the fifth chapter of *Onegin*. [. . .] One had to see his mother's joy: she cried like a child and affected us all. My husband was also in the seventh heaven – I thought that their embraces would never end.' A few days later she added a postscript: 'I have now spent the evening with Pushkin which I told you about earlier. I liked him very much, he is very nice, we got to know each other quite well, Anton took pains over it, since he loves Aleksandr like a brother. What pleased me the best was that in his manner, his habits and his tone he is extraordinarily like his brother Lev, whom I love with all my heart.'[74] But both the Delvigs and Pushkin's parents soon left St Petersburg to spend the summer in Reval, the fashionable resort on the Baltic.

Pushkin had taken rooms in Demouth's Hotel, on the Moika

Embankment, just off the Nevsky Prospect, 'a poor suite, consisting of two rooms, where he led a strange life. He stayed in all morning – which for him began late – and if he was alone read, lying in bed. If he had a visitor, he would get up and sit at a little table with toilet requisites, and, while conversing, would clean, clip and file his nails, which were so long they could have been called claws.'[75] In this fashionable hostelry he stood out, as one visitor noted, in clothes that were obviously not of St Petersburg cut, and an extremely odd hat. He was soon busy reviving old and cultivating new friendships, writing, and making plans for the publication of his works. 'Pushkin is with us every day: this stops him playing the rake,' Karamzin's widow, Ekaterina Andreevna, remarked.[76] She had preserved the tradition of her late husband's literary salon and received informally every evening in her apartment on Mokhovaya Street. The guests sat on chairs which were arranged along the walls of the room; in the centre was an oval table; and tea was dispensed by Ekaterina Andreevna's stepdaughter, Sofya, hence known as the 'Samovar-pasha'. She was a pretty, talkative, unconventional girl, who smoked and had a passion for English novels. 'She possesses genuine liveliness and unassumed mischievousness, graciously moderated by a certain respect for the decencies,' remarked Baratynsky.[77] Her stepmother, Ekaterina Andreevna, had been the first in a succession of older women whose relationship with Pushkin was of a quasi-maternal nature. During this visit to St Petersburg another was added to the line: Elise Khitrovo.

Born in 1783, she was the favourite daughter of Field-Marshal Kutuzov. At nineteen she had married her father's aide-de-camp, Count Ferdinand Tiesenhausen, who was killed at the battle of Austerlitz while rallying Russian troops.* Her second husband, Major-General Nikolay Khitrovo, whom she married in 1811, became the Russian chargé d'affaires in Florence in 1815, but died four years later. Of her two daughters by Tiesenhausen – both striking beauties – the younger, Dolly, in 1821, at the age of seventeen, married an Austrian diplomat, Count Karl-Ludwig Ficquelmont, who was twenty-seven years older than her, and six years older than her mother. In July 1829 he became the Austrian ambassador

* His death was used by Tolstoy as the basis for the episode in *War and Peace* in which Andrey Bolkonsky is wounded at Austerlitz

in St Petersburg. Elise had returned to Russia in the summer of 1826, and soon became well-known in St Petersburg society. Though generous, warm-hearted, and staunch and loyal in her friendships, she possessed a number of minor eccentricities which made her, in some respects, a comic figure. Extremely proud of her father, she signed her letters – invariably written in French, since her Russian was abominable – 'Elise Hitroff, née princesse Koutousoff-Smolensky' – a title with which she had certainly not been born, since her father had not been created prince until after her second marriage. Though, unlike her daughters, she was far from beautiful, she was extremely proud of her shoulders, bust and back, exposing them as far as decency permitted at balls and routs. One society wit, gazing at the vast expanse of flesh, remarked: 'It is high time to draw a veil over the past.'[78]

No sooner had she met Pushkin than she fell desperately in love with him, expressing her feelings with a kind of almost hysterical exaltation. The emotion contained a maternal element: she is constantly solicitous about the state of his health: when he dislocated his foot in February 1828, which confined him to bed for a week or so, a spate of notes ensued. But the emotion was only partly maternal: Pushkin was at times hard put to keep her at arm's length. His feelings for her were ambivalent. As always,

Elise Khitrovo

he was morbidly sensitive to the possibility of appearing comic – as could easily have happened, for she made no secret of her adoration. He had recourse, therefore, to gently ironic ridicule. She became known among his friends and acquaintances as 'bare Liza', or as Erminia – the name of the princess of Antioch in Tasso's *Jerusalem Delivered*, who cherishes a hopeless and self-sacrificial love for the poem's hero, Tancred. Yet at the same time she was intelligent, cultured, and very well-read; she took an especially keen interest in contemporary French literature. In addition, through her long sojourn in diplomatic circles, she was formidably knowledgeable on European politics. As their correspondence shows, he took her views on literature and politics seriously – she was, perhaps, the only woman of his acquaintance of whom this could be said. He relied on her for the latest news, and she kept him supplied with books, periodicals and newspapers. In 1830, after he had left St Petersburg for Moscow, and she learnt that he was proposing to get married, she wrote: 'Forbid me to speak to you of myself, but do not deprive me of the happiness of being your commissionaire. I will talk high society, foreign literature – the probability of a change of ministry in France with you, alas, I am at the source of everything, I lack only happiness!'[79]

Since returning from exile, Pushkin had taken to serious gambling. Occasionally he won: sending Sobolevsky part of a debt, he remarked: 'This is hard-earned money, won at cards in the sweat of my brow from our friend Poltoratsky.'[80] More often he lost. In St Petersburg he took to visiting his old friend and former colleague at the Foreign Ministry, Count Aleksandr Zavadovsky. Zavadovsky had a villa on the Vyborg side – the suburb on the north, or right bank of the Neva – where high stakes were played for every night. Pushkin had fallen, too, into the hands of some professional gamesters – Ostolopov and Shikhmakov, according to a Third Department agent – with whom he often gambled in his rooms at Demouth's.

Even without his losses at cards, his finances were in a bad way: 1827 was not a good year for him as far as publishing was concerned. The previous autumn he had entrusted the second chapter of *Eugene Onegin* to Sobolevsky, rather than sending it to Pletnev in St Petersburg. This provoked an injured and pathetic letter in which Pletnev, after complaining that no one was giving him works to publish any more, asked what he should do with the manuscript of *The Gypsies*, which had passed the censor some months earlier. Disregarding the implicit plea, Pushkin gave this poem also to Sobolevsky. But he insisted that the price be set at six roubles – which, for a slim duodecimo brochure of forty-six pages, four of which were blank, seemed steep. 'He's written *The Gypsies* and is now haggling over it like a gypsy,' the bookseller Smirdin remarked to Boris Fedorov, a writer and journalist. 'And it's printed strangely – there are some blank pages among the printed ones.' 'That's typographical romanticism,' Fedorov replied.[81] It did not do well, partly perhaps because large portions had already appeared in *Pole Star* in 1825, and in the almanac *Northern Flowers* in 1826. 'My Gypsies are not selling at all,' he complained to Sobolevsky in July; and in September

Pletnev wrote: 'Not a single bookseller wants to buy your Gypsies: they all say that they have still got a whole shelf of the old ones.'[82] Sobolevsky was more successful with *The Robber Brothers*, a romantic narrative poem Pushkin had begun in 1821, but of which he had written only some two hundred lines: it had appeared in its entirety in *Pole Star* for 1825. The whole edition – 2,400 copies – was sold to the Moscow bookseller Shiryaev for fifteen hundred roubles. And in October Pushkin reluctantly sold Smirdin the right to bring out second editions of *Ruslan and Lyudmila*, *The Prisoner of the Caucasus* and *The Fountain of Bakhchisaray*. For this he received ten thousand roubles, half of Smirdin's projected gross receipts. Had he republished them himself, he would have made more, but only over a period of time. Smirdin was still advertising the editions in 1834.

Meanwhile Pletnev continually urged him to bring out more chapters of *Eugene Onegin*. 'Nothing produces money so easily as Onegin, brought out in parts, but regularly, every two or three months. That is already proved *a posteriori*,' he wrote. 'By God's grace, it is already all written. It only needs copying, and releasing. But then you have an attack of spleen. You say to the public in a freakish fit: here are the Gypsies for you; buy them! But the public, to spite you, won't buy it and waits for Onegin and Onegin.'[83] Pushkin, who now had the next three chapters ready for publication, eventually yielded. He gave Chapter Three to Pletnev. It was held up for a time, because, through Sobolevsky's inefficiency, copies of Chapter Two were unavailable in St Petersburg, but eventually appeared in October. It was followed, at the beginning of February 1828, by Chapters Four and Five, published together, and in March by Chapter Six. All sold well, and all were received well by the press: 'Where was he able to find these passionate expressions with which he expresses the languor of first love?' asked the *Northern Bee* of Chapter Three, in which *Son of the Fatherland* found 'many genuine, inimitable beauties'.[84] On Chapters Four and Five, however, the *Athenaeum*, a Moscow journal, printed an unsigned article (apparently by M.A. Dmitriev), which regressed to the pedantic nit-picking of the reviews of *Ruslan and Lyudmila*. 'The analysis of these chapters printed in the Athenaeum,' Pushkin later wrote, 'surprised me by its excellent tone, excellent style and by the oddity of its objections. The most common rhetorical figures and tropes brought the critic to a stand: can one say *the glass fizzes* instead of *the wine fizzes in the glass? the fireplace breathes* instead of *smoke comes from the fireplace?* Are not *jealous suspicion** and *treacherous ice* too bold? What do you think this means: *boys/With their skates noisily cut the ice?* The critic guessed, however, that it meant: boys run over the ice in skates.'[85]

On 27 July 1827 he left St Petersburg for Mikhailovskoe on what an English rake of that period would have called a repairing lease. '[Pushkin] has decamped to the country out of annoyance (or perhaps grief), having lost all that he had with him: 7 thousand!!' wrote Andrey Ivanovsky, a civil servant in Benckendorff's Third Department.[86] 'I am in the country and hope to write a great deal, I will be with you at the end of autumn,' he informed Delvig. 'So far inspiration is lacking, and I have meanwhile taken to prose.'[87] The prose was *The Blackamoor of Peter the Great*, the never-completed novel based on the life of Abram Gannibal. Vulf rode over from Trigorskoe to see him. 'I mounted a shaky porch and entered the tumbledown cabin of the pre-eminent Russian poet. I saw him, in a red Moldavian fez and dressing-gown, at his work-table, on which were strewn all the requisites of an admirer of fashion's dressing-table; on it also lay, in friendly proximity, Montesquieu, a volume of the *Bibliothèque de campagne*,† and the Journal of Peter I; Alfieri, Karamzin's monthlies and an interpretation of dreams were to be seen too, concealed among half a dozen almanacs.'[88] Inspiration finally came. 'No sooner does the divine word/Touch his acute ear,/Than the soul of the poet starts,/Like an awakened eagle,' he wrote in 'The Poet' on 15 August.[89]

He left Mikhailovskoe on 13 October. 'Arriving at Borovichi at twelve in the morning, I found another traveller lying in bed. He was holding the bank, playing against a hussar officer. I had dinner meanwhile. In paying I ended up five roubles short, punted them on a card, and, card by card, lost 1,600. I paid up somewhat crossly, borrowed 200 roubles and drove off extremely annoyed with myself. – At the next station I found Schiller's *The Visionary*, but had hardly managed to read the first

---

* Pushkin has copied a mistake made by the critic: the phrase is 'jealous indignation' (V, xliv, 12).

† *Bibliothèque de campagne, ou Amusements de l'esprit et du coeur*, an anthology, twelve volumes of which were published in Amsterdam between 1745 and 1762.

pages, when four troikas with a military courier suddenly drove up. "Poles, I suppose?" I said to the landlady. – "Yes," she replied. "They're taking them back now."* I went out to look at them.'

> One of the prisoners stood leaning against a pillar. Up to him came a tall, thin and pale young man with a black beard in a frieze overcoat, and in appearance a real Jew – indeed, I took him for a Jew, and the inseparable concepts of Jew and spy produced their usual effect on me. I turned my back on him, thinking that he had been summoned to Petersburg as an informant. Seeing me, he looked at me with animation. I involuntarily turned to him. We gaze intently at one another – and I recognize Küchelbecker. We threw ourselves into each other's arms. The gendarmes dragged us apart. The courier took me by the arm with threats and oaths – I did not listen to him. Küchelbecker was taken ill. The gendarmes gave him water, put him in a carriage and galloped off. – I drove off in the other direction. At the next station I learnt that they had come from Schlüsselburg – but where were they being taken?[90]

It was the first time Pushkin had seen Küchelbecker since 1820. Since the failure of the Decembrist revolt he had been kept in solitary confinement in the fortress at Schlüsselburg – situated where the Neva flows out of Lake Ladoga – and was now being transferred, with two other Decembrists, to the fortress at Dünaburg (now Daugavpils in Latvia). He remained in solitary confinement until 1835, when he was sent as an exile to Siberia.

Küchelbecker

Disappointed by his failure to become influential on the *Moscow Herald*,† Pushkin still

---

* Pushkin is assuming that the occupants of the troikas were members of the Polish Patriotic Society, which had had links with the Decembrists.

† He had gradually distanced himself from the journal, with which his relations became strained at the beginning of 1828. In January it printed some twenty stanzas of the seventh chapter to *Eugene Onegin*; but with so many mistakes that Pushkin, in annoyance, gave the extract also to Bulgarin's *Northern Bee*. The stanzas appeared in this journal in February, embellished with a derisive footnote: 'This extract was printed in a magazine with inexcusable mistakes. At the wish of the esteemed Author, we insert it in the *Northern Bee* with

hankered after literary journalism, and longed to have a periodical of his own. For the time being he made do by assisting Delvig in the preparation of the next number of *Northern Flowers* – hardly the same thing, however, because this appeared only once a year. Work on it brought him into contact with Orest Somov, a freelance journalist, and Delvig's close collaborator. A native of the Ukraine, and one of the very few to earn a living solely by the pen, Somov had been a friend of Ryleev, and had been imprisoned for a short time after the Decembrist revolt. The indolent Delvig found him invaluable, but Pushkin initially mistrusted him, since at this time he was also working for Bulgarin's *Northern Bee*: and, indeed, with his hangdog mien and red-rimmed eyes he scarcely inspired confidence.* Two years later, however, when both were involved in the production of Delvig's *Literary Gazette*, Pushkin's mistrust gave way to an appreciation of Somov's industry and he saw much of him. 'Somov and Pushkin are our regulars, they come every day, since they are my husband's closest collaborators,' Sofya Delvig wrote in 1830.[91]

At the beginning of December Mickiewicz arrived in St Petersburg, causing, according to a Polish journalist, 'an unprecedented sensation. Russians and Poles hasten to demonstrate their attention to him. We are having a continuous carnival here: dinners go on beyond midnight, one after another. Mickiewicz cannot manage to accept all the invitations.'[92] However, he did accept Pushkin's invitation to a dinner in his honour on 10 December in the Hotel de Paris on Malaya Morskaya Street. A week later Pushkin took him to dine with his parents. Over the next few months they met continually: on 8 January 1828 both attended a literary lunch given by Bulgarin; on 30 April Pushkin, who had moved back to Demouth's, entertained Mickiewicz in his rooms there. 'The day before yesterday I spent the evening and night at Pushkin's with Zhukovsky, Krylov, Khomyakov, Mickiewicz, Pletnev and Nikolay Mukhanov,' Vyazemsky told his wife. 'Mickiewicz improvised in French prose and astonished us, not so much of course by the form

---

corrections. The iteration of A.S. Pushkin's verses (N.B. with his permission) can never be superfluous' (*Severnaya pchela*, 19 February 1828).

* He was in fact right not to trust him, since he appears to have furnished details of Pushkin's doings to the Third Department: 'Here is the first news of him [Pushkin] from ͏͏͏ ͏͏͏ ͏͏͏͏͏͏,' ͏͏͏ ͏͏͏͏ ͏͏͏͏ to Benckendorff in March 1829 (Lemke, 493).

of his phrases, as by the power, richness and poetry of his thoughts. For instance, he compared his thoughts and feelings, which he had to express in a foreign language, with a child, dying at its mother's breast, with a fiery mass burning underground without a volcano for its eruption. These improvisations have a remarkable effect. He himself was agitated in the extreme, and we all listened trembling and in tears.'[93] On 11 May Mickiewicz and others dined with A.A. Perovsky and listened to Pushkin reading *Boris*; he was present again a week later when Pushkin gave another reading at the Laval mansion on the English Embankment. And in mid-June Mickiewicz returned the hospitality he had received with a dinner at the Vauxhall in Ekateringof Park. The guests included Vyazemsky, Pushkin, Delvig, Polevoy and Mukhanov. One of the few Poles present was a friend of Mickiewicz from Vilna, Stanislaw Morawski. He had not met Pushkin before, though he had seen a portrait, which had not impressed him: the features were 'uninteresting', and the whole inspired 'a certain revulsion'. He was assured, however, that it was an exact likeness. Pushkin in the flesh proved no more attractive. 'The carelessness of his attire, his dishevelled hair (he was somewhat bald) and side-whiskers, the distorted soles, and especially heels of his shoes, were evidence not only of a lack of attention to his appearance, but also of slovenliness. Mickiewicz was also not a lover of dandyism, but in his negligence there was dignity, nobility, and something sublime.'[94]

Ekaterina Ushakova's fears that Pushkin would not return to her seemed only too justified: not only did he give no indication of wishing to revisit Moscow, but his behaviour suggested that he had completely forgotten about her. In December the Vorontsovs were in St Petersburg, and for a short time Pushkin renewed his relationship with Elise. To record their trysts – they met four times in the week of the twelfth to the eighteenth – he resurrected the little French memorandum-book she had given him in Odessa. The following February he began a short affair with Anna Kern, who was now living in St Petersburg. But before then his sister, Olga, had forcibly brought the idea of marriage back to his mind.

Olga was now thirty, and seemed destined to become an old maid. At the beginning of January 1828, however, Nikolay Pavlishchev, whom she had known for some time – he had been at school with Lev, and was five years younger than her – asked for her hand in marriage. He was a civil servant in the Ministry of Education, was poor, 'far from attractive and utterly prosaic'.[95] Her parents refused to countenance his suit, and forbade him the house. When, two weeks later, the lovers met at a ball and danced a cotillion together, Nadezhda Osipovna hurried out of the card-room and angrily pushed her daughter away from Pavlishchev. Olga, her sensibilities outraged, promptly fainted. The following day she sent her suitor a note agreeing to an elopement. At one in the morning of 25 January she stole out of the house, joined Pavlishchev in a sleigh, and drove to the Holy Trinity church in the Izmailovsky Regiment,* where they were married. Returning home, she sent for Pushkin – who had known nothing of her intentions – and asked him to inform their parents. After three hours of heated discussions, during which Sergey Lvovich became so over-excited that it became necessary to summon a barber to bleed him, the parents agreed to accept the marriage, though with no very good grace. 'My friend Mrs Pavlishcheva seems very miserable,' Vyazemsky told his wife in April. 'Her family cannot be brought to open their arms to her husband.'[96] The newly-weds moved into the Delvigs' flat, vacant since Delvig had been sent to Kharkov by the Ministry of the Interior, where he was now employed.

Before exile Pushkin had known the Olenins well. He had first met Anna Kern at their house on the Fontanka in 1819, and at that time had been a frequent visitor to their country villa at Priyutino, less than an hour's ride to the north of the capital. They had four children: Petr, a guards officer, Aleksey – a year older than Pushkin, and known to him and Vyazemsky as 'Aleksey Junior', or simply 'Junior' – Varvara, who was already married, and Anna, known as Annette. In 1819 she had been a pale eleven-year-old, the spoilt youngest child of the family. When he saw her again in the winter of 1827 at a ball given by Elise Khitrovo, she was one of the city's beauties, a small, graceful, nineteen-year-old blonde. 'Among the poet's singularities was that of having a passion for small feet, which in one of his poems he confessed to preferring to beauty itself,' she wrote in her diary, and, referring to herself in the third person, added, 'Annette combined an acceptable appearance with two things: she had eyes which were sometimes pretty and sometimes

* The district between the Izmailovsky and Tsarskoselsky (now Moskovsky) Prospects was generally called the Izmailovsky Regiment, since the the the barracks of the Izmailovsky Guards were here.

stupid. But her feet were indeed very small and almost none among the young people of society could get into her shoes. Pushkin noticed this advantage and his avid eyes followed young Olenina's feet over the slippery parquet.' For her part, Annette was enthralled by the sight of 'the most interesting person of his time and the most distinguished in the career of letters'.[97] Soon he was head over heels in love with her, ornamenting his manuscripts with her initials and her name, writing it sometimes forwards, sometimes backwards – 'ettenna eninelo', 'eninelo ettenna' – and sometimes inscribing what he hopes will be her future signature: 'Pouchkine Annette', 'Annette Pouch'.[98] 'The Olenin girl is quite a lively little piece,' Vyazemsky told his wife on 17 April. 'Pushkin calls her a little dragoon and is courting this little dragoon.' On Sunday 20 May he and Mickiewicz drove out to Priyutino. 'There we found Pushkin with his lover's grimaces. The country

Anna Olenina

is quite pleasant, especially for Petersburg: there is sufficient movement in the views, the elevations, the water, forest etc. But on the other hand the gnats make this place a veritable hell. I have never seen such a quantity of them [. . .] Pushkin was covered in bites and, besieged by the gnats, exclaimed tenderly, "How sweet".'[99]

At the end of May Vyazemsky, about to leave St Petersburg, invited a number of his friends to a 'farewell picnic'.[100] This took the form of an excursion to Kronstadt on one of the paddle-steamers – then called 'pyroscaphs' – that plied regularly between the island and the capital. Among those who took part were Pushkin, Mickiewicz, Annette and her brother Junior, Griboedov,* and Nikolay Kiselev, the younger brother of Elizaveta Ushakova's fiancé Sergey, and himself another of Annette's suitors. The boat left at 9 a.m. Another passenger on board was the

---

* Having played a significant part in the peace negotiations with Persia, he had returned to St Petersburg in March, bringing with him their result, the Treaty of Turkmenchay. There had been a ceremonial reception for the treaty on 14 March; Griboedov was generously rewarded and appointed the Russian plenipotentiary minister in Persia, whither he returned on 6 June, and where he was killed the following January. While in St Petersburg he stayed at Demouth's Hotel, and naturally saw much of Pushkin.

English portrait-painter George Dawe. He had been in St Petersburg since 1819, having been invited by Alexander I to paint a series of portraits of the generals engaged in the war with Napoleon for a special 'military' gallery of the Winter Palace. Now, having completed nearly four hundred portraits of Russian officers (at a thousand roubles apiece), full-lengths of Wellington, Kutuzov and Barclay de Tolly, and an equestrian portrait of Alexander twenty feet high, he was on his way home and was travelling to Kronstadt to take the London packet. He knew Pushkin, and, seeing him now, took out his pad and began a sketch of his head. Noticing this, Pushkin produced two impromptu stanzas, 'To Dawe, Esqr'. 'Why does your sublime pencil/Sketch my Negro profile?' he enquired. Dawe would be better employed drawing Annette: 'Only of youth and beauty/Should genius be the admirer.'[101]

They had fine weather on the way to Kronstadt, but began the return journey in a thunderstorm, with strong winds and pelting rain. 'You should have seen how everyone ran about, rushed into the cabins, the noise, the shrieks, the pushing and shoving,' Vyazemsky told his wife; 'here one fat Englishwoman falls off the ladder, but on to the deck, not into the sea, there a Frenchwoman is pulled out of a boat and through a port-hole into the ship [. . .] Olenin the son drinks twenty-one roubles worth of porter and vodka by himself. It is sublime. Pushkin sulks, frowns like the weather, like love.'[102] Thirty years later Annette recollected the trip in a letter to Vyazemsky: 'Do you remember those happy times, when we were young and gay, and in good health? When Pushkin, Griboedov and you accompanied us on the Neva steamer to Kronstadt. Ah, how beautiful everything then was and life flowed like a rapid, noisy stream!'[103]

But he could easily be distracted from the pursuit of Annette. Rogation Day was celebrated in St Petersburg as the beginning of spring: a religious procession took place round the walls of the Peter-Paul fortress, prayers were said against flood, and the populace took to the Neva in boats. On this day in 1828 – 18 April – Pushkin and Vyazemsky followed the custom, though ice was still coming down the river from Lake Ladoga. 'Pushkin and I were getting into a boat when two ladies came up and one asked us in French whether we would allow them to come with us, for fear of going by themselves,' Vyazemsky told Princess Vera. 'We, of course, agreed. And what should happen? They turned out to be a procuress with one of her girls. The procuress recognized Pushkin from his portrait exhibited at the Academy.* And so this is how the Russian God made fun of our devout and poetic journey. At the quay of the fortress we parted with our vile prose, but not before Pushkin asked permission to call on them, but I, as Christ is my witness, did not, and we went wandering about the fortress for two hours.'[104]

This was hardly a serious entanglement, but his relationship with Agrafena Zakrevskaya was. A year younger than Pushkin, she was a tall, statuesque beauty with black hair and eyes, who at eighteen had married Arseny Zakrevsky, a thirty-two-year-old army officer: dull in the extreme, but an excellent administrator who had a very successful career. Agrafena could hardly have been more different. She was a creature of fits and humours, eccentric and unconventional, and capable of the most freakish behaviour. In 1823 Zakrevsky, now a lieutenant-general, was made governor-general of Finland. His wife became legendary in Helsingfors society, allowing her eccentricities full play and flaunting a succession of lovers. Returning after a jaunt with Prince Lvov, one of Zakrevsky's aides-de-camp, she described him in the book of arrivals as: 'Prince Chou-Chéri, Crown Prince of the Kingdom of the Moon, with part of his court and half of his harem'.[105] Baratynsky, who was then stationed in Finland, became one of her victims. The experience scarred him, and he gives a bitterly hostile portrait of her as Princess Nina in his narrative poem *The Ball*.† 'How omnipotently attractive/ Was her vivid beauty!' he writes, and warns those called to her 'luxurious bosom': 'Flee her: she has no heart! [. . .] Her heat is the heat of a drunken maenad,/The heat of fever – not the heat of love.'[106]

In 1828 Zakrevsky became Minister of the Interior and moved with his wife to St Petersburg; Pushkin met her that spring. In a fragment of prose fiction, composed several months later, he portrays her as Zinaida Volskaya, with whom the hero embarks on an affair; 'not supposing that frivolity could be combined with strong passions, he foresaw a relationship without any important consequences, an extra woman in

---

* This was the portrait painted by Orest Kiprensky in May–June 1827; it depicts Pushkin with a plaid shawl over his right shoulder. In the top right of the portrait is a statuette of a muse, holding a lyre.
† Published jointly with Pushkin's *Count Nulin*, under the title *Two Stories in Verse*, in December 1828.

the list of his flighty mistresses, and coldbloodedly planned her conquest. Perhaps, if he could have imagined the storms that awaited him, he would have relinquished the triumph, since a man of fashion finds it easy to sacrifice his pleasures and even his vanity for the sake of indolence and decorum.'[107] But Pushkin did not imagine the storms, had not read Baratynsky, and was soon tempestuously involved with Agrafena. On 7 May Vyazemsky, who had dubbed her the 'bronze Venus', wrote to his wife, 'Yesterday at the Avdulins' ball [Pushkin] completely cut me out with Zakrevskaya, but I showed no jealousy.'[108] In 'A Portrait', composed in July, Pushkin compares her to 'a lawless comet/In the calculated orbit of the spheres'.[109] Vyazemsky quoted these lines in a letter to Turgenev, adding, '[Pushkin] has spent the whole summer spinning in the vortex of Petersburg life, hymning Zakrevskaya.'[110] The eleventh of August was Annette's twentieth birthday. 'O goodness, how old I am,' she wrote, 'but what can be done? [. . .] Pushkin, or Red Rover,* as I have called him, arrived as usual. He is in love with Zakrevskaya. He speaks of her all the time, in order to make me jealous, but at the same time in a low voice says various tender things to me.'[111]

The passion soon burnt itself out. In July Vyazemsky had been in Penza, where he had met a Mr Beketov, a cousin of Matvey Sontsov, who had married Pushkin's aunt. Beketov, he told Pushkin, affected to see a double entendre in the line from *Eugene Onegin* where the poet speaks of ladies 'With the *Well-Intentioned* in their hands' (III, xxvii) – a reference to the journal of that name. 'He thinks,' Vyazemsky continued, 'that you are thrusting into the ladies' hands that which we have between our legs. I told him that I would pass this commentary on to you and was sure that you would dote on the Sontsov family because of their cousin's conjecture. But the *well-intentioned* is a splendid name. By the way, what is Junior's *well-intentioned* getting up to?'[112] When Pushkin replied, catching up the joke, the affair with Agrafena was over. 'If it were not for your bronze Venus, I would have died of boredom,' he wrote. 'But she is consolingly funny and sweet. I am writing verse to her. And she has promoted me to the rank of pander (to which I am drawn by my wonted inclination and the present state of my

---

* A reference to the eponymous hero of James Fenimore Cooper's pirate novel, *The Red Rover* (1827).

Well-Intentioned, about which could be said that which was said of its printed namesake: truly the intention is good, but the execution is terrible*).'[113] 'I had already heard that you were hovering around my bronze Venus,' Vyazemsky wrote in his reply, 'but to penetrate her one would need a bronze well-intentioned.'[114] The problem with Pushkin's well-intentioned might have been as much physical as psychological. The procuress whom he and Vyazemsky had ferried across the Neva had turned out to be Sofya Ostafevna, the madam of a well-known St Petersburg brothel. In November, sending Delvig a poem for *Northern Flowers*, he apologized for not having yet composed a reply to some verses addressed to him by Anna Gotovtseva, a Kostroma poet, adding: 'I have completely lost the art of paying compliments: I find it as hard to penetrate a madrigal as a cunt. And it's all Sofya Ostafevna's fault.'[115]

Despite these distractions, he continued to pursue Annette, and in August formally requested her hand: a request that was immediately and unceremoniously turned down by her parents. Whatever his eminence as a poet, he was not the son-in-law that a respectable family, particularly one so highly placed in society as the Olenins, could have wished for. He possessed no capital, no property; his income was insecure and fluctuating; his reputation was dubious in the extreme: not only was he known to be a gambler and a rake, but he was also politically suspect. Olenin, as a member of the Council of State, knew all about the 'André Chénier' affair, and knew, too, about the accusation of lewd blasphemy recently brought against Pushkin in connection with *The Gabrieliad*.† As for Annette, though flattered by the attention of 'the most interesting person of his time', she could not have been less in love with him, writing in her diary: 'God, having endowed him with unique Genius, did not grant him an attractive exterior. His face was expressive, of course, but a certain malice and sarcasm eclipsed the intelligence visible in his blue, or rather say glassy eyes. A Negro profile acquired from his mother's side did not embellish his face. And add to this dreadful side-whiskers, dishevelled hair, nails like claws, a small stature, affectation in his manners, an arrogant attitude to the women whom he chose

---

* Pushkin is quoting the poet and wit M.V. Milonov's *mot* on the journal.
† See page 281.

to love, the peculiar nature both of his natural and assumed character, and boundless self-esteem.'[116] In any case, her heart was wholly occupied by a handsome colonel, Prince Aleksey Lobanov-Rostovsky, who was to receive the Cross of St George and be promoted major-general for his part in the storming of the Turkish fortress of Varna. But he never proposed, and in the end Annette did not marry until 1840: her husband, Fedor Andrault, was the illegitimate son of Count Langeron, the former governor of Odessa.

Even without the failure of his marital hopes, the year had been an unhappy one. Earlier, on 26 May, his twenty-ninth birthday, he had composed one of his darkest lyrics:

> Vain gift, chance gift,
> Life, why wert thou given me?
> Or why by mysterious fate
> Art thou condemned to punishment?
>
> Who with inimical power
> Called me forth from nothingness,
> Filled my soul with passion,
> Agitated my mind with doubt? . . .
>
> There is no goal before me:
> The heart is empty, the mind idle,
> And the monotonous sound of life
> Oppresses me with melancholy.*[117]

---

* The poem was published in *Northern Flowers* for 1830, and caught the attention of Filaret, the Metropolitan of Moscow, who, Vyazemsky told Turgenev, 'parodied or rather palinoded Pushkin's verses on life, which he found at the house of their common friend, Elise Khitrovo, who burns with Christian love for the one, and with pagan for the other' (*OA*, III, 192–3). Filaret's palinode – an ode in which the author retracts something said in a former poem – begins: 'Not in vain, not by chance/Was life given me by God,/Not without the mysterious will of God/Is it condemned to punishment' (*PSS*, III, 507). Elise sent it to Pushkin, who thanked her ironically: 'Lines by a Christian, a Russian bishop in response to some sceptical couplets! That's really a piece of luck' (To E.M. Khitrovo, first half January 1830; XIV, 57), and addressed an equally ironic reply, 'In hours of amusement or idle boredom . . .', to Filaret, in which, struck by the latter's 'majestic voice', he repents, sheds 'floods of tears', and concludes: 'The soul, scorched by thy fire/Has renounced the dark of earthly vanities,/And in holy terror the poet/Hearkens to the seraph's harp' (III, 212).

The first of the year's setbacks had occurred the previous month. In March the war with Persia had ended with Russia making large territorial gains in Transcaucasia, acquiring Erivan and Nakhichevan, that is to say Persian Armenia (Western Armenia still remained under Turkish rule). Pushkin's imperialistic enthusiasms had made him a supporter of the war – 'I have simply fallen in love with him [Nicholas I],' he wrote, 'He has suddenly invigorated Russia/With war, hopes and labours'[118] – and he was delighted at its victorious conclusion. Meanwhile the cause of Greek independence had been set back by the arrival there of a strong Egyptian army under the command of Ibrahim Pasha, son of the Sultan's vassal Mohammed Ali. However, on 20 October (NS) 1827 a joint British, Russian and French fleet under Admiral Codrington, without authorization from the Allied governments, destroyed the Egyptian fleet at Navarino Bay, thus cutting Ibrahim off from his supplies and reinforcements. The Sultan reacted by calling the Moslem faithful to a Holy War, and repudiating the Convention of Akkerman, signed with Russia in October 1826. As well as giving Serbia, Wallachia and Moldavia a degree of autonomy, this had allowed Russian ships to navigate Turkish waters, and to pass the Straits. Nicholas waited until the successful conclusion of the war with Persia, and then, on 14 April, declared war on Turkey. On the twenty-fifth he left St Petersburg for the Balkan front; on the same day troops of the Second Army under Wittgenstein crossed the Prut, while Paskevich commenced operations against the Turks in Transcaucasia.

Initially the war aroused great patriotic fervour. Officers clamoured for postings to the active armies, and even Vyazemsky and Pushkin, though totally without military experience, applied for permission to join Wittgenstein's forces. 'Every man thinks meanly of himself for not having been a soldier,' Dr Johnson remarked. Of Pushkin's male acquaintances, most of those of the previous generation had fought – some with great distinction – in the Napoleonic wars. Even the despised Bulgarin had been decorated, both by the Russians and the French. Now his own generation had begun to go to war: Nikolay Raevsky had been promoted major-general for his conduct during the Persian campaign, and little Lev had gained the reputation of a dashing cavalry officer in Raevsky's regiment. Vyazemsky encouraged Pushkin to apply. 'He leads nothing but a social life here,' he told Turgenev, 'and Petersburg could have ruined him. Martial life will do him to a turn and will nourish him with what is material. Up to now his poetry has been chiefly concerned with himself.'[119] But both were turned down. 'I asked to be attached to headquarters, or to our acquaintance Count Pahlen, who will administer the principalities of Moldavia and Wallachia when our troops occupy them; but to judge by the letter, that is the reply, one would have thought I had demanded a brigade in the active army,' Vyazemsky wrote in annoyance to his wife.[120] He did not realize that both he and Pushkin were still regarded with suspicion by the authorities. 'Believe me, my dear General,' Grand Duke Constantine had written to Benckendorff on 14 April, 'that in view of their previous behaviour, no matter how much they might try now to demonstrate their loyalty to His Majesty's service, they are, in my view, not at all people on whom one can, even in the least, rely'; adding, a fortnight later, 'their request, believe me, had no other aim than to find a new field for the dissemination with greater success and greater ease of their subversive principles, with which they would have soon gained many proselytes among the young officers'.[121]

Pushkin received Benckendorff's letter telling him that there were no vacancies on 20 April. Cast down by the news, he spent that evening at Zhukovsky's, where a plan was mooted to travel that summer 'to London on a pyroscaph, from London to spend three weeks in Paris', and to return in August. 'Pushkin, Krylov, Griboedov and I arranged to set out on this European foray,' Vyazemsky told his wife.[122] But this was an idle, after-dinner scheme which no one took seriously, apart from Pushkin. The following day he replied to Benckendorff. Accepting 'with reverence' the emperor's decision, he continued: 'Since for the next 6 or 7 months I will probably remain idle, I would wish to spend this time in Paris, something which perhaps I would not succeed in doing subsequently. If Your Excellency would deign to solicit for me from the Sovereign this valuable permission, you would do me a new and genuine favour.'[123] Benckendorff found himself at a loss. As a bureaucrat, he was astounded by the grotesque nature of Pushkin's request: it was as if a child, refused a slice of cake, should then demand the entire cakestand. He could not turn down the petition without referring it to Nicholas, but the emperor was at the front. He therefore dispatched Ivanovsky – one of his subordinates who had some acquaintance with Pushkin – to try to persuade him to withdraw the request.

Ivanovsky, accompanied by a friend, went round to Demouth's, where he found Pushkin in bed: chagrin – or over-indulgence – had brought on a bilious attack. He began by trying to convince the poet that Nicholas had had his best interests at heart; did not want to expose him to danger; would have had to give him the rank of cadet, which would have caused difficulty; probably would have allowed him to attach himself to Diebitsch's or another's staff. After a good deal of this, inter-mixed with flattery, Pushkin began to grow more cheerful. Ivanovsky's master-stroke was to suggest that he should join Paskevich's eastern campaign. 'A splendid thought,' exclaimed Pushkin, now fully recovered. Could he take it that the request to visit Paris had been withdrawn, Ivanovsky enquired. Pushkin agreed, though 'a melancholic gloomy cloud passed over his brow'. Ivanovsky's companion, who had observed the encounter with interest, remarked, as they left the hotel, how aston-ished he had been by Pushkin's rapid changes in mood.[124] Today these would cause him to be classed as a manic-depressive, his financial improvidence and compulsive gambling being adduced as corroborative evidence. In the event he did not apply for permission to travel to the army in Transcaucasia: other preoccupations soon distracted him.

The next setback came towards the end of the summer. In May two domestic serfs of the retired staff-captain V.F. Mitkov, in a petition to the Metropolitan of St Petersburg, complained that 'their master was corrupting them in the understanding of the Orthodox Christian faith they professed by reading to them from his manuscript book a certain depraved composition with the title of "The Gabrieliad", and that they herewith submitted to His Eminence the Metropolitan that same book'.[125] The Metropolitan, Serafim, a reactionary zealot, brought the matter to the attention of the civil authorities; it was then reported to Nicholas, who ordered it to be investigated. At the beginning of August Pushkin was summoned before the St Petersburg military governor-general, Pavel Kutuzov, and questioned about the poem. Asked whether he was the author, he replied categorically that he was not; he had seen the poem for the first time in 1815 or 1816 while at the Lycée and had taken a copy of it. He did not know what had happened to this copy; he had not seen it since and it was no longer in his possession.

Pushkin was no doubt extremely disconcerted – and highly annoyed – by the unexpected reappearance of this youthful indiscretion. But a moment's thought should have told him that a childish reliance on the virtues of stout denial was unwise. After all, he had never made any particular secret about his authorship. He had sent a copy to Vyazemsky,* and must have known that many others had been made and circulated. In 1822 S.S. Petrovsky – whom Pushkin had never met – wrote to Sobolevsky: 'Pushkin has written a poem The Gabrieliad or the love of the archangel Gabriel for the Virgin Mary';[126] and in 1825 Yakushkin had discussed the poem in a letter to Chaadaev in terms which suggested they had both read it. Pushkin's authorship was even known in official circles: in March 1826 the gendarme colonel Ivan Bibikov – a flowery stylist – wrote to Benckendorff from Moscow, warning against the dangers of exiling young poets and journalists, who, 'finding themselves alone in these deserts, separated, so to say, from all intellectual society, deprived in the springtime of their life of all hope, distil the gall of their discontent in their writings, and flood the empire with a mass of seditious verses which carry the torch of revolt into every class and which attack with the perfidious and dangerous weapon of ridicule the sanctity of religion – that restraint which is indispensable for all peoples and in particular the Russians', adding in a footnote to the last phrase: 'See A. Pushkin's work The Gabrieliad.'[127]

Pushkin's testimony was sent to Nicholas, who ordered Count P.A. Tolstoy, the commander-in-chief of St Petersburg and Kronstadt, to obtain a written statement. Tolstoy passed the order to Kutuzov, who summoned Pushkin to his office again on 19 August. When asked from whom he had received the poem he produced the following statement: 'The manuscript circulated among officers of the hussar regiment, but from which of them exactly I obtained it I cannot at all recall. I burnt my copy, probably in 1820. I make so bold as to add that in none of my works, even those of which I most repent, is there a trace of unbelief or blasphemy of religion. I find all the more regrettable therefore the opinion that ascribes so miserable and shameful a work to me.'[128] In a draft of the statement he had toyed with the idea of saddling the poet and dramatist Prince Dmitry Gorchakov, who had died in 1824, and

---

* On an edition of Pushkin's poems, published in Berlin in 1870, which contained extracts from the poem, Vyazemsky noted: 'I should have in my old papers a complete manuscript of "The Gabrieliad", done in Pushkin's own hand, which he sent me. It must be burnt, which I will bequeath my son to do' (Ibid.. (19p) 199)

had been known as an atheist and freethinker, with the work. He put the idea into practice when writing to Vyazemsky. 'The Gabrieliad has finally reached the government; it is being attributed to me; I have been denounced, and I will probably answer for another's pranks, if Prince Dm. Gorchakov does not appear from the other world to defend his rights to his own property.'[129] He knew this would not deceive Vyazemsky; the aim was rather to mislead the police, should the letter be opened and read, and to instruct Vyazemsky what to say, should he be examined.

Tolstoy forwarded Pushkin's statement to Nicholas, who sent back an order: 'Count Tolstoy is to summon Pushkin to his presence and tell him in my name that, since I know Pushkin personally, I believe his word. But I desire that he should assist the government to discover who could have composed something so vile and insulted Pushkin by issuing it under his name.' The meeting took place on 2 October. When the emperor's orders were made known to Pushkin, 'after considerable silence and thought he asked: would he be permitted to write directly to His Imperial Majesty, and, having received an affirmative answer, immediately wrote a letter to His Majesty, and, sealing it, handed it to Count Tolstoy'.[130] 'When questioned by the Authorities,' he had written, 'I did not consider myself obliged to confess to a prank as shameful as it was criminal. But now, when questioned directly by the person of my Sovereign, I declare that *The Gabrieliad* was composed by me in 1817. Throwing myself on the mercy and magnanimity of the tsar, I am Your Imperial Majesty's loyal subject Aleksandr Pushkin.'[131] It will be noticed that, while admitting himself to be the author, he has endeavoured to mitigate his guilt by passing the poem off as an adolescent's transgression: it had been composed in 1821, not 1817. The letter was sent, unopened, to Nicholas. A fortnight later Pushkin received a personal reply from the emperor, who brought the investigation to an end on 31 December by affixing a resolution to the dossier: 'This case is known to me in detail and has been completely concluded.'[132] Pushed to the wall, Pushkin had had to confess, in humiliating fashion, that he had written the poem and that his testimony had been a lie from beginning to end. It had been a degrading experience, which immeasurably strengthened Nicholas's hold over him.

Of the other participants in the affair Mitkov had been exempted from any further investigation in July. He disciplined the two serfs who had informed on him, Nikita Gorbunov and Spiridon Abramov, by dispatching them to the army as conscripts: the term of service was then twenty-five years. For good measure Gorbunov was also given an official flogging at the police-station.

'They say that Pushkin, to console himself from the vicissitudes of love, has been gambling and has lost all his money. He has the spirit of a poet, but not the character,' Sofya Karamzina, the 'Samovar-Pasha', wrote to Vyazemsky in June.[133] Over the next six months, as his emotional life became ever more complicated, his addiction to gambling became ever more marked, and was noted with distress by his acquaintances. 'He will misuse his opportunities as much as possible, and, I must confess, I cannot watch without sadness the brilliance of such a glittering talent compromising itself at the card-table,' commented Princess Aleksandra Golitsyna in November.[134] And, the following March, after Pushkin had left St Petersburg for Moscow, Sofya wrote again: 'We were not sorry to see him go, since he had become unpleasantly morose in society, spending days and nights gambling with, it is said, a gloomy rage. And his mien and his pale face, like Béverlei's,* were not at all pleasant.'[135]

'While Kiselev and the Poltoratskys† were here I continued that manner of life which I have sung in the following manner,' he had told Vyazemsky in September,

> 'But on rainy days they often met.
> Doubling, the mother-fuckers, from 50 to 100.
> And they would lose and chalk it up.
> So they occupied themselves on rainy days.'‡[136]

Had he contented himself with adversaries such as these, amateurs like himself, his losses would have been moderate. But now, as well as the sessions with professional gamesters in his room at Demouth's and at

---

* Eponymous hero of *Béverlei* (1768), a tragedy about a gambler by the French dramatist Bernard-Joseph Saurin (1706–81).

† Nikolay Kiselev, Annette Olenina's suitor, and his cousins by marriage, Aleksey Pavlovich and Mikhail Aleksandrovich Poltoratsky, themselves cousins, whom Pushkin had met in Kishinev.

‡ He used these lines, omitting the obscenity, as the epigraph for the first chapter of *The Queen of Spades*.

Zavadovsky's villa, he had taken to playing for high stakes at the St Petersburg English Club. This had been founded in 1772 by an English merchant, Francis Gardner, and membership had initially been confined to the English business community. By the end of the century it was also being used by the Russian nobility, and had gradually become an exclusive – Bulgarin was blackballed in 1827 – gentlemen's club, whose premises were a single-storey merchant's residence on the Moika Embankment. Pushkin was elected in 1832; before then he visited it as a guest. An English traveller, who dined there in 1852, found its members refreshing themselves 'with porter and champagne mixed in large jugs'.[137] Here he played with the cuirassier Mikhail Sudienko, one of Bencken- dorff's aides-de-camp, and the twenty-five-year-old Ivan Yakovlev – to whom, in the spring of 1829, he lost 6,000 roubles. Yakovlev could afford to indulge a passion for cards, being the grandson of a millionaire tax-farmer. A little later, in Moscow, Pushkin fell into the clutches of a professional gamester, Vasily Ogon-Doganovsky, to whom he lost the huge sum of 24,800 roubles.

By the end of September 1828 he was contemplating another sojourn in the country. Society would be wanting at Mikhailovskoe: Arina Rodionovna had died that summer; and there were no neighbours in residence at Trigorskoe. He thought of going to Malinniki, Praskovya Osipova's estate near Tver, together with her and her daughter Annette, but Vulf unexpectedly showed himself a stickler for propriety: 'I saw Pushkin, who wants to travel with my mother to Malinniki, which is very disagreeable to me, because from this the good name of my mother and sister will suffer, and this is harmful to my sister for several other reasons,' he confided to his diary.[138] Nevertheless, having celebrated the anniversary of the Lycée's founding with seven former schoolfellows on 19 October, Pushkin set out for Malinniki in the early hours of the following morning. Ekaterina Karamzina, Praskovya's rival for the post of Pushkin's surrogate mother, also disapproved of the visit: 'One must hope that the country will inspire him again to something sublime, although I am distressed that he should have left to spend all this time at his friend's estate, rather than his own, where isolation would have had a greater effect on his imagination than the society of some good provincial lady, who can provide nothing more than a few scenes for *Onegin*, of which there are enough already.'[139]

Pushkin remained in the country until the end of November, enjoying the attentions of Praskovya, her daughters and nieces, and their neighbours: 'Here there are lots of pretty wenches (or maids, as Boris Mikhailovich orders them to be called*); my relations with them are Platonic, and as a result I am getting fat and improving in health.'[140] One in particular caught his eye: 'Mariya Borisova is a flower in the desert, a nightingale among the birds of the forest, a pearl in the sea and I am resolved to fall in love with her in a day or two,' he told Vulf.[141] He flirted desperately, too, with Zizi Vulf. None of these flirtations, however, engaged him deeply; his heart still belonged to Annette, and he had been deeply wounded by his rejection. For him autumn was always the time of the year most conducive to composition; and, despite his other preoccupations, that autumn in St Petersburg, when the weather had been appallingly bad for weeks on end, had been immensely productive: just before leaving he had completed the first draft of a new narrative poem, *Mazepa* – a title changed, just prior to publication, to *Poltava*. At Malinniki, on 27 October, he composed a dedication to it addressed to Annette:

> ... will the poet's dedication,
> As once his love,
> Before you without reply
> Pass, again unacknowledged?[142]

At the same time he addressed to her the best-known of all his lyrics.

> I loved you: love still, perhaps,
> Is not quite extinguished in my soul;
> But let it no longer alarm you;
> I do not want to distress you in any way.
> I loved you silently, hopelessly,
> Tortured now by shyness, now by jealousy;
> I loved you so sincerely, so tenderly,
> May God grant you be so loved by another.[143]

---

* A reference to Boris Fedorov's review, in his journal *St Petersburg Observer*, of Chapters Four and Five of *Eugene Onegin*, in which he objected to the fact that Pushkin called young noblewomen 'maidens', and a simple peasant girl 'a maid'

In 1830, when his love had finally turned to bitterness; and when, too, he was anxious to prove to his future wife – a beautiful girl, somewhat inclined to jealousy – that his former passion no longer existed, he caricatured Annette and her father in the draft version of a stanza in Chapter Eight of *Eugene Onegin*, calling her 'a sickly and hunchbacked doll', accompanied by 'her scoundrel father/A nothing on little legs'.[144]

He left Malinniki for Moscow in the first week of December 1828, and by the sixth was installed at the Hotel du Nord, on Glinishchevsky Lane, just off the Tverskaya. Pogodin called on him the next day, and was given the manuscript of *Poltava* in order to make a fair copy for submission to Nicholas. Pushkin gave a reading of the poem a little later at Sergey Kiselev's apartment on Povarskaya Street, in the presence of his host, Vyazemsky, Tolstoy the American, and a young army officer and amateur poet, Aleksandr Bashilov. The occasion was not an unqualified success: Bashilov 'got drunk at dinner and during the reading threw up nearly all over Tolstoy'.[145]

He remained in Moscow for a month; during this time, Vyazemsky told his wife, 'his most constant visits were to the [Rimsky]-Korsakovs and the gypsies'.[146] Now, as in 1826, the attraction at the Rimsky-Korsakovs was their daughter Aleksandra. In May 1827 she had been taken to the Caucasus by her mother, Mariya Ivanovna, to whom Pushkin had entrusted a letter for Lev, then serving in Georgia: 'My letter will be brought to you by M.I. Korsakova, an extraordinarily sweet representative of Moscow. Travel to the Caucasus and meet her – but please don't fall in love with her daughter.'[147] They had spent over a year in the Caucasus: 'The Korsakova woman hasn't had a single moment without an adventure,' wrote one Moscow gossip. 'Somewhere she was fallen on by hillmen and robbed to the skin; then some neutral prince [. . .] tried to carry Sasha [Aleksandra] off, and, having failed, asked for her hand, offering 300 thousand roubles immediately in earnest of a dowry.'[148]

The fashion of visiting the gypsy quarter of Gruziny – it lay just to the west of Tverskaya-Yamskaya Street, beyond the Triumphal Gate – to spend the night drinking, watching the dancing and listening to the singing had begun in the time of Catherine II. Noblemen and merchants spent vast sums on this amusement and on their gypsy mistresses – Nashchokin had one; Tolstoy the American married his. In 1820 Pushkin had urged his fellow-member of the *Green Lamp*, Vsevolozhsky, to visit the gypsies while in Moscow, tempting him by imagining the scene:

> ... the Egyptian maids
> Fly and twist before you;
> I sense their shrill songs,
> Moans of languor, wails, wild screams;
> Their frenzied movements,
> The fire of their furious eyes ...[149]

Now, and in the course of future visits, he got to know well the choir conductor, 'that old sod, Ilya the gypsy',[150] and one of the best-known singers, eighteen-year-old Tatyana Demyanova, whom Yazykov fell in love with two years later, dedicating several poems to her.

During this visit Pushkin saw little of Ekaterina Ushakova, to whom he had been so close during his previous stay: she now had an acknowledged suitor. 'Yesterday we had lunch at Vasily Lvovich's with the Ushakovas, the beauties of the Presnya, but do not imagine that this was a lunch for Aleksandr's engagement,' Vyazemsky wrote to his wife on 19 December. 'Although he might fall in love for auld lang syne, Gorchakov's Dolgoruky* is ensconced there and it looks very like a marriage.'[151] At the end of the month Pushkin paid five roubles for admission to a public ball in the Kologrivov mansion on the Tverskaya, organized by the well-known dancing master Petr Iogel (whose classes he had attended as a child), where he was entranced by the sight of a tall, auburn-haired vision in a simple white dress with a gold circlet in her hair. After learning that she was the sixteen-year-old Natalya Nikolaevna Goncharova, he asked Tolstoy the American, a close acquaintance of the family, to present him to her mother, Natalya Ivanovna. Though Pushkin did not know it at the time, he had a far better chance of success as a suitor with the Goncharovs than he had had with the Olenins. They did not belong to the old aristocracy; they did not occupy a high position in society, nor had they any influence within it – though Natalya's maternal great-aunt, Natalya Zagryazhskaya, *née* Countess Razumovskaya, a lady-in-waiting and Dame of the Order

---

* Aleksandr Dolgoruky (or Dolgorukov), a former officer, now a civil servant, and a minor writer. Vyazemsky's description is a reference to the fact that he was known to have enjoyed the patronage of Prince Gorchakov, the Minister of ...

of St Catherine, was still, as she had been since the time of Paul, a powerful figure at the court. But, despite this connection, the family was in decline, both socially and financially; and there was in addition something slightly louche about its recent history.

The Goncharovs had been tradespeople in Kaluga until the early eighteenth century. But during Peter the Great's reign Natalya's great-great-grandfather, Afanasy Abramovich, had made them rich and noble, setting up a canvas factory and paper mill on a river to the north-west of the town. Goncharov paper was considered to be the best in Russia, and he enjoyed a virtual monopoly in supplying Peter's new fleet with sailcloth. He died a multimillionaire, owning many factories and mills, and a host of estates – the chief of which, near the site of his first enterprise, was Polotnyany Zavod: the Canvas Factory. His son, Nikolay, died young, and the whole estate passed to his grandson, Afanasy Nikolaevich, who showed himself as adept in spending money as his grandfather had been in amassing it. When he died in 1832 he left debts of half a million roubles. He enlarged the mansion at Polotnyany Zavod and filled it with French furniture and Venetian glass; extended the park, adding bowers, grottoes and classical statues at every turn of the walks; built orangeries and pineries; and set up a stud farm, constructing an immense manège for the training and exhibition of his thoroughbreds. His only child, Natalya's father Nikolay, born in 1787, had artistic leanings and some musical talent. In 1804 he had joined the Foreign Ministry in St Petersburg.

Natalya Goncharova

On the maternal side Natalya's grandfather, Lieutenant-General Ivan Zagryazhsky, was a man of some eccentricity. While stationed at Dorpat he had an affair with the young Ulrike von Posse, who had been married at seventeen, but had left her husband four years later. When she became pregnant, he brought her back to his estate – Yaropolets, near Tver – and, abandoning her to the care of his wife, Aleksandra, settled permanently in Moscow. Ulrike gave birth to a daughter, Natalya, in 1785, and died six years later. Aleksandra Zagryazhskaya brought up Natalya as one of her own children. When she moved to St Petersburg to put her daughters – Sofya and Ekaterina – under the protection of her powerful sister-in-law, Natalya Kirillovna, she took Natalya with her; all three girls became maids-of-honour to the Empress Elizabeth, Alexander I's wife. Like her mother Ulrike, Natalya was a beauty; she caught the attention of the empress's lover, Aleksey Okhotnikov, an officer of the Chevalier Guards. He was murdered in October 1806, supposedly on the instance of the Grand Duke Constantine, and in January 1807 Natalya married Nikolay Goncharov. There is a hint of recompense for some undisclosed service in the nature of the wedding, whose brilliance seems inconsonant with the social position and birth of the bride and groom: it took place in the presence of the emperor, empress, dowager empress – who before the ceremony had adorned Natalya's bridal headdress with diamonds – two grand dukes, and two grand duchesses.

The couple moved to Moscow, where Nikolay became secretary to the governor. Meanwhile Afanasy Nikolaevich's wife, tiring of his extravagances, had left him. He went abroad for some years; during his absence Nikolay managed the factories and succeeded in repairing some of the damage done by his father. However, Afanasy returned in 1812, bringing with him a French mistress, Madame Babette, known in the family as 'the Parisian laundress'. For some time the whole family lived together at Polotnyany Zavod, but then Afanasy took business affairs wholly into his own hands, and Nikolay, together with his wife and six children – Dmitry, Ekaterina, Ivan, Aleksandra, Natalya and Sergey – moved back to Moscow. Here they settled in a large house which, with its outbuildings, gardens and grounds, occupied nearly a block on Nikitskaya Street, beyond the Nikitsky Gate. At this time Nikolay began to show signs of mental instability, though he seems not to have been clinically insane, as was previously thought, but was rather an alcoholic depressive. Whatever the cause, he ceased to appear in society, and took no further part in business or family affairs. Such was the state of the family when Pushkin made their acquaintance. For the moment he took matters no further.

11

COURTSHIP
1828–31

> I am marrying, that is, I am sacrificing
> independence, my carefree, capricious independence,
> my luxurious habits, aimless journeyings, my
> solitude, my inconstancy.
>
> (VIII, 406)

O N 5 JANUARY 1829 Pushkin left Moscow for St Petersburg. At Tver he turned off the main road and drove to Malinniki, where he found Vulf and a house full of girls. 'I concluded an offensive and defensive alliance with him against the beauties,' Vulf noted, 'as a result of which my sisters called him Mephistopheles and me Faust. But Gretchen (Katenka Velyasheva), despite Mephistopheles' advice and Faust's wooing, remained cold: all our efforts were in vain.' The two set out together for St Petersburg on the evening of the sixteenth. 'At the post-stations, while the horses were being changed, we played chess, and while travelling spoke of contemporary domestic events, of literature, life, women, love and so on. Pushkin speaks very well; his ardent perceptive mind grasps subjects rapidly; but these very qualities can cause his judgement of matters to be superficial and one-sided. He gets to know the characters of the people he meets extraordinarily quickly; and no one knows women as he does. Because of this, without possessing any external advantages, which always influence the fair sex, he gains their favours by his brilliant wit alone.' They arrived in the capital at eight in the evening on the eighteenth, and drove straight to Andrieu's restaurant on the Malaya Morskaya, where 'all the people of the best *ton* dine'.[1]

Paul's widow, the dowager empress Mariya Fedorovna, had died the previous October, and three months of strict mourning had been observed in court circles in St Petersburg. This came to an end just after Pushkin's arrival, when the first dance of the season was given by Elise Khitrovo. A nineteen-year-old maid of honour, Aleksandra Rosset, whose black eyes had charmed Vyazemsky the previous year, was among the guests. 'Elise behaved abominably, she wore a white dress, very décolleté;* her plump shoulders were fully exposed; on her index finger she wore the ribbon of St George and Field-Marshal Kutuzov's watch and kept saying: "He wore this at Borodino". Pushkin was at this dance and stood in a corner behind the other gentlemen. We were all in black dresses. I said to Stephanie:† "I terribly want to dance with Pushkin." "All right, I will choose him in the mazurka," and she did in fact go up to him. Abandoning his hat he followed her. He could not dance. Then I chose him and asked: "Which flower will you have?" "That

Aleksandra Rosset

which is your colour" was the answer, which sent us into raptures. Elise went into the drawing-room, graciously lay down on the sofa and summoned Pushkin.'[2]

Aleksandra was the daughter of an Italian, who, after serving in the Russian army, had worked as a civil servant under Richelieu in Odessa. He died in 1813, and his half-Prussian, half-Georgian widow soon married again. Her second husband managed through his connections to avoid the expense of educating his stepchildren: the four boys were enrolled in the Corps-des-Pages, while Aleksandra became a boarder in the Catherine Institute for daughters of the nobility. By her attainments there she attracted the attention of the dowager empress, the institute's patron, who secured her a place at court. 'At that time in St Petersburg there bloomed a certain maiden, and all of us, more or less, were prisoners-of-war of this beauty [. . .] Some one among us called the dark, southern, black-eyed beauty Doña Sol – the chief personage in Hugo's Spanish

---

* She should still have been in mourning, as were the maids-of-honour.
† Stephanie Radziwill, another maid of honour

drama,'* Vyazemsky wrote.[3] He was soon one of her most devoted captives. 'We are spending this summer in Reval,' Sofya Karamzina wrote to a friend in April 1829, 'and I have a premonition that Vyazemsky will visit us there, all the more since with us is travelling that clever sweet maid-of-honour, Rosset, whom last year he could only go and admire in the theatre. What will it be like to live in the same house as her!'[4] She was undoubtedly beautiful: small and dark, with delicate features and immense black eyes. At the same time she had extraordinary vivacity and charm, was highly intelligent, witty and amazingly well-read – though there was not the slightest hint of a blue-stocking about her. 'Her modest maid of honour's cell on the fourth floor of the Winter Palace became the scene of a constant assembly of all the celebrities of the literary world of that time.'[5] Among these literary admirers, all of whom addressed verses to her, were, besides Vyazemsky, Zhukovsky – who called her a 'heavenly little devil' and offered for her hand, though he was forty-six to her nineteen – Vasily Tumansky, Khomyakov, Sobolevsky and, in later years, Lermontov. She cut an equally wide swathe at court, where her conquests included the Grand Duke Michael and even, it was rumoured, Nicholas himself.

Pushkin and she became close friends, and he saw much of her in Tsarskoe Selo and St Petersburg until 1835, when her diplomat husband, Nikolay Smirnov – they had married in 1832 – was posted to the Russian embassy in Berlin. But there is not a hint of anything more intimate in their relationship, despite the later suspicions of Pushkin's wife: 'I am not making love to [Countess Nadezhda] Sollogub, as Christ is my witness; nor to Smirnova either,' he reassured her in May 1834, adding, to allay any doubt, 'Smirnova is terribly big with child and will give birth in a month.'[6] Nor did Pushkin ever consider her as a possible wife. Given his susceptibility to beauty, this indifference is odd: but a trait that for her admirers gave an added, irresistible piquancy to her seductiveness left him unaffected. 'That inaccessible atmosphere of chastity, modesty, that fragrance that surrounds a beautiful woman, never surrounded her, even in the bloom of her youth,' one captive noted. Vyazemsky enlarges the comment, writing: 'Women usually have a poor understanding of lowness and vulgarity; she understood them

---

* Victor Hugo's play *Hernani* (1830).

and rejoiced in them, as long as, of course, they were not lowly low and vulgarly vulgar.'[7] While she was the most attractive of companions, with whom he could, as with Vyazemsky or Sobolevsky, crack a salacious joke, or enjoy risqué literature,* Pushkin did not consider her as a possible mistress, still less a wife.

However, he did not remain long in Petersburg. When Ivanovsky had come to see him the preceding spring to discuss his petitions to accompany the army or go to France, he had – so Pushkin believed, or affected to believe – implicitly given him Benckendorff's permission to travel to the Caucasus and join Paskevich's army. Pushkin now made use of it. On 4 March the St Petersburg postal director Konstantin Bulgakov gave him a travel warrant for the journey from St Petersburg to Tiflis and back. The following day he left St Petersburg for Moscow, where he put up at the Hotel du Nord. He had been meditating the trip for some time: the previous May Vyazemsky had written to his wife: 'Pushkin is going to the Caucasus and further, if he succeeds.'[8] Vyazemsky may merely be referring to an intention to follow the army into Turkey; but he could be hinting at a crackbrained scheme that Pushkin had concocted – as impractical as, and even more nebulous than those he had hatched with Vulf at Mikhailovskoe – to escape from Russia by crossing into Persia and making his way to Tabriz, not far from the frontier, where he would find several Western diplomatic missions. Russians were, however, not popular in Persia at that time, and recent events in Teheran – Moscow was talking of nothing else – might have given him pause. Griboedov had returned to Persia in September, stopping in Tiflis to marry Princess Nina Chavchavadze. On 30 January, urged on by the mullahs, a crowd of fanatical Moslems, whose fury at the exactions necessary to pay the indemnity to Russia stipulated by the Treaty of Turkmenchay was further exacerbated by the fact that Griboedov had given asylum to three Christians (two Armenian women from the harem of the Shah's son-in-law, and a Georgian eunuch of

---

* In 1836–7 she had a passionate affair with Nikolay Kiselev, earlier Annette Olenina's suitor. Once, when they were in Baden together, he asked her: 'Have you ever read Les historiettes galantes of Tallemant des Réaux?' 'Of course,' she replied, 'and they gave me great pleasure, especially "The Answers of M. Cosmus", and I know "The Story of an Infantry Captain". It was Pushkin who pointed them out to me, as well as the works of Rivarol, Chamfort and Voltaire's Tales' (Smirnova-Rosset, 487).

the Shah's harem), broke into the Russian mission in Teheran and slaughtered all those present save one: the young secretary to the legation, Ivan Maltsov. Griboedov's body was so mutilated that it could only be recognized by the crooked little finger, wounded in a duel with Yakubovich in 1818.

'You probably know that at the present moment Pushkin is clambering about the Caucasus,' Sofya Karamzina informed the Vyazemskys on 20 March. 'That is the latest lunacy that has entered his head.'[9] In fact, he was still in Moscow, and that evening had called with Wiegel on Aleksandr Bulgakov, the brother of the St Petersburg postal director. They spent a very pleasant evening, had supper with the family, and did not leave until two in the morning. 'He admired the

Griboedov

children and Katya's singing; she sang two of his poems, set to music by Genishta and Titov,' Bulgakov wrote to his brother. 'He is travelling to Paskevich's army to experience the horrors of war, will serve as a volunteer, perhaps, and will sing of all this. "Oh, don't go!" Katya said to him: "Griboedov was killed there." "Don't worry, madam: is it likely they will kill two Aleksandr Sergeevichs in the same year? One is enough!" But Lelka paid him a fine compliment. "Byron went to Greece and died there; don't go to Persia, one similarity with Byron is sufficient." Well said, my little Snub-nose! Pushkin was struck by this consideration.'*[10]

He had been elected – also on 20 March – to the Moscow English Club, which had its premises in a mansion on the Bolshaya Dmitrovka.† It was a more high-minded institution than its St Petersburg brother: Nicholas was wont to enquire what the club's opinion on some new government measure might be; while Wiegel wrote sarcastically: 'A member of the Moscow English Club! O, that is a creature of a completely special kind, which has not its like either in Russia, or any other

---

* Katya and Lelka are Bulgakov's two daughters: Katerina, just nineteen, and fifteen-year-old Olga. Griboedov and Pushkin had the same Christian name and patronymic.
† In April 1831 it moved to the Razumovsky palace on the Tverskaya.

land. The chief, distinguishing trait of its character is confidence in its own omniscience.'[11] Pletnev wrote to congratulate him on his election, sending ten copies of *Poltava*, which he had just seen through the press.

'A. Pushkin's new poem has come out, but with the title "Poltava", not "Mazepa",' Vasily Lvovich told Vyazemsky. 'I think that A. Pushkin was mistaken in changing the title, but, all the same, his poem is an excellent work.'[12] Pushkin had first been fascinated by the story of the Ukrainian hetman in 1824, when he had read Ryleev's *Voinarovsky* and vainly sought Mazepa's grave in Charles XII's camp at Varnitsa. His increasing preoccupation with history had rekindled the interest; in Mazepa he saw a figure very like that of the protagonist of his historical drama *Boris Godunov*: a ruthless and cunning intriguer who, in his quest for power, commits crimes that return to haunt him. The attempt in the poem to blend three different genres: the romantic tale, the historical epic and – in the description of Peter at Poltava – the triumphal ode is not, perhaps, wholly successful, yet at the same time the language – often consciously archaic, and very different from the lighter style of *Onegin* or *Count Nulin* – is more powerful and compelling than in any of his previous narrative poems. The portrayal of Peter is particularly of note.

> From his tent
> Surrounded by a crowd of favourites,
> Emerges Peter. His eyes
> Shine. His countenance is terrible.
> Movements rapid. He is splendid,
> In all he is like the wrath of God!
> (III, 182)[13]

He is the avatar of kingship, devoid of human traits, semi-divine. Here for the first time the Petrine theme – one of the most important in Pushkin's work – is given full expression. Pushkin was surprised by the poem's reception: 'Poltava, which Zhukovsky, Gnedich, Delvig, Vyazemsky preferred to everything I had written up to then, was not a success,' he wrote later. 'Perhaps it did not deserve to be, but I was spoilt by the reception given to my earlier, much weaker compositions.'[14] Indeed, his honeymoon with the critics was now over. The reception given to *Poltava* foreshadowed the even more hostile reception of succeeding works.

Though he had left St Petersburg for the south with some precipitancy, he dallied for nearly two months in Moscow before continuing his journey. He gave various reasons for his procrastination: sometimes the state of the roads, sometimes illness. In fact, he had fallen in love once again – with Natalya Goncharova, whom he was pursuing tenaciously. The Ushakova girls saw much of him at this time: partly, perhaps, because the route to their house took Pushkin past Natalya's windows. Ekaterina's suitor, Dolgorukov, was no longer in evidence, and her relationship with Pushkin had modulated into one of affectionate friendship – he gave her an inscribed copy of *Poltava*. Nevertheless, her magnanimity was tried when Pushkin, with characteristic tactlessness, dilated on Natalya's physical attractions, or discussed at length the chances of his success. The three turned his pursuit into a joke, referring to Natalya as 'Kars', after the reputedly impregnable Turkish fortress. Still, despite its reputation, Paskevich had taken it the previous June, so there might yet be hope for Pushkin. On 1 May he put his fortunes to the test when, on his behalf, Count Tolstoy the American asked Natalya Ivanovna for her daughter's hand in marriage. 'Pushkin was not directly refused, but the response was that one should wait and see, that their daughter was still too young and so on.'[15] He penned an ecstatic letter to Natalya Ivanovna:

> I should write to you on my knees, shedding tears of gratitude, now that Count Tolstoy has brought me your response: this response is not a refusal, you allow me hope. However, if I still murmur, if sadness and bitterness mix with my feelings of happiness, do not accuse me of ingratitude; I understand the prudence and tenderness of a Mother! – But pardon the impatience of a sick heart, drunk with happiness. I leave instantly, I take with me in the depths of my soul the image of that celestial being who owes her existence to you.[16]

He kept his word, and left that night. On the way south he made a detour through Kaluga and Belev to call on General Ermolov, the former commander-in-chief in the Caucasus, whose estate was near Orel. In the epilogue to *The Prisoner of the Caucasus* Pushkin had praised Ermolov for his ruthless pacification of the region. Now, on meeting him, he was impressed by his appearance: 'a tiger's head on Hercules's torso'.[17] From

Orel Pushkin rejoined the main road south, and, passing through Elets and Voronezh, arrived in Novocherkassk a few days later. Here, to his delight, he met two St Petersburg acquaintances, who were also travelling to Tiflis: Count Vladimir Musin-Pushkin and his Swedish brother-in-law, Baron Emil Stjernvall-Walleen.* Pushkin was happy to join them, all the more as they were travelling in some luxury. Their conveyance was an immense britzka belonging to Musin-Pushkin, 'a kind of fortified settlement, which we have named *Comfort*. In its northern quarter wines and provisions are stored. In the southern – books, greatcoats, hats etc., etc. On the east and west it is defended by guns, pistols, musketoons, sabres and the like. At each post-station a portion of the northern supplies is unloaded, and so we could not pass the time in better fashion.'[18]

Ermolov

While *Comfort*'s horses were being changed at a post-station on the road to Stavropol, Pushkin wandered into a Kalmyk encampment and entered one of their tents: 'A young Kalmyk girl, very far from bad-looking, was sewing and smoking tobacco. A dark, ruddy face. Crimson lips, pearl-like teeth. [...] "What are you sewing?" "Trousers." "For whom?" "For me." "Kiss me." "I can't, I'm shy." Her voice was extraordinarily pleasant. She gave me her pipe and began to eat with all her family. Tea with mutton fat and salt was boiling in the pot. I don't believe any nation's cuisine can produce anything filthier. She offered me her ladle – I did not have the strength to refuse. I drank it down, trying not to breathe – asked for something to eat with it – and was given a piece of dried horse-flesh. I swallowed this with great pleasure. After this exploit I thought I had a right to a reward. But my proud beauty hit me over the head with a musical weapon, similar to our balalaikas. Tiring of Kalmyk hospitality, I left the tent and drove on.'[19]

On 13 May they entered Georgievsk. Pushkin spent the next day

* The Stjernvall-Walleen sisters, Aurore and Emilie, were celebrated beauties. Aurore, to whom Baratynsky and Vyazemsky addressed poems, married the millionaire P.N. Demidov, and, after his death, Karamzin's son Andrey. Emilie, after whom Pushkin was to dangle in the 1830s, was Musin-Pushkin's wife; his elder brother Ivan had married Mariya Urusova, who had been the object of Pushkin's admiration in Moscow in 1827.

re-visiting the spa at Pyatigorsk, where he had stayed with the Raevskys in 1820. By the sixteenth they were in Ekaterinograd, where they had to wait for an escort along the Georgian military highway. 'Our caravan, consisting of about 500 people, collected at the assembly point. The drum began to beat, and we set off. In front travelled a cannon, surrounded by foot soldiers – its match was lit, and they kindled their pipes at it – and after it came a procession of coaches, britzkas, and the waggons of soldiers' wives, moving from one fortress to another, and behind them squeaked an endless string of two-wheeled carts. At either side were herds of horse and oxen, and about them galloped guides in felt cloaks with shaggy caps and lassos.'[20] In Vladikavkaz, which they reached on 21 May, the cannon was left behind, as the road began to rise into the mountains. They stopped for the night in Lars, where Pushkin discovered a manuscript copy of *A Prisoner of the Caucasus*: he read it, he confessed, with pleasure – it was undoubtedly immature, but he had managed to capture the manners and scenery of the region. Near the village of Kazbek they met a carriage with a military escort. Its occupant was the Persian court poet Fazil Khan, the vanguard of an embassy sent by the Shah from Teheran to apologize for the sacking of the Russian mission, and to make some recompense for the deaths of Griboedov and his colleagues. The Shah's sixteen-year-old grandson, Khusrau Mirza, headed the embassy; he carried with him as gifts eighteen books for the St Petersburg library and a famous Indian diamond of 88 carats, known as the 'Shah'. The officer commanding the escort made the two poets known to one another. 'Through the interpreter I was beginning a high-flown Eastern greeting, partly carried away by my innate sense of mockery. But how ashamed I was, when Fazil Khan answered my inappropriate intricacies simply, with the wit and courtesy of a decent man.'*[21]

The following day they began the climb to the summit of the Krestovy Pass, the highest point of the road. For the ascent a team of oxen

---

* Fazil Khan, Khusrau Mirza's tutor, was not an official member of the embassy and hence was travelling separately. In 1830 the almanac *Snowdrop* contained a 'Translation of an ode, composed in St Petersburg by Fazil Khan, the poet of Prince Khusrau Mirza, for presentation to His Majesty the Emperor'; in the same year Count Khvostov published in the *Neva Almanac* a poetic epistle, 'To Fazil Khan. On the occasion of Robertson's balloon ascent, at which the author chanced to be together with the Persian poet'.

had to be harnessed to Musin-Pushkin's britzka. Preferring not to wait, Pushkin mounted a horse and rode up through the snow, accompanied by Colonel Ogarev, the engineer in charge of repairs to the military highway. Passing the granite cross on the summit, erected as a memorial to Peter the Great, he began the descent into the valley of the Aragva in Georgia, when 'a breath of the fragrant South suddenly begins to waft over the traveller'.[22] Between Pasanauri and Ananuri he passed the main body of the Persian embassy, and arrived in Tiflis shortly before midnight on the twenty-seventh. None of his friends was in Tiflis; they were all with their regiments in Turkey. He wrote to Nikolay Raevsky, asking him to get Paskevich's permission to join the army, and eventually left Tiflis on 10 June. He spent that night at a Cossack post. The following day, according to the account of his travels he wrote in 1835 – *A Journey to Erzerum during the Campaign of 1829* – after crossing a stream near the fortress of Gergery, he had a noteworthy encounter 'immortalized in one of the most famous images in Russian literature'.[23] 'Two oxen, harnessed to a cart, were coming up the steep road. A few Georgians accompanied the cart. "Where are you from?" I asked them. "From Teheran." "What are you conveying?" "*Griboed.*" It was the body of the murdered Griboedov, which they were taking to Tiflis.'[24]

The image is, however, fictional: the cortège – of which Pushkin gives an inaccurate description – had passed through Gergery several weeks earlier. Nowhere in Pushkin's work or his correspondence, other than here, in the *Journey to Erzerum*, composed six years later, can be found any mention of this dramatic and remarkably coincidental encounter with the body of his dead friend – the most striking event of the journey.*

On the thirteenth Pushkin caught up with the army beyond Kars; it was advancing towards Erzerum. He had a joyful reunion with his brother and with Nikolay Raevsky, whom he had not seen since the Crimea. That evening Raevsky presented him to Paskevich, who welcomed him warmly: he hoped that his brilliant campaign would be immortalized in verse. He was to be disappointed. 'The mellifluous lyres

---

* 'It is not important whether this meeting with Griboedov's body was real, or whether it was an artistic construction, brilliantly executed by Pushkin. Readers are convinced that the meeting took place, and the researcher should not destroy great illusions, but has the duty to remind the . . . that of poets in Russia' (Мурьянова, 11.)

of our best poets have long ceased to resound in praise of feats of arms,' he wrote plaintively to Zhukovsky in 1831. 'So the brightness of the memorable events of the Persian and Turkish wars has grown dim.'[25]

Other friends were to be found in the camp. Vladimir Volkhovsky, a fellow-pupil at the Lycée, was now a colonel and the expedition's quartermaster-general: they met immediately after Pushkin's arrival, when, bearded and covered with dust, Volkhovsky stopped for a moment's conversation. Among Raevsky's officers was a gaming acquaintance, Rufin Dorokhov, whom Pushkin had known in St Petersburg before exile. A notorious hothead, he had been reduced to the ranks for brawling, duelling and wearing civilian dress, but had recently regained his commission for his reckless bravery in action. And Pushkin was particularly pleased to see again, for the first time since 1820, Mikhail Pushchin, the younger brother of his bosom friend at the Lycée. Though, unlike Ivan, Pushchin had not been a Decembrist, he had had some knowledge of the conspiracy. For this he had been stripped of his rank and posted, as a private, first to Siberia and then to the Army of the Caucasus. He had a brilliant military mind and made himself indispensable to Paskevich during the Persian and Turkish campaigns, conducting the army's reconnaissance, and planning its line of march. Badly wounded at the storming of the Turkish fortress at Akhalzikhe the previous August, he had just been promoted lieutenant.

But Pushkin had not travelled to Turkey to renew old acquaintanceships: he thirsted for martial glory, or at least the experience of war. His wishes were fulfilled on the day after his arrival, as the official history of the campaign records:

The skirmish of 14 June 1829 is remarkable because our famous poet A.S. Pushkin took part in it [. . .] When the troops, having completed an arduous march, were resting in the Inzha-Su valley, the enemy suddenly attacked our forward line. The poet, hearing in his proximity for the first time the sounds of war, could not restrain a surge of enthusiasm. In a poetic impulse he immediately sprang out of the headquarters, mounted a horse, and in a minute was among the outposts. Major Semichev, an experienced officer whom General Raevsky dispatched in pursuit of the poet, had difficulty in overtaking him, and was obliged to remove him forcibly from the Cossack front line just as Pushkin, animated by that courage so characteristic of a new recruit, seizing a lance from one of the dead Cossacks, galloped against the enemy cavalry. It can be imagined how extremely astonished our men of the Don were, seeing before them an unknown hero in a cloak and a round hat.[26]

self-portrait

This was, however, his first and last experience of battle. The Turkish army retreated steadily before Paskevich, and on 27 June yielded Erzerum without offering resistance.

Pushkin had enjoyed the life of the camp – 'A cannon-shot would wake us at daybreak. Sleep in a tent is remarkably healthy. At dinner we washed down our Asiatic shashlyk with English beer or champagne cooled in the snows of the Taurus'[27] – and was sorry to leave it. He moved into the rooms recently occupied by the harem of the Seraskier, the Turkish commander-in-chief, and occupied himself in sight-seeing. Osman Pasha, a Turkish notable and a prisoner in Tiflis, in a letter to Paskevich had expressed concern as to the safety of his harem. When Paskevich sent an officer to investigate, Pushkin accompanied him, and saw 'five or six round heads with black inquisitive eyes' gazing at him from a high window. Though all were pleasant-looking, he was disappointed that none was a beauty. The interpreter on the visit was a Russian officer with an unusual history. At eighteen he had been captured by the Persians, castrated, and had served for twenty years as a eunuch in the harem of one of the Shah's sons. 'He spoke of his misfortunes, of his life in Persia with touching simplicity,' Pushkin noted. 'His testimony was invaluable from a physiological point of view.'[28]

Plague had broken out in the town, and Pushkin determined to bring his stay to an end. On 18 July Paskevich gave a farewell dinner in his honour, and presented him with a Turkish sabre. By 10 August he was in Vladikavkaz once more. Here, waiting for the convoy, he found Pushchin and Dorokhov on their way to the Caucasian spas. After he had given Pushchin a pledge not to play cards while they were in company, the three set off together. They spent the journey companionably drinking their way through a case of hock given to Pushkin by Raevsky. No sooner had they arrived in Pyatigorsk than Pushkin sat down to faro with Dorokhov and a chance-met officer in the Pavlovsky Life Guards, Vladimir Astafev. The gamblers were later joined by Vasily Durov, the mayor of the small town of Sarapul, halfway between Kazan and Perm – an odd character, full of fantastic schemes for making money, who amused and astonished Pushkin with stories of his adventures. A few days later Pushkin – penniless, having lost all his money to Astafev – turned up at Pushchin's lodgings in Kislovodsk. He stayed for nearly a month. Borrowing money for travel, he eventually left in the second week of September taking Durov with him. From Novocherkassk he wrote back to Pushchin to tell him that Durov had turned out to be a cheat; that he had lost 5,000 roubles to him, which he had had to borrow from the ataman of the Don Cossacks; and that he was abandoning him and going on to Moscow alone.

The emperor first learnt of Pushkin's journey from the *Tiflis Gazette*, which on 28 June devoted an article to the poet's stay in the city. Years later Nicholas was still incensed by this exhibition of what he considered to be gross ingratitude: Pushkin had promised to reform, but immediately afterwards 'galloped off to the Caucasus without my knowledge or my permission!'[29] He dictated a resolution that Benckendorff took down in pencil. '[Pushkin] is to be asked who gave him permission to go to Erzerum, firstly it is beyond the frontier and secondly he has forgotten that he must inform me in advance of everything that he does at least as far as travelling is concerned this means that the next time he will be assigned a residence.' The last words are a threat to confine him again, as at Mikhailovskoe. On 1 October Benckendorff wrote to General Strekalov in Tiflis ordering him to interrogate Pushkin, adding that he should not omit to remark that 'this behaviour could be considered wilfulness and could attract disadvantageous attention'.[30] But by this time Pushkin had long since left the Caucasus. He arrived in Moscow on 20 September, and took rooms at the Hotel d'Angleterre, just off Tverskaya Street. Learning this, Benckendorff repeated the questions in a letter of 14 October, which, however, did not catch up with Pushkin until November, when he was in St Petersburg. On 10 November he produced an obsequious apology. He did not explain why he had travelled to Tiflis; once there, however, he wrote, 'I could not resist the desire to see my brother who is serving in the Nizhny Novgorod dragoons and from whom I had been separated for five years.' He therefore obtained permission to join the army from Nikolay Raevsky, 'a friend of my childhood'. After these two specious statements – he had spent several days with Lev two years earlier; he was at least fifteen when he first met Raevsky – he concluded: 'I am conscious how false my position was and how foolish my behaviour, but at least there was nothing in it but foolishness. The idea that it could be attributed to any other motive would be unbearable. I would rather suffer the most severe disfavour than seem an ingrate in the eyes of him to whom I owe everything, to whom I am ready to sacrifice my existence, and this is no mere phrase.'[31]

It was generally thought that Pushkin's journey to Erzerum had been prompted by the desire to collect material for his next work. The *Tiflis Gazette*, remarking that Pushkin's visit to the Caucasus had produced *The Prisoner of the Caucasus*, and that to the Crimea *The Fountain of Bakhchisaray*, continued: 'Now our reading public unites the pleasantest of expectations with A. Pushkin's sojourn in the camp of the Caucasian warriors* and asks: what will our beloved poet, the witness of bloody battles, bestow on us from the military camp?'[32] Like Paskevich, the reading public was to be disappointed. Pushkin's journey resulted in no triumphal odes or lengthy military epics, but only – with the exception of a poem addressed to Natalya Goncharova, 'On the hills of Georgia lies night's darkness . . .'[33] – in two or three slight and unimportant lyrics. Several critics voiced their disillusionment. Bulgarin's *Northern Bee* – which was conducting a feud with Pushkin at the time – began a review of the seventh chapter of *Eugene Onegin*: 'And so our hopes have vanished. We thought that the author of Ruslan and Lyudmila had hastened to the Caucasus to slake his thirst with the sublime emotions of Poetry, to enrich himself with new impressions and in sweet verses to transmit to posterity the great exploits of the modern Russian heroes. We thought that the great events in the East, astonishing the world and winning for Russia the respect of all civilized nations, would awaken

---

* A reference to Zhukovsky's poem on the campaign of 1812, 'A Bard in the Camp of Russian Warriors'

the genius of our Poets – but we were mistaken! The celebrated lyres have remained silent, and in the desert of our poetry Onegin has appeared again, wan, weak.'[34]

The hoped-for work did not appear until 1836, and was not verse, but prose – the *Journey to Erzerum*. In other respects, too, it was not what his readers might have expected. Though a brilliant and original piece of travel writing, it was wholly unconventional, a world apart from the official history of the war. Pushkin does not scruple to play with reality, and depicts the hostilities in episodic, fragmentary form, portraying himself as an uncomprehending innocent wandering over the battlefield, adumbrating Stendhal's description of Fabrice del Dongo at Waterloo in *The Charterhouse of Parma*, or Tolstoy's of Pierre Bezukhov at Borodino in *War and Peace*. Of an action on 19 July he writes: 'The regiments formed up; the officers placed themselves at the head of their platoons. I remained alone, not knowing which way to ride, and let my horse go as it pleased. I met General Burtsov, who summoned me to the left flank. What is the left flank? I thought, and rode on.' And, rather than picking out the glorious and the heroic, he delights in the comic and surreal. A party of Armenians come to ask for assistance against the Turks, who have driven off their cattle. 'Colonel Anrep, not fully understanding what they wanted, imagined a Turkish force was in the hills, and with one squadron of the Uhlan regiment galloped off in that direction, informing Raevsky that there were 3,000 Turks in the hills. Raevsky set off after him, in order to reinforce him in case of danger. I considered myself attached to the Nizhny Novgorod Regiment, and with great annoyance galloped to the relief of the Armenians. Having travelled some 20 versts, we rode into a village and saw several laggard uhlans, who, dismounted, with naked swords, were pursuing a number of chickens. Here one of the villagers explained to Raevsky that it was a matter of 3,000 head of cattle, which the Turks had driven away two days before.'[35]

Immediately on arrival in Moscow, Pushkin hurried round to the Goncharovs. He found the children at breakfast, but Natalya refused to see him without her mother, who was still asleep. He returned at a more conventional hour, and in the course of the next two weeks called on them repeatedly. However, he spent most of his time at the Ushakovs, where the company was infinitely more amusing and more pleasant. He told the sisters of his travels and adventures, illustrating them in Elizaveta's album with drawings of people in Eastern dress. In it he sketched a view of Erzerum, adding the inscription: 'Erzerum, taken – another hand has here inserted "by me A.P." – with the help of God and the prayers of Ekaterina Nikolaevna on the 27 June in the year of our Lord 1829.'[36] He poked affectionate fun at Elizaveta, who the following April was to be married to Colonel Sergey Kiselev, by punning on the name of her fiancé – *kisa* in Russian means pussy-cat – and making several drawings of her accompanied by a large fat cat. In one Elizaveta, wearing a married lady's cap and spectacles, is singing the aria 'Una voce poco fa' from Rossini's *Barber of Seville*, while the cat, also in spectacles, conducts from the top of her music stand. Behind her are four more cats, of graduated size, their tails to the spectator – presumably the couple's progeny. On two separate pages of the album he wrote down in pencil two lists of women's names – one sixteen names long, the other twenty-one – the so-called Don Juan list of his past loves. The shorter list – perhaps that of the more serious involvements – ends with the name Natalya.[37] He kept the sisters informed on the progress, or otherwise, of his wooing, and complained to them about the difficulties of dealing with Natalya Ivanovna, his beloved's mother. In Elizaveta's

Natalya's mother

album he drew a large portrait of her with a severe, frowning black face; underneath Elizaveta has written 'Mamma Kars'. In fact, the courtship was going very badly. 'What torments awaited me on my return!' Pushkin wrote to Natalya Ivanovna the following spring. 'Your silence, your cold air, Mademoiselle Natalie's welcome, so indifferent, so inattentive ... I did not have the courage to speak out, I left for Petersburg with death in my soul.'[38]

The despondency was short-lived. Setting out for St Petersburg on 12 October, he turned off again to Malinniki, where he found Annette Vulf by herself, nursing a head cold and reading the Irish poet Thomas Moore. Together they sent a jocosely facetious letter, with suggestive overtones, to her brother Aleksey. He stayed some days with Annette's uncle, Pavel Vulf, at Pavlovskoe. Here, on 2 November, he wrote 'Winter. What can we do in the country?'

> I greet
> The servant who brings me a morning cup of tea
> With questions: is there a thaw? has the storm subsided?
> Is there powder-snow or not? and can one leave
> The bed for the saddle.

He rides out; the dogs catch two hares; but on his return excruciating boredom sets in, only relieved by the appearance of a neighbour and her two daughters:

> in the dusk the girl comes out on the porch:
> Neck and breast are open, and the blizzard in her face!
> But northern storms do not harm the Russian rose.
> How ardently burns a kiss in the frost!
> How fresh is a Russian maiden in the snow dust![39]

Netty Vulf, 'tender, languorous, hysterical, *plumper Netty*', whom in 1825 Pushkin regretted 'having seen, and even more not having possessed', was by herself on her parents' neighbouring estate, Bernovo.[40] He visited her there, and expunged the previous regrets. 'I am astonished at the graciousness with which Netty is exercising the rights of hostess at Bernovo,' Aleksey Vulf wrote to Annette. 'It would be impossible to extend hospitality to one's guests further than she has done.'[41]

During Pushkin's absence Elise Khitrovo's younger daughter, Dolly, had arrived in St Petersburg with her husband, Count Ficquelmont, the newly appointed Austrian ambassador. Her salon in the embassy on Dvortsovaya Embankment was soon as well-known as that of her mother. Elise Khitrovo's 'mornings (which in fact took place between one and four in the afternoon) and the evenings of her daughter, Countess Ficquelmont, are ineradicably engraved in the memory of those who had the good fortune to participate in them', Vyazemsky wrote. 'The whole of European and Russian topical life, political, literary and social, was echoed in these two related salons [...] One could gain information on all the questions of the day, beginning with a political brochure and a speech in parliament by a French or English orator, and ending with a novel or dramatic work by one of the favourites of that literary epoch. [...] And what was best of all, this universal, oral, conversational newspaper was given its direction and edited by two dear, sweet women.'[42] Dolly and Pushkin met on 10 December, when he attended a large dinner at the embassy. 'The author Pushkin converses in a charming manner – without pretension, with fire and emotion – one could not be more ugly – he is a mixture of the physiognomy of a monkey and a tiger,* he is descended from an African race – there are still some hints of it in his eye and there is something savage about his look,' she noted in her diary.[43]

At this time St Petersburg was celebrating the successful conclusion of the war with Turkey: by the Treaty of Adrianople Russia had made territorial gains in the Caucasus and at the mouth of the Danube; had been given full liberty for navigation and commerce in the Black Sea; and the autonomy, under Ottoman suzerainty, of Serbia, Moldavia and Wallachia had been confirmed. The crown princes of both Prussia and Sweden spent the winter in the capital, and were present at one of the most glittering events: a costume ball on 4 January at the Anichkov Palace, at which – according to the French chargé d'affaires, Baron Bourgouin – 'the gods and goddesses of Olympus appeared, the first in rich and elegant costumes, the second in comic attire. Russian or French verses were recited or sung by these allegorical figures,' who addressed themselves to the empress.[44] Dolly's sister, Countess Ekaterina Tiesenhausen, was to appear as Cyclops, and turned to Pushkin for a suitable verse. Sending her a neatly turned trifle, he added: 'You will, of course, Countess, be a true Cyclops. Accept this platitude as a proof of my perfect submission to your orders. If I had a hundred heads and a hundred hearts, they would all be at your service.'[45] Dolly was disappointed by the spectacle, though 'Cathérine as Cyclops and Annette Tolstaya† as Neptune were both delicious'.[46]

Soon Pushkin was automatically included in the revels. 'We will definitely make our *masked* expedition tomorrow evening – we will

---

* This description goes back to Pushkin's days at the Lycée; in the protocol of the Lycée anniversary meeting on 19 October 1828 he refers to himself as 'Pushkin the Frenchman (a mixture of a monkey and a tiger)' (*Rukoyu Pushkina*, 733). He had, presumably, thus characterized himself to Dolly in the course of their conversation.

assemble at 9 at mamma's,' Dolly wrote on 11 January. 'Come there with a *black domino* and a *black mask* – we will not need your carriage, but we will need your servant – ours would be recognized. We count on your wit, dear M. Pushkin, to animate all this. You will have supper afterwards with us and then I will renew my thanks.'[47] Afterwards she noted in her diary: 'Yesterday the 12th we gave ourselves the pleasure of going in dominoes and masks to different houses, there were eight of us, Mamma, Cathérine, Mme de Meyendorf and me – Heeckeren, Pushkin, Skaryatin, and Fritz. We went to the English ambassador's, the Ludolfs' and the Olenins', and we had great fun, though Mamma and Pushkin were immediately recognized – we came back to have supper at home.'*[48]

Pushkin's friendship with the Ficquelmonts opened the doors to diplomatic circles in St Petersburg. A list of acquaintances on whom he intended to leave his visiting card at the New Year includes the Ficquelmonts; the French ambassador, the duc de Mortemart, and the secretary of the French legation, Théodore-Joseph de Lagrenée; Lord and Lady Heytesbury at the English embassy; the Count and Countess Ludolf at the embassy of the Kingdom of the Two Sicilies; and the Spanish ambassador, Don Juan Miguel Paëz de la Cadena. An English traveller, the dandy Tom Raikes, in his *Visit to St Petersburg* (which takes the form of letters to a friend) begins his ninth letter, dated 24 December 1829 (NS), 'I met last night at Baron Rehausen's [the secretary to the Swedish legation] the Byron of Russia; his name is Pouschkin, the celebrated, and, at the same time, the *only* poet in this country. His fame is established and unrivalled; no competitor attempts to win the laurel from his brow. His poems are read with delight by his countrymen, who alone can appreciate their merit; and his labours are not without reward, – he can always command ten roubles for every line from his publisher [. . .] I could observe nothing remarkable in his person or

---

* Heeckeren, the Netherlands minister in St Petersburg, was to play an important part in Pushkin's later life; Mme de Meyendorf – Betsy, one of Dolly's close friends – was the daughter of the previous Netherlands ambassador and was married to a civil servant in the Department of Trade; twenty-two-year-old Grigory Skaryatin was an officer in the Chevalier Guards; Prince Fritz Lichtenstein a member of the Austrian embassy. The party visited the residence of the English ambassador, Lord Heytesbury, on the English Embankment; that of Count and Countess Ludolf, the embassy of the Kingdom of Two Sicilies, also on the English Embankment; and the Olenins on the Fontanka.

manners; he was slovenly in his appearance, which is sometimes the failing of men of talent, and avowed openly his predilection for gambling: the only notable expression, indeed, which dropped from him during the evening was this, *"J'aimerais mieux mourir que ne pas jouer"* [I would rather die than not gamble].[49] In January Pushkin attended a ball given by the French ambassador. Nicholas caught sight of him, and was annoyed by his appearance. In the margin of a letter from Benckendorff the emperor jotted down: 'Apropos of that ball. You ought to tell Pushkin that it is improper for him *alone* to be in civilian dress, when we are all in uniform, and that he should at least get himself court uniform; henceforth, in similar circumstances, let him do this.'[50]

The cheerfulness brought on by the sojourn in Malinniki had soon been dissipated. 'I arrived in Petersburg the other day,' he wrote to Elizaveta Ushakova's fiancé, Sergey Kiselev. 'My address is *At Demouth's*. How are you? How are our friends? In Petersburg there's heartache, heartache . . .'[51] He had been hard hit by the rejection – as he conceived it to be – that he had received from Natalya and her mother. As before in similar circumstances, his thoughts turned to foreign places. He had known, on and off since 1818, the scientist, inventor, Sinologist and expert on Central Asia Baron Schilling von Canstatt, a civil servant in the Foreign Ministry. Schilling had been one of the party on the excursion by pyroscaph to Kronstadt in the summer of 1828, and Pushkin had sketched his portrait in Elizaveta Ushakova's album – a stout, jolly gentleman with a double chin, wearing spectacles and something remarkably similar to a baseball cap. Schilling had introduced him to another Orientalist, Father Iakinf, who had presented Pushkin with a copy of a book on Tibet that he had translated from the Chinese. When Pushkin met both again, at the end of 1829, he learned that they were planning an expedition, financed by the Foreign Ministry, to eastern Siberia and China to study the Buryat nation and to investigate the possibilities of trade with Peking. This – or indeed any foreign excursion – seemed just the thing to take his mind off Natalya – or so he hoped.

> Let us go – he wrote – I am ready; wherever you, my friends,
> Wherever you might think of going, I am ready
> To follow you everywhere, fleeing the haughty maiden.[52]

On 7 January 1830 he wrote to Benckendorff: 'While I am still neither married, nor attached to the service, I would wish to travel, either to France, or to Italy. However, if this is not granted, I would request the favour of visiting China with the mission that is about to travel there.' 'His Majesty the Emperor has not deigned to acquiesce in your request to travel abroad,' Benckendorff replied on the seventeenth, 'believing that this would excessively derange your pecuniary affairs, and at the same time distract you from your occupations. Your desire to accompany our mission to China cannot be put into effect either, since all the members have already been designated, and cannot be changed without informing the court at Peking.'[53] Pushkin had, finally, to reconcile himself with the realization that Nicholas would never allow him to leave the country: he made no more requests of this kind. At the time, however, he had little chance to brood over the disappointment or its implications, for he was soon wholly involved in two emotionally demanding experiences, one public – a bitter feud with Bulgarin; the second private – the reappearance in his life of Karolina Sobańska.

Bulgarin was a notorious figure with a chequered career. Born in 1798 near Dorpat to a family of Polish squires, he had been educated at cadet school in St Petersburg, had entered a hussar regiment and had fought against the French in 1806–7 – being wounded and decorated at the battle of Friedland – and the Swedes in 1808. But in 1811 he had been cashiered for unsatisfactory conduct and for some time had lived in penury in Reval, supporting himself, according to his detractors, by begging and petty theft. He then joined the French army's Polish legion, fought in Spain, and in the Russian campaign of 1812, when he was awarded the Legion of Honour. In 1819 he returned to St Petersburg, became a journalist, and in 1825 founded the *Northern Bee*, which he edited and published until his death in 1859. This appeared twice a week (daily after 1831), and was the only non-official paper allowed to print political news, which appeared without editorial comment. The

Bulgarin

government's favourable attitude to the paper was a reward for its unquestioning acceptance of official policy, and for Bulgarin's invaluable services to the Third Department, which he regularly supplied with reports and denunciations. In appearance he was gross and unattractive, and was alleged to have married a former prostitute.

Somewhat to the disgust of the more fastidious Vyazemsky, Pushkin had in the past been not unfriendly towards Bulgarin, and had indeed even published several poems in the *Northern Bee*, which had continually lauded his work. But towards the end of 1829 his attitude changed. Dmitry Dashkov, a former Arzamasite, had been Deputy Minister of the Interior from 1826; and in March 1829 became Deputy Minister of Justice. In these capacities he was on occasion consulted by Benckendorff, and saw some of the Third Department files. Through him other Arzamasites – Zhukovsky, Pushkin and Vyazemsky – learnt of Bulgarin's connection with the Third Department. As a result they began, somewhat ostentatiously, to draw their skirts away from his publications and from those of his close collaborator, Grech. This led, in return, to attacks on them in the *Northern Bee* and its allies – Grech's *Son of the Fatherland* and Polevoy's *Moscow Telegraph*. At the same time the idea that Pushkin had so long cherished – that of establishing their own literary journal – took on a far more concrete form, now that these others were no longer a haven for their own work.

On 23 December Pogodin, who kept his friend Shevyrev – then in Rome – acquainted with developments on the literary scene, wrote: 'A five-day paper is being organized in Petersburg; its collaborators are: Delvig, Pushkin, Vyazemsky, Somov, Zhukovsky, with the aim of acting against Polevoy and Bulgarin.'[54] The first number of the paper, entitled the *Literary Gazette*, appeared on Wednesday, 1 January 1830, and every five days thereafter. The editor was Delvig; but from the third number (of 11 January) to the twelfth (of 25 February) it was edited by Pushkin with the assistance of Somov, since Delvig was in Moscow: 'Send Delvig to me as soon as possible, if you're not coming yourself,' Pushkin wrote to Vyazemsky at the end of January. 'It's boring editing the Gazette alone, with the help of Orest, my intolerable friend and comrade.'[55] A prefatory page at the beginning of the first number set out the newspaper's programme and sent a message to Bulgarin: 'Writers who have published for the past six years their works in the *Northern Flowers* will continue also to participate in the *Literary Gazette*. (Of course, Messrs journal editors, being occupied with their own periodical publications, will not be among this paper's contributors.)'[56] Bulgarin could not miss the implication: he had contributed to *Northern Flowers* for the past three years, and was the only journal editor to have done so. He attempted a feeble riposte in the next number of the *Northern Bee*, claiming that two – obviously imaginary – writers, former contributors to *Northern Flowers*, had asked him to announce that they would not be writing for the *Literary Gazette*. A little later, annoyed by the reception of his novel *Ivan Vyzhigin*, he took a general swipe at the other camp. 'For our home-grown Walter Scotts, Goethes, Byrons, Johnsons and Aristophaneses the main crime of *Vyzhigin* is that it *is selling*, not mouldering on the shelf together with their *immortal* works.'[57] All this was good clean fun, but what followed was much dirtier.

Pushkin had not relinquished hope of publishing *Boris Godunov*. Before leaving for the Caucasus he had entrusted it to Zhukovsky in the hope that he would be able to obtain permission, but had been disappointed. On 7 January he raised the matter again with Benckendorff. 'It would be embarrassing for me, given my lack of fortune, to do without the 15 thousand roubles that my tragedy could bring me, and I would be sad to give up the publication of a work that I had long meditated and with which I am most satisfied.' Benckendorff replied on the seventeenth, promising a definite reply in the near future, and on the twenty-first returned the manuscript, asking Pushkin to change 'a few, completely trivial places' and then to resubmit it.[58]

It had been known for some time that Bulgarin had written an historical novel, *Dmitry the Pretender*, which had the same subject as Pushkin's play. Excerpts from the work had appeared the previous year and its publication as a separate work was imminent. Pushkin now knew not only of Bulgarin's connection with the Third Department, but also that the journalist had been given access to the manuscript of *Boris* by Benckendorff.* As a result he had come to believe that Bulgarin had plagiarized his play in writing *Dmitry*, and that Benckendorff was now temporizing over its publication in order to give a free run to his agent's

---

* Indeed, he might even have seen Bulgarin's report on it. In a draft of the letter to Benckendorff of 7 January he wrote 'the political ideas [of the play] are completely monarchic' (XIV, 269). This repeats Bulgarin's judgement in his report on *Boris*, echoing it so closely – 'The spirit of the whole work is monarchic,' he had written (Lemke, 608) – as to suggest that Dashkov, or another, had shown the report to Pushkin.

novel. 'My tragedy will probably not be at all successful,' he wrote later, after the publication both of *Dmitry* and of *Boris*. 'The periodicals are full of malice towards me. For the public I no longer possess what is chiefly attractive: youth and a novel literary name. In addition, the main scenes have been printed or distorted in the *imitations* of others. Opening Mr Bulgarin's novel at random, I find that he too has Prince V. Shuisky coming to tell the tsar of the appearance of the Pretender. I have Boris Godunov speaking in private with Basmanov about the abolition of the order of precedence – Mr Bulgarin as well. All this is dramatic invention, not historical record. But great minds think alike.'[59] It was not long before Bulgarin himself got to hear of the accusation. On 18 February, just after the publication of *Dmitry the Pretender*, he wrote to Pushkin: 'With the greatest astonishment I have heard from Olin* that you have apparently been saying that I *stole* your tragedy *Boris Godunov*, put *your verse* into prose, and took from *your tragedy* scenes for *my* novel! Aleksandr Sergeevich! Look to your fame! Is it possible to lay such a cock and bull story at my door? I have not read your tragedy (I assure you of this on my honour. I have been told the content and, I must confess, do not agree with much. I can produce those who told me.), apart from the printed extracts, but have only heard of its composition from those who have read it, and from you. In the main, in character and action, as far as I can judge from what I have heard, we are complete *opposites*.'[60]

Dmitry the Pretender was reviewed in the *Literary Gazette* on 7 March. The piece, which was unsigned, was written by Delvig, now returned from Moscow. Pushkin had declined the task, saying 'in order to criticize a book, it is necessary to read it, and I cannot rely on my strength'.[61] Though Delvig did not charge Bulgarin with plagiarism, he did make two malicious comments directed more at the author than the book. He refers to 'the biased preference, everywhere displayed, for the Polish people over the Russian'; and writes: 'History has not spared Dmitry the Pretender; she has exposed his vices and foolhardiness to the full light of day: but why burden in addition the terrible memory of him

---

* Valerian Olin, St Petersburg translator, journalist and editor, who published a poem by Pushkin in the 1830 edition of his almanac *A Little Pocket-book for Amateurs of Russian Antiquity and Literature*.

with a calumny? Where, in what secret chronicles has it been discovered that he was Sapieha's spy?* What purely literary purpose induced the author to endow him with this undeserved title?'[62] The first comment implied that Bulgarin's first loyalty was to Poland, rather than Russia. The second was more pointed: Bulgarin had made Dmitry a spy, not for literary reasons, but because the profession was the one he knew most about.

Bulgarin was enraged by the review, which he attributed to Pushkin. Both accusations flicked him on the raw. That of being a spy affected his standing in the literary world, but was best ignored, especially since it happened to be true. The charge that he was a Polish patriot, however, threatened his profitable relationship with the government, both as employee of the Third Department, and as editor of the *Northern Bee*: in both capacities he had assiduously proclaimed himself an ardent supporter of nationalism and monarchism. He replied on 11 March with 'An Anecdote', a ponderous, long-winded allegory. Which of these two writers, he asked, was more worthy of respect, 'firstly: a native Frenchman [i.e. Pushkin], serving Bacchus and Plutus more assiduously than the Muses, who in his works has revealed not a single noble thought, not a single elevated feeling, not a single useful truth, whose heart is cold and mute, like an oyster, whose head, a kind of rattle, stuffed with blaring rhymes, has not given birth to a single idea; who [. . .] stones everything sacred with his rhymes, boasts to the mob of his free-thinking, while surreptitiously crawling at the feet of the mighty, in order to be allowed to attire himself in an embroidered kaftan [. . .]; secondly, a foreigner [i.e. Bulgarin] who during his life has betrayed neither his principles nor his character, who was and is true to duty and honour, who loved his country before its union with France and after its union loves it together with France; who has paid France with his own blood for its hospitality on the field of battle, and now pays it tribute through the sacrifice of his mind, his feelings and ardent desire to see it great, powerful, and cleansed of all moral ailments, who writes only that which he is ready to say to anyone's face, and says what he is glad to publish.'†[63]

---

* Leo Sapieha, chancellor of Lithuania, and the Polish ambassador in Moscow.
† The reference to the 'embroidered kaftan' to be obtained by 'crawling at the feet of the powerful' suggests that Bulgarin had learnt from Benckendorff of the emperor's command that Pushkin should provide himself with a court uniform.

To most of the paper's readers the target of Bulgarin's crude sarcasm was obvious. 'Recently Bulgarin in his *Northern Bee* covered Pushkin with mud: called him senseless and a villain who was depraving the people, and even a blackguard, hanging round ante-rooms in order to get an embroidered coat!! What do think of that?' one of Shevyrev's correspondents wrote to him on 18 April. 'Of course, he said all this allegorically, but in such a way that any peasant would understand whom it referred to.'[64]

Bulgarin followed this attack with a bludgeoningly hostile review of Chapter Seven of *Eugene Onegin*, which had just been published. Nicholas was one of the *Northern Bee*'s more faithful readers. On the day this article appeared he visited Benckendorff, who was then ill, at his apartment on the Malaya Morskaya. On returning to the Winter Palace he sent him a note: 'I forgot to tell you, my dear friend, that in today's number of the *Bee* there is again a most unjust and most vulgar article directed against Pushkin; there will apparently be a continuation to this article: I suggest that you summon Bulgarin and forbid him henceforth to publish any criticism whatsoever of literary works; and, if possible, forbid his paper.' Benckendorff was quick to come to the defence of his agent. He had found 'nothing personal against Pushkin' in Bulgarin's article; the two authors had enjoyed good relations with each other for the past two years, but Bulgarin's pen, 'always loyal to the authorities', had been indignant at Pushkin's failure to hymn 'the great events which had immortalized the recent years' – the Russian victories over Turkey: this was a cunning hit at Pushkin's journey to Erzerum which, as he knew, had angered Nicholas. He attached to his letter a copy of the *Literary Gazette*'s review of *Dmitry the Pretender* – a book which defended monarchism and legitimacy – to show what provocation Bulgarin had had to endure. Nicholas's reply surprised him. The emperor was halfway through *Dmitry* – Benckendorff had assumed he was unacquainted with it – and was largely in agreement with the arguments of the review. '*For myself* I have *inwardly* thought exactly the same,' he wrote. 'This story, in itself, is more than sufficiently vile as not to be adorned with legends which are disgusting and unnecessary to the interest of the main events. So in this respect the criticism is, I think, just. On the other hand, there are only facts and very little sense in the criticism of *Onegin*, although I do not completely excuse the author, who would have done much better not to abandon himself completely to this type of literature, very amusing but far less noble than *Poltava*. However, if this criticism continues then I, for fairness' sake, will forbid it everywhere.'[65] Nicholas must have been distracted by some other piece of business, or Benckendorff persuaded him to take no action, for the *Northern Bee* continued to publish criticism; and, indeed, on 1 April printed the second half of Bulgarin's review.

Pushkin had been in Moscow since 12 March; the *Northern Bee* therefore reached him some days after its publication. When the number containing Bulgarin's 'Anecdote' arrived, he was shocked by the depth of malevolence it revealed, and appealed to Benckendorff. 'Mr Bulgarin, who says he has some influence with you, has become one of my most rabid enemies because of a review which he has attributed to me. After the infamous article which he has published on me, I believe him capable of anything. I have to inform you of my relations with this man, because he could do me infinite harm.' Benckendorff's reply was unhelpful and scarcely honest: 'As for Mr Bulgarin, he has never spoken to me of you, for the good reason that I only see him two or three times a year, and have only seen him recently to reprimand him.'[66] Even before writing to Benckendorff, however, Pushkin had hit on a brilliant way of turning Bulgarin's allegorical method back upon the author: on 16 March Pogodin noted in his diary that Pushkin had offered him an article on 'Bulgarin's denunciations and tale-bearing' for the *Moscow Herald*, but, 'seeing that I did not want to use it, took it back'.[67] Pushkin sent the article to Delvig, and it appeared in the *Literary Gazette* on 6 April.

> In one of the numbers of the *Lit. Gazette* the memoirs of the Parisian executioner were mentioned; the moral compositions of Vidocq, the police detective, are a no less disgusting, no less curious phenomenon.*
>
> Imagine a man without a name or a refuge, living by daily denunciations, married to one of those unfortunate creatures

---

* The spurious memoirs of Charles Henri Sanson (1740–93), the guillotineer during the Reign of Terror in France – whom Pushkin calls, erroneously, 'Samson' at the end of his article – appeared in 1829; one of its two authors, Louis François l'Heritier de l'Ain (the other was Balzac), was also responsible for the equally spurious, immensely popular memoirs (4 vols, Paris, 1828–9) of François Eugène Vidocq (1775–1857), a famous criminal who became chief of the French secret police. Pushkin was obviously acquainted with the work.

whom his office obliges him to keep under surveillance, an arrant scoundrel, as shameless as he is vile, and then imagine, if you can, what the moral compositions of such a man must be.

Vidocq in his memoirs calls himself a patriot, a good Frenchman, as if Vidocq could have a fatherland! He asserts that he served in the army, and that he was not only allowed, but instructed, to change his coat in all kinds of ways, and even now flaunts the Legion of Honour ribbon, arousing in coffeehouses the indignation of honourable poor wretches on half-pay. He insolently boasts of the friendship of the well-known dead, who had dealings with him (who has not been young? and Vidocq is an obliging, useful fellow). He speaks of good society with extraordinary pomposity, as though he were allowed entry to it, and severely criticizes well-known authors, partly hoping for their contempt, partly from calculation: Vidocq's views of Casimir Delavigne, of B. Constant must be interesting precisely because of their absurdity.

Who could believe it? Vidocq has his pride! He flies into a rage on reading journalists' unfavourable opinion of his style (the style of M. Vidocq!). When this occurs he writes denunciations of his *enemies*, accuses them of immorality and freethinking, and speaks (not as a joke) of nobility of emotion and freedom of opinion: his irritability, which would be amusing in any other hack, is consoling in Vidocq, for from it we see that human nature, in its vilest degradation, still preserves reverence before concepts which are sacred to the human race.

An important question arises:

The works of the police-spy Vidocq, of the executioner Samson and of others do not offend either established religion, or the government, or even morality in the usual meaning of this word; at the same time it is impossible not to admit that they are extremely offensive to public decency. Should not the civil power turn its sage attention on this new form of temptation, which has completely escaped the foresight of the legislature?[68]

Few readers of the *Literary Gazette* would have been puzzled by Pushkin's lampoon: its subject was immediately obvious. He rammed home the comparison between the shady policeman and the shady journalist with an epigram:

> The disaster is not that you're a Pole:
> Kosciusko's a Pole, Mickiewicz's a Pole!
> If you like, be a Tatar, –
> I see no shame in this either;
> Be a Jew – that's no disaster;
> The disaster is that you're Vidocq Figlyarin.*[69]

On 25 April Vyazemsky sent a copy of this to Turgenev in Paris, explaining that it was 'in answer to a filthy little article by Bulgarin in the *Northern Bee*, in which Pushkin [...] is called a gambler, a drunkard, a freethinker before the mob and a toad-eater before the mighty'.[70] The identification of Bulgarin with Vidocq was a stroke of genius: soon it had caught on widely. The St Petersburg book-seller Lisenkov did a roaring trade in portraits of Bulgarin labelled 'Vidocq' until his stock was confiscated. Witty though Pushkin's two works are, they are, like Bulgarin's, wholly personal. On reflection he might have considered that it was neither edifying nor profitable to follow his enemy into the gutter: more calumnies were bound to follow.

Bulgarin's reply came at the beginning of August, with a letter in the *Northern Bee* that purported to be from a correspondent in Germany: 'Byron's lordship and his aristocratic escapades, combined with God knows what manner of thought, have driven many poets and rhymesters in various countries out of their minds, and they have all begun prating about their 600-year-old nobility! [...] An anecdote is being told about how some Poet in Spanish America, also an imitator of Byron whose mother or father – I cannot remember which – was a Mulatto, began to claim that one of his ancestors was a Negro Prince. In the town Rathaus it was discovered that long ago there was a lawsuit between a skipper and his mate about this Negro, whom each of them claimed,

---

* The surname Figlyarin, formed from *figlyar*, 'clown', had been in general use as a rhyming nickname for Bulgarin for a number of years: it had made its first appearance in the *Ladies' Journal* in 1826.

and that the skipper proved that he had bought the Negro for a bottle of rum. Who would have thought then that a poet should claim this Negro. Vanity of vanities.'[71]

This was a clear personal attack on Pushkin, the first half referring to his paternal and the second to his maternal ancestry. Bulgarin was hardly likely to know Pushkin's family history, or that he was inclined to boast of his 600-year-old nobility: he was given the information for the pasquinade by Uvarov, the former Arzamasite, who, though professing friendship for Pushkin, secretly disliked him. Though the attack might have been considered a fair riposte for the insinuation, in the Vidocq article, about the former profession of Bulgarin's wife, this was naturally not the view taken by Pushkin. He replied to it with the poem 'My Genealogy', in which, as well as hitting out at Bulgarin, he defined his own social position, in the process disparaging – perhaps injudiciously – the new aristocracy. He is not, he remarks ironically, an aristocrat: that title is nowadays reserved for nobility of a more recent creation than his own: families which are, for example, descended from a pancake-seller, or the valet of Paul I (he is referring to the Menshikovs and the Kutaisovs). He, the 'descendant of ancient boyars', is now a *meshchanin*, a petty bourgeois. In a postscript he replies to the attack on the other side of his family, turning the anecdote against its author: a skipper did acquire Gannibal, but that skipper was Peter the Great, and 'the purchased blackamoor' became 'the tsar's confidant, not his slave'. He ended the poem with another unkind reference to Mrs Bulgarin:

> Inspired Figlyarin decided:
> I was a bourgeois among the nobility.
> But what is he among his respected family?
> He? ... He is a nobleman on Bourgeois Street.[72]

Meshchanskaya [Bourgeois] Street was a well-known red-light district of St Petersburg.

In November 1831 Pushkin, who wished to include the poem in a new collection of his verse, wrote to Benckendorff explaining the circumstances of its composition. 'Since indecency had been taken so far as to speak of my mother in a feuilleton which should have been purely literary, and since our newspapermen do not fight duels,' he

wrote, 'I considered it my duty to answer the *anonymous* satirist, which I did in verse, and in no uncertain terms. I sent my reply to the late Delvig,* asking him to print it in his paper. Delvig advised me to suppress it, remarking that it would be ridiculous to defend oneself, pen in hand, against attacks of this kind and to parade aristocratic sentiments when one is, all in all, no more than a gentleman-bourgeois, if not a bourgeois-gentleman.' Benckendorff passed the letter on to Nicholas, who replied: 'You may tell Pushkin that I am in complete agreement with the opinion of his late friend Delvig: insults which are so low and vile as those applied to him dishonour him who makes them and not him to whom they are addressed. The only weapon against them is *contempt*; that is how I should have behaved in his place. As to his verses, I find them witty, but filled more with venom than anything else. For the honour of his pen, and above all, of his *reason*, he would have done better not to circulate them.'[73]

Pushkin had first seen Karolina Sobańska in the governor of Kiev's drawing-room on 2 February 1821. They had met again in Odessa two years later: the close friendship formed then might have become something more intimate and passionate, had not Pushkin been distracted, first by Amaliya Riznich, then by Elise Vorontsova. Now, in the winter of 1829–30, they met for the third time in St Petersburg. Dispirited by his reception at the Goncharovs in Moscow, Push-kin had given up any hope of making Natalya his wife. At the end of January he wrote to Vyazemsky with, it seems, genuine indifference, 'Is it true that my Goncharova is getting married to the Archival Meshchersky? What is Ushakova, who is mine as well doing?'[74] In this mood he fell an easy victim to Sobańska's attractions. She collected autographs – her collection was eventually to include, among others, those of Pitt, Wellington, Madame de

Karolina Sobańska

Staël, Chateaubriand, Mickiewicz and Benjamin Constant – and asked Pushkin to contribute his signature to her album. On 5 January 1830 he did more than this. 'What good is my name to you?' he wrote,

---

* Delvig had died in January 1831.

It will die, like the melancholy sound
Of a wave breaking on a distant shore,
Like night's noises in the dense forest.
On the album page
It will leave a dead trace, like
The pattern of an epitaph on a tombstone
In an unknown language.
What good is it? Long forgotten
In new, stormy emotions,
It will not evoke in your soul
Peaceful, tender memories.
But . . . on a day of grief, in the silence
Pronounce it, pining;
Say: someone remembers me,
There is in the world a heart, in which I live . . .[75]

On Sunday 2 February he wrote to her, 'Today is the 9th anniversary of the day that I saw you for the first time. That day decided my life. The more I think of it, the more I see that my existence is inseparable from yours; I was born to love you and follow you – any other care on my part would be error or folly; away from you I have felt nothing but remorse for a happiness I have been unable to assuage. Sooner or later I shall have to abandon everything and come and fall at your feet.'[76]

Suddenly, however, his hopes of marrying Natalya were reanimated. Vyazemsky had seen her and her mother at a ball given by Prince Dmitry Golitsyn, the military governor-general of Moscow, at his house on the Tverskaya. Mindful of his friend's interests, he had asked an acquaintance to engage her for a dance, and, if possible, try to find out how Pushkin's chances stood. The response was very favourable; they sent their greetings, and Vyazemsky passed them on when he came to the capital early in March to take up a post at the Ministry of Finance. Full of optimism again, Pushkin left for Moscow immediately, taking only the time to inform his friend of the relationship with Sobańska, whom Vyazemsky soon met. 'Sobańska is clever, but too grand,' he told his wife on 7 April. 'Ask Pushkin whether she is always like this, or only with me and on first acquaintance.'[77] Pushkin's precipitate departure aroused suspicions that he was contemplating another clandestine trip

'I will be very glad to know that the reasons prompting this action are sufficiently valid to excuse it,' Benckendorff wrote. 'But I consider it my duty to inform you that all the unpleasant consequences to which you might be subjected must be ascribed to your own conduct.'[78]

The joyful anticipation with which he set out soon gave way, on the journey south, to gloomier doubts and forebodings. Did he really want to exchange the carefree, unconstrained life of a bachelor – which, after all, he had only fully enjoyed since leaving Mikhailovskoe – for that of a married man, burdened with cares and responsibilities? The two women in his life represented the alternatives, Sobańska standing for bachelordom, Natalya for marriage. Which was he in love with? Could a decision here solve the other dilemma? The trouble was that they were so different, so much the opposite of each other in almost every characteristic, that it was only too easy to love both simultaneously, if in very different ways. Sobańska, four years older than he, was a voluptuous, experienced woman: dazzlingly charming, cosmopolitan, well-read, with an insider's knowledge of politics and a fine brain. Compared to her the eighteen-year-old Natalya, though slim and virginally beautiful, was a provincial simpleton, with little knowledge of literature and less of the world. Nor was she distinguished by her intellect: 'Aleksey Davydov came to the Assembly with us and found Kars [Natalya] rather stupid. During the mazurka he stood behind her chair for more than an hour,' Ekaterina Ushakova – perhaps a not wholly unprejudiced observer – had told her brother.[79]

Though he had left in such haste, now, racked with indecision, he turned aside to Malinniki and stayed for three days with Praskovya Osipova. He eventually arrived in Moscow on the evening of 12 March, and, as he wrote to Vyazemsky, 'straight from the carriage landed at a concert where all Moscow was present'.[80] This was a charity concert, given in aid of the Moscow Eye Hospital; 'all Moscow' included Nicholas I, brought to the city by a hubbub over the dismissal of an actress – Mme Alfred, a favourite of the public – from the French theatre. The first people Pushkin saw were Natalya and Vyazemsky's wife, Princess Vera. Later that month he wrote to Vyazemsky again: 'My letter will be delivered to you by [Ivan] Goncharov, brother of the beauty: you can now guess what troubles me in Moscow.'[81] But Vyazemsky, privy to his friend's emotional entanglements, had already guessed. 'The other day

I received a letter from Pushkin brought by Goncharov,' he told Vera; 'holding the unopened letter in my hand and talking to him, I thought: well, is this the announcement to me of his marriage? I had to give in and opened the letter.'[82] But it contained no announcement.

Indeed, Pushkin was conducting a very desultory courtship, not daring to make a direct proposal, since he feared in almost equal measure both acceptance and rejection. As before, he spent far more time with the hospitable Ushakovs than at the Goncharov house: his assiduity in visiting the sisters caused his intentions to be misinterpreted. 'They say that he [Pushkin] will marry the elder Ushakova (the younger is betrothed to Kiselev) and that he has grown noticeably more staid,' Pogodin wrote to Shevyrev.[83] Ekaterina herself knew perfectly well that he would not marry her; but she was as much in the dark as anyone else about his real intentions. 'About our autocratic poet I will tell you that he is hopelessly in love (or probably is pretending to be out of habit) with the younger Goncharova,' she wrote to her brother. 'Here they say that he is getting married, some even that he is married. But he dined with us today, and does not seem to have that good intention, but one cannot be sure of anything. His brother Lev arrived from the Caucasus and called on us, he is very charming and polite and had an excellent campaign, is covered in medals. Here is his *bon mot* about Aleksandr Sergeevich, composed when he saw him running after Kars's carriage on Novinsky Boulevard: He is fettered,/Enchanted/Completely Goncharovized.'*[84]

Pushkin's time was not taken up wholly with courtship. The Moscow literary world saw much of him. On 22 March he dined at Pogodin's; Yazykov was among those present, and he met for the first time Sergey Aksakov – later famous for his *Family Chronicle* (1856), a thinly fictionalized portrayal of life in Orenburg province at the close of the eighteenth century – and the journalist and critic Nikolay Nadezhdin, the son of a village priest of Ryazan province, who founded his own journal, the *Telescope*, the following year. Pushkin had been much annoyed by Nadezhdin's review of *Poltava*, and his first, somewhat

---

* Lev had been given four months' leave from the Caucasus on 14 December 1829; he had been promoted lieutenant and awarded the orders of St Anna and St Vladimir. The wit of his *bon mot* comes from the rhyme *ocharovan* ('enchanted')/*ogoncharovan* ('Goncharovized')

snobbish impression of the writer's person was equally unfavourable: 'He seemed to me extremely common, *vulgar* [Pushkin uses the English word] boring, arrogant and wholly without decency. For example, he picked up a handkerchief which I had dropped.'[85] That night, after leaving Pogodin's, Pushkin attended a service held for Batyushkov, who was thought to be on the point of death (in fact, he did not die until 1855). Now incurably insane, he was living in Moscow in the care of his aunt, Ekaterina Muraveva. Pushkin had not seen him since November 1818, when he had been one of the party who bade farewell to the poet on his departure for Naples. 'The choristers sang moderately,' noted Batyushkov's doctor, 'but their singing from a distance affected the patient. The doors were open, and the sounds carried to him; he lay motionless on a divan with closed eyes and did not even stir when a candle was placed on the table by him. The poet Aleksandr Pushkin, who was present during the service together with Muraveva and Princess Vyazemskaya, approached the table near which the patient lay, and, moving the candle, with animation began to speak to him, but he did not stir and said not a word, and did not even notice the people standing in the hall. He probably thought he was hearing the song of archangels.'[86]

As in Odessa, Pushkin confided his emotional problems to Vyazemsky's wife, Princess Vera, who passed his confessions on to her husband. Hoping to resolve his dilemma one way or the other, Pushkin had told Natalya and her mother about his infatuation with Sobańska. The news astonished Vyazemsky. 'Surely he cannot be thinking of marriage, but if he is, how can he play the fool? One can tease a woman whom one is pursuing by pretending to be in love with another, and base hopes of conquest on her vexation, but how can one think that a girl will marry, or a mother give her daughter's hand in marriage to an inconstant fop, who was seeking consolation for his grief? What was the Goncharovs' reply? However, the more I think about it, the more convinced I become that you are making a fool of me.' Pushkin's behaviour seemed so unbelievable that for the next few weeks he rejected out of hand any idea of his marriage. 'You keep writing rubbish to me about Pushkin's marriage: he's not got the slightest thought of marriage,' he told Vera rudely on 21 April;[87] on the same day, in a long letter to Turgenev in Paris, he wrote: 'Pushkin is now in Moscow; here everyone says that he is getting married, but this is probably nonsense.'[88]

It was, however, far from nonsense, and Vyazemsky was behind the times. On 5 April Pushkin had finally resolved to put his fate to the test, and had written to Natalya's mother. As a request for her daughter's hand the long letter, written in French, was somewhat unconventional: after recollecting the peripetias of his acquaintance with Natalya, Pushkin went on to analyse in detail his shortcomings as a suitor.

> Only habit and a long intimacy could gain me the affection of Mlle your daughter; I can hope to attach her to me in the course of time, but I have nothing to please her; if she consents to give me her hand, I shall see in this nothing but the proof of the calm indifference of her heart. But, surrounded with admiration, homage, seductions, will this calmness last? She will be told that an unfortunate fate alone has prevented her from forming other bonds, more fitting, more brilliant, more worthy of her, – perhaps these remarks will be sincere, but she will assuredly believe them to be so. Will she not have regrets? Will she not regard me as an obstacle, a fraudulent ravisher? Will she not hold me in aversion? God is my witness that I am ready to die for her, but having to die in order to leave her a dazzling widow and free to choose a new husband – this idea – is hell.
>
> Let us speak of fortune; I set little store by that. Mine has sufficed me up to now. Will it suffice me, married? for nothing in the world would I endure that my wife should know privation, that she should not be where she is invited to shine, to amuse herself. She has the right to demand it. To satisfy her I am ready to sacrifice on her behalf all the tastes, all the passions of my life, a completely free and adventurous existence. Still, will she not murmur if her position in the world is not as brilliant as she merits and which I would wish for her?
>
> Such are, in part, my anxieties. I tremble lest you should find them only too reasonable. There is yet another which I cannot resolve to commit to paper.[89]

The anxiety he could not commit to paper, that made him an even less suitable applicant for Natalya's hand, was his anomalous and uncomfortable position vis-à-vis the government and, in particular, the emperor.

In one sense Pushkin's transparent honesty is wholly admirable:

he wished to leave the Goncharovs under no illusions regarding his circumstances. Yet at the same time another motive can be dimly sensed. He cherishes the hope – unacknowledged perhaps even to himself, existing only at a subconscious level – that his suit will be refused, and he will be able, without any pang of conscience, to tell himself that fate did not wish him to become a married man, and return to the life of a bachelor and to Sobańska. But Mrs Goncharova was not deterred; the family's financial situation had deteriorated since Pushkin had first made Natalya's acquaintance, and she was pleased by the prospect of marrying off one of her three daughters. The following day, Easter Sunday, Pushkin called on the Goncharovs, made a formal proposal for Natalya's hand, and was accepted. Shortly thereafter cards were sent out to announce that the official ceremony of betrothal would take place on 6 May. He did not see Sobańska again. Immediately after the proposal Pushkin hastened to write to his parents.

> I wish to marry a young person whom I have loved for a year – Mlle Natalya Goncharova. I have her consent, that of her mother. I ask for your blessing, not as an empty formality, but in the intimate persuasion that this blessing is necessary to my well-being – and may the latter half of my existence be more consoling for you than my sad youth.
>
> Mme Goncharova's finances being very disarranged, and depending in part on those of her father-in-law, this matter is the only obstacle that stands in the way of my happiness. I have not the strength to think of renouncing it. It is far more easy for me to hope that you will come to my help.[90]

Sergey replied immediately and – for once – with some generosity:

> Blessed be yesterday a thousand and another thousand times, my dear Aleksandr, for the letter which we received from you. It filled me with joy and gratitude. Yes, my boy. That is the word. – I had long forgotten the sweetness of the tears I shed while reading it. May Heaven lavish all its blessings on you and on the dear companion who will complete your happiness. – I would have liked to write to her, but do not yet dare to do so, for fear of not yet having the right. I await Lev with more

impatience than ever, in order to speak of you to him or rather that he might speak to me. Olinka [Olga] was with us at the moment we received your letter. You can imagine the effect which that had on her . . .

Let us turn to what you say to me, my dear friend, about what I can give you. You know the state of my affairs. – I have a thousand serfs, it is true, but two-thirds of my estates are mortgaged with the Foundling Home. – I give Olinka about 4,000r a year. Of the estate of my late brother which fell to my share I still have 200 serfs entirely unencumbered, I give you for the time being full and complete use of them. They might produce an annual income of 4,000r and with time might give you more.*

Pushkin's mother added a postscript:

Your letter, my dear Aleksandr, filled me with joy, may Heaven bless you, my dear Friend, may the prayers which I address it for your happiness be heard, my heart is too full, I cannot express all that I feel, I would like to hold you in my arms, to bless you and tell you in person how much your happiness means to my existence. I am sure that everything has come about as your desires wished. Mademoiselle Goncharova will be as dear to me as all of you my children.[91]

Pleased with his father's generosity, Pushkin, in a letter to Princess Vera about a French novel – Jules-Gabriel Janin's *L'Âne mort et la femme guillotinée* (1829) – broke off a disquisition on love to announce it, and the fact of his marriage, to her: 'First love is always an affair of emotion: the more stupid it is, the more delicious memories it leaves,' he wrote. 'The second is an affair of sensuality, you see. The parallel could be taken much further. But I have not the time. My marriage with Natalie

---

* The Foundling Homes in Moscow and St Petersburg were instructed in 1772 to make loans to noblemen on the security of their estates; in this capacity they were usually referred to as the Board of Guardians, after the governing body of the institution. The 'estate of my late brother' was Kistenevo, near Sergey's estate of Boldino in Nizhny Novgorod province; he had inherited it from his half-brother, Petr Lvovich, a retired lieutenant-colonel of artillery, who had died in 1825. Though Sergey had indeed promised Olga 4,000 roubles a year after her marriage, in the first year he gave her only 2,000, in the two succeeding years 1,500, and even less thereafter.

(who in parenthesis is my hundred and thirteenth love) is decided. My father is giving me 200 peasants which I shall pledge at the pawnshop, and pledge you, dear Princess, to be my sponsor at the wedding.'[92] Meanwhile Vyazemsky had been celebrating the engagement with Pushkin's parents. 'Your letters, which I read there,' he wrote on his return from dinner, 'convinced me that my wife was not mystifying me and that you really were a bridegroom. Come to my arms, bridegroom! But what convinced me most of all of the genuineness of your marriage was the second, extra bottle of champagne, with which your father regaled us after getting your last letter. I saw then that it wasn't a joke. I could have not believed your letters, his tears, but could not not believe his champagne. I congratulate you from the bottom of my heart.'[93]

Pushkin could not proceed with the marriage until he had allayed the third anxiety of his letter to Mrs Goncharova. On 16 April he wrote to Benckendorff:

I am to marry Mlle Goncharova whom you must have seen in Moscow, I have her consent and that of her mother; two objections have been made to me: my fortune and my position with respect to the government. As to my fortune, I was able to answer that it was sufficient, thanks to His Majesty who has given me the means of living honourably from my work. As for my position, I have not been able to conceal that it is false and dubious. Excluded from the civil service in 1824, this stigma remains with me. Having left the Lycée with the rank of 10th class, I never received the two ranks which came to me by right, my superiors neglecting to put me forward and I not caring to remind them. It would be hard for me now to return to the civil service in spite of all my good will. A completely junior position, such as my rank permits me to occupy, could not suit me. It would distract me from my literary pursuits which provide my livelihood and would only cause me senseless and useless annoyance. Mme Goncharova is afraid to give her daughter to a man who could have the misfortune of being in the Emperor's disfavour ... My happiness depends on a word of good will from Him for whom my devotion and gratitude are already pure and without limits.[94]

Benckendorff replied on 28 April.

> His Imperial Majesty, having heard with benevolent satisfaction
> the news of the marriage you are about to enter into, deigned
> to observe with regard to it, that he was pleased to believe that
> you had certainly examined yourself well before taking this step,
> and that you had discovered within yourself those qualities of
> heart and character necessary for a woman's happiness, and
> especially for a woman as amiable and as interesting as Mlle
> Goncharova.
>
> As for your individual position vis-à-vis the government, I
> can only repeat to you that which I have told you so many
> times; I find it perfectly in your interests; there can be nothing
> false or dubious in it, unless you yourself wish to make it such.
> His Majesty the Emperor, in wholly paternal solicitude for you,
> sir, deigned to charge me, General Benckendorff, not as head of
> the gendarmerie, but as the person in whom he pleases to place
> his confidence, to observe you and guide you by my counsel; no
> police have ever been ordered to keep a watch on you. The advice
> I have from time to time given you, as a friend, can only have
> been useful to you, and I hope that you will become still more
> convinced of this. What then is the shadow to be found over
> your position in this respect? I authorize you, sir, to show this
> letter to all those whom you believe should see it.[95]

The letter contained one downright lie. Though Pushkin was not under
continuous surveillance, a watch was kept on him, and reports concerning it regularly crossed Benckendorff's desk. However, his reassurances
satisfied Pushkin; he was especially pleased by the news that the tsar
had taken an interest in his marriage and had remembered Natalya.
Nicholas had met her in 1829, at a ball given to celebrate the imperial
family's visit to Moscow for the Christmas festivities, and had congratulated her on her performance in a *tableau vivant*: 'The little Goncharov
girl was ravishing in the role of Dido's sister,' Aleksandr Bulgakov had
told his brother.[96]

'His Majesty has done me the honour of indicating to me his benev-
olent satisfaction at the marriage I am about to enter,' Pushkin told his
parents, quoting Benckendorff,[97] and to Benckendorff himself wrote, 'It

is to the solicitude of Your Excellency that I owe the new favour with which the Emperor has honoured me: I beg you to accept the expression of my profound gratitude. Never in my heart have I been unaware of the benevolence, dare I say wholly paternal, which His Majesty has had towards me; never have I wrongly interpreted the interest which you have always kindly shown to me; my request was only made to reassure an apprehensive mother, further affrighted by calumny.'[98] Benckendorff was away from St Petersburg at the time, and the letter was forwarded by von Fock, who wrote, 'I annexe to my missive a scrap of a letter from our famous Pushkin. These lines characterize him perfectly in all his thoughtlessness, all his careless frivolity. Unfortunately he is someone who thinks of nothing but is ready for everything. His actions are guided by momentary impulse.'[99]

Meanwhile Pushkin was enjoying the privileges of an accepted suitor: on 15 April he took Natalya to a masquerade at the Noble Assembly, and on 3 May they were present at a charitable performance of Kotzebue's tragedy *Misanthropy and Repentance* in the Assembly's Grand Hall. But he did not seem a particularly happy man. Nadezhda Ozerova, the twenty-year-old daughter of the senator Petr Ozerov, wrote to a friend in St Petersburg; 'I must confess, my dear angel, that this play by Kotzebue bored me to death with its length and insipidity [...] By way of interesting acquaintances Goncharova was there with Pushkin. To judge by his physiognomy one would think that he was annoyed at not being refused as he had thought he would be. It is said that they are already engaged, but no one knows whom this comes from; it is alleged too that mother Goncharova was strongly opposed to her daughter's marriage, but that the young person persuaded her. She seems to be very taken with her intended, but he has as glacial an air as before, though he plays the lover.'[100] As he became closer acquainted with the family and with his future mother-in-law, his forebodings about the future increased. Natalya Ivanovna was not a pleasant woman. She was stupid, insensitive and tactless, and combined meddlesomeness with dictatorial high-handedness. Inclined to hysterics if her will was thwarted, she was in everything swayed solely by emotion, and hence completely insusceptible to arguments which derived from common sense or from logic. Natalya's father, Nikolay Afanasevich, thought to be mentally ill, was rarely to be seen and played no part in family affairs.

To arrange the marriage settlement Pushkin therefore turned to her grandfather, Afanasy Goncharov, who had sent the couple his blessing and congratulations when the engagement had been announced. In the third week of May he accompanied Natalya and her mother to Polotny-any Zavod, Afanasy's estate in Kaluga province, some hundred miles to the south-west of Moscow. He was impressed by the splendour of the surroundings, and pleased by the success of the mission: Afanasy promised to share a village, Katunka in Nizhny Novgorod province, between his three granddaughters – each would receive 280 serfs; while her mother would make over to her 200 serfs in Yaropolets, the estate in Moscow province she had inherited from her father. Pushkin was flattered, too, when on 26 May, his birthday, Ivan Antipin, a Kaluga book-seller, and his friend Faddey Abakumov, tramped the eleven miles from town to offer their congratulations on the occasion and express their high opinion of his work. But the visit also had consequences which were to cause him some inconvenience.

Natalya's grandfather had – possibly after learning of the interest taken in the marriage by the emperor – conceived a wholly erroneous impression of the connections the poet possessed in St Petersburg. As a result, when Pushkin returned to Moscow at the end of May, leaving Natalya at Polotnyany Zavod, he took with him two commissions – which, given the circumstances, he could hardly refuse. Afanasy, finan-cially embarrassed, had asked him to assist in securing a large loan from the state; he also wished Pushkin to obtain permission from the tsar to sell a large bronze statue of Catherine II. Originally com-missioned by Potemkin from a foundry in Berlin, it had been acquired by Afanasy's father, who intended to erect it to commemorate the empress's visit to Polotnyany Zavod in 1775. This was, however, never done, and the statue had lain in the estate's cellars for the past thirty-five years.

The question of the statue was easily resolved. Nicholas readily acceded to Pushkin's proposal, put in a letter to Benckendorff, that 'his late august grandmother [should] get us out of our [financial] predicament'.[101] The loan proved more difficult. At one point the sugges-tion was made that it should be secured by a mortgage on the factory, but Pushkin felt unable to take the responsibility of agreeing to this without the consent of the heirs to the estate. Afanasy became impatient at his lack of success. 'From the letter which I have had the honour to receive,' Pushkin replied in September, 'I note with extreme regret that you suppose me to be insufficiently zealous. Please accept my excuse. I did not dare to take it upon myself to intercede in your affair only because I feared a refusal, were I to approach the emperor or ministers at an inappropriate moment. My relations with the government are like spring weather: one minute rain, the next sun. And just now a cloud has appeared . . .'[102] He advised Afanasy to make an approach through Benckendorff; whether this was successful or not, Pushkin heard no more of the matter.

The statue, however, reappeared when Natalya inherited it after Afanasy's death in 1832; it proved as much of a white elephant to the Pushkins as it had to Afanasy. In March, almost as soon as it had been delivered to their lodgings in St Petersburg, Pushkin offered it to a rich friend, Ivan Myatlev. 'Congratulations to your sweet and charming wife on her weighty acquisition, what's it like having the great Catherine as an eavesdropper?' Myatlev replied. 'The idea of buying the statue has not quite ripened within me, but I should think you're in no hurry to sell it, it doesn't need feeding, and meanwhile my affairs will improve, and I will be in a better state to obey my whims.'[103] In June Pushkin suggested to Benckendorff that the government might wish to acquire the statue for 25,000 roubles – a quarter of its original cost – to erect at Tsarskoe Selo. Benckendorff passed the letter on to the Minister of the Court, Prince P.M. Volkonsky, who had the statue inspected by four professors from the Academy of Arts – one, the sculptor Samuil Galberg, was to take Pushkin's death-mask. They thought it a fine work of art, probably worth more than the price asked. However, Pushkin heard nothing from Volkonsky; the following February, therefore, he got Natalya to write to the minister. This did produce a reply: the offer was turned down. Only after Pushkin's death was the statue finally disposed of: in 1846 it was erected outside the cathedral in Ekaterinoslav.

On 16 July 1830 he left for St Petersburg: 'Pushkin has galloped off to Piter to print Godunov,' Yazykov told his brother.[104] He did want to discuss publishing matters with Pletnev, but had also other business to transact: especially the transfer of the 200 serfs from his father to himself. 'Aleksandr arrived on Saturday,' Sergey Lvovich told Olga. 'He found me sitting on a bench on the Nevsky Perspective near the library. – He had just dismounted from his carriage and was going to us on foot. – And so we, embracing, gesticulating, chatting, walked home arm in arm.'[105] At his parents' apartment Pushkin found Lev, who, however, left for Moscow the following day.

While in St Petersburg he called on his fiancée's eighty-three year-old great-aunt, Natalya Kirillovna Zagryazhskaya, an imposing figure. 'I arrive, I have myself announced, she receives me at her toilette, like a very pretty woman of the last century,' he reported to Natalya. 'You are the one who is marrying my grand-niece? – Yes, madame, – How is that? I am extremely astonished; I have not been told, Natasha has written me nothing about it. (She was not speaking of you, but of your mamma.)' Pushkin explained that the marriage had only just been decided upon. 'She repeated to me the Emperor's compliments to your address – and we parted very good friends.' A day or two later he wrote to Natalya again. 'You are awaited here with impatience. The ladies ask to see your portrait, and do not pardon me for not having it. I console myself by spending hours in front of a blonde Madonna who is as much like you as two drops of water, and whom I would have bought, if she did not cost 40,000 roubles.'[106] This was a Virgin and Child, attributed to Raphael, on exhibition at Slenin's bookshop on the Nevsky. From their first meeting he had imagined a resemblance between Natalya and a typical Madonna of the Renaissance. 'I am marrying a red-haired Madonna with a squint,' he had remarked – Natalya was near-sighted – and would later refer to her as 'my squinting Madonna'.[107] 'He is enchanted with his Natalie, and speaks of her as of a Divinity,' his mother told Olga.[108]

He was in tearing high spirits throughout the month he spent in St Petersburg. 'He has never been so charming, so full of verve and gaiety in his conversation – it is impossible to be less pretentious and more witty in the way one expresses oneself,' Dolly Ficquelmont noted in her diary.[109] Though shortly after his arrival he had written to Natalya: 'Petersburg already seems very dull to me, and I expect to cut my stay as short as I can,'[110] he soon changed his mind, discovering how pleasant it was to be once again a carefree bachelor, no longer subject to the whims and tantrums of a future mother-in-law. At the beginning of August he added a postscript to a letter Vyazemsky had written to his wife: 'I confess to my shame that I am amusing myself in St Petersburg and hardly know how or when I shall return.'[111] One of the amusements was to repeat, together with Delvig, the diversions of their youth. They were both members of a party that made a trip one evening to Krestovsky Island.* Here, as they had been wont to do ten years earlier, they kicked up a terrible bobbery, accosting and insulting harmless holiday-makers – much to the disapprobation of Delvig's cousins, the seventeen-year-old Andrey and twenty-year-old Aleksandr, who, thinking such behaviour unseemly, especially in the presence of Delvig's wife and infant daughter, endeavoured unsuccessfully to restrain them.

Vyazemsky had matters to attend to in Moscow, and when he left on 10 August, Pushkin took the opportunity to accompany him in the diligence. Delvig went with them as far as Tsarskoe Selo, where they dined with Zhukovsky. They stopped for a short time in Tver to visit Fedor Glinka, a fellow-member of the *Green Lamp*, who had been exiled to the town for his part in the Decembrist revolt. During the journey Vyazemsky was able to observe Pushkin's eating habits at close quarters and later made a note on them. 'Pushkin was not at all a gourmand,' he wrote. 'He even, I think, did not value and had no understanding of the mysteries of the art of cuisine, but for some things he was extraordinarily greedy. I remember how on the road he ate, almost in one gulp, twenty peaches which he had bought in Torzhok. Dried apples often suffered at his hands as well.'[112]

On their arrival Pushkin learnt that his uncle was dangerously ill. He called round to see him, and was present a week later when he died, on 20 August. 'Poor Uncle Vasily!' he wrote to Pletnev. 'Do you know his last words? I come to see him, find him unconscious; coming to, he recognized me, was melancholy and silent for a little while, then: *how boring Katenin's articles are!* and not another word. What about that? That's what it means to die an honourable warrior, on your shield, your war-cry on your lips!'[113] In the absence of his parents, Pushkin took upon himself all the arrangements for the funeral, sending out a

---

* A foreign visitor describes Krestovsky Island as 'peculiarly the resort of the lower classes of St Petersburg; hither flock the Mushik [peasant] and Kupez [merchant] in gay gondolas, to enjoy, in the woods, their national amusements of swings and Russian mountains, and here on holidays smokes on the grass under every pine-group the favourite *samovar*, round which may be seen encamped a party of long-beards, gossiping, singing, and clamouring' (J.G. Kohl, *Russia*. London, 1842, 178).

faire-part in his name and that of Lev. The service took place in the Church of St Nikita the Martyr, on Staraya Basmannaya Street, and Pushkin then followed the coffin on foot across the city to the Donskoy monastery, where Vasily was buried. The funeral was attended by 'a deputation of the whole of literature, of all the schools, all the parties'.[114]

'The wedding will not take place before the month of September,' Pushkin's mother had noted in July.[115] But the period of mourning for Vasily Lvovich which Pushkin, as a close relative, had to observe forced a postponement. More worryingly, his precarious financial circumstances threatened to be a permanent obstacle to the union. In a letter to Natalya's grandfather he claimed that the unexpected burden of having to pay the expenses of his uncle's funeral had disrupted his financial arrangements. Perhaps; but this was a fleabite compared to his other obligations. Earlier that year, when it appeared that his suit would be successful, he had instructed Pletnev to enter into an agreement proposed by the St Petersburg book-seller Smirdin. By this Smirdin acquired, for four years, all the remaining copies of everything Pushkin had published up to now: nearly ten thousand volumes which – if all were sold at the printed price – would bring in just under 60,000 roubles. In return the book-seller was to pay Pushkin six hundred roubles a month for the four years of the agreement – 28,800 roubles in all, or just under half the value of the books. It is obvious that the agreement was all in Smirdin's favour: he not only did not have to produce a lump sum at once, but also stood to make a large profit on the arrangement. But Pushkin was desperate for a regular income in order to reassure the Goncharovs as to his financial security. The payments were, it is true, regular, but only for four years; and it was wholly irresponsible to suggest, as he had done, that this income was sufficient for the expenses of married life. His position had, however, improved since then: he had acquired 200 serfs from his father, while Natalya's mother and grandfather had promised her 480. The return on these, added to Smirdin's payments, would produce annually approximately 20,800 roubles – a reasonable competence.* But his gambling debts alone could easily swallow up more than a year's income.

---

* Estimating the annual *obrok*, or quit-rent, at 20 roubles a serf. In fact, those promised by the Goncharovs never materialised.

To take only the first eight months of the present year: in February he had paid Mikhail Sudienko 4,000 roubles which he had lost to him at the St Petersburg tables; he still owed Ivan Yakovlev 6,000 – but perhaps Yakovlev, being a millionaire and in Paris, would not press him for the money. In May Pletnev deducted a thousand roubles from his receipts from sales to pay a card debt to Prince Nikolay Obolensky, a distant relative of the Pushkins and a well-known card-sharp. Between the fifteenth of that month and the beginning of June Pushkin wrote ten letters to Pogodin, begging, with ever-increasing urgency, for a loan of 5,000 roubles to pay a debt incurred at the gaming-table. In the end Pogodin lent him two thousand. And while in Moscow he lost 24,800 roubles to the professional gamester Vasily Ogon-Doganovsky. To pay off these debts and begin married life in solvency he required a capital sum: the only way of acquiring this would be to mortgage his 200 serfs.

However, he was not the only person whose affairs were in disarray. The Goncharovs, too, were financially embarrassed, and Natalya's mother, finding it impossible to raise the sum required for her daughter's dowry, was anxious to put off the marriage for a time. In addition, gossip and rumours about Pushkin's former life and his reputation as a rake and a gamester had come to her and Natalya's ears – 'hence tiffs, caustic insinuations, unreliable reconciliations,' he told Pletnev.[116] Natalya's name-day was 26 August, and the Goncharovs gave a ball that evening. He called on them the following day to take his leave before setting out for his father's estate at Boldino, in Nizhny Novgorod province, to be inducted into the possession of his serfs. He saw Mrs Goncharova; the hostility between the two suddenly ignited, resulting in a row of epic proportions. 'I am leaving, having fallen out with Mme Goncharova,' he told Vera Vyazemskaya. 'On the day after the ball she made the most ridiculous scene you can possibly imagine. She said things to me which in all conscience I could not listen to. I do not know yet whether my marriage has been broken off, but the occasion is there, and I have left the door wide open.' And to Natalya he wrote, with some irony: 'I am leaving for *Nizhny*, uncertain of my fate. If Mme your mother has decided to break off our marriage and you to obey her, I will subscribe to all the motives which she wishes to give for this, even if they are as reasonable as the scene which she made yesterday and the insults which she pleases to lavish on me. Perhaps she is right and I was wrong in believing for a moment that happiness was made for me. In any case you are perfectly free; as for myself, I give you my word of honour to belong to no one but you or never to marry.'[117]

On 29 August, in company with Vyazemsky, he visited Prince Yusupov's estate at Arkhangelskoe. It was the day of the patronal festival, and a French artist, Nicolas de Courteille, who was living on the estate, did a pen and sepia wash drawing of the ceremony. Yusupov, seated and attended by a negro servant, is receiving the tribute of a kneeling peasant. In the background are Vyazemsky and Pushkin, both seated, the former wearing glasses and with crossed legs; the latter in striped trousers, with left elbow on his knee and chin in his hand, looking pensive – as well he might. Two days later he left for Boldino.

He made a rapid journey, passing through Vladimir, Murom and Arzamas – the sleepy provincial town which had lent its name to the literary society of his youth – and arriving in Boldino on or about 3 September. The road crossed a wooden bridge over a little river, the Azanka, and began the ascent of a steep hill, turning in the process into the village's main street. Near the top it opened out into a wide, sloping marketplace. Here was the village tavern and, to the right, Vasily Lvovich's manor.* On the summit of the hill, in an open space, stood the white-painted stone Church of the Assumption, built by Pushkin's grandfather in 1789. Low wooden peasant huts with straw roofs clustered about it. Opposite was an oak paling behind which were a pond and the manor house. The surroundings were very unlike those at Mikhailovskoe: there was no park, with bowers and alleys, no garden, no flower-beds; merely a bare patch of ground with one or two trees. The house itself was a barrack-like, wooden building, some seventy-five feet long and forty deep, with nine rooms on the ground floor and two on the mezzanine. It had not been used since the time of Pushkin's grandfather. It still contained his furniture: an icon of the Virgin Mary, six armchairs, twenty-four chairs, two card-tables, two dining-tables, four sofas, an old-fashioned cupboard with drawers underneath and shelves with a glass front on top, a glass-fronted corner cupboard, a cupboard with

---

* The brothers had divided the village on inheriting it from their father; Vasily's portion, encumbered with huge debts, was eventually put up for auction by the mortgagee in 1835, when it was bought by an hussar colonel, Sergey Zybin.

drawers in the storeroom, a commode with three drawers and two mirrors. One might have expected Pushkin to stay at Kistenevo, six miles to the north-east, the village to which his serfs belonged, but the house there had been pulled down after the death of its owner, Sergey's half-brother Petr.

'With the course of time the ancestral domains of the Belkins were split up and fell into decay,' Pushkin wrote in the unfinished *History of the Village of Goryukhino*, on which he worked during his stay at Boldino.[118] He was thinking as much of the Pushkins as of the fictional Belkins: they had been important landowners in the region since the sixteenth century; his grandfather had still possessed a large estate, but it had been divided among his children and portions sold off: 'The grandfather was rich, the son is needy, and the grandson goes begging,' he had written in another fragment of fiction.[119] However, he found the conditions at Boldino extremely propitious for composition. 'Autumn is approaching,' he had written to Pletnev before leaving Moscow. 'This is my favourite season – my health usually becomes stronger – the time of my literary labours begins.' And a week after his arrival he wrote again: 'Ah, my dear fellow! How charming the country is here! imagine: steppe after steppe; of neighbours not a soul; ride as much as you like, write at home as much as you fancy, no one will interfere.' He was much happier, too: he had received 'a very sweet letter' from Natalya, promising to marry him even without a dowry. Yet on the whole he was glad she was not with him: 'You cannot imagine how cheering it is to play truant from one's betrothed, and sit down and write verses.'[120] He was, indeed, amazingly productive. Before receiving Natalya's letter, still sunk in the gloom with which he had left Moscow, he had written the magnificent 'Elegy':

> The burnt-out gaiety of reckless years
> Lies heavy on me, like dull crapulence.
> But, like wine – the older the sorrow of past days
> Is in my soul, the stronger it is.
> My path is cheerless. I am promised toil and sorrow
> By the future's restless sea.
>
> But, o my friends, I do not wish to die;
> I wish to live, in order to think and suffer;

>And I know, that I shall have pleasures
>Among the sorrows, cares and anxieties:
>At times be again intoxicated by harmony,
>Shall weep tears over my creation,
>And perhaps – on my sad sunset
>Love will shine with a parting smile.[121]

After hearing from her, he turned to more cheerful prose: the stories that were to make up *The Tales of the Late Ivan Petrovich Belkin* flowed from his pen: 'The Undertaker' – who plies his profession in a house on the Nikitskaya, opposite the Goncharov mansion – was completed on 9 September, 'The Postmaster' on the fourteenth, and 'The Lady-Peasant' on the twentieth.

His formal registration as owner of 200 serfs at Kistenevo progressed, too, with marvellous celerity. He sensibly turned for advice to his neighbours, the Ermolovs, whose estate was at Chernovskoe, some miles to the north of Kistenevo, on the Arzamas high-road. The family was headed by the widowed matriarch Pelageya Ivanovna, one of whose ten children, Olga, was married to the president of the district court, Aleksandr Dyadyukin. On 11 September Pushkin sent a servant, Petr Kireev, with an application for the transfer of the serfs to the court at the district town, Sergach; and on the sixteenth, following Dyadyukin's instructions, the district assessor Grigorev travelled to Kistenevo to induct Pushkin into his property. This did not, however, complete all the necessary formalities. The two hundred serfs had to be individually identified, and documents had to be prepared for submission to the Foundling Home as security for the mortgage Pushkin hoped to obtain. Petr Kireev travelled backwards and forwards between Boldino and Sergach, and Pushkin himself, somewhat to his annoyance, had to ride twice – on 19 September and on 4 October – to the little town, with its '11 streets, no squares or pavements, 15 bridges across ravines and the river Sergachka, 3 churches, of which one stone. Four official buildings, two stone, two wooden. 341 dwelling-houses, all wooden. Factories: 7 brickworks, one tannery. 5 shops and a liquor store. A hospital with 10 beds, and no educational establishments.'[122]

During his second visit, as well as attending to his own business, he had a deed of manumission drawn up for one of the Boldino serfs. This was the bailiff's daughter, Olga Kalashnikova, whom he had got with child when at Mikhailovskoe, and to whom he was now making belated reparation. The deed could not be executed immediately, since Olga was formally the property of Pushkin's mother; Pushkin took it away with him when he left Boldino, and promptly forgot about it. Olga timidly reminded him of his promise in a postscript to one of her father's letters, and her freedom was eventually registered with the district court at Lukoyanov on 2 June 1831. She had taken the liberty of jogging his memory, because she had a suitor – Pavel Klyucharev, a petty nobleman with thirty serfs, an assessor with the Lukoyanov district court who held the rank of titular councillor. They were married on 18 October: it is amusing to note that, since Olga through her marriage acquired noble status and took her husband's rank, she was now theoretically Pushkin's social superior and would go in to dinner before him.

'Around me is Cholera Morbus,' Pushkin had told Pletnev on arrival in Boldino. 'Do you know what kind of beast that is? I'm afraid it will swoop down on Boldino and eat us all up – before you know, I'll be off to see Uncle Vasily, and you'll be writing my biography.'[123] Pushkin was incorrect: it was not cholera morbus – an ailment which was probably not cholera at all – but the far more virulent Asiatic or Indian cholera which had appeared in the border provinces of Orenburg and Astrakhan in 1829, and had moved irresistibly westwards. In 1831 it reached St Petersburg – where over 7,000 died – and spread as far north as Archangel; while in Poland one of its victims was Grand Duke Constantine. From here the disease devastated Europe, crossed the Channel, killed 6,000 in London in 1830 to 1831, and eventually made its way to North America.

Pushkin had known of the epidemic before leaving for Boldino, but had not wished to put off his journey. 'I set out with the nonchalance for which I was indebted to my residence among Asiatics. They do not fear the plague, relying on fate and on certain precautions, and in my mind cholera was related to plague as an elegy is to a dithyramb.'[124] He preserved his insouciance in Boldino, even after cases of cholera began to occur in the province. 'I would have liked to send you my sermon to the local peasants about cholera; you would die of laughter, but aren't worthy of this gift,' he told Pletnev.[125] He mentioned this sermon two years later to Anna Buturlina, the wife of the governor of Nizhny Novgorod, with whom he dined on a visit to the town in September 1833.

'What did you do in the village, Aleksandr Sergeevich?' she asked. 'Were you bored?' 'I had not the time, Anna Petrovna. I even gave sermons.' 'Sermons?' 'Yes, in church from the pulpit, about the cholera. I admonished them. Cholera has been sent to you, my children, because you do not pay the quit-rent, and get drunk. If you continue in your ways, you will be whipped. Amen!'[126]

Measures for dealing with the epidemic were put into force in the region in mid-September. The chief – and almost wholly ineffective – recourse was to establish barriers round the larger towns and between provinces, which travellers were not allowed to pass until they had spent fourteen days in quarantine. Having completed his affairs, Pushkin wished to return to Moscow: but this would involve, he told Natalya, passing through no fewer than five – fourteen, in another letter – quarantines, which he optimistically thought would take at least a month. On 30 September he drove over to see Princess Golitsyna, whose estate lay on the high-road some thirty versts from Boldino, to get the latest news and suggestions as to the best route: since she was a Muscovite she would, he thought, be well informed.* The following day he learnt that 'the cholera had reached Moscow; that the emperor was in the city; and *that all its inhabitants had abandoned it* [and] that *it was forbidden both to enter or to leave Moscow*'.[127] The first piece of news raised anxieties as to Natalya's safety; the third somewhat allayed them, and, in conjunction with the fourth, convinced him there was no point in travelling to Moscow, especially if she were not there.

Nicholas's behaviour in visiting the stricken city was greatly admired, and added much to his popularity. Pushkin, too, found the gesture wholly admirable: 'What of our Sovereign?' he wrote to Vyazemsky. 'Stout fellow! You wait, he'll pardon our convicts yet [i.e. the Decembrists] – God grant him health.'[128] That October he paid the tsar a subtle compliment in 'The Hero', a dialogue between the Poet and his Friend. Who is your hero? the Friend asks; Napoleon, answers the Poet; not for his victories and triumphs, but for his visit to the plague hospital in Jaffa in 1799. The lines are an oblique reference to Nicholas's visit to Moscow: a suggestion Pushkin emphasizes by affixing to the poem the

---

* Which of the numerous members of the Golitsyn family this princess was, is unknown. Kuprivanova (91–6) sums up the arguments for and against a number of candidates, and suggests Princess Natalya Grigorevna Golitsyna

note: '29 September 1830; Moscow' – not the time and place of its composition, but the date of the tsar's arrival in the city. In the final section the Friend, following Bourrienne's *Mémoires*, dismisses the story of Napoleon shaking hands with the plague victims as a myth. The Poet responds indignantly: 'No!/Dearer to me than a host of base truths/Is the delusion that ennobles us.'[129]

Nicholas had put his Minister of the Interior, Count Arseny Zakrevsky – the much-cuckolded husband of the 'bronze Venus' – in charge of measures against the epidemic. On 26 September he issued a circular to the affected provinces from his headquarters in Penza. After noting that the epidemic was spreading and criticizing the efficiency of the cordons – the barriers between provinces – he wrote: 'Cordon service is an obligatory duty for the inhabitants and an inescapable service for all members of the gentry, which none have the right to refuse; and they should also, prompted by nobility, hasten to aid their neighbour when first asked or nominated.' There followed instructions on the appointment of temporary officials to deal with the epidemic. On 13 October the Lukoyanov marshal of nobility, Vladimir Ulyanin, submitted a report of the appointments he had made. In the list of the twelve ward curators – the most junior position – appeared 'the collegial secretary A.S. Pushkin'.[130] Pushkin did not wish to be interrupted in his work by the duties of the post, nor did he wish to be tied to Boldino until the epidemic had passed. 'I had all the difficulty in the world in getting out of it,' he commented.[131]

Meanwhile he had begun to worry about Natalya. 'My betrothed has stopped writing to me, and where she is, and how she is, up to now I don't know,' he wrote to Pletnev. 'What about that? That is, my dear Pletnev, though I'm not the type, to coin a phrase – but it is coming to the point where I'll put my head in a noose. Even verse won't come into my head, though it's a marvellous autumn, with rain and snow, and mud to the knee. I don't know where my lass is; I hope she's left plague-stricken Moscow, but where's she gone? Kaluga? Tver? To Bulgarin's at Karlovo?'[132] Though the tone was joking, the anxiety was real. 'I don't know where and how my betrothed is. Do you know, can you find out? For God's sake find out and write to me,' he asked Pogodin.[133] At the end of October he at last heard from her, though her letter was far from satisfactory: 'Your letter of 1st October I received on the 26th,' he wrote. 'It distressed me for many reasons: first, because it took no fewer than 25 days; 2) that on the first of October you were still in Moscow, which had been long infected by the plague; 3) that you had not got my letters; 4) that your letter was shorter than a visiting-card; 5) that you are obviously angry with me, while I am the unhappiest of creatures without that. Where are you? how are you? I wrote to Moscow, but no one replies.'[134]

On 7 November he made another attempt to reach Moscow, having learnt that there were only three real quarantines, and he was unlikely to be held up for a fortnight at each. Arriving at the first, at Sevasleika, on the east bank of the River Oka, opposite Murom, he was told he would only have to wait for six days. But then his travel warrant was demanded and a dialogue ensued. '"Are you travelling on official business?" – "No, on personal, most urgent business." – "Then please drive back to the other road. You are not allowed through here." – "Has this been going on long?" – "About three weeks." – "And these swine of governors don't let it be known?" – "It's not our fault, sir." – "Not your fault! Does that make it any better for me?"' He was forced to return. 'And that is how I covered 400 versts without leaving my lair.'[135] Back in Boldino he resolved that his next attempt would be copper-bottomed, supported by all the necessary documentation. He turned to a neighbour at Chernovskoe, Dmitry Yazykov, the gendarme colonel responsible for the cordon at Nizhny Novgorod, who supplied him with a travel permit for the journey from Boldino to Moscow, while the ward curator contributed a certificate that Boldino was free of cholera – indeed, there had been no cases of the disease in the village.

In the meantime he had received another, longer letter from Natalya. She had got it into her head that the Princess Golitsyna Pushkin had visited at the end of September was young and pretty; that Pushkin had not been at Boldino, but had been staying with her – and, no doubt, carrying on with her. To disabuse her he laid out his doings in detail. 'You thus see (if you deign, that is, to believe me), that my stay here is forced, that I am not living at Princess Golitsyna's, although I have paid her a visit.' 'Your last letter reduced me to despair,' he wrote a week later. 'How could you have had the courage to write it? How could you have believed that I remained confined at Nizhny [Novgorod] because of that cursed Princess Golitsyna? do you know that Princess Golitsyna? By herself she is as big as all your family, including me.'[136] At the end of November he left Boldino again, only to be stopped at Plotava, the Moscow quarantine station on the Vladimir road. But he was no more than seventy-five versts from his goal. 'Here I am in quarantine and for the moment I desire nothing more,' he wrote to Natalya. 'This is what we've come to – we're glad when we're placed under arrest for two weeks in a weaver's filthy hut on bread and water.'[137] However, the arrest was much shorter: on 5 December he finally arrived in Moscow.

Pushkin had told Pletnev that the autumn was a productive time of the year for him, but he cannot have dreamt how productive it would be. There was something about Boldino: the house, its situation, the climate; the isolation: the freedom from the intrusion of friends, family, fiancée or fiancée's family; all this – combined, perhaps, with the stark realization that his life was about to change completely, with worries about marriage, money, Natalya – engendered a psychological state extraordinarily favourable to composition. His creative genius was unlocked, and during the three months at Boldino a stream of works poured forth. In prose he wrote all the stories that comprise the *Tales of the Late Ivan Petrovich Belkin*, and *The History of the Village of Goryukhino* – a parody of Polevoy's *History of the Russian People*, which he had reviewed in the *Literary Gazette* in January. In verse he composed some thirty lyrics; *The Little House in Kolomna* – a short comic narrative poem in the manner of *Count Nulin*; the *Little Tragedies* – the four short dramatic pieces *Mozart and Salieri*, *The Covetous Knight*, *A Feast in the Time of Plague* (a translation of part of Act I scene iv from John Wilson's *City of the Plague*), and *The Stone Guest*, a re-working of the Don Juan story. He also finished *Onegin's Journey*, originally intended as Chapter Eight of the poem, and wrote Chapter Nine – which eventually became the eighth and last chapter. And on 19 October – the anniversary of the Lycée's opening, always a significant date in Pushkin's life – he burnt – as a note on the last page of the manuscript of 'The Snowstorm' tells us – the unfinished tenth chapter of the work, which was to tell of Eugene's involvement with the Decembrists.

'I am overgrown with side-whiskers, have had my hair cut *en brosse* – have become staid and stout – but this is yet nothing – I am engaged, my dear fellow, engaged and getting married!' he wrote from Moscow to his old Kishinev friend, Nikolay Alekseev, now on General Kiselev's staff in Bucharest. Sergey Kiselev, Elizaveta Ushakova's husband, enclosing Pushkin's letter in a packet to his brother, added a postscript on a separate sheet: 'Pushkin is marrying the Goncharov girl,' he wrote. 'Between ourselves, a heartless beauty, and it seems to me that he would be glad to conclude an indemnity agreement!'[138] During Pushkin's absence rumours had been circulating that the engagement was at an end. 'Pushkin is living in his Nizhny Novgorod village, but his fiancée is in Moscow!' Baron Rozen wrote to Andrey Podolinsky. 'They say that his marriage has fallen through; his fiancée loves him, but his future mother-in-law does not approve of our amiable poet and holds against him all the sins of his early youth!'[139] 'I found my mother-in-law full of animosity towards me, and had difficulty coping with her – but thank God – managed,' Pushkin told Pletnev on 9 December.[140] He busied himself in letting his friends know that the rumours were groundless. 'As for the news that my engagement has been broken off, it is false and is due only to my long absence and my habitual silence with my friends,' he informed Elise Khitrovo.[141] Not all welcomed the news. 'The rumour that Pushkin had been turned down by his fiancée, to the general pleasure of the whole of the literary public, turns out to be false!' Baratynsky wrote to Yazykov.[142]

He had taken rooms at the Hotel d'Angleterre: his arrival was noted by the police, who put him under surveillance. However, he spent little time there. After the reconciliation with Mrs Goncharova, he was required on most days to squire her and Natalya to a service at one or other of Moscow's cathedrals, and in the remaining time to be in constant attendance on them. 'I will come to see you,' he wrote to Vyazemsky in Ostafevo at the end of December. 'But today and tomorrow I am on duty with my fiancée in Moscow.' He repeated the metaphor – not wholly a joke – a fortnight later. 'I will try to get leave and come to you for the name-day. But I do not promise to.'[143] He did escape for a short time on New Year's Eve. 'I saw the New Year in with the gypsies and with Tanyusha [Demyanova], a real drunken Tatyana. She sang a song, composed in the gypsy camp, to the tune of *The Sleigh Came*: "Davydov and his nostrils,/Vyazemsky and his spectacles,/Gagarin and his whiskers/Frightened the girls/And drove them all away etc." '*[144]

---

* 'Drunken Tatyana' is the heroine of a well-known popular song; *The Sleigh Came*, a traditional folk-song. Apart from Vyazemsky, those mentioned are Dmitry Davydov, a well-known hussar and poet; and Prince Fedor Gagarin, Vyazemsky's brother-in-law.

Nashchokin was undoubtedly present that evening. His mistress, Olga Soldatova, who lived with him in his chaotically untidy apartment in the Arbat district, was one of the gypsy singers, and Nashchokin continually dragged Pushkin off to their performances. During that winter the two became very close. Their finances – consisting mostly of gaming debts – were inextricably tangled; ready cash, at a premium with both, was looked upon as common property, and each, raising a loan from a money-lender, would share the proceeds with the other. Pushkin, about to set off for church with Natalya and her mother, sent Nashchokin a note: 'I am just going to pray to God and took the last hundred with me. Find out, please, where my Tatar lives, and, if you can, get a couple of thousand on your behalf.'[145] The Tatar was a money-lender and merchant from whom Pushkin had bought a shawl – the traditional engagement gift – for Natalya.

Elise Khitrovo had sent him a packet of foreign journals and books, enabling him to catch up on events in Europe – he had heard nothing while at Boldino. 'The French have almost ceased to interest me,' he told her. 'The revolution ought to be over but each day new seeds are thrown on it. Their king [Louis Philippe], with his umbrella under his arm, is too bourgeois.'[146] The only interest that he retained was in the trial in December of Polignac, the ultra and fanatical reactionary whose appointment as prime minister by Charles X had provoked the July Revolution. He had bet a bottle of champagne with Vyazemsky on the outcome, and lost when Polignac was sentenced to life imprisonment, rather than execution. 'Do not forget to bring, or to send the champagne,' wrote Vyazemsky, who was expecting him at Ostafevo.[147] Events in France were, however, overshadowed by those closer to home.

The success of the July Revolution, together with Belgium's secession from the United Netherlands had fostered thoughts of independence in Poland. An abortive attempt on Grand Duke Constantine's life in November led to an almost accidental slide into armed insurrection; by the end of January, after the publication of a manifesto calling for the restoration of the eastern territories and claiming that the Poles were defending the liberties of all Europe, Poland had an independent government headed by Adam Czartoryski, and was at war with Russia. News of the revolt reached Moscow at the beginning of December. It immediately aroused all Pushkin's nationalistic pride, his fierce, not to say rabid imperialism – all the more so as to his mind Poland was an inalienable part of the empire. 'A humiliated Sweden and an obliterated Poland, these are Catherine's main claims on the gratitude of the Russian people,' he had written in 1822.[148] 'He was a most passionate enemy of the Polish revolution and in this respect, as a Russian, was practically a fanatic,' Zhukovsky commented after his death.[149] On 9 December he gave his first reaction to the events in a letter to his usual correspondent on political matters, Elise Khitrovo. After the uprising had been suppressed, the privileges granted by Alexander, including the constitution, would have to be withdrawn, he affirmed, and continued:

> ... Do you know the scathing remark of the Marshal your
> father? When he entered Vilna, the Poles came to throw them-
> selves at his feet. Get up, he said to them, remember that you
> are Russians. We can only pity the Poles. We are too powerful
> to hate them, the war which is about to begin will be a war of
> extermination – or should be. Love of one's fatherland, such as
> it can exist in a Polish soul, has always been a gloomy emotion.
> Look at their poet Mickiewicz.[150]

Not all Pushkin's friends shared his views. To them he appeared to have abandoned the values of Europe and civilization and regressed to a primitive, crude and reactionary Russian nationalism. Nikolay Turgenev described him in a letter to his brother Aleksandr as 'a barbarian'. 'Your conclusion regarding Pushkin is justified,' Aleksandr replied: 'there is indeed still some barbarism in him, and Vyazemsky took him severely to task in Moscow for Poland [...] It is only about Poland that he is a barbarian.'[151] Vyazemsky took Pushkin to task during one of his visits to Ostafevo that winter: he was there on 16 December, when he found the family alone, and again on 4 January, when he drove out in a party together with Denis Davydov, Nikolay Mukhanov, Prince Nikolay Trubetskoy, Prince Boris Svyatopolk-Chetvertinsky and his wife Nadezhda, Vyazemsky's sister-in-law. 'Some neighbouring ladies came over in the evening, a drunken fiddle struck up, and off went the dance,' Vyazemsky noted in his diary. 'But I did not allow the mazurka to be danced: it is a seditious dance' – being Polish, of course.[152] There was certainly conversation about Poland that evening. Then and later Pushkin revealed those views and attitudes of which Vyazemsky wrote: 'There sometimes manifested itself in him that feeling which it would be sinful to term patriotism, but was closer to pharisaism'; and of which he elsewhere commented: 'Although [Pushkin] was not at all a slavophil, he often showed himself an adherent of those ideas, sympathies, arguments and especially those enmities which are, so to say, those of a Russia turned in on itself, that is, a Russia which does not recognize Europe and which has forgotten that it is a member of Europe, that is the pre-Petrine Russia.'[153]

Pushkin found a more sympathetic listener in Elise; he reiterated his views to her later that month: 'The question of Poland is easy to decide. Nothing can save her but a miracle and there are no miracles. Her salvation is in despair, *una salus nullam sperare salutem*,* which is nonsensical. Only a convulsive and general exaltation could offer the Poles any chance whatsoever. So the young people are right, but the moderates will win and we will have a Warsaw province, which we should have had 33 years ago.'[154]

On 13 January the Polish Sejm had declared that Romanov rule in Poland was now over and that the Polish throne was vacant; on the twenty-fifth Nicholas replied with a manifesto. 'This insolent disregard of all rights and vows, this obstinacy in evil-doing has filled to overflowing the measure of offence; the time has come to employ force against those who know no repentance, and we, calling on the aid of the Most High, the Judge of actions and intentions, have ordered our loyal troops to march on the insurgents.'[155] 'The emperor's last proclamation is admirable,' Pushkin wrote to Elise. But the idea that one or more of the European powers might intervene in support of Polish independence worried him, and was to do so recurrently in the next few months. For the moment, however, he was comforted by the fact that the new French government – in direct disregard of the agreement reached at the Congress of Vienna – had announced that it would not allow foreign intervention in the internal affairs of Belgium: an attitude which, he hoped, would also be taken with regard to Russia. 'It appears that Europe will only be a spectator of our actions,' he wrote. 'A great

* An adaptation of Virgil's line, 'There is only one salvation [for the vanquished] – to hope for no salvation' (*Aeneid*, ii, 354).

principle has emerged from the womb of the revolutions of 1830: the
principle of Non-intervention which will replace that of legitimacy,
violated from one end of Europe to another.' So far France had contented itself with sending to St Petersburg, as a special envoy, the duc
de Mortemart, who had been ambassador there from 1828 to 1830 and
had established good relations with Nicholas; it was hoped he would be
able to influence Russian policy towards Poland. 'So M. de Mortemart
is in St Petersburg, another agreeable and historical man in your society,'
he remarked enviously to Elise. 'How I long to be back there again and
how sick I am of Moscow and its Tatar uselessness.' He ended the letter
with the words '*delenda est Varsovia*', 'Warsaw must be destroyed', a
variation of Cato's dictum on Carthage.[156] He desperately wanted to be
back in the Ficquelmont salon in St Petersburg, at the hub of events,
hearing the latest news, listening to and taking part in intelligent and
knowledgeable conversations on current affairs. By comparison Moscow
was a provincial backwater, ill-informed, out-of-date, and taking a
malicious, unpatriotic pleasure in the misfortunes of the nation. 'Nowadays there is no popular opinion in Moscow,' he wrote two years later;
'nowadays the disasters or the glory of the fatherland find no response
in this heart of Russia. It was sad to hear during the recent Polish
insurrection the gossip of Moscow society. It was nauseating to see
a heartless reader of French newspapers smiling at the news of our
setbacks.'[157]

Boris Godunov had finally appeared towards the end of December, just
over five years after its completion. 'I am thinking of writing a foreword,'
Pushkin had informed Pletnev in May. 'My fingers are itching to squash
Bulgarin. But would it be proper for me, Aleksandr Pushkin, appearing
before Russia with Boris Godunov, to start talking about Faddey Bulgarin? It seems improper. What do you think? Decide.'[158] On Pletnev's
advice he abandoned the idea. From Boldino he sent him a dedication:
'To the Memory, Precious to Russians, of Nikolay Mikhailovich Karamzin, this work, inspired by his Genius, is dedicated with reverence
and gratitude by A. Pushkin'.*[159] This arrived too late to be set up in

---

* 'You want a *plan* [of the play]?' he had written to Vyazemsky in 1825. 'Take the end of
the Xth and all the eleventh volume [of Karamzin's *History*], there's the *plan* for you' (to
P.A. Vyazemsky, 13 and 15 September 1825, XIII, 227).

type with the rest of the manuscript, but Pletnev had it printed off as a separate sheet, which was then tipped-in to the book after the title page. Anxious to pay off his debts and cover his marriage expenses, Pushkin felt he could not wait for receipts from the play to dribble in from the book-sellers. He therefore turned again to Smirdin, who bought the entire print-run – probably 2,400 copies – for 10,000 roubles, and also reimbursed Pletnev for the costs incurred in production.

Four hundred copies of the play were sold in St Petersburg on the morning of publication. 'They write to me that my Boris is having a great success: a strange thing, an incomprehensible thing! at least I never expected it,' he wrote to Pletnev. 'What can be the cause? Reading Walter Scott? the voice of connoisseurs, of which elect there are so few? the clamour of my friends? the opinion of the court? – Whatever it might be – I do not understand the success of my tragedy. It's very different in Moscow! here they regret that I've gone so completely, completely downhill.'[160] The opinion of the court was certainly favourable: 'His Majesty the Sovereign Emperor has deigned to instruct me to inform you that he deigned to read with especial pleasure your work: Boris Godunov,' Benckendorff wrote. 'With the feeling of the most profound gratitude I had the honour to receive the Sovereign Emperor's favourable opinion on my historical drama,' Pushkin replied. 'Written during the last reign, Boris Godunov owes its appearance not only to the particular protection with which the sovereign has honoured me, but also to the freedom boldly granted by the monarch to Russian writers at such a time and in such circumstances when any other government would have endeavoured to constrain and fetter the publishing of books.'[161]

On 18 January 1831 Pushkin was staggered and distressed to learn of the death of Delvig from fever four days earlier in St Petersburg; the news was confirmed by a letter from Pletnev describing the rapid progress of the illness, which seems to have been typhus. Delvig had been depressed for some months. In October he had published a quatrain by Casimir Delavigne on the July Revolution in the *Literary Gazette*. He had been summoned to Benckendorff's office, sworn at, and the newspaper had been banned. Though Benckendorff later half-heartedly apologized and allowed the *Gazette* to resume publication (Delvig could not, however, be named as editor, and Somov took his place), the incident had caused

Delvig to sink into apathetic gloom – a state exacerbated by his marital problems. The previous year Aleksey Vulf had seduced Sofya Mikhailovna: 'I did not possess her completely, because I did not wish to, – conscience did not allow me to treat a man like the baron in such a way,' he noted virtuously in his diary. Though Vulf was now an officer in the Prince of Orange's Hussars ('a regiment chosen by me exclusively on account of the uniform, the best in the army'[162]), and was stationed in the south of Russia, his place in Sofya Mikhailovna's boudoir had been taken by Sergey Baratynsky, the poet's younger brother, a handsome young medical student.*

Pushkin immediately informed Vyazemsky of their friend's death, and on the twentieth called on Sofya Mikhailovna's father, Mikhail Saltykov, to give him the news, but had not the heart to do so. The following day he wrote to Pletnev: 'This is the first death I have mourned. Karamzin towards the end was estranged from me, as a Russian, I deeply regretted him, but no one in the world was closer to me than Delvig. Of all the ties of childhood he alone remained in view – our poor little band collected round him. [. . .] Yesterday I spent the day with Nashchokin, who was deeply affected by his death – speaking of him, we called him the late Delvig, and this epithet was as strange as it was terrible. Nothing can be done! We must agree to it. The late Delvig. So be it.' He wrote again ten days later, suggesting that he, Pletnev and Baratynsky should set down their memories of Delvig: 'Let the three of us write the life of our friend, a life rich, not with romantic adventures, but with beautiful feelings, clear, pure reason and hopes.'[163] Nothing came of the proposal, but his memory was celebrated more ephemerally. 'Yesterday we had a wake for Delvig. Vyazemsky, Baratynsky, Pushkin and I, sinful as I am, dined together at Yar's,† and the event passed off without excessive drunkenness,' Yazykov wrote to his brother on 28 January.[164]

In the meantime Pushkin had been preparing for married life. On 23 January he signed a six-month lease for a brick, two-storey house on

---

* Sofya Mikhailovna married Baratynsky secretly, less than six months after Delvig's death, and spent the rest of her life on her husband's estate in Tambov province. 'She and her husband fight like cat and dog,' wrote Pushkin's sister Olga in 1835. 'He, on the pretext of visiting his patients, travels from village to village and is away for months at a time; then he returns, his wife from rage becomes pregnant, and he leaves again' (*PIES*, XVII–XVIII, 169).

† Tranflat Petrovich Yar had opened a French restaurant on the Kuznetsky Moot in 1826.

the Arbat, paying half of the rent – 1,000 roubles – in advance. The ground floor and mezzanine were retained by the landlord; Pushkin and Natalya would occupy a freshly decorated apartment on the first floor, consisting of hall, drawing-room, study, bedroom and boudoir. In the yard were the kitchen, laundry, stable, carriage-house and servants' quarters. With Nashchokin's assistance he engaged a number of servants: a butler, Aleksandr Grigorev; a valet, Nikifor Fedorov; a housekeeper, Mariya Ivanovna; a cook, and one or two others. Natalya would bring a ladies' maid with her. He moved out of his hotel room and into the apartment at the beginning of February.

He was simultaneously engaged in sorting out his financial affairs, in order to start married life with a clean slate. Of the ten thousand received from Smirdin for *Boris*, five thousand had immediately gone to Sofya Mikhailovna to pay off a debt owed to Delvig. Knowing that she was far from well-off, Pushkin had asked Pletnev to enquire whether she would sell the Kiprensky portrait of him which Delvig had commissioned. She agreed; Pletnev paid her a thousand roubles, and sent the remaining four thousand, in two instalments, to Pushkin. At the end of January the loan on the two hundred Kistenevo peasants was finally approved. He had taken out a thirty-seven-year mortgage, would receive 200 roubles a soul, and would have to pay 2,400 roubles a year in interest. On 29 January he withdrew the whole loan, 38,000 roubles (a thousand had to be left in the account, and expenses amounted to another thousand). 'I have mortgaged my 200 souls, and got 38,000 – and here is its distribution,' he wrote to Pletnev. '11,000 to my mother-in-law, who insisted that her daughter should have a dowry – the money is as good as gone. 10,000 to Nashchokin, to help him out of evil circumstances: sure money. There remains 17,000 for settling-in and a year's living.'[165] He was absolutely right in his judgement of the relative security of the payments. He never saw a copeck of the dowry that had been promised by Natalya's grandfather. Nashchokin, however, whose promissory notes Pushkin had redeemed from a money-lender, paid him back in December.

The wedding had been arranged for Wednesday, 18 February. The closer this day approached, the more gloomy became his views on married life. On 10 February, sending his old friend Krivtsov a copy of *Boris*, he wrote:

I am married – or almost. Everything that you could say to me in favour of bachelor life and against marriage, all this I have already thought over. I have cold-bloodedly weighed up the advantages and disadvantages of the situation I have chosen. My youth passed raucously and fruitlessly. Up to now I have lived not as people usually live. I have had no happiness. Il n'est de bonheur que dans les voies communes.* I am past 30. At thirty people usually marry – I am acting as people usually do, and I shall probably not repent of it. Besides I am marrying without rapture, without childish enchantment. The future appears to me not in roses, but in its austere nakedness. Misfortunes will not astonish me: they enter into my domestic calculations. Any joy will be unexpected.[166]

His behaviour gave rise to new rumours about the marriage. On 28 January Olga Bulgakova, who two years before had tried to persuade Pushkin not to go to Persia, had married Prince Aleksandr Dolgorukov. The newly-weds gave a ball on 15 February; Pushkin was present, but not Natalya. The following day Olga's father, that inveterate gossip Aleksandr Bulgakov, wrote to his brother in St Petersburg: 'Rumours have been going round the town again that Pushkin's marriage is breaking up; it must become clear soon: Wednesday is the last day on which a wedding is possible. It is said that the fiancée is unwell. He was at our ball, was noticed, danced, and vanished after supper. Where is Pushkin, I asked, and Grigory Korsakov answered seriously: He has been here all evening, and now he has gone to see his betrothed. A nice thing to visit a sick girl at 5 in the morning! Nothing good can be expected, it seems; I think that not just for her, but for him too it would be best if the marriage did not take place.'[167]

On 16 February the gypsy singer Tanya Demyanova called on Nashchokin and his mistress Olga.

We had scarcely greeted each other, – she later recollected – when a sleigh drew up to the porch and Pushkin entered the hall. He saw me from the hall and cries: 'Ah, my joy, how glad I am to see you, greetings, my dearest' – kissed me on the cheek

* 'There is no happiness except on the ordinary paths'; a slight misquotation from the last ꞮꞮꞁ꞊ Ꝺ Ꝏ Ꝏꞁ꞊ Ꝏꞁ꞊ (1801) – it should read 'Il n'y a de bonheur...'

and sat down on the sofa. Sat and fell into thought, and, as if serious, propped his chin on his hands and looked at me. 'Sing me,' he says, 'Tanya, something for luck; you've perhaps heard I'm getting married?' – 'How could I not hear, God grant you happiness, Aleksandr Sergeevich!' 'Well, sing something, sing!' – Give me, say I, the guitar, Olga, and we will sing for the gentleman! . . . she brought the guitar, I began to strum, thinking what to sing . . . Only my own heart wasn't happy then; because I had my own sweetheart, – he was a married man, his wife had taken him away from me, forcing him to live with her in the country all winter – and I was very miserable because of this. And, thinking of this, I sang Pushkin a song, – although it's considered a betrothal one, I shouldn't have sung it then, because it's said that it's unlucky:

Oh, mother, what is raising dust in the field?
Mistress, what is raising dust?
The horses have run wild . . . But whose horses, whose horses?
The horses of Aleksandr Sergeevich . . .

I sing this song, and I myself could not be more sad, and feel it and convey it in my voice, and what will happen, I don't know, I can't raise my eyes from the strings . . . And suddenly I hear Pushkin begin to weep loudly. I lifted my eyes, and he has his head in his hands and is crying like a child . . . Pavel Voinovich rushed to him: 'What is it, what is it, Pushkin?' 'Oh,' he says, 'her song turned my insides over, she does not forecast joy for me, but a great misfortune!' And after that he did not stay longer, but drove away without taking his leave of anyone.[168]

On the seventeenth he invited ten or so friends – among them were Lev, Vyazemsky, Nashchokin, Baratynsky, Yazykov, Denis Davydov, and Ivan Kireevsky – to the Arbat flat. 'Pushkin probably has a bachelor dinner today and did not invite me. Vexing,' Pogodin noted in his diary. Later he added to the entry: 'I called and wished him happy. Baratynsky and Vyazemsky were there discussing moral good.'[169] Fresh salmon was served, and much drink consumed. 'On the evening before his wedding Pushkin held a so-called stag-party, or, better said, a farewell drunken orgy to bachelor life,' Yazykov remarked. His observation was based on personal knowledge. Two years later Davydov, in a letter to him about his poetry, wrote: 'At Pushkin's stag-party I, drunk, spoke to you about this, but you were so drunk that you will hardly remember it.' Vyazemsky declaimed a poem written for the occasion; unfortunately, only a few lines survive:

> Pushkin! Tomorrow you're married!
> Bachelor life farewell!
> Dash the bachelor cup to the ground
> But tomorrow don't fire a blank cartridge . . .*[170]

Pushkin, who had been sad and silent all evening, stole away early to see Natalya.

The couple had hoped to marry in Prince Sergey Golitsyn's private chapel, but Filaret, the Metropolitan of Moscow, had forbidden it. Instead, the ceremony took place in the Church of the Ascension at the Nikitsky Gate, in the parish where the Goncharovs lived. There was almost a hitch at the last minute: Natalya's mother sent Pushkin a hurried message to say that she had no money for a carriage, and the wedding would have to be postponed. The messenger returned with a subvention to cover the fare. The wedding breakfast took place in the new apartment. The ten-year-old Pavel Vyazemsky was astonished by the *dernier cri* decoration of the Pushkins' drawing-room: lilac flock wallpaper, embossed with a design of flowers. Yazykov got drunk again; Nashchokin took him back to his apartment where he made a bumbling pass at Tanya Demyanova and was turned down flat.

'Is it true that Baratynsky is getting married?' Pushkin had asked Vyazemsky in May 1826, writing from Mikhailovskoe. 'I fear for his mind. Lawful cunt is a kind of warm cap with ear-flaps. The whole head vanishes in it. You are perhaps an exception. But even there I am convinced that you would have been far cleverer, if you had been a bachelor ten years longer. Marriage castrates the mind.'[171] He was about to find out whether he was right. Another fear for the future had been expressed the previous year by Aleksey Vulf, who, in a little village in Kherson province, had just learnt of his promotion to cornet and was

* The pun in Vyazemsky's lines is unfortunately untranslatable: *kholostoy* means both 'bachelor' and 'blank', as in 'blank cartridge'.

meditating on life, when he heard from his sister that Pushkin was engaged to be married. 'I wish him happiness,' he wrote in his diary, 'but do not know whether it is possible to hope this, considering his morals and his manner of thought. If *tit for tat* is part of the order of things, then how many horns will he have to wear, poor chap, which is all the more probable as his first task will be to debauch his wife. I hope that I am wrong in all this.'[172]

MARRIED LIFE
1831–33

Our age is mercantile; in this iron age
Without money there is no freedom.
'Conversation of a bookseller with a Poet'

(II, 329)

'I AM MARRIED – and happy; my only desire is that nothing in my life should change – I can expect nothing better. This state is so new for me that I seem to have been born again,' Pushkin wrote to Pletnev a week after the wedding.[1] He was astonished and delighted to discover that he had lost nothing in abandoning the experienced embraces of a Sobańska or Zakrevskaya for Natalya's virginal charms.

No, I do not prize violent pleasure,
Sensual rapture, madness, frenzy,
Moans, the young bacchante's screams,
When, writhing snakelike in my arms,
With a burst of ardent caresses and with biting kisses
She hastens the moment of the final convulsion!

O, how sweeter are you, my meek one!
O, how excruciatingly blissful I am with you,
When, yielding to lengthy entreaties,
You, tender, give yourself to me without ecstasy,
Demurely cold, to my rapture
You scarcely respond, heed nothing,

And then grow animated, more and more –
And finally involuntarily share my flame!*[2]

The newly-weds led a busy social life. On 20 February they attended a ball given by Princess Shcherbinina; on the twenty-second a charitable masquerade at the Bolshoy Theatre in aid of the victims of cholera; on the twenty-fourth a masquerade at the Noble Assembly; and on the twenty-seventh they themselves gave a small ball in their new apartment. The eighty-year-old Prince Yusupov, the addressee of Pushkin's poem 'To a Grandee', written the previous April, was one of the guests, as was the egregious Bulgakov, who wrote to his brother: 'Pushkin gave a capital ball yesterday. Both he and she entertained their guests splendidly. She is lovely, and they are like two turtle-doves. God grant that this may continue always. Everyone danced a great deal, and since the company was small, I also danced at the request of the beautiful hostess, who engaged me herself, and on the orders of old Yusupov: "I too would have danced, if I had had the strength," he said. The supper was excellent; everyone thought it strange that Pushkin, who had lived solely in hostelries, should suddenly have acquired such an establishment. It was nearly three when we left.'[3] And on Sunday 1 March they, with some forty others, celebrated the end of Shrove-tide with a sleigh-ride organized by Sergey and Nadezhda Pashkov, at whose house on Chistoprudny Boulevard the company afterwards partook of pancakes.

'Since his marriage he [Pushkin] is quite a different man – sensible, reasonable, adoring his wife,' Praskovya Osipova was told by a Moscow relative. 'She is worthy of this metamorphosis, for they say that she is as clever as she is beautiful, the bearing of a goddess, with a charming countenance; and when I meet him, next to his beautiful wife, I am involuntarily reminded of the portrait of that very clever and intelligent little animal, which you will guess without my naming it.'[4] The animal is of course that which Pushkin himself used as a comparison – a

---

* Pushkin could not publish this extraordinary poem, a technical *tour-de-force* in which one woman is described almost entirely through nouns, the other through verbs, in view of its unabashed mimicry of two sexual climaxes. There is here perhaps an echo of Sterne's remark in *A Sentimental Journey* – 'there is nothing unmixt in this world; and some of the gravest of our divines have carried it so far as to affirm, that enjoyment itself was attended even with a sigh – and the greatest *they knew of* terminated *in a general way*, in little better than a convulsion' – of which Pushkin had earlier commented: 'Intolerable observer! he should have kept it to himself; many would not have noticed it' (XI, 52).

monkey. Natalya and Pushkin were certainly very different from one another: she was eighteen to his thirty-one, beautiful where he was ugly, and tall where he was short: he did not like standing next to her, saying

Natalya

jokingly that he found it a lowering experience. Bulgakov compared them to Venus and Vulcan. Not everyone found her attractive, however. Vasily Tumansky, Pushkin's friend and fellow-poet from Odessa, called on the happy couple at the beginning of March. 'Pushkin rejoiced at my arrival like a child,' he wrote to his cousin, 'insisted that I dine there, and very sweetly introduced me to his comely wife. However, do not imagine something extraordinary. She is a pale little, pure little girl with regular features and sly eyes, like any grisette. It is clear that she is still gauche and stiff. [...] That she has no taste is obvious from her ugly attire; that she has no cleanliness or order was shown by the soiled napkins and tablecloth and the confusion of the furniture and crockery.'[5] But critical comments were rare: most could find no fault in Natalya.

Nevertheless, happiness was not wholly unalloyed. Lev, as so often before, was being annoyingly feckless. He had prolonged his leave from the Caucasus on pretence of illness, but now could not put off any longer his return to the regiment. However, like most young officers, he longed to take part in the Polish campaign. On his behalf Pushkin petitioned Benckendorff and persuaded Elise Khitrovo to use her interest at court. 'Everything had been decided,' he wrote to Lev on 6 April. 'They were only awaiting a reply from Count Paskevich, when Benckendorff received *an unfavourable report* on you from Moscow. I have no intention of making moralizing remarks; but if you had not been a rattle, and had not got drunk with French actors at Yar's, you would probably already be on the Vistula.'[6] In fact, Pushkin was too pessimistic: Lev was transferred to the Finland dragoon regiment in May, in time to take part in the final crushing of the revolt. But this was a mere pin-prick, a passing annoyance, trivial beside the problems that Natalya's family was causing.

Her grandfather, Afanasy Goncharov, had promised to share his Nizhny Novgorod estate at Katunka between Natalya and her two sisters:

each would receive 280 serfs, worth 112,000 roubles (at 400 roubles a soul), producing an income of 5,600 roubles a year (at 20 roubles a soul). However, the estate was encumbered with a mortgage of 185,691 roubles: this had to be paid off before the serfs could be transferred to the new owners. Pushkin had no hope of raising Natalya's share of this sum, and her sisters had, of course, even less. Afanasy then suggested that Pushkin might administer the estate. There was nothing Pushkin less wanted to do; he turned it down, on the grounds that 'the debts and arrears might increase, and the estate might be completely lost', and proposed instead that Afanasy should give Natalya a power of attorney to receive her share of the income, and a promissory note, which would not be valid during Afanasy's life ('God grant that it might remain such for many years!'), giving Natalya a prior claim on the serfs over any other creditors.[7] Afanasy had the documents drawn up, but discovered that it was impossible to put them into effect since he was passing over his legal heir, Natalya's father.

Nor was Pushkin ever repaid the 11,000 roubles he had lent the Goncharovs for Natalya's dowry. 'It is impossible to rely on my mother-in-law and my wife's grandfather,' he wrote to Pletnev, 'partly because their affairs are in ruin, partly too because one should not rely on anyone's word. At least on my part I have acted honourably and more than disinterestedly. I am not boasting and not complaining – since my little wife is a darling not only in outward appearance, and I do not consider what I had to do as a sacrifice.'[8] But the matter continued to rankle, and the sum increased when he mentioned it again. 'Grandfather is a swine; he is marrying off his third concubine with a dowry of 10,000, but can't pay me my 12,000 – and gives nothing to his granddaughter,' he wrote to Nashchokin that autumn.[9] The fine set of diamonds that Mrs Goncharova gave Natalya on her marriage was, it is true, some compensation – or would have been, had she received the jewellery itself, rather than a receipt from the Moscow Foundling Home with whom it had been pledged. Pushkin redeemed the jewels, but financial difficulties soon forced him to pawn them again, this time with Nikita Weyer, the French vice-consul in Moscow, a money-lender with whom he and Nashchokin had many dealings. He was never able to redeem them again.

Worst of all was the constant, nagging irritation of Natalya's mother.

The marriage, it seemed, had made no difference to her: on the contrary, it offered further possibilities for making herself intolerable. While continuing to malign Pushkin to his wife without respite, she was now also able to interfere dictatorially in the couple's household arrangements. A month of this was more than enough for Pushkin. 'I have no intention whatsoever of remaining in Moscow, the reasons for this are known to you – and every day are added new ones,' he told Pletnev on 26 March. They would leave after Holy Week and go, not to St Petersburg, but to Tsarskoe Selo. 'Blessed thought!' he exclaimed. 'I would thus spend the summer and *autumn* in inspirational solitude, near the capital, surrounded by dear memories and similar comforts. And houses there must be cheap now: there are no hussars, no court – many empty apartments. I would see you, my dear, every week, Zhukovsky too – Petersburg is at hand – living is cheap, no need for a carriage. What could be better?'[10] 'My brother is coming to settle here in May,' Olga wrote to her husband, 'so there are more expenses, if not for a carriage, then for clothes. I don't want to look like a frump compared to my sister-in-law, who is said to be excessively elegant.'[11] Meanwhile relations with Mrs Goncharova had gone from bad to worse. Aleksandr Polivanov, a retired lieutenant-colonel of the Chevalier Guards, who was a neighbour of the Goncharovs at Polotnyany Zavod, had begun to pay court to Natalya's sister, Aleksandra. He turned to Pushkin for assistance in his suit; the latter pleaded his case in a letter to Afanasy, asking him, however, not to tell Mrs Goncharova of his intervention. However, she came to hear of it, and flew into a hysterical rage, accusing her son-in-law of going behind her back to interfere in family affairs. 'For God's sake rent me a lodging – there will be the two of us, 3 or 4 men and 3 women servants,' Pushkin implored Pletnev in the second week of April.[12] They could not leave immediately, as Pushkin was still trying to come to some arrangement with Afanasy about the Nizhny Novgorod estate, but on 15 May they decamped hastily, leaving Nashchokin to send their furniture and servants after them, and, arriving in St Petersburg on the eighteenth, put up for the time being at Demouth's Hotel. A month later, from the safe sanctuary of Tsarskoe Selo, Pushkin wrote to his mother-in-law:

I was obliged to leave Moscow in order to avoid troublemaking of a kind that in the long run could have jeopardized mine than my peace of mind; I was being depicted to my wife as an odious person, greedy, a vile usurer, she was told: you are a fool to allow your husband etc. You will admit that this was to preach divorce. A wife cannot decently let herself be told that her husband is despicable, and the duty of mine is to submit herself to what I choose. It is not for a wife of 18 to govern a man of 32. I have shown patience and tact, but it appears that both have been imposed upon. I love my peace of mind and will know how to assure myself of it.

When I left Moscow you did not see fit to speak to me of business; you preferred to make a witticism on the possibility of divorce, or something of the kind. However, it is essential for me to know definitely what you have decided on with regard to me. I do not speak of that which you had intended to do for Natalie; that has nothing to do with me and I have never thought of it in spite of my greediness.*

I mean the 11,000 roubles that I lent you. I am not asking for them to be paid, and am in no way pressing you. I only want to know exactly what arrangements you see fit to make, so that I may make mine accordingly.[13]

Once his anger had expressed itself, he calmed down, and Natalya was able to persuade him not to send the letter: it might have put an end for good to intercourse between him and his mother-in-law.

During the week the couple spent in St Petersburg Pushkin introduced Natalya to his parents and to his sister. 'They adore each other,' Olga wrote to her husband; 'my sister-in-law is quite charming, pretty and beautiful and witty, and at the same time quite a child.'[14] He also took her to meet Elise Khitrovo, employing the occasion to borrow Stendhal's The Red and the Black from his hostess – 'I am enchanted by it,' he told her a day or two later, putting in a request for Hugo's Notre-Dame when she should have finished it.[15] Dolly Ficquelmont was with her mother when the Pushkins made their call; she had heard Pushkin calling his bride-to-be 'a red-haired Madonna with a squint' the previous year, and could now test the truth of this description. 'She

---

* Pushkin is referring to the 200 serfs which Mrs Goncharova had promised Natalya from her estate at Yaropolets, and which never materialized.

is a very young and beautiful person,' she wrote in her diary, 'slender, svelte and tall – the countenance of a Madonna, extremely pale, with a sweet, timid and melancholy air – eyes a clear and transparent browny-green – not a squinting, but an uncertain gaze.'[16]

Dolly Ficquelmont

On 25 May they moved to Tsarskoe Selo, and installed themselves in the lodging Pletnev had rented: a pretty little wooden house on the corner of Kolpinskaya and Kuzminskaya Streets, looking out over the park of the Alexander Palace. Their belongings soon arrived from Moscow, and they settled down to the quiet existence Pushkin had hoped for. In the mornings he would work in his study on the mezzanine, and in the afternoons they would walk together in the parks. But his 'inspirational solitude' was soon disturbed. There were domestic problems: he was obliged to sack the butler, Aleksandr Grigorev, who was discovered to be swindling, not only the Pushkins, but also the local tradesmen. 'On his retirement Aleksandr Grigorev received from me as a testimonial a box on the ear,' Pushkin told Nashchokin, 'that gave him the idea of carrying out a revolt and he appeared here with military forces, that is, with a constable; but this led to his own downfall; for the shopkeepers, having found out about everything, would have had him thrown into jail, from which I magnanimously delivered him.'[17]

During the months at Tsarskoe he corresponded much with Nashchokin; his finances were soon in as parlous a state as they had been earlier, and Nashchokin, whose own obligations were inextricably entangled with those of his friend, was endeavouring to negotiate favourable terms for the repayment of the huge card debt Pushkin owed to Vasily Ogon-Doganovsky. He did not succeed; and Pushkin, writing to him at the beginning of October to suggest a final resort, commented, 'I am ashamed not to be punctual, but I am completely undone: marrying, I thought to spend three times as much as before, it turns out to be ten times as much.'[18] Yet, despite his situation, he was apparently contemplating the purchase of a little estate – Savkino, between Mikhailovskoe and Trigorskoe. 'May you live happily and peacefully and may I one day once again find myself in your neighbourhood!' he wrote at the conclusion of a letter to Praskovya Osipova at Trigorskoe, adding: 'And apropos of that, if I did not fear to be indiscreet, I would beg you, as a good neighbour and very dear friend, to let me know whether I might acquire Savkino, and on what terms. I would build a cottage there, place my books in it, and come to spend several months of the year next to my good and old friends.' Praskovya could imagine nothing more pleasant than having him once again fixed in the district, and, in a series of letters, deluged him with information about the proprietors of Savkino, and about other possible purchases in the neighbourhood. She had, perhaps, not given sufficient weight to the next sentences in his letter: 'What say you, Madame, to my castles in Spain or my cottage at Savkino? As for me, the idea enchants me, and I return to it constantly.'[19] It was only an enchanting dream: there was no possibility that he could ever put it into effect.

He was, however, meditating various schemes for increasing his income. While involved with the *Literary Gazette* he had been extremely envious of the success of Bulgarin's *Northern Bee*, which made a profit of eighty thousand roubles a year, while the *Gazette* struggled to cover its expenses. The reason for the *Bee*'s popularity was that it was allowed to print foreign and domestic political news, being supplied with the latter by the Third Department. In July 1830 he had indeed drawn up a memorandum, pointing out that the *Bee*'s success gave its literary opinions undue weight, and requesting permission to print foreign news in the *Gazette*. But this had got no further than a draft, and Delvig's death had put an end to the idea. Returning to it now, he conceived the plan of founding an entirely new newspaper, and drew up a provisional scheme of its contents: it would have sections devoted to foreign and domestic politics; to foreign and domestic literature; a *feuilleton*; a theatre column; a list of books received, and advertisements. Such a newspaper would not be independent, but, restricted to print only such information as the government supplied, would become to some extent its mouthpiece. This prospect caused Pushkin no qualms whatsoever. Indeed, he went further: 'I offer my journal to the government – as a weapon in its action on public opinion,' he wrote at the conclusion of his plan.[20]

Secondly, he was minded, while not abandoning literature, to refashion himself as a historian. He might not rival Karamzin, but he could certainly outdo Polevoy, whose *History of the Russian People* he had criticized severely in the *Literary Gazette*, and had parodied in the *History of the Village Goryukhino*. He had long had aspirations in this genre, dating back at least to 1822, when he had thrown down a few notes on eighteenth-century Russian history; more recently the research necessary for the composition of *Boris Godunov* and *Poltava* had required an immersion in two historical epochs, and the latter work had in particular turned his attention towards the figure of Peter the Great, the creator of modern Russia. Finally, he felt he could now apply for reinstatement in the civil service, and even for the promotion to which his length of service entitled him.

At the beginning of June he tentatively broached the newspaper project to von Fock, Benckendorff's assistant. The latter was delighted by the news. It would be a splendid coup for the Third Department were Pushkin to become the editor of a quasi-governmental newspaper like the *Northern Bee* and a propagandist for the regime. And no cunning intrigue, no persuasion of any kind had been required: the poet had offered his services voluntarily, had put his own head on the block. He sent Pushkin a fulsome reply: 'In wishing you the most brilliant of successes in your enterprise, I will certainly be one of the first to rejoice in it and to congratulate the public on the fact that a talent as distinguished as yours will contribute to procure for it as much pleasure as instruction.'[21] But if the project were to succeed, it would be necessary to find an official protector for the paper who would act as the conduit between it and the government: the Third Department was unsuitable, partly because of its reputation, partly because of its connection with the *Northern Bee*. A little later Pushkin heard from Wiegel – now in St Petersburg – who made, as if of his own accord, a suggestion. 'The project of a political and literary journal is charming, I have been giving it much thought,' he wrote. 'I have sought and have, I believe, found a way for its execution which is at once sure and noble. You know M. Uvarov, once an Arzamasite [. . .]; your project has been communicated to him, he approves it, he applauds it, he is enchanted by it, and will speak of it to the General [Benckendorff] whenever you desire [. . .] He seized on the idea of your project with ardour, I would even say with childlike glee. He promised, he swore to co-operate in its execution;

now that he knows you to hold good principles, he is ready to adore your talent, which up to now he only admired.' Wiegel concluded by enumerating other prizes that Uvarov swore could fall into Pushkin's lap now that he was known to hold 'good principles': 'In his impatience he wishes to see you an honorary member of his Academy of Sciences; the first vacant chair in Shishkov's Academy should be destined for you, reserved for you; as a poet, you have no need to serve, but why should you not be at court? If a crown of laurels decorates the forehead of the son of Apollo, why should a key not decorate the backside of the descendant of an ancient and noble race?'*[22]

It was clear that official permission would be given for the newspaper, and Pushkin now wrote to Benckendorff, linking this proposal with his other hopes.

The genuinely paternal solicitude of the Sovereign Emperor deeply touches me. Already heaped with His Majesty's benefactions, I have long been irked by my inactivity. My present rank (the same as that with which I left the Lycée) unfortunately presents an obstacle in the profession of the civil service. I was in the Foreign Ministry from 1817 to 1824; for my length of service I should have had two further ranks, those of titular [councillor] and collegial assessor; but my former superiors omitted to put me forward. I do not know whether it is possible for me to receive that to which I am entitled.

If the Sovereign Emperor were pleased to make use of my pen, I would strive with punctiliousness and zeal to fulfil the will of His Majesty and am ready to serve him to the best of my abilities. In Russia periodical publications are not the representatives of different political parties (which do not exist with us) and the government does not need to have its official journal; but nevertheless public opinion needs to be guided. I would take on with happiness the editorship of a *political and*

---

* Uvarov, now a highly placed official in the Ministry of Education, had been president of the Imperial Academy of Sciences since 1818; Shishkov was president of the Russian Academy, founded in 1783 on the model of the French Academy: Pushkin was elected a member in January 1833. In the last sentence Wiegel is referring to the court position of chamberlain, the back of whose uniform was embroidered with the symbolic key of the office. Pushkin was appointed to the inferior office of gentleman of the chamber in January 1834.

literary journal, that is one in which political and foreign news were printed. Around it I would unite writers with talent and in such a way would bring close to the government those useful people who are still shy of it, supposing it without cause to be an enemy to enlightenment.

The permission to occupy myself with historical research in our state archives and libraries would correspond even more with my activities and inclinations. I would not dare and do not wish to take on the title of Historiographer after the unforgettable Karamzin; but I could in time fulfil my long-held wish to write a History of Peter the Great and his successors up to the Emperor Peter III.[23]

On the letter Benckendorff jotted down Nicholas's decision in pencil – 'Tell Count Nesselrode that the Sovereign orders him to be taken into the Foreign Ministry with permission to rummage in the old archives in order to write a History of Peter I. The Count should enquire as to Pushkin's salary or fix it himself'[24] – and immediately conveyed it verbatim to Pushkin. The latter was overjoyed, writing to Nashchokin, 'This autumn I shall occupy myself with literature, and this winter shall bury myself in the archives, access to which the Tsar has allowed me. The Tsar is very gracious and kind to me. Before you know it, I'll be a favourite'; and, the following day, 22 July, to Pletnev: 'By the way I shall give you a piece of news (but let it remain, for many reasons, between ourselves): the Tsar has taken me into his service – but not government office or court or military service – no, he has given me a salary, opened the archives to me, so that I can rummage there and do nothing. This is very kind of him, isn't it? He said: Since he is married and is not rich, one must keep his pot on the boil. Damn it, he is kind to me.'[25] His official reinstatement in the Foreign Office, however, did not take place until November, when he was given one step up in rank, to the ninth grade, that of titular councillor. He was not to be promoted again. His salary – 5,000 roubles a year – was first paid in July 1832, and then only after the intervention of another Arzamasite, Dmitry Bludov, now Minister of the Interior.*

* Bludov had an amusing conversation on this subject with Nesselrode, who began: 'I
[   ] wish the salary to be paid by Benckendorff.' 'Why not by you? Does it matter

Despite Pushkin's initial enthusiasm for the newspaper project, he rapidly cooled towards it. He remembered the labour that had gone into looking after the *Literary Gazette*, a smaller enterprise, and how six weeks of it had been more than enough for him. Editing the new paper would be a full-time occupation: when would he find the leisure for literature and history? At the beginning of September he wrote to Vyazemsky: 'There's no use even thinking of a political paper, but we could try a monthly, or four-monthly, three times a year, journal – there's one problem: *without fashion* it won't sell, and *with fashion* we'd be on a level with Shalikov, Polevoy etc. – which would be shameful.' He received a sarcastic reply, containing an indelicate pun. 'What kind of fashions would they be, if you are thinking of a four-monthly, or three times a year journal? Where would our fashions be up to the moment? Kamchatka perhaps? And there's no use even thinking of a monthly: we do not lead a sufficiently righteous life for our monthlies to be always on time.'[26]

Though Pushkin dropped the idea then, financial difficulties forced him to revert to it the following spring. On 28 April 1832 Olga told her husband that Pushkin was intending to bring out a daily political paper: 'My poor brother is about to defile his poetic genius and defile it solely in order to satisfy the daily material needs; but judging by what he has told me in describing his hopeless position, Aleksandr cannot do otherwise.'[27] In May he wrote to Benckendorff about the project, sending him a copy of the memorandum he had originally drawn up for the *Literary Gazette*. Permission for the paper – to be called the *Diary* – was given by Bludov at the Ministry of the Interior – much to Uvarov's annoyance, since he felt that this was a matter for the Ministry of Education, which was responsible for censorship. It was to begin publication in September and come out three times a week. Pushkin's enthusiasm for the project lasted through the summer: on 4 July Nikolay Mukhanov, a civil servant at the Ministry of Education, noted in his diary: 'Called on Pushkin. Saw Pletnev there and a very remarkable statue of the Empress Catherine. We spoke of his newspaper; he has the most sensible views: anti-liberal, anti-Polevoy, hates the spirit of our

whether it comes out of one drawer or the other?' 'So as to *avoid setting a bad example*.' 'For heaven's sake,' exclaimed Bludov, 'if such an example were to give birth to nothing more than a new *Fountain of Bakhchisaray* it would be worth it' (*PVVS*, II, 221).

journals.' The conversation was renewed the next day at Mukhanov's, when Pushkin repeated the ideas of his letter to Benckendorff the previous year: 'The aim of his journal, as he sees it – is to show the government that it can do business with decent people, rather than with literary scoundrels, as has been the case up to now.' A few days later in the ministry Mukhanov discussed Pushkin's project with Uvarov, who, no longer involved, dismissed it with scorn: 'He maintains that Pushkin cannot publish a good journal, since he has not the character, nor the perseverance, nor the practical preparation necessary for a journal. In a way he is right.'[28]

Pushkin himself was not unaware of these deficiencies, and for practical assistance had been counting on Somov, who had looked after that side of affairs on the *Literary Gazette*. It was a severe blow, therefore, when, while putting together a new number of *Northern Flowers*, the proceeds from which were to go to Delvig's widow, he detected Somov in some financial irregularity and was forced to sack him.* Casting around for a new collaborator, he came across the twenty-seven-year-old journalist and civil servant Narkiz Tarasenko-Otreshkov, who not only had the required practical knowledge, but was even willing to put some money into the enterprise. Despite this happy find – Pushkin was unaware that Tarasenko-Otreshkov had connections with the Third Department – his commitment began once again to wane. Meeting Grech in the street, he suggested – as Grech with some amazement reported to his partner Bulgarin – a collaboration between them: he would take over *Son of the Fatherland* and turn it into a review on the European model. But a few days later he had changed his mind: he wanted Grech to become his associate on the *Diary*, which would be printed on Grech's press. His inability to make up his mind convinced Grech – who, with Bulgarin, feared the loss of the *Northern Bee*'s monopoly – that he was not a serious rival. 'I am not at all afraid of Pushkin's paper,' he wrote to Bulgarin. 'It will be worse than the *Northern Mercury*.'[29] Unsuccessful with Grech, Pushkin turned again to Tarasenko-Otreshkov, and, before leaving for Moscow on 17 September, gave him a power of attorney to raise funds, find a printer, and rent an office for

---

* Somov's crime turned out to be poor arithmetic, rather than peculation. See his letter to Pushkin of 10–24 January 1833 (XV, 10–3)

the paper. In Moscow he endeavoured, without success, to drum up contributors and articles. 'My head spins when I think of the paper,' he wrote to Natalya. 'How on earth shall I cope with it? May God give Otryzhkov* health. Perhaps he will manage.'[30] But on his return to St Petersburg he once again abandoned the project. 'Everything has turned out happily,' Grech told Bulgarin on 16 November. 'Pushkin has come to his senses and will publish neither a journal or a newspaper.' A week later Vyazemsky wrote to Turgenev: '[Pushkin's] paper now will certainly not come about, at least not next year. It's a pity. The Grech-Bulgarin gang of literary canaille remains as strong as before.'[31]

The cholera epidemic that had imprisoned Pushkin at Boldino reached the north in the summer of 1831; the first cases in St Petersburg occurred in mid-June. On 21, 22 and 23 June riots took place on Sennaya Square: the populace, angered by the measures taken against the disease, and believing they were being poisoned by the doctors, sacked a temporary hospital and killed some of the medical personnel. Pushkin was impressed by Nicholas's conduct on this occasion, as he had been earlier by the emperor's visit to the cholera-stricken Moscow. 'The Emperor appeared in the midst of the rebels,' he told Praskovya. 'One person writes to me: "The Sovereign spoke with the people. The mob listened on its knees – silence – the Tsar's voice alone *like a holy bell* resounded on the square." He lacks neither courage nor oratorical talent; this time the disturbance was calmed, but the disorders have since been renewed. Perhaps grape-shot will have to be employed.'†[32] He was equally impressed by Nicholas's visit to the Novgorod military colonies in July to quell the cholera riots there; these had lasted for ten days and led to serious loss of life. 'The Sovereign called the regiment into the manège, ordered the priest to read a prayer, kissed the cross and addressed the mutineers. He cursed them, declared that he could not pardon them, and demanded that they give up the ring-leaders. The regiment gave its word. Witnesses speak with rapture and astonishment of the bravery

---

* 'Belcher': Pushkin is punning on Tarasenko-Otreshkov's surname.
† Pushkin's correspondent was Baron E.F. Rozen; the phrase in italics is a quotation from *Boris Godunov*, part of the advice given by the dying Boris to his son Fedor: '. . . the voice of the tsar should not/Lose itself emptily in the air;/Like a holy bell, it should only herald/ Great sorrow or a great festival' (VII, 90).

and spirit of the Emperor,' he wrote.[33] But in general Pushkin did not approve of this method of suppressing public disorder, nor had he sympathy for the mob. 'The people should not become used to the countenance of the tsar as to a common occurrence,' he remarked. 'Police reprisals alone should intervene in the agitations of the streets, – and the voice of the tsar should threaten neither grape-shot nor the knout. The tsar should not personally approach the people. The mob will soon cease to fear his mysterious power and will begin to pride itself on its relations with the Sovereign.'*[34]

Immediately after the first appearance of cholera Pushkin's parents had fled to Pavlovsk, leaving Olga alone in the capital: her husband was with the administration of the army in Poland. Her attempts to rejoin them were frustrated by the extremely strict quarantine cordon set up on the road to Tsarskoe Selo, beyond which lay Pavlovsk. She finally managed to evade this by leaving in the middle of the night and taking a roundabout route. But, arriving in Pavlovsk and not knowing the whereabouts of her parents' lodging, she knocked up a neighbour, Mrs Arkharova, who reported her to the police. As a result she was sent back to St Petersburg under guard, while her parents were put into quarantine and could not leave their house for a fortnight. Annoyed by the escapade, Pushkin sent her a sharp reprimand. 'Aleksandr [. . .] has become as grumpy as a woman in labour,' she wrote to her husband. 'He sent me such an impertinent and foolish letter, that I would rather be buried alive than let it pass to posterity.'[35]

The court, too, had left St Petersburg at the beginning of the epidemic, going first to Peterhof and then to Tsarskoe Selo, where it arrived in July. 'Tsarskoe Selo is full of excitement and has turned into the capital,' Pushkin told Pletnev.[36] Natalya, in a white dress and hat, with a red shawl round her shoulders, often walked in the park with Pushkin,

---

* Pushkin's view of the nature of kingship agreed with that of the Grand Duke Michael; in his diary he records a conversation of December 1834: 'I had a long conversation with the Grand Duke. We began with newspapers. "Imagine what rubbish they've printed in the *Northern Bee*: about the emperor's sojourn in Moscow. The *Bee* writes: 'The Sovereign Emperor, having visited the cathedrals, returned to the Palace and from the top of the Red Staircase bowed low (low!) before the people.' Not satisfied with that, the fool of a journalist continues: 'How delightful it was to see the Sovereign bowing his sacred head before the citizens of Moscow!' – Don't forget, this is read by shopkeepers." The Grand Duke is right, and the journalist is, of course, an ass' (XII, 334)

or rambled there by herself when he was at work. She caught the attention of Nicholas, who had admired her in a *tableau vivant* in Moscow in 1829, and of Alexandra, the empress. 'I have just been with Countess Kochubey,' she wrote to her grandfather in Polotnyany Zavod on 13 July. 'She overwhelmed me with kindness, asked me for news of all the family, and ended by offering me her services should I have need of them. She has been charged by the Empress to tell me that Her Majesty wishes to see me and that she would appoint a time for this. When I told the countess that I would be embarrassed to come all alone to the court, she had the kindness to tell me that she would do all she could to present me herself. I can no longer walk peacefully in the gardens, for I have learnt from a maid of honour that their Majesties wished to know the time at which I walked, in order to meet me; so I choose the most isolated parts.'[37] 'She has been presented to the Empress, who is enchanted by her,' Olga told her husband.[38]

Though the arrival of the court disturbed the tranquillity that Pushkin had hoped for, some compensation was offered by the fact that it had brought to Tsarskoe Selo two close friends – Zhukovsky, in his capacity as tutor to Nicholas's son, the future Alexander II, and the maid-of-honour Aleksandra Rosset. Zhukovsky lived in the Alexander Palace, very near the house Pushkin had taken. 'Pushkin is my neighbour and I see him frequently,' he wrote to Turgenev. 'Since you told me that my mouth waters when I gaze at his wife, I cannot avoid imagining myself as a great dane, that sits and dozes, watching while something very tasty is being eaten in front of it, and from each side of its muzzle hang two long streamers of saliva. But Pushkin's little wife is an adorable creature.'[39]

Pushkin saw even more of Aleksandra: she called on the Pushkins most mornings, and, after greeting Natalya, would leave her downstairs, occupied with a book or her embroidery, and go up to Pushkin's study to listen to his latest lines. She would often stay for a meal – 'cabbage or green soup with hard-boiled eggs, large rissoles with spinach or sorrel, and for dessert white gooseberry preserve'[40] – before returning to her duties. Natalya was inclined – both now and later – to be jealous of the other woman's intimacy with Pushkin. In return, Aleksandra felt some contempt for Natalya, who, she thought, had a mind that did not rise above gossip and fashion.

Zhukovsky and Pushkin visited Aleksandra almost every evening, sitting in her room in the Great, or Catherine Palace from seven o'clock until nine, when she had to attend the empress. Zhukovsky had been in love with her; had indeed proposed to her; but his feeling had subsided into friendly affection: he sent her charming, witty letters; and, after she had quarrelled with him and driven him from her room one evening, returned the next day with a peace-offering in the form of a set of comic classical hexameters. How could he, unworthy dog that he was, regain her favour?

> Will you order, that I should allow
> The skin to be stripped from my noble body, to sew you
> A dozen warm galoshes, so that, when walking on grass,
> You should not wet your little feet?[41]

At the end of July the empress gave her consent to Aleksandra's engagement to Nikolay Smirnov, a civil servant at the Foreign Office, who had been recently attached to the Russian mission in Florence. Vyazemsky, learning of this, became alarmed, remembering that he had sent her some very imprudent letters. 'Ask her, Doña Sol that is, to burn before her marriage all my poetry and prose; that she still has them I know, for she showed them to someone for a laugh,' he wrote to Pushkin, who replied: 'I was at Doña Sol's yesterday; she has not got your letters here; she is not going to burn them and accuses you of being fatuous. The fact is that she is extraordinarily sweet, clever, and mimics General Lambert's wife and the German chamberlain – to perfection.'*[42]

Zhukovsky had recently hit on a rich vein of composition: 'Zhukovsky is still writing away,' Pushkin told Vyazemsky; 'he acquired six notebooks, and began six poems at once; he has really got the flux. It is a rare day when he doesn't read me something new; he must have written a whole volume this year [. . .] I too am ill of the trot; the other day I shat a thousand-line fairy-tale; another is rumbling in my belly.'[43] The fairy-tale Pushkin refers to is his 'Tale of Tsar Saltan', written in friendly competition with Zhukovsky's 'Tale of Tsar Berendey'. A young writer from the Ukraine, Gogol-Yanovsky (he was soon to drop the second part of his surname), whom Pletnev had introduced to Pushkin

---

* General Karl Lambert and his wife Ulyana were Pushkin's neighbours at Tsarskoe Selo.

in May, was staying in Pavlovsk, and would often walk the three miles of dead-straight road over to Tsarskoe Selo to be with the two poets. Later that year he wrote to a friend: 'I spent the whole summer in Pavlovsk and Tsarskoe Selo [. . .] Almost every evening we met – Zhukovsky, Pushkin, and I. O, if only you knew what delights came from the pens of these wights. Pushkin's [. . .] were Russian folk-tales – not like *Ruslan and Lyudmila*, but completely Russian [. . .] Zhukovsky's were also Russian folk-tales, some in hexameters, some simply in tetrameters and, what a miracle! Zhukovsky was unrecognizable. A new, expansive poet has, it seems, appeared, and a purely Russian one. There is nothing of the previous German.'[44]

The war with Poland was still very much an abiding concern with Pushkin. Though there could only be one outcome, he shared the general discontent with the extremely slow progress of the campaign. 'The freedom of speech amazes me. Diebitsch is openly and very severely criticized,' he wrote to Vyazemsky on 1 June.[45] A little earlier, 'at a moment when it was permissible to be discouraged',[46] in 'Before the sacred tomb' – that of Kutuzov in the Kazan cathedral – he had appealed to the commander's shade to 'Appear, breathe enthusiasm and ardour/ Into the regiments you left!'[47]

On 14 May the Polish army under General Skrzynecki met Diebitsch's forces at Ostrołęka to the north-east of Warsaw. Both sides had around 6,000 casualties, but the Poles, defeated, retreated towards Warsaw. 'Skrzynecki was in this battle,' Pushkin informed Vyazemsky. 'Our officers saw him gallop up on his white horse, change to a chestnut, and begin giving orders – they saw him, wounded in the shoulder, drop his sword and fall from his horse, saw his suite rush towards him and remount him. Then he began singing *Poland has not perished yet* and the suite joined in, but then a bullet killed a Polish major in the crowd, and the singing broke off. All this is fine from a poetic point of view. But all the same they have to be crushed, and our slowness is excruciating.' The advance was held up when Diebitsch died of cholera on 29 May; Paskevich, appointed in his stead, did not arrive in Poland until 13 June, and then took his time in preparing the final assault. As before, Pushkin was much exercised by the possibility of intervention by a Western power, which would lead, he feared, to a European war. He expressed his anxieties in the letter to Vyazemsky: 'For us the Polish revolt is a family affair, an ancient, hereditary quarrel; we cannot judge it by European impressions, no matter what our manner of thought might otherwise be. But Europe must have general objects of attention and partiality, they are necessary both for the peoples and the governments. Of course, it is to the advantage of practically all the governments to keep in this case to the principle of non-intervention, that is, to avoid getting a hangover from another's excesses; but their peoples are straining at the leash and baying. Before you know it, Europe will be at us. How lucky that we did not get involved last year in the latest French row!* Otherwise one good turn would deserve another.'[48] Count Komarovsky, who had married Venevitinov's sister, came across him in the park, looking gloomy and preoccupied. Reading the papers worried him, he said: did Komarovsky not realize that things were as dangerous now as they had been in 1812? He was more optimistic in July: 'It looks as if the affair will blow over without a European war. God grant that it may,' he remarked to Nashchokin, though the anxiety surfaced again at the beginning of August. 'The Polish affair seems to be coming to an end, but I'm still afraid: a general battle, as Peter I said, is a very dangerous thing. And if we besiege Warsaw (which will demand a large number of troops), then Europe will have the time to interfere in an affair which is not hers. However, France won't butt in by herself; England has nothing to quarrel with us about, so perhaps we'll scramble through.'[49]

On 25 August the Russian army reached the outskirts of Warsaw, and the city surrendered two days later. Paskevich's dispatch – 'Warsaw is at the feet of Your Imperial Majesty'[50] – arrived in Tsarskoe Selo on 4 September. 'We were all dining together at the common maid-of-honour table,' Aleksandra Rosset wrote. 'A servant ran across from the Alexander Palace and announced the joyful and terrible news. We all had relatives and acquaintances: my two brothers were at the storming of Warsaw. We rushed over to the Alexander Palace as we were, without our hats and parasols.'[51] Seeing Pushkin's servant, she told him to pass the news on to his master, but in this she had been forestalled by Countess Lambert. As a symbolic gesture, Paskevich had chosen as his messenger

* The French revolution in July 1830.

Prince Aleksandr Suvorov, a cavalry captain, and grandson of Russia's most famous general, who himself had taken Warsaw in 1794. Pushkin approvingly recorded in his diary Suvorov's reception: '"How many men are there left in the Suvorov regiment?" the emperor asked Suvorov. "300, Sire." "No, 301: you are its colonel."'[52]

To celebrate the victory he and Zhukovsky brought out together a little sixteen-page brochure, *On the Taking of Warsaw*. It contained one poem by Zhukovsky, 'An Old Song to a New Tune', and two by Pushkin, 'To the Slanderers of Russia', and 'The Anniversary of Borodino' – Warsaw had fallen on this date. It appeared with remarkable speed: the poems were presented to Nicholas on 5 September, the censor's permission was given on the seventh, and on the fourteenth the booklet was already on sale, at a price of two roubles, at Smirdin's bookshop.

'To the Slanderers of Russia', written on 16 August, before the end of the revolt, repeated the arguments Pushkin had set out in his letter to Vyazemsky, addressing them chiefly to Lafayette and other deputies who in the French Chamber had attacked Russia's policy in Poland – 'Leave us alone: this is a dispute of Slavs between themselves, / An old, domestic quarrel, already weighed by fate, / A question which you will not solve,' he wrote.[53] 'The Anniversary of Borodino', written immediately after the news of the capture of Warsaw, reiterates the ideas of the previous poem, paying tribute, too, to Paskevich, who had been wounded in the assault – some compensation for the fact that Pushkin's muse had ignored his triumphs in Persia and Turkey. Both poems are the expression of that chauvinist, imperialist element in Pushkin, previously manifested in the epilogues to *The Prisoner of the Caucasus* – to which Vyazemsky had taken such exception – and *The Gypsies*, and brought out with such vehemence by the Polish revolt.

The reception given to *On the Taking of Warsaw* was diverse. The poems were naturally much admired at court, and Pushkin's favourite poet, Count Khvostov, sent him some verses entitled 'To A.S. Pushkin, Member of the Russian Academy, 1831, on the Occasion of Reading His Poem on the Slanderers of Russia', with an accompanying letter which welcomed the poem but added: 'Having been convinced by mournful experience that the depraved hearts of envious rebels are hardened and that their ears do not hear the harmonies of the sons of Apollo, I confine myself to the hope that your renowned lyre should in preference sing of Russia's ancient and recent heroes.'[4][51]

He also received praise from a very unexpected quarter. Before he had left Moscow Chaadaev had given him two of his *Philosophical Letters*; Pushkin had promised to try, with Bludov's help, to get them published in St Petersburg. Throughout the summer they had corresponded about the scheme, made impossible by the cholera epidemic, and eventually Pushkin, after giving the letters to Zhukovsky to read, returned them to Chaadaev with some non-committal remarks relating rather to their form than their content. Now Chaadaev, having learnt of Pushkin's intention to write a history of Peter, and having read the poems, wrote on 18 September: 'I have just seen your two pieces of verse. My friend, never have you given me so much pleasure. At last you have become a national poet; you have at last discovered your mission. [. . .] The piece addressed to the enemies of Russia is especially admirable; it is I who tell you this: there are in it more thoughts than have ever been said or done for a century in this country.' What is astonishing, indeed extraordinary about these remarks, is that Pushkin's poems represent views which are completely opposed to all Chaadaev's ideology: in the *Philosophical Letters* he is a completely Europocentric thinker, contrasting civilized and unified Europe with backward and self-isolated Russia.†[55]

As might be expected, Vyazemsky disliked the verses extremely, making a series of irritated comments about them in his diary during the second half of September. 'If we had freedom of the press, the thought would never have come into Zhukovsky's mind, and Pushkin

---

* Khvostov's description is premature: Pushkin did not become a member of the Academy until January 1833.

† 'This postscript contradicts not only everything in general that Chaadaev wrote and thought; it contradicts the very essence of the letter to which it was added! Do we have here a pathological spiritual breakdown or a disgusting, ugly lie? Something else comes to my mind: fear of censorship [. . .] and, simultaneously, devilish irony' (Lednicki (1954), 82). In fact, Chaadaev appears genuinely to have held the views he expresses in the postscript. On 26 September Turgenev wrote to his brother from Moscow: 'Last week we [Turgenev and Vyazemsky] dined in the English Club with Chaadaev, and afterwards had a heated argument about the merit of the verses by Pushkin and others, which here everyone has been reading the past week – "On the Taking of Warsaw" and "Epistle to the Slanderers of Russia". We somewhat attacked Chaadaev for his opinion of the verses' (Veresaev (1936), II, 117–18). Vyazemsky earlier, in a letter to Pushkin of 14 July, had expressed the view that Chaadaev was a little touched' (XIV, 190).

would never have dared, to sing of Paskevich's victories [. . .] There is not a single page of the *Journal des Débats* which does not have an article written with greater fire and greater eloquence than Pushkin's lines in "The Anniversary of Borodino".' And to Elise Khitrovo he wrote, repeating the arguments he had put forward in criticizing *The Prisoner of the Caucasus*, 'Let us not imitate savages, who dance and sing around bonfires of their enemies. Let us become Europeans again, to atone for verses which are utterly not of a European kind. How these verses saddened me. Authority, public order must sometimes carry out sad, bloody obligations. But the poet, thank God, is not obliged to sing of them. [. . .] Such poetry is a terrible anachronism and debases its own beautiful talents.'[56]

'With what lively sympathy it ['To the Slanderers of Russia'] was applauded in St Petersburg,' wrote Wiegel. 'In Moscow, however, [. . .] it was called an immense blot on his poetic fame.'[57] Here it was commonly thought that he had written the poems to ingratiate himself with the emperor, or in return for the latter's generosity – 'Go and hymn the government for taking such measures if your knees itch and you feel an irresistible urge to crawl with the lyre in your hands,' Vyazemsky had commented acidly.[58] The poems caused a rift between Pushkin and the *Moscow Herald* writers: typical of their views is a letter written by one of the 'archive youths', Nikolay Melgunov, to Shevyrev in Italy: 'It annoys me that you should praise Pushkin for his latest doggerel. He has become so disgusting to me as a person, that I have lost any respect for him, even as a poet. Since one is inseparable from the other. I do not speak of the Pushkin who wrote "Godunov" and the rest – that was another Pushkin, that was a poet who gave great hopes and tried to justify them. The present Pushkin is a man who has stopped halfway along his path and who, instead of gazing directly into the face of Apollo, looks from side to side and seeks other gods to whom he may offer his talent in sacrifice. Pushkin has fallen, fallen, and, I confess, I am extremely sorry about it. O, ambition and cupidity!'[59]

This criticism is undoubtedly unfair to Pushkin. He was extremely grateful to the emperor for reinstating him and allowing him access to the archives. But he was not trying to curry favour by sycophantically echoing governmental propaganda: though the views he expresses in the two poems may be criticized, they are undoubtedly his own; they, and his attitude generally to the Polish revolt, stem naturally from a deep-seated and deeply emotional patriotism. Vyazemsky was more just when, immediately after Pushkin's death, he wrote: 'In the Polish revolt we can tell from his poems if he was a liberal in regard to the Poles and the French. These poems are not triumphal, occasional odes: they are the effusion of intimate feelings and deeply rooted opinions and convictions.'[60]

The end of the Polish campaign was marked by an immense military parade on the Field of Mars in St Petersburg. 'The review and the whole ceremony were splendid,' Nicholas wrote to Paskevich in Warsaw. 'There were 19,000 troops and 84 guns, the weather was magnificent and the spectacle extraordinary.'[61] He commissioned the artist Grigory Chernetsov to produce a painting of the scene: the huge canvas – eleven feet by seven – was not completed until 1837; on it were depicted, as spectators of the parade, 223 members of St Petersburg society, with Krylov, Zhukovsky, Gnedich and Pushkin – whose measurements Chernetsov took the following April – as the capital's literary representatives.

In mid-October the Pushkins – Natalya was now pregnant – left Tsarskoe Selo for St Petersburg. They took an apartment on Voznesensky Prospect, by the Izmailovsky Bridge over the Fontanka, but, dissatisfied with it, moved in a few weeks to a more fashionable address on Galernaya Street, just behind the English Embankment: the rent here was 2,500 roubles a year, half Pushkin's civil service salary. Olga, who was having difficulty paying her rent, and could not move in with her parents, since their lodgings were too small, wrote to her husband on 23 October: 'Aleksandr, who, when he arrived, proposed that I should move in with them, has not renewed this offer and even if he did, I would not accept it: the kind of life which they will lead does not suit me: they receive too many people which would scarcely amuse me, and my friends are not theirs.'[62]

Natalya made her St Petersburg debut at a rout given by the Ficquelmonts at the Austrian embassy on 25 October. 'She is of great beauty and there is something poetic about her person,' Dolly wrote in her diary. 'Her figure is superb, her features regular, her mouth gracious and her gaze – though vague – is pretty – there is something sweet and delicate in her physiognomy – I do not yet know how she converses, amidst 150 people one scarcely converses, but her husband says she is witty. As for him, he is no longer a poet when she is there – yesterday he seemed to me to experience all those little sensations of agitation and emotion felt by a husband who wishes his wife to be a success in society.'[63] He need not have worried, for her success was immediate; she was much noticed at a ball given by the Kochubeys two weeks later. '[Pushkin's] wife has appeared in high society, where she was very well received; she pleased everyone by her manners and her expression, in which there is something touching. I met them yesterday walking on the English embankment,' Baron Mikhail Serdobin wrote to his half-brother, Baron Boris Vrevsky, on 17 November.*[64] 'As for my sister-in-law, she is the woman most in fashion here,' Olga informed her husband. 'She is in the highest society and it is generally said that she is the most beautiful; she has been nicknamed *Psyche*.'[65] Natalya had joined the select circle of such renowned society belles as Countess Elena Zavadovskaya (thought to be 'that Cleopatra of the Neva' of Chapter Eight of *Eugene Onegin*), Countess Stephanie Wittgenstein (née Radziwill, Aleksandra Rosset's friend and fellow maid-of-honour), Princess Sofya Urusova, the emperor's mistress, the Swedish beauties Countess Emilie Musina-Pushkina and her sister, Aurore Stjernvall-Walleen, and Mariya Pashkova – a close friend of Dolly, who thought her the most beautiful of all. Dolly's initial enthusiasm for Natalya faded somewhat as she grew to know her better. The following September, after a ball given by the Beloselsky-Belozerskys on Kamenny Island, she wrote in her diary: 'Madame Pushkina, the poet's wife, has the greatest success – one could not be more beautiful nor look more poetic – and yet she is far from witty, and even seems to have little imagination.' But she always gave her beauty its due, noting, after a rout she herself had given in November 1832, 'The most beautiful there yesterday, however, was Madame Pushkina, whom we call the poetic, not so much because of her husband as because of her celestial and incomparable beauty. She has a face before which one could stay for hours, as before a perfect work of the Creator.'[66] Count Vladimir Sollogub, an impressionable eighteen-year-old in the autumn of 1831, later wrote: 'In my life I have seen many beautiful

---

* Serdobin and Vrevsky were the illegitimate sons, by different mothers, of Prince A.B. Kurakin; in July Vrevsky had married Praskovya Osipova's daughter, Zizi Vulf.

women, have met many women even more charming than Mrs Pushkin, but I have never seen a woman who combined to such perfection classically regular features and figure. She was tall, with a fabulously narrow waist, and luxuriously developed shoulders and bust, and her small head, like a lily on its stem, swayed and graciously turned about on her slim neck; I have never seen since such a beautiful and regular profile, and her complexion, her eyes, her teeth, her ears!'[67]

Though Pushkin was gratified with his wife's reception, it did have considerable drawbacks: the more socially successful she became, the greater became the expenses necessary to her situation – in particular, those of her toilette. Help here came from Ekaterina Zagryazhskaya, Natalya's aunt (her mother's half-sister), who conceived a great fondness for her beautiful young niece. Over the next few years she not only provided most of Natalya's many ball-gowns, but also contributed generously to the family's expenses. In 1831 she was fifty-two; a maid-of-honour for twenty-five years, she possessed influence at court and had a wide acquaintance in high society: no better cicerone could have been found to guide the inexperienced Natalya through its intricacies and to instruct her in its etiquette. Pushkin was extremely grateful to her – 'I send my respects to Katerina Ivanovna and kiss her hand with the tenderness of an Ermolov'[68] – and continually urges Natalya to follow Ekaterina Ivanovna's advice. He, too, found her a sympathetic confidante: 'Yesterday your aunt called on me and chatted with me in her carriage; I complained about my way of life to her, and she consoled me,' he told Natalya.[69] But in one respect they came to differ radically: Ekaterina Ivanovna believed Natalya was born to be a queen of St Petersburg society, to glitter brilliantly at a ball or rout. She therefore fiercely opposed Pushkin, when, convinced that high life in St Petersburg was as much a drain on his creativity as on his finances, he suggested from time to time that the family might live in the country.

Pogodin had come to the capital that autumn, and on 20 October 1831 noted in his diary: 'Evening at Zhukovsky's [. . .] Gnedich, Pushkin and Odoevsky – read their fairy-tales – jokes and filthy stories [. . .] Pushkin for some reason was very out-of-sorts.'[70] Pushkin had reason to be morose, both then and later: from now on, until the end of his life, he was never to be free of financial embarrassment. This was not, as had been the case in the past, primarily due to gambling losses, but to the attempt to live a life that was beyond his means. The shifts and expedients, never less than annoying, sometimes humiliating in the extreme, to which he had to have recourse, occupied – especially when he took on, as he later did for a time, the finances of his parents and siblings – a wholly disproportionate amount of his time and energy. For secure income he could rely only on the 5,000 roubles in salary from the Foreign Office, 600 roubles a month from Smirdin (which would come to an end in May 1834) and the varying amounts of quit-rent from the serfs at Kistenevo: 3,600 roubles in 1831, and probably about the same amount in the following three years, after which Pushkin yielded the income to his sister. To cover the rest of his expenses he had only his irregular literary earnings – chiefly the fees paid by the literary journals to which he contributed poems, stories and articles. These were usually small, since the journals had a small circulation; but in 1834 the bookseller Smirdin founded the *Library for Reading*, a monthly journal for 'Belles-Lettres, Science, Art, Commerce, News and Fashion'. This, aimed primarily at the provincial reading public, had up to 7,000 subscribers, and could afford to pay its best-known contributors not only fees which were immense for the time – Pushkin was popularly supposed to receive ten roubles a line (which popular report turned into a gold piece a line) for verse – but also a thousand roubles for the right to put their names on the cover.* But even with this assistance, his income came nowhere near covering his outgoings, and he had to borrow money right and left, in large or small sums, from friends and acquaintances, from professional and amateur money-lenders. On his death his debts amounted to nearly 100,000 roubles. His servants' wages

---

* According to a – probably apocryphal – anecdote, Natalya obtained even more for her husband. 'I called on Aleksandr Sergeevich for a manuscript, bringing the fee,' Smirdin is supposed to have related. 'When I went into his study, Aleksandr Sergeevich said, "My wife has taken my manuscript, go to her, she wants to see you herself," and he took me to her; we knocked on the door; she said "Come in" – Aleksandr Sergeevich opened the door and went away; I did not dare to cross the threshold, because I could see a lady standing in front of a looking-glass, with one knee on a stool, and the maid was lacing up her satin corset. "Come in, I'm in a hurry to get dressed," she said. "I summoned you to tell you that you won't get the manuscript from me, until you bring me a hundred in gold instead of fifty. My husband sold you the poem too cheaply."' (Gordin, A.M. and M.A., 258.) The poem referred to is presumably 'The Hussar', published in the first number of the *Library for Reading*. It has been calculated (Smirnov-Sokolsky, 337) that Pushkin's total earnings – including his salary, but excluding income from the estate – over the period 1820–37 amounted to 255,180 roubles, of which he received 122,800 from Smirdin.

had not been paid, nor his subscription to the English Club, and, besides the outstanding loans, he was in debt to tradespeople of every description: grocers, butchers, poulterers, firewood suppliers, livery-stable owners, carriage-makers, watch-menders, wine-merchants, tailors, milliners and mantua-makers. Though these bills for the most part represented household expenses during the months before his death, others had been running for much longer: his account with Bellizard the booksellers, with Dixon's English bookshop, and with the furniture-makers the brothers Gambs, for example, dated back to soon after his marriage.

But in the autumn of 1831 all this was still in the future; he was by no means under the hatches yet, and indeed hoped that *The Tales of Belkin*, which he had written at Boldino, and which were published in October, would relieve the more urgent of his financial exigencies. On sending the manuscript to Pletnev in July, he had, with excessive optimism, calculated that he might clear ten thousand roubles. In fact, the proceeds from 1,200 copies at five roubles each, after deducting printing costs and commission, were less than half the sum he had hoped for.

He displayed an uncharacteristic timidity in putting the *Tales*, his first prose work to be published, before the public. When he had mentioned them to Pletnev, saying that they made Baratynsky 'neigh and kick about', he added that they would have to be published anonymously, otherwise 'Bulgarin would abuse them'.[71] The work appeared, therefore, without Pushkin's name, under the title *Tales of the Late Ivan Petrovich Belkin, edited by A.P.* The disguise was transparent, all the more so since Pushkin had told Pletnev to 'whisper my name to Smirdin, so that he can whisper it on to purchasers'.[72] When he republished the *Tales* in 1834 he did so under his own name.

A.P., the imaginary editor, is but the last step in an elaborate hierarchy of narrators. A number of people – Titular Councillor A.G.N, Lieutenant-Colonel I.L.P., the steward B.V, and the spinster K.I.T. – relate stories, portions of which they themselves have been told by others, to Belkin, who sets them down; his manuscript, after his death, falls into the hands of A.P., who turns to Belkin's next-of-kin and heiress, Mariya Trafilina, for information as to the author. Since she did not know Belkin, she directs him to an unnamed neighbour, who in a letter gives some description of his late friend. The combination of the testimonies of all these artless individuals, most of whom have no knowledge of literature, paradoxically produces a work of extreme artistic sophistication, which is at the same time distinguished by an extraordinary literariness. Unbeknownst to his narrators, Pushkin seasons the stories with implicit or explicit references to, or echoes of, a large number of contemporary or earlier authors, and parodies, among others, such genres as the Gothic tale and the Sentimental story. Parody is indeed the driving force of the tales, and is combined with Pushkin's favourite literary device, itself a form of parody: the subversion of the reader's expectations. After the repeated – perhaps sometimes crude – use of the device in *Ruslan and Lyudmila*, it is absent from the southern poems, but recurs again in *The Gypsies* and *Count Nulin*; here it is everywhere, constantly suggesting denouements which do not arrive. Only a sophisticated literature, Pushkin believed, was capable of producing or appreciating parody: it was one of the qualities for which he particularly admired English literature. 'England is the motherland of caricature and parody [. . .],' he wrote in 1830. 'The art of imitating the style of well-known writers has been brought to perfection in England [. . .] This type of jest demands a rare flexibility of style; a good parodist is a master of all styles, but our writers are hardly masters of one.'[73] He was proved right by the reception of the *Tales*, which was extremely lukewarm: their subtlety was completely unappreciated. 'These are farces, laced in a corset of simplicity,' Polevoy remarked in the *Moscow Telegraph*, while in the *Northern Bee* Bulgarin commented, 'There is no fundamental idea in the Tales of Ivan Petrovich Belkin. Reading them is like eating a sweet – they're forgotten immediately.' And in 1846 Belinsky, in the last of his long articles on Pushkin's work in *Fatherland Notes*, wrote: 'In 1831 were published *The Tales of Belkin*, coldly received by the public, and even more coldly by the press. Indeed, though it cannot be said that there is nothing at all good in them, all the same these tales are not worthy of either the talent or the name of Pushkin.'[74]

By the winter of 1831 it had become clear to Pushkin that the tangle of his and Nashchokin's financial affairs could only be resolved if he intervened personally. He left St Petersburg for Moscow on 3 December, hoping that settling the business would also enable him to redeem Natalya's diamonds. 'Aleksandr galloped off to Moscow before St Nicholas's day, and as usual, completely unexpectedly, telling only Natasha and declaring that he absolutely had to see Nashchokin and not at all on poetic business, but on far more material business – prosaic,' Olga wrote to her husband. 'Just what the financial affairs are, on account of which he absconded from here, I cannot learn from him, and will not ask his wife.'[75] Writing to Natalya, Pushkin made a joke of the discomfort of the journey in the diligence with two companions. One was 'a Riga merchant, a good German, who was choked with phlegm every morning, and hawked it up for a good hour in a corner of the post-station. The other was a Memel Jew, travelling at the other's expense. You can imagine what jolly company. The German was religiously drunk three times a day and twice a night. The Jew amused him during the journey with pleasant conversation, for example narrating *Iwan Wijiguin** to him (*ganz charmant!*).'[76]

He stayed with Nashchokin, though he had some difficulty on arrival in discovering the latter's new apartment – he had moved to a single-storey wooden house in Gagarinsky Lane (now Ryleev Street), off the Prechistenka. Here Pushkin found his friend living in his usual manner: 'His home is such a jumble and confusion that one's head spins,' he told Natalya. 'He has all kinds of people with him from morning till evening: gamblers, retired hussars, students, attorneys, gypsies, spies, especially money-lenders. Everyone is admitted; everyone has to see him; they all shout, smoke pipes, eat, sing, dance.'[77] More civilized company was provided by Vyazemsky and Aleksandr Turgenev. 'Evening with Pushkin at Vyazemsky's,' the latter noted in his diary. 'Conversation with him and Vyazemsky about England, France, their authors, their intellectual life etc.'[78] Turgenev wisely refused an invitation to a party at Nashchokin's, which Pushkin himself found not wholly enjoyable: 'Yesterday Nashchokin gave us a gypsy evening,' he wrote to Natalya. 'I have become so unused to this, that my head is still aching from the shouting of the guests and the singing of the gypsy girls.'[79] While in Moscow he carefully avoided the Goncharovs: he had no desire, he told Natalya, to have the obligatory scene with her mother, who was still telling all Moscow how mercenary he was.

Pushkin's financial dealings – the business which had brought him to Moscow – were only partially successful; Nashchokin's affairs were

---

* Bulgarin's novel *Ivan Vyzhigin*.

in such a tangle that little could be done about them. But he did pay back the money he had borrowed in January, enabling Pushkin to come to an accommodation with one of his principal creditors, Luka Zhemchuzhnikov. In July 1830 he had given Zhemchuzhnikov a bill for 12,500 roubles to cover his card losses. This did not fall due until July 1832, but Pushkin wanted to have as few debts hanging over his head in married life as possible. He now paid Zhemchuzhnikov 7,500 roubles on account, and must have persuaded him to be satisfied with this and to let the bill run, for it was not presented until after Pushkin's death, when his trustees paid the remaining 5,000, together with 1,389 roubles in interest. He did not manage, however, to redeem Natalya's jewels: 'I don't intend to wait for the Golconda diamonds, but will take you out in beads at the New Year,' he told her.[80] He left Moscow on 24 December.

Yazykov had seen something of Pushkin during his stay and had learnt of his financial affairs, of which he deeply disapproved. 'Between ourselves,' he wrote to his brother, 'Pushkin came here not on purely literary business, or rather not on business, but for gambling deals, and found himself in most loathsome society: among hacks, swindlers and fleecers. This always happens to him in Moscow. He lives more decently in Petersburg. It is obvious, brother, that the saying marriage changes a man is untrue!'[81] Pushkin, however, maintained that on the contrary he had changed. In a letter of January 1832 to Mikhail Sudienko, now living in the country, with whom he had often gambled at the St Petersburg English Club, he wrote: 'I must tell you that I have been married about a year, and that in consequence my mode of life has changed completely, to the indescribable chagrin of Sofya Ostafevna* and the parasites of the Chevalier Guards. I have not touched cards and dice for more than two years.'[82] But at the time he was hoping to borrow a large sum from Sudienko, and hence was somewhat economical with the truth. He had, no doubt, given up brothels, and perhaps he played less than before, but he never abandoned cards completely. Indeed, Aleksandr Strugovshchikov, a young writer who met Pushkin in the autumn of 1831, wrote in his memoirs: 'I played with him several times for quite high stakes, and no better gentlemanly simplicity, courtesy and tact can be desired than that which reigned in our settlings-up (although

* The madam of a St Petersburg brothel, whom he had met in the spring of 1828.

he often lost, he always brought the money the following day).'[83] Though the promissory note for 10,000 roubles which he gave to Prince Nikolay Obolensky on 9 January 1832 might have represented a loan, it was more probably a loss at cards; while a note of his debts, jotted down in August 1836, includes 5,000 roubles owed at cards.

Whenever he was separated fom Natalya, he wrote to her, frequently and regularly. She replied, with, it seems, equal frequency, but her letters have unfortunately not survived.* The tone of Pushkin's side of the correspondence is given by the five letters that he wrote to her during this visit to Moscow. They are dotingly affectionate, intimate (later letters are not without indecencies), amusing, full of gossip, of chiding admonitions and of worries about her well-being. During this first separation he is especially concerned that his servants, Vasily and Aleshka, appear to be taking advantage of her during his absence. 'Tell the servants that I am very dissatisfied with them,' he writes. 'I ordered them not to worry you, but they, I see, have rejoiced at my absence. How dared they admit Fomin,† when you did not want to receive him? and you are a fine one, too. You dance to their tune; pay money when anyone asks; our house-keeping won't survive like that.'[84] On returning from his next trip to Moscow he was, his father wrote, because of Natalya's laxness, 'obliged to give a good beating to that well-known drunkard Aleshka for his exploits and send him back to the country'.[85]

But during this first separation his chief anxiety concerns Natalya's pregnancy. 'Since I left you, I am constantly somehow afraid for you,' he writes. 'You won't stay at home, you'll go to the palace, and before you know you'll have a miscarriage on the hundred and fifth step of the grand staircase. My darling, my wifekin, my angel! do me this favour: walk about the room for two hours a day, and take care of yourself [...] If you go to a ball, for God's sake don't dance anything except quadrilles.' He repeats the injunctions in the next letter, but then has disturbing news from Natalya: 'What is this *vertige*?' he asks. 'Fainting-fits or nausea? Has the midwife seen you? Have you been let blood? All this terribly worries me. The more I think, the more clearly I see that it was stupid of me to leave you. If I'm not there you'll do something

* On the fate of her letters see S.V. Zhitomirskaya, 'K istorii pisem N.N. Pushkinoy', *Prometey*, VIII, 148–65.
† Perhaps Nikolay Ilich Fomin, a writer and bookseller.

silly. Before you know you'll have a miscarriage. Why don't you walk? You gave me your word of honour that you'd walk two hours a day.'[86]

His admonitions had, of course, little effect on Natalya. 'I found my wife healthy, despite her girlish imprudence,' Pushkin wrote to Nashchokin on his return to St Petersburg – 'she dances at balls, exchanges compliments with the Sovereign, and skips off the porch. I must take the wench in hand.'[87] During his absence she had attended a ball given by Prince Kochubey; and on 19 December she went to a ball at the Anichkov Palace, where the emperor engaged her in conversation. Another young guest, Princess Varvara Repnina, wrote home to her mother: 'The only ladies to attract my attention at the ball were Mrs Pushkina, the poet's wife – she is really magnificent; I prefer her to Countess Zavadovskaya, and then the Ribeaupierre girls. Oh mama, how charming they are!'*[88] It was a signal honour to have been invited to the Anichkov Palace: of the balls here Korff noted: 'To these evenings an especially privileged company was invited, known in upper circles as *la Société d'Anitchkoff*, and whose composition, determined not so much by the ladder of the official hierarchy, as by the closeness to the royal family, rarely changed.'[89] Natalya could not, however, be a regular visitor since neither she nor Pushkin held a position at court.

While Pushkin was in Moscow the artist Aleksandr Bryullov had painted a watercolour of Natalya, the only portrait executed during Pushkin's lifetime. She is wearing a pink-and-white ball dress with leg-of-mutton sleeves. Her waist is extraordinarily small; her bare shoulders rise from a froth of lace and ribbon; her hair is intricately braided on top of her head; she has long, pendant ear rings and on her head a circlet of pearls with a pendant *à La Belle Ferronnière* over her forehead. She looks demurely down, yet at the same time there is more than a hint in her expression of the nineteen-year-old minx. Pushkin, besotted as he was, had of course no hope of taking her in hand. Despite her pregnancy, they continued to lead a hectic social life. 'My sister-in-law, Natasha, will soon be a mother and will be, I assure you, a most tender and exemplary mother,' Olga wrote to her husband. 'But it is a pity that she does not look after herself at the moment. According to her, she is obliged to spend almost every evening at the play or at a rout,

---

* The three daughters of Aleksandr Ribeaupierre, the Russian ambassador to Prussia.

and thus spends nights without sleep. Aleksandr rages against this, but, having cursed a good deal, always yields to her insistence that they have to go out, and leaves with his wife to yawn all night at balls.'[90]

Pushkin was inducted for the second time into the Foreign Office on 27 January 1832, taking an oath and affirming that he 'belonged to no Masonic lodge nor to any secret society either within the empire or outside it';[91] and on 18 February, the first anniversary of his wedding, he was introduced to its archives by Bludov. It was clear that the authorities viewed his new role as historiographer favourably: the previous day he had received a personal gift from the emperor, conveyed through Benckendorff: *The Complete Collected Laws of the Russian Empire from 1649* in fifty-five volumes, intended as an aid to his research. And when, thanking Benckendorff for 'this precious sign of the tsar's benevolence to me', he requested permission to use Voltaire's library – acquired after the French writer's death by Catherine II – in the Hermitage, this was immediately accorded.[92]

On 19 February the book-seller Smirdin, to celebrate his move from the Moika Embankment to the Nevsky, next to the Lutheran church of St Peter, gave a large banquet in the new premises. The whole of St Petersburg literary society was present. At the table Pushkin had opposite him Bulgarin and Grech. Between these two sat Vasily Semenov, who had been a year junior to Pushkin at the Lycée, and was now one of the St Petersburg censors. Pushkin leant across and remarked loudly, 'You're just like Christ at Golgotha today, Semenov' – Christ, of course, had been crucified between two thieves. Bulgarin was incensed, but Grech took the insult in good part, and a little later himself came out with a bold witticism when he proposed the health 'of our sovereign the emperor, the author of that splendid work, the Censorship Statute'.[93] The moment was preserved by Bryullov, whose sketch of Grech proposing the toast, champagne-glass in hand, was reproduced as the frontispiece to the first number of Smirdin's almanac *House-Warming*, the idea for which had been conceived at the banquet.*

Grech's remark was all the more bold in that the literary world had

---

* Vyazemsky, in a letter to Turgenev, expressed his dislike of the illustration 'where next to Zhukovsky is Khvostov, where I am in profile, but Bulgarin in full phiz' (OA, 4, 250).

just been shocked by an example of Nicholas's arbitrary exercise of his power as supreme censor. A new journal, the *European*, had been founded by Ivan Kireevsky in Moscow at the beginning of the year. He had secured Zhukovsky, Yazykov, Baratynsky, Khomyakov and Turgenev as collaborators, while Pushkin and Vyazemsky had promised their support. The first two numbers were favourably received. Pushkin congratulated Kireevsky on them, praising especially – 'at long last we have got genuine criticism' – his 'Survey of Russian Literature for 1831'.[94] But Nicholas, prompted by Benckendorff (who in turn had been prompted

Grech

by Bulgarin), after perusing Kireevsky's articles, declared that the author, under the guise of writing about literature, was in fact writing about politics. He ordered the journal to be closed, since its editor had shown himself to be 'not a right-thinking and not a reliable person'.[95] Zhukovsky was related to Kireevsky (his half-sister was Kireevsky's grandmother). He had lived with the family when Kireevsky was a child, and had been influential in the latter's education, becoming extremely fond of the young man. He now endeavoured to persuade the emperor to rescind his decision. But his intercession was unavailing. Chagrined, and in poor health, he applied for a year's leave to take the waters at Ems.

He left on 18 June, accompanied by Turgenev and Sergey Vikulin, a casual acquaintance, who was travelling to Scotland to meet his fiancée, a Miss Mclean.* Vyazemsky, Pushkin, and Vasily Engelhardt – Pushkin's old gaming companion, to whom he had addressed the poem 'I have escaped from Aesculapius' in 1819 – saw the travellers off, accompanying them on the pyroscaph to Kronstadt. 'The steamer left at one,' Turgenev wrote in his diary. 'I sat on the deck – watching the receding shore, and leaving no one, apart from graves, in Petersburg, since Zhukovsky was with me. He leant for a moment on me and sighed on my behalf for our native land: he alone sensed that I could not return . . . Petersburg, its

---

* Vikulin, a pious but somewhat unbalanced young man, had retired from the Life Guards Dragoons six years earlier because of ill-health; since then he had often travelled to Europe. His engagement to Miss Mclean may have been a figment of his imagination; in 1844, in Devonshire, she refused to marry him: he went mad and died four years later.

suburbs, were far away; I summoned Pushkin, Engelhardt, Vyazemsky, Zhukovsky and Vikulin to breakfast and champagne in the cabin – and there became animated with sadness and my loneliness in the world . . . My brother was far away . . . Pushkin reminded me that I was not yet beyond Kronstadt, where we arrived at four.* We embarked on another steamer: *Nicholas I*, on which I had travelled to Russia a year ago; we dined badly, but drank well, at seven I parted with Engelhardt and Pushkin: they returned to Petersburg; Vyazemsky remained with us, envying our lot.'96

Zhukovsky's absence – he did not return to Russia until the following September – was a sad loss for Pushkin: the two had become very close since the previous summer in Tsarskoe Selo. He missed the well-known Saturday literary gatherings in Zhukovsky's huge, low-ceilinged study on the fourth floor of Shepelevsky House;† he missed their tête-à-tête discussions; he missed Zhukovsky's help and advice, which, with the latter's knowledge of the court, could be invaluable; and he missed, too, although he was perhaps unaware of this, Zhukovsky's steadying influence.

At the beginning of May, though Natalya was very near her term, the Pushkins had moved to a new apartment on Furshtatskaya Street, near the Tauric Gardens, furnishing it in part with mahogany furniture from the warehouse of the Gambs brothers, cabinet-makers to the court: six stools, a writing-table covered in red morocco, a swivel chair, a low armchair, and a sofa. On 19 May their first child, a girl, was born: they named her Mariya. 'I have just come from Khitrovo,' Pushkin wrote to Vera Vyazemskaya a fortnight later. 'She could not be more touched by Batyushkov's state – she offers to come herself to attempt the ultimate remedy, with a self-abnegation which is really admirable.‡ Apropos of self-abnegation: imagine, my wife has been maladroit enough to give birth to a little lithograph of me. I am in despair at it, in spite of all my self-conceit.'97

---

* Pushkin was presumably warning Turgenev that, over-animated by champagne, he was being injudicious in his remarks: Turgenev's brother, Nikolay, was of course a proscribed Decembrist, who had only escaped imprisonment by remaining abroad.

† This building was immediately next to the Winter Palace; it was replaced by the New Hermitage, built in 1839–51.

‡ Batyushkov's doctor had suggested that his patient's mental state might be improved by sexual intercourse; but Pushkin is doubtless joking about Elise's willingness to offer herself as the remedy.

Afanasy Nikolaevich, Natalya's grandfather, had come to St Petersburg that spring. In an attempt to redeem his financial situation, he was petitioning the tsar for permission to sell the entailed estates, and for a subsidy to keep his factories from bankruptcy. While these requests were slowly passing through the civil service bureaucracy, he was amusing himself in the capital, buying expensive presents for his concubines in Polotnyany Zavod – though he was now seventy-two, and ill to boot. He came to see Natalya on 22 May, bringing with him 500 roubles for his great-granddaughter, and was present at the child's christening – in the Cathedral of St Sergius, on the Liteiny Prospect – on 7 June: the godparents were Sergey Lvovich and Ekaterina Zagryazhskaya. Soon after returning to Moscow he learnt that his petitions had been unsuccessful; he died shortly afterwards, on 8 September.

Pushkin, worried about Natalya's inheritance, and wishing, too, to take out a second mortgage on the Kistenevo serfs, hurried off to Moscow, arriving there on 21 September, and instead of staying with Nashchokin put up at the Hotel d'Angleterre: a wise decision, for the latter's household was even more chaotic than before. Two new hangers-on had appeared, 'an actor, who used to play second suitors, but now struck by paralysis and gone completely stupid, and a monk, a convert from the Jews, hung about with fetters, who imitates the Jewish synagogue for us, and tells us suggestive stories about the Moscow nuns'.[98]

With Afanasy's death Natalya's elder brother, Dmitry, a Foreign Office official, had become the *de facto* head of the family. But he could not take charge of the estate until the legal heir, his father Nikolay, had been recognized by the courts as incompetent. This took place on 1 November, when Dmitry was named as his father's guardian. His mother, Natalya Ivanovna, had declined the office and renounced all claim on the Goncharov estate, no doubt fearing that otherwise her own estate at Yaropolets might become security for the Goncharov debts. Before his death Afanasy had given her, for his granddaughters, promissory notes – liens on the Goncharov property – for 100,000 roubles, in lieu of the estate he had promised them. She sold these for 60,000 in cash, but neither repaid Pushkin the 11,000 she owed him, nor shared the proceeds among her daughters. Dmitry proved a poor businessman, never succeeding in ridding the lands and factories of their burden of debt. In the end the only inheritance Natalya received from her grandfather was the statue of Catherine II and, spread over the years 1832 to 1836, the sum of 6,288 roubles and 9 copecks, with a final payment of 1,597 roubles 27½ copecks in 1837.

On applying to the Moscow Foundling Home for a second mortgage, Pushkin discovered that he would need documents other than those he already possessed. He wrote to Kalashnikov, the bailiff at Boldino, ordering him to have them drawn up and sent to Nashchokin; then, giving his friend a letter of attorney to act on his behalf, on 10 October hurried back to St Petersburg and Natalya. Kalashnikov was unconscionably slow in obtaining the paperwork. Only on 18 January 1833 did he inform Pushkin that the necessary documents had been sent to Nashchokin: he had had to travel four times to Nizhny Novgorod, and three to Sergach: his expenses amounted to 271 roubles. Pushkin gave Nashchokin a month to conclude the affair, and then wrote asking him to pay Delvig's father-in-law, Senator Mikhail Saltykov, 2,525 roubles – a debt he was embarrassed not to have settled earlier – out of the sum raised by the mortgage, and to send the rest to him. He was, however, too sanguine. The letter crossed with one from Nashchokin, telling him that the new certificate was useless: the Foundling Home would only give a second mortgage if the landowner possessed at least five desyatins of land for each mortgaged serf; Pushkin had less than three. Furthermore, the figures given in the latest document did not agree with that used to secure the first mortgage. Pushkin obviously did not understand the proviso, thinking it was only necessary that the documents should agree. At the end of November that year Nashchokin wrote to him in some irritation: 'Your bailiff came and corrected the paper – but they still will not give you any money – as I wrote and told you I know not how many times you have to have five desyatins a soul, and he has again only got three – before it was two.'[99] The attempt to raise a second mortgage had finally to be abandoned.

Pushkin's correspondence with Natalya during his short stay in Moscow reveals a change in their relationship. During his first absence he had worried about her ability to cope with domestic affairs. Reassured on this score, he now worries, not that the household will fall into chaos because of her timidity, but that her lack of timidity will reduce it to chaos. 'I see you waging war without me at home, engaging new servants, breaking carriages, checking the accounts, milking the wet-nurse, Well done, you smart wench!' he writes with affectionate irony.*[100] But a new concern emerges: almost every letter from Moscow takes Natalya to task, sometimes seriously, more often jokingly, for her flirtatiousness. 'It is not good that you are engaging in various flirtations,' he writes; 'you should not have received Pushkin,† firstly because he has never called on us when I was there, and secondly, though I am sure of you, one must not give society grounds for gossip.' 'You flirt with the whole diplomatic corps,' he remarks in another letter, and couples this concern with anxiety for her health: 'By the way, see if you are with child, and in this case look after yourself from the beginning. Do not go riding, but find some other way of flirting.'[101] From now on in his letters to her he will constantly, almost obsessively, harp on this aspect of her behaviour. Sometimes he forbids flirtation – 'Do not flirt with Sobolevsky', 'Do not flirt with the tsar' – at other times has no objection to it – 'I allow you to flirt to your heart's content,' he writes.[102]

He arrived back in St Petersburg suffering from what he believed to be rheumatism. He complained of it in a letter to his father, who passed on the news to Olga and her husband. 'Rheumatism in his leg made itself felt before he left Moscow, and, judging by his letter, Alexandre is suffering terribly. Outwardly the leg is normal: no redness, no swelling, but hellish inward pain makes him a martyr, he says that the pain goes through his whole body, and is especially in his right hand, which is why his handwriting is feeble and illegible [. . .] Without acute pain he can neither lie, nor sit, nor stand, least of all walk; he was obliged to leave home [. . .], leaning on a stick, like an 80-year-old.'[103]

His affliction could hardly have been more malapropos, since activity was demanded of him. He had discovered, as he had feared, that Natalya had managed to produce complete confusion in the household. Apologizing to Nashchokin for not having sent him the wherewithal to pay off a debt, he wrote: 'Let this be my justification for unpunctuality. When I got here, I found great disorders in my house, was obliged to

---

* Natalya had informed Pushkin that their carriage had broken down when she was using it. 'My coachbuilder is a rascal,' he replied. 'He charged me 500 r. for repairs and a month later the carriage might as well be scrapped' (To N.N. Pushkina, 25 September 1832; XV, 31).

† Probably Colonel Fedor Matveevich Musin-Pushkin of the Life Guards Hussars, who was distantly related to Natalya.

turn off servants, change cooks, and finally to rent a new apartment, and consequently to use those sums which otherwise would have been inviolable.'[104] The new apartment was much nearer the centre, on the corner of Bolshaya Morskaya and Gorokhovaya Streets. On the third floor, it consisted of twelve rooms and a kitchen. Included in the rent of 3,300 roubles a year were a coach-house, a stable with three stalls, a small woodshed, an ice-house and an attic for drying washing. Three of the rooms were hung with French wallpaper, and five had parquet floors. The landlord was Petr Zhadimerovsky, a well-known merchant, who owned a considerable amount of property in St Petersburg. The Pushkins settled in at the beginning of December, bringing their furniture with them and in addition buying from the Gambs brothers a large mahogany-framed psyche-glass for Natalya's boudoir, which cost 550 roubles.

She was now pregnant once more – 'I don't know what he does with his spinster muse, but with his lawful wife he labours for posterity, she is with child again,' Vyazemsky told Zhukovsky, who was now living in a village on the shore of Lake Geneva.[105] However, the condition was as yet scarcely noticeable, and certainly did not prevent her from attending balls that winter. The season came to a climax at Shrove-tide, the week before Lent. On 6 February 1833 the Ficquelmonts gave a ball at the Austrian embassy at which the royal family was present. Nicholas, wearing, in compliment to his host, the uniform of an officer in the Hungarian hussars, singled out Pushkin and engaged him for some time in conversation about his work on Peter the Great. Such gracious public condescension was taken by those present as a signal mark of the emperor's favour. Pushkin immediately exploited the situation, approaching the Minister of War, Count Aleksandr Chernyshev, and asking him for access to the archives of the General Staff. Chernyshev promised his assistance.

Pushkin had spent the earlier part of the day in rather different fashion, attending the funeral of Gnedich, who had fallen victim three days earlier to the influenza epidemic that was sweeping St Petersburg. Most of the literary figures of the capital were present, and Pushkin, together with Krylov, Vyazemsky, Pletnev and others, carried the coffin from the church to the cemetery at the Alexander Nevsky monastery. After the ceremony he contributed to a subscription to raise a monument to the writer. A somewhat farcical note was given to the proceedings by the behaviour of Count Khvostov, who, 'during the whole service gave out his poems and spoke at the top of his voice, so that at the end of the ceremony Krylov said to him: "You were more audible than the Gospels"'.[106]

On 8 February, Ash Wednesday, the Minister of the Court, Prince Volkonsky, gave a masquerade ball in the Department of Imperial Domains on the Dvortsovaya Embankment, which began at half past nine and ended at six. 'Yesterday's masquerade was splendid, brilliant, diverse, hot, stifling, exhausting, prolonged,' Vyazemsky wrote.[107] Natalya 'appeared in the costume of the Priestess of the Sun, and had much success. The Emperor and Empress approached her and praised her costume, and the Emperor declared her the Queen of the Ball.'[108] Immediately afterwards, however, she went down with influenza, and spent the first week of Lent in bed.

Pushkin's friends disapproved of his new way of life. 'You are right to despise such loafers as Pushkin, who does nothing except in the morning go through old letters in his filthy trunk, and in the evening take his wife around balls, not so much for her pleasure, as for his,' Pletnev wrote to Zhukovsky; he was echoed by Gogol: 'One meets Pushkin nowhere, except at balls. So he will fritter away his whole life, unless some chance, or rather necessity, drags him into the country.'[109] Gogol's first sentence can hardly be taken literally; he did not move in this elevated society, and had no chance of meeting Pushkin at a ball. And both did Pushkin a rank injustice in implying that it was of his choice that he led this kind of life. It was not, though he undeniably enjoyed some aspects of high society: the company of cultured and civilized diplomats, or of beautiful and charming women, for example. But, as he complained to Nashchokin, the drawback was that he could not live this life and at the same time finance it: 'Worries about life keep me from boredom. But I do not have leisure, that careless, free bachelor life necessary for the writer. I whirl about society, my wife is in high fashion – all this demands money, I obtain money through labours, and labours demand solitude. Here is how I plan my future. In the summer after my wife's lying-in, I will dispatch her to her sisters in the Kaluga village, and myself will journey to Nizhny, and perhaps to Astrakhan.'[110]

Though these criticisms were unfounded, an unprejudiced observer might have censured other elements of Pushkin's behaviour, in particular the unabashed fashion in which, not long after his marriage, he began to court other women. 'Countess [Emilie Musina-] Pushkina is in beauty this year,' Dolly Ficquelmont had noted in her diary in November, 'she glitters with a new brilliance thanks to the homage which the poet Pushkin gives her.'[111] On 26 May he bought a two-day pass to Kronstadt, ostensibly to see off Sergey Kiselev, Elizaveta Ushakova's husband, but in reality to bid farewell to Countess Nadezhda Sollogub, who was leaving for Europe on the same boat. The previous autumn he had dedicated a poem to the beautiful eighteen-year-old (she was the niece of his fellow lycéen, Prince Gorchakov): 'No, no, I must not, dare not, may not/Yield madly to love's turmoil.'[112] For Natalya this new flame replaced Aleksandra Rosset as an object of jealous suspicion; a suspicion heightened by the fact that Pushkin in his letters, like a man in the grip of an obsessive passion, seemed to find it impossible not to keep mentioning Nadezhda's name. His attempts to reassure her – 'Why, wifekin, do you want to compete with Countess Sollogub? You're a beauty, an Amazon, but she's just skin and bone'[113] – failed in their effect: Natalya did not wish to be reminded that she, now a wife and mother, was no longer an adorably virginal, ethereally beautiful young girl like her rival. The following year Andrey Karamzin wrote to Princess Vyazemskaya: '[Mrs Pushkina] is angry with Mary [the Vyazemskys' daughter] because of [...] her friendship with Countess Sollogub; the constancy of her hatred for the latter makes one weep with laughter.'[114] Another object of Pushkin's admiration was the blonde beauty Amaliya Krüdener, the illegitimate daughter of the Bavarian ambassador to St Petersburg, who had married a Russian diplomat when she was only sixteen. She was later the favourite of Nicholas I. 'Yesterday there was a party at the Ficquelmonts,' Vyazemsky wrote to his wife at the beginning of August. 'It was quite jolly. Pushkin alone was palpitating with his interest of the moment, blushing, when he gazed at the Krüdener woman, and constantly hanging around her.'[115] There is no doubt that he was deeply in love with Natalya, but this did not mean he could not also fall in love with others of different charms, court them, dedicate verse to them, and even, possibly, embark on a relationship with them.

'To begin with [his] wife was terribly jealous, but then became indifferent and accustomed to her husband's infidelities,' Princess Vyazemskaya recollected. 'She herself remained faithful to him, and everything passed off lightly and frivolously.'[116]

Financial problems became acute at the end of February, when two schemes on which Pushkin had pinned much hope – the re-mortgaging of the Kistenevo serfs and the sale of the statue of Catherine II, which together would have brought in 35,000 roubles – collapsed simultaneously. There was one item on the credit side: Smirdin was about to pay him 12,000 roubles for the first complete edition of *Eugene Onegin*, which would come out in March. This was less than half of the 25,000 he might make, were he to publish the work himself, but he could not afford to wait until the following May, when his agreement with the book-seller would come to an end. This sum would not keep him afloat for long, and other expedients were necessary. In a letter to Natalya's brother Dmitry he suggested the latter should borrow, on the security of the Polotnyany Zavod estates, 35 or 40,000 roubles from Prince Vladimir Golitsyn – whom he had already sounded out on the matter – and should then lend him 6,000 roubles of this sum. He concluded the letter by bringing up the matter of the serfs which his mother-in-law had promised: 'You know that Natalie was to have 300 souls from her grandfather,' he wrote; 'Natalya Ivanovna told me at first that she would give her 200. Your grandfather was unable to do it, and I did not even count on it; Natalya Ivanovna feared lest I should sell the land and give her a disagreeable neighbour; it would be easy to remedy that; one would only have to insert a clause in the settlement to the effect that Natalie would not have the right to sell the land. It is with much repugnance that I broach this subject, because at bottom I am neither a Jew nor an usurer, though I have been called both of these, but what can one do? If you think that there is nothing in this letter which might offend Natalya Ivanovna, then show it to her, if not, speak to her of it, and give up as soon as you see that it is unpleasant to her.'[117] The situation must have been grave indeed, if Pushkin was willing to swallow his pride and make a servile approach for help to his mother-in-law – especially after his earlier high-minded assertion that the promised serfs had nothing to do with him, and that he had no intention of ever referring to them.

The letter did not produce the serfs, nor did Dmitry fall in with

Pushkin's suggestion. Though Natalya was his favourite sister, and he was very happy to send her a little page from Polotnyany Zavod ('He as yet does not have a decent appearance and is squatting by the stove in the kitchen; his red livery will be ready tomorrow Sunday 12 March,' she told him), or comply with her request for a landau from the Polotnyany Zavod coach-house ('Please let the landau be fashionable and handsome, for God's sake try, and I shall try to marry you off to X'*), he sensibly declined to involve himself in his brother-in-law's chaotic financial affairs.[118] Pushkin was thus forced to turn elsewhere. On 22 April he borrowed 6,500 roubles from the money-lender Vasily Yurev; on 26 June he approached Aleksandr Ananin, a translator in the Ministry of Marine, for a loan of 2,000 roubles; and on 12 July gave the bookseller Ivan Lisenkov a promissory note for 3,000 roubles.

He was not the only member of the family in trouble: at the end of February he received a rambling letter from his brother Lev, then in Warsaw, begging for help. Bored with peace-time soldiering, Lev had applied for retirement. According to him – though his narrative is far from clear, and one cannot but suspect that some material part of the story has been concealed – his application had been held up, and he had been struck off the roll of his regiment for failing to report for duty. The exclusion – even though it meant he would forgo the promotion usually awarded on retirement – would not have worried him, had it not been a barrier to entry into the civil service, and Lev had now decided to become a diplomat: 'My wish is,' he wrote, 'to be with the mission in Greece or in Persia; I would have liked to be in Egypt, but it seems difficult to get a place there.' Could Pushkin therefore plead his case with Paskevich, now on his way to St Petersburg?[119]

Pushkin's parents had learnt of Lev's problems much earlier. They were very anxious about him, and particularly concerned as to how he would support himself without his pay as an officer. Luckily for their peace of mind, they were unaware that he had already run up large

---

* Natalya is referring to Countess Nadezhda Chernysheva, the youngest daughter of the Goncharovs' neighbours at Yaropolets: a tall girl, as swarthy as a gypsy and vividly beautiful. Dmitry, then twenty-five, though very much in love, had little chance of success: he had not inherited the good looks of his family, was slightly deaf, and had a bad stammer. In addition the Chernyshevs were extremely rich, and occupied a high position in society. He persevered in his courtship, but received a definitive refusal in 1836.

debts in Warsaw. After taking advice from friends, Sergey Lvovich wrote to Paskevich, and, scraping together with great difficulty fifteen hundred roubles, sent them to Lev. For some reason Pushkin did not wish to ask a favour of Paskevich; instead he spoke to the Minister of War, Chernyshev, and Lev's position was regularized: on 23 May Sergey Lvovich joyfully informed him of this. However, Lev took no immediate steps to enter the Foreign Office, but remained in Warsaw, leading a pleasantly dissolute life, until October. Aleksey Vulf, who was also in Poland with his regiment, noted in his diary: 'Lev is just the same [. . .] and is, unhappily, completely penniless. He had the frivolity to lose not only all the money he got from his father and borrowed from others, but more besides, which makes him difficult to help.'[120] Push-kin thought that Lev had probably made a mistake

Lev Pushkin

in leaving the army, though he had no very high opinion of his brother's abilities in any sphere. That autumn, after Lev had come to St Petersburg and was without occupation, he wrote to Natalya from Boldino: 'What is my brother doing? I do not advise him to enter the civil service, for which he has as little aptitude as he has for the military, but he does at least have a healthy arse, and would go further in a saddle than on an office chair.'[121]

On 7 January 1833 Pushkin had been elected a member of the Russian Academy. Its meetings took place every Saturday, and Pushkin attended his first on 28 January, when a batch of entries for the new Academy dictionary was discussed. 'The other day Pushkin was at the Academy and related killingly funny things about the unseemliness of the proceedings,' Vyazemsky told Zhukovsky, 'Katenin has been elected a member and bawled his head off. They are meditating a new edition of the dictionary. Pushkin was most of all disappointed with the lunch, which consisted of some unpleasant Russian salad as hors d'oeuvre ("five pieces of smoked salmon with onion," according to Pletnev) and a variety of vodkas. He wants his first motion to be that they should hire a good cook and buy some good French wine.'[122] Despite the unappealing nature of the lunch, Pushkin continued to attend, going to one or two meetings a month.

All this, combined with the social whirl, not only cut into his time, but also created an atmosphere that was less than propitious for poetic composition: he needed peace, quiet and isolation. Nevertheless, he was far from idle. Since the previous spring he had been regularly visiting the Foreign Ministry archive. And the previous October he had begun work on a novel, later entitled *Dubrovsky*. This was by no means his first essay in the genre. Though he had published only one prose work, the *Tales of Belkin*, he had begun and abandoned a number of others. Most consisted of nothing more than some scattered notes, and a few opening pages. *The Blackamoor of Peter the Great* – an historical novel, much influenced by Scott – had progressed somewhat further. But, after completing six short chapters with no sign of any plot, he had given up the project. The new novel was based on a story he had heard from Nashchokin. A White Russian nobleman, having lost his estate in a lawsuit with a rich neighbour, had taken to the forest with a band of peasants, become a robber and outlaw, and had terrorized the district until eventually captured. Pushkin began the novel – originally called *Ostrovsky* – with great enthusiasm. At the beginning of December he wrote to Nashchokin, 'I have the honour to announce to you that the first volume of Ostrovsky is finished and will be sent to Moscow in a few days for your inspection and the criticism of Mr Korotky' – Korotky, a civil servant at the Foundling Home and a friend of Nashchokin, had supplied Pushkin with details of a lawsuit for the novel.[123] Progress slowed in the New Year, as it became clear that the novel had the same weaknesses as *The Blackamoor*. Scene succeeded scene without any real narrative drive and without, too, any hint of a developing plot. At the beginning of February Pushkin laid the manuscript aside and did not return to it.

His archival research had engendered a fascination with a subject as yet untouched by Russian historians – the peasant revolt of 1773–4, which at its height had set almost all east and south-east Russia ablaze. Its leader was a Don Cossack, Emelyan Pugachev, who claimed to be Catherine II's husband, Peter III, assassinated in 1762. Before embarking on *Dubrovsky*, Pushkin had toyed with the idea of making Mikhail Shvanvich, an officer and adventurer who had thrown in his lot with the revolt, and to whom Pugachev had given the title of secretary of state, the hero of a novel. Now, after giving up *Dubrovsky*, he returned to this plan, on 31 January jotting down a note for a novel in which Shvanvich would be the central figure. It had suddenly occurred to him that he could combine both his interests: he could, at one and the same time, write a history of the Pugachev rebellion and a novel with this event as its setting.

From Mikhail Delarue, a minor poet who had been a close friend of Delvig, and was a civil servant at the Ministry of War, he had learnt that much material on the revolt was contained in the General Staff archives, both in St Petersburg and in Moscow. It was with the view of gaining access to this that he had approached the Minister of War, Chernyshev, at the Ficquelmonts' ball. However, since he judged that the revolt was still a delicate subject, and that research on it might be frowned upon by the authorities, he had told Chernyshev that he needed the material in order to write a biography of Suvorov. He was a poor dissembler: when, two days later, Chernyshev wrote to enquire which documents he would like to see, he requested, in the first place, the report of the inquiry on Pugachev – though Suvorov had been involved merely in the final stage of the suppression of the revolt – and, only secondly, the general's official reports for the campaigns of 1794 and 1799. Later he did not bother to sustain the pretence, since Chernyshev showed no interest in what he read. Whether it was because Pushkin's requests were made through the minister, or because they were handled by Delarue, they were processed with a zeal and efficiency wholly uncharacteristic of Russian bureaucracy. A continuous stream of bulky, leather-bound dossiers flowed in to his study. He threw himself on them with eager enthusiasm.

In the space of ten days, between 25 February and 8 March, he worked his way through two huge folios containing over a thousand pages of documents – catalogued as 'various secret papers and Pugachev's manifestos in his own hand'.[124] Copying out whole documents, making extracts from others, summarizing, digesting, and throwing down a mass of notes, he laid the foundation for his history of Pugachev. Naturally, he did not confine himself to archival sources. Pavel Svinin, the editor of *Fatherland Notes*, sent him the manuscript of the memoirs of Aleksandr Khrapovitsky, Catherine's secretary of state, and from Grigory Spassky, a historian of Siberia and well-known bibliophile, he borrowed a manuscript copy of P.I. Rychkov's eye-witness account of the six-month siege of Orenburg by the rebels, from October 1773 to March 1774. By July, however, he had realized that he would have to see some of the chief centres of the uprising – Orenburg and Kazan – for himself; he had learnt from Yazykov's brother, Aleksandr, of an Orenburg landowner who had interesting material on Pugachev, and he might be able to glean useful information from other local inhabitants. Furthermore, he could combine this journey to Russia's eastern provinces with another visit to Boldino, which lay not too far off his direct route, and which, he hoped, might have the same magical effect on his inspiration as it had done in the autumn of 1830. He wrote to Benckendorff, asking for permission to make the journey and to use the local archives. In reply he received a letter from Mordvinov, Benckendorff's deputy since von Fock's death in August 1831, enquiring as to the purpose of the journey. 'For the past two years I have occupied myself with historical researches alone,' he replied, 'without writing a single purely literary line. I need to spend two months in absolute isolation, in order to rest from these most important occupations and complete a book, which I began long ago, and which will provide me with money, of which I am in need. I myself am ashamed to spend time on vain occupations, but what can be done? They alone give me independence and the means of living with my family in Petersburg, where my labours, thanks to the Sovereign, have a more important and useful goal [...] Perhaps the Sovereign will wish to know precisely what book I wish to finish writing in the country: it is a novel, most of the action of which takes place in Orenburg and Kazan, and this is why I would like to visit both these provinces.'[125] Pushkin was still anxious not to reveal his intention, and his reply was far from honest. His main purpose was to write his history of the revolt, the first draft of which he had already completed; and the novel – which was eventually to become *The Captain's Daughter* – far from being begun long ago, had hardly been embarked on. However, a week later, on Saturday 5 August, as if to justify the assertion, he did scribble down a few notes outlining a possible plot.

That he was in need of money was, however, absolutely true. Indeed, he had just incurred further expense by renting for the summer a villa near the fashionable suburb of Novaya Derevnya, on the mainland, where the Pletnevs had a summer residence. This was one of the elegant row erected by Fedor Miller, the former butler to Alexander I and Nicholas, along the bank of the Black River, which flowed into the northernmost arm of the Neva. '[The villa] is very pretty, the garden is big and the house is very big, fifteen rooms and an attic,' Pushkin's mother wrote to Olga. 'Natalie is well, she is very pleased with her new residence, all the more as it is only a step away from her aunt, who is living on the farm with Natalya Kirillovna [Zagryazhskaya].'*[126]

Here, on 6 July, Natalya gave birth to a son. Pushkin had wanted to call him Gavril, after his ancestor of Boris Godunov's time, but Natalya insisted that he should be called Aleksandr, after his father. The christening took place on 20 July, at the Church of the Birth of John the Baptist on Kamenny Island. Nashchokin, who had come from Moscow expressly for the occasion, was the child's godfather, and Natalya's aunt, Ekaterina Zagryazhskaya, the godmother. After the ceremony there was a small party at the villa. Two days earlier Pushkin had prepared for it by ordering three bottles of champagne, three of Château-Lafite, a bottle of Sauternes and a bottle of port from his French wine-merchant, F. Raoult. Natalya's mother, aroused to unwonted generosity by the birth of a grandson, sent her daughter a thousand roubles. 'Aleksandr is enchanted with his red-headed Sasha,' his parents wrote to Olga. 'He is always present when he is undressed, put in his cot, and lulled to sleep, he listens to his breathing; before leaving he makes the sign of the cross over him three times, kisses his little forehead, and stands for a long time in the nursery, admiring him.'[127]

Three years earlier, at Boldino, Pushkin had made a note on the back of the manuscript of an unfinished poem. It read: '9 May 1823 Kishinev – 25 September 1830 Boldino'; beneath, having performed the subtraction, he had written '7 years, 4 months, 17 days' – the length of time (he was a day out) taken for the composition of his best-known and best-loved work, the novel in verse, *Eugene Onegin*. The complete work had finally been published by Smirdin in March. It received little attention in the press, though Polevoy, in the *Moscow Telegraph*, welcomed

---

* The farm was a small imperial residence, used by courtiers and visitors to the court: '[The Prussian prince] will live on the farm, beyond the Stroganov villa, where Kochubey and Zagryazhskaya lived in the summer,' K.Ya Bulgakov wrote to his brother in May 1834 (*RA*, 1904, I, 420).

it from a 'mercantile' point of view: to buy the eight chapters separately would have cost forty roubles, but the complete novel cost only twelve. 'Hail to the Poet,' he exclaimed, 'who has taken pity on the empty pockets of the reading public.'[128]

Like all Pushkin's narrative works, *Eugene Onegin* has an exceedingly simple plot. In May 1820 the hero, the twenty-five-year-old Onegin, leaves St Petersburg for the estate in the country he has inherited from an uncle. Here he meets the young poet Vladimir Lensky. Lensky is in love with Olga Larina; her elder sister, Tatyana, falls in love with Onegin, and confesses her feelings in a letter, only to be rejected. At Tatyana's name-day party on 12 January 1821 Onegin pays outrageous court to Olga; Lensky challenges him to a duel and is killed. Onegin leaves, and journeys to Astrakhan, the Caucasus, the Crimea and Odessa – his travels are described in a fragmentary chapter, printed as an appendix to the main narrative. In the autumn of 1824 he returns to St Petersburg and meets Tatyana again. She is now married and occupies a high place in society. He falls in love with her, and confesses his feelings in a letter, only to be rejected.

This Tatyana, the society hostess of Chapter Eight – 'a faithful reproduction/*Du comme il faut . . .*', in whom is to be found nothing of that which 'In high London society/Is called *vulgar*' (VIII, xiv–xv) – is an idealized portrait of Pushkin's conception of a lady of the first fashion, an epitome of *bon-ton*: on which, he hoped, his young betrothed might model herself. On his second visit to Boldino, in October 1833, he wrote to Natalya: 'Describe for me your appearance at balls, which, as you write, have probably begun already – and, my angel, please, do not flirt. I am not jealous, and I know that you will not go too far; but you know how I hate everything that smacks of the Moscow miss, everything that is not *comme il faut*, everything that is *vulgar* . . . If on my return I find that your sweet, simple aristocratic tone has changed, I will divorce you, I swear to Christ, and out of misery will go for a soldier.'[129]

Like the *Tales of Belkin*, *Eugene Onegin* is a work of extraordinary literariness, crammed with references to Russian, Western, and classical authors and their works. Indeed, it can almost be read as literary history, an account of the evolution of literary taste in Russia over the preceding few decades, presented synchronically, with each of the three main characters personifying a stage in this evolution. Tatyana is a devotee of the sentimental novel – which she reads in French – seeing Onegin as an amalgam of all her favourite heroes, and herself of their heroines; Lensky, educated at Göttingen, is a German romantic: Pushkin mimics his style in describing his mediocre verse (II, vii–x), and gives us, as a sample of it, the elegy Lensky composes on the eve of the duel (VI, xxi–xxii); finally, Eugene, as Tatyana discovers by poring over the books in his study, is an admirer of Byron, and Pushkin, who has earlier taken a dig at that poet –

> Lord Byron, by an opportune caprice,
> Clothed in gloomy romanticism
> Even hopeless egoism
>
> (III, xii)

– now takes another at Eugene for posturing as a Byronic hero:

> Can he be an imitation,
> An insignificant phantom, or else
> A Muscovite in Harold's cloak,*
> A commentary on another's whims,
> A complete lexicon of fashionable vocabulary? . . .
> Is he not, perhaps, a parody?
>
> (VII, xxiv)

Beyond Byron stands Pushkin himself, who gives us an account of his peregrinations with the Muse (VIII, i–vi) since his days at the Lycée, and whose poem subsumes and surpasses that which has preceded it.

Despite Pushkin's less than favourable view of Byron, it is obvious that the conception of *Eugene Onegin* owes a good deal to the other poet's *Don Juan*, which Pushkin much admired. In execution, however, the poem was more influenced by Sterne's *Tristram Shandy*, which Pushkin appears – from a letter to Zhukovsky of December 1816 – to have read originally in French at the Lycée. Like *Tristram Shandy*, *Eugene Onegin* is notable for the number and variety of its digressions. To characterize them Pushkin could have appropriated Sterne's comment:

> The machinery of my work is of a species by itself; two contrary motions are introduced into it, and reconciled, which were

---

* The hero of Byron's poem, *Childe Harold's Pilgrimage*.

> thought to be at variance with each other. In a word, my work
> is digressive, and it is progressive too, – and at the same time.
> [...] Digressions, incontestably, are the sunshine; – they are
> the life, the soul of reading; – take them out of this book for
> instance, – you might as well take the book along with them.
>
> (*Tristram Shandy*, I, xxii)

Like Sterne, Pushkin plays with his readers: *Eugene Onegin*, confusingly, points in two different directions at the same time. On the one hand, it artlessly invites us to regard the narrative as life, rather than art, by such ingenuous devices as introducing real personages – the author, Kaverin, Vyazemsky – to the characters, or claiming that the author possesses the manuscripts of Lensky's last poem and of Tatyana's and Onegin's letters. Yet at the same time the narration itself is acutely self-conscious: not only does it call attention to its own artificiality with comments on, for example, rhyme and vocabulary, but the very virtuosity with which Pushkin handles the Onegin stanza with its complex rhyme scheme emphasizes its status as art, rather than life. This inner contradiction leaves us, in the end, unsure in our view of the work, sure only that it cannot be read simply as the story of Eugene and Tatyana.

Pushkin's departure for Orenburg was delayed when Natalya, nursing her newly-born son, fell ill with mastitis. He eventually left in his own carriage on 17 August, accompanied by Sobolevsky, who had returned from a five-year stay in Europe the previous month. Vyazemsky thought him much improved: he had acquired a reddish-blond beard and moustache, an emerald-green short tail-coat, and a fashionable air. He had brought several books for Pushkin with him, including the fourth volume of Mickiewicz's works, published in Paris in 1832, which was banned in Russia. In it he had written: 'To A.S. Pushkin, for diligence, achievement and good behaviour.'[130]

They had difficulty in leaving the city. The Neva was very high, and a northerly gale was blowing: it was feared that the river would again inundate the city, as it had done in November 1824. The Troitsky pontoon bridge was closed, and Pushkin had to make a wide detour, crossing much higher up. Of the trees that lined the road to Tsarskoe Selo he counted more than fifty that had been uprooted by the wind. They arrived in Torzhok on the nineteenth, and put up – as Pushkin usually did when journeying between St Petersburg and Moscow – at the hotel kept by the Pozharsky family, whose name has been immortalized by the pork cutlets for which the establishment was famous.

The following day, after 'breakfasting gloriously', he wrote to Natalya. Telling her of the journey, he continued: 'Write to me about your mastitis and everything else. Don't spoil Masha, look after your own health, don't flirt on the 26th. You'll say there's no one to do it with! All the same, don't flirt.' The twenty-sixth of August was Natalya's name-day, but the date was also the anniversary of the battle of Borodino, which was always celebrated by a ball at court. Natalya's supposed rejoinder is a reference to the tsar, who this year would not be present: he had left St Petersburg on 15 August for a meeting at Münchengrätz in Bohemia with the Austrian emperor, Francis I, and Crown Prince Frederick William of Prussia. 'I am turning off to Yaropolets,' Pushkin continued, 'leaving Sobolevsky alone with a Swiss cheese.'[131] The latter was bound for his own estate, Teploe, while Pushkin, with some misgivings, was on his way to call on his mother-in-law.

His next letter, however, did not come from Yaropolets. 'You will never guess, my angel, whence I am writing to you,' he began. 'From Pavlovskoe; between Bernovo and Malinniki, about which I have probably told you much. Yesterday, turning on to the country road to Yaropolets, I discovered with pleasure that I would go past the Vulf estates, and decided to visit them. At eight in the evening I arrived at my good Pavel Ivanovich's, who was as overjoyed to see me as if I had been kin.' Pushkin was not being quite honest with Natalya: it was not by chance that he passed the Vulf estates, for the route he was taking to Yaropolets was not the most direct – he would have done better to stay on the high-road as far as Tver. But if he had hoped to renew old acquaintances, he was to be disappointed. 'Of my old girl friends I found only the grey mare, on which I rode over to Malinniki; but she no longer dances under me, or is spirited, and in Malinniki instead of all the Annettes, Evpraksiyas, Sashas, Mashas etc., there lives only Praskovya Aleksandrovna's manager, Reichman, who treated me to a schnapps or two.'[132]

He eventually arrived in Yaropolets late in the evening on Wednesday the twenty-third, and was received with open arms by Natalya Ivanovna. This unexpectedly cordial reception was partly due to the fact that she wished to ask him for a favour. Like her father-in-law, Afanasy, she had formed a totally erroneous impression of his influence in St Petersburg, which she hoped he would exercise on behalf of the Goncharov business. After he had left she wrote to her son: 'You should have found Aleksandr Sergeevich there [in Moscow], which would make me very glad. He is very disposed to be of use to you in your dealings with the government'; and, a few days later, 'It is essential for you to meet him, so that he can help with the business difficulties'.[133] But her attitude to her son-in-law had also changed markedly since the arrival of her first grandchildren. 'I spent Thursday with her,' Pushkin told Natalya. 'We spoke much of you, of Mashka, and of Katerina Ivanovna [Zagryazhskaya]. It seems to me that she is jealous of your attachment to her; but although she complained about the past as usual, it was with less bitterness. She very much wants you to spend next summer with her.'[134]

Natalya Ivanovna no longer lived in Moscow; leaving her mentally disturbed and alcoholic husband to the care of the children, she had taken up permanent residence at Yaropolets, which – after some property exchanges with her half-sisters – she had inherited, together with 1,396 serfs, in 1823. Its handsome neoclassical mansion had been built at the end of the eighteenth century by Aleksandr Artemevich Zagryazhsky, her grandfather, who had also laid out the large park in the English style and enclosed it with a massive Gothic wall. But Natalya Ivanovna cared little for appearances, and was characteristically miserly in keeping up the estate. 'She lives very quietly in great isolation in her ruined palace, and grows vegetables over the ashes of your ancestor Doroshenko, to whom I went to pay my respects,' Pushkin wrote.*[135] He was much impressed by the library, which occupied, together with the billiards room, the first floor of the mansion, and contained Aleksandr Artemevich's collection of books. For his historical research he borrowed several dozen, together with some copies of the *St Petersburg Gazette* for the 1750s and 60s. They filled two crates, which, with a selection of jams and fruit liqueurs, were sent off to St Petersburg by Natalya

---

* Petr Dorofeevich Doroshenko (1627–98), hetman of the Ukraine, and Natalya's great-great-great-grandfather, who was given a large grant of land, including Yaropolets, by the Regent Sophia.

Ivanovna. He had been shown round the demesne by her manager, Semen Dushin, who was suspected by the Goncharov children of being more concerned with feathering his own nest than looking after the estate. But Natalya Ivanovna would hear no criticism of him: this, together with her preference for living here rather than in Moscow, gave rise to the suspicion that the relations between them were more intimate than those which usually obtain between employer and employee.*

Leaving Yaropolets late in the evening on 24 August, Pushkin slept in his carriage, and arrived in Moscow the following day at noon. He had intended merely to pass through Moscow, but was kept there for several days while his carriage, which had suffered on the country roads round Pavlovskoe and Yaropolets, was repaired. On Natalya's birthday, 27 August, he spent the evening with Nashchokin: 'And what an evening! champagne, Lafite, flaming punch with pineapple – and all to your health, my beauty,' he told her. The following day he met Nikolay Raevsky in a bookshop: '"You dirty dog," he said to me tenderly, "why haven't you come to see me?" "You beast," I answered with feeling, "what have you done with my Little Russian manuscript?"† After that we drove off as though nothing had happened, with him holding me by the collar in sight of everyone to prevent me from jumping out of the carriage.' Pushkin finally left on 29 August; Nashchokin saw him off with 'champagne, punch, and prayers'.[136]

He arrived at Nizhny Novgorod on the morning of 2 September, called on the governor, Major-General Buturlin, and took in the sights. It was disappointing to find that the vast annual fair, which made the town the commercial centre of Russia, had just ended. But he walked down to its site – the sandy spit of land formed by the confluence of the Oka and Volga – and strolled about the rows of empty shops and warehouses, which reminded him of 'the departure from a ball, after the Goncharovs' carriage has already left'.[137] The following day he dined with the Buturlins, and left immediately afterwards for Kazan. The roads were good, the weather magnificent: 'Hot days, with a touch of frost in

---

* A rumour as to this relationship presumably lies at the basis of Sobolevsky's crude description of Natalya Ivanovna's life at Yaropolets: 'She drinks the whole day, and fucks all the lackeys' (Bartenev, 64).

† A copy of *Istoriya rusiv* [*History of the Russians*], at that time erroneously ascribed to the Ukrainian author Georgy Konissky. See *PKZh*, 140.

the mornings – what luxury!' However, he was anxious about Natalya. 'My angel, I think I have acted stupidly in leaving you and beginning a nomadic life again.'[138] How was her health? He was glad that she would have the company of her eighteen-year-old brother Sergey, whose regiment – the Kiev Grenadiers – had recently been posted to St Petersburg. Her other brother, Ivan, who was twenty-three, and a lieutenant in the Life Guards Hussars, was also in the capital, but was as little to be relied upon, and as prone to get into scrapes, as Lev. At the moment he was trying to avoid being coerced into marriage. 'It's obvious from everything that the whole family exploited his disturbed condition to lure him into their toils [. . .] Money will have to be paid. If the girl is not with child, the misfortune is not too great. I shouldn't think there will be a duel with the father or the cobbler-uncle.'[139]

However, Pushkin's chief anxieties were, as usual, financial. How had Natalya coped when the accounts came in? 'I can vividly imagine the first of the month,' he wrote. 'Parasha, the cook, the coachman, the apothecary, Mme Sichler etc. pester you for what is owed them, you haven't enough money, Smirdin makes excuses to you, you're worried – get angry with me – and I deserve it.'*[140] In fact, the situation was even worse than his vivid imagination could conceive. Dissatisfied with the apartment they had moved into in December, Natalya had rented another, on the first floor of a house on Panteleimonskaya Street, near the Summer Garden. The new apartment consisted of ten rooms, with a kitchen and two servants' rooms in an annexe in the courtyard, a stable with six stalls, a coach-house, a hay-loft, an ice-house, a wine-cellar, a laundry shared with the other occupants, and a section of the attic for hanging washing. Unfortunately, it was considerably more expensive than the other: 4,800 roubles a year instead of 3,300. And, to her horror, after signing the contract, she discovered that she had to pay four months' rent – 1,600 roubles – in advance. She could just manage to cover this with the money Pushkin had left her, but was then penniless, with nothing for the normal household expenses over the next few months. In desperation she wrote to her brother Dmitry. 'As regards money I have a favour to ask you, which will perhaps surprise you, but

---

* Parasha was the children's nurse; Mme Sichler, a fashionable milliner, had a shop on Bolshaya Morskaya Street. At the beginning of 1835 Pushkin noted that she was owed 3,500 roubles (Perepiska Pushkina, 980.)

there is nothing else to do. I am at the moment in such a difficult position and cannot apply to my husband, whose whereabouts I do not know, because he is travelling about Russia and only at the end of September or beginning of October will be on his Novgorod estate. That is why I am so bold as to beseech you to help me in the embarrassing position in which I find myself, by sending at least a few hundred roubles, if, of course, that is not difficult for you. Otherwise refuse me outright and do not be angry that I have asked you for this favour.' She ends with a joking reference to his unhappiness in love: 'Be assured, dear friend, that only necessity compels me to resort to your generosity, since otherwise I would never have dreamt of disturbing you at a time when you are almost on the point of shooting yourself.'[141] Dmitry generously sent her 500 roubles. The affair did not have a lasting effect on her: she was soon blithely ordering from Gambs Frères a mahogany divan on castors, covered in crimson camlet, for the new apartment. But then they, of course, did not demand immediate payment.

Natalya's precipitancy had another unfortunate consequence, as Pushkin discovered when he returned to St Petersburg at the end of the year. There had been some irregularity in the manner in which the lease of the previous apartment had been terminated, and the landlord, Zhadimerovsky, took the Pushkins to court for the remainder of the rent: 1,063 roubles 33¼ copecks. In April 1835 he won his case, but Pushkin refused to pay, offering instead seven of his Kistenevo serfs. The matter dragged on, and only after Pushkin's death was Zhadimerovsky paid by the trustees to the estate.*

As he approached Kazan, entering the region over which Pugachev had held sway, he began, while changing horses, to ask the local villagers about the rebellion. In a little pocket-book, with a green paper cover, he jotted down in pencil stories such as that told him by the post-master of a station between Cheboksary and Kazan: 'Pugachev was riding past a hay-cock – a little dog rushed out at him – he ordered the hay-cock

---

* Pushkin's 200 Kistenevo serfs had been mortgaged in 1831 and none of these could therefore be used to pay off Zhadimerovsky. However, he describes the seven as being free from debt: if this is correct, they must have been among those added to the estate by the 8th census revision of 1833, which recorded 226 souls at Kistenevo (see M.I. Kalashnikov's letter of 2 May 1834; XV, 138). Even so, it is questionable whether he would have had the right to dispose of them, for Sergey Lvovich had made over to him only the usufruct of the estate.

to be taken apart. They found two young ladies – after some thought, he ordered them to be hanged.'[142] He reached the town late at night on 5 September. The next morning he discovered with pleasure that Baratynsky was staying at the same hotel. The other poet had been visiting his wife's family at their nearby estate, and was about to return to Mara, the Baratynskys' demesne in Tambov province. On meeting his friend, however, he put his departure off for a day.

Kazan had been stormed and burnt by Pugachev on 12 July 1774. Pushkin visited the scenes of the fiercest fighting, and questioned the townspeople about the event, taking down their narratives in his pocket-book. He spent the evening with Baratynsky, who, just before leaving the next morning, introduced him to Karl Fuchs, a German doctor and amateur local historian. They got on well together, and Pushkin promised to call on him later that day. Meanwhile he took a droshky out to the site of Pugachev's camp, inspected the locality where the battle between the rebels and the relieving forces, commanded by Michelsohn, had taken place, visited the fortress, and returned to the town to write up his notes. He dined with the Pertsov family – the husband, Erast, was a St Petersburg literary acquaintance, author of the satire *The Art of Taking Bribes*; Pushkin admired his light verse, in which, according to Vyazemsky, there was 'a good deal of pepper, salt and gaiety'.[143] After dinner, about six in the evening, he called on the Fuchses, and, following a conversation about the revolt, was taken by the doctor to see a seventy-nine-year-old merchant, Leonty Krupenikov, who had been a prisoner of the rebels, and who recollected seeing Pugachev approaching him 'on horseback, accompanied by fifty Cossacks dressed in long blue caftans'.[144]

Later, when Fuchs was called away to a patient, Pushkin was entertained by his wife Anna. She was a friend of Baratynsky and Yazykov and herself wrote verse, which had appeared in the Kazan journal, the *Transvolga Ant* (presumably named thus in imitation of Bulgarin's *Northern Bee*). Her salon was the centre of the town's cultural life. At Pushkin's request, she read him poems dedicated to her by Baratynsky and Yazykov, and some of her own verse. Pushkin was pressed to stay for supper, and remained with them until after one. During their conversation he introduced the subject of animal magnetism, or mes-

merism, in which he was clearly very interested; this was succeeded by a discussion of visitations by spirits, of fortune-telling, and of super-stitions: he was obviously already meditating the subject of *The Queen of Spades*, which he was to compose at Boldino that autumn.

He left Kazan for Simbirsk at seven the next morning, dashing off a hurried note to Mrs Fuchs before his departure: 'With heartfelt thanks I send you my address and hope that your promise to visit St Petersburg was not merely a civility. Please accept, dear madam, the expression of my deep gratitude for the affectionate reception of a traveller, to whom his momentary stay in Kazan will long be memorable.'[145] She, mean-while, had got up at five to compose a poem on 'the passage of a famous guest' through Kazan.[146] On completion she sent it round to the hotel, but Pushkin had already left. Four days later he wrote to Natalya: 'I landed for the evening at the home of a forty-year-old *blue stockings* [sic; he uses the English term], an unendurable woman with waxed teeth and filthy fingernails. She opened her notebook and read me some two hundred verses, without turning a hair. Baratynsky has written verse to her and with astonishing shamelessness has extolled her beauty and genius. I expected every moment that I would be compelled to write in her album – but God was merciful, however she took my address and threatens me with a correspondence and a visit to Petersburg.'[147] The letter was far from veracious, and hardly just to his hostess, who was only in her late twenties, and considered pretty, but he wished to forestall any jealousy on Natalya's part.

Late in the afternoon of 9 September he drove into Simbirsk, and, putting up at the hotel, immediately paid a visit to the governor, Alek-sandr Zagryazhsky, a distant relation of Natalya. A pleasing depiction of his arrival is given by Constance Hablenz, then a thirteen-year-old, who that evening, together with the governor's daughter, Liza Zagryazhskaya – whom Lev was to marry in 1843 – and other girls, was attending a dancing class in the mansion. 'Suddenly there entered the hall a gentleman of short stature, in a black tail-coat, with curly brown hair, and a pale, or rather mulatto pock-marked complexion: he seemed very ugly to me then [. . .] We were all sitting on our chairs, and when he gave us a general bow we curtsied to him; in a few minutes we had all got to know him and asked him to dance with us; he immediately agreed, went up to the window, took a pistol from his coat-pocket, and, putting it on the window-ledge, waltzed with each of us for a turn or two.'[148]

The following day was occupied with research: Pushkin walked round the town – compared to Kazan, it seemed very much a provincial backwater – and sought the reminiscences of its inhabitants. He had expected to see Yazykov here, and was disappointed by his absence; the next afternoon he set out for the poet's family estate at Yazykovo, some sixty-five versts to the west of Simbirsk. He arrived towards evening – on country roads his carriage covered about ten versts (between six and seven miles) an hour – but found there only his friend's eldest brother, Petr Mikhailovich. He was a genial, cultured man, to whom Pushkin immediately took a great liking. Together they spent a pleasant evening discussing the revolt; Yazykov generously presented Pushkin with his manuscript of Rychkov's unpublished history of the siege of Orenburg: valuable in itself, and invaluable to the historian of the revolt. Pushkin had seen a copy in St Petersburg, and had made an eleven-page précis, but had had to return it to its owner. The next day he drove back to Simbirsk, dined with the governor, and set out for Orenburg.

But two days later he was in Simbirsk again: the road along the west bank of the Volga had proved unsuitable for his light travelling carriage, and there had, too, been other problems. 'I had just got to the highway, when a hare ran across it in front of me. The devil take it, I would have given much to have hunted it down,' he complained to Natalya: to have a hare cross one's path was an infallible presage of misfortune. But this was not all. 'At the third station they began to put my horses to – I suddenly notice there are no postillions – one is blind, the other drunk and has hid himself. Having kicked up as much of a row as I could, I determined to return and take another road.'[149] He stayed another day in the town to dine with the middle Yazykov brother, Aleksandr, in the family's town house: the other guests included Major-General Grigory Bestuzhev, whom Pushkin, when at the Lycée, had known as a dashing young hussar; Ivan Arzhevitinov, Aleksandr Turgenev's cousin, who had lost a leg at Borodino; and the brothers Petr and Apollon Yurlov, two local squires, to whose house the party adjourned after dinner, where Pushkin, who was 'in very good form, [. . .] astonished all those present with his wit'.[150]

He finally left at dawn on 15 September, crossing the Volga and travelling down the eastern bank. While waiting for the ferry he sketched in his pocket-book the scene behind him – the ground rising towards

Simbirsk, with the wooden Smolensk church on the summit of the nearest eminence, and, on the left, at a distance, a large house with a garden behind – probably that which had belonged to Karamzin's brother, Vasily. Three days later he arrived in Orenburg. He was now in the region which had been the centre of the uprising; Orenburg itself, still fortified by an earth rampart and ditch, had changed little since the time of Pugachev. Here he found a friend: Vasily Perovsky, the newly appointed governor, who offered him hospitality in his villa outside the town. Pushkin had first met Perovsky – one of the four illegitimate sons of Count Razumovsky – in St Petersburg, after leaving the Lycée, and had seen much of him in recent years: he had been one of Aleksandra Rosset's admirers, though he had never offered for her. Had he done, she would certainly have turned down Smirnov's proposal: 'Perovsky was very handsome, brave, kind, and he also had two thousand souls, he would have been a generous patron to my brothers.'[151]

While at the governor's Pushkin was overcome by a momentary attack of homesickness. 'How are you, wifekin? Do you miss me? I am lonely without you,' he wrote to Natalya. 'If I wasn't ashamed to, I'd come straight back to you, not having written a single line.' But he cheered himself up in the course of the letter, enumerating the sins of his servant Gavrila Kalashnikov, Olga's brother – 'Imagine the tone of a Muscovite clerk, stupid, garrulous, drunk every other day, eats my travel provision of cold grouse, drinks my Madeira, spoils my books and at the post-stations calls me now a count and now a general' – and congratulating himself on his chastity – 'How well I'm behaving! How satisfied you would be with me! I'm not courting young ladies, not pinching station-master's wives, not flirting with Kalmyk girls – the other day I turned down a Bashkir maiden, despite my curiosity, very excusable in a traveller.'[152]

Meanwhile Perovsky had summoned Grebenshchikov, the ataman of the Cossack settlement at Berdy, some five miles outside Orenburg, and ordered him to prepare for Pushkin's arrival by assembling together those members of the settlement who remembered the revolt. He also instructed Vladimir Dahl, a civil servant attached to his office, to put himself at Pushkin's disposal during his stay. The choice of Dahl was not arbitrary: he, too, knew Pushkin from St Petersburg. Of half-Danish, half-German parentage, he had been educated at the Naval Cadet School and served for a short time with the Baltic and Black Sea fleets, but, disliking the sea, turned to medicine. As an army surgeon he had taken part in the Turkish and Polish campaigns; he had, however, a difficult personality, and, forced to abandon a medical career, entered the civil service. Pushkin had made his acquaintance the previous year, when, under the pseudonym 'Cossack Lugansky', he had brought out a collection of Russian folk-tales. He later became famous as a lexicographer, when, in the 1860s, he published his four-volume *Dictionary of the Living Russian Language*.

On the morning of the nineteenth Dahl called for Pushkin. They drove through the town together, and Dahl pointed out the sites connected with the siege: the bell-tower of St George's Church, on which the rebels had mounted a cannon to bombard the garrison, the remains of earthworks between the Orsky and Sakmarsky gates, and the wood on the far bank of the Ural River, where a force of insurgents had hidden before endeavouring to cross the river on the ice and storm the unfortified side of the citadel. Later the conversation turned to literature. 'You cannot believe how much I want to write a novel, but no, I can't,' Pushkin told him. 'I have begun three – I begin splendidly, but then lack patience, and cannot cope.' He spoke, too, of Peter the Great – the idea of *The Bronze Horseman* was already germinating within him – and of his future: 'Up to now I still cannot understand and comprehend intellectually that giant: he is too huge for us short-sighted ones, and we are still too close to him – one has to move away two centuries – but I understand him emotionally; the longer I study him, the more astonishment and reverence deprive me of the means of thinking and judging freely. [. . .] But I will make something out of this gold. O, you will see: I will yet accomplish much! My comrades, you know, have grown grey or bald to no purpose, but I have only just finished sowing my wild oats; you did not know me in my youth, such as I was; I did not live as one ought to live; as I look back, I see the stormy horizon behind me . . .'[153]

On arrival at Berdy – Pugachev's headquarters from November 1773 to March 1774 – they found a number of Cossacks waiting for them in the ataman's house; among them was Nikolay Kaidalov, the sixteen-year-old son of a Moscow merchant, who described the occasion:

[Pushkin] was wearing a tightly buttoned up frock-coat; over it a frieze overcoat with velvet collar and cuffs, on his head was a crumpled felt hat. On each hand he had a ring – on the left thumb, and on the right index finger. His finger-nails were long, like shovels. There was something extraordinarily original about his figure and his manners.

On entering the room Pushkin sat at the table, took out a notebook and pencil and began questioning the old men and women and writing their stories in it. Finally the questions ceased, he got up, thanked Grebenshchikov and the old people, to whom he distributed a few silver coins, and left for Orenburg.

I would remark that the superstitious old men and women did not like him; he produced an unfavourable impression on them by not taking his hat off when he entered the room, not crossing himself before the icons, and by having long nails; for this they termed him Antichrist; some even did not want to take his money (which was bright and new), calling it Antichrist's and believing it to be false.[154]

Enquiring about other villagers who might remember Pugachev, Pushkin and Dahl were directed to the hut of Arina Buntova, who, when fourteen or fifteen, had been one of the Pretender's concubines. 'In the village of Berdy, where Pugachev was quartered for six months, I had *une bonne fortune* – I found a 75-year-old Cossack woman, who remembers those times as we remember 1830,' he told Natalya.[155] She showed them the hut in which Pugachev had lived, described him, and sang them three songs about him.

The next day the two set out for Uralsk, the starting-place and the centre of the rebellion. Their route, along the Orenburg Fortified Line on the right bank of the Ural, followed that taken – in the reverse direction – by Pugachev's first campaign. They passed the sites of the little forts with their wooden stockades, which, one after another, had been stormed by the rebels, and their garrisons, unless they pledged allegiance to Pugachev, cut to pieces or hanged. At Fort Tatishcheva the eighty-three-year-old Matrena Dekhtyareva told him the story of its capture, which he later incorporated in his *History of Pugachev*:

The wounded Elagin [the fort's commander] and Bilov himself resisted desperately. At last the rebels broke into the smoking ruins. The commanders were seized. Bilov was beheaded. Elagin, a stout man, was skinned; the villains extracted his fat, and smeared their wounds with it. His wife was hacked to pieces. Their daughter [. . .] was led before the victor, as he was ordering her parents' execution. Pugachev was struck by her beauty, and took the unhappy girl as one of his concubines, sparing her seven-year-old brother for her sake. Major Velovsky's widow, who had fled from Fort Rassypnaya, was also at Tatishcheva. She was strangled. All the officers were hanged. Some soldiers and Bashkirs were taken into the field and executed with grape-shot. The others had their heads shaved in the Cossack fashion, and were impressed into the rebel forces.[156]

Gathering more testimonies on the way, Pushkin and Dahl arrived in Uralsk on the evening of the twenty-first. They were greeted by Colonel Vasily Pokatilov, the ataman of the Cossack host, and put up in the official residence. The next morning Pushkin inspected the old town, visiting the house in which Pugachev had lived, and the little citadel, heroically defended throughout the rebellion by its Russian garrison, under the command of Colonel Simonov and Captain Krylov – the father of the poet. 'The local ataman and the Cossacks received me famously, gave two dinners for me, drank my health deeply, competed with one another in giving me all the information I needed – and regaled me with fresh caviare, prepared in my presence.'[157] Among those he met was Father Vasily Chervyakov, who was still firmly convinced that the leader of the rebellion had been the Emperor Peter III. 'Aleksandr Sergee-vich Pushkin explained to me that he was a pretender, the Don Cossack Emelyan Pugachev, who had taken the name of the late emperor,' he later said, 'but I do not believe this. How can these young people know what happened in olden times!'[158]

This autumn at Boldino, Pushkin believed, would be as productive as that three years earlier. 'I already feel the spell coming over me – even in the carriage I am composing, so what will I do on my bed?' he had written to Natalya from Orenburg, referring to his favourite posture for writing: in bed, with his notebook propped on his knees.[159] But the circumstances of his arrival, on the evening of Sunday 1 October, were not propitious: 'On entering the Boldino boundaries, I met some priests, and was as furious with them, as I had been with the Simbirsk hare. All these meetings are not for nothing' – to have a priest, let alone several, cross one's path was even more unlucky than meeting a hare.[160] However, he immediately started work on *Pugachev*, putting his notes in order, and recasting the chapters he had written earlier in St Petersburg. He soon settled into a routine of life. 'You ask how I live and whether I have improved in looks?' he wrote to Natalya. 'Firstly, I have grown a beard; [. . .] 2) I wake at 7, drink coffee, and lie abed until 3 [. . .] At 3 I ride, at 5 into the bath and then dine on potatoes and buckwheat porridge. I read till 9. There's my day for you, and all are alike.'[161] A secret police report confirms this eremitic existence: 'The aforesaid Pushkin [. . .] during the whole time of his sojourn occupied himself exclusively only with writing, he called on none of his neighbours and received no one.'[162] Among the locals, however, there circulated a rather more romantic conception of his existence. 'Do you know what they say of me in the neighbouring provinces? This is how they describe my activities: when Pushkin writes verses – before him stands a decanter of the *finest* liqueur – he downs a glass, a second, a third – and then begins to write!'[163] But he had not yet got into the vein of composition which he had known before in Boldino: three weeks after his arrival, on 21 October, having questioned Natalya about the children – 'Just how is my toothless Puskina? O, these teeth! And how is red-haired Sasha? And from whom did he get the red hair? I did not expect that of him'* – he went on: 'Of myself I will tell you that I am working in a lazy, slipshod way. My head has been aching for days, spleen has been gnawing me; today is better. I have begun much, but have no enthusiasm for anything; God knows what is happening to me.'[164]

The season had begun in St Petersburg, and Natalya's letters were full of fashionable intelligence. She was wearing her hair in a different way, *à la* Ninon de Lenclos.† 'I want to see you with your hair dressed *à la* Ninon so much I don't know what to do; you must be marvellously sweet,' he wrote.[165] And she had acquired a suitor: Nikolay Ogarev, a twenty-one-year-old second lieutenant in the Life Guards Horse

* Pushkin's brother, Lev, had red hair.
† Straight hair, parted in the middle, falling to the shoulders in ringlets.

Natalya

Artillery. 'Who else besides Ogarev is paying court to you?' he asked. 'Send me a list in alphabetical order.'[166] He did not object to his wife having admirers. On the contrary, he would have been disappointed if she had not: he was proud of her beauty, and proud that it was admired by others; it was, too, flattering to his self-esteem to know that others envied him the possession of one of the most desirable women in St Petersburg. But he did object strongly to flirtatious behaviour: it was low, vulgar, the kind of thing one found in Moscow, and could lead to something worse. One of Natalya's letters suggested that she had been indulging in it, and in his next he delivered a stinging homily to her on the subject:

I want to scold you a little. You seem to have properly overdone the flirting. Look: it's not for nothing that flirting is not in fashion and is considered a sign of bad *ton*. There's little sense to it. You are glad that dogs run after you, as after a bitch, raising their tails like a poker and sniffing your arse; that is really something to be glad about! It is easy, not only for you, but even for Praskovya Petrovna,* to get scoundrelly bachelors to run after you; all you have to do is to noise it about: I, you say, am very keen on it. That's the whole secret of flirtation. *Where there's a trough, there'll be swine.* Why receive men who are courting you? You don't know whom you'll come across. Read A. Izmailov's fable about Foma and Kuzma.† Foma fed Kuzma with caviare and herring. Kuzma began to ask for a drink, but Foma wouldn't give him one. So Kuzma thrashed Foma for being a scoundrel. From this the poet draws the following moral: Beauties! Don't feed men herring, if you don't want to give them something to drink; otherwise you may run into a Kuzma. Do you see?[167]

---

* Probably Vyazemsky's sixteen-year-old daughter.

† 'The Forbidden Beer', printed in the *Neva Almanac* for 1829.

In his next letter, written a week later, after a half-apology for his harshness, he reverts to the same subject:

> I shall repeat to you a little more gently, that flirtation leads to nothing good; and though it has its pleasures, nothing so rapidly deprives a young woman of that without which there is neither domestic felicity nor tranquillity in one's relations with society: *respect*. There's no point in rejoicing over your conquests. That whore whose coiffure you've borrowed (NB you must be very pretty with that coiffure; I was thinking about it tonight), Ninon, used to say: On the heart of every man is written: *to the easiest to get*. After that, pride yourself, if you will, in seducing men's hearts.

Not wholly persuaded that reason would convince her, he went on to appeal to her emotionally:

> Think this over well and don't worry me needlessly. I shall leave soon, but will stay in Moscow for some time on business. Wifekin, wifekin! I travel the highways, live in the remote steppe for three months at a time, stop in nasty Moscow, which I hate – for what? For you, wifekin; so that you can be tranquil and can sparkle to your heart's content, as is fitting at your age and with your beauty. But you must take care of me, too. To the troubles, inseparable from a man's life, do not add family worries, jealousy, etc, etc. – not to speak of *cuckoldry*, about which I read a whole dissertation in Brantôme a few days ago.*[168]

Pushkin was somewhat disingenuous here. He did miss Natalya and the children, did worry about her, but at the same time he enjoyed the travel, the new scenes, the marvellous sense of something approaching bachelor freedom; and, above all – for once again the miracle had occurred, brought about by some inexplicable concatenation of circumstances – the sensation that he was creating at the full stretch of his genius.

'I recently got into a writing mood, and have written a mass of stuff,' he had told Natalya the previous week; 'I shall bring you a lot of verses,' he wrote now, 'but don't noise it abroad: otherwise the alma-

* Pushkin is referring to Brantôme's *Vie des dames galantes* (1665–6).

nacists will worry me to death.'[169] He wanted to get the best price for his work from Smirdin, rather than giving it to Odoevsky or Sobolevsky, both of whom had asked him to contribute to almanacs they were putting together – neither project came to anything. Odoevsky had, however, given him some pleasant news: Zhukovsky, 'grown young and healthy again', had returned to St Petersburg.[170] Sobolevsky's letter, with its requests for contributions – 'commands, contracts for made to measure verse' – is typical of its author: 'For Christ's sake, Aleksandr Sergeevich, verse and prose, prose and verse, for dinners, for wine, for horses, for tarts, and for God knows what else. The fact is that I have vowed by 1 May to earn or extort 20,000,' he wrote; and, thinking as usual of his stomach, added in conclusion: 'Do bring some dried sterlet; it's extremely good; and some cured sturgeon would not come amiss, either. It should all be wrapped in bast and tied beneath the carriage; it wouldn't get in the way.'[171]

Baratynsky later called the results of this Boldino autumn 'incredible'.[172] In under six weeks, between 1 October and 9 November, Pushkin finished the *History of Pugachev* and wrote *The Bronze Horseman*, possibly his masterpiece; a short story, *The Queen of Spades*; *Angelo*, a re-working, as a narrative poem, of Shakespeare's *Measure for Measure*, of which he later said to Nashchokin, 'My critics [. . .] think that this is one of my weak compositions, whereas I have written nothing better';[173] two imitations of the verse folk-tale, *The Tale of the Fisherman and the Fish*, and *The Tale of the Dead Tsarevna and the Seven Heroes*; two translations of ballads by Mickiewicz; and a handful of short poems, including the impressively powerful 'God grant that I go not mad', and the great lyric 'Autumn (A Fragment)', with its depiction of Boldino existence and of its own composition:

> And thoughts seethe bravely in my head,
> And light rhymes run towards them,
> And fingers call for a pen, a pen for paper,
> A moment – and verse will freely flow.
> So, motionless, a ship sleeps in a motionless sea,
> But hark! – suddenly the mariners dart, crawl
> Up, down – and the sails are swollen, full of wind;
> The hulk starts and parts the waves.[174]

On 9 November he left for Moscow. Here he put up with Nashchokin, whom he had to ask for another loan, bringing his debt to his friend up to four thousand roubles. He found him in a profound domestic crisis. Since 1829 he had been living with his gypsy mistress, Olga Soldatova, by whom he had had two children, a son and a daughter. Pushkin had acted as the daughter's godfather, and had written sympathetically to Nashchokin when she died in infancy: 'My poor god-daughter! In future I shall not stand god-father to your children, dear Pavel Voinovich; I do not bring luck.'[175] Now, however, Nashchokin had fallen in love with, and wished to marry Vera Nagaeva, the twenty-two-year-old illegitimate daughter of a distant relative, Aleksandr Nashchokin. When he informed Olga of this, she went into a prolonged fit of hysterics, while he sat in silence listening to 'her groans – feigned madness – oaths, curses – and the like'.[176] At the end of the year he fled secretly to the country, married Vera on 2 January, and settled with her for the time being in Tula. Here his financial circumstances became extremely straitened, and for the next six months he bombarded Pushkin with appeal after pathetic appeal begging for repayment of the loan. 'I have written five letters to you – each one more touching than the previous. The first I wrote to you – when I had – only a hundred and fifty roubles left, the second when there remained – five roubles, the third when I was in debt – over a hundred roubles besides rent for the lodging – the fourth when the landlord – exchanged his pleasant manner to me for a harsh one. At the time of the fifth I had already sold everything there was to sell, four times cheaper than the real price, owed over a thousand roubles, and did not dare to go downstairs – however stuffy the rooms were, because the landlord was as harsh as before – and drunk to boot.'[177] Pushkin eventually sent him a thousand roubles on 19 June.

During this short visit to Moscow – three or four days at most – Pushkin saw practically no one. Kireevsky, in a letter to Yazykov, found an ingenious reason for this unsociability: 'He showed himself nowhere, because he was travelling *with a beard*, in which he wished to appear before his wife.'[178] Had he gone into society, he would have had to shave. He did, however, call several times on Avraam Norov, a writer and senior civil servant – he became the Minister of Education in the 1850s – whom he had first met in St Petersburg before exile; they had last seen each other in July, at a dinner for I.I. Dmitriev, when those present had subscribed for a memorial to Karamzin at Simbirsk. Norov, a great bibliophile, had a splendid library, in which Pushkin took the opportunity of checking some references in his *Pugachev*. He also acquired from him – Norov was disposing of the rarest items in his collection before leaving for Egypt and the Holy Land – a copy of Radishchev's *Journey from Petersburg to Moscow* (1790), for which he paid two hundred roubles. Though this was a fine copy, bound in red morocco, with marbled end-papers and gilded fore-edge, its value lay in its association: it was that which had been used in the Secret Chancery to indict Radishchev, and contained numerous notes in red pencil made by Catherine II. Pushkin made a note of its price and its history on the fly-leaf.* This acquisition undoubtedly inspired the *Journey from Moscow to Petersburg*, on which he embarked immediately after his return to St Petersburg: the narrator retraces Radishchev's route in the opposite direction, comparing his picture of contemporary Russia with that of his predecessor.

He left Moscow on 17 November, giving a lift to Vera Nagaeva's sixteen-year-old brother Lev – Lelinka, as his sister called him affectionately – who was going to St Petersburg to take up a post as a clerk in the civil service. 'Lelinka did not disturb me,' he told Nashchokin, 'he is very nice, i.e. silent – our whole relationship was limited to my pushing him away with my elbow, when he leant on my shoulder at night.' Pushkin's servant was a less pleasant companion. 'When I left Moscow, my Gavrila was so drunk and so enraged me, that I ordered him to get down from the box, and left him on the highway in tears and hysterics.' The next morning Nashchokin found him sleeping on the staircase outside his apartment, and packed him off after his master. Pushkin arrived back on the evening of the twentieth, and found that Natalya was, as might have been expected, not at home, but at a ball. 'I went round for her – and carried her off home, like a uhlan carrying off a provincial young lady from the name-day party of the town governor's wife.'[179]

---

* Copies of Radishchev's work were in any case rare, since it had been suppressed after the first edition.

THE TIRED SLAVE

1833–34

It's time, my friend, it's time! the heart pleads for peace –
Day flies after day, and each hour bears away
A particle of life, and you and I together
Make plans to live, but before we know it – shall suddenly be dead.
There is no happiness in the world, but there is peace and freedom.
Long have I dreamt of an enviable lot –
Long have I, a tired slave, contemplated flight
To a distant home of work and unsullied pleasures.

(III, 330)

A FEW DAYS AFTER returning to St Petersburg Pushkin bought a new notebook: large and heavy, half-bound in brown leather, with stout board covers. A leather flap on the front cover ended in a metal hasp, which engaged with a lock on the back. On Friday 24 November he began to keep a diary in it. It might have been thought that, given the privacy ensured by the lock, he would have set down here his most intimate thoughts and feelings. Almost the opposite is true: the diary is dry and factual, consisting for the most part of notes of social events, of conversations at dinners and routs, with occasionally a sentence or two of comment. He writes as dispassionately of the incidents of his own life – only rarely does a note of emotion emerge. Like the monk Pimen in *Boris Godunov*, he sees himself as the chronicler of his times. However, it is not the large historical events, but the smaller that he records: the details that convey the flavour of the age, the kind of testimony he had recently sought to elicit from the survivors of the

Pugachevshchina, material which the historian can find in no official source. After listening one evening to Natalya Kirillovna Zagryazhskaya's stories and anecdotes about Elizabeth and Catherine II, he wrote: 'The Empress is writing her memoirs . . . Will they reach posterity? Elisaveta Alekseevna wrote hers, they were burnt by her lady-in-waiting; Mariya Fedorovna also – the Emperor burnt them by her command – What a loss!'*[1] A typical entry is that of 27 November:

> Dinner with Engelhardt – conversation about Sukhozanet, appointed commander of all the corps. It is apparently in order to give a different turn to these establishments, said Engelhardt. The uniform for ladies – velvet, embroidered with gold – is very much condemned, especially at the present time of poverty and disaster.[2]

General Sukhozanet, an artillery officer, had lost a leg in the Polish campaign; unfit for active service, he had received several appointments, including that of Director of the Corps-des-Pages. In a later entry Pushkin makes it clear why he was thought peculiarly unsuitable for this post – and reveals the indelicacy of Engelhardt's witticism – calling him 'a Pederast and an inveterate gambler'.[3] The 'uniform for ladies' refers to the new court dress – an imitation of the costume of peasant women – which was to be worn on ceremonial occasions: the first such occasion would be St Nicholas's Day, 6 December, the emperor's name-day. Pushkin thought its introduction inappropriate at a time when, because of the failure of the harvest, peasants were threatened with starvation, while landowners – other than the richest – found themselves in straitened circumstances. In this he was unwittingly in agreement with the Third Department. 'The less well-off families complain that the order has come at a time when all are more or less embarrassed and behind with their revenues because of the bad harvest,' Mordvinov wrote to Benckendorff. 'And then the time given is so short – There will be immense competition between orders; velvet, embroidery will become considerably dearer. – The women are in complete insurrection.'[4] Nevertheless the reform went ahead. The *Northern Bee*, describing the ceremony on the morning of the sixth, remarked, 'All the ladies [. . .] were

* Elizaveta Alekseevna (née Princess Luise of Baden) was the wife of Alexander I; Mariya Fedorovna (née Princess Sophie of Württemberg) the wife of Paul I.

wearing today for the first time the national Russian costume sanctioned for them by His Imperial Majesty: married ladies in costumes with trains, cut in the fashion of sarafans, and kokoshniks with gauze veils, and unmarried in dresses of the same kind with short sleeves and with Russian kerchiefs on their heads. Ladies-in-waiting wore dresses of green velvet embroidered with gold, and maids-of-honour of crimson velvet.'*5 Pushkin's mother had made an early call that morning on a friend, Mrs Arkharova: she knew that the latter's daughter, Aleksandra Vasilchikova, and two great-nieces, Natalya Obreskova and Nadezhda Sollogub, were coming round to show off their new costumes before the ceremony. She spent the evening, from five until past midnight, in the gallery of the Winter Palace, watching the ball below.

She and Sergey Lvovich had returned from Mikhailovskoe, where they had spent the summer and autumn, on 22 November, putting up temporarily at the Hotel de Paris. Pushkin, Natalya and Lev called on them two days later; they came from dinner at the Karamzins (it was Ekaterina Andreevna's name-day), where Pushkin had been pleased by the sight of an apparently younger, and certainly healthier Zhukovsky. 'Yesterday I saw Natalie, she is looking very well, although she has got thinner,' Nadezhda Osipovna wrote to Olga, 'they all three were going to a large party at the Ficquelmonts. Lev was very elegant and completely drenched in scent.'6

There was at this time a slight froideur between the elder Pushkins and their son and daughter-in-law. Natalya, they thought, had been deplorably careless in forwarding letters for themselves and Olga which had been directed care of Pushkin's St Petersburg address, while Pushkin himself had been deplorably remiss in corresponding with them: they had not heard from him for months, and it was only by chance that Sergey Lvovich had learnt of his journey to the Ural. '[Aleksey] Vulf considerably astonished us,' he told Olga at the beginning of November, 'by informing us that Aleksandr was in Orenburg. What is there for him to do in that land of Huns and Heruls?'†7 As always, Lev was their

---

* A sarafan is a kind of tunic dress, buttoning down the front, while the kokoshnik worn at court was described by the Marquis de Custine, who visited Russia in 1839, as 'a kind of tower, formed of rich stuff, and something resembling in shape the crown of a man's hat, lowered in height, and open at the top' (Marquis de Custine, *Empire of the Czar*. New York, 1989, 165).

† The Heruls were a Germanic tribe, said to have come originally from Scandinavia, who appeared on the shores of the Black Sea in the third century AD, when, in conjunction

favourite child: when, at the beginning of December, they moved into an apartment in Gagarinskaya Street, the best room – 'very cheerful, gets the sun, has two windows, and the walls are a splendid green' – was kept for him.[8] However, he showed no inclination to move from Engelhardt's Hotel on the Nevsky, where he had put up on arriving from Warsaw in October and where he remained until April, even though the rooms cost two hundred roubles a week.*

On 28 November the Pushkins were at the première of Casimir Delavigne's melodrama, *Les enfants d'Édouard* (i.e. the princes in the Tower), performed in French, and afterwards attended a rout with dancing given by Sergey Saltykov in his house on the Malaya Morskaya. He gave a soirée of this kind every Tuesday throughout the winter. The following evening they went to a ball given by Major-General Buturlin and his wife, Elizaveta Mikhailovna, where Pushkin had an interesting conversation on foreign policy with John Bligh, the English chargé d'affaires, with whom he dined a fortnight later. On 15 December Prince Kochubey and his wife gave a splendid ball at their house on the Fontanka, at which the emperor was present, but not the empress, who was indisposed. 'Countess Shuvalova was amazingly beautiful,' Pushkin noted in his diary. She was Polish by birth – in a later entry he calls her 'a Polish coquette and hence very indecent'[9] – and Vyazemsky, with his predilection for Polish beauties, was for some time very taken with her. 'She was born a rose without thorns,' he wrote to Turgenev.[10]

Pushkin immediately plunged back into the literary life of the capital. On 25 November, together with Natalya, he called on Prince Odoevsky, who with his wife Olga Stepanovna (née Lanskaya), known as the beautiful Creole, received guests in their apartment on Moshkov Lane every Saturday evening after the theatre. He was soon, too, a regular visitor again to Zhukovsky's Saturdays at Shepelevsky House; there, on 16 December, he heard a German declaimer, Karl Kizewetter, reciting scenes from *Faust* to a piano accompaniment. He was unimpressed. And on 2 December Gogol called on him and read him his new work,

---

with the Goths, they invaded the Roman empire. The mention does credit to Sergey Lvovich's knowledge of history, as well as his alliterative art.

* The hotel was in a huge building on the Nevsky Prospect, the property of Pushkin's friend Vasily Engelhardt; it also contained a restaurant and halls in which concerts and public masquerades and balls were given.

'The Story of how Ivan Ivanovich quarrelled with Ivan Nikiforovich', which Pushkin found 'very original and very amusing'.[11] He and Zhukovsky saw much of Gogol during this time. The latter was eager to exchange the unpleasant climate of St Petersburg for the more salubrious one of his native Ukraine, and hoped to be appointed to the chair of history at the newly established University of St Vladimir in Kiev; both had agreed to intercede with Uvarov, the Minister of Education, on his behalf. On 21 December Pushkin called at his apartment on the Malaya Morskaya in connection with this, but, not finding him at home, left a note. Two days later Gogol replied, regretting his absence; he would have called on Pushkin the following day, had he not fallen ill. 'A cold has taken it into its head to associate itself with my haemorrhoidal virtues, and I have now a regular horse-collar of handkerchiefs on my neck,' he wrote. Wishing to convince Pushkin of his suitability for the chair, he added, with more than a soupçon of Ukrainian braggadocio, 'I exult in advance, when I imagine with what a swing my work will go in Kiev. I shall bring into the light of day many things, not all of which I have read to you. There I will finish my History of the Ukraine and Southern Russia, and will write a Universal History, which, in its proper form, does not unfortunately yet exist, either in Russia or even in Europe.'[12]

Pushkin's chief concern on his return, however, was to publish as advantageously as possible the works he had brought back from Boldino. He summoned Smirdin, and laid down his conditions. Vasily Komovsky, a civil servant in the Ministry of Education, and a friend of the Yazykov brothers, wrote to Aleksandr Yazykov at the beginning of December: 'Pushkin has returned from Boldino and has brought back, rumour has it, three new poems. I was present when Smirdin returned to his shop after seeing him, and very

Gogol

sorrowfully complained of him: for these three little works, which, he says, will not make more than three sheets [i.e. 48 pages], Aleksandr Sergeevich is demanding 15,000 roubles! This baron has no bad imagination.'[13] Pushkin's demand was not, however, as Komovsky implies, one that might have been made by Baron Münchhausen. Given the profit that Smirdin was likely to make from his new magazine, the *Library for*

Reading – The Bronze Horseman was intended to be the centrepiece of its first number – he could afford to pay Pushkin at this rate; and did agree to it. For Pushkin, however, the money would only tide him over his immediate financial emergencies.

Copying out *The Bronze Horseman* in his most legible handwriting, on the best Goncharov paper, he sent the poem to Benckendorff on 6 December, asking for permission to publish it; at the same time requesting that the pieces destined for Smirdin's magazine might be submitted to the ordinary censor together with the contributions by other authors. He ended by confessing that instead of the historical novel, set in the time of Pugachev, he had written a history of the revolt: could he submit it for the emperor's consideration? 'I do not know whether it will be possible for me to publish it, but dare to hope that this historical fragment will be of interest to His Majesty especially in connection with the military actions of the time, which up to now are scarcely known.'[14]

'On the 11th I received an invitation from Benckendorff to present myself to him the following morning,' he noted in his diary. 'I went. *The Bronze Horseman* was returned to me with the Sovereign's comments. The word *idol* [*kumir*] has not passed the Imperial censorship; the lines

> And before the younger capital
> Old Moscow has faded,
> As before the new empress
> The widow in imperial purple –

have been crossed out. In many places (?) has been placed, – all this makes a big difference to me. I was forced to alter the conditions with Smirdin.'[15] The tsar had agreed, however, that his other works could be submitted to the normal censor, and had asked to see the Pugachev manuscript. Although Pushkin here intimates that his main concern, if he cannot publish *The Bronze Horseman*, is the loss of income involved – a view he repeats a few days later in a letter to Nashchokin – in fact, the disappointment cut much deeper. He needed to bring out an important work to maintain his reputation. To the younger generation of writers and critics he was beginning to appear as someone who had little to say to them, whose day was past. The following November Belinsky, in one of a series of articles entitled 'Literary Reveries' which appeared in *Rumour*, a 'news and fashion' supplement to Nadezhdin's *Telescope*, wrote:

Pushkin reigned for ten years: *Boris Godunov* was his last great achievement; in the third part of the complete collection of his verse* the notes of his harmonious lyre died away. Now we no longer recognize Pushkin: he has died, or, perhaps, only fallen for a time into a swoon. Perhaps he is no longer with us, or perhaps he will rise from the dead; this question, Hamlet's *to be or not to be* is hidden in the mists of the future. At least, to judge by his fairy-tales, his poem *Angelo*, and his other works published in *House-Warming* and the *Library for Reading*, we must mourn a bitter, irretrievable loss.[16]

Depressed, Pushkin fell into a state of apathetic inertia. He abandoned work on the *Journey from Moscow to Petersburg*, which had been progressing well, and laid *The Bronze Horseman* aside. On 14 December, two days after the manuscript had been returned to him, he spent the evening with the Smirnovs and Arkady Rosset, Aleksandra's brother. He read the poem to them and told them of the emperor's criticisms. 'I do not know why,' Smirnov later wrote in his journal, 'but it can only be out of caprice that at the moment he is depriving us of his poem *The Bronze Horseman* (the Peter the Great monument), since those corrections which the tsar asks for are justified and will not spoil the poem, which, moreover, is weaker than his others.'[17] Smirnov, however, was no artist: he did not realize that Pushkin could not bring himself to tamper with the poem, simplifying and degrading it. Aleksandr Turgenev understood something of this. 'Pushkin read me his new poem on the flood of 1824,' he noted in his diary the following autumn. 'It is charming; but his censor, the emperor, crossed out many lines, and he does not want to publish it.'[18] It was only in 1836, when he needed material for his new journal, the *Contemporary*, that Pushkin took up the poem and began to revise it in the light of the tsar's criticisms, only to abandon the task before its completion. It was, therefore, never published during his lifetime, though the prologue, without the four lines quoted in Pushkin's diary to which the emperor had taken exception (and without the final five lines which introduce the following section), appeared in the December 1834 number of Smirdin's *Library for Reading*, with the title 'Petersburg. An excerpt from a poem'.

---

* Published in 1832.

> On the shore of desolate waves
> He stood, full of lofty thoughts,
> And gazed afar.
>
> $(1-3)^{19}$

The opening lines of the prologue to *The Bronze Horseman* depict Peter the Great as, according to legend, on 16 May 1703, while an eagle flew overhead, he laid two pieces of turf together to form a cross, saying: 'Here shall be a city'. A hundred years later the desolate, uninhabited site has flowered; St Petersburg has replaced Moscow as Russia's capital. A storm is getting up as Eugene, a minor civil servant, returns to his lodging in Kolomna on the evening of 6 November 1824. Because of the weather the pontoon bridges across the river will be removed, and he will be separated for several days from his beloved, Parasha, who, with her widowed mother, lives on Vasilevsky Island. The next morning the Neva suddenly overflows its banks, causing the worst flood since the city's foundation. Eugene takes refuge on one of the marble lions at the entrance to Prince Lobanov-Rostovsky's new palace, on the corner of Peter Square, whence he stares desperately over the Neva towards Vasilevsky Island and Parasha. Before him, its back towards him, stands Falconet's equestrian statue of Peter. Later that day the flood recedes; Eugene crosses to Vasilevsky Island, where he finds that Parasha's house and its inhabitants have been swept away. Few traces of the flood can be seen when the next day dawns; civil servants go to work as usual; and there can be no more striking testimony to the resumption of normal life than the fact that

> Count Khvostov,
> The poet, beloved by the heavens,
> In immortal verses already sang
> Of the disaster of the Neva's shores.
>
> $(344-7)^*$

Unlike the rest of St Petersburg's inhabitants, Eugene does not return to normal life. His reason shattered by the loss of Parasha, he abandons

---

* Pushkin is here making a sly intertextual joke at his own expense. The description of Khvostov is taken from a poem to Pushkin by a young poet from Kostroma, Anna Gotovtseva, who addresses him as 'The glory of our days, the poet beloved by the heavens'; her work, and Pushkin's 'Reply to A.I. Gotovtseva' both appeared in *Northern Flowers* for 1829.

his lodging and wanders about the city. About a year later chance brings him again to Peter's statue. Blaming the emperor, 'by whose fateful will/ The city was founded by the sea', for his misfortune, he threatens the statue, but, imagining it has turned its head towards him, flees, and throughout the night hears behind him the heavy gallop of its unrelenting pursuit. Later, on one of the small uninhabited islands in the Neva, a house, washed up by the flood, is discovered: Eugene's corpse lies on its threshold.

Before leaving St Petersburg that autumn Pushkin had copied into one of his notebooks three poems in Polish by Mickiewicz from the volume Sobolevsky had given him.* These were part of the cycle entitled 'Digression' [*Ustęp*], appended to the third part of Mickiewicz's Romantic drama *Forefathers' Eve* [*Dziady*]. Pushkin still greatly admired Mickiewicz as a poet – they had not, of course, met since May 1829, when Mickiewicz left Russia for Europe. In their political views, however, they were totally opposed. While Mickiewicz was an untiring apostle for Polish independence, Pushkin believed with equal fervour that the country should remain part of the Russian empire. The recent war had brought this difference to a head. The third part of *Dziady*, completed in 1832, in which Mickiewicz gives Poland, with its Christian qualities of self-sacrifice and redemption, a messianic role in Europe, and the poems of 'Digression', a bitingly satirical political polemic directed against Russian autocracy and its incarnation in stone, St Petersburg, were inspired by the conflict. Pushkin was naturally angered at the attack on Russia and its capital, and deeply wounded by the final poem, 'To Muscovite Friends'.† In this, Mickiewicz, after mourning the fate of his Decembrist friends, Ryleev – hanged – and Bestuzhev – exiled – continues:

Others perhaps have been touched by a fiercer heavenly punishment;
Perhaps one of you, disgraced by public office or a medal,
Has surrendered his free soul forever to the Tsar's favour
And today bows obsequiously at his threshold.

---

* According to Senkovsky, the editor of the *Library for Reading*, Pushkin 'in mature years had taught himself Polish to that degree necessary to read works of literature and poetry' (*Rukoyu Pushkina*, 550). His library contained two Polish grammars and two Polish dictionaries.
† 'Do Przyjaciół Moskali'. On the title Lednicki comments: 'The appellation *Moskal* is a derogatory one. Therefore, the meaning [. . .] of the title of this dedicational poem is: 'To Enemy Friends' (Lednicki (1955), 137).

Perhaps with mercenary tongue he praises his triumph
And rejoices in the martyrdom of his own friends,
Perhaps in my country he bleeds with my blood
And to the Tsar boasts of his damnation as of services.[20]

These scathingly vituperative lines are only too obviously aimed at Zhukovsky and Pushkin, execrated among Poles for their publication *On
the Taking of Warsaw*. In August 1834 – a year after the composition of
The Bronze Horseman – Pushkin, still smarting from these insults, began,
but never completed, a poem on Mickiewicz. The tone is one of pained,
but ironic resignation. 'He lived among us/Amidst a tribe, alien to him,
but/Did not harbour malice towards us in his soul, and we/Loved him,'
he began. 'But now/Our pacific guest has become our enemy – and
with poison/Fills, to please the violent mob,/His verses.'[21]

Nevertheless, he had cause to be grateful to Mickiewicz, for the
latter's 'Digression' was undoubtedly the main stimulus for the creation
of *The Bronze Horseman*. Viewed as a reply to Mickiewicz, the poem is
an unabashed celebration of the recent triumph of Russian imperialism,
and Eugene's futile revolt an allegory of the equally futile revolt of the
Poles. Of course, Pushkin's enthusiasm for Russian imperialism was not
confined to its manifestation in Poland. The poem can also be seen in
more abstract terms, as a meditation on imperialism in general, at
the centre of which stands the double figure of Peter and his statue,
simultaneously both identical and different, beneficent and sinister, suggesting the ambiguous nature of power and the inhumanity which is
an inevitable concomitant of imperial greatness. 'Peter I did not fear
popular Freedom, the unavoidable consequence of enlightenment, since
he trusted in his power and despised humanity perhaps even more than
Napoleon,' Pushkin had written in 1822.[22]

In 1909 the poet and critic Valery Bryusov pointed out that the most
striking quality of *The Bronze Horseman* was the discrepancy between
the story and the content. If we find it difficult to believe that *Eugene
Onegin* is only about the relationship between Eugene and Tatyana, in
no way can we convince ourselves that the whole meaning of *The Bronze
Horseman* is subsumed in Eugene's loss of Parasha and his madness.
The fact that the title does not refer to Eugene, the presence of so much
in the poem not directly related to him, and, above all, the manner in

which we are encouraged to see incidents and characters as allegories and symbols – all this has proved irresistible to critics, who, in a search for a hidden meaning, have written far more on *The Bronze Horseman* than on any other work by Pushkin. Perhaps the greatness of Pushkin's achievement is to be measured by the fact that the poem has shown itself to be infinitely accommodating to interpretation.[23]

The emperor's unfavourable treatment of *The Bronze Horseman* was followed almost immediately by a mark of his favour, which, paradoxically, was as unwelcome to Pushkin, and was to trouble him more. On 30 December Count Nesselrode informed the Minister of the Court, Prince Volkonsky, that the emperor had been graciously pleased to confer on Titular Councillor Pushkin the office of gentleman of the chamber. 'My brother first heard of his appointment as gentleman of the chamber at a ball given by Count Aleksey Fedorovich Orlov,' Lev recollected. 'This so infuriated him that his friends had to take him away into the count's study and try to pacify him in every way possible. I do not think it proper to repeat here everything the enraged poet, foaming at the mouth, said about his appointment.'[24] Smirnov uses the same verb: the appointment 'infuriated' Pushkin;[25] and Vulf, who spent a few days in St Petersburg at the beginning of February and had not seen his friend since 1829, found him 'little changed by marriage, but powerfully indignant with the tsar for dressing him in a uniform coat'.[26] Pushkin himself made a curiously dispassionate note about his appointment in his diary on 1 January 1834: 'Two days ago I had the title of gentleman of the chamber conferred on me – (which is somewhat unbecoming to my years). But the court wanted Natalya Nikolaevna to dance at the Anichkov.'[27]

The comment succinctly expresses the main reasons for Pushkin's anger. Firstly, the office was one which was usually given to much younger men: Nikolay Remer, who became a gentleman of the chamber at the same time as Pushkin, was seven years younger; Pushkin's brother-in-law, Dmitry Goncharov, had been twenty-one when he received the favour. And Pushkin, who feared nothing more than appearing ridiculous, was very conscious of the fact that, dressed in the uniform of the office, he would cut a ludicrous figure by the side of the handsome, fresh-faced young men who would be his new colleagues. And would not wits – a most disquieting thought – draw a satirical parallel between himself and Khvostov, who, after marrying Suvorov's niece, had obtained preferment through his uncle-in-law: 'Being not young at all, ugly and clumsy, he had conferred on him the office of gentleman of the chamber – an envied post although usually given to eighteen-year-old noble youths. This seemed so strange to the court that some people dared remark on it to Catherine. "What could I do," she answered, "I can refuse nothing to Suvorov: I would have made the gentleman a maid of honour had he asked." '[28] Secondly, though this was not the kind of recognition he wished for, it was at least recognition, and was the first favour he had received. Yet it had come to him not for his work, not for his services to literature, but because he had a beautiful wife with whom the emperor wished to flirt at the intimate balls held in the Anichkov Palace. She – now pregnant again – was overjoyed: 'As a piece of news I can inform you,' her mother-in-law wrote to Zizi Vrevskaya on 4 January, 'that Aleksandr has been appointed gentleman of the chamber. Natalie is in raptures, because this gives her access to the court. Meanwhile she dances somewhere every evening.' And on 26 January she told Olga: 'Natalie's presentation at court was an immense success, she is the only one talked about, at the Bobrinskoy ball the emperor danced the French quadrille with her and sat next to her at supper. They say that at the ball in the Anichkov palace she was enchanting.' 'Natalie is at every ball,' she wrote two months later, 'always beautiful, always elegant, everywhere much caressed; she comes home every day at 4 or 5 in the morning, dines at 8, and rises from the table to do her toilette and hurry off to a ball.'[29]

His friends found the news of his appointment amusing. 'Pushkin has been delivered of – do you know what? You'll never guess! – Gentleman-of-the-chamberdom!' Vyazemsky wrote facetiously to Turgenev; and in the same vein to Dmitriev, 'I also forgot to congratulate your Excellency, as chief chamberlain of our poets at the radiant court of Phoebus, on a new gentleman of the chamber – the poet Aleksandr Pushkin.'[30] On 7 January Pushkin noted in his diary that he had met Grand Duke Michael at the theatre, and the latter had congratulated him on the appointment: 'I humbly thank Your Highness,' he had replied. 'Up to now all have laughed at me, you are the first to congratulate me.'[31] But the witticisms gradually died down; towards the end of the month Sofya Karamzina wrote to a friend: 'Pushkin was very much afraid of bad jokes about his unexpected appointment as gentleman of the chamber, but now he has calmed down, drives to balls, and takes pleasure in the triumphant beauty of his wife.'[32]

His initial annoyance at his appointment as gentleman of the chamber had been exacerbated by his conviction that Nicholas had purposely intended to insult him. Why could he not have been made chamberlain, as Vyazemsky had been two years earlier? Wiegel had practically promised him this in the summer of 1831, during the discussions about the projected newspaper. It is of course true that Nicholas could have appointed him to the superior office, but to do

Vyazemsky

so would have been to violate the general presumption that this was reserved for those of higher rank – a presumption given legal force in a ukase of June 1836, by which appointment as chamberlain was restricted to civil councillors and above, and as gentleman of the chamber to titular councillors and above. Pushkin, as a titular councillor, only just qualified for gentleman of the chamber status; there was a huge gap between this rank, the ninth, and the fifth, that of civil councillor. To begin with he did not appreciate the point, and made his dissatisfaction almost discourteously plain. At his first meeting with the emperor in the new year – at the Bobrinskoy ball – he noted that 'the Sovereign did not speak to me about my appointment as gentleman of the chamber, and I did not thank him'.[33] But the matter was explained to him, and by March he was writing to Nashchokin, 'Of course, in making me a gentleman of the chamber, the Sovereign was thinking of my rank, not of my years – and I am sure had no thought of wounding me.'[34]

The office brought with it other vexations. The first was that of the green and gold uniform – the 'striped caftan', as he later contemptuously called it.[35] He swore that he could not afford it, and therefore could not take up the office. This obstacle was overcome by Smirnov. 'Learning from my tailor that the new uniform of Prince Wittgenstein, who had transferred to military service, was for sale, and that it would fit Pushkin well,' he writes, 'I sent it to him with a note, saying that I had bought him the uniform, but that it was up to him either to take it, or to cause me a loss by leaving it on my hands. Pushkin took the uniform and went to court.'[36] The next difficulty was knowing when to wear it. On 23 January he took Natalya to the Anichkov Palace for the first time. 'I arrived in uniform,' he recorded in his diary. 'I was told that the guests were in tail-coats – I left, leaving Natalya Nikolaevna, and, having changed, went to S.V. Saltykov's soirée – the Sovereign was displeased, and began to speak of me several times: "He might have given himself the trouble to go and put on a tail-coat and return. Reproach him for it"' – an injunction obviously addressed to Natalya.[37] For guidance through the complex maze of court etiquette he turned to Aleksandra Smirnova-Rosset, but even with her help and that of old Countess Bobrinskaya,* 'who always lies for me and gets me out of trouble',[38] could not avoid the occasional faux-pas. At the end of the year he turned up with Natalya for a ball at the Anichkov wearing – correctly – his uniform tails, but carrying a tricorn hat with a plume, instead of a round one. He was given a substitute, but it was 'so greasy with pomade, that my gloves were soaked and turned yellow'.[39]

'Last month was very lively,' Pushkin noted at the end of February – 'a multitude of balls, routs etc.'[40] He had been interested to see Yakov Skaryatin, one of the assassins of the emperor Paul in 1801: Zhukovsky later told him that it had been Skaryatin's scarf with which the emperor had been strangled.† As usual, the climax of the season was its final

---

* Née Baroness Ungern-Sternberg, she was the widow of Count Aleksey Grigorevich Bobrinskoy, the illegitimate son of Catherine II and Grigory Orlov.
† Browning obliquely describes the murder in 'Waring', though placing it, incorrectly, in Moscow:

> Or who, in Moscow, toward the Czar
> With the demurest of footfalls
> Over the Kremlin's pavement, bright
> With serpentine and syenite,
> Steps, with five other Generals
> That simultaneously take snuff,
> For each to have pretext enough
> To kerchiefwise unfold his sash
> Which, softness' self, is yet the stuff
> To hold fast where a steel chain snaps,
> And leave the grand white neck no gash?

Browning happened to be in St Petersburg that spring: he left London on 1 March in the suite of the Russian consul general, Chevalier George de Benckhausen, and returned

week. 'What a Shrovetide!' Konstantin Bulgakov wrote to his brother in Moscow on 26 February. 'Balls every day. Today at the Shuvalovs, tomorrow at the Lazarevs, and the French actresses are giving a masquerade for the benefit of some widow, for whom a collection is also being taken; on Wednesday at the Austrian ambassador's, on Friday at Prince Volkonsky's, on Saturday there's a children's masquerade in the palace, and on Sunday, they say, a little ball in the Anichkov Palace.'[41] Not a member of court, he was wrong about this last: on Sunday 4 March there was not one, but two balls at the Anichkov – one in the morning, beginning at half past twelve, and one in the evening, beginning at half past eight. Natalya was at the first; Pushkin joined her at nine for the second, observing that many of the guests now arriving were jealous of those already there. During the evening that misfortune occurred which Pushkin had feared during Natalya's first pregnancy. 'Suddenly I see that she is not feeling well – I take her away, and on getting home she miscarries,' he told Nashchokin.*[42] 'Thank God! Shrove-tide is over, and with it the balls,' he noted with some fervour in his diary.[43] Natalya, young and healthy, soon recovered, and in the middle of April Pushkin packed her off with the children to Polotnyany Zavod for the summer, where her sisters were, he wrote, 'suffering terribly from my mother-in-law's caprices'.[44]

The disadvantages of Pushkin's new position became more apparent after the season had ended: as a gentleman of the chamber he was expected to be present at most court functions. Like a number of his colleagues, his devotion to duty was minimal: at Easter Nicholas, noting that many chamberlains and gentlemen of the chamber had been absent from the services in the court church, ordered them to be reprimanded. Pushkin, however, disregarded the summons to appear before Count Litta, the senior court chamberlain. Henceforth he tended to plead illness as a means

---

on 1 May. During his visit he admired the frozen Neva, which gave him a scene or two for an unfinished play, 'about a fair on the Neva, and booths and droshkies and fish-pies and so forth, with the Palaces in the background' (John Maynard, *Browning's Youth*. Cambridge, Mass., 1977, 128); saw 'Florid old rogue Albano's masterpiece' (*The Ring and the Book*, XI, 272) – a representation of Europa and the bull – in the Hermitage; and met a King's Messenger called Waring, who gave his name to the poem's protagonist.

* Natalya had apparently been unaware that she was pregnant; on 9 March Pushkin's mother, giving Olga news of the miscarriage, added 'so now she is lying still in bed, after skipping around all winter and, finally, all Shrove-tide, when she was two months pregnant. In vain did I say she was pregnant. Her aunt maintained the opposite, and her niece continued to dance. Now they are astonished that I was right' (*Mir Pushkina*, I, 212).

of escape, though he was sorry to have done so on the occasion of the tsarevich's majority, since, he told Natalya, 'I did not see the historical scene and in old age shall not be able to speak of it as a witness.'[45]

There were, however, some advantages to be gained from his new position: for one thing, his relationship with the emperor became much easier. Though Nicholas was inclined to make Pushkin's misadventures with his uniform the subject of his wit, he would often engage him in conversation – 'On Sunday at the ball in the concert hall the Sovereign talked with me for a long time; he speaks very well, not confusing the two languages [French and Russian], not making common mistakes and employing real expressions,'[46] Pushkin noted – and he took too a great interest in what Zhukovsky whimsically referred to as 'The History of Mr Pugachev':[47] 'It is a pity I did not know you were writing about him,' Nicholas said; 'I would have introduced you to his sister, who died three weeks ago in Erlingfoss fortress', to which Pushkin added the exclamation 'Since 1774!' The tsar was mistaken: it was Pugachev's daughter Agrafena, not his sister, who had died in Finland. In February he returned the manuscript to Pushkin with some 'very sensible' comments, and, when Pushkin applied through Benckendorff for a loan of 20,000 roubles to cover the publication costs, immediately agreed, making only the proviso that the title should be changed to 'The History of the Pugachev Rebellion'.[48]

A draft of the letter to Benckendorff shows that Pushkin had originally contemplated asking for 15,000 roubles, but, thinking he could use some of the loan to pay off his mounting debts, increased the figure to 20,000 – an action which was, if not fraudulent, at least questionable. The loan was interest-free, and was to be paid back in two equal instalments in March 1835 and March 1836. When Dmitry Knyazhevich, an official of the Ministry of Finance, wrote to inform him that he could collect the money from the Treasury, he made a note of some of the debts on the back of the letter: 3,000 to Natalya's aunt; 3,900 to Ivan Yakovlev – a card debt incurred in 1829; 3,000 to Smirnov; 2,000 to the book-seller Lisenkov – he had borrowed 3,000 the previous July on a bill which had fallen due in January, when he had paid back only 1,000; 1,500 to Prince Obolensky – doubtless a gambling debt; 300 to Pletnev. Beneath these figures are four other sums with no indication of what they represent. If all, as seems likely, are monies owed, the total is 24,200 roubles. The printing of *Pugachev*, by the press attached to the Second Department of the Imperial Chancery – whose director was Mikhail Yakovlev, Pushkin's friend from the Lycée – cost 3,291 roubles and 25 copecks; in addition, Pushkin had to pay some 2,200 roubles for paper, and nearly 3,000 for the engraving and printing of a portrait of Pugachev; he may, therefore, have had something over 10,000 roubles left to cover debts of more than twice that amount.

He took pleasure, too, in the fact that his new office led to a closer acquaintance with the Empress Alexandra Fedorovna – the former Princess Charlotte of Prussia – whom he had long admired. In a stanza of the eighth chapter of *Eugene Onegin* – later omitted from the final version – he had described her, then a Grand Duchess, dancing with her brother-in-law, Alexander I, at a ball in the autumn of 1824:

> into the close circle, fallen silent,
> Like a winged lily,
> Swaying, enters Lalla Rookh,*
> And above the obeisant crowd
> Shines with regal head,
> And quietly weaves and glides
> A star-like Grace among the Graces.[49]

He was officially presented to her on 8 April. 'There were twenty of us [...] I was the last on the list. The empress came up to me laughing: "It's too ridiculous for words! ... I was racking my brains wondering which Pushkin would be presented to me – it turns out to be you! ... How is your wife?" [...] I love the empress terribly, despite the fact that she is already 35 and even 36.'[50] She was in fact thirty-five.

Of the other members of the imperial family Nicholas's brother, the Grand Duke Michael, was, if not a friend, at least a very friendly acquaintance: a number of conversations between the two on subjects ranging from the Decembrist revolt to hereditary baldness are recorded in Pushkin's diary. And, like others, on meeting Michael's wife, the attractive and intelligent Grand Duchess Elena – formerly Princess Charlotte of Württemberg – he was immediately captivated. 'Last Sunday I

---

* The empress had been known as Lalla Rookh since her appearance as Moore's heroine at a court masquerade in Berlin in January 1821 – an event celebrated by Zhukovsky in his poem 'Lalla Rookh'.

was presented to the Grand Duchess,' he wrote to Natalya at the beginning of June. 'I drove to Her Highness's on Kamenny Island in that pleasant disposition of spirit in which you are accustomed to see me when I don my magnificent uniform. But she was so sweet that I forgot both my unhappy role and my vexation.'[51] The censor Krasovsky, known for his reactionary views, was presented at the same time. '"It must be a trial to have to read everything that appears," the Grand Duchess said to him. "Yes, Your Imperial Highness," he answered, "present-day literature is so detestable that it is a torture." The Grand Duchess left him as soon as possible and talked with me about Pugachev.'[52]

Another pleasing event in a year not rich in this respect was the reception of his Hoffmannesque short story, *The Queen of Spades*, which had appeared anonymously – though all knew that Pushkin was its author – in the March issue of Smirdin's *Library for Reading*. At the beginning of April, when the periodical had reached the more remote districts of Russia, he was pleased to receive an affectionate and flattering letter from his friend and fellow-poet Denis Davydov, then living on his estate in Simbirsk province, one of whose *bons mots* he had used as the epigraph for the second chapter of his story. 'For pity's sake! What kind of devilish memory is this?' Davydov wrote. 'God knows when, in passing, I told you my answer to M.A. Naryshkina about the lady's maids who are fresher, and you put it word for word as the epigraph to one of the parts of *The Queen of Spades*. Imagine my astonishment, and even more my delight in living in your memory, in the memory of Pushkin, once the dearest of drinking companions, and always my own, my one and only poet! My heart really overflowed with happiness, as though I had received a note from a woman I loved.'[53]

'My *Queen of Spades* is in high fashion – gamblers are punting on the trey, seven and ace,' Pushkin himself noted in his diary. 'At the court a likeness was discovered between the old Countess and Princess Natalya Petrovna [Golitsyna], but it appears that no offence has been taken.'*[54] That gamblers should have taken an interest in the story was

---

* Princess Natalya Petrovna Golitsyna, known as the *princesse moustache*, was then ninety-three; like the countess, she had 'been in Paris in the time of Louis XVI, had been very well received by the unfortunate queen, Marie Antoinette, and had left Paris shortly before the revolution' (*Dnevnik*, 132). Her mansion on the corner of the Bolshaya Morskaya and Gorokhovaya Streets was considered to be the first house in St Petersburg

unsurprising, for it seemed to offer a means of outwitting chance. Its hero, Hermann, becomes obsessed by the belief that an old countess possesses the secret of an infallible means of winning at faro. By making up to her young ward he gains entry to her house and, in order to extort the secret, threatens her with a pistol, causing her to expire. On the night after her funeral he is visited by her apparition and told that he will win by betting on the three, seven and ace. He stakes his savings on the three; wins, and stakes all on the seven; wins, and stakes all, as he thinks, on the ace – but loses, because he has, inadvertently, or under the influence of some malign force, chosen the queen of spades: the card winks at him with a grin and to his horror he sees a likeness between it and the countess. The shock drives him mad: though it could be plausibly maintained that he has been mad from the outset of the story, and that the shock has merely made his condition apparent. Certainly his rumination, early in the narrative, on one way of obtaining the secret – 'Get introduced to her, insinuate myself into her favour, – perhaps become her lover, – but all that demands time – and she is eighty-seven, – she could die in a week, – in two days'[55] – displays the rationality of a lunatic, though Pushkin is also amusing himself at his character's expense. He had made the same joke earlier in a letter to Natalya from Boldino: 'On the road I dangled only after old women of seventy and eighty – and didn't even look at young sixty-year-old trollops.'[56]

The Queen of Spades has, especially in recent years, attracted much critical attention – perhaps almost as much as *The Bronze Horseman*, and possibly for the same reason: what is, on the face of it, a simple story presents difficulties and suggests possibilities which go far beyond its ostensible subject.[57] Generally speaking, readings fall into two categories, whose nature was adumbrated in 1880 by Dostoevsky in a letter to an aspiring authoress: 'At the end of the tale, that is, having read it, one does not know what to think: did this vision emanate from Hermann's nature, or was he really one of those who have contact with another world, a world of evil spirits hostile to man.'[58] In other words, on the one hand are those who see the story as realistic, and give a psychological explanation for events; on the other those for whom it is fantastic and the events supernatural. But both readings run into difficulty: the realistic-psychological finds itself confronted with the rationally inexplicable, and the fantastic-supernatural with the far too easily rationally explicable. In the end, it is difficult not to suspect that the story is a paradox, uniting two mutually contradictory views: the literary equivalent of one of those prints by Escher that conflate two mutually contradictory perspectives; a conscious, tongue-in-the-cheek refutation of the sententious truism with which the final chapter of the story opens: 'Two immovable ideas cannot exist together in the moral sphere, just as two bodies cannot occupy the same space in the physical world.'[59]

When Natalya had left St Petersburg in April she had gone first to Moscow. Here she had been reunited with her sisters Ekaterina and Aleksandra, whom she had not seen since her departure three years earlier. Her mother, who had quarrelled with her two elder daughters, was at Yaropolets. 'What's to be done with your mother?' Pushkin wrote. 'If she won't come to see you, go and see her for a week or two, although that is extra expense and extra trouble. I am terribly afraid of family scenes for you.'[60] Natalya took his advice, and, taking the children with her, travelled to Yaropolets at the end of the first week of May. Her mother, touched by the sight of her grandchildren, sent an almost gracious letter to Pushkin. 'I will begin by thanking you heartily for the happiness you have given me by allowing your wife to come to see me with the children,' she wrote. 'My only regret is the short stay which she proposes to make here, however, as it is an arrangement agreed between you, I cannot oppose it [. . .] Your children are charming and are beginning to get used to me, although on their arrival Masha screamed at her grandmother.'[61] At the end of May Natalya left her mother's estate for Polotnyany Zavod, where she was to spend the summer together with her sisters and her elder brother, Dmitry. She and the children were not put up in the mansion, which adjoined the cloth mills, but in a guest house in the grounds: a two-storey, wooden building with fourteen rooms, one of which – unusually for that time – was a bathroom.

From St Petersburg Pushkin sent her a series of tender and affectionate letters, full of admonitions, sometimes serious, but more often humorous. He is worried about her health: 'I am sending you [. . .] the prescription for the drops. Do me a favour, do not forget to read Spassky's instructions and follow them' – Ivan Spassky was the Pushkins' family doctor in St Petersburg. 'Don't ride wild horses (I most humbly beseech Dmitry Ivanovich about this),' he jokes, and, more seriously: 'Don't dare to go bathing – have you gone mad?' He sends her advice on looking after the children: she is not to let her sisters spoil Masha, they are to 'pay no attention to her tears and screams, or otherwise she will give me no peace'; her father is not to see the children: 'In his condition he cannot be relied upon. Before you know it, he'll bite Masha's little nose off.' She is not to be worried that Sasha's wet nurse has turned out to be addicted to drink: 'The boy will become accustomed to liquor, and will be a fine fellow in the manner of Lev Sergeevich.' A few weeks later, however, he reproaches her for not having dismissed the woman. 'How can you keep a drunkard by the children, believing the promises and tears of a drunkard?'[62]

As with many men, the experience of fatherhood had a profound effect on Pushkin. From his letters to Natalya it is obvious that he is no longer the Voltairean freethinker he once was, but has reverted to the beliefs of his childhood. He almost invariably ends with some variation of the formula 'I kiss and bless you and the children', often adding 'Christ be with you', or 'the Lord bless you'. These are, of course, conventional expressions, but they are ones which would have been unlikely to drop from the pen of the author of the blasphemous *Gabrieliad*, or from that of the man who boasted he had been taking lessons in 'pure atheism' from a deaf English philosopher. Another passage makes it clear they are far from meaningless: 'Having scolded you [for going to Kaluga against his advice], I take you tenderly by the ears and kiss you – thanking you for praying to God on your knees in the middle of your room. I pray too little to God and hope that your pure prayers are better than mine, both for me, and for us.'[63]

'I allow you to flirt to your heart's content,' he wrote to Natalya: a magnanimous gesture, for he had continually to defend himself against her accusations that he was dangling after Nadezhda Sollogub. But he had come to realize that Natalya was not at heart a promiscuous flirt. He had no real objection to decorous dalliance with the emperor at the intimate little balls – there were rarely more than a hundred couples – in the Anichkov Palace, and thought that, having become accustomed to this heady success, she would scorn to fly at humbler game. When, to tease him, she pretended to have acquired a suitor at Polotnyany

Zavod, he wrote: 'About which neighbour do you write me sly letters? with whom do you frighten me? I see from here what it is. A man of about 36; a retired military man, or an election official. With a paunch and wears a peaked cap. Has 300 souls and is going off to remortgage them – on account of the poor harvest. And on the eve of his departure he sentimentalizes before you. Isn't that it? And you, my wench, for lack of *him* [i.e., Nicholas] or another, choose even this fellow as an admirer: very sensible.' But she took the joke rather too far. 'I have nothing to say about your flirtatious relations with the neighbour,' he wrote. 'I gave you permission to flirt myself – but it is absolutely not necessary for me to read a sheet covered on both sides with a detailed description of it.'[64]

He saw nothing of Nadezhda Sollogub, he told Natalya, for he was leading a very quiet life, not going into society, but seeing to the printing of *Pugachev* and working hard on his history of Peter the Great. He had so got out of the habit of social intercourse as to become almost uncouth. 'Yesterday when I entered the well-lit ballroom with its elegant ladies, I became as embarrassed as a German professor. I had difficulty in finding the hostess; had difficulty in muttering a word. Then, looking around, I saw there weren't so many people and it was a simple ball, not a rout. [...] So I ate my fill of ices and drove home – at one o'clock.'[65] His life was, perhaps, not quite as eremitic as he gave Natalya to believe. When 'The Last Day of Pompeii', a picture by Karl Bryullov (brother of Aleksandr, who had painted Natalya's portrait) that had been much admired when shown in Milan and Paris, was put on exhibition in George Dawe's former studio in the Winter Palace, Pushkin was among those who thronged to see it. Impressed, he began a poem describing the same spectacle, but got no further than the fourth line. He was also seeing Elise Khitrovo almost every day. 'He is very busy in the mornings,' his mother told Olga, 'then he goes for recreation to the [Summer] Garden, where he walks with his Erminia; the constancy of the young person withstands all ordeals, and your brother is exceedingly ridiculous.'[66]

She was much missed, he told Natalya: 'In society many ask about you and long for you to return. I say that you have gone to dance in Kaluga.'[67] Though Pushkin might pass her absence off with a joke, it seemed suspicious to some. 'The rumours which people continually repeat concerning Aleksandr make me feel sick,' Sergey Lvovich wrote to Olga. 'Do you know that when Natalie had a miscarriage they said that it was as a result of the beatings he had given her! For goodness sake, how many young women go to see their relatives, and spend 2 or 3 months in the country! Does anyone find fault with them? But he and Lev can do nothing without being criticized.'[68]

Towards the end of April, in a letter to Natalya, Pushkin had written, apropos of the celebrations marking the majority of the tsarevich, the future Alexander II:

I do not intend to present myself to the heir with congratulations and greetings; his reign is in the future; and I probably shall not see it. I have seen three tsars: the first ordered my cap to be taken off, and scolded my nurse on my account; the second was not gracious to me; although the third drafted me as a chamber page in my declining years, I do not wish to exchange him for a fourth; better let well alone. We will see how our Sashka gets on with his born in the purple namesake; I did not get on with mine. God grant he may not follow in my footsteps, write poetry and quarrel with tsars! Then he wouldn't outdo his father in verse, but neither would he tilt at windmills.[69]

The letter was opened by the police in Moscow, copied, and forwarded to Benckendorff, who brought it to Nicholas's attention. The tsar was furious. Pushkin openly admitted that he lied in order to escape court ceremonies; displayed an obvious contempt for his office of gentleman of the chamber, referring to himself derisively as a 'chamber page' – a rank given only to boys; and was critical of tsars in general, in particular of Nicholas's predecessors, his father, Paul, and his brother, Alexander I. Luckily Nicholas showed the letter to Zhukovsky, who managed to calm his indignation and persuade him that it was harmless. On 10 May Pushkin wrote in his diary: 'The emperor was displeased that I had not shown myself touched and grateful by my appointment as gentleman of the chamber. – I can be a subject, even a slave, – but will not be even the Lord God's lackey and fool.* However, what profound immor-

---

* The sentiment is an adaptation of a remark made by Lomonosov in a letter to I.I. Shuvalov of 19 January 1761; Pushkin also quotes it – inexactly – in his *Journey from Moscow to St Petersburg* (XI, 254).

ality there is in the usages of our government! The police unseal a husband's letters to his wife and take them to the tsar (a well brought up and honourable man) to read, and the tsar is not ashamed to admit this – and to put in motion an intrigue worthy of Vidocq and Bulgarin! No matter what you say, it is no easy thing to be an autocrat.'[70]

The incident continued to rankle; on 18 May he wrote to Natalya:

> I did not write to you because I was angry – not with you, but with others. One of my letters fell into the hands of the police and so on. Look, wifekin: I hope that you will give no one my letters to copy; if the post unseals a husband's letter to his wife, that's their affair, and what's unpleasant is that the secrecy of family relationships is intruded upon in a filthy and dishonourable manner; but if you were to blame it would be very painful for me. No one should know what may take place between us; no one should be received in our bedroom. There is no family life without secrecy. I write to you, not for the press; and you should not receive the public in your privy. But I know that that cannot be; and I've long ceased to be surprised by swinishness in anyone.[71]

Of course, he does not really believe that Natalya would allow his letters to be copied; he is, rather, warning her that, since they are liable to be opened, she should be careful in her remarks, and simultaneously is taking a dig at the officials who, he imagines, are reading the letter. Over the course of the next few weeks he rarely writes to her without including a caustic sentence or two aimed at the police. 'Be cautious,' he tells her, 'probably your letters too are being unsealed: the security of the State demands it.'[72]

His initial indignation with Nicholas's behaviour gradually died down, though he still experienced unconquerable revulsion at the thought that officials were prying into his private life, eavesdropping on his and Natalya's intimacies. 'I have ceased to be angry with *him* [i.e. Nicholas],' he wrote to Natalya on 11 June, 'because, *toute refléxion faite*, he is not to blame for the swinishness which surrounds him. Living in a privy, one willy-nilly becomes accustomed to shit, and its stench ceases to bother one, regardless of the fact that one is a *gentleman*. Oh, to get away in the fresh air.'[73] The ever present, ever increasing financial distress brought about by life in the capital had always been a powerful argument for moving to the country, an argument now strengthened by his new dislike for the city as the seat of imperial power, the centre of gossip and intrigue. 'Do you really think that swinish Petersburg isn't repulsive to me?' he asked Natalya. 'That I like living here amid lampoons and denunciations?'[74] And there was another reason to move: earlier that year he had taken over the responsibility of managing the family estates. Boldino was almost terminally run down: to reverse its decline demanded a resident, not an absentee landowner. 'Oh, to spit on Petersburg, to hand in my resignation, to get away to Boldino and live as a country gentleman!' he exclaimed.[75]

Retirement was, he persuaded himself, the only sensible solution to his problems. 'The difficulties with the estate enrage me,' he told Natalya. 'With your permission it will, I think, be necessary for me to resign and to put aside with a sigh my gentleman of the chamber's uniform, which so pleasantly flattered my self-esteem, and in which, unfortunately, I haven't managed to play the fop.'[76] Throughout June his intention gradually hardened, as he became more and more depressed by his present existence, a depression exacerbated by Natalya's absence. 'I am having firm thoughts about resignation,' he told her, confessing in the same letter a lapse into earlier habits. 'I am wholly at fault towards you in a money matter. I had money ... and gambled it away. But what could I do? I was so full of spleen that I had to amuse myself somehow. *He* is to blame for everything; but God be with him; if only he would let me retire to the country.'[77] In fact, Pushkin had already taken a decisive step without informing Natalya: on Monday 25 June, under the influence of a particularly black mood, he had sent a short, almost peremptory note to Benckendorff at Peterhof, where the court had taken up its summer residence earlier that month:

> Since family affairs necessitate my presence sometimes in Moscow, sometimes in the provinces, I see myself obliged to retire from the service and beg Your Excellency to obtain for me permission for this.
>
> I would ask, as a final favour, that the authorization which His Majesty deigned to grant me, that of visiting the archives, be not withdrawn from me.[78]

At Peterhof the empress's birthday on 1 July was celebrated by a ball at the palace. On the following evening there was a more intimate celebration at the Villa Alexandriya, the empress's private residence. During the course of the evening Zhukovsky was shocked to learn from Nicholas of Pushkin's request. On returning to his room he dashed off an irritated letter:

> The Sovereign has again spoken to me about you. If I had known in advance what induced you to apply for retirement, I could have explained it all to him, but since I myself do not understand what could have forced you to commit this idiocy, there was nothing I could reply to him. I only asked: *is it impossible somehow to put this right?* – Why should it be impossible? he replied. I never detain anyone, and shall allow him to retire. But in that case everything will be finished between us. He can, however, still take his letter back. – This genuinely touched me. But act as you think best. In your place I would not doubt for a moment how to act.[79]

He gave the letter to Bludov to take to St Petersburg; Pushkin received it the next morning, on Tuesday 3 July.

He was already having second thoughts about his action, and his misgivings were much reinforced by Zhukovsky's account of his conversation with the emperor. If he persisted, he would lose his position at court (and, what was much more important, Natalya would lose hers); they would lose their position in society; he would lose his privileged relationship with the emperor; he would lose the possibility of favours such as the recent loan for the publication of *Pugachev*. Was the sacrifice of all this worth the ability to live in self-imposed exile at Boldino as a country gentleman? On consideration he thought not; he therefore sent Benckendorff another short note. 'A few days ago I had the honour to address myself to Your Excellency to obtain from you the permission to retire from the service. Since this step was improper I beg you, Count, to take it no further. I would rather appear to be inconsistent than ungrateful.'[80] It was only after dispatching this he received Benckendorff's reply to his first letter. This spelt out the threat implied in the emperor's words to Zhukovsky, 'in that case everything will be finished

I laid the original of your letter of 25th inst. before the Sovereign Emperor, and His Imperial Majesty, not wishing to detain anyone against their wishes, ordered me to inform the Vice-Chancellor of the gratification of your request, an order which I shall fulfil.

However, to your request that in retirement you should be granted the right to visit the state archives to gather material the Sovereign Emperor did not express his approval, since this right can only be granted to those who enjoy the especial trust of the authorities.[81]

On the same day – 3 July – Zhukovsky wrote a longer letter to him, in less haste. 'You really are a stupid fellow, I am convinced of that now,' he began. 'Not only stupid, but your conduct is also indecent: how could you, when about to put into effect what you had so artfully cooked up, not say a word to me about it, neither to me, nor to Vyazemsky – I cannot understand it.' And indeed it was peculiar. On 22 June – three days before Pushkin's first letter to Benckendorff – Zhukovsky had paid a short visit to St Petersburg and had dined with Vyazemsky and Pushkin. Yet the latter had not given the slightest hint that he was meditating so momentous a step. 'Stupidity, vexatious, egotistical, unutterable stupidity!' was Zhukovsky's conclusion. In Pushkin's place, he would immediately write, as honestly and straighforwardly as possible, a letter to the emperor himself, accusing himself of stupidity, explaining the reasons for his action, and expressing 'that sentiment of gratitude which the Sovereign fully deserves'. He was to write immediately, and send the letter to Benckendorff. 'I never imagined that there was still the possibility of remedying that which you were pleased so recklessly to spoil. If you do not avail yourself of this possibility, then you will be that bristly animal, which feeds on acorns and with its grunts offends the ears of every well brought up gentleman; put plainly, you will be acting badly and stupidly, you will ruin yourself for your whole life and will deserve your own and your friends' disapprobation.'[82]

Elise Khitrovo delivered this letter to Pushkin on the following day – Wednesday the fourth. Pushkin immediately replied, telling Zhukovsky that he had written to Benckendorff to withdraw his request, and that he had received Benckendorff's reply to his first letter, forbidding him access to the archives. 'This grieved me in all respects,' he wrote. 'I submitted my resignation in a moment of depression and annoyance with everything and everyone. My domestic circumstances are difficult; my position is not a cheerful one; a change of life is almost a necessity. I did not have the courage to explain all this to Count Benckendorff – for this reason my letter must have seemed dry, whereas it was simply stupid. But I certainly did not have the intention to bring about what has happened. To write a letter directly to the Sovereign I truly do not dare – especially now. My justifications would be like petitions, and he has already done so much for me.' He would instead write another letter to Benckendorff.[83]

'I am extremely grieved,' he wrote, 'that my thoughtless petition, forced from me by unpleasant circumstances and vexatious, petty troubles, could appear to be insane ingratitude and opposition to the will of him who until now has been rather my benefactor than my sovereign. I shall await the determination of my fate, but in any case, nothing will alter the sentiment of my deep devotion to the tsar and of filial gratitude for his previous favours.'[84] At nine the next morning – Thursday 5 July – Zhukovsky called on Benckendorff to plead his friend's cause. He brought with him the letter Pushkin had written to him the previous day. In the course of the conversation he gave it to Benckendorff as offering some explanation of Pushkin's motives. The meeting, however, was inconclusive: Benckendorff could not promise that Nicholas would allow Pushkin to withdraw his resignation. Later that day he sent Zhukovsky Pushkin's second and third letters of 3 and 4 July. Zhukovsky read them with incredulity, and the following morning, before leaving to see Benckendorff again at eleven, sent Pushkin an angry letter. 'I really do not understand what has happened to you; you seem to have become an idiot; you should either be living in the madhouse, or should order yourself a good flogging to set your blood in motion [. . .] Surely you cannot have forgotten how to write; surely you do not consider it beneath yourself to express some kind of feeling to the Sovereign? Why subtilize? Be simple. The Sovereign is grieved by your action; he considers it ingratitude on your part.'[85] By now Pushkin was feeling harassed beyond measure by the affair. 'I really don't understand myself what is happening to me,' he replied. 'To take retirement, when it is demanded by circumstances, the future fate of my family, my own peace of mind – what kind of crime is that? what ingratitude? [...] Now, why are my letters dry? And why should they be running with snot? In the depths of my heart I feel myself in the right before the Sovereign; his anger grieves me, but the worse my position is, the colder and more constrained is my language.'[86]

On the same day he composed a third letter to Benckendorff in which he strove to answer the charge of ingratitude. In fact, this, and those from and to Zhukovsky, were supererogatory: the matter had been decided on Thursday the fifth, when Beckendorff sent a memorandum to Nicholas. Enclosing copies of Pushkin's letter to him of the third, and to Zhukovsky of the fourth, he wrote: 'Since he confesses that he simply committed an act of stupidity, and prefers rather to appear inconsistent than ungrateful, then (since I have as yet informed neither Prince Volkonsky, nor Count Nesselrode of his resignation) I assume that Your Majesty would be pleased to regard his first letter as though it had not existed. Before us is the measure of the man; it is better that he should be in service, rather than left to himself!!' On this Nicholas minuted: 'I pardon him, but summon him before you to explain to him once again the whole senselessness of his behaviour and what it might have resulted in; that which might be pardonable in a twenty-year-old madcap is not excusable in a man of thirty-five, who is married and the father of a family.'[87]

It had been an unedifying affair, from which no one emerged with much credit, with the possible exception of Zhukovsky. His insistence that Pushkin should express his gratitude towards the tsar – even though Pushkin was far from entertaining the sentiment – may appear unduly sycophantic to the modern sensibility, but it recognized the reality of the situation. And he did labour unceasingly to extricate Pushkin from the situation in which his foolishness had landed him. For it was extraordinarily foolish not to have consulted Zhukovsky and Vyazemsky before sending in his resignation, and even more extraordinarily foolish – or naive beyond belief – to have couched his request in so brusque a form, while simultaneously imagining he would be able to retain the privileges he had been given. And the foolishness was compounded by the fact that his *démarche* occurred so soon after the contretemps in May, which appeared to have taught him nothing about the emperor's character. Yet Pushkin in normal circumstances was very far from being either foolish or naive. However, when pressures upon him – financial, social, domestic – became unendurable, he did not, as others might, lapse into apathetic resignation, but, in the grip of a kind of sullen rage, became incapable of rational thought or action, and lashed out indiscriminately at anyone or anything, caring little – on the contrary rather hoping – that he might, like Samson at Gaza, bring the whole edifice of his life crashing about him. His behaviour here adumbrates his behaviour in the spring of 1836, when, in the space of a few weeks, he nearly became involved in three duels, or in the winter of 1836-7, when he put into motion the train of events that led to his final, fatal duel.

'The past month was a stormy one,' he noted in his diary. 'I almost quarrelled with the court, but all turned out well in the end. However, it will be remembered against me.'[88] The episode – together with the incident concerning his letter to Natalya – brought to an end the improvement in his relations with Nicholas.

Though he had ignored the emperor's susceptibilities in submitting his resignation, he was not so completely lost to good sense as to be equally heedless of Natalya's feelings: he therefore carefully kept her in the dark. Since she had left, he had written to her on an average twice a week. After his first note to Benckendorff, however, he suddenly sent her – as if to expiate feelings of guilt – three letters in three days, in none of which does he mention his resignation. Then, after receiving Benckendorff's reply, he fell silent, and did not write to her again until 11 July, by which time the affair had been settled. Even then he referred to his action only in general terms. 'A few days ago I almost did something disastrous,' he wrote, 'I almost quarrelled with *him* – and I funked terribly, which made me melancholy.' It was not until the fourteenth that he could resolve to tell her what he actually had done. 'The other day,' he wrote, 'I was overcome by spleen: I handed in my resignation. But I got such a scolding from Zhukovsky, and such a dry discharge from Benckendorff, that I funked, and asked for Christ's and God's sake that my resignation be not accepted. And you're even glad of it, aren't you? It'll be all right if I live another 25 years or so; but if I turn up my toes in less than ten, then I do not know what you will do, and what Mashka and especially Sashka will say. There will be little consolation for them in the fact that their papa was buried as a fool, and that their mama was so terribly pretty at the Anichkov balls.'[89]

Natalya would certainly have complained had she been told that her dancing days were over and that she had to move to a dilapidated wooden house on a run-down estate at the back of beyond. Life in the country had no attractions for her. The following May, after Pushkin had paid a short visit to Trigorskoe and Mikhailovskoe, Annette Vulf wrote to her sister Zizi Vrevskaya: 'He is enchanted with country life and says that it makes him want to settle there, but his wife has absolutely no desire to do so and then again he would not be allowed, I think.'[90] Had his resignation been accepted, Natalya would have been doubly annoyed because this would have put an end to a scheme which she had concocted with her sisters. Their quarrel with their mother and her withdrawal to Yaropolets had severely curtailed their social life, lessening their hopes of obtaining a husband. They were, therefore, extremely eager to move to St Petersburg where Natalya – who, though younger, was a married woman – could sponsor them in society and introduce them to circles far more glittering than those which they had known in Moscow. Natalya's first thought was to try to get them appointments as maids-of-honour. 'Why do you want to install your sisters in the palace?' Pushkin objected. 'In the first place you will probably be refused; and in the second, if they are accepted, then think what vile gossip will spread around swinish St Petersburg.' She then suggested that Ekaterina and Aleksandra should come and live with Pushkin and herself in St Petersburg. 'Hey, wifekin! look here,' he wrote. 'Here's my opinion: a family should be *alone* under *one* roof: husband, wife, children while they are small; parents, when they are extremely old. Otherwise there's no end of trouble, and no domestic peace.'[91] But he could not resist her persuasions, and a little later wrote to say that he had taken a larger apartment – the lodging in the Batashev mansion on the Dvortsovaya Embankment just vacated by the Vyazemskys: they had left for Italy, hoping the change in climate would improve the health of their seventeen-year-old daughter Praskovya.*

On 4 August Pushkin applied for three months' leave to visit the Nizhny Novgorod and Kaluga provinces 'for domestic reasons'.[92] He left on the sixteenth or seventeenth, travelling through Moscow, where he stopped only for four hours. Long enough, however, to call in at a

* It did not: she died in Rome in March 1835.

ball, astonishing Lev by his sudden appearance, and meeting his old friend and rival for the affections of Elise Vorontsova, Aleksandr Raevsky, whom he found 'made stupid by rheumatism in his head'. He was travelling post, without a servant, and was lucky to escape without injury from an ugly incident on the road. 'In Tarutino some drunken coachmen almost killed me. But I got my own way. Why call us robbers? they said to me. We've been given our freedom, and a pillar has been put up to us.'*[93] He was in Polotnyany Zavod by the twenty-first, in time to celebrate Natalya's name-day on the twenty-sixth, and her birthday on the twenty-seventh.

The family was together for a fortnight. During this time Pushkin visited another Goncharov estate some thirty-five miles away – little Nikulino, with only eighty serfs, which was being sold at auction to pay off some of the family's debts. He must have liked the property, for in October he gave the Goncharovs' former bailiff, S.G. Kvasnikov, a power of attorney to bid on his behalf at the auction. How he expected to finance the purchase is unclear. Perhaps he hoped to reach some compromise with the Goncharovs by giving up the claim to the 11,000 roubles he was owed by his mother-in-law. But Nikulino turned out to be part of the entailed property, and had to be withdrawn from sale.

In the first week of September he accompanied Natalya and her sisters to Moscow. This time his visit was slightly less fleeting. He saw something of Turgenev. 'I galloped to the theatre, to the box taken by Pushkin, his wife and his sisters-in-law,' the latter noted in his diary on 8 September. The next day he called on the family. Pushkin read him some pages of *Pugachev*, which impressed him as containing 'much that was curious and original'.[94] That evening Pushkin left for Boldino. Natalya paid a short visit to her mother at Yaropolets, taking only Masha – rather to Natalya Ivanovna's annoyance – with her. On 25 September she and the children, her two sisters, and her brother Dmitry, left

---

* Tarutino is a village on the Moscow–Kaluga road, then part of the estate of Count Sergey Rumyantsev. It had been the scene of a fierce battle against the French on 6 October 1812. To mark the event Rumyantsev petitioned the tsar for permission to free the peasants of Tarutino and of the neighbouring Granishcheva – 439 souls in all – and make over to them the land they had been cultivating. In return they were to erect a monument to commemorate the Russian victory. The monument was consecrated in June 1834; it bore the inscription: 'On this spot the Russian army, led by Field-Marshal Kutuzov, saved Russia and Europe'.

for St Petersburg. 'Natalie is pregnant again, her sisters are with her, and are going snacks with them in renting a very fine apartment,' Nadezhda Osipovna wrote to Olga in November. 'He [Pushkin] says that it suits him as far as the expenses are concerned, but incommodes him a little, as he does not like to change his habits as head of the household.'[95]

The Pushkin family finances had always been precarious, and over the years had become steadily worse. As mortgage succeeded mortgage, more and more of the income from Boldino was diverted to interest payments, which were, however, often avoided and ignored. This habit had nearly led to catastrophe in the autumn of 1831. 'My father is in terrible straits,' Olga had written to her husband from St Petersburg: 'he is in danger of having his property sold under the hammer, and yet he is going to rent a house here.'[96] Impending disaster did not convince Sergey Lvovich to change his way of life, nor was he capable of managing his household. 'He is robbed, pillaged on all sides; his retainers are veritable locusts: imagine: 15 people!' Olga lamented.[97] Though Pushkin continually suggested that he and Nadezhda Osipovna should retire to Mikhailovskoe for some years, Sergey ignored his advice, complaining that everything was the fault of his bailiff, Mikhail Kalashnikov, believed by the family members to be dishonestly enriching himself at their expense. 'I could wish nothing better than to know you were in Boldino, auditing the accounts of that rascal bailiff,' he wrote to Lev;[98] while Olga, recapitulating his finances to her husband, concluded, 'God knows whether he will receive anything from that archthief his bailiff, who alone is gorged with money and prospers to our misfortune.'[99] Kalashnikov may, however, have been maligned: he died a poor man; and the causes of the decline, apart from the burden of the mortgages, seem to have been inefficiency and indolence, rather than dishonesty, combined with a general fall in the price of grain – it was all arable farming at Boldino.

In the autumn of 1833, however, Sergey Lvovich, driven by desperation to act completely out of character, took a decisive step, sacking Kalashnikov, and replacing him with Iosif Penkovsky, a White Russian squire. He had been recommended by Nadezhda Osipovna's cousin, Ekaterina Melander, whose estate at Sukhopoltsevo, near Ostrov, he had managed while her husband was in the army. As a fellow-member of the gentry, he would have to be paid a good deal more than Kalashnikov – one, later two, thousand roubles a year instead of one or two hundred – but the expense would be worthwhile if the fortunes of the estate could be turned round. Armed with Sergey Lvovich's power of attorney, and bearing with him the hopes of the elder Pushkins, Penkovsky set off for Boldino in the second week of October. Apologizing to Olga for failing to send her a remittance, Nadezhda Osipovna wrote on 21 October: 'Papa is in despair, but I live in hope: the new manager will soon be in Boldino, and I hope he will exert himself to collect what we need to relieve us, and make a good impression from the start.'[100]

Pushkin, who had just returned from his journey to Orenburg, was in Boldino when Penkovsky arrived, and oversaw the handing over of the estate to the new manager. The Boldino peasants seized the opportunity to present a petition to him complaining of Kalashnikov's conduct: dictatorial, arbitrary and leading to the ruin of the estate. Nevertheless Pushkin, perhaps still experiencing a residue of guilt for his seduction of the bailiff's daughter, retained him as the manager of his serfs in Kistenevo.

Ever since his first visit to Boldino in 1830 he had dreamt of reuniting the family's scattered patrimony. During this stay, in 1833, he began to consider how this might be accomplished. The first step would be the acquisition of Vasily Lvovich's Boldino estate, which was now in the hands of the mortgagee, the Foundling Home. Sergey Lvovich was the legal heir, but had no hope of paying off the mortgage, and therefore would probably have to renounce the inheritance. Pushkin, however, had hopes of persuading the Foundling Home to agree to some kind of accommodation. To achieve this he would have to become a landed proprietor himself by taking over his father's estate – which might also lead to an improvement in the family finances. He discussed his plans with Nashchokin in November, and on the twenty-fourth wrote to him from St Petersburg, 'I have seen my father, he is very glad of my proposal to take over Boldino.'[101] The scheme was, of course, even more chimerical than his plans to buy a property of his own, as he finally had to realize. It turned out that, in addition to the mortgage, his uncle's estate was burdened with promissory notes for 110,000 roubles, which Vasily Lvovich had given to his common-law wife, Anna Vorozheikina, and his daughter by her, Margarita, since he was legally unable to leave the property to them. This put it completely out of Pushkin's reach. When it was eventually sold at auction in 1835, it went for 230,000 roubles.

Though he had to abandon these hopes, in the end he was nevertheless forced to take over responsibility for Boldino. 'My circumstances have become even more difficult and here's why,' he wrote to Nashchokin towards the end of March 1834. 'The other day my father sends for me. I arrive – find him in tears, mother in bed – the whole house in terrible agitation. "What's the matter?" – "The estate is being inventoried." – "You must pay the debt as soon as possible." – "The debt has already been paid. Here's the manager's letter." – "Then what's the trouble?" – "We have nothing to live on until October." – "Go to the country." – "We haven't the means." What's to be done? I shall have to take the estate in hand, and fix an allowance for my father. New debts, new troubles.'*[102] He could not stand by and let the property be lost to the family, as Vasily Lvovich's had been.

On 13 April he wrote to Penkovsky in unexpectedly businesslike fashion:

> My father has been pleased to place at my complete disposal the management of his estate; therefore, confirming the power of attorney given by him to you, I notify you that henceforth you are to refer directly to me with regard to all business concerning Boldino. Send me immediately an account of the monies forwarded by you to my father since you entered on the management, also those borrowed by you and those used in payment of debt, and in addition how much unsold grain remains, how much uncollected quit-rent, and how much (if any) arrears. You should also commence a homestead inventory of Boldino, so as to complete it by September.[103]

He prepared for the accounting tasks that lay ahead by making a little booklet from sixteen sheets of foolscap writing paper, folded in two. On the outside leaf he wrote 'Accounts in connection with the manage-

---

* Taking the inventory of an estate was a preliminary to distraining upon it for the non-payment of debt. The procedure, or the threat of it, was nothing new for Boldino. One of Penkovsky's first tasks, the previous November, had been to defer the execution of an inventory in respect of an earlier debt, while the following September Olga wrote to her husband: 'Imagine, last year the estate was inventoried five times!' (*PIES*, XVII–XVIII, 165.)

ment of Boldino and Kistenevo 1834'.[104] The first entries in it, dated 6 and 9 April, are debits of 666 roubles – a quarter's rent for his parents' apartment – and of 200 roubles, given to them in cash; to these he added 550 roubles he had already laid out on their behalf: money sent to Olga in Warsaw and that paid as wages to their servants. For the moment he could afford to let the account go into the red: he was relatively flush, having just received the 20,000 roubles intended to pay for the printing of *Pugachev*. But if this went on his parents' debts, it meant an end to his hopes of using it to extinguish his own.

Sergey Lvovich's distress had been caused not only by the inability to cope with his own debts, but also – which, perhaps, affected him even more – by the inability to cope with those Lev had run up, for which he was continually being dunned. On 6 April, therefore, he wrote joyfully to Olga: 'His [Lev's] Warsaw debts will be paid. Aleksandr is taking the responsibility for them on himself, as it is becoming very difficult for me.'[105] This immediately provoked a letter from Olga's husband, Nikolay Pavlishchev, who was to become Pushkin's most annoying correspondent. 'Having learnt from Sergey Lvovich's letters that you were taking on the task of paying Lev Sergeevich's debts and providing my wife with an annual allowance,' he wrote, 'I consider it necessary to give you my view of these two subjects.' He requested payment of Lev's debt to him – 1,539 zloty 5 groszy, including interest – and enclosed an approximate schedule of Lev's other debts, which the 'bold captain' – as he was known in the family – had drawn up before leaving Warsaw. This included a restaurant bill from which it appeared that during six weeks in the autumn of 1833 Lev had got through sixty-three bottles of wine and one of rum. 'Your father,' Pavlishchev continued, 'speaking of the allowance with which you would annually provide my wife, writes that *in the first year* you could not give more than 1,500 roubles, but might give more in future years. In balancing my expenses up to now against the support promised by Sergey Lvovich, I am forced to ask: from just what point will this *first year* begin?' Although Sergey had promised Olga an allowance of four thousand a year, he had never paid the full amount; indeed in the last twenty months they had received no more than 1,500 roubles.[106]

Meanwhile Sobolevsky had obtained for Pushkin a detailed schedule of Sergey Lvovich's mortgages with the Foundling Home. The total borrowings amounted to 176,906 roubles 95 copecks, on which the annual interest was 11,826 roubles 50 copecks; these payments were 11,045 roubles 92 copecks in arrears, though this did not take into account Penkovsky's most recent payment. 'My friend the book-keeper', Sobolevsky wrote, had pointed out that this sum should be paid as soon as possible.[107] On 4 May Pushkin replied to his brother-in-law, setting out these figures. The income from Boldino, he thought, might be twenty-two thousand a year. After paying the interest there would be some ten thousand left: fifteen hundred for Olga and the same for Lev would give Sergey Lvovich seven thousand, which, he wrote, 'would be sufficient for him, but there are arrears to the government, private debts, Lev Sergeevich's debts, and my father has already received and spent part of this year's income. Until I have brought these confused matters into order and become familiar with them, I can and do not promise Olga Sergeevna anything. My situation allows me to take nothing from the income of my father's estate, but I cannot and am not in a position to add money *of my own*.' In a postscript he added, 'In one month *from my money* I have paid 866 roubles for my father and 1,330 for Lev Sergeevich: more I cannot do.'*[108]

Sobolevsky had, however, discovered a gleam of light in the darkness: seventy-four of Sergey Lvovich's Kistenevo serfs were free from debt, and could be mortgaged for 250 roubles each. Pushkin put this in train, but it was a protracted process, and it was not until 20 July that he received 13,242 roubles – the remainder had been withheld to pay off the arrears – from the Foundling Home. On the twenty-third he sent Pavlishchev 837 roubles in payment of Lev's debt. Meanwhile, on 11 June, he had packed his parents off to Mikhailovskoe, after paying 678 roubles for the repair of their carriage, and giving them 600 roubles in cash. 'My parents do not know that they are a hair's breadth away from total ruin,' he wrote to Praskovya Osipova a little later. 'If they could take it upon themselves to stay for several years at Mikhailovskoe, matters might be sorted out, but that will never happen.'[109] He was already

---

* He had forced Lev to move out of Engelhardt House and into their parents' apartment: the 1,330 roubles were the rent for Lev's room at the hotel. He had also paid his brother's restaurant bill of 260 roubles. In fact, his statement was incorrect: he had not paid the hotel account, but had given Engelhardt a bill payable at twelve months. He did not take it up when it fell due, and it was eventually redeemed after his death by his trustees.

beginning to feel sorry he had taken on the responsibility. 'My head's going round and round,' he wrote to Natalya. 'I rue the day I took over the estate, but what could I do? It wasn't for me, but for the children.' The other members of the family, with their constant demands for money, were a sore trial: 'Lev Sergeevich and my father are making me very angry, and Olga Sergeevna is already beginning to make me angry.' 'I am being pestered unmercifully,' he complained in June and repeated the complaint a few weeks later: 'Here I am being pestered and enraged without mercy.' Natalya had been against the project from the start. 'How right you were,' he told her, 'that I should not have taken these troubles on myself, for which no one will say thank-you, and which have already spoilt so much of my blood that all the leeches of our house can't suck it out of me.'[110]

Though he might have got rid of his parents for the time being, a more burdensome incubus was still present in the form of his brother, who refused to acknowledge the seriousness of the situation and, as soon as one old debt was paid, blithely ran up another. 'Lev Sergeevich is behaving very badly,' Pushkin wrote to Natalya. 'He hasn't a copeck, but loses 14 bottles of champagne at a time playing dominoes at Dumé's. I say nothing to him, because the man is, thank God, 30; but I'm sorry for him and annoyed.'[111] He paid the restaurant's bill – 220 roubles – and gave his brother two hundred and eighty in cash.

Lev had carried out his intention of joining the Foreign Office in April. He hoped to be posted to Georgia, where he had enjoyed himself so much when in the army. When it became clear that this would not happen, he abruptly resigned, and at the end of July set off for Georgia independently, extracting 950 roubles from Pushkin for travel expenses. He travelled slowly: in mid-August he was still in Moscow, where he met with Aleksandr Raevsky. The two left together for the south, but had got no further than Kharkov when winter set in. He did not reach Tiflis until mid-February 1835; his reinstatement hung fire, and he amused himself during his idleness by giving dinners and running up debts. Although he might have taken part in some expedition as a volunteer – 'there he is, fighting against the mountaineers at this very moment,' Olga told her husband in September[112] – his appointment as staff-captain in a Cossack regiment was not gazetted until the following July.

Two of Lev's debts had particularly worried Sergey Lvovich. The first was the account of Hut's restaurant on Miodowa Street in Warsaw, where Lev had entertained his fellow-officers of the Finland Dragoons before leaving Poland. Pushkin had no sympathy for the problems of Polish restaurateurs, and ignored the bill, which was not paid until the end of the 1840s. The second debt was extremely embarrassing. While in Poland Lev had borrowed 2,000 paper roubles and 300 in gold from Aleksandr Pleshcheev, an artillery colonel, and a good friend of Pushkin, as well as of Lev. Pushkin paid 1,500 roubles in December, but ignored requests for the rest of the loan. This produced, two years later, an unpleasant letter from Pleshcheev himself, asking for the money he had lent 'your scamp of a brother'. 'It is time for you, Aleksandr Sergeevich, to settle your accounts with me. I got your brother out of a hole, and you don't even answer my letters; you paid part of the debt, but as it were deny the rest; you are not so poor, and I not so rich, that you cannot afford to pay, or that I can afford not to demand.'[113] Lev had incurred another large debt in November 1833, when he had given Ilya Boltin a bill for a card debt of 10,000 roubles. Possibly because it would not fall due for four years, Pushkin managed, through Sobolevsky, to buy it up for only 2,500 roubles in December. After dealing with debts of this size, it must have been almost a relief to pay Lev's tailor's bill, a mere 391 roubles.

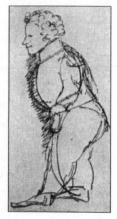

Lev

While dealing with the intricate finances of Sergey Lvovich and Lev, Pushkin had not let the management of the estate itself escape his attention. On 7 May Penkovsky had responded to his letter of 13 April in some detail, setting out the *corvée* and quit-rent obligations of the serfs. He was, he added, sowing spring oats, as the weather was very favourable. The winter crop would be poor, since Kalashnikov had used poor quality seed. He wrote again on 15 May: as yet it was impossible to estimate, as Sergey Lvovich had requested, this year's income; half the winter rye was good, half bad, while the spring sowing had not yet begun to show. He had sown two desyatins of poppies and four of hemp. 'May I take the liberty of suggesting,' he went on, 'that your personal presence this summer in Boldino village would be indispensably necessary for the disposition of the fields, from which section awkward woods should be cleared for plough-land (25 desyatins are needed for the next winter crop), for the inspection of the sown fields, and for the examination of the condition of the peasants.' A fortnight later he wrote again, sending 400 roubles of quit-rent, which Pushkin set as a credit against the 4,474 roubles he had so far expended.[114]

After Kalashnikov's missives, a welcome note of brisk efficiency emanates from Penkovsky's letters. However, Pushkin could not believe that his father had for once, possibly for the first time in his life, taken a sensible decision.* 'I could have confidence neither in Mikhail [Kalashnikov], nor in Penkovsky, in view of the fact that I knew the first, and did not know the second,' he commented later.[115] He therefore determined to put his own man in place, and, on the advice of Aleksey Vulf, approached the German agronomist Reichman, who had managed Malinniki for Praskovya Osipova, and who had treated Pushkin to 'a schnapps or two' when he had called there the previous August. Praskovya was horrified. 'So you have put faith in the recommendation of Mr Alexis Vulf,' she wrote caustically. '*Alexis* who is nothing more than an innocent as far as economy is concerned – a greenhorn – who after finding his estate without a crust of bread – his fields badly cultivated, his peasants without food – could call Mr Reichman a good economist!!!' Pushkin needed an honest and practical Russian, not a dishonest German. 'I have good reason to believe that in spite of the poverty in which Reichman left our lands – he did not abandon them with empty pockets. Believe me.' A week later she wrote again to reiterate her warning: 'He was in charge at Malinniki – for 4 years – at Niva for three – and left 500 souls in desperate straits.' She took the opportunity of reminding Pushkin that his parents owed her nearly two thousand roubles: she would be grateful if he could let her have the money in December, to pay the interest on her mortgage.†[116]

---

* Sergey Lvovich could, in fact, hardly have chosen better: despite a barbarous prose style, Penkovsky proved to be an exemplary intendant, who managed the estates to the great satisfaction of the Pushkins until May 1850.

† The debt, it seems, was not paid: in May 1836 Praskovya's daughter, Zizi Vrevskaya, wrote to her brother, Aleksey Vulf, 'Boris [Baron Vrevsky, her husband] is very busy. Pushkin has not paid him, but asks him to wait until the journal [the *Contemporary*] brings in the 2 thousand: so that will be God knows when, and his journal, they say, is no great success' (ДДД, II, 149, 199).

Reichman arrived in Boldino on 30 May, read his credentials to the peasants on 4 June, but left less than a week later, taking 125 roubles from Penkovsky for travel expenses. On 22 June he was back in Tver. 'You recommended Mikhail Ivanov [Kalashnikov] to me but I found nothing reliable in him, through him your peasants have become completely destitute,' he wrote. 'And I in fact learnt all this not only from your peasants, but also from impartial neighbours living in the vicinity. [. . .] After I found all this out I myself did not know what to do, but since Osip Matveevich [Penkovsky] is a decent man and is bringing order into everything I left the management to him again. But I was convinced that if I were to manage together with Mikhail Ivanov I could foresee nothing good. [. . .] It would be better to agree to give up this place so as not to cause a loss to you and your peasants.'[117] 'I have depressing news from the estate,' Pushkin told Natalya. 'The new manager I sent found everything in such disorder that he refused the management and left. I'm thinking of following his example. He is a clever fellow, and Boldino could make a mess of another five years.'[118]

The attempt to install Reichman had been injudicious. Penkovsky had obviously believed that his post was secure for several years: in his first letter he had told Pushkin that he was intending to renew the floor, reconstruct the stoves, and replank the roof of the house at Boldino. On 12 June he wrote, 'The arrival of the new manager caused me great dismay, and even more the ignorance of the reason why I had seemed to you incapable of the management of your estate despite my unremitting labours.'[119] However, Reichman's praise of the manager, the obvious improvement in the estate that Pushkin saw when in Boldino in September, and the equally obvious preference of the peasants for the new regime, caused him to confirm Penkovsky in his post. He sent him a power of attorney to replace that given by Sergey Lvovich, at the same time countersigning, without comment, the very generous schedule of allowances which he had submitted.*

* He could keep a pair of horses, and was allowed yearly 24 *chetverts* [1 *chetvert* = 210 litres] of hay and corn as fodder; his other annual allowances included '4 *chetverts* of rye, three of barley, 4 *chetveriks* [8 *chetveriks* = 1 *chetvert*] of peas, one *chetvert* and 4 *chetveriks* of buckwheat, six *poods* [1 *pood* = 16.38 kilograms] of oatmeal, 10 *funts* [40 *funts* = 1 *pood*] of rice, fifteen of semolina, 3 *poods* of salt, 8 of beef, 3 of pork, three of butter, 10 turkeys, 15 geese, 20 ducks, 30 chickens, 4 calves, 5 sheep, 10 piglets, 400 eggs, 2 *poods* 20 *funts* of tallow candles, 6 *vedros* [1 *vedro* = 12 litres] of strong liquor' (*Rukoyu Pushkina*, 769–70).

The two powers of attorney are almost identical; there is, however, one interesting difference between them concerning the manager's disciplinary powers. In that given by Sergey Lvovich the relevant sentence reads: 'Should any of the peasants or domestic serfs be disobedient or found guilty of a crime, they should be handed over without partiality to the court and I should be informed.' Pushkin's formulation is harsher and more arbitrary: 'Should any of the peasants or household serfs be of bad conduct, harmful to the estate, they should be at any time handed over as a quittance against the next conscription; should they be unfit, they should be handed over without quittance, and I should be informed beforehand.'[120] Conscriptions into the army, introduced by Peter the Great, had been frequent, but irregular up to 1830, after which date each village could normally expect to supply a draft – the size of which depended on the number of souls it comprised – every other year. During most of the eighteenth century service had been for life, but this was reduced to twenty-five years in 1793, and to twenty years, plus five in the militia, in 1834. Landowners could, however, reduce a village's obligation by turning serfs over to the army and receiving a 'recruit quittance' against a future conscription: many took advantage of this to rid themselves of their malefactors. When Pushkin had been in Boldino in 1833, he had received a petition from the village elders in which, among other requests, they had asked him to send five thieves who were 'unfit to be on the estate' off as recruits.[121] The request impressed Pushkin, who ordered Penkovsky to carry it out. In the unfinished *Journey from Moscow to Petersburg*, begun after his return from Boldino, he reveals himself to have become a keen advocate of the system, remarking that choosing conscripts according to rota, a method 'which a number of landowner-philanthropes support, should not exist as long as our gentry rights exist. It is better to use these rights for the good of our peasants, and, removing from their midst harmful rascals, persons deserving severe punishment etc., make of them useful members of society. It is senseless to sacrifice a useful peasant, an industrious, good father of a family, and spare a thief and an impoverished drunkard – out of respect for some arbitrarily accepted principle.'[122] Practice, unfortunately, did not correspond with theory: of the five offered to the army, three were rejected on medical grounds and one ran away.

At the same time as confirming Penkovsky at Boldino, Pushkin had given him the management of his portion of Kistenevo, sacking the unfortunate Kalashnikov. Although, after mortgaging the Kistenevo serfs in 1831, he had enquired anxiously as to the procedure for making interest payments – 'Be so good as to explain to me how one pays the [Foundling] Home,' he wrote to Nashchokin. 'Must I come myself? Or send someone a power of attorney? Or send the money by post?'[123] – in the end, with a financial fecklessness worthy of his father or brother, he had paid no interest whatsoever since taking out the loan. As a result one of Penkovsky's first tasks was to inform Pushkin that the local assessor for the nobility was about to carry out an inventory of the property prior to distraining on it for the accumulated arrears, 7,200 roubles. Should he, he asked, pay off the debt from the income of Boldino? Pushkin replied decisively on 10 November: 'I have received your letter of 30 October and hasten to answer it. *My debt* to the Foundling Home I will pay myself, and you should not spend a copeck of the Boldino revenue on it.'[124] Penkovsky managed to defer payment until the following February, but then, finding it impossible to obtain any further grace, and having received neither money nor instructions from Pushkin, was obliged to satisfy the Foundling Home out of the Boldino revenue.

By the end of 1834 there was little left of the proceeds from the loan Pushkin had obtained in July. In January 1835 his mother wrote to Olga: 'Do not blame Aleksandr if he has sent you nothing up to now; it is not his fault and not ours, Léon's debts have completely brought us to extremity. Mortgaging our last property, Aleksandr paid what your brother owed, and this amounted to 18,000,'* and her father added, 'I cannot conceal from you that Léon's frivolity and indifference to our means in running up debts which he could never pay, and because of which I had to mortgage my last remaining free peasants, caused and still causes me great distress. He continues to spend money heedlessly even after learning that it was our last resource. That put Aleksandr in a position where it was impossible for him to give us what was strictly necessary.'[125] When this letter reached Warsaw, it caused considerable anxiety to Pavlishchev, who saw the family estate being dissipated in

---

* An exaggeration: those of Lev's debts paid by Pushkin only amount to this sum if the bill for 10,000 given to Boltin is included at its face value, not at the amount – 2,500 roubles – Pushkin paid to redeem it.

order to pay Lev's debts, thus lessening his wife's future inheritance. This anxiety was compounded by another. 'Having a fair knowledge of Sergey Lvovich's domestic affairs, I cannot contemplate with equanimity your intention to refuse to manage the estate,' he wrote to his brother-in-law at the end of January. Were Pushkin to do so, then, sooner or later, Boldino would go under the hammer. He proposed a means of avoiding this. Lev's extravagance was, he believed, partly due to the fact that he had no property of his own. Let his portion be separated off and given to him; managing it would teach him financial prudence, and, if he were to run up debts, would do so on the security of his own property: the estate itself would be protected against further depredations. It seems extraordinarily sanguine of Pavlishchev, who had observed at first hand the remarkable facility Lev displayed for living beyond his means, to trust in the efficacy of this remedy. His real aim emerges in the final sentences. 'I know that this management is a burden to you, but what can be done? – However, were my wife to be given her portion, I would have a reason to take leave for six months or so, to travel to Boldino, and, while busying myself there with our portion, to put your communal part in order.'[126] At the end of April, having waited four months vainly for a reply, he wrote again to reiterate his plea that Olga's portion should be put into her hands before it was all spent on Lev.

Pushkin was in fact thinking of giving up the management. He had cleared off the majority of the debts; he could contribute nothing to the running of the estate: under Penkovsky's efficient management the interest was being paid on time, and the manager had recently put forward a scheme, immediately approved by Pushkin, to do away with quit-rent assessments, replacing them by a universal *corvée*, which, he calculated, would raise the income to 30,000 a year. Pushkin accepted, too, Pavlishchev's suggestion that Lev and Olga should have their portions of the estate, even sharing the view that this might reform Lev. Writing to his brother that April, he set out the sums that had been dispensed on the latter's behalf, and continued: 'Since my mother has been very ill [Nadezhda Osipovna had fallen ill the previous October, and was still far from well] I am still looking after affairs in spite of a thousand unpleasantnesses. I count on giving them up at the first opportunity. I shall try then to let you have your share of the lands and peasants. Probably you will then busy yourself with your affairs and will lose your indolence and your facility of living from one day to the next.'[127]

At the beginning of May he put these views into practice in a letter to Penkovsky. 'By agreement with my father,' he wrote, 'the income from Kistenevo from now on is assigned exclusively to my brother Lev Sergeevich and my sister Olga Sergeevna. Consequently send all the income from my share to wherever my sister or her husband Nikolay Ivanovich Pavlishchev requests; and the income from the other half (less the interest due to the Home) send to wherever Lev Sergeevich orders. Boldino remains my father's.'[128] The following day he wrote to Lev and to Pavlishchev setting out this new arrangement. He had, he told Pavlishchev, been unable to divide up the estate: 'You know our family circumstances; you know how difficult it is for us to accomplish anything sensible or business-like' – Sergey Lvovich had presumably proved recalcitrant. For the time being Olga would have to content herself with the income, less interest, from the 200 serfs at Kistenevo.[129]

Pushkin did not divest himself immediately of responsibility for the family finances. At the beginning of June his mother told Olga that they wanted to spend the summer in Pavlovsk. 'But our move,' she wrote, 'depends on Aleksandr, it is necessary for him to give us the means for this.'[130] The entries in Pushkin's home-made account-book come to an end that month, with a payment of 175 roubles to Sergey Lvovich's tailor, but he still held the purse-strings in July: on the twelfth Nadezhda Osipovna complained to Olga from Pavlovsk that life there was 'not cheerful, since your brother forgets that we cannot live on air'.[131] Shortly afterwards, with nothing remaining to disburse, he left his parents to their own resources. However, much to his annoyance, it seemed impossible to convince the family that he no longer had anything to do with the management of the estate. Most pertinacious in believing the contrary was Pavlishchev, who bombarded him with letters about Olga's portion at Kistenevo and the income from it. By December Pushkin was leaving them for Sobolevsky to read, and in January Olga wrote to her husband from St Petersburg: 'I am very annoyed with you for having written to Aleksandr: it only succeeded in stirring up his bile; I cannot recollect ever having seen him in such a dreadful mood: he shouted loud enough to make himself hoarse that he would rather give up everything he possessed (including, perhaps, his wife) than again have to deal with Boldino, the manager, the Foundling Home, etc., etc., that all you had to do was to address yourself to Penkovsky, that it was his business to be informed of affairs, that he is paid for that, that he must *know about everything*. He did not read your letter, he gave it to me after opening it, but without looking inside. His anger in fact seemed quite comic to me, so much so that I very much wanted to laugh. He seemed so like my father.'[132] Pavlishchev did, it was true, have some justification for raising the subject: Olga's income was forwarded through Sergey Lvovich, who often took the opportunity to divert it to his own use.

Pushkin's accounts are not easy to follow, and his arithmetic is often eccentric. Nevertheless it appears that at the end of the episode he was not out-of-pocket, especially after taking into account the fact that the Boldino estate had paid the arrears of interest on his mortgage. His income would, it is true, be slightly reduced by making over the Kistenevo revenues to Olga – but only slightly: the serfs produced about 3,600 roubles a year, two-thirds of which went on paying the interest, leaving a net income of only 1,200 roubles. 'Of course this is neither a sacrifice on my part, nor a favour, but a calculation for the future,' he wrote to Pavlishchev on telling him the news. 'I myself have a family and my affairs are not in a good state.'[133] The remark is somewhat enigmatic, since it is hard to see how giving up 1,200 roubles a year can be seen as an investment in the future, but Pushkin is, presumably, thinking of Pavlischev's earlier argument: the involvement in the estate of his sister and brother-in-law is an insurance against it being dissipated to pay Lev's bills; a means, therefore, of preserving his children's inheritance.

Though materially Pushkin's losses might have been insignificant, in other, less tangible respects they were incalculable. To the difficulties involved in managing the estate – dealing with Penkovsky, with Kalashnikov, with the Boldino peasants, the Kistenevo peasants, with the Foundling Home – were added the problems of his parents' subsistence, of Lev's debts, of the financial insecurity of his sister and her husband, and, of course, of his own financial worries. All this still further frayed a temper and mood already worn ragged by his appointment as gentleman of the chamber, by the perlustration of his correspondence, and by the repercussions resulting from his attempt to resign. The concomitant expenditure of time, of effort, and, above all, of nervous energy left little over for composition. In the autumn of 1834 he spent two weeks at Boldino: the scene and the season of two earlier periods of miraculous inspiration and creation, now filled with the mundane occupations of the landowner. On 15 September he wrote to Natalya: 'The first snow met me in the village and now the yard in front of my little window is all white; this is very friendly of it, however, I have not yet begun to write, and am taking up my pen for the first time to chat with you. I am glad to have got to Boldino; it seems there will be less trouble than I expected. I should very much like to write something. I don't know whether inspiration will come.' His letter was interrupted by the arrival of Petr Bezobrazov, the husband of Vasily Lvovich's daughter Margarita, who had come to the village in the hope of saving something from Vasily's estate. 'Ugh, I had difficulty in getting rid of him. He sat with me for two hours,' Pushkin wrote after his departure. 'We each tried to overreach the other – God grant that I overreached him in practice; in words I think I did.' This was not the only interruption. 'Just now some peasants were with me, with a petition; I was obliged to try and overreach them, too – but they surely will overreach me ... Although I have become a terribly good politician since I've been reading *The Conquest of England by the Normans.** What's this now? A peasant woman with a petition. Good-bye, I'm going to hear what she wants.' A little later he finished the letter. 'Well, wifekin, some humour. A soldier's wife asks me to register her son as one of my peasants, but, says she, he's been registered as a bastard, although, says she, she gave birth to him only 13 months after her husband was taken as a recruit, so how can he be a bastard? I shall bestir myself for the honour of the insulted widow.'[134] The sole result of this, his last visit to Boldino, was a fair copy of *The Tale of the Golden Cockerel*, dated 20 September 1834.

---

* Augustin Thierry, *Histoire de la conquête de l'Angleterre par les Normands*: Pushkin had the third edition (4 vols, Paris, 1830) in his library.

14

A SEA OF TROUBLES
1834–36

To be
Accountable to no one, to serve and indulge
Only oneself, before authority or livery
To bend neither conscience, nor thoughts nor one's neck;
To wander hither and thither at one's whim,
Marvelling at the divine beauties of nature,
And before the creations of art and inspiration
Trembling joyfully in the raptures of emotion.
– That is happiness! Those one's rights!

(III, 420)

PUSHKIN'S LAST STAY IN BOLDINO came to an end on
1 October 1834. On that day he left for St Petersburg, where he
arrived on the fourteenth. He had broken his journey for a short
time in Moscow, and, while there, had driven over to Yaropolets for
the day. His mother-in-law had taken him to call on her neighbours,
the Chernyshevs, hoping he might promote her son Dmitry's suit of
their daughter Nadezhda, but he was reluctant to be involved, having
burnt his fingers once before when acting as a matchmaker for the
Goncharovs. 'We visited the Chernyshevs together,' Natalya Ivanovna
told Dmitry, 'again with the good intention of advancing your affair,
but did not manage to say anything about it.'[1] She did, however, manage
to say a good deal about her other children to Pushkin. 'She told
him God knows what slanders about us,' Ekaterina Goncharova wrote
to Dmitry, 'and in addition asserted that it was us who had incited
Tasha [Natalya] not to take her son with her when she visited mother

last; we just knew that would be another thing we would be blamed for.'[2]

Natalya's two sisters were delighted to have escaped from their mother and from the provincial stuffiness of Moscow. 'We have been twice to the French theatre and once to the German,' Ekaterina informed Dmitry, 'to a party at Natalya Kirillovna [Zagryazhskaya]'s, where we were terribly bored, and to a rout at Countess Ficquelmont's, where we were introduced to some persons of society, and a number of young people requested to be introduced to us, and consequently we hope that we will have partners for our first ball. We pay numerous visits, which doesn't amuse us much, and *they look at us as if we were polar bears* – wanting to know what kind of creatures are these "sisters of Madame Pushkina", since this is just how Countess Ficquelmont presented us to some ladies at her rout.'[3] There was a slight indignity in owing their social acceptance to their younger sister, still only twenty-two. Ekaterina, known in the family as Koko, was twenty-five; Aleksandra, or Azya, twenty-three. 'Her two sisters are very sweet, but far inferior to Natalie in respect of beauty,' Sergey Lvovich told Olga after meeting them for the first time.[4] Nevertheless, they were certainly not unattractive. Like Natalya, both were tall. Ekaterina, thin and somewhat gawky, had, with her black eyes and hair, the look of a Georgian girl. Aleksandra had a fuller figure, but a sallow complexion, while that slight strabismus which made Natalya's gaze so enchantingly mysterious had with her become a definite squint.

From St Petersburg they assailed Dmitry with a torrent of requests and commissions. Could he send them more money? Could he write to Andreev, the Goncharovs' agent in Moscow, reminding him to send on the trunk with their ball dresses? Could he send some home-made strawberry jam from Polotnyany Zavod? Ekaterina, through her aunt's influence, had been

Aleksandra Goncharova

appointed as a maid-of-honour, but was remaining with the Pushkins, rather than moving into the palace: could he therefore send one of the domestic serfs to act as her lady's maid? And – a request by which all the sisters set great store – would he please send them by the New Year a carriage from the Polotnyany Zavod coach-house, 'having had it repainted in very dark damson with black fittings and upholstered with framboise silk'.[5] Dmitry was extraordinarily dilatory in fulfilling this last request. It was not until nine months later, in June 1835, that Aleksandra could write: 'The carriage arrived safely and we are infinitely grateful to you for it; we have already driven out in it, and although Auntie finds it abominable because of the springs, we have become used to it, so everything is fine.'[6] That summer the Pushkins had again taken a villa on the bank of the Black River, and the two sisters often rode out in the vicinity – Dmitry had sent them their favourite saddle-horses. 'Here we have the reputation of splendid riders,' Ekaterina wrote. 'In a word, when we ride out you cannot imagine how on all sides and in every language they go into raptures over the beautiful horsewomen.' 'Our talents in the art of horsemanship have made a great stir, which much embarrasses us,' she added.[7] After recovering from childbirth, Natalya joined them on Matilda, a black eight-year-old English thoroughbred mare.

The most important social event they had attended in the winter of 1834 was the ball given on the emperor's name-day, 6 December – the day on which Ekaterina became a maid-of-honour. 'The ball was splendid in the highest degree, and I came home very tired,' she wrote, 'but the beautiful Natalie was completely exhausted, although she danced no more than two French dances. But I must tell you that she was very obedient and very sensible, for dancing had been forbidden her.* She danced a polonaise with the emperor; he, as always, was very kind to her, although he scolded her a little on account of her husband, who had reported himself sick so as not to have to wear his uniform. The emperor told her that he perfectly well understood the nature of his illness, and since he was delighted she was with them, Pushkin should be all the more ashamed of not wanting to be their guest; however, madame's beauty served as a lightning conductor and averted the storm.'[8]

That winter Pushkin was avoiding, as far as possible, formal social occasions. 'Since January I have been very much occupied with Peter,' he wrote in the New Year. 'I have been three times to balls; and have left them early. I am little occupied with court gossip. A fig for posterity.'[9]

But he had been seeing much of his friends, and especially of Turgenev, who had returned to Russia the previous May. He remained in St Petersburg until December, when he left for Moscow, then travelling on to Vienna. The two dined, together with Zhukovsky, at the Smirnovs on 6 and 17 November; on the thirteenth Turgenev watched a performance of Delavigne's *Les enfants d'Édouard* from the Pushkins' box at the theatre; on the sixteenth they were both guests at Ekaterina Karamzina's birthday party; and on the twenty-ninth both were present at a dinner given by Count Bobrinskoy. 'I courted our sweet and clever hostess with wit and reminiscences,' Turgenev recorded in his diary, though also noting: 'The Lucullan feast and three dishes with truffles oppressed me.'[10]

Turgenev had fallen into disfavour with the emperor for abandoning his career in the civil service, and for his ceaseless efforts to obtain the rehabilitation of his brother Nikolay, still proscribed as a Decembrist. As a result, those Arzamasite friends who were now highly placed civil servants – Bludov, Uvarov and Wiegel among others – shunned his company. This was to be expected, and, though not pleasant, was bearable. But he was hurt when others exhibited the same caution. On 1 December he made an aggrieved note in his diary. 'The emperor and empress were at the Mikhailovsky Theatre [...] And the Pushkins did not invite me into their box ... So, farewell, my friends, serviles and liberals alike. "I must to the woods!"'*[11] But he soon forgave Pushkin. On 10 December, with Gogol and others, they spent a pleasant evening at Zhukovsky's: the gathering did not break up until three in the morning. And from Moscow in January he wrote to Zhukovsky with the request that Pushkin should send to him in Vienna, through the Foreign Office, a copy of *Pugachev*, 'with an autograph, in memory of the sacred olden days'.[12] At the end of February he wrote again to say that the Russian ambassador, Dmitry Tatishchev, had been reading *Pugachev*, and that the book was now going the rounds among the Russian community. 'Tell the poet-historian,' he added, 'that the homonymous countess (née Urusova) sends her regards.' He was referring to the

---

* Turgenev is employing the vocabulary of Spanish politics: 'servile' was a hostile designation applied (in 1820 and later) by Spanish liberals to royalists. The quotation is from Pushkin's unfinished narrative poem *The Robber Brothers* (1821–2): the words are uttered by one of the brothers as the two, chained together, languish in prison.

ambassador's niece, Mariya Musina-Pushkina, with whom Pushkin had been in love in 1827–8. And from Rome, at the beginning of April, he wrote: 'I am sending you and Pushkin each a tortoise-shell lyre from beneath the skies of Virgil,' and ended the letter 'from the Aeolian Harp' – his *Arzamas* nickname.[13]

The press of the Second Department had completed the printing of *Pugachev* in November; on the twenty-third Pushkin wrote to Benckendorff: 'I would like to have the happiness of presenting the first copy of the book to the Sovereign Emperor, adding to it some notes which I decided not to include, but which may be of interest to His Majesty.'[14] On the twenty-fifth the *Northern Bee* informed its readers that the *History of the Pugachev Rebellion* was on sale at Glazunov's bookshop on the Nevsky for 20 roubles a copy, or 22 with postage. A number of presentation copies had been produced, bound in morocco with moiré endpapers, gilded fore-edge and gold-leaf lettering. One was destined for the tsar; Nashchokin received another.

The work's reception was disappointing. 'Aleksandr's work on the Pugachev revolt has come out,' Sergey Lvovich told Olga in January. 'Its style is very powerful and it is very interesting. The periodicals say nothing about it and do not even mention it.'[15] In fact, that month it was reviewed in *Son of the Fatherland* by Vladimir Bronevsky, a retired major-general and author of a history of the Don Cossacks. He was disappointed by the book, which he described as a 'still-born child'; it was full of inaccuracies, and he regretted that it had been 'painted in a limp, cold and dry fashion, and not with the fiery brush of a Byron'.*[16] In February Pushkin's friend Baron Rozen contributed a much more favourable review to the *Northern Bee*. 'How strange is the desire of those who expected from Pushkin a History written with a flaming pen, the brush of a Byron!!' he wrote, emphasizing his astonishment with a double exclamation point. 'That our great poet was able not to be a poet in his History,' he continued, 'is precisely why he deserves the highest praise, and demonstrates how well he understands the immutable bounds of each of the fine arts.' Pushkin, he concluded, 'has given us a complete picture of that mournful episode of a happy and great

---

* Pushkin devoted a long article in the third number of the *Contemporary* (1836) to a detailed and ironic rebuttal of Bronevsky's criticisms.

reign. A sage economy in and an elegant arrangement of material; a precise, genuinely artistic chiaroscuro, and, finally, an inimitable conciseness of style, in which not a single redundant epithet can be found, – all this is gratifying proof of a great historical talent.'[17]

But Rozen's praise could not ensure the work's commercial success. Though in January Pushkin wrote to Nashchokin, 'Pugachev has become a good, punctual quit-rent payer, Emelka Pugachev my quit-rent peasant! He has brought me in money enough, but since I've been living in debt for two years, nothing's left in my pockets, it's all gone to pay off debts,' it soon became depressingly obvious that he had been deluding himself.[18] The work was not popular, and sold badly. In September he received a note from his Lycée friend Mikhail Yakovlev, now director of the Second Department's press, who had overseen its printing. 'I am sending you Pugachev,' the latter wrote. 'I have hired for *five roubles* two carts, but could not load everything into them and so an official horse has been provided for assistance. Please pay the men for the transport.'[19] The carts contained the unsold remainder of the edition in unbound sheets: on Pushkin's death 1,775 copies out of the 3,000 printed were discovered in his apartment. He had hoped to make some 40,000 roubles out of the book, but, after paying the printing costs and giving the book-sellers a discount, cannot have received much more than 16,000. And since he had borrowed 20,000 from the state to finance the publication, the end result was a loss of 4,000.

Pushkin himself attributed the work's unpopularity to his refusal to pander to the public taste. 'It is being berated, and deservedly,' he told Dmitriev, to whom he had sent a copy of the book. 'I wrote it for myself, not believing I would be able to publish it, and strove only for the clear exposition of somewhat confused events. Readers love anecdotes, details of a locality, etc.; but I consigned all that to the notes. As for those sages who are indignant with me for representing Pugachev as Emelka Pugachev, and not as Byron's Lara, I willingly refer them to Mr Polevoy, who undoubtedly, for a reasonable price, will undertake to idealize this person in the very latest fashion.'[20] But this was far from the truth: he had written the book for publication, and had very much hoped to clear his debts with the proceeds. In his diary he attributed its lack of success not to its lack of Byronic romance, but to the machinations of an enemy. 'In public my Pugachev is being much abused, and what is worse, is not selling,' he wrote. 'Uvarov is a great villain. He cries out against my book, calling it a subversive work.'[21]

Sergey Uvarov, the president of the Academy of Sciences since 1818 and Minister of Education from April 1834, was a classical scholar of some distinction, who had corresponded with Goethe and Friedrich Schlegel. He was also a brilliant civil servant, much impressing Speransky, who wrote of him that he was a 'splendid man, both in mind as in heart', being 'noble, clever, and, of Russians, the leading *scholar* in Russia'.[22] His character, however, did not match his capabilities: vain, self-seeking, unscrupulous and dishonest, he was arrogant towards his inferiors and servile to those above him. His path and Pushkin's had crossed a number of times in the past. Uvarov had been present in the audience at the Lycée when Pushkin had read his 'Recollections in Tsarskoe Selo' before Derzhavin in January 1815, but the two only became acquainted some years later in St Petersburg, when both were members of *Arzamas*. In October 1831 he had sent Pushkin his French rendering of 'To the Slanderers of Russia', accompanying it with a fulsome letter whose metaphorical whimsy recalls the language of the *Arzamas* gatherings. 'An invalid, who has long forgotten the path to Parnassus, but who has been enraptured by your splendid, genuinely *popular* verses,' he wrote, '*has done his best* to imitate them in French. He has not concealed from himself all the dangers of competing with you, but, inspired by you, wished once again, perhaps for the last time, *to fix his European bayonet*.' Pushkin, equally fulsome, echoed Uvarov's style in his reply, referring to 'the splendid, genuinely inspired verses, which it pleased your modesty to call an imitation', and continuing: 'My verses served you as a simple theme for the development of a genial fantasy. It remains for me to thank you from the heart for the attention shown me, and for the force and fullness of the thoughts which you have magnanimously ascribed to me.'[23]

When Pushkin was in Moscow the following September, Uvarov invited him to attend a lecture at the university. Ivan Goncharov, then a student, was among the audience. 'Suddenly this genius, this glory and pride of Russia – was but five paces from me! I could not believe my eyes. The lecture was being given by Davydov, the professor of the history of Russian literature. "Here you have the theory of art," said Uvarov, turning to us students and indicating Davydov "And here is art itself," he added, indicating Pushkin. He brought out this phrase, obviously prepared beforehand, with some éclat.'[24] On 10 April 1834 Pushkin noted in his diary: 'Yesterday evening at Uvarov's – tableaux vivants – we sat for a long time in darkness. S.* was not there – deadly boredom. After the tableaux a waltz and a quadrille, a bad supper.'[25] And in May that year he petitioned Uvarov – unsuccessfully – on Gogol's behalf for the chair of history at the newly established St Vladimir University in Kiev.

Outwardly the relationship seems perfectly amicable: though not intimates, they were yet closer than mere social acquaintances. But beneath the surface Uvarov did harbour a jealous resentment of the other: it had been he who had furnished Bulgarin with the details of Pushkin's ancestry for his pasquinade in the *Northern Bee*. He carried this hostility over into his official duties. Under Alexander I censorship had become the responsibility of the Ministry of Education; and in 1828 a reorganization of the system had established as its highest authority the Chief Directorate of the Censorship, the *ex officio* chairman of which was the Deputy Minister of Education. In this capacity Uvarov had been chagrined to discover that the special dispensation given to Pushkin by the tsar meant that his works escaped normal censorship. On 9 April 1834 the censor Nikitenko attended on the minister. 'I presented him with a composition or translation by Pushkin, *Angelo*,' he noted in his diary. 'Formerly the sovereign himself examined his longer poems, and I did not know whether I had the right to censor them. Now the minister has ordered me to act in relation to Pushkin on the regular basis. He read *Angelo* himself and demanded the exclusion of several lines.'[26] Two days later, after Pushkin had received the censored manuscript, Nikitenko made a caustic comment: '[Pushkin] is in a rage: Smirdin pays him a chervonets [a 10-rouble gold piece] a line, therefore he loses here a few score roubles. He has demanded that dots be inserted in place of the omitted lines, so that Smirdin should have to pay him for the dots as well!'[27]

It was, no doubt, vastly annoying to be subjected by Uvarov to a further censorship; and equally annoying no doubt that the minister should have orchestrated the chorus of disapproval with which *Pugachev*

* Presumably Nadezhda Sollogub.

was received – 'Pushkin is being abused for his Pugachev,' Pogodin had noted in his diary soon after publication.[28] Nevertheless, Pushkin's reaction seems excessive. In his diary he attacks not only Uvarov, but also the latter's friend, Prince Mikhail Dondukov-Korsakov (brother of Nikolay Korsakov, who had been at the Lycée with Pushkin). Though Uvarov was married, with four children, he was known to be homosexual, and Dondukov-Korsakov, also married (he had been given imperial permission to adopt the name and title of his wife, Princess Dondukova), was commonly believed to be his lover. It was difficult otherwise to understand why Uvarov should have jobbed him into the position of curator of the St Petersburg Education District (and *ex officio* chairman of the St Petersburg Censorship Committee) – a post for which he possessed no obvious qualifications. As chairman he had informed Pushkin of Uvarov's decision to apply the regular censorship to his works. '[Uvarov's] minion Dondukov-Korsakov (a fool and a Sodomite) persecutes me with his censorship committee,' Pushkin fulminated in his diary. 'Apropos of Uvarov: he is a great scoundrel and charlatan. His depravity is well-known. He was so base as to run errands for Cancrin's children. They said of him that he began as a whore, was then a nurse, and became President of the Academy of Sciences much as Princess Dashkova became President of the Russian Academy. He stole crown firewood and even now still has outstanding debts (he has 11,000 souls), and used artisans employed by the state to carry out his own work etc. etc. Dashkov (the minister), who used to be his friend, meeting Zhukovsky arm in arm with Uvarov, took him to one side, saying: you should be ashamed to walk with such a man in public!'*[29]

---

* Uvarov had formerly worked under the Minister of Finance, Count Georg Cancrin: Pushkin could have had the story either from Turgenev, who in 1824 wrote to Vyazemsky, '[Uvarov] knows all Cancrin's wet-nurses and gives his children their pap' (*OA*, III, 33), or from Wiegel, who commented that Uvarov 'tried to ingratiate himself into Cancrin's favour, caressed his children and went into their nursery and inquired about their health so often that he was taken for some kind of doctor and the children showed him their tongues' (*Letopisi GLM*, 1 (1936), 535). But these, and the other rumours about Uvarov, were well-known in St Petersburg society. Princess Ekaterina Dashkova was appointed President of the Russian Academy by Catherine II in 1783, owing the position more to favouritism than merit. Prince Dmitry Dashkov, the Minister of Justice, had also been a member of *Arzamas*.

About this time Pushkin took a fling at Uvarov's father in one of the collection of mainly historical anecdotes he entitled – in English – 'Table-talk'.* An aide-de-camp to Catherine II and commander of the Life Guards Grenadiers, Semen Fedorovich Uvarov was, according to Wiegel, best known for his virtuosity on the bandura (a Ukrainian stringed instrument resembling a large mandolin), which he would play while simultaneously dancing the hopak: for this skill Potemkin dubbed him 'Senka the bandurist'. Pushkin's anecdote runs:

Dondukov-Korsakov

Suvorov observed fasts. Potemkin once said to him, laughing: 'I see, count, that you want to ride into heaven on the back of a sturgeon.' This joke, it goes without saying, was received rapturously by his highness's courtiers. A few days later one of Potemkin's most servile toad-eaters, called by him Senka the bandurist, had the idea of repeating to Suvorov himself: 'Is it true, your excellency, that you wish to ride into heaven on a sturgeon?' Suvorov turned to the humorist and said to him coldly: 'Know that Suvorov sometimes puts questions, but never answers any.'[30]

Pushkin's discontent with the situation and his anger with those he believed to be responsible for it continued to smoulder. 'I have had the misfortune to incur the enmity of the minister of education, as well as that of Prince Dondukov, né Korsakov. Both of them have already made me feel this in quite a disagreeable manner,' he wrote in the draft of a letter to Benckendorff.[31] Early that year the vice-president of the Academy of Sciences, A.K. Shtorkh, had fallen ill, and on 7 March Uvarov appointed Dondukov-Korsakov as his temporary replacement, an appointment which became permanent with Shtorkh's death on 31 October. To contemporaries Dondukov-Korsakov seemed to have even fewer qualifications for this post than for the others he held. 'It has been a black year for our academies,' Pushkin wrote to Dmitriev: 'no

---

* He published eleven (out of forty-nine) in the third issue of the *Contemporary*, though not this one.

sooner had Sokolov passed away in the Russian Academy than Dondukov-Korsakov appeared as vice-president in the Academy of Sciences.
Uvarov is a conjuror, and Dondukov-Korsakov his puppet. Someone
said that where one goes, there goes the other; one does somersaults on
the rope, the other beneath him on the floor.'*³² He expressed his
feelings with a scabrous epigram:

> In the Academy of Sciences
> Sits Prince Dunduk.†
> It's said that such an honour
> Is unbefitting to Dunduk;
> Why then does he sit?
> Because he is an arse-hole.³³

This juvenile piece of wit might have relieved Pushkin's feelings, but it
was hardly likely to improve the situation. Its composition was all the
more recklessly self-indulgent as he was hoping to bring out several
more works in the near future. The two volumes of his collected narrative
poems, which came out in August, and for which Smirdin paid him, it
is calculated, 12,000 roubles, had to be presented to the censorship
committee, but this did not present a problem, since all the works had
been published before.‡ He was anxious, however, to follow these with
the *Journey to Erzerum*, which he had successfully submitted to the
emperor through Benckendorff in April.§ But had this work now also
to be censored in the normal way? On 28 August he turned to the Chief
Directorate of the Censorship itself for a ruling. From Mikhailovskoe
at the beginning of October he wrote to Pletnev to enquire whether the
Journey had passed the censor, and what the Committee's reply had
been to his 'most humble petition'. 'Will the little donkey Nikitenko
and the bull Dunduk really kick and butt me to death? They won't
get rid of me so easily, though.'³⁴ He began drafting a complaint to

* P.I. Sokolov, the permanent secretary of the Russian Academy, and editor of the
St Petersburg Gazette, had died on 9 January 1835.
† Pushkin frequently refers to Dondukov-Korsakov as 'Dunduk', 'blockhead'.
‡ The first volume contained *Ruslan and Lyudmila, The Prisoner of the Caucasus* and *The
Fountain of Bakhchisaray*; the second *The Robber Brothers, The Gypsies, Count Nulin, Poltava,
The Little House in Kolomna* and *Angelo*.
§ He later gave up the idea of a separate edition, since he needed material for the *Contempor-
ary*, in the first number of which the *Journey* appeared.

Benckendorff. 'The Committee has not honoured my petition with an answer,' he wrote. 'I do not know in what way I could have deserved such neglect – but not a single Russian author has been more oppressed than I.'[35] Though the Censorship Directorate had considered Pushkin's letter at its meeting on 9 September, it was not until the end of the month that Uvarov replied. Manuscripts which had the emperor's permission for publication could be printed independently; all other works intended for publication had to be referred to the Censorship Committee. This letter, which Pushkin appears not to have received until his return to St Petersburg on 23 October, did in fact confirm his view of the situation. However, by now he had convinced himself that he was the victim of a persecution campaign: sullen and resentful, he longed to lash out at his enemies, regardless of the consequences to himself. And a heaven-sent opportunity to do just this now occurred.

While he had been in Mikhailovskoe, Count Dmitry Nikolaevich Sheremetev, perhaps the richest landowner in Russia, had fallen ill on his estates near Voronezh. The great-grandson of Field-Marshal B.P. Sheremetev, one of Peter the Great's generals, he had inherited, on coming into the family estate, over three and a half million roubles, 210,000 serfs and some 600,000 desyatins of land, which included the famous estates of Kuskovo and Ostankino outside Moscow. He had no immediate family, but Uvarov's wife, Ekaterina Alekseevna, was his cousin. 'A false rumour had begun to spread here about the death of the wealthy Sheremetev, who is in Voronezh,' Vyazemsky told Turgenev. 'In the Committee of Ministers someone said that he had scarlet fever. "And you, you've got expectation fever," said Litta in his stentorian tones, turning to Uvarov, who is one of Sheremetev's heirs.'*[36] On learning the news, Uvarov had hurried round to the Sheremetev palace on the Fontanka and had ordered that seals should be placed on all the property. Sheremetev, however, recovered. Inspired by this ludicrous episode, Pushkin composed in November the poem 'On Lucullus's Recovery', and giving it the misleading sub-title 'An imitation of the Latin', sent it off to the *Moscow Observer*. Both editor and censor were misled, and the poem appeared at the end of December.

---

* Count Giulio Litta, chairman of the Fourth Department (State Economy) of the Council of State.

After addressing in the first two stanzas a young – Sheremetev was thirty-one – nabob on his death-bed, surrounded by gloomy doctors and praying servants, Pushkin turns to his heir, who has already placed seals on the property, thinking

> 'Now I'll no longer
> Nurse magnates' children;
> I myself will be a magnate too;
> Since in the vaults there's enough to spare.
> Now honesty can be the best policy!
> I won't fiddle my wife out of money,
> And will forget how to steal
> The firewood of the crown!'

But the invalid recovers; his friends rejoice; his servants kiss each other; his bailiff forcibly ejects the heir, for whom the poet predicts ultimate discomfiture: the young man will marry and have a son.[37]

The *Moscow Observer* reached St Petersburg in the middle of January 1836, and caused a sensation. 'Pushkin has written a kind of pasquil on the minister of education, with whom he is very angry because the latter has subjected his works to the regular censorship,' Nikitenko recorded in his diary on 17 January. 'He once boasted that he would without fail get one of the local censors confined to the guard-house, especially me, whom he cannot forgive for "Angelo". It looks as though he will achieve this end in Moscow, for the piece has caused a great stir in the town. No one has the slightest difficulty in recognizing Uvarov in it.'[38] The minister certainly recognized himself, for the poem threw him into a paroxysm of rage. Nikolay Terpigorev, an official at the Ministry of Education, overheard him roaring that Pushkin's works should be allotted 'not one, but two, three, four censors'.[39] The outburst proved insufficiently cathartic, for he followed it with a complaint to the emperor about the poem, channelled through Benckendorff. On Nicholas's orders Benckendorff summoned Pushkin to his office and gave him a severe reprimand.

Pushkin's friends differed in their view of the poem. Turgenev was enraptured by it. 'My thanks to the translator from the *Latin* (a pity it's not from the *Greek*!*),' he wrote to Vyazemsky from Paris. 'The

* A reference to Uvarov's homosexuality, known as 'the Greek vice'.

biographical stanza will serve as an epigraph for the whole life of the apostate Arzamasite. Another would be forgotten, but Pushkin has branded him with immortal obloquy. – Eternal torture serves the thief right!'[40] Zhukovsky, however, deplored the work. Writing to Benckendorff after Pushkin's death, he refers to 'those unhappy verses to Lucullus, for which not you alone, but all his friends harshly upbraided him'.[41] Nikitenko summed up public opinion. 'The whole town is engaged with "Lucullus's Recovery",' he wrote on 20 January. 'Uvarov's enemies are reading the piece with delight, but the majority of the cultured public are dissatisfied with their poet. In fact, Pushkin has gained little with this poem in terms of public opinion, which, despite all his pride, he nevertheless much values.'[42]

Uvarov's thirst for revenge was still unabated. He now hit on a means both of embarrassing Pushkin, and of deflecting attention from himself. Among his and Pushkin's acquaintance was a middle-aged diplomat, Varfolomey Bogolyubov – 'a crafty, agile old fellow, with a repulsive, satanic physiognomy, who wore two stars and was known to be a creature of Uvarov's'.[43] Like the minister, he was homosexual.

Prompted by Uvarov, Bogolyubov began to put about the rumour that Prince Nikolay Repnin, who also stood to profit from Sheremetev's death (he and Uvarov had married sisters), had expressed himself in an exceedingly offensive manner about 'Lucullus's Recovery'. Furious, Pushkin penned a stiff note in the third person to Repnin. This would have been equivalent to a challenge, had he sent it, but he respected Repnin, twenty years his senior, a general of cavalry, who had been until recently governor-general of Little Russia.* The final version was more emollient. 'As a Gentleman and father of a family, I must watch over my honour and the name which I must leave to my children,' he wrote. 'I have not the honour of being personally known to Your Excellency. Not only have I never offended you, but for reasons known to me, I have up to now had for you true feelings of respect and gratitude. However, a Mr Bogolyubov has repeated in public remarks which are insulting to me, and as coming from you. I beg Your Excellency to be

---

* The brother of the Decembrist Sergey Volkonsky. The difference in surname between the brothers is explained by the fact that, Field-Marshal Prince N.V. Repnin having no male issue, Alexander I ordered the senior of his grandsons to adopt the name 'so that a noble family should not die out' (Veresaev (1937), II, 155).

good enough to let me know where I stand. No one knows better than I the distance which separates us: but you, who are not only a great lord, but also the representative of our ancient and genuine nobility to which I too belong, will, I hope, understand without difficulty the imperious necessity which has dictated this step to me.'[44] The letter is somewhat gnomic, since he cautiously omits any mention of the poem itself, lest by doing so he should insult Repnin again; at the same time he endeavours to establish a bond between them on the grounds of their ancestry – a bond which would exclude the parvenu Uvarov.

A few days later he received a reply from Repnin, who had had no difficulty in understanding Pushkin's veiled remarks:

> Flattering to me as certain expressions in your letter are, I must tell you frankly that it distressed me, since it showed that you, dear sir, did not scorn tales so inimical to my principles. I see Mr Bogolyubov only at the house of S.S. Uvarov and have no relations with him, and never in his presence said anything in relation to you, all the more after reading your epistle to Lucullus. I must tell you sincerely that your genial talent will bring benefit to the fatherland and fame to you when it hymns Russian faith and loyalty, not when it insults honourable people.[45]

Pushkin replied the next day, thanking Repnin for his letter. 'It is impossible for me not to admit that Your Excellency's opinion regarding compositions which are insulting to the honour of a private individual is completely just,' he wrote. 'It is difficult to pardon them even when they are written at a time of distress and blind vexation. As the amusement of an idle or depraved mind they would be unforgivable.'[46]

He was beginning to regret having written the poem; a regret that was aggravated by the actions of a French émigré, Alphonse Jobard. The latter had taught French to the girls at the Smolny Institute. He had then been appointed professor of Greek, Latin and French literature at the University of Kazan, but had been deprived of his post in 1824 after causing a series of scandals by accusing – probably with justice – the local education authorities of corruption and gross mismanagement. Since then he had deluged, first the curator of the Kazan Education District, and then the Minister of Education with petitions, making such a nuisance of himself that several – unsuccessful – attempts had been made to declare him insane. He seized with joy on 'Lucullus's Recovery', and, translating it into French, sent it to Uvarov together with a 'dedicatory epistle', in which he announced that, 'having firmly decided to acquaint Europe with this remarkable work, I intend to send this translation, together with all the commentaries which may be required for an understanding of the text, to Brussels to my brother, a lithographer, typographer, book-seller and editor of the newspaper *L'Industriel*'.[47] At the same time he circulated copies of the translation and letter in Moscow. One fell into the hands of Denis Davydov, who sent it on to Pushkin, writing: 'The translation is pretty bad, but has amusing passages, as for the letter, I laughed like an idiot when I read it. This Jobard is a malicious beast, who has adroitly pecked to death the Stork, brought down by the Falcon.'[48]

In March Pushkin received another copy from Jobard himself, together with a letter in which the Frenchman asked him to decide the fate of the work. In reply Pushkin congratulated him on his 'charming translation', which was 'as pretty as it was malicious'; however, he begged him not to publish it in Belgium; 'I am sorry,' he added, 'to have published a piece which I wrote in a moment of bad humour. Its publication incurred the displeasure of someone whose opinion is dear to me, and whom I cannot defy without ingratitude and stupidity.'*[49] Jobard agreed, but added that he had sent copies both to his brother in Belgium and to his father in France so that 'if I do not obtain the justice which I claim, dead or alive, I shall be avenged by the publication of this tissue of injustice, violence and infamy, of which I have been the victim for so many years'.[50]

It was true that in the autumn of 1835 Pushkin had reason to feel harassed and persecuted: beside the problems of censorship he had other, even weightier troubles on his mind. Yet, though in this 'time of distress and blind vexation' it was no doubt satisfying in the extreme to hold Uvarov up to scorn in 'On Lucullus's Recovery', in the circumstances it was an act of irresponsible folly to publish the poem. By doing so he succeeded, for the sake of a momentary triumph, in worsening relations with the emperor; in turning Uvarov into an open, implacable enemy – which was to have consequences for the censorship of his

---

* He is presumably referring to Nicholas I.

work, especially of the *Contemporary*; and, finally, in alienating a large number of his readers. In September 1836 Aleksandr Karamzin, in a long letter to his brother Andrey, then travelling in Europe, mentioned that Nikolay Mukhanov had 'the previous evening seen Pushkin, whom he found terribly low in spirits, repenting that he had written his vindictive pasquil, and sighing for the lost favour of his public'.[51] 'I am no longer popular,' he told the French writer Loeve-Veimars that summer.[52]

Pushkin's irritable annoyance over the censorship was partly due to the fear that a change might affect his income. His financial situation, never secure, was growing worse with every month, as he slid further and further into debt. In May 1834 he borrowed a further 4,000 roubles from Ivan Lisenkov, who kept a new and secondhand bookshop on Sadovaya Street in St Petersburg; in June 1836 8,000 roubles from Prince Nikolay Obolensky; in September 1836 10,000 from Vasily Yurev; and, between 1 April 1835 and his death, 15,960 roubles from Aleksey Shishkin, a retired colonel of engineers – according to Sobolevsky, 'the kindest and most honest of usurers'[53] – on the security of three necklaces of Oriental pearls with gold clasps, two Turkish shawls, one white, one black, a quantity of table silver, some of which belonged to Natalya's sister Aleksandra and some to Sobolevsky, a coffee pot and a Breguet watch. Nor did he scruple to touch his friends and relatives for loans, large and small. In January 1835 he borrowed 4,900 roubles from Nikolay Smirnov, Aleksandra Rosset's husband; while on his death he owed 2,500 roubles to his sister-in-law Aleksandra, 500 to the composer Mikhail Wielhorski and 3,000 to Ekaterina Karamzina, the historian's widow. Others were less accommodating. Towards the end of 1835 Natalya wrote to her mother asking her for an allowance of 200 roubles a month; Natalya Ivanovna refused, on the grounds that her finances were not prospering. Aleksandra, telling Dmitry of this, waxed indignant: 'It is really shameful that mother will do nothing for them, it is an unpardonable lack of concern, all the more as Tasha wrote to her recently and she did nothing but give advice, which doesn't cost a penny and doesn't make sense.'[54]

Earlier that year Pushkin had made several attempts to improve matters. There was nothing new about his schemes: all had been tried, with little or no success, in the past. At the beginning of April he resurrected the newspaper project of 1831. 'I should like to be the editor of a newspaper similar in everything to the *Northern Bee*, and as for purely literary articles (such as lengthy critiques, tales, novellas, narrative poems, etc.), which cannot be accommodated in a feuilleton, I would wish to publish them separately, a volume every three months, in the manner of the English Reviews.'[55] The idea of a review (he uses the English word) was a new one; as a collaborator he had enlisted Prince Odoevsky, who had earlier contributed both to the *Literary Gazette* and to several issues of *Northern Flowers*. Odoevsky had grandiose views; the title of the new periodical, he suggested, should be 'The Contemporary Chronicler of Politics, Sciences and Literature, containing a survey of the most noteworthy events in Russia and other European states, in all branches of political, scientific and aesthetic activity from the beginning of the third (the last) decade of the 19th century'. 'We must find an epigraph,' he added, 'I can't live without one.'[56]

On 16 April Pushkin called on Benckendorff to discuss the project; a few days later, at a second meeting, he was told that the emperor had refused to allow the newspaper. The decision came as a surprise: after all, in 1832 Nicholas had approved an almost identical scheme. But since then he had formed doubts as to Pushkin's loyalty, and had cooled towards him. He had not been amused by the poet's deplorably cavalier attitude towards his duties as gentleman of the chamber. In addition, there had been the incident of the intercepted letter, followed almost immediately by the bungled attempt at resignation.

Pushkin was not overly disappointed. Though he regretted the loss of an opportunity to put his finances on a secure basis, he did not feel himself cut out to be a Bulgarin. 'This metier is not mine and is repugnant to me in many respects,' he had written.[57] Instead he began, with Pletnev's assistance, to put together an almanac – 'Let us call it Arion or Orion; I love names which have no meaning' – which was to contain, among other material, the *Journey to Erzerum* and Gogol's short story 'The Carriage'.[58] However, nothing came of the project, and Pushkin soon reverted to the idea of the quarterly, writing to Benckendorff at the end of December: 'I would like during next year, 1836, to publish 4 volumes of purely literary (such as stories, poems etc.), historical, scientific articles, and also of critical analyses of Russian and foreign literature; similar to the English quarterly Reviews.'[59] The emperor gave his permission, and in April 1836 the first number of the *Contemporary* was published. Three further numbers followed that year; another number had been prepared by Pushkin before his death: this, together with three further issues, was brought out by Vyazemsky, Zhukovsky, Odoevsky, Pletnev and Kraevsky in 1837.

The review had originally been conceived as a supplement to the 'political and literary newspaper' whose profits would clear Pushkin's debts; by publishing one without the other he had, with that financial acumen and flair for business so characteristic of the Pushkins, turned a profit-making enterprise into one which would, almost infallibly, result in a loss. With extraordinary, baseless optimism – 'he hopes it will bring him not less than 60,000 [roubles]!' Olga wrote in January'[60] – he ordered 2,400 copies of the first issue (the very popular *Library for Reading* had a print-run of 5,000), and repeated the order for the second. For the third he halved the quantity, and reduced it to 900 for the fourth. An inventory of his possessions, taken after his death, records 109 unsold complete sets of the journal; an unrecorded number of the first and second issues was burnt by order of the trustees. The *Contemporary* had, therefore, some 790 subscribers.* The subscription for all four issues was 25 roubles, which would have produced an income of 19,750 roubles – from which must be deducted twenty per cent for those copies sold through book-sellers. Against this sum must also be set the cost of the paper – 2,935 roubles, of printing – approximately 3,860 roubles, of binding – 552 roubles, incidental expenses, and, above all, the fees paid to contributors, which, it has been calculated, could hardly have been less than 20,000 roubles. In other words, by the end of 1836 the enterprise must have pushed him some ten thousand roubles further into debt. In addition, of course, he had deprived himself of the income his works would have made if published elsewhere, since all now appeared in the *Contemporary*. Smirdin, he told Nashchokin in January, before the launch of the journal, had offered him 15,000 a year to give it up and to write for the *Library for Reading*. It would have been sensible to accept the offer: he would have been 25,000 roubles a year better off, without even taking into account the payments he would have received

---

* In September 1836 Aleksandr Karamzin, in a letter to his brother, writes: 'Pushkin has 700 subscribers. Not a lot'; according to A.F. Voeikov, he had 'fewer than a hundred and fifty subscribers outside St Petersburg' (*PVPK*, 119, 967).

for individual works. But he could not bring himself to do so. 'Senkovsky [the editor of *Library for Reading*] is such a beast, and Smirdin such a fool – that it's impossible to have anything to do with them.'[61]

His initial reaction on being refused permission to publish a newspaper had been to turn to the alternative means of improving his circumstances: by cutting expenses, rather than increasing income. 'I am thinking of leaving St Petersburg and going to the country, if only I will not bring displeasure on myself by this,' he told his brother-in-law on 2 May 1835.[62] The displeasure was, of course, that of Nicholas, which Pushkin had incurred the previous summer by his attempt at resignation. There were other, more practical problems: where, for example, was the family to live? Boldino was the back of beyond, there were no friendly neighbours there, and in any case the manor house, such as it was, was occupied by Penkovsky and his family. Mikhailovskoe was also impossible. 'Aleksandr is going to the country for three years, without knowing where,' Sergey Lvovich wrote to Olga. 'As I hope that we will be able, if God lets us live, to go to Mikhailovskoe next year, it is impossible for us to yield it to Aleksandr for all that time. To deprive ourselves of this last consolation does not at all enter into our calculations.'[63]

Although Natalya's pregnancy was very near its term, on 2 May Pushkin 'having an imperative necessity to be absent in Pskov province for 28 days',[64] applied for leave, and on the fifth left St Petersburg. 'As a piece of news I will tell you,' his mother wrote to Olga on 7 May, 'that the day before yesterday Aleksandr left for *Trigorskoe*, he should return in less than 10 days for Natalie's lying-in. You might perhaps think that it is a matter of business, – not at all: it is solely for the pleasure of travelling, – and in such bad weather! We were extremely astonished when he came to say good-bye the day before his departure. His wife is very saddened by this. One has to admit that your brothers are real oddities and will never give up their oddnesses.'[65] Praskovya Osipova was equally surprised. 'On 8 May Aleksandr Sergeich Pushkin unexpectedly arrived at Trigorskoe. He stayed until the twelfth and travelled back to St Petersburg,' she noted.[66] He rode over to Golubovo to see Zizi Vrevskaya and her husband on the ninth, spent three pleasant days at Trigorskoe – 'Lord, how wonderful it is here with you!' he told Praskovya's fifteen-year-old daughter Mariya. 'But there, in Petersburg,

what boredom often suffocates me!'[67] – and arrived home on the fifteenth: Natalya had given birth to a son a day earlier.

The motives for this sudden trip are inexplicable. Certainly no
'imperative necessity' summoned him to Trigorskoe: he had no business
to transact there. And surely he cannot have undertaken the journey

'solely for the pleasure of travelling', as
his mother maintained. Annette Vulf's
explanation, in a letter to her sister Zizi,
seems no closer to the mark. 'You were
astonished by Pushkin's arrival and could
not conceive the aim of his journey,' she
wrote: 'But I think that it was simply
to make a trip to see you and Mother,
Trigorskoe, Golubovo and Mikhailovskoe, for I too can see no other plausible

Praskovya Osipova

reason. It cannot be possible that he should have undertaken a journey
in such weather in order to speak to Mother about the two thousand
roubles he owes her.'[68] He could have wanted to discuss buying an estate
with Praskovya: she had been very helpful in 1831 when he had for
a moment contemplated the purchase of little Savkino, next door to
Trigorskoe. But the discussion could have been carried out by correspondence, and, if it had taken place, surely her daughters, Annette and Zizi,
would have known. His behaviour, in fact, seems bizarre, and can perhaps only be rationalized as the result of marital discord, highly emotional in its nature, and possibly connected with, or exacerbated by, the
presence of the Goncharov sisters. It is clear that he wanted above all
to get away from St Petersburg and from the final stages of Natalya's
pregnancy. He behaved in exactly the same manner the following May,
leaving St Petersburg three weeks before Natalya's lying-in, and arriving
from Moscow a few hours after she had given birth to a daughter. But
the similarity between the two episodes is coincidental, for this time he
had a genuine excuse for his absence – he needed to drum up support
for the *Contemporary* in Moscow – while the extremely affectionate
letters he wrote to Natalya during those weeks argue strongly against
any rift in their relationship on this occasion.

'On Tuesday, at 7 or 8 in the evening Natalie was delivered of a son,
whom they have called Grigory it is not quite clear to me why,' Sergey

Lvovich told Olga, thinking perhaps that his name should have been given to his second grandson. 'Natalie gave birth a few hours before Aleksandr's arrival,' his wife added, 'she was already expecting him, however no one knew how to tell her about it, and, truly, the pleasure of seeing him so excited her that she was ill for the whole of the day.'[69] Natalya's violent reaction suggests the emotional resolution of a quarrel. Pushkin considered it worthy of mention in a letter to his mother-in-law. 'I am happy to congratulate you on your grandson Grigory, and to commend him to your favour,' he wrote. 'Natalya Nikolaevna gave birth to him safely, but was in pain for longer than usual – and now her condition is not wholly good – although, thank God, there is no danger at all. She gave birth in my absence, I had been obliged to travel to the Pskov estate on business, and returned the day after her delivery. My arrival alarmed her, and she suffered all day yesterday; today she is better.'

He went on to a less pleasant subject. 'Yesterday we received from you the box with the hat together with a note which I have not shown my wife so as not to distress her in her condition,' he wrote. 'It appears that she did not carry out your commission satisfactorily, and from the note she might conclude that you were angry with her.'[70] Natalya's sister Aleksandra glosses this remark in a letter to their brother. 'Imagine what a trick mother played on us. Do you remember that unfortunate hat which we ordered for her? Well, she found it too bright and returned it to us with a note full of rage addressed to Tasha. But we lost nothing, because Auntie bought it from us; so mother doesn't suspect that she did us another favour. But what wilfulness.'[71]

The news of another grandson improved Natalya Ivanovna's temper. She sent a sum of money as a present for his christening on 22 May. Thanking her, Pushkin wrote that the gift 'arrived very opportunely'. They needed a new cook, he went on: those in St Petersburg were all 'spoilt and unbelievably expensive'. Did she have one she could spare in Yaropolets? He would have to be 'good, honest, and of undebauched behaviour'. He concluded with news of her eldest grandchild, now three, and already displaying some of the traits which were to cause Tolstoy to base Anna Karenina partly upon her: 'Masha is asking to go to a ball, and says that she has already learnt to dance from the dogs. You see how quickly they grow up with us; before you know it she will be engaged.'[72]

Natalya's convalescence was more prolonged than on previous occasions, but this did not prevent her from planning her social life. On 8 June Nadezhda Osipovna told Olga that she 'was still weak; she only left her room recently and cannot think of reading or working, she has large schemes as far as amusement is concerned, she is getting ready for the Peterhof festival which will be on the first of July'.[73] Pushkin had rented the villa on the Black River again, and they moved there in the middle of the month. By 1 July, the empress's birthday, Natalya was fully recovered. The festival was splendid. 'The fireworks were magnificent, no, I am wrong, they were illuminations, there were no fireworks,' wrote Nadezhda Osipovna. 'They say that Natalie was miraculously beautiful, and, truly, after the last childbirth she has become more beautiful than ever.'[74]

Meanwhile Pushkin had been meditating on his future. He was anxious, as he had told Pavlishchev, not to incur Nicholas's displeasure, and certainly wished to avoid a repetition of the previous year's episode, when he had had to withdraw his resignation with grovelling apologies, for fear of losing access to the archives, indispensable for his work on Peter the Great. Yet he was desperately in need of money, and desperately in need of leisure in which to write. Only a large loan, or permission to live for three or four years in the country – preferably both – could, he thought, stave off complete financial disaster. He felt, too, that the tsar, having forbidden him to redeem his finances by publishing a newspaper, was morally obliged to assist him in some other way. He drafted a letter to Benckendorff:

> My project not having the approval of His Majesty, I confess that I feel myself relieved of a great burden. But also I see myself obliged to have recourse to the favour of the Emperor who is now my sole hope [. . .] To pay all my debts and be able to live, to arrange my family's affairs, and be at last free to abandon myself without worries to my historical works and my occupations, it would suffice for me to find a means of borrowing 100,000.

The emperor had been good enough to give him a salary of 5,000 roubles. 'This sum represents the interest on a capital of 125,000. If, instead of my salary, His Majesty would do me the favour of giving me the capital as a *loan* for ten years and without interest – I would be perfectly happy and peaceful.'[75]

On reflection he realized that the sum was ludicrously large: even if he were morally entitled to it, he had absolutely no hope of obtaining it. He turned to the alternative solution. On 1 June he again wrote to Benckendorff. Life in St Petersburg was 'horribly expensive'.

> I see myself in the necessity of cutting short expenditures which only lead me into running up debts and which prepare for me a future of inquietude and embarrassment, if not of destitution and despair. Three or four years of retirement to the country would give me the possibility of returning to Petersburg to resume those occupations which I still owe to the favour of His Majesty.

Mindful of the effect his letter of the previous year had had upon Nicholas, he added:

> I would be in despair if His Majesty could suppose in my desire to move away from Petersburg any motive than that of absolute necessity. The least sign of displeasure or of suspicion would suffice to retain me in the position I occupy, since, in a word, I would rather be embarrassed in my affairs than lost in the opinion of him who has been my benefactor, not as Sovereign, not from duty and from justice, but from a free sentiment of noble and generous benevolence.[76]

His idea was to retire to Boldino with his family for several years. Though he talked much of the scheme, his friends and family treated it with some scepticism. '[Aleksandr] says that it is impossible for him to live here and that he must go away to the country for several years, – but I do not believe that Natalie would agree to this,' Annette Vulf commented.[77] And at the beginning of June his mother had remarked: '[Natalie] wants to take a villa on the *Black River*, but does not want, as her husband wishes, to travel further afield, – in a word, what woman wants, God wants.'[78] In fact, it all depended on the emperor's decision. On the first page of Pushkin's letter he wrote in pencil: 'There are no obstacles to him going where he wants, but I do not know how he proposes to reconcile this with his service. He should be asked whether he wants to resign, as otherwise there is no possibility of granting him leave for this length of time.'[79] Benckendorff communicated the remark to Pushkin, who replied: 'I abandon my fate completely to the Tsar's will, and desire only that His Majesty's decision be not a sign of disfavour to me and that entry to the archives, when circumstances allow me to remain in Petersburg, be not forbidden to me.'[80] After seeing Nicholas, Benckendorff minuted: 'If he needs money, His Majesty is willing to assist him, he should tell me; if he needs to be at home, he can take four months' leave.'[81] On 22 July Pushkin called on him to discuss these proposals, but, not finding him in, entrusted his views to a letter. In five years in St Petersburg he had, he wrote, contracted 60,000 roubles of debt. He had been obliged to take his family's finances in hand, which had embarrassed him so much that he had had to renounce an inheritance (he is referring to his uncle's portion of Boldino, but the account bears little semblance to reality). His only recourse was to take out a large loan – which was impossible – or to retire to the country. 'Gratitude is for me not a painful sentiment,' he concluded; 'and, certainly, my devotion to the Emperor's person is not affected by any reservations of shame or remorse; but I cannot conceal from myself that I have absolutely no right to His Majesty's benefactions, and that it is impossible for me to ask for anything.'[82] On the letter Benckendorff made another minute: 'The emperor offers him 10 thousand roubles and 6 months' leave at the end of which he will see whether he should resign or not.'[83] This was not ungenerous, since the money was a gift, rather than a loan, but it would not go far in clearing Pushkin's debts. On 26 July, therefore, he wrote again to Benckendorff:

It pains me when I receive an unexpected favour to demand two others, but I have resolved to have recourse in complete frankness to him who has deigned to be my Providence. Of my 60,000 in debts, half are debts of honour. To pay them I see myself obliged to contract usurious debts, which will double my embarrassment, or even put me in the necessity of having again recourse to the generosity of the Emperor.

I therefore beg His Majesty to do me a full and complete favour: first, in giving me the possibility of paying off these 30,000 roubles; and, second, in deigning to allow me to consider

Natalya Nikolaevna Pushkina, Pushkin's wife, by A.P. Bryullov, 1831-2

Aleksandra Smirnova-Rosset
by N.M. Alekseev, 1844

V.A. Zhukovsky by
E.R. Reitern, 1832

The St Petersburg flood of 1824 by an unknown artist

Falconet's Bronze Horseman by M.F. Damame-Demartrais, 1799

LEFT Ekaterina Goncharova, Pushkin's sister-in-law and Georges d'Anthès's wife, by J.B. Sabatier, 1838

BELOW Aleksandra Goncharova, Pushkin's sister-in-law, by an unknown artist, 1830s

Pushkin by Thomas Wright, 1837

ABOVE Baron Heeckeren
by Krichuber-Höfelich,
1843

RIGHT Baron Georges
d'Anthès by Thomas
Wright, 1834-7

RIGHT Idaliya Poletika
by P.F. Sokolov, 1828

BELOW Count V.A.
Sollogub by an
unknown artist, 1830-5

Pushkin's death mask, taken on 29 January 1837

that sum a loan, and, in consequence, causing the payment of
my salary to be suspended until my debt be liquidated.[84]

In claiming that half the money he owed consisted of debts of honour
– a statement of dubious veracity – Pushkin no doubt hoped that
Nicholas would consider the settlement of gentlemanly obligations more
urgent than the payment of a book-seller's or a dressmaker's bill. He
may have been right, for on 29 July Benckendorff minuted: 'The
Emperor accords him 30 thousand roubles, suspending, as he requests,
his salary.'[85] On 1 August he informed the Foreign Office that Pushkin
had been given four months' leave, and on the same day advised Count
Cancrin at the Finance Ministry that the emperor had approved an
interest-free loan of 30,000 roubles. Pushkin did not leave for the
country until 7 September; ten days earlier Olga, who, together with
her ten-month-old son Lev was now living with the older Pushkins in
Pavlovsk, had written to her husband in Warsaw: 'Yesterday Aleksandr
came to see me with his wife. They are no longer going to the Nizhny
estate, as Monsieur proposed, because Madame will not hear speak of
it, and he will content himself by spending some *days* at Trigorskoe,
while she will not budge from Petersburg.'[86]

Pushkin received the emperor's loan
from the Finance Ministry just before
leaving St Petersburg. But he was taken
aback to find that it consisted only of
18,231 roubles 67 copecks instead of the
30,000 he had expected. The eagle-eyed
accountants at the ministry had noticed
that he had not made the first repayment
– ten thousand roubles – of the loan he
had been given for the publication of
Pugachev. They had therefore deducted
this amount, together with interest of
268.33. In addition, the new loan was sub-

Cancrin

ject to a five per cent tax for the benefit of invalid servicemen. Much
annoyed, on 6 September he wrote to Cancrin, begging for the balance,
and obligating himself to pay interest on the first loan until he could
redeem it completely. From Mikhailovskoe, where he had arrived on

10 September, he wrote to Natalya, 'How is our expedition? have you seen Countess Cancrin and what is the answer?'[87] He was hoping that she could persuade the countess to plead his cause with her husband, the minister. Whether as a result of this démarche or not, on 10 October Cancrin informed Benckendorff that, following Pushkin's petition, he had laid the matter before the emperor who had agreed that the arrears of the earlier loan and the interest on it should not be subtracted from the 30,000; however, Pushkin could not be exempted from the five per cent invalid tax.

Pushkin arrived in Mikhailovskoe on 10 September; on the thirteenth he rode over to Golubovo to see the Vrevskys. He played chess with the baron, giving him a knight, for Vrevsky was not a strong player; borrowed some volumes of Scott: the French translation by Defauconpret, published in Paris in the 1820s – 'I am reading Walter Scott's novels, over which I am in rapture,'[88] – and learnt from Zizi that her stepsister, Aleksandra Bekleshova, had recently come over from Pskov to pay them a visit, and was expected again in the near future. At Mikhailovskoe during his exile Aleksandra – Sashenka – had had an adolescent infatuation with him, which he had not scrupled to exploit. He hurried back to Trigorskoe and, sitting across from Masha Osipova, Sashenka's half-sister, to whom she bore a striking resemblance, sent her a letter. 'My angel, how sorry I am to have missed you, and how happy Evpraksiya Nikolaevna made me when she said that you were thinking of coming to our district again! For God's sake, come; at least for the twenty-third.* I have for you three baskets of confessions, explanations and odds and ends. It would be possible, at leisure, to fall in love as well.'[89] On the nineteenth he went to Golubovo again, and stayed the night, but Sashenka was not there, nor did she come to Trigorskoe for Praskovya Aleksandrovna's birthday. At the beginning of October Zizi wrote to her brother Aleksey with sardonic cynicism: 'On his arrival here the poet was very jolly, guffawing and jumping about as he used to do, but now seems to have fallen again into melancholy. He was impatiently expecting Sashenka, apparently hoping that the ardour

---

* The birthday of Sashenka's stepmother, Praskovya Osipova.

of her feelings and the absence of her husband would reinvigorate his ageing physical and moral forces.'[90]

Largely responsible for the melancholy was his financial situation, which was still preying on his mind, and for which the emperor's loan had been only a temporary alleviation. Brooding over the recent correspondence with Bencken-dorff, and the failure of *Pugachev*, he wrote to Natalya: 'You cannot imagine how vividly the imagination works when we sit alone in four walls, or walk through the woods, when no one prevents us from thinking, thinking until our

Aleksandra Bekleshova

head spins. And what do I think of? This is what: what are we going to live on. My father won't leave me the estate; he has already squandered half of it; your estate is a hair's breadth away from ruin. The tsar won't allow me to register as a squire or a journalist. God knows I can't write books for money. We haven't a penny of sure income, but sure expenditure of 30,000. Everything depends on me, and on auntie. But neither I nor auntie is immortal. God knows what will become of this. Meanwhile, it makes one sad.'[91] A week later he was still brooding over the same topic. 'The sovereign promised me a *Gazette*, but then forbade it; he forces me to live in Petersburg, but does not give me the means to live by my labours. I am wasting my time and my spiritual strength, throwing my hard-earned money out of the window, and see nothing in the future. My father is squandering his estate, with as little pleasure as calculation; your folks are losing theirs because of the stupidity and carelessness of the late Afanasy Nikolaevich. What will come of it? God knows.'[92]

He was worried, too, about Natalya. 'Yesterday I saw the moon on my left side, and began to be very disturbed about you.' To see the moon in this way presaged misfortune:

> Suddenly glimpsing
> The young, two-horned moon's face
> In the sky on her left side,
> She [Tatyana] shuddered and paled.
> *Eugene Onegin* (V, v–vi)

He had received no letters from her: they were held up, he discovered, because they were misaddressed. 'How deliciously stupid your address is! To Pskov province to the village Mikhailovskoe. Oh, my dear! But to what district you don't say. And I expect there's more than one Mikhailovskoe; and if there's only one, then who knows where it is. What a scatter-brain!'[93] And when letters did arrive, they did not make very joyful reading. 'My darling, yesterday I received two letters from you; they distressed me greatly. What is Katerina Ivanovna [Zagryazhskaya] ill with? You write *fearfully ill*. Therefore there is danger?' There had been a fire in the apartment, 'probably caused,' he wrote, 'by the negligence of your ladies-in-waiting, who are having a good time in my absence! Thank God it confined itself to the curtains.'[94] Natalya's ladies-in-waiting are her maids, of which there were four. Though servants' wages were derisory, Pushkin's finances cannot have been helped by his fondness – in this he took after his father – for surrounding himself with a large domestic staff. Besides the maids, the family had two nannies, a wet-nurse, a cook and his assistant, a butler, a valet, and several other men servants.

If Natalya was not giving him bad news, she was scolding him. He endeavoured, with affectionate mockery, to laugh her out of her bad humour. 'My dear wifekin,' he wrote,

we have here a filly which goes both in harness or under the saddle. Excellent in every way, but should something on the road frighten her, she will take the bit between her teeth, and will carry you over hill and dale for ten versts – and you have no hope of stopping her until she tires herself out.

I have received, my angel of meekness and beauty! your letter, in which you deign, taking the bit between your teeth, to kick out with your sweet and elegant little hoofs, shod by Madame Katherine.* I hope that you have now tired yourself out and calmed down. I expect decent letters from you, in which I can hear you and your voice – and not abuse, which I in no way deserve, since I am behaving like a shy young maid.[95]

* Proprietress of a fashionable dress shop.

But he was seldom in a jesting mood: his anxieties were drying up inspiration. 'I am continually worried and am writing nothing, though time is passing,' he told Natalya on 21 September; and, four days later: 'Imagine, up to now I haven't written a line; and all because I am not tranquil.' 'I spend my time very monotonously,' he added on the twenty-ninth. 'In the mornings I get nothing done, but just beat the wind. In the evenings I ride to Trigorskoe, burrow in old books and munch nuts. And I am not thinking of writing either poetry or prose.' Only on 2 October was he able to issue a more favourable report: 'Since yesterday I have begun to write (touch wood!).'[96] 'We have been to Svyatye Gory,' Vrevsky wrote to Vulf. 'While there I paid a visit to the Poet, who has been settled at Mikhailovskoe for three weeks, and has already been to see us several times at Golubovo. I found him at one o'clock in the afternoon still in his dressing-gown and busy writing I know not what – perhaps his history of Peter the Great, for around him were huge bundles of documents.'[97] But ten days later Pushkin was telling Pletnev dispiritedly, 'I would be glad to come to you in November, all the more as I have never had in all my life such a fruitless autumn. I am writing, but am making a hash of it. For inspiration one must have spiritual tranquillity, and I am not tranquil at all.'[98]

At times he was acutely depressed. His anxieties and frustrations were compounded by a more general melancholy brought on by contemplating the passage of time. 'In Mikhailovskoe I found everything as of old,' he wrote to Natalya, 'except that my nurse is no longer there, and that by the familiar old pines there has grown up, during my absence, a young pine family, the sight of which I find annoying, just as sometimes I find annoying the sight of young Chevalier guardsmen at balls where I no longer dance. But there's nothing to be done; everything around me tells me that I am growing old, and sometimes even in a pure Russian tongue. For example, yesterday I met with a peasant woman I know, to whom I couldn't help saying that she had changed. To which she replied: and you too, my protector, have grown old and ugly.'[99] The following day he composed '... Again I have visited...', one of the few poems produced during this stay at Mikhailovskoe. It concludes with an address to the annoying 'young pine family':

Greetings, young
And unfamiliar generation! not I
Will see your powerful later growth,
When you will outgrow my acquaintances
And conceal their aged heads
From the passer's eye. But may my grandson
Hear your welcome rustle, when,
Returning from a gathering of friends,
Full of happy and pleasing thoughts,
He passes by you in the night's darkness,
And remembers me.[100]

The gloomy vexation of the letter has been transmuted in the poem into the serene and mature acceptance of inevitability: of the passage of time and the succession of generations.

He had taken four months' leave, from 27 August to 23 December, but cut his stay short, arriving back in St Petersburg on 23 October. Frustration and lack of inspiration would probably have caused him to leave early – 'Aleksandr [. . .] was bored to death at Trigorskoe,' Olga told her husband[101] – but in the event he was summoned back by the news that his mother was seriously ill: 'I found my poor mother at death's door.'[102] She had come from Pavlovsk to find a lodging in St Petersburg for the winter, and had collapsed when calling on an old family friend, Varvara Knyazhnina. Given up as a hopeless case by two doctors, Rauch and Spassky, she had been nursed at the Knyazhnins for ten days, and had shown some improvement – attributable, Olga thought, to Dr Markelov's pills, which she had recommended: 'Markelov's pills have resuscitated her!' she wrote triumphantly in November.[103] Nadezhda was so much better, indeed, that she could be moved to the new apartment which she and Sergey Lvovich were to share with Olga and her baby Lolo. This was a small and uncomfortable – but cheap – lodging on the corner of Shestilavochnaya Street (now Mayakovsky Street) and Grafsky Lane.

It was a doubly unpleasant homecoming for Pushkin. 'In this sad situation I also have the affliction of seeing my poor Natalie the target of society's hatred,' he told Praskovya Osipova. 'It is said everywhere that it is dreadful that she should be so elegant, when her father and mother-in-law have nothing to eat, and when her mother-in-law is dying in the house of strangers. You know how things really are. Strictly speaking, one cannot say that a man who has 1,200 peasants is poverty-stricken. It is my father who has something, and I who have nothing. In any case, Natalie has nothing to do with this; it is I who should be responsible. If my mother had decided to stay with us, Natalie, as a matter of course, would have taken her in. But a cold house, full of brats and crowded with company, is scarcely suitable for a sick person. My mother is better off in her own home. I found that she had already moved; my father is in a very pitiable state. As for me, I am worried to death and bewildered.'[104]

Nadezhda Osipovna had first fallen ill over a year earlier. The previous October she had written to Olga from Mikhailovskoe: 'Papa has been suffering from spasms for several weeks, I am telling you about them, because he is already better – otherwise we would not be preparing to leave. But he suffered greatly and, unfortunately, I had a rash and was so weak that I could hardly move and could hardly give him the help he needed.' Though Sergey Lvovich's ailment was far less serious than that of his wife, he is far more detailed – more, perhaps, than Olga might have desired – in his description of it. 'Not to mince matters,' he wrote, 'for many days I could evacuate only by means of an enema and was very afraid I might grow used to this, like those XVIIIth century ladies who performed this degrading operation on themselves every morning, in order to have a fresh complexion.'[105] Nadezhda Osipovna had still not recovered when they set off for St Petersburg. The journey brought on a fever: for three weeks she was too ill to move into the lodging they had taken, but had to remain at Demouth's Hotel, where they had put up on arrival. Zizi Vrevskaya called on them in their apartment at the end of January, writing to her husband, 'Yesterday I gave Madame Pushkin a mantelet which gave her much pleasure. It is true that it was a little expensive – 60 roubles, but what could I do? She had been wearing a little jacket all the time and then I wanted to give her pleasure with something. Her health is very bad: the doctor is asking for a consultation and they have no money to pay the specialists and so he [Sergey Lvovich] keeps putting it off.'[106] From Warsaw Olga anxiously followed the progress of her mother's illness – 'She has neither spasms nor pain, but is yellow, though slightly less so than before, and weak'[107] – a succession of partial recoveries, inevitably followed by relapses. She recommended valerian tea and tar-water. Nadezhda Osipovna riposted with an infallible specific against teething pains, from which Lolo was suffering. Olga should 'rub his gums once or twice with blood from a cock's comb, but it must be a black cock'. 'I advised Natalie to do this,' she continued, 'and her children's teeth have come through in the most successful manner in the world.'[108] Pushkin was pessimistic about the outcome. On 2 May he wrote to Lev: 'Our mother was dying; now she is better, but not completely. I do not think she can live long.' And on the same day he told Pavlishchev: 'My mother is better, but she is by no means as well as she thinks; the doctors do not hope for a complete recovery.'[109] In July 1835 the elder Pushkins moved to Pavlovsk for the summer – Nadezhda Osipovna's illness made the journey to Mikhailovskoe unthinkable – and at the end of August Olga arrived from Warsaw. 'I am at last with my family, caressed and pampered together with my child, as you can imagine,' she wrote to her husband. 'I live in the house itself, have two little rooms, it is all I need, and I would be quite tranquil, were it not for the ill health of my mother, whom I find changed beyond all that I could imagine; she says she is well, but her feeble state much alarms me.'[110] Sergey Lvovich had at last managed to scrape together enough to pay the fees of a consultation, which had established the nature of the illness. 'The whole trouble, according to them [the doctors], arose from an affected liver,' Nadezhda Osipovna wrote. 'The griefs and worries which I have long experienced, and which have reduced me to this state, were the moral cause.'*[111]

Many – perhaps most – of these griefs and worries were contributed by her adored and spoilt younger son, Lev. In October one of his letters extremely distressed his parents. 'It is thanks to this letter from Léon that Mother had this relapse,' Olga remarked bitterly. 'He pretends that he is absolutely destitute, and that in order to consign this letter to the post he had to have recourse to a humiliating step, etc. He's lost count of the 20,000 roubles paid on his behalf, and besides that my parents send him what they can; but far from being destitute, he lives at Tiflis

* The most likely diagnosis is cancer of the liver.

like someone with ten thousand to spend. M. Rosseti* who has just arrived from there told my sister-in-law this. And my poor Mother nearly died! As soon as she read this letter she became completely yellow and had an attack of fever which obliged her to take to her bed and that very day she began to bring up the little that she managed to swallow.'[112] Lev's view of matters was rather different. 'He [Pushkin] is just like my father. They look upon their payment of my debts as a sum of money they have given to me. I thank him for paying them, but I'm nevertheless dying of hunger.'[113] Henceforth Pushkin, on Olga's advice, opened Lev's letters to his parents, only passing on those which were unlikely to distress Nadezhda Osipovna.

Her condition gradually worsened over the next few months; on 11 March 1836 Olga wrote to her husband: 'Mother is very ill; she has perhaps only a few days to live. When you receive this letter, she will without doubt no longer exist; the doctor has told me that everything may end this week [. . .] My father's despair torments me beyond all I can say: he cannot control himself, he sobs in her presence, – this frightens her, torments her. I have tried to tell him, – he shouted at me, he forgot that I, I was losing a mother. In truth I do not know what to do. Alexandre only makes brief appearances, like the others; I am quite alone with her.'[114]

Nadezhda Osipovna died at eight in the morning on 29 March, Easter Sunday. The funeral service took place in the Cathedral of the Transfiguration on Preobrazhenskaya Square; in the cathedral register the cause of death was given as consumption. On 8 April Pushkin left St Petersburg and accompanied his mother's body to the Svyatogorsky monastery near Mikhailovskoe. Here, on 13 April, she was buried in the Cathedral of the Assumption, near the graves of her parents, Osip and Mariya Gannibal. While at the monastery Pushkin reserved a plot for himself next to his mother's grave, paying the necessary fee. He spent the evening with his friends at Trigorskoe. From Mikhailovskoe the following morning he wrote to Pogodin about the *Contemporary*; then drove to Golubovo, whence he sent a cheerful letter to Yazykov: finding here Aleksey Vulf, that 'student and hussar in retirement, moustached

* Klementy Rosset, one of Aleksandra's four brothers, who had been attached to the Independent Caucasian Corps from 1833 to 1835.

agronomist, Lovelace of Tver', had reminded him of the time ten years before, in June 1826, when the three of them had been together at Trigorskoe.[115] Late that evening he and Vrevsky set off for St Petersburg, where they arrived on the sixteenth.

Sergey Lvovich was not present at the funeral: perhaps he was too prostrate with grief to travel. 'You cannot believe how pitiful Sergey Lvovich is, so that one cannot bear to look at him,' Annette Vulf wrote to Zizi. 'He is now a body without a soul.'[116] At the end of the month Penkovsky wrote to Pushkin: 'Yesterday I received a letter from Sergey Lvovich from which I understood that he was in a terrible state after your late mother and my benefactress Nadezhda Osipovna, in which he writes – *I do not know where to lay my head*. On that I ventured to suggest to Sergey Lvovich that he should leave St Petersburg and move to Boldino, that there he could find various kinds of pleasure in agriculture and could live tranquilly, wanting for nothing.'[117] Sergey Lvovich did spend a short time at Boldino in the summer – it was only the second time he had ever visited the estate – before going to stay with his sister and brother-in-law, the Sontsovs, at Korovino, their estate in Ryazan province. In the autumn he moved to Moscow.

Immediately after Nadezhda Osipovna's death the question of the disposal of her estate at Mikhailovskoe arose. As is often the case with inheritance matters involving several family members, the process degenerated into a long, unpleasant succession of wrangles. Superficially matters were simple, as the division of the estate was laid down by law: Olga was to receive 1/14th; Sergey Lvovich 1/7th (which, in fact, he ceded to Olga); and Lev and Pushkin were to share the remainder – receiving, therefore, 11/28ths each. However, the beneficiaries could only receive their respective shares if either the estate were to be sold, or one of them were to buy the others out, becoming its sole owner.

Olga's husband had arrived from Warsaw a few hours after his mother-in-law's death. Since the road to Warsaw passed not far from Mikhailovskoe, he suggested that he and Olga, on their way back to Poland, should stay for a month or so on the estate to look into its management and attempt a valuation. He wrote to his superior, Field-Marshal Paskevich, to request leave; and, at the same time, reflecting that, while acting on Olga's behalf, he might require Lev's support, sent a letter to Tiflis asking for a power of attorney. Lev had this document drawn up and registered on 5 May in the Tiflis district court: 'I most humbly beg you, Dear Sir, [. . .] to take the estate under your management and receive the income collected from it: and if you find it necessary or advantageous, you may sell, mortgage, or, if you wish, give it away,' it read in part.[118] The Pavlishchevs arrived at Mikhailovskoe in mid-June. Olga was far from well; the fact that her symptoms seemed to be replicating those of her mother was extremely worrying: she had a terrible cough, perpetual fever, bilious attacks, and a yellow complexion. But she was cured by a local witch-doctor, who whispered over glasses of wine, which she then drank, and who ordered her to use the bath-house.

Pushkin had now definitely decided to keep Mikhailovskoe for himself, buying out his brother and sister. On 3 June he wrote to Lev:

Here is a brief calculation of our proposed division:
80 souls and 700 desyatins of land in Pskov province are worth
(at 500 roubles a soul instead of the usual value of 400)   40,000 r.

Of this is excluded a 7th share for our father	5,714
And a 14th share for our sister	2,857
Total	8,571

Our father has refused his share and given it
    to our sister.

For our share there remains to divide equally	31,429 r.
Your share comes to	15,715

Pushkin was not only generously rounding-up Lev's share to the nearest rouble, but also – and far more generously – adding 8,000 roubles to the value of the estate by setting a higher price than normal on each serf. He concluded by advising his brother to buy up any outstanding promissory notes before his creditors got wind of his inheritance, and suggesting that he might wish to receive his share in three yearly instalments.[119] Lev replied in his usual carefree manner at the beginning of July. 'I don't know whether Mikhailovskoe should be mortgaged or sold, and I don't care a hang about it; as long as there is money, and you promise me that. What could be better?' He had given no promissory notes, and had, in any case, nothing to buy them up with. His debts – chiefly for lodging and food – might amount to 2,000 roubles. He enclosed a power of attorney, so that Pushkin could proceed with the transfer of the estate.[120]

A few weeks after writing to Lev, Pushkin sent a similar letter to Pavlishchev. This crossed with a lengthy missive in which Pavlishchev gave the results of an exhaustive audit which he had carried out on the bailiff's accounts. From this, he wrote, 'it can be seen that last year the bailiff gave your father 630 roubles, set 720 roubles against expenses, and stole 3,500 roubles. This is terrible thievery: and what is its cause? it comes from, firstly, that the bailiff is a thief; and, secondly, that he, receiving according to your father's direction 300 roubles in salary and about 260 roubles in various provisions, cannot feed with this himself, his wife, five children and two women (who are in service with him, from the village).' In addition the bailiff – Ringel, a German – was an extremely bad manager, who had let the estate go to rack and ruin. He had summoned the man, sacked him, and had taken over the management of the estate.[121]

Pushkin had no sooner thanked his brother-in-law for his efforts, than he received another, equally long letter, provoked by his proposals for the division of the estate, which, Pavlishchev felt, were demonstrably unfair to the other beneficiaries – Olga and Lev. 'Your valuation at 500 r. a soul has, if you will allow me to say so, no basis.' This was followed by a short lesson in basic economics: 'The value of every estate is determined by the income it produces.' Pushkin was wrong in saying that the estate consisted of 700 desyatins; it consisted of 1,965, and should produce an income of 3,600 roubles. This would give it a capital value of 80,000 roubles; each of the 80 serfs would then be worth, not 500, but 1,000 roubles. Allowing for the depredations of future bailiffs, theft, and bad harvests would bring the sum down to 70,000. 'This is the closest and lowest valuation,' he wrote, adding sententiously, 'That is how valuations are done, Aleksandr Sergeevich.' However, if Pushkin bought the estate, he was willing to lower the valuation by a further six thousand to 64,000. Olga would then get just over 13,700 roubles, and Lev 25,000. He had already written to Lev to inform him of these suggestions. If Pushkin did not wish to acquire the estate, it should be immediately put on the market at 70,000.[122]

'Pavlishchev tells me that he is not agreeable to selling his share of Mikhailovskoe for the sum you offer; consequently there will be a hitch.'

Lev wrote. But he did not seem to be unduly disturbed, nor was he inclined to align himself with Pavlishchev, as the latter might have hoped. However, reminding Pushkin that he had now been reinstated in the army, he asked whether, since he had not the wherewithal to equip himself for the coming campaign, his brother might see his way to advancing the first instalment of his share of the estate.[123]

Pavlishchev had also written to Sergey Lvovich. His letter was an amalgamation of the two to Pushkin: the first half enumerating the iniquities of the former bailiff; the second dilating on his revised valuation of the estate, and emphasizing the consequential increase in Olga's share. 'Of course,' he wrote, '13 thousand is not a large sum (for Aleksandr Sergeevich, for example, who just for his apartment pays as much as I receive in salary); but in my situation it is a crust of bread against a rainy day. At the same time, while observing Olga's benefit, I have preserved too the interest of Lev Sergeevich, who sent me his power of attorney: he will surely thank me if instead of 15 thousand he receives on my valuation 25 thousand.'[124] By implying that Pushkin's carelessness, not to say self-interest, was threatening to reduce the amounts which Olga and Lev, Sergey Lvovich's favourite children, might legitimately hope to receive from the estate, Pavlishchev was hoping to enlist his father-in-law's support. He had not reckoned on the latter's delicate sensibilities, nor his self-centredness. 'M. Pavlishchev's letter, full of details on the management of Mikhailovskoe and on the division of your mother's estate, rent my soul and broke my heart – I passed a sleepless night. It is so indecent, written even with the greatest discourtesy, with no consideration, either for my position, or for the scant time that has passed since my bereavement.'[125]

By his machinations Pavlishchev had succeeded, not only in alienating his father-in-law, but also in souring relations between himself and Olga. On 10 August Zizi Vrevskaya wrote to her brother: 'Poor Olga Sergeevna is still very unwell. Her coughs and chest pains were cured by the peasant with his whispers and his baths. But the day before yesterday they came to ask us to send for the apothecary, because she was suddenly having faints and being sick.* I think that probably

---

* Olga was, as she later realized, pregnant: she gave birth to a second child, Nadezhda, on 23 May 1837.

Pavlishchev angered her by something, for they are still arguing about the sale of Mikhailovskoe. He won't go lower than 800 roubles a soul, and she is afraid through this to fall out with Aleksandr, on whom all her hope lies, [. . .] she argued with him until she wept, and he became incensed and said a lot of rude things to her. He wants Aleksandr to give up his share, he likes Mikhailovskoe very much and asserts that it will give him 10 thousand or more.'[126]

Pavlishchev was, however, growing desperate. He was extremely pressed for money, and time was not on his side. He had to be back in Warsaw on 15 August, but could not leave without some money to pay off his creditors. Though he had applied for a month's sick leave, reports from Warsaw of Paskevich's displeasure forced him to cave in before receiving Pushkin's reply. On 21 August he accepted the first valuation of 40,000, begging Pushkin to bring or to send at least 2,500 roubles of Olga's share as soon as possible. On the twenty-eighth, having received a reply, he wrote: 'And so the affair of the division of the inheritance between us is at an end. I expect you here and 2,500 roubles, without which, as I hear from Warsaw, it is impossible for me to leave.'[127]

'They [the Pavlishchevs], poor people, are in a miserable state,' Zizi wrote on 10 September. 'Paskevich ordered him to be told that if he did not immediately appear in Warsaw, he would be dismissed; by the next post the order was repeated, with very unpleasant additions, and they have not got a penny. Olga Sergeevna has taken to her bed because of these troubles, he went to Ostrov to get money, but could not supply rye, which he has not got, and which he had to borrow from his neighbours. Aleksandr Sergeevich doesn't come and doesn't write. This egoism is unpardonable.'[128] Pavlishchev took matters into his own hands. As an advance on Olga's share he collected as much quit-rent as possible, sold off what produce was available – 'Boris [Vrevsky] lent him 25 chetverts of rye, I lent him 50, Mikhailovskoe furnished him with 83, which makes 158, and off he goes to Ostrov and sells it to Mr Kiryakov,* the colonel of the regiment: and gets for it almost 2000,' lamented Praskovya Osipova[129] – and decamped for Warsaw with Olga on 11 September.

Pushkin did not return to the subject of the estate until 20 October,

---

* Vasily Yakovlevich Kiryakov: the husband of Pelageya Melandya, Olga's second cousin.

when he wrote to his father, '[Olga's] husband after irritating me with totally useless letters no longer shows any sign of life when it's a matter of putting his affairs in order. Send him, I beg you, a power of attorney for the share which you have given to Olga.'[130] Pushkin had spoken too soon, for a few days later he received another of Pavlishchev's long letters, crammed with detail, to which was annexed an inventory and valuation of the movable property at Mikhailovskoe. He had discovered that Olga was entitled to a larger share of this than of the immovable property: after recalculation and subtraction of what they had already had, he determined that she was still owed 6,578.80 roubles. Could Pushkin possibly let them have 1,578 roubles now, and the remaining 5,000 in January 1838? And if he would like to acquire four horses, given to Olga by Sergey Lvovich, for 300 roubles, could he make that 1,878? Darker clouds were gathering round Pushkin's head at this time; he had, too, no money to spare. Only in January did he send Pavlishchev a note, containing, Olga remarked, 'only a few lines for my husband, scrawled in haste in reply to a letter written as long ago as July, and which he completely misunderstood, not having taken the trouble to read to the end, and made no mention of two others which my husband has written from here. It is obvious that he is extremely busy and in a very bad temper.'[131] 'Let Mikhailovskoe be sold,' he had written. 'If they give a good price for it, it will be better for you. I will see whether I am able to keep it for myself.'[132]

This seemingly contradictory statement is the elliptical expression of a new plan, which he had expressed in a letter to Praskovya Osipova. 'Do you want to know what my wish would be? I would have liked you to be the owner of Mikhailovskoe, and to reserve for myself the house and garden with a dozen domestic serfs.'[133] Praskovya replied energetically: 'Pavlishchev is a real villain and a lunatic to boot – I do not want Mikhailovskoe and since you are the son of my heart I want you to keep it – do you hear? ... And have the patience to read me – fate preserves it for you.' He was to buy out Olga and Lev at 500 a serf, taking out a mortgage to do so; the income would be more than three thousand, which would pay the interest easily. But he should not forget that the estate owed her and Vrevsky two thousand roubles for rye.[134] After the experience with Boldino, however, Pushkin had no desire to take up estate management again. His plan to keep only the house and grounds began to seem feasible when, at the beginning of 1837, both Zizi's husband Vrevsky, and the latter's half-brother, Serdobin, expressed interest in acquiring the estate. Pushkin's death put an end to these schemes.

On 11 October 1833 the St Petersburg Gazette informed its readers of the arrival at Kronstadt from Lübeck three days earlier of the packet Nicholas I. Among its passengers was Baron Heeckeren, who was returning to his post as the minister for the Netherlands in St Petersburg; he was accompanied by a young Frenchman, Baron Georges d'Anthès, whom he had met on his way through Germany; learning that the other was also travelling to Russia, and discovering in him a distant relative – both were connected, on their mothers' side, to the von Wartensleben family – he had taken him under his wing.

Jacob Derk Anne Borchard Baron van Heeckeren van Enghuysen, lord of Beverweerd en Odijk, belonged to one of Holland's oldest noble families. Born in 1791, he had served in the Dutch navy during the Napoleonic wars. In 1815, after the establishment of the Kingdom of the Netherlands, he joined its diplomatic service, and was posted as secretary to the embassy in Stockholm. He later became the chargé d'affaires in St Petersburg after the recall of the then minister, Baron Verstolk van Soelen, and in March 1826 presented his letters of credence as the latter's successor. A close friend of the Foreign Minister, Nesselrode, he was a respected and influential member of the diplomatic corps. His reputation suffered a blow, however, when he was discovered to be abusing the privilege of the diplomatic bag: in 1833 the Ministry of Trade informed the Foreign Ministry that 'for some time considerable quantities of goods have been imported by Heeckeren'.[135] These duty-free goods, ranging from wines to furniture, were far more than he could have required for personal use, and he made a large profit by their sale. Generally disliked for his meddlesomeness and penchant for intrigue, and feared for his caustic tongue, he had gradually fallen out with most of St Petersburg society. When Dolly Ficquelmont had met him in the autumn of 1829, she had at first not taken to him; he had a 'thin, false, unsympathetic face'. Later she had changed her mind. 'I have become very used to his company which I find witty and amusing, I cannot and hope that society is wrong about his character,' she noted in her diary. In February 1830 Dolly went to a ball at his house – 51, Nevsky Prospect – 'a little miniature, but a jewel of elegance', and when that May he paid a visit to Holland she remarked that 'he will leave a large gap in our salon, of which he was a very pleasant habitué'.[136] Princess Lieven, returning to St Petersburg in 1834 after twenty-two years in England, would write to Earl Grey: 'Among the Corps Diplomatique the *gens d'esprit* are M. de Ficquelmont the Austrian Ambassador and M. de Heeckeren, the Dutch minister.'[137] Pushkin had met him – as he had met most members of the diplomatic corps – through the Ficquelmonts. But the two were no more than bowing acquaintances.

Georges d'Anthès, Heeckeren's protégé, came from Alsace. The family fortunes had been established at the beginning of the eighteenth century by Jean Henri d'Anthès, a wealthy ironmaster, ennobled in 1731, whose estate at Soultz, near Mulhouse, became the family seat. His great-grandson, Joseph Conrad d'Anthès, married in 1806 Countess Marie-Anne-Louise von Hatzfeldt; their third child and first son, Georges, was born in Colmar on 5 February 1812. In 1829 he entered the Saint-Cyr military academy, but was forced to leave the following year after the July revolution, being, like the majority of the cadets, a partisan of Charles X. He returned to Soultz, where he found his father having difficulty – the family wealth had declined over the generations – in supporting five other children, together with a small tribe of close relatives. D'Anthès determined to seek his fortune elsewhere, and left for Prussia, where he hoped to obtain a place through family connections. In Berlin he was offered a non-commissioned officer's rank in the army, but declined it; he obtained, however, a letter of recommendation from Prince William, Nicholas's brother-in-law,* and with it pressed on to Russia, where he also had influential relatives: two great-aunts on his mother's side. One, a von Hatzfeldt, had married a Nesselrode; another, Countess Charlotte Musina-Pushkina, née von Wartensleben, was the widow of Count Aleksey Musin-Pushkin, who had been the Russian ambassador in Stockholm and London.

On arrival in St Petersburg d'Anthès put up at the English Inn

---

* The two were in fact connected twice through marriage: Nicholas's wife, the Empress Alexandra, was William's sister; William's wife, Augusta of Saxe-Weimar-Eisenach, was Nicholas's niece.

on Galernaya Street, and presented his letters of recommendation to Major-General Adlerberg at the Ministry of War. The latter passed his papers on to General Sukhozanet, and at the beginning of January informed d'Anthès that his examination for entry into the Guards would take place soon after Epiphany; the general, he added, 'hopes to polish it off in a morning, if only all the professors can be free at the same time'. A postscript indicates that Nicholas had taken a personal interest in d'Anthès's application: 'The emperor asked me whether you were learning Russian,' Adlerberg wrote. 'I replied yes on the off chance. I believe I recommended you to take a Russian teacher.'[138] The examination took place at the end of January. D'Anthès, who was exempted from three subjects – Russian literature, military regulations and military law – passed the remainder, and on 8 February was commissioned as a cornet in the Chevalier Guards. 'Baron d'Anthès and the Marquis de Pina, two Chouans, will be taken into the Guards directly as officers,' Pushkin had noted in his diary a few days earlier. 'The Guards are grumbling.'*[139]

Though d'Anthès was promoted lieutenant in January 1836, he was a far from exemplary soldier. 'On joining the regiment d'Anthès proved to be not only very weak at drill, but in addition a very undisciplined officer, and remained such throughout his whole service with the regiment: sometimes he would "get in his carriage" after the guard had been mounted, when "generally not one of the officers would leave"; sometimes, on parade, "as soon as the regiment had been stood at ease, he would take the liberty of lighting a cigar", sometimes "in bivouac, despite the order that officers should only appear in uniform, he would emerge in his nightshirt, with his coat over his shoulders". When drilling "he would correct his troop too loudly", which, however, did not prevent him from "not maintaining the proper distance" and before the command at ease sitting "completely slumped in his saddle" [...] This is not to mention his absences from guard duty, his unpunctuality on parade and so on ... D'Anthès was punished 44 times during his three years' service with the regiment.'[140]

---

* Chouan was a name given to those partisans who after 1793 fought in the west of France against the Republic and First Empire; hence a polemical appellation for supporters of the Bourbons. The Marquis de Pina, like d'Anthès a legitimist, was commissioned not in the Guards, but as an ensign in a line regiment, King Frederick William III's Grenadiers, from which he was cashiered in 1837 for theft.

The regiment provided the bodyguard of the imperial family, and d'Anthès was brought into close contact with the emperor and empress. He is mentioned several times in the empress's diary: she considers that, with his somewhat coarse, free and easy manners, he is a bad influence on a fellow-officer, the young Aleksandr Trubetskoy, for whom she had a distinct *tendre*. According to d'Anthès Nicholas's attitude was somewhat different. 'The emperor too was gracious towards me and conversed with me for a good quarter of an hour, much to the displeasure of many people who were bursting with jealousy,' he told Heeckeren on 8 December 1835. 'At the last Anichkov ball his majesty was extremely affable and conversed with me for a very long time,' he wrote three weeks later. 'All this took place to the great despair of all those present, who would have eaten me alive, if eyes could bite.'[141]

The young officer – 'one of the *handsomest of the guards*, and one of the most fashionable men,' commented Olga[142] – was an immediate social success, and had soon a wide circle of acquaintances in high society and in the diplomatic and literary worlds, becoming – surprisingly, since he was by no means cultured – a frequent visitor to the Karamzins and the Vyazemskys. Tall, with blond hair and blue eyes, distinguished by the romantic aura of a royalist exile, he was particularly successful with the opposite sex. But he did not make the most of his opportunities. Pavel Vyazemsky describes him as 'a practical, commonplace, good fellow, a joker, not at all a Lovelace or a Don Juan, who had come to Russia to make a career. His philandering offended none of the decencies of St Petersburg high society.'[143] He acquired a mistress – a married woman whose identity is unknown – to whom he refers in his letters as 'my Spouse'. The cognomen suggests that there was little romance about the liaison, and little that was romantic in d'Anthès's nature. Such as there was was reserved for his patron, Heeckeren, with whom his relationship had become ever closer.

The minister had begun to treat his protégé as though he were his own son from their arrival in St Petersburg. He had exerted all his influence on the other's behalf, writing to his father to assure him that d'Anthès would be given a commission in the Guards, and offering to defray the expenses of his equipment: at this time d'Anthès was too hard up even to be able to renew his exiguous civilian wardrobe, going 'to parties in a black tail-coat and grey breeches with red piping, not wishing for such a short time to replace his worn-out black trousers'.[144] 'I have just learnt from Georges of his appointment, and of everything that you have had the generosity to do for him – I cannot thank you and express my gratitude to you enough,' the elder d'Anthès replied. 'Georges owes his future existence to you alone, Baron, and is conscious of this, he looks upon you as his father and I hope he will be worthy of you.'[145]

Of this somewhat surprising relationship Trubetskoy – with whom d'Anthès shared quarters in Novaya Derevnya during the summer exercises of 1837 – remarked in a memoir written fifty years later: 'I don't know what to say: whether he [d'Anthès] lived with Heeckeren, or Heeckeren with him ... At that time buggery was widespread in high society. To judge by the fact that d'Anthès continually pursued ladies, it must be assumed that in his relations with Heeckeren he only played a passive role.'[146] By the beginning of 1835 Heeckeren had become passionately attached to the younger man – a feeling reciprocated by d'Anthès – and urgently sought a means by which they might live together without provoking prurient gossip. A severe illness early that year forced him to leave Russia in May to recuperate: he was not able to return for over a year. During this time he visited d'Anthès's family in Soultz, and, while in the Netherlands, investigated the possibility of legally adopting the other as his son. This proved impossible, for the relationship between them was not one recognized as a basis for adoption by the relevant articles of the French civil code (which remained in force in the Netherlands until 1838). However, Heeckeren successfully petitioned the King of the Netherlands, William I, to grant d'Anthès Dutch nationality, to admit him to the Dutch nobility, and allow him to change his name to Heeckeren. Though naturalization was immediate, incorporation into the nobility and the change of name would not come into effect until, at the earliest, May 1837.*

On his return to Russia, however, Heeckeren contemptuously ignored this stipulation, together with the fact that he had not been able to adopt

---

* D'Anthès's Dutch nationality was annulled retrospectively in December 1837 on the grounds that he had continued to hold a commission in the Russian army without obtaining the king's permission. After much discussion between the Supreme Council of Nobility and the Minister of Justice in Holland his incorporation into the nobility and his change of name were allowed to stand. On this episode see the excellent article by J.C. Baak and P. van Panhuys Polman Gruys, 'Les deux Barons de Heeckeren: documents néerlandais', *Revue des études slaves*, XVII (1937), 18–45, and *Russkii*, 79–108, 471–447.

d'Anthès. On 22 May he wrote a letter of bare-faced mendacity to the Foreign Minister, Nesselrode. 'I have the honour to inform your Excellency that I have legally adopted as my son Baron Georges-Charles d'Anthès and that, by the decision of His Majesty the King of the Netherlands dated 5 May 1835, the Supreme Council of the Nobility recognized his right to bear my name, my title, and my arms.' Could Nesselrode therefore ensure that henceforth he would be described on the regimental roll and elsewhere as Baron Georges-Charles de Heeckeren?*[147]

Both in Holland and in St Petersburg this pseudo-adoption was considered most peculiar and aroused much speculation. In the aftermath of the events of January 1837 Prince William of Orange wrote to his uncle, the tsar: 'No one here has been able to understand with what significance, and with what aim d'Anthès's adoption by Heeckeren took place, above all since Heeckeren maintains that they are not related by any tie of blood.'[148] At about the same time Aleksandr Karamzin was telling his brother: '[d'Anthès] was adopted by Heeckeren for reasons which even now are still entirely unknown to the public (which avenges itself for this with conjectures).'[149] One such conjecture was reported by P.D. Durnovo (son-in-law of Prince Volkonsky, the Minister of the Court), who after a rout at the Nesselrodes in November 1836 noted in his diary: 'The young man is the illegitimate son of the Dutch king.'[150] A fuller form of this rumour had it that d'Anthès was 'the son of Heeckeren's sister and the King of Holland, who had been adopted by his rich uncle'.[151] These rumours undoubtedly had Heeckeren as their source – 'one of the officials at the Dutch embassy, Gevers, would openly say that their ambassador was lying when he let it be known in society that the young man was his illegitimate son.'[152] He preferred to calumniate the morals of his monarch, even of his sister, rather than let himself and d'Anthès be suspected of the 'Greek vice'.

'My life is very monotonous,' Pushkin had written to Natalya in May 1834, when she was at Polotnyany Zavod. 'I dine at Dumé's at about 2, so as to avoid the bachelor crowd. I spend the evenings at the club.'[153] He did not succeed in avoiding bachelors completely, for one day that

---

* From now on, in contemporary letters, memoirs and official documents d'Anthès is usually referred to as Heeckeren. To avoid confusion I shall, however, continue to call him d'Anthès.

summer, while sitting at the restaurant's table d'hôte, he struck up an acquaintance with d'Anthès; and, when dining there a little later, introduced him to his old Lycée friend Konstantin Danzas, now a staff-captain in the Independent Caucasian Corps: the three were to meet again, less amicably, on the afternoon of 27 January 1837.

During the summer of 1835 the court was frequently in residence at the palace on the Elagin island; the Chevalier Guards were encamped at Novaya Derevnya, on the mainland to the north. Here too was 'the new establishment of Struve for mineral waters, a magnificent house, with elegant saloons, and promenades under cover [. . .] a favourite resort of the fashionable world of the islands'. This 'mock Carlsbad' had a separate suite for the royal family; the empress often visited it, for a walk in the mornings, or a ball in the evening.[154] 'I remember,' wrote Nikolay Kolmakov, then a nineteen-year-old law student, 'at one of these balls Aleksandr Sergeevich Pushkin and his beautiful wife Natalya Nikolaevna were also present [. . .] The ball ended. Natalya Nikolaevna, waiting for her carriage, stood leaning against a column by the entrance, while young officers, mostly Chevalier guardsmen, surrounded her, showering her with compliments. A little to one side, near another column, stood a pensive Aleksandr Sergeevich, taking not the slightest part in the conversation.'[155]

By the autumn d'Anthès had made the acquaintance of Natalya and her sisters, and had become one of the trio's *cavalieri serventi*. 'What can I tell you that is interesting? Our life goes on,' Aleksandra wrote to her brother at the beginning of December. 'We dance quite often, we ride at Bistrom's* every Wednesday; and the day after tomorrow we are having a grand carousel: with the most fashionable young men and the most beautiful and charming young persons. Do you want to know who? I will name them for you. Let us begin with the ladies, as this is more polite. First of all, your two beautiful sisters, or your two beauties of sisters, for the third . . . can only hobble about; then Marie Vyazemskaya and Sophie Karamzina; the cavaliers are: Valuev – *a model young man*, d'Anthès – a Chevalier guardsman, A. Golitsyn – an artilleryman, A. Karamzin – an artilleryman; it will be wonderful.'†[156]

---

* The proprietor or manager of the manège near the Engineers' Palace.
† Natalya could 'only hobble about', because she was pregnant. Petr Valuev, a civil servant who later became Minister of the Interior, married Mariya Vyazemskaya in May 1836, the

In November, in a postscript of a letter to Heeckeren, d'Anthès had written: 'I almost forgot to tell you I am breaking off with my Spouse and hope to inform you of the ending of my romance in my next.'[157] Two months later, on 20 January 1836, he revealed the reason for this action.

> My very dear friend, I am truly at fault in not replying immediately to the two kind and amusing letters you sent me, but you see the night is spent dancing, the morning at riding-school, and the afternoon asleep – that has been my life for the past fortnight and will be for at least as long in the future, but what is worse than all that is that I am madly in love! Yes, madly, for I do not know which way to turn. I will not tell you her name, because letters can go astray, but remember the most delicious creature in Petersburg and you will know her name, and what is most horrible about my position is that she loves me too, and we cannot see each other, it has been impossible up to now, for the husband is revoltingly jealous [. . .] I would do anything in the world for her, just to give her pleasure, for the life I lead has been for some time a continual torture. To love one another and only to be able to speak of this between two figures of a quadrille is terrible: I am perhaps wrong in confiding all this to you and you will consider it stupidity, but my heart is so big and so full that I have need to pour things out a little. I am sure that you will pardon this folly, I agree that it is one, but it is impossible for me to think straight, although I very much need to, for this love poisons my existence. But don't worry, I am prudent and I have been so to such an extent that up to now the secret belongs only to her and to me.

The delicious creature, as a transparent hint later in the letter made clear, was Pushkin's wife, Natalya Nikolaevna. The confession over, d'Anthès turned to more prosaic matters: 'The only present which I'd like you to get for me in Paris is gloves and socks of filoselle, a cloth made of silk and wool, very pleasant and warm to wear, which aren't,

---

two Karamzin brothers, Andrey and Aleksandr – it is not clear to which Aleksandra is referring – were ensigns in the Life Guards Horse Artillery; Aleksandr Golitsyn was a staff-captain in the same regiment.

I think, very expensive.'[158] It was naive to imagine the infatuation could remain a secret. On 5 February the maid-of-honour Mariya Mörder, an inquisitive and romantically-minded twenty-one-year-old, described in her diary a ball given by the ambassador of Naples and the Two Sicilies, George di Butera e Radoli, and his wife Varvara. 'The rarest flowers filled the air with tender fragrance [...] It was a veritable magic, enchanted castle. [...] In the crowd I noticed d'Anthès, but he did not see me. It was possible, moreover, that he was simply not in the mood. It seemed to me that his eyes expressed anxiety – he was looking for someone, and, suddenly darting to one of the doors, disappeared into the next room. In a minute he appeared again, but now with Mrs Pushkin on his arm. My ears caught the words: "Leave – do you really want to, madame? – I don't believe it – that wasn't your intention . . ." The expression with which these words were spoken left no doubt as to the correctness of the observations I had made earlier – they were madly in love! Having spent not more than half an hour at the ball, we made our way towards the door: the baron was dancing a mazurka with Mrs Pushkin – how happy they seemed at that moment! . . .'[159] Three days earlier d'Anthès had written to Heeckeren. 'I believe I love her more than I did two weeks ago! In a word, it's an obsession, my dear, which never leaves me, which is with me when asleep and when awake [...] I have more reasons for happiness than ever, because I have managed to be received in her house, but to see her alone is almost impossible, I think, and yet absolutely imperative.'[160] There is no doubt that Natalya was flattered, indeed moved by d'Anthès's impetuous onslaught. 'He aroused her,' Pushkin later admitted.[161] But that she returned his love may be doubted. 'I enjoy being with him. I simply like him,' she told Vera Vyazemskaya: a prosaic corrective to d'Anthès's romantic effusions.[162] Mariya Mörder, as is obvious from her account, is herself infatuated with d'Anthès – 'he is astonishingly handsome,' she sighs to her diary[163] – and only has eyes for him: her account bears out d'Anthès's description of his emotions, but says nothing of Natalya's.

During the course of one of the numerous balls that took place during the week of Shrove-tide d'Anthès endeavoured to take the relationship a step further, seeking – as he told Heeckeren – to persuade Natalya to commit adultery:

My dear friend, now the carnival has ended and with it part of my torments; I really believe that I am a little calmer now that I don't see her every day; and then all the world can no longer come and take her by the hand, the waist, dance and talk with her, as I myself do; and that even better than me, because they have a clearer conscience. It is stupid to say it, but it turns out, something I'd never have believed, that it was from jealousy that I was continually in an irritated state which made me so unhappy. And then we had an explanation, the last time I saw her, which was terrible, but which did me good. This woman, who is generally supposed to be far from clever, I don't know whether it is love that gives her it, but it would be impossible to put more tact, grace, and intelligence than she did into this conversation, and it was difficult to maintain, since it was a matter of no less than refusing to violate her duties for a man whom she loves and who adores her; she described her situation to me with such lack of constraint, asked my pardon with such naïveté, that I was really conquered and could not find a word to reply. If you knew how she consoled me, for she knew I was suffocating and was in a terrible state, and when she said to me: 'I love you as I have never loved, but never ask more than my heart, for all the rest does not belong to me and I can only be happy in honouring all my duties, pity me and love me always as you do now, my love will be your recompense'; I tell you, I believe that I would have fallen at her feet to kiss them had I been alone, and I assure you that since that day my love for her has grown even more, but it is now no longer the same thing: I revere her, I respect her, as one reveres and respects a being to whom all one's existence is bound.[164]

There is no reason to doubt that d'Anthès made an attempt on Natalya's virtue, nor that she rejected him, softening her refusal with some show of affection. But his creative imagination seems to have been at work in the description of the scene, putting into Natalya's mouth a wretched pastiche of Tatyana's speech to Eugene in the final chapter of *Eugene Onegin*. D'Anthès's subsequent behaviour is the most convincing argument against the veracity of his account. Utterly devoid of both the reverence and the respect he declared he felt for her, it is the behaviour of a rejected lover, whose passion is not returned, rather than that of one secure in the love of his mistress, and only prevented by her virtue from enjoying her favours to the full.

Heeckeren had been horrified by d'Anthès's letters. Knowing Pushkin's reputation, he feared the possibility of an appalling scandal, while his jealousy had been aroused by the young man's rhapsodic descriptions of his love for Natalya. He begged d'Anthès to break off the relationship, which was bound to become the subject of gossip. 'As God is my witness,' d'Anthès replied, 'on receiving your letter I had already taken the decision to sacrifice the woman for your sake. My resolve was great, but your letter was so kind, it contained so much truth and tender friendship, that I did not hesitate for a moment; from that instant I have completely changed my behaviour to her: I have avoided her as assiduously as I sought her earlier; I have conversed with her with all the indifference of which I am capable, but I think that, if I had not got your letter by heart, I would not have had the spirit. This time, thank God, I conquered myself, and of the uncontrollable passion, which I spoke of in all my letters to you, and which devoured me for six months, there remains in me only devotion and tranquil admiration for the creature who made my heart beat so strongly.' He rejected indignantly Heeckeren's assertion that Natalya had already sacrificed her virtue to another. 'I believe that there are men who have lost their heads over her, she is lovely enough for that, but that she should have submitted to them, no! She has not loved anyone more than me, and recently there have been innumerable occasions when she could have given me everything – and, my dear friend – never anything! never in life!' Natalya was then in her seventh month of pregnancy. At the end of March he wrote to Heeckeren again: he had spoken to her only four times in three weeks. 'I have to say frankly,' he continued, 'that the sacrifice which I have made for your sake is immense. To keep one's word so resolutely one must love as I love you.'[165]

Heeckeren's prediction that d'Anthès's pursuit of Natalya would become one of the *on dits* of St Petersburg society was soon proved true. 'I was going to a ball at court when the Grand Duke and Heir joked with me about her,' d'Anthès confessed.[166] Nor was the rumour confined to court circles. Olga, writing to her father later that year, remarked that '[d'Anthès's] passion for Natalie was a secret for no one. I knew all about it when I was in St Petersburg and joked about it to him.'[167] Pushkin knew of it too: it added one more worry to the burden of troubles that oppressed him in the first months of 1836. Chief of these, of course, was his mother's long illness. As far as his work was concerned, the scandal caused by 'On Lucullus's Recovery' had exacerbated his problems with the censorship, and much increased the difficulty of launching the *Contemporary*. And in the background was the constant, nagging ache of insolvency. At the beginning of the year his known debts amounted to nearly 80,000 roubles, a sum that increased month by month, as expenditure exceeded income. He had hoped that he would make money from the *Contemporary*, had budgeted on it: 'His wife has already on its future profits rented a villa on Kamenny Island, more than twice as expensive as last year's,' Annette Vulf wrote to her mother.*[168] The quarterly turned out, however, to be a further drain on his resources. He seemed incapable of reducing his expenses. Although he already had two carriages, one two-seated, the other four, a chaise and a travelling calash, in June he acquired from the coach-maker Aleksandr Drittenpreis another four-seated carriage costing 4,150 roubles. In March the book-sellers Bellizard et Cie presented a bill for 2,172.90 roubles, some items of which had been outstanding since 1834. Pushkin paid them 975 roubles at the end of April, but could not resist calling in whenever he passed their establishment on the Nevsky and adding another item or two to his account. In May, for example, he bought 44 volumes, including the complete works of E.T.A. Hoffman, translated into French, Sismondi's history of the fall of the Roman empire in French (he read the first five pages), Bulwer-Lytton's *Rienzi*, and Thomas Hamilton's *Men and Manners in America*, both in French translations. Lacking ready money to pay the most necessary household expenses, he was reduced to undignified and demeaning expedients, repeatedly raising small loans on the security of Natalya's or Aleksandra's personal possessions. The contemplation of his problems produced gloom and bitterness; feeling that fate and his enemies were conspiring against him, he was inclined, as before, to lash out indiscriminately at

---

* This was a villa belonging to F.I. Dolivo-Dobrovolsky, into which the family moved at the beginning of May 1836 – Pushkin was in Moscow at the time. See Mikhail Yashin, 'Dacha na Kamennom ostrove', *Neva*, 1965, 2, 187–203.

the world. His irritability reached its peak early in February 1836, when, within the space of a week, he issued two challenges to duels and came close to a third – this last was his exchange of letters with Prince Repnin over 'Lucullus'.

The previous year he had helped the former domestic bursar of the Lycée, Efim Lyutsenko, an untalented littérateur who was in financial difficulties, to bring out his translation of a tale in verse by Wieland, agreeing – generously, but misguidedly – to make the book more saleable by putting his own name on the cover. When it appeared anonymously at the beginning of 1836, the title-page read: 'Vastola or the Wishes, a story in verse by Wieland. In three parts. Published by A. Pushkin.'* The absence of a translator's name, together with the ambiguity of the verb, persuaded many that this was Pushkin's own work, all the more so as the 1834 collection of his stories employed the same formula, being entitled 'Stories, published by Aleksandr Pushkin'. Readers were dumbfounded, therefore, to discover a work which bore little semblance to poetry and was, moreover, written in the style of 'the times of Tredyakovsky and Sumarokov', as Belinsky remarked. Reviewing Vastola in Rumour, the supplement to Nadezhdin's Telescope, he came to the conclusion that Pushkin could not be the translator. If, for charitable motives, he had lent his name to some poverty-stricken rhymester, he had gone too far: the action was comparable to the 'soft-heartedness of the head of a department, who refuses to sack a drunken, lazy and stupid clerk, not wishing to deprive him of a crust of bread'. Osip Senkovsky, the editor of the Library for Reading, took the same view. If Pushkin had 'hired his name out, so that the book would sell better', this would be 'contrary to all our notions of charity'. But, annoyed that Pushkin had defected from his journal to launch the Contemporary, he went further than Belinsky, ridiculing the work, and Pushkin's part in it, and concluding that the only honourable way out was for Pushkin to recognize the poem as his own and include it in his collected works.[169]

These criticisms, in particular that of Senkovsky, got under Pushkin's skin. He published a reply in the first number of the Contemporary, remarking that 'up to now no one has been forbidden to print the

---

* Wieland's title is Pervonte, oder die Wünsche; Lyutsenko uses the name of the heroine, rather than the hero.

works of others, with the agreement or at the request of the author. This is called to *publish*; a clear expression; at least up to now no other has been thought of.'[170] But it could not be denied that he was responsible for the misunderstanding. He would have liked to forget the episode; unfortunately this proved to be impossible. On 3 February two young men, Semen Khlyustin and Grigory Nebolsin, called on him. Khlyustin was the nephew of Tolstoy the American; the family estate bordered on that of the Goncharovs, and he was therefore a close acquaintance of Natalya and her sisters. During the conversation Khlyustin tactlessly quoted a phrase from Senkovsky's review to the effect that Pushkin had deceived the public. Touched to the quick, Pushkin flew into a rage, shouting that he could not tolerate people who repeated 'the idiocies of swine and blackguards like Senkovsky'.[171] Khlyustin, considering himself insulted, replied in kind and left: his stiff farewell salute was ignored. Summoning Sobolevsky, Pushkin sent him off to obtain an apology or to arrange a meeting. But Sobolevsky, not thinking the matter urgent, delayed his visit, enabling Khlyustin to shoot off a letter the following morning demanding satisfaction for the insults he considered he had received. A duel was only averted by Sobolevsky's emollient intervention.

On the day after this incident – 5 February – Pushkin composed his stiffly polite letter to Prince Repnin, and, in the same week, sent a grossly insulting missive to Count Vladimir Sollogub, which could not fail to provoke a challenge and *rencontre*. The previous winter, unhappy in love, the twenty-two-year-old Vladimir – cousin of Nadezhda Sollogub – had asked to be posted away from St Petersburg, and had been sent to Tver. On the eve of his departure he had attended a rout at the Karamzins, where Natalya and her friend, Mariya Vyazemskaya, had teased him so unmercifully about his lovesick demeanour that he had been provoked into a stinging rejoinder. A garbled version reached Pushkin, according to which Sollogub had not only insulted Natalya, but had also implied that she was conducting a flirtation with Adam Lenski, a handsome Pole, renowned for the elegance of his mazurka. He wrote to Sollogub, demanding an explanation, but the letter never reached its destination. It was only towards the end of January that Sollogub was informed of the rumours by Andrey Karamzin and learnt that Pushkin, having had no reply, was now accusing him of cowardice. He hastened to write to him, denying any *arrière pensée* in speaking of

Lenski, but refusing to retract his remark to Natalya, and declaring himself ready to give Pushkin satisfaction at any time the latter might appoint. Pushkin's reply – the letter mentioned above – ran:

> You have given yourself useless trouble in giving me an explanation which I did not ask for. You have allowed yourself to utter impertinences to my wife and have boasted of it. The name which you bear and the society you frequent oblige me to demand satisfaction for the indecency of your conduct.[172]

Pushkin's last self-portrait, drawn on a draft of the letter to Sollogub

Adding that he could not be in Tver until the end of March, he gave the letter to Khlyustin – now a friend once again – to deliver on his way to Moscow.

'There was nothing to be done,' Sollogub writes; 'I began to prepare for a duel, bought pistols, chose a second, put my papers in order and began to wait and waited for three months in vain.'[173] Although Pushkin had proposed to travel to Moscow early in the year to work in the archives on Peter the Great – 'Aleksandr is leaving tomorrow for Moscow with Ivan Goncharov,' Olga wrote on 18 February[174] – his mother's illness and the difficulties involved in bringing out the first number of the *Contemporary* caused the journey continually to be postponed. It was not until 29 April that he was able to depart. On 1 May he arrived in Tver, but Sollogub had left the previous day for his mother's estate. He had, however, taken the precaution of leaving a note for Pushkin with his second, Prince Kozlovsky. The next day Pushkin resumed his journey to Moscow, arriving at Nashchokin's apartment in Vorotnikovsky Lane after midnight. Sollogub returned to Tver on 4 May, and learnt to his horror that he had missed Pushkin, who, he feared, might accuse him of cowardice again. Calling for a post troika, he galloped off to Moscow, and knocked Pushkin up at dawn. 'He came out to me in a dressing-gown, still half-asleep, and began to clean his extraordinarily long nails.' The conversation was at first cool: Pushkin enquired as to Sollogub's second; his was Nashchokin. A discussion of the *Contemporary* began to melt the frost. 'The first number was too good,' Pushkin remarked, 'I will make the second more boring: one mustn't pamper the public.' Nashchokin then emerged, also half-asleep, with dishevelled hair. Sollogub 'looking at his peaceable countenance, I involuntarily came to the conclusion that not one of us wanted a bloody denouement, and that the point was how we were all to extricate ourselves from this stupid situation without losing our dignity.'[175] In the end Sollogub wrote a letter of apology to Natalya which Pushkin promised not to make use of, unless he were accused of allowing his wife to be insulted. He and Sollogub parted amicably; indeed, the incident led to a much closer friendship between them than before.

For the time being his embittered and resentful irritation had passed, though it was to return, in more virulent form, some months later. The rumours about Natalya had not altered his relationship to her: his letters from Moscow are as tenderly and teasingly affectionate as ever. Had he been concerned about her flirtations, it would have been impossible for him to joke as he did on 6 May, when, after retailing to her some comically exaggerated items of Moscow gossip, he continued, 'and about you, my darling, some talk is going about which I'm not getting completely, because husbands are always the last in town to find out about their wives, however, it appears that you have reduced someone to such despair by your coquetry and cruelty that in consolation he has set up a harem of budding actresses. This is not good, my angel: modesty is the best adornment of your sex.'[176] The 'someone' was Nicholas I.

Though Pushkin's main purpose in coming to Moscow had been to work in the archives on his history of Peter, he found his time taken up mainly by the concerns of the *Contemporary*, whose first number had been published on 11 April, though permission for the journal had been given three months earlier, on 10 January. The long delay was partly due to censorship difficulties. 'As the censor of the new journal the curator [Dondukov-Korsakov] has appointed Krylov, the most cowardly, and hence the strictest of our fraternity,' Nikitenko noted in January. 'They wanted to appoint me, but I earnestly requested to be excused this: dealing with Pushkin is too burdensome'; adding in April: 'Pushkin is being cruelly oppressed by the censorship. He has complained of Krylov and has requested another censor to assist the first. He has been given Gaevsky. Pushkin repents, but it is too late. Gaevsky is so terrified of the guardhouse, where he was confined for a week, that now he has doubts as to whether news of the kind that such-and-such a king has died can be printed.'[177] Too timid to take decisions themselves, the censors continually referred articles to the committee; this delayed approval, and Pushkin found himself frequently corresponding with its chairman, Dondukov-Korsakov. Though the latter had invited Pushkin to address himself directly to him in cases of difficulty, he proved little amenable to persuasion: 'One's allowed to argue with the censorship, but not with Your Grace,' Pushkin noted in annoyance on the back of one of his letters.[178]

In editing the *Contemporary* he had the assistance of his old literary associate Pletnev, of Prince Odoevsky, whom he had recruited as a collaborator the previous year, and of Andrey Kraevsky, to whom he had been introduced by Odoevsky. Though the twenty-six-year-old Kraevsky was at the time financially embarrassed, forced to supplement his meagre salary as a civil servant at the Ministry of Education by giving private tuition, he asked no remuneration for delivering manuscripts to the printers, correcting proofs, and carrying out the other menial tasks he was given. His ambition was to edit his own literary journal; he hoped, by acquiring Pushkin's good will, to enlist him as a contributor. And, indeed, when he took over from Voeikov the editorship of the literary supplement to the *Russian Invalid* at the beginning of 1837, Pushkin gave him an unpublished lyric, 'Aquilon', which appeared in the magazine on 2 January. After Pushkin's death he wrote to Odoevsky, asking whether he could have in memory of the poet 'his yellow cane with the button of Peter the Great's coat set in the knob'. 'If the trustees cannot comply with my feeling of affection for the departed,' he added, 'then let them give me the cane for the debt Pushkin always considered he owed me for the *Contemporary*: during the whole year, as you know, I received not a copeck from him.'*[179]

While Pushkin was in Moscow the three were preparing the second

---

* Kraevsky, 'the Methuselah of Russian journalism', edited *Fatherland Notes* from 1839 to 1868. He was the illegitimate son of an illegitimate daughter of General Nikolay Arkharov, governor-general of St Petersburg under Paul; his mother, according to Grech, 'having brought into the world the great publisher of *Fatherland Notes*, herself did not know whose son he was, since she had had many collaborators in editing him. A White Russian blackguard called Kraevsky gave him his surname in return for the mother's favours. She later married another blackguard, a certain Major von Pahlen, and, having lost her nose in some campaign with Venus, set up a girls' boarding-school in Moscow' (Grech, 150–1).

number of the *Contemporary*, communicating with him through Natalya, who in turn relayed his instructions to them – Vyazemsky would jokingly refer to her as 'Madam Co-editor'.[180] Despite her advanced pregnancy, she was much involved in the journal's affairs, though perhaps more concerned with the quality of its income than with that of its contents. One of Pushkin's aims in coming to Moscow was to persuade the booksellers there to stock the journal. 'I am going out to busy myself with the *Contemporary*'s affairs,' he wrote to her on 11 May. 'I fear that the booksellers may take advantage of my softheartedness and secure some concessions in spite of your strict instructions. But I will try to demonstrate a noble firmness.'[181] However, he could not bring himself to apply a commercial spirit to a commercial enterprise. 'I have spoken to Pushkin about sending the *Contemporary* to Moscow on commission,' Kraevsky wrote in October. 'He hummed and hawed. His carelessness would enrage a lamb!'[182] It was not so much carelessness as fastidiousness, a dislike of belonging to the world of Senkovsky, Grech and Bulgarin. 'I see that it is imperative for me to have an income of 80,000,' he wrote to Natalya. 'And I will have. I haven't engaged in speculation in a journal for nothing – though it's just the same as night-soil collection, which Bezobrazov's mother wanted the monopoly of: cleansing Russian literature means cleansing privies and depending on the police.'[183]

He also hoped to acquire new contributors in Moscow, being interested particularly in recruiting some of the *Moscow Observer* writers and, from Nadezhdin's *Telescope*, the young, up-and-coming critic Vissarion Belinsky. But he had to tread carefully, for the editors of the *Observer* had not forgotten that he had palmed 'On Lucullus's Recovery' off on them as 'an imitation of the Latin'; while relations between the *Observer* and Belinsky had been cool since the latter's recent attack on that journal in the *Telescope*. 'I flirt with Moscow literature as best I can, but the Observers don't love me,' he told Natalya; and, immediately after his return to St Petersburg wrote to Nashchokin, 'I left you two spare copies of the *Contemporary*. Give one to Prince Gagarin, and send the other in my name to Belinsky (NB keep it quiet from the Observers) and have him told that I am very sorry I did not manage to see him.'[184] In the end, of the *Observer* writers only two old friends, Yazykov and Baratynsky, contributed a poem each to the *Contemporary*. He did not make a further approach to Belinsky, whose reception of the journal had been decidedly cool. There was too little in it, he thought, and it was to appear too infrequently. Of the contents he damned with faint praise Pushkin's 'Feast of Peter the Great' and 'The Covetous Knight', and remarked of the *Journey to Erzerum* that it was 'one of those articles which are excellent not on account of their content, but of the name with which they are signed'. Zhukovsky's 'Night Parade' was, however, 'a genuine poetic pearl', while the most interesting article, in his view, was the unsigned 'On activity in journal literature in 1834 and 1835'.[185] The anonymity concealed Gogol, whose piece was a robust attack on most other Russian periodicals, though its chief target was the *Library for Reading* and its editor Senkovsky, who was ridiculed both for his criticism and for the fiction he wrote under the pseudonym Baron Brambeus. Senkovsky had perhaps somehow got wind of the article, for when the current number of the *Library for Reading* appeared at the end of March, a few days before the publication of the *Contemporary*'s first volume, it contained a note on the new journal. Pushkin had founded it, Senkovsky asserted, because he envied the success of the *Library for Reading*; it would be devoted to abusive polemics, 'the lowest and most loathsome form of prose after rhymed pasquils' – an obvious hit at 'On Lucullus's Recovery'. The article concluded with a direct warning to Pushkin: 'Have a care, incautious genius!'[186]

At the time Senkovsky was on bad terms with the *Northern Bee*; Bulgarin was therefore happy to publish in this newspaper a vigorous, but anonymous reply to these charges, written by Odoevsky. But this did not mean that he had become reconciled with Pushkin; he was merely biding his time. At the beginning of June he devoted a long article – it appeared in serial form, in three successive numbers of the *Northern Bee* – to the *Contemporary*. The journal was 'prejudiced and unjust', he concluded, and was 'acting not in the spirit of common literary good, not in the spirit of the times, but in a partisan and fussily annoying spirit'. The contents of the first number were 'worthless', with the exception of the travel sketch 'The Valley of Azhitugay'.* He was

---

* By Sultan Kazy-Girey, a Circassian, and a cornet in the Caucasian Mountain troop of the Horse Guards. As a serving officer, Kazy-Girey was forbidden to publish literary works without the permission of the authorities. Both he and Pushkin were reprimanded for not observing this regulation.

particularly severe on Turgenev's letter from Paris, which he dismissed as 'incoherent prattle'.[187]

It was due to Vyazemsky that Turgenev's letters to him from Paris were published in the *Contemporary*. 'I read your letter on Saturday at Zhukovsky's, who on Saturdays summons the literary fraternity to his Olympian attic,' he wrote in December. 'There were Krylov, Pushkin, Odoevsky, Pletnev, Baron Rozen etc., etc. All cried with one voice: "What a pity there isn't a journal into which could be poured all this boiling, succulent bouillon made from the up-to-the-minute innards of today!"'[188] The journal was provided by the foundation of the *Contemporary*; unfortunately, critics tended to agree with Bulgarin, rather than with the literary fraternity. For Belinsky Turgenev's piece was 'that kind of badly written note to a friend, on various scraps of paper, which is neither coherent nor entertaining'.[189] And even Aleksandra Smirnova-Rosset, reading in Berlin a copy of the *Contemporary* sent to her by Vyazemsky, could not refrain from exercising her wit at Turgenev's expense in her letter of thanks. He was, she told Vyazemsky, a man 'who comprehends all sciences and knows everything'; in his article he 'strings together famous names and recommends books he has not read'.[190] Turgenev himself was incensed by the publication of what he considered to be a private letter. 'I never expected such almost criminal frivolity from you and such indiscretion,' he wrote indignantly to Vyazemsky.[191]

Pushkin left Moscow in the early hours of 21 May, after a farewell dinner with Nashchokin who gave him a turquoise ring – a talisman against violent death – and a necklace for Natalya. 'I arrived at my villa at midnight on the twenty-third,' Pushkin wrote to him a week later from Kamenny Island, 'and on the threshold learnt that Natalya Nikola-evna had safely given birth to a daughter Natalya a few hours before my arrival. She was asleep. The next day I congratulated her and gave her, instead of a chervonets, your necklace, over which she is in rap-tures.'[192] The ground floor of the villa was extremely damp, and Natalya's aunt forbade her to leave her room on the first floor for nearly a month, even though she had soon recovered from her confinement. It was not until 24 June that she relented, and allowed her niece to go for a drive, accompanied by her sisters on horseback. Three days later, on Sunday the twenty-seventh, the new baby was christened at the Church of the

Birth of John the Baptist on the island. The godparents were Natalya's aunt and Count Mikhail Wielhorski.

On the journey back to St Petersburg Pushkin had been accompanied by the artist Karl Bryullov, who had returned to Moscow that January after thirteen years in Italy. The two had met in the studio of the sculptor Ivan Vitali and had taken an instant liking to one another. 'What a lucky fellow Pushkin is!' the painter exclaimed. 'He laughs so heartily his guts can almost be seen!'[193] Pushkin had much admired Bryullov's painting 'The Last Day of Pompeii' when it had been exhibited in the Winter Palace in the summer of 1834, and was now greatly impressed by the sketch for a painting – never completed – entitled 'The Taking of Rome by Genseric'. He discussed with the artist the possibility of using as a subject a scene from the life of Peter the Great, but he also hoped that Bryullov would follow the example of his elder brother Aleksandr, who had painted Natalya's portrait soon after their marriage. 'I have already managed to visit Bryullov,' he had written to her on 4 May. 'I found him in the studio of some sculptor with whom he is living. I liked him very much. He is depressed, fears the Russian cold etc., longs for Italy, and is very discontented with Moscow. I saw some sketches he had begun, and thought of you, my delight. Surely I'll have a portrait of you, painted by him! It is impossible that, having seen you, he should not want to paint you.'[194]

The friendship continued in St Petersburg, and Pushkin often called in at Bryullov's studio in the Academy of Arts, on the embankment of Vasilevsky Island. Not long after their return he invited the painter to supper in the villa. 'I was in low spirits, did not want to go and for a long time refused. But he was more stubborn than I and dragged me off with him. His children were already asleep. He woke them and brought them out to me one at a time in his arms. This did not come naturally to him, I found it sad, and it gave me a picture of strained family happiness. I lost my patience and said: "Why the devil did you marry?" He replied: "I wanted to travel abroad, but I wasn't allowed to, I was in a situation where I didn't know what to do, and I got married."'[195] Pushkin paid his last visit to Bryullov's studio on 25 January 1837, when he and Zhukovsky, leafing through the artist's portfolio, were much amused by a drawing entitled 'Arriving for a ball at the Austrian envoy's in Smyrna'. 'Pushkin could not part with the sketch, laughed until tears came and asked Bryullov to give him the treasure, but the sketch already belonged to Princess Saltykova, and Karl Pavlovich, assuring him that he could not have it, promised to draw him another. Pushkin was inconsolable: he knelt before Bryullov with the sketch in his hands and began to beseech him: "Give it to me, my dear fellow. You know you won't draw another for me, give me this one." '[196] Bryullov did not give it to him; nor had he painted Natalya's portrait. Four days later Pushkin was dead.

Once back in St Petersburg Pushkin found the problem of dealing with the censorship as intractable as ever. The second number of the *Contemporary* was an advance commemoration of the twenty-fifth anniversary of the 1812 campaign. Published at the beginning of July, it contained the memoirs of Nadezhda Durova, who, disguised as a man, had served as an officer in the uhlans during the campaign; an article by Vyazemsky, 'Napoleon and Julius Caesar'; and a review of Edgar Quinet's narrative poem *Napoléon*. To these he had intended to add 'The Taking of Dresden', an article by Denis Davydov. Davydov's troops had captured the city in March 1813, when he had, on his own initiative, concluded a two-day armistice with the French commander. Accused of disobeying orders, he was relieved of his command by the corps commander, General Wintzingerode, and would have been court-martialled, had it not been for the intervention of Alexander and Kutuzov. The article was a defence of his actions and an attack on Wintzingerode, who, he believed, had acted out of jealousy. It had to be submitted to the military as well as the civil censors, and publication – despite a personal application to Dondukov-Korsakov – was forbidden. 'Pity we couldn't print it in *Contemporary* No 2, which will be all full of Napoleon,' Pushkin wrote to Davydov. 'How fitting it would have been there to butcher General Wintzingerode at the foot of the Vendôme column as a propitiatory sacrifice!'[197] After many more dealings with the censors – 'I do not know what offence has been committed by Russian writers, who are not only submissive, but also of themselves in agreement with the spirit of the government. But I do know that they have never been so oppressed as now'[198] – and a long correspondence with Davydov, the article, 'castrated by military censorship',[199] appeared in the fourth number of the *Contemporary*, which came out in November.

Contributors posed problems of a different kind: dealings with 'the cavalry maiden', Nadezhda Durova, took up a vast amount of time. Pushkin should perhaps have been forewarned, for she was the sister of that odd fantasist, Vasily Durov, with whom he had gambled in Pyatigorsk on his return from Erzerum. In 1806, at the age of twenty-three, Durova had abandoned her husband and three-year-old son and, dressed as a man, attached herself to a Cossack regiment. The following year she enlisted in the Royal Polish Uhlans and fought in the Prussian campaign. When her sex was discovered, Alexander I allowed her to remain in the army, giving her the name Aleksandr Aleksandrov and a cornet's commission in the Mariupol Hussars. In 1811 she transferred to the Lithuanian Uhlans and fought throughout the 1812 campaign, eventually retiring with the rank of staff-captain in 1816, when she was awarded a pension for life.

In June 1835 her brother had written to Pushkin to enquire whether he would be interested in publishing her memoirs. She was a well-known figure, and, given the piquant nature of her exploits, the book would no doubt sell well. Pushkin replied positively, but the manuscript went astray in the post, provoking a flurry of letters, necessitating replies, from Durova herself. In its stead her brother sent Pushkin, in March 1836, her memoirs of the 1812 campaign. Even before reading the manuscript he agreed to publish the work in the *Contemporary*, paying 200 roubles a sheet. For separate publication he suggested putting the two works together, which would produce a 'thicker, and hence dearer book'. '*The Complete Memoirs*,' he added, 'will probably sell well after I have trumpeted them in my journal. I am prepared either to buy them, or publish them on the author's behalf.' He had the manuscript copied, and, on the bottom of the letter, scribbled: 'I have just read the copied Memoirs: a delight! lively, original, splendid style. An undoubted success.'[200]

On 6 June Durova – who still dressed as a man and referred to herself as one – arrived in St Petersburg. Pushkin called on her at Demouth's Hotel the following day, bringing with him the proofs of her article, 'The Memoirs of N.A. Durova', to which he had written a short preface. 'We see with amazement,' it concluded, 'that the tender fingers, which once gripped the bloody hilt of a uhlan's sabre, also wield a swift, picturesque and fiery pen.'[201] Immediately after he had left, taking with him the manuscript the post had failed to deliver, she sat down to write to him. She was distressed that he had revealed her name: would it not be possible to remove the article from the journal, unite it with the memoirs she had just given him, and publish both under the title 'Memoirs of the Russian Amazon known under the name of Aleksandrov written by her own hand'? Pushkin was appalled at the suggestion. Her article was the centrepiece of the number: 'What has happened to Durova's memoirs? Has the censor passed them? They are essential to me – without them I'm sunk,' he had written to Natalya from Moscow in May.[202] Nevertheless he concealed his agitation. He doubted, he wrote, whether it would be possible to remove the article, as the copies were being bound. As for its title, his 'sincere and disinterested' opinion was to leave it as it was. '*The Memoirs of an Amazon* is somehow too affected, mannered, reminiscent of German novels. *The Memoirs of N.A. Durova* is simple, sincere and noble. Be brave – embark on a literary career as valiantly as on that which brought you fame.' In a postscript he offered her the use of his empty town apartment.[203]

She sent a servant round to enquire whether she might move in, but to her surprise he returned with the news that Pushkin had given up the lodging, which now had another tenant.* This seemed strange to Durova, but she said nothing of it to him when he arrived to take her to dinner at the villa. The other guests were Pletnev, Pushkin's sister Olga, and his two sisters-in-law: Natalya was still keeping to her room. The five-year-old Mariya had been allowed to dine with the adults. 'Whom would you rather marry, me or papa?' Pletnev asked her. 'You and papa,' she replied. 'But what about our guest,' asked Pushkin, 'do you love him, would you like to marry him?' 'No, no!' she answered hurriedly. Durova noticed that Pushkin had gone red. 'Surely he could not believe that I would be insulted by the words of a child,' she thought.[204]

Reassured about the *Contemporary* article, she now began to importune Pushkin about the publication of her complete memoirs. At their first meeting he had incautiously told her that the tsar was his censor:

---

* A misunderstanding: the Pushkins had indeed vacated Vyazemsky's old apartment when they had moved to their villa. But they had, against their return, taken out a lease on a smaller, cheaper apartment on the floor above: the concierge was presumably unaware of this.

Durova took this to mean that Nicholas read everything he published, whether by himself or another. 'When you show my memoirs to the tsar,' she wrote, 'simply say to him that I have sold them to you, but not that I myself am here; an incomprehensible terror overcomes me at the thought of our sovereign!' Why had he not yet done this, she enquired indignantly a fortnight later. 'You will say that he is not at home, he is on manoeuvres! Go there, he will surely be in a good humour there, and my memoirs will not anger him.' And why had no progress been made in their publication? If nothing happened before the end of the month, she would take the manuscript away from him.[205] 'I thank you very much for your frank and decisive letter,' Pushkin replied. 'It is very pleasing, because it bears the genuine stamp of your ardent and impatient character.' Explaining, in polite and conciliatory fashion, what was happening to her manuscript, and promising to send at the beginning of July the 500 roubles he still owed her, he concluded: 'Whether you sell them [the memoirs] or print them yourself, please entrust me with all the pains of publication, proof-correction and so on.'[206] This was perhaps – given his other preoccupations – taking chivalry too far. Pletnev thought so. 'You are wrong to entrust the publication of your memoirs to Aleksandr Sergeevich,' he told her. 'He has difficulty in coping with his own affairs; he will take it on from politeness, but it will be a burden to him.'[207] Persuaded by this, and by Pushkin's slowness in dealing with the work, she gave it to a relative, I. Butovsky, who published it later that year with the title *The Cavalry-Maiden*. 'So I had the stupidity to deprive my memoirs of their most brilliant adornment . . . their greatest glory – the name of the immortal poet!' she later lamented.[208]

Financial problems, never far from the forefront of Pushkin's mind, now exacerbated by the running sore of the *Contemporary*, became pressing again in the summer. On 1 June he borrowed 8,000 roubles from Prince Nikolay Obolensky. And in July Natalya wrote to her brother:

> You know that as long as I was able to do without help from home I did so, but now my situation is such that I consider it even my duty to assist my husband in that difficult situation in which he finds himself; it is not fair that the whole burden of

keeping my large family should fall on him alone, and that is why I am compelled, dear brother, to resort to your kindness and magnanimous heart, in order to implore you to appoint me, *with mother's help*, an allowance equal to that which my sisters receive, and, if possible, let me have it before January, that is from next month. I openly confess to you that we are in such a calamitous situation that there are days when I do not know how to carry on the household, my head spins. I very much do not want to disturb my husband with all my little domestic troubles, I already see how sad and depressed he is, cannot sleep at night, and, consequently, in such a state is not able to work to provide us with the means for existence: in order to compose, his head must be free. And you therefore will easily understand, dear Dmitry, that I have turned to you to help me in my extreme need. My husband has given me so many proofs of his delicacy and disinterestedness that it will be quite just if I for my part try to alleviate his situation; the allowance you appoint me will at least go on the children, and that is a noble aim. I am asking you for this favour without my husband's knowledge, for if he knew of it, despite the straitened circumstances in which he finds himself, he would prevent me doing it. So do not be angry with me dear Dmitry for the immodesty in my request, be assured that only extreme necessity gives me the courage to pester you.[209]

This hardly seems the letter of a woman interested in nothing but her fashionable toilette and her social success; nor of one who would have been seduced by the attractions of a d'Anthès. Touched by this epistle, and, perhaps, softened by his own happiness – on 29 July he married Princess Elizaveta Nazarova in Tula – Dmitry agreed to give her an allowance, at the same time offering his brother-in-law some advice: he should apply for a long leave and move to the country. It was advice Pushkin would have been only too pleased to take, had it been possible.

Though the allowance might have eased for Natalya the problem of coping with the daily household expenses, it could not affect the overall financial position. At the beginning of August Pushkin turned again to Shishkin, borrowing 7,000 roubles on the security of Sobolevsky's table silver, which the latter had left with him before going abroad. Immediately afterwards, in gloomy mood, he drew up a schedule of his most pressing debts, rounding the figures to the nearest hundred roubles. He owed 3,500 to Madame Sichler, who kept a fashion shop on the Bolshaya Morskaya; 500 to his tailor, Conrad Rutsch; 700 to Brügel, another tailor, who furnished the servants' liveries; 400 to Dumé's restaurant; 400 to his wine-merchant; 1,000 to Nicholls and Plincke, whose English shop on the Nevsky was considered the best in St Petersburg; and he had lost 5,000 roubles at cards. Then there were the debts to his friends, the loans from money-lenders, the interest on his mortgages. The total came to 41,300 roubles.

THE FINAL CHAPTER
1836–37

To every day, to every year
I am used to bid farewell with a thought,
Attempting to divine among them
The anniversary of my coming death.

Where, too, will fate send me death?
In battle, travel, on the waves?
Or will the neighbouring valley
Receive my cold dust?

And though to the insentient body
It matters not where it rots,
Nevertheless closer to my loved places
I would wish to rest.

And at the entrance to the grave
Let young life play,
And let indifferent nature
Shine with eternal beauty.

(III, 194–5)

'I HAVE BEEN OBLIGED to leave the Batashev house, whose caretaker is a rascal,' Pushkin wrote to his father in October.[1] In its stead he had, on 1 September, signed a two-year lease at a rent of 4,300 roubles a year for an apartment on the Moika Embankment, near the Konyushenny Bridge. The house – the present number twelve – belonged to Princess Sofya Volkonskaya, the sister of the exiled Decembrist Sergey Volkonsky. The grand apartment of the *piano nobile* was occupied by one of Pushkin's acquaintances, Fedor Lubyanovsky,

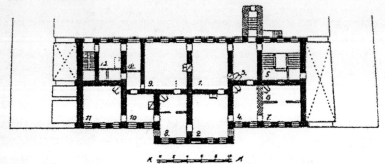

Reconstruction of the plan of the apartment on the Moika Embankment
(from A. A. Platonov, *Poslednyaya kvartira Pushkina v ee proshlom i nastoyashchem*.
Leningrad, 1927)

1. Study
2. Drawing-room
3. Vestibule
4. Dining-room
5. Main staircase
6. Larder

7. Pantry
8. Bedroom
9. Nursery
10,11. Rooms of A.N. and E.N. Goncharova
12,13. Servants' quarters

a senator and privy councillor, the former governor of Penza. Beneath, on the ground floor, was the Pushkins' flat, into which they, together with the children, the Goncharov sisters and the servants moved on 12 September. It consisted of eleven rooms, with a kitchen, laundry and servants' quarters in the basement. There was a stable with six stalls, a barn and hayloft, and a 'dry cellar for wines'.[2]

Entering the house by the front door, one found oneself at the foot of the main staircase; at the head of the first flight of eight stairs was a landing with, on the left, the door to the Pushkins' apartment. This led into a vestibule; immediately opposite was the door of Pushkin's study, which looked out, not upon the Moika, but on the courtyard at the rear of the house. It was a medium-sized room, with bookcases lining most of the far and rear walls, where a double-sided extension formed a bay; in this stood a mahogany divan on castors, upholstered in crimson camlet. The centre of the room was occupied by a very large, plain table usually covered with books and papers. On it stood a brass inkstand ornamented with the figure of a negro leaning on an anchor: the inkwells themselves had the form of cotton bales. It had been a New Year's present from Nashchokin in 1831: 'I am sending you your ancestor with inkwells which open and show that he was a man with second sight,' he had written.[3] By the windows was a 'mahogany mechanical Voltaire armchair with reading-stand upholstered in red morocco', bought, no doubt as a birthday present for Pushkin, from Gambs Frères on 25 May 1835:[4] its mechanical qualities consisted of an adjustable back and sliding foot-rest. In it Pushkin read and wrote, wearing 'an old, cheap dressing-gown, of the kind usually sold by Bokharan hawkers'.[5]

Had one turned left in the vestibule and walked through the far door towards the front of the house, one would have found oneself in the dining-room with, to the left, a pantry. A door in the right-hand wall, close to the windows, led into the drawing-room, longer than the other by reason of a bay. This continued into the next room, Natalya's and Pushkin's bedroom. Beyond this were Aleksandra's and Ekaterina's rooms, a store-room, full of unsold copies of *Pugachev* and the *Contemporary*, and servants' quarters with, beyond them, the service stairs. The nursery was behind the bedroom and beyond Pushkin's study: like the latter it looked out on the courtyard.

For some months d'Anthès had kept to the vow he had made in March. He avoided meeting Natalya in society, and ceased frequenting those houses where he might meet her. 'D'Anthès no longer appears and has only given proof of his existence by sending us a pot of Paris pomade,' Sofya Karamzina wrote to her brother Andrey on 27 May.[6] But self-indulgence, rather than self-discipline was his forte, and he was too fond of society to lead the life of a hermit for long. In the same letter Sofya had told her brother of a projected excursion by omnibus the following day to Pargolovo, a resort to the north of St Petersburg. Besides Sofya herself, the party would consist of her half-sister Ekaterina, who had married Prince Petr Meshchersky in 1828, the Goncharov sisters, Ivan Maltsov, and Prince Nikolay Trubetskoy. However, from Ekaterina we learn of an addition to the party. 'We had obtained permission from the chatelaine of Pargolovo, Princess Butera, to have her elegant villa opened for us, and it was in a beautiful salon, wonderfully cool and balmy with the scent of flowers, that we partook of an excellent picnic dinner we had brought with us. Nikolay Trubetskoy had attended to the costly provision of the wines, and had done this amply and generously. The Crémant and the Sillery flowed like water down the throats of our cavaliers, who all rose from table redder and gayer than when they had sat down, d'Anthès above all, and Maltsov, who rattled on unceasingly without pity for our ears.'[7]

By the end of the first week in June d'Anthès was again a fixture in the Karamzin salon. 'We have visitors every evening, d'Anthès almost daily,' Sofya wrote. '[He is] tormented by two training sessions a day (the grand duke* having discovered that the Chevalier Guards do not know how to sit a horse), but is nevertheless gayer and more amusing than ever, and often finds the means to accompany us on our cavalcades.' His visits became less frequent after the Karamzins removed to Tsarskoe Selo for the summer, and Sofya was therefore pleased to see him at the fête given at Peterhof on 1 July to celebrate the empress's birthday. 'He was coming nonchalantly down the stair when he saw me,' she wrote, 'then he took the rest at a jump and ran towards me, blushing with satisfaction.' Later, after a cold dinner, they went arm in arm to watch the fireworks, when, she wrote, he 'much amused me with his jokes, his gaiety, and even with his outbursts of emotion, which are also very comic (still for the beautiful Natalie)'.[8]

Since the end of March d'Anthès had become an assiduous visitor to the house of Princess Baryatinskaya, whose son Aleksandr, a lieutenant in the Life Guards Cuirassiers, was a close friend. But the attraction of the house lay rather in Aleksandr's pretty sister, the seventeen-year-old Mariya. The Baryatinskys were one of the first, and one of the richest families in St Petersburg, with a high idea of their own consequence. So high, indeed, that the princess had made it clear to one of society's most eligible young men and the empress's favourite, Prince Aleksandr Trubetskoy, that he would not be welcome as a suitor for her daughter's hand: his father had, she thought, made a *mésalliance* in marrying the daughter of the Vilna police chief. But she appeared to welcome d'Anthès's frequent visits, and Mariya, as is obvious from the entries in her diary, was much taken with him.

On 3 July the Chevalier Guards moved to Krasnoe Selo for the summer manoeuvres, but this did not interrupt d'Anthès's intercourse with the Baryatinskys, who were spending the summer at Pavlino, their estate on the Peterhof road. During the following weeks there was a continuous succession of balls, fêtes champêtres and parties at the vari-

---

* Michael Pavlovich, commandant of the corps of guards regiments.

ous imperial residences of the region: Peterhof, Strelna, Ropsha, Krasnoe Selo and Znamenskoe. 'We danced. I enjoyed myself. Waltz with d'Anthès, but not the mazurka,' Mariya noted of one ball; and of another at Ropsha wrote that d'Anthès engaged her for the mazurka, another Chevalier Guards officer, Grigory Skaryatin, for the waltz, and Aleksandr Trubetskoy for the first quadrille. In her diary she records d'Anthès's compliments and his flirtatious raillery, teasing her about the fate of her bouquet, which, he avers, will be quarrelled over by her numerous Chevalier Guards admirers.[9]

On 31 July a fête with fireworks to mark the end of the manoeuvres had been arranged at Krasnoe Selo. This was to be Natalya's first social engagement since her lying-in. Accompanied by her sisters and the wives of three Chevalier Guards officers, she arrived at Pavlovskaya, where the regiment was encamped, at four in the afternoon. They were given 'a splendid dinner' in a tent especially prepared for them, but otherwise the evening was not a success. Rain brought about the cancellation of the fireworks and forced them to take refuge in the quarters of Captain Petrovo-Solovovo, whose wife was one of the party. And although the empress, on learning of their arrival, immediately invited them to the ball in her tent, since, as Ekaterina wrote to her brother, 'we were all in high-necked dresses and outdoor shoes, and in addition some of us were in mourning, no one went and we spent the whole evening at the windows of the hut, listening to the brass band of the Chevalier Guards'.[10] At the dinner d'Anthès had seen Natalya for the first time since March. No wonder that Mariya Baryatinskaya, who was one of those in the empress's tent, should have written in her diary: 'I did not enjoy myself very much at the ball.' But she soon recovered, enjoying herself very much when d'Anthès and two other officers dined at Pavlino two days later, and even more the following evening when Princess Baryatinsky gave a ball to bid farewell to the regiment.[11]

From Krasnoe Selo the Chevalier Guards moved to Novaya Derevnya on the north, or Vyborg bank of the Neva. With the regiment bivouacked there and the empress in residence at the Elagin Palace, the capital's social centre of gravity moved to the islands, much to the relief of the Goncharov sisters. 'Our Islands are still very little animated because of the manoeuvres,' Ekaterina had written in July. 'They end on the fourth and then there will be balls at the waters and dance evenings, but now we only have *conversazioni*, at which one can die of boredom. Yesterday there was one such at Countess Laval's, where we almost gave up our souls to God from boredom. Today we were supposed to be going to the Sukhozanets, where it would have been just the same, but since we are sensible people we decided that one should not overindulge in such pleasures.'[12]

The move gave d'Anthès the opportunity to recommence his pursuit of Natalya. In addition to seeking her out in society he began to send her 'quite often books and theatre tickets accompanied by short notes, [. . .] among which were some whose expression might have aroused his [Pushkin's] susceptibility as a husband'.[13] Pushkin later dismissed them contemptuously as 'twaddle'.[14] Mariya Baryatinskaya could not but notice that she had been supplanted, and reacted with injured pride. 'The Rauchs invited A. Trubetskoy and d'Anthès to sit at our table. I said hardly a word to them,' she wrote of a ball at Pavlino in the middle of August. And, when on 5 September a ceremonial parade of the Chevalier Guards was followed by a ball and dinner at the Elagin Palace at which the Pushkins were present, she refused to follow the example of the empress and, like others, don a guardsman's uniform jacket. 'There is no one to whom I would wish to show this compliment,' she remarked. D'Anthès, seeing the richest prize on the matrimonial market slipping away from him, endeavoured to remedy matters by calling at the Baryatinskys' town house and charming Mariya's mother. 'He confessed that he was a devoted admirer of beauty, that there was no mother who was as beautiful as she, and no daughter more charming than I etc. He sent his most respectful regards to me,' Mariya noted drily.[15]

But he immediately turned back to Natalya. He was becoming daily more obsessed with her, and daily more outrageous in his behaviour towards her. As a sop to the social proprieties, he had begun in public to court her sister, Ekaterina. She was only too eager to take his attentions at their face value, since for some time she had been far less than indifferent to him. But this charade deceived neither society nor Pushkin. Together with his ever more pressing financial worries, his difficulties with the censorship, and the ill-success of the *Contemporary*, the realization that d'Anthès had renewed his addresses to Natalya produced in him that state of heightened irritability he had known earlier in the year; this time, however, it was combined with an unconcealed hostility towards the young Frenchman. The situation was perhaps most difficult for Natalya, who had to tread a narrow path between two unbalanced – at least in respect of their relationship to her and to one another – personalities. With hindsight it is easy to say – as many of Natalya's contemporaries later did – that she should have rejected d'Anthès out of hand. But she had rejected him once, only to find that he was now behaving as though that event had never taken place. Perhaps she should have snubbed him annihilatingly in public. But how would this have been interpreted in society, and how would d'Anthès have reacted? The resulting scandal could have ruined her reputation. In any case, she was still fond of him, he still amused her. Nor did she want to spoil her sister's chances of happiness. Yet, on the other hand, the more complaisant she showed herself towards d'Anthès, the more dangerous Pushkin's sullen irritation became. In the end she did nothing, hoping, as many would in her predicament, that sense and good manners would prevail, and that the situation would eventually resolve itself peacefully.

On 17 September Sofya Karamzina celebrated her name-day. That afternoon Pushkin with his wife and sisters-in-law drove out to Tsarskoe Selo, calling at the English shop on the Nevsky to buy an album for twenty-five roubles as a present. Besides Pushkin, Natalya and her sisters – 'all three dazzling in elegance, in beauty and with unbelievable waists' – the dinner guests included d'Anthès, two of the Rosset brothers, Arkady and Aleksandr, the Vyazemsky teenagers, Pavel and Nadezhda, and Zhukovsky. Later in the evening other friends and neighbours arrived, to make, as Sofya told her brother, 'a proper ball, and a very gay one too, to judge by everyone's countenance, with the exception of that of Aleksandr Pushkin, always melancholy, abstracted and worried'. 'His depression makes me depressed,' she continued. 'His wandering, wild, distrait gaze rests only, with disquieting attention, on his wife and on d'Anthès, who continues exactly the same farce as before: inseparable from Catherine Goncharova and from afar making eyes at Natalie, with whom, however, he finished by dancing the mazurka, and it was pitiful to see Pushkin's face opposite, framed in the door, silent, pale and menacing. My God, how stupid it is!' When Countess Stroganova arrived, Sofya, knowing that Pushkin much admired her (she was the former Natalya Kochubey, one of his Lycée loves), asked him to entertain her. Blushing, he agreed, only to stop short and return ill-humouredly. 'Well?' asked Sofya. 'No, I won't go, that count's sitting there already.' 'What count?' 'D'Anthès, Heeckeren or whatever.'[16]

Natalya Stroganova

The autumn season in St Petersburg had now begun. The previous week the Chevalier Guards had moved to their barracks in the city, between Voskresenskaya and Zakharevskaya Streets; Vera Vyazemskaya, after a prolonged stay on Norderney, returned to her apartment on Mokhovaya Street towards the end of the month; and on 14 October, when the first snow fell, the Karamzins left Tsarskoe Selo for St Petersburg. 'Since we have been here the weather has been terrible,' Sofya told her brother, 'snow, rain and mud, so that one can't go out; it has given me a headache, a cold in my head and on my chest, and consequently I'm in a temper, whereas in Tsarskoe I was not ill once.' Their friends had taken the first opportunity to call at their apartment on Mikhailovskaya Square. 'We have taken up our town way of life again,' she wrote, 'our evenings, at which Natalie Pushkina and d'Anthès, Catherine Goncharova, with Alexander [Rosset] by her side, Alexandrine [Goncharova], with Arkady [Rosset] by hers, have from the first day taken up their usual places.'[17]

Sofya is describing the evening of the fourteenth: though she did not know it, that seating plan was not to be repeated. Between then and the evening of the sixteenth d'Anthès made another determined assault on Natalya's virtue, sending her a letter, concocted with Heeckeren's assistance, in which he pleaded with her to leave Pushkin and go away with him. She rejected the proposal out of hand, making it clear in addition that he would no longer be a welcome visitor to their apartment. Balked here, d'Anthès turned again to Mariya Baryatinskaya, persuading Captain Petrovo-Solovovo's wife to ascertain indirectly whether a formal proposal would be acceptable. 'He would be in despair, if he were to be refused,' she told Mariya's cousin. But by now Mariya had taken her admirer's measure. 'I would be the unhappiest creature if I had to marry him. He amuses me, that is all,' she wrote. 'And maman learnt from Trubetskoy that Mrs Pushkina rejected him. Perhaps that is why he wants to get married. *Out of spite!* . . . I will know how to thank him, if he dares suggest it to me.'[18]

At the end of September Pushkin and Natalya had visited the Academy of Arts for the annual exhibition of works by the graduating class of students. He was much taken by two statues depicting peasant youths. 'Thank God, at last we have folk sculpture too in Russia,' he exclaimed, and, inspired by the statue of a knucklebone-player, composed an impromptu quatrain in elegiac couplets, which he gave to the sculptor, Nikolay Pimenov. The twenty-year-old Ivan Aivazovsky, winner of the gold medal for painting, later famous for his seascapes, was introduced to him. 'I took a good look at him and even remember what the charming Natalya Nikolaevna was wearing. The poet's beautiful wife had on a black velvet dress with a corsage of plaited black braid and real lace, a large, pale-yellow straw hat with a large ostrich feather, and long white gloves.'[19]

On 3 October the Moscow *Telescope* published anonymously a Russian translation of the first of Chaadaev's *Philosophical Letters*, originally written in French. A few days later Pushkin received from the author an offprint of the article. It was not a new piece of work: the letters had been written between 1828 and 1830. Pushkin had read them in manuscript when in Moscow in 1830–31; had indeed taken two with him to Tsarskoe Selo, and had unsuccessfully attempted to get them published. In this first letter Chaadaev, who saw religion as the motive force of history, and Roman Catholicism as the proper form of religion, argued that Russia had, unlike the nations of Western Europe, no history, no culture and no tradition because it had received its Christianity from Byzantium, and had sided with the latter in the church schism of 1054. In a letter to Metternich the Austrian ambassador, Count Ficquelmont, wrote that the article 'fell like a bomb amidst Russian vanity and those principles of religious and political pre-eminence to which the capital is much inclined';[20] while Herzen later remarked that it 'shook the whole of intellectual Russia'.[21] 'Daily, from morning to noisy evening (which Chaadaev, Orlov, Sverbeev, Pavlov and others spend with me in vehement and thundering argument) I am deafened by my own debates and those communicated from other salons about this philippic,' Turgenev told Vyazemsky, who, like Baratynsky, was preparing a refutation of Chaadaev's views.[22] The prevailing reaction was indignation. 'He says a lot of fine things about Russia,' Sofya Karamzína wrote to her brother, '"an unhappy country with neither past, present nor future", a country in which there is not a single thinking person, a country without a history, in which only two giants have arisen, Peter I, who threw over it the mantle of civilization in passing, and Alexander, who crossed Europe as a conqueror, leading a mass of men whose apparent virtue, courage, was no more than cowardly docility, men who were only "human by their face, but without any physiognomy"! What do you think of all these horrors? Not bad for a Russian!'[23]

On 19 October Pushkin composed a letter to Chaadaev. He had been charmed to reread the article, though astonished to see it translated and printed. 'As for the ideas,' he continued, 'I am far from being entirely of your opinion.' Chaadaev's argument throughout is almost wholly abstract; Pushkin does not attempt to refute it on the same plane, but, rather, to question it by adducing historical fact. The church schism might have cut Russia off from the rest of Europe, he admitted, but she too had a mission: acting as a bulwark between Europe and the Mongol invasion she had saved Christian civilization. 'Each nation goes through a period of stormy emotion, passionate unrest, thoughtless and pointless action,' Chaadaev had written. Only of Russia was this not true. 'To begin with – savage barbarism, then rude ignorance, then pitiless and humiliating foreign dominion, whose spirit was later inherited by our national authority, – such is the mournful history of our youth.'[24] 'As to our historical nullity, I decidedly cannot be of your opinion,' Pushkin riposted. 'Are not the wars of Oleg and Svyatoslav, and even the apanage wars, that life of adventurous effervescence and ruthless and pointless activity which characterizes the youth of all nations?' Nor did he agree with Chaadaev's observations on the present state of Russia. 'Do you not find (with your hand on your heart) something impressive in Russia's present situation, something which will strike the future historian? Can you believe that he will place us outside Europe? Although I am personally heartily attached to the Emperor, I am far from admiring everything I see around me; as a man of letters I am embittered; as a man of prejudices, I am offended – but I swear to you on my honour, that not for anything in the world would I wish to change my fatherland, nor to have any other history than that of our ancestors, such as God has given to us.' But, he concluded, much in Chaadaev's letter was profoundly true. 'It must be admitted that our social existence is a sad thing. That this absence of public opinion, this indifference for all that is duty, justice and truth, this cynical contempt for the thought and dignity of man, are truly distressing. You have done well to say it out loud. But I fear that your historical opinions might do you harm . . .'[25]

Three days later Klementy Rosset, Aleksandra's brother and an officer of the General Staff, sent Pushkin a note. 'Immediately on returning home I learnt of the following circumstance, which I hasten to communicate to you as an addendum to our conversation. The Emperor has read Chaadaev's article and found it absurd and extravagant, saying that he was sure "that Moscow did not share the insane opinions of the Author", and has instructed the governor-general Prince Golitsyn to inquire daily as to the health of Chaadaev's wits and to put him under governmental surveillance, to dismiss the censor and ban the journal. I am informing you of this so that you can reread the letter you have written to Chaadaev, or better postpone sending it by post.'[26] Pushkin took Rosset's advice and laid the letter aside, jotting on the final page: 'A raven does not peck out a raven's eye – a Scottish proverb, quoted by Walter Scott in *Woodstock*.'*[27]

Rosset was well-informed: his note accurately conveys the substance of the dispatch, approved by the emperor, which Benckendorff sent to the military governor-general of Moscow on 22 October. In addition all Chaadaev's papers were confiscated, while Nadezhdin, the editor and publisher of the *Telescope*, was sent to St Petersburg under police escort – he was later exiled to Ust-Sysolsk (now Syktyvkar) in the extreme north-east of Vologda province. Chaadaev, officially deemed insane, and virtually under house arrest, fell into deep depression. 'They say that Chaadaev has been strongly shaken by the misfortune which has befallen him,' Turgenev wrote to Vyazemsky on 3 November. 'He has given up his horses, sits at home, has suddenly grown terribly thin, and with some kind of blotches on his face.' And, four days later, added: 'He never leaves the house. I'm afraid that he might really become mad.'[28] Pushkin, anxious about his friend, slipped an enquiry about him into

---

* Pushkin's memory was slightly at fault. The remark occurs in the preface to *Woodstock*, and runs: 'Hawks, we say in Scotland, ought not to pick out hawks' eyes, or tire upon each other's quarry.'

a letter to Davydov. 'You ask about Chaadaev?' the latter replied. 'I cannot tell you anything about him at first hand; I never used to call on him, and do not call on him now. I always considered him well-read and without any doubt an extremely clever charlatan in a constant paroxysm of self-esteem, – but with as much spirit and character as a blonde coquette, in which I was not at all mistaken. Stroganov [the chairman of the Moscow censorship committee] related to me the whole of his conversation with him; everything from beginning to end! How he, seeing calamity unavoidable, confessed to him that he had written this pasquil on the Russian nation immediately after returning from foreign parts, at a time of insanity, during attacks of which he had made attempts on his own life; how he had endeavoured to lump all the blame on the journalist and the censor – on the first because he had charmed him (Nadezhdin charmed!) and enticed from him permission to publish this pasquil, – and on the other because he had let it through.'[29]

October the nineteenth, the day on which he had written to Chaadaev, was a significant date in Pushkin's calendar: it was the day on which the Lycée had been opened in 1811. On that day the members of the first intake were accustomed to hold an annual reunion, usually in Mikhail Yakovlev's St Petersburg apartment. Exile had prevented Pushkin's presence in the first years after leaving school, but he had been one of the gathering in 1828, in 1832 and again in 1834. And, if unable to take part in the celebration, he had at times celebrated the event with a poem: in 1825, when at Mikhailovskoe, he had written the impressive '19 October' –

> The wood sheds its crimson dress,
> The frost silvers the faded field,
> Day peeps out as though against its will
> And hides behind the rim of the surrounding hills.
> Blaze, hearth, in my eremitic cell;
> And you, wine, friend of autumnal cold,
> Spill over my breast the comfort of inebriation,
> The momentary oblivion of bitter pain.
>
> (II, 424)

and for the reunion of 1831, which he had failed to attend, though in St Petersburg at the time, he composed 'The more often the Lycée celebrates . . .'[30]

The coming celebration was particularly significant, in that it was the twenty-fifth anniversary of the Lycée's foundation. Egor Engelhardt, the school's former director, who kept up a very friendly relationship with many of his former pupils (though not with Pushkin: 'I never see Pushkin, even in the street he avoids meeting me,' he complained[31]), and who appears to have attended some of the reunions, put forward the suggestion that on this occasion there should be a joint celebration by the first three intakes. Yakovlev, writing to inform Modest Korff of the suggestion, said that he had discussed it with others of their vintage and that 'it had been decisively resolved that: *according to previous custom the first year to graduate should celebrate alone.* Let Egor Antonovich, as the Lycée's former director, unite under his banners the second, third and later years, and give honour and praise to the Lycée's existence, but let him leave us oldsters in peace.' Korff disagreed: a joint reunion, he was sure, would be 'incomparably *more jolly*'; and, since there would be many more people, for the same subscription Yakovlev would be able to 'make the celebration more poetic by, for example, hiring musicians to play during dinner'. But he would be happy for the matter to be put to a vote.[32] The result was an unambiguous endorsement of Yakovlev's view. Pushkin, sending his and four other votes all in favour of exclusion, wrote: 'There is no point in changing the ancient customs of the Lycée for the twenty-fifth jubilee. This would be a bad omen. It has been said that even the last Lycéen will celebrate 19 October *alone*. It is not a bad idea to reiterate that.'*[33]

Myasoedov, once the dolt of the class, now a rich landowner with an estate in Tula province, had come up to St Petersburg beforehand; on the fifteenth he gave a sumptuous dinner for his friends. Four days later the reunion itself took place in Yakovlev's apartment, 'on the Ekaterininsky Canal in the former house of the Bible Society', beginning at half past four, and finishing at half past nine.[34] Eleven of the original lycéens were present: Yudin, Myasoedov, Grevenits, Yakovlev, Martynov, Pushkin, Illichevsky, Komovsky, Steven and Danzas. Minutes were kept of each meeting, and when composed by Pushkin, could fall embarrassingly into schoolboy facetiousness. On this occasion he wrote:

* A reference to '19 October': 'Which of us in old age the day of the Lycée/Will have to celebrate alone?' The answer would be Prince Aleksandr Gorchakov, who, outliving all his classmates, died in 1883.

The above-mentioned Gentlemen of the Lycée gathered in Yakovlev's house and feasted in the following manner:

1) They dined well and loudly
2) They drank three healths (*toasts* as they are called abroad)
   a) to the twenty-fifth anniversary of the Lycée
   b) to the prosperity of the Lycée
   c) to the health of those absent
3) They read letters once written by the absent brother Küchelbecker to one of the comrades
4) They read ancient minutes, songs, and other papers in the Lycée Archive kept by elder Yakovlev –
5) They remembered old times at the Lycée.

After some school songs, Pushkin stood up to read his poem on the twenty-fifth anniversary of the Lycée, but 'had only just begun to recite the first verse, when tears began to stream from his eyes. He could not continue reading.'[35]

> There was a time: our young celebration
> Was brilliant, noisy, and wore a crown of roses,
> And the clink of glasses was mingled with songs,
> And we sat crowded closely together.
> Then, carefree ignoramuses in our souls,
> We all lived more lightly and more boldly,
> We all drank the health of hope
> And of youth and all its ventures.
>
> Now is not the same: our riotous celebration
> With passing years, like us, has lost its devil,
> Become meek, grown quiet and staid,
> The clink of toasting goblets is muffled;
> Between us conversation does not flow so playfully.
> We sit further apart and more sadly,
> And laughter sounds less frequently amid the songs,
> And more often do we sigh and fall silent.[36]

Three days before the Lycée reunion, on Friday 16 October, Natalya, unaccompanied by Pushkin, had spent the evening at Vera Vyazem skaya's salon. Among the other visitors was d'Anthès. The encounter was embarrassing for both, but it was d'Anthès who suffered the more. He was on duty the following day, when he wrote to Heeckeren from Captain Bethancourt's quarters in the Chevalier Guards barracks:

> Dear friend, I wanted to speak to you this morning, but had so little time it wasn't possible. Yesterday I happened to spend the whole evening alone with the Lady in question, but when I say alone, I was the only man at Princess Vyazemskaya's for almost an hour. You can imagine my state, I finally pulled myself together and played my part quite well and was even quite merry. In short I held out well until 11, but then my energy gave out and I was overcome by such weakness that I only just managed to leave the room, and once on the street began to weep like a great fool, which besides relieved me greatly, as I was suffocating; then, when I got back to my room, it turned out I had a raging fever, didn't sleep a wink during the night and nearly went mad with mental suffering.

That evening Natalya would be, he knew, at the rout given by the Bavarian ambassador, Count Maximilian Lerchenfeld-Köfering. He implored Heeckeren to abandon the card-room and find an opportunity to have a private conversation with her.

> I think you ought to go up to her openly and say to her, so that her sister can't hear, that you absolutely must talk to her seriously. Then ask her whether she happened to be at the Vyazemskys yesterday; when she answers yes, you say that you thought so and that she can do you a great favour; you tell her what happened when I came home yesterday as though you had seen it yourself, that my servant became frightened and woke you at two in the morning, that you questioned me a lot, but could get nothing out of me,* and that you're convinced that I had a quarrel with her husband, and that you're turning to her to avoid a calamity (her husband wasn't there). This will

---

* In the margin here d'Anthès added: 'But you didn't need my words, you yourself had guessed that I'd lost my head because of her, and observing the change in my behaviour and character had convinced you of it, and therefore it was impossible that her husband hadn't noticed it too.'

only prove that I haven't told you anything about the evening, and that is absolutely necessary, for it must seem as if with regard to her I am not being open with you and that you are only asking her as a father concerned about his son: it wouldn't be bad if you could hint in the conversation that you think relations are much more intimate than they are, for in vindicating yourself you will find the opportunity to give her to understand that they should at least be such judging by her behaviour to me [...] On no account must she suspect that she is being cozened, she must see in your action only a very natural feeling of anxiety about my health and my future, and you must ask her urgently to keep it a secret from all, especially me. It would be better if you didn't immediately ask her to receive me, you could do that the next time, and be careful not to use expressions which were in that letter.*[37]

This is an extraordinary letter to write about a woman with whom one is ostensibly in love. To take the least heinous offence first, it is hardly the act of a gentleman to ask one's father (if only by adoption) to act as pander to further one's attempt at adultery. And the cynical proposal to manipulate Natalya's emotions by what is not far short of blackmail is extremely distasteful. To the present-day forensic psychologist, however, the letter would be of extreme interest. Taken together with d'Anthès's behaviour in the preceding months and during the following weeks, it would be clear evidence that this is a classic case of the 'stalker' syndrome; in particular of that sub-group in which the individual refuses to admit, despite all evidence to the contrary, that a relationship is over. D'Anthès cannot have concealed his feelings as successfully as he thought, for it must have been after this evening that Vera Vyazemskaya forbade him the house.

His 'raging fever' proved not to be emotional, but physical: he went down with a pulmonary infection – he had a constitutionally weak chest – and was reported as sick in the regimental orders from 19 to 27 October. Nevertheless Heeckeren carried out the commission, seeking

* A reference to the letter, written with Heeckeren's help, and sent to Natalya between the fourteenth and the sixteenth of the month, in which d'Anthès implored her to leave Pushkin.

out Natalya at the Lerchenfelds, and endeavouring to seduce her on d'Anthès's behalf – without success. 'Like an obscene old woman you would go and spy on my wife from every corner to speak to her of your son,' Pushkin later wrote in an – unsent – letter to the ambassador, 'and when, ill with the pox, he was confined to his home by treatments, you would say, vile that you are, that he was dying of love for her; you would mumble to her: give me back my son.'[38]

During the summer of 1831 in Tsarskoe Selo Natalya had met her second cousin, Idaliya Poletika, for the first time, and the two had immediately become close friends, both having, according to Aleksandra Smirnova-Rosset's caustic comment, nothing in their heads besides 'finery and gossip'.*[39] Idaliya was now in her late twenties; her husband, Aleksandr Mikhailovich, was an officer in the Chevalier Guards. He had recently – on 15 October – been promoted colonel, but previously had commanded the fifth squadron of the regiment, in which d'Anthès was a lieutenant. Idaliya thus knew d'Anthès, and was indeed extremely attached to him. She had also been very friendly towards Pushkin: in October 1833, at the close of a letter to Natalya from Boldino, he had written: 'Tell Poletika that I will come in person for her kiss, as they say they won't accept them in the mail.'[40] However, at some point her affection had turned to inveterate and long-lasting hatred. As late as 1888, when she was living in Odessa, she announced her intention of going to spit on a newly erected statue of Pushkin. One explanation given for this sudden swing from amity to hate is that Pushkin 'ignored

---

* Idaliya was the natural daughter of Count Grigory Stroganov and the Portuguese Countess Juliana d'Eca (née Oyenhausen), who had left her husband for Stroganov, then Russian ambassador to Spain and Portugal. They married in 1826, after the death of Stroganov's first wife. While abroad he had had the reputation of an irresistible ladykiller, renowned for the number of his conquests; so much so indeed that in Byron's *Don Juan* Donna Julia, the hero's first lover, quotes her rejection of his advances as a striking testimony to her virtue:

> Did not the Italian *Musico* Cazzani
> Sing at my heart six months at least in vain?
> Did not his countryman, Count Corniani,
> Call me the only virtuous wife in Spain?
> Were there not also Russians, English, many?
> The Count Strongstroganoff I put in pain,
> And Lord Mount Coffeehouse, the Irish peer,
> Who killed himself for love (with wine) last year.
>
> (I, cxlix)

the unprepossessing Idaliya Grigorevna's effusions of love and once, while riding in a carriage with her, offended her in some way'.[41] Idaliya was not 'unprepossessing' – she was on the contrary remarkably attractive, as her portraits show – but she was also not famous for her virtue. Indeed, her reputation was such that some months earlier the regiment's commander, Major-General Grünewaldt, had felt himself licensed to make a crude joke at her expense. This so incensed one of her admirers, Lieutenant Petr Savelev, that he had leapt upon his superior officer and endeavoured to strangle him with a pistol lanyard. He had been reduced to the ranks and transferred to a dragoon regiment stationed in the Caucasus.* Given her promiscuity, it is not difficult to conceive that she might have offered herself to Pushkin: rejection, or inadequacy in performance, could easily have been responsible for the virulent dislike which replaced the earlier affection. And when the opportunity arose to do him a bad turn, while simultaneously obliging d'Anthès, she grasped it with both hands.

On 2 November she invited Natalya to her apartment in the officers' quarters on Zakharevskaya Street. Natalya accepted the invitation, but later that day turned up at the Vyazemskys, breathless and full of indignation. When she arrived at the Poletikas' apartment, she recounted, she had been shown into the drawing-room to find there not Idaliya, who had gone out, but d'Anthès. 'He had taken out a pistol and threatened to shoot himself, if she did not give herself to him,' Princess Vera later related. '[She] did not know how to escape his importunities; she wrung her hands and spoke as loud as she could.'[42] Luckily, Idaliya's four-year-old daughter, Elizaveta, wandered into the room; and, using her as a shield, Natalya was able to escape. Whatever her earlier feelings for d'Anthès had been, this remorseless persecution by father and son had by now expunged any trace of love. But as yet she had not been able to bring herself to tell Pushkin of what she had undergone, for fear of what the consequences might be. Two days later, however, she had no choice.

---

* On 6 May, in a letter to Natalya from Moscow, Pushkin wrote: 'What Moscow says about St Petersburg, that's something funny. For example: you have a certain *Savelev*, a Chevalier guardsman, a splendid young man, in love with Idaliya Poletika, for whose sake he gave Grüenewaldt a slap in the face. Savelev will be shot in a couple of days. Imagine how miserable Idaliya is!' (To N.N. Pushkina, 6 May 1836; XVI, 112.)

The anonymous letter

At about nine in the morning on Wednesday 4 November the newly instituted town postal service delivered an envelope to the apartment on the Moika Embankment. Posted the previous day, it contained an anonymous letter, which ran (the original is in French):

The Grand Crosses, Commanders and Chevaliers of the Most Serene Order of *Cuckolds*, gathered in grand chapter under the presidency of the venerable Grand Master of the Order, His Excellency D.L. Naryshkin, *have unanimously nominated Mr Aleksandr Pushkin coadjutor to the Grand Master of the Order of Cuckolds and historiographer of the Order.*

Permanent Secretary: Count I. Borch[43]

Dmitry Naryshkin, who occupied the court position of Chief Master of the Hunt, was the best known, and probably the most complaisant cuckold of the age. He was married to Princess Mariya Svyatopolk-Chetvertinskaya – 'her beauty was so perfect, that it seemed unnatural, impossible'[44] – who had been for many years the mistress of Alexander I, bearing him three children. The mention of Iosif Borch, a translator at the Foreign Office, was a hit closer to home. His wife, Lyubov, known usually as Emma, was a distant cousin of Natalya – her mother was a Goncharov. Both had a louche reputation. Pushkin, encountering their carriage, remarked to a friend: 'There go two exemplary couples. The wife, you know, sleeps with the coachman, and the husband with the postilion.'*[45]

That same morning identical copies of the letter were delivered to Princess Vyazemskaya, Mikhail Wielhorski, Klementy Rosset, the Karamzins, Elise Khitrovo, and Aleksandra Vasilchikova, Sollogub's aunt – this last obviously intended for Sollogub himself, who was staying with her. These were all in a double cover, with Pushkin's name on the inner, sealed envelope. The Vyazemskys, Wielhorski, Rosset and the Karamzins, no doubt suspecting, as Princess Vera remarked, that this contained 'something insulting to Pushkin',[46] opened it. Vyazemsky's first thought was to throw the paper in the fire, but he changed his mind, resolving, with his wife, to keep it a secret. In February 1837 he enclosed a copy in a long letter to Grand Duke Michael Pavlovich, in which he set out the events of Pushkin's last months. Wielhorski eventually sent his letter to Benckendorff. The Rossets, on the advice of their flatmate Nikolay Scalon, a lieutenant on the General Staff, for the moment did nothing and kept silent. So did the Karamzins, who appear to have destroyed their copy. Sollogub, thinking that the sealed envelope might contain something about his earlier brush with Pushkin, took it round, unopened, to the latter's flat. Pushkin looked at the enclosure. 'I knew it!' he said. 'Give me your word of honour not to say anything to anyone. It is a vile slander against my wife. Though it's like getting shit on one's hands. It's unpleasant, but one washes one's hands, and

* Andrey Karamzin met Emma – 'the pretty Borch', he calls her – in Baden-Baden in July 1837 and was very taken with her, engaging her for the mazurka and riding out with her. He found Borch himself less attractive. 'The sour face of her ugly runt of a husband depressed the whole of the company,' he wrote (*Starina i novizna*, 17 (1914), 310, 320).

that's an end to it.'[47] He read Sollogub the letter he had written to Elise Khitrovo, who had also sent him the envelope she had received without opening it.*

After Sollogub's departure Pushkin saw Natalya. She confessed to him the whole history of her relationship with d'Anthès: the initial flirtation; his growing infatuation; her attempt, at Shrove-tide, to sever the connection; his renewed pursuit of her in the autumn, turning eventually into persecution; his letter, begging her to abandon Pushkin; Heeckeren's poisoned whispers; the threats, the attempts at blackmail; and, finally, the encounter at Idaliya Poletika's two days earlier. She showed him, too, some of the notes he had sent her during the course of the relationship. However, he never doubted for a moment Natalya's innocence; nor, in light of the events of the preceding weeks, can we. D'Anthès's behaviour is not that of a successful lover whose liaison has come to an end, but that of a rejected, desperate, and psychologically unbalanced suitor. Pushkin's reaction was immediate: he sent d'Anthès a cartel, challenging him to a duel.

The authorship of the anonymous letter has not been incontrovertibly established.[48] Pushkin believed that it came from Heeckeren and said as much in an – unsent – letter to Benckendorff. Pushkin's friends in general shared this belief. In a memoir written in 1842 Nikolay Smirnov, Aleksandra Rosset's husband, noted: 'Only one thing is beyond doubt, that is, that Heeckeren was their author. What followed showed that the Sovereign did not doubt this, and it is said that the police had indisputable proof of it.'[49] This 'indisputable proof' has never been discovered in the files of the Third Department, though in the 1850s Pavel Miller, Benckendorff's private secretary from 1833 to 1844, in a short, not wholly accurate note on Pushkin's death, commented: 'D'Anthès resolved to take his revenge on him [Pushkin] by dis-

---

* Pushkin's letter to Khitrovo has not survived; from her reply she appears to have got hold of the wrong end of the stick: 'No, my dear friend, for me it is completely scandalous – I assure you it has reduced me completely to tears – I believed I had done enough good in the world not to be at all involved in such horrible calumnies! – On my knees I beg you not to speak of this stupid affair to anyone at all – I am astonished to have such a malicious enemy – as to your wife, dear Pushkin, she is an angel and she has only been attacked in order to make use of my voice and wound me to the heart!' (*Prometey*, X, 257.)

honouring her [Natalya]. A vile means, worthy of a blow – Baron Heeckeren with that aim wrote several anonymous letters, which he sent to two or three of Pushkin's acquaintances. – The paper, format, handwriting and ink of these letters were completely identical.'*[50] But here again Heeckeren's authorship is only asserted, not proved.

Heeckeren himself violently protested against the accusations. 'There is another grievance on the subject of which it is doubtless thought that I would not stoop to justify myself, and so it has not been positively articulated, however my name has been linked to the scandal of the anonymous letters!' he wrote to Nesselrode the following March. 'And in whose interest could this weapon of the most cowardly assassin, of the poisoner be employed? Was it in that of my son, of Mr Pushkin, of his wife? I blush merely from being able to bring myself to ask this question.'[51] The point he is here – somewhat obscurely – making is an important one. If he were the author of the letters, what could his aim possibly be? He could not have wanted to become involved in a scandal, and, as the events of the next few weeks were to show, was willing to go to almost any lengths to prevent a duel. Yet these were the most likely results which the letters would produce. And to see them, as many have done, as an integral part of some well-laid, Machiavellian plot conceived by Heeckeren is plainly absurd.† Their obvious aim is to cast a slur on Natalya's reputation, and to make a mock of Pushkin. Heeckeren could, one supposes, have wanted to do this to take revenge on Natalya for her rejection of d'Anthès, thinking that while the letters might enrage Pushkin, they would not provoke him to a duel. Indeed later those who knew only of the letters were surprised at the outcome. 'Khomyakov justly considers that Pushkin was tired of life, and that he used the first excuse to rid himself of it, since, according to him, a lampoon is not an offence for which one fights,' Vladimir Mukhanov

* Miller's remarks are based on a comparison between the two copies of the letter in the Third Department's possession. One was that sent to Wielhorski; the provenance of the second is unknown.

† Vyazemsky's belief that 'diabolical traps, diabolical snares were set for Pushkin and his wife', and that d'Anthès was urged on 'by the infernal machinations of his father' (*RA*, 1879, II, 253; 1900, I, 392) seems as implausible as Anna Akhmatova's more recent contention that Heeckeren, wishing to separate d'Anthès and Natalya, was convinced that Pushkin 'on receiving such a letter, would immediately take his wife away from St Petersburg, send her to her mother in the country (as in 1834) – or anywhere and everything would end peaceably' (Akhmatova, 127)

noted in his diary in February.[52] Pushkin himself seems at first to have been of the same opinion: 'I cannot be insulted by an anonymous letter,' he told Sollogub. 'If someone spits on my coat from behind, it is then my valet's business to clean the coat, not mine.'[53] But this was before he had heard Natalya's confession: that was the cause of the challenge, not the anonymous letters. Heeckeren was dishonest, duplicitous and malevolent, but he was also far from stupid. Had he been the author, he would undoubtedly have realized that the letters would precipitate the discovery of all that had taken place between d'Anthès and Natalya, tipping the balance and making a duel almost inevitable. Since the author of the letters did not make this deduction, or, having made it, ignored it, he – or she – cannot have been Heeckeren. Aleksandr Karamzin saw events more clearly than the majority of Pushkin's friends – and Pushkin himself – when he wrote to his brother in March: 'If it is Heeckeren who is the author of these letters – that would be an atrocious and incomprehensible absurdity on his part.'[54] Heeckeren was, too, the representative of the Dutch king in St Petersburg: were he to be discovered to be circulating anonymous letters slandering Russia's foremost poet and his wife, a favourite of the emperor and empress, his diplomatic career would be at an end. That, surely, would be too great a sacrifice to make even to soothe the pique of an adopted son.

Pushkin was, apparently, not the only person to receive a letter of this kind. Aleksandr Trubetskoy, in his – not wholly trustworthy – recollections of Pushkin and d'Anthès, recorded in 1887, remarks: 'At that time a few young pranksters – among them Urusov, Opochinin, Stroganov, my cousin – began sending out anonymous letters to cuckolded husbands.'*[55] Nor was the letter an original composition. In December Sollogub was shown by d'Archiac, an acquaintance at the French embassy, 'several printed forms with various comic diplomas for various absurd titles'. D'Archiac, continued Sollogub, 'told me that Vienna society had amused itself the whole winter by circulating similar hoaxes. Among them was also a printed version of the diploma sent to Pushkin. So the vile joker, who caused his death, did not even invent

---

* Trubetskoy's recollection is supported by the ambassador of Baden-Württemberg, Christian von Hohenlohe-Kirchberg, who in a dispatch from St Petersburg of December 1836 wrote: 'Troubling the serenity of families by sending anonymous letters has already been a regrettable custom for some time here' (quoted in Vitale, 129).

his joke, but got a version from some member of the diplomatic corps and copied it.'[56] All the recipients of the letter, with the exception of Elise Khitrovo, were closely connected to the Karamzins. Vyazemsky was Ekaterina Karamzina's half-brother; the Rosset brothers were very close friends of Aleksandr and Andrey Karamzin; Sollogub had been a fellow-student of the Karamzin brothers at Dorpat University; Mikhail Wielhorski had been for years a family friend of the Karamzins and the Vyazemskys. The sender, therefore, probably was acquainted with Trubetskoy's circle of young guards officers, had connections in diplomatic circles, was a frequent visitor to the Karamzin salon, and – which excluded Heeckeren – had called on the Rosset brothers at home: only this could explain the detailed address on the envelope addressed to Klementy Rosset, which read: 'At Sanftleben's house, on the left, on the third floor'.[57] He also knew that Pushkin, though not, like Karamzin, an officially appointed historiographer, was being paid a salary to work on a history of Peter the Great, and was, of course, cognizant of the gossip concerning d'Anthès and Natalya. And, above all, he was a malicious prankster, with no particular like of Pushkin, who delighted in stirring up mischief.

One person fits this description admirably: the twenty-year-old Prince Petr Dolgorukov, known as 'the Lame' – a deformed foot caused him to limp – a civil servant at the Ministry of Education, whom Count Adlerberg saw, at an evening party in the winter of 1836–7, 'standing behind Pushkin indicating d'Anthès to someone and at the same time putting up his forefingers and curling them like horns'.[58] Klementy Rosset had immediately suspected that the letter had been concocted by Dolgorukov together with his flatmate, the twenty-two-year-old Prince Ivan Gagarin. Shortly after receiving it he called on the two in their apartment on Millionnaya Street, where he found them at dinner. 'In the presence of the servants he said nothing,' Gagarin later wrote, 'but as soon as we had risen from table and passed into the other room, he took out of his pocket the anonymous letter addressed to Pushkin [. . .] Then a conversation took place between us; we wondered who could have written the pasquil, with what aim, and what the consequences might be.'[59] Rosset's suspicions were shared by many others; but were first expressed openly in 1863, in a pamphlet on Pushkin's death composed by Aleksandr Ammosov. Both Dolgorukov and Gagarin hastened to deny the accusation. Since then Gagarin, who left Russia in

1843 and became a Jesuit priest, has come to be thought innocent. Dolgorukov, on the other hand, whose later career includes other instances of anonymous letter-writing, still seems by far the most likely perpetrator. Comparisons of his handwriting with that of the anonymous letters have, however, proved inconclusive, and as yet no conclusive proof of his guilt – or innocence – has been discovered.[60]

Whoever the sender of the anonymous letters was, it seems highly unlikely, to say the least, that he (or she) was acting in concert with Heeckeren, as has been maintained. All the arguments against Heeckeren's involvement apply with equal force to a hypothetical conspiracy between Heeckeren and another. Tempting as it is to see a causal link between d'Anthès's rejection in Idaliya Poletika's drawing-room and the dispatch, the following day, of the anonymous letters, impartial logic can only view this succession of events as coincidence; a coincidence, however, which was to have tragic consequences.

When Pushkin's challenge arrived at the Dutch embassy on the morning of Thursday 5 November d'Anthès was on guard duty. The letter – addressed presumably to 'Baron Heeckeren' – was opened by the minister. Horrified by the contents, he hesitated for some time before deciding what to do. At about midday he called on Pushkin. Explaining that as yet d'Anthès, still on duty, knew nothing of the matter, he accepted the challenge on his behalf, but asked for a delay of twenty-four hours before taking matters further. Pushkin agreed.

Meanwhile Natalya had got in touch with her brother, Ivan, an officer in the Life Guards Hussars, stationed at Tsarskoe Selo. Ivan hurried to St Petersburg, was told to give Zhukovsky an urgent message, and hurried back to Tsarskoe Selo. The following day, 6 November, was the feast day of St Paul, the patron saint of Ivan's regiment, which was to be marked by a ceremonial parade attended by the tsar and tsarevich, followed by a banquet in the Alexander Palace. Ivan managed to see Zhukovsky, but only at the cost of being late for the parade and being put under arrest for several days. Zhukovsky himself had been invited to the banquet, but, ignoring this, set off for St Petersburg, arriving at the Pushkins just before noon. He had only been there a few minutes when Heeckeren was announced. Thinking it best to allow the two a tête-à-tête conversation, he left.[61]

Heeckeren now pleaded with Pushkin for another week's grace. He spoke of 'his paternal feeling for the young man, to whom he had devoted his whole life, with the aim of assuring his well-being'. But now 'the whole edifice of his hopes would be razed to the ground at the very moment when he considered his labour at an end'. Though he had accepted Pushkin's challenge on d'Anthès's behalf, he had not, as yet, told the other of it.* Pushkin, 'touched by the emotion and tears of the father', magnanimously agreed to give him, not a week's, but a fortnight's grace.[62] On Heeckeren's departure Zhukovsky reappeared. When he explained the reason for his presence, Pushkin showed him the anonymous letter and told him of the challenge sent to d'Anthès. He had, however, he added, just agreed to wait a fortnight before proceeding further. Zhukovsky was immensely relieved: not only did the concession suggest that Pushkin's hand was not itching for the feel of a pistol butt, but the delay also allowed for extensive *pourparlers* between an intermediary and each of the two sides. He spent the rest of the day with Vyazemsky and with Wielhorski – with whom he was staying – being careful not to mention the affair to either. In the evening he was brought a letter from Ekaterina Zagryazhskaya, Natalya's aunt, asking him to call on her the following morning.

The conversation with Zhukovsky had brought the anonymous letter back to the forefront of Pushkin's mind. He began to brood over its wording, teasing out the malicious innuendoes. Did his appointment as 'coadjutor' to Naryshkin suggest a similarity between them? Was he believed to occupy the same position vis-à-vis Nicholas as Naryshkin had vis-à-vis Alexander? It was true that the emperor had been a great admirer of Natalya ever since first meeting her at Tsarskoe Selo in the summer of 1831, constantly singling her out at court. He had made a joke of it to Nashchokin, describing Nicholas as 'dangling after her like some stripling officer; of a morning he purposely drives past her windows several times, and in the evening, at a ball, asks why her blinds

---

* This is commonly thought to be a lie (see e.g. Abramovich (1994a), 81); d'Anthès's guard duty had ended at noon the previous day, and Heeckeren would have had ample time to talk to him. However, I find it on the contrary very plausible. Heeckeren's one desire was to postpone the duel in the hope of eventually persuading Pushkin to withdraw the challenge. D'Anthès, whatever his faults, was no coward. If he learnt that Heeckeren was pleading for a week's grace, he might see this as an aspersion of his honour and declare himself willing to fight immediately.

are always down'.[63] And Natalya, for her part, would flirt abominably with the emperor. He had had to upbraid her affectionately for this on many occasions; the relationship had indeed become a standing joke between them. But he was absolutely sure that there was nothing more to it than this.* Nevertheless, rumour might hint at a more intimate liaison. And it was as much against rumour as against reality that he had to defend himself and Natalya. Furthermore, had there not been stories that Naryshkin's complaisance had not gone unrewarded, that he had profited financially from his wife's infidelity? Might not similar stories circulate about him, and might they not be even more damaging than those about Naryshkin? After all, there was no proof that Naryshkin had received anything from Alexander, but he had had from Nicholas a loan of 20,000 roubles for the publication of *Pugachev* in March 1834, and of 30,000 in September 1835 to pay off his debts. Thinking of this, he composed a letter to the finance minister, Count Cancrin.

Dear Sir, Count Egor Frantsovich,

Encouraged by the indulgent attention with which your excellency has already deigned to favour me, I take the liberty of disturbing you with a most humble request.

According to the arrangements of which your excellency's ministry is aware, I stand indebted to the Treasury (without security) for 45,000 roubles, 25,000 of which must be repaid by me in the course of five years.†

Now, wishing to pay my debt in full and immediately, I discover one obstacle to this, which can easily be removed, but only by you.

I possess 220 souls in Nizhny Novgorod province, of which 200 are mortgaged for 40,000. By the arrangements of my father,

---

* Nicholas seems not always to have pressed his flirtations to their logical conclusion. Aleksandra Smirnova-Rosset in a diary entry for March 1845 notes that, towards the end of a ball at the Anichkov Palace, she was sitting with Amaliya Krüdener, one of his favourites, watching him flirting animatedly with another, Countess Elizaveta Buturlina. 'You supped with him, but today the last honours are for her,' she said. 'He is a strange man,' Amaliya replied. 'These things nevertheless have to have a result, but with him there is never an end, he hasn't the courage for it, he has a peculiar idea of fidelity. All these games with her prove nothing' (Smirnova-Rosset, 9).
† When asking for a loan, Pushkin had suggested that he forwent his salary of 5,000 roubles a year, which would go towards paying off the debt. The debt of 45,000 he refers to is thus 20,000 plus 30,000 less one year's salary.

who bestowed this estate on me, I do not have the right to sell them during his lifetime, although I can mortgage them either with the Treasury or with private individuals.

But the Treasury has the right to recover what is due to it, regardless of any private arrangements, as long as those have not been imperially confirmed.

In payment of the aforesaid 45,000 I take the liberty of offering this estate, which surely is worth that much and probably even more.

I take the liberty of troubling your excellency with another request which is important to me. Since this matter is extremely insignificant and may fall within the scope of a normal procedure, I most earnestly beg your excellency not to bring it to the attention of the Sovereign Emperor, who in his magnanimity probably would not desire such a repayment (although it is in no way a burden to me), and might perhaps order that my debt be forgiven, which would put me in an extremely difficult and embarrassing position: since in such a case I would be constrained to refuse the Tsar's favour, which could seem an impropriety, pointless braggadocio, or even ingratitude.

With the most profound respect and complete devotion I have the honour to be, dear sir, Your Excellency's most humble servant.[64]

Pushkin was in effect proposing the cancellation of his debt to the Treasury by the expropriation of an estate which belonged to his father (any interest in which he had already forfeited by giving up the revenue to his sister). And, while riding roughshod over the laws of property and inheritance, the Treasury was at the same time to keep its actions hidden from the tsar. The grotesque illogicality and ludicrous impracticality of the proposals reveal, more than anything else, how psychologically confused and disturbed Pushkin was at the time. While, over the next few months, when dealing with subjects which did not touch on his own personal position, he was able to act normally and bring his intellect sensibly and incisively to bear, at other times he could fall into a state bordering on lunacy. Cancrin replied diplomatically a fortnight later; he considered 'the acquisition by the Treasury of landowners' estates in general inconvenient, and in any such case imperial permission must be sought'.*[65]

On the next morning – Saturday 7 November – Zhukovsky called on Ekaterina Zagryazhskaya in response to her note of the previous evening. She had learnt of the situation from Natalya, and had also been appealed to by Heeckeren, who hoped to enlist her influence with the Pushkins. Appalled at the threat to her niece's reputation, she now begged Zhukovsky to do his utmost – though he needed no urging – to avert the duel. From here he went to the Dutch embassy to see Heeckeren. He found him alone: d'Anthès was again on guard duty.† Zhukovsky began to explain what his relationship with Pushkin was, and how it came about that he was acting as an intermediary in the affair without – at the moment – the latter's knowledge. He was, he said, ignorant of what had preceded the challenge. At this point Heeckeren cut him short. His adopted son – he mendaciously hinted that they were also linked by ties of blood – was in love, not with Natalya, but with her sister. 'Aleksandra?' asked the astonished Zhukovsky. No, not Aleksandra, but Ekaterina. D'Anthès had 'been begging his father to consent to their marriage, but he, finding the marriage unsuitable, had not given his consent, now, however, seeing that further obstinacy on his part had led to a misunderstanding which threatened to have grievous consequences, he had, finally, given his consent'.[66]

This, though Zhukovsky did not know it, was an obvious lie: d'Anthès had had no thoughts of marrying Ekaterina. The scheme had been concocted by Heeckeren with the aim of preventing a duel. If d'Anthès was in love with Ekaterina, he could hardly have been pursuing Natalya; and Pushkin therefore could have no reason for calling his future brother-in-law out. Earlier Heeckeren had put this plan to d'Anthès: once he had obtained the fortnight's grace, there was no

---

* After Pushkin's death the debt was cancelled by Nicholas. 'The Sovereign Emperor,' the chairman of the trustees wrote to Natalya, 'has again deigned to pour forth his munificence on your family, by imperial order striking from the accounts of the State Treasury those particular sums given to your late husband, and remitting their exaction from the deceased's estate or the pension of his heirs, as should occur according to the obligations which he gave' (*Arkhiv Opeki Pushkina*, 119).

† At a regimental inspection on 4 November he had carried out his duties as troop commander so inefficiently that Major-General Grünewaldt gave him five extra guard duties, on 6, 8, 10, 12 and 14 November; guard duty was from noon to the following noon.

reason to keep the other any longer in the dark. But it was only after he had painted, in the blackest terms, the consequences, both for his and for d'Anthès's career, of fighting a duel with so well-known a figure as Pushkin, that his protégé had reluctantly consented to the stratagem.

Zhukovsky was overjoyed by this extraordinary news. Giving Heeckeren his word to do everything he could to stop a duel, he hurried back to Pushkin and told him of what he had learnt. To his astonishment Pushkin was not at all pleased; on the contrary he flew into a violent rage. He was annoyed with Zhukovsky for interfering, but his rage was directed at d'Anthès and Heeckeren, who, he believed, had taken a coward's way out by inventing this proposal of marriage. He now told Zhukovsky something of the history of Natalya's relationship with d'Anthès, keeping back those episodes which might have harmed her reputation. But there was still enough to horrify Zhukovsky, who agreed that d'Anthès's behaviour provided more than sufficient provocation for a challenge. Nevertheless, he urged Pushkin to accept this honourable way out. Pushkin adamantly refused: he would not be cheated of his prey. In addition, the marriage proposal was clearly a sham, on which d'Anthès would renege as soon as the challenge was withdrawn. Eventually Zhukovsky left, and went round to Wielhorski's apartment on Mikhailovskaya Square; that evening both Heeckeren and d'Anthès visited him there. Zhukovsky told them of Pushkin's intransigence and delicately suggested that the marriage proposal would have more weight were it to be repeated before a witness: such as the sisters' aunt, Ekaterina Ivanovna Zagryazhskaya, who, though not a Goncharov, could be considered to represent the family. The following morning, Sunday 8 November, he called on her to report progress. She greeted his news enthusiastically: here was a means of averting an encounter which also gave her niece the opportunity of making an advantageous marriage. She sent a note to Heeckeren; he came round later – Zhukovsky had left by then – and reiterated the proposal.

Over the course of the next few weeks Ekaterina Ivanovna, anxious as she was about the well-being of her nieces, was to take an active part in the negotiations over the affair. The rooms she occupied in the Winter Palace became a kind of neutral ground where Zhukovsky and the Goncharov sisters could meet with Heeckeren and d'Anthès. It was presumably here that Heeckeren pressed into Natalya's hands the letter which, he proudly told Nesselrode, 'I demanded from my son, a letter addressed to her and by which he declared that he renounced pursuing any claims on her. And the bearer of that letter was I myself, who put it into her own hands.'[67] It is somewhat curious, and indicative of Heeckeren's view of morality, that he should take credit for obtaining from d'Anthès a vow that he would act as normal decency required. And it was after one of Heeckeren's visits some days later to Ekaterina Ivanovna that his note to d'Anthès, on guard duty again, elicited the following reply:

> My very dear friend, I thank you for the two notes you sent. They calmed me a little, which I needed, and am writing these few words to you to tell you again that I rely wholly on you, whatever decision you might take, being convinced in advance that in all this business you will act better than I.
>
> My God, I don't hold it against the woman and I am happy to know that she is at ease, but it is gross imprudence or madness, which I moreover do not understand, nor what her purpose was. A note tomorrow to let me know if anything new happened during the night, you don't say either whether you saw her sister at her aunt's and how you know that she confessed to the letters [. . .] In all this Catherine is a good creature who is behaving admirably.[68]

It is clear from this that Ekaterina, overcome by the possibility of marriage to the man with whom she has been hopelessly in love, has switched her loyalties completely. She has been retailing to Heeckeren information she can only have obtained from Natalya, telling him that her sister had shown Pushkin those letters from d'Anthès, 'whose expression might have aroused his susceptibility as a husband' – news which has disquieted their author: no one likes to have their love letters read by a third party, especially if that third party is the lover's spouse.

From Ekaterina Ivanovna Zhukovsky went to see Pushkin. He found him in a quieter mood, even subdued: when Zhukovsky began to speak to him of his obligations to his family, his friends, to literature, he burst into tears. But he still – even after learning that Heeckeren was to repeat the marriage proposal to Ekaterina Ivanovna – refused to accept that it was genuine, and would not withdraw the challenge.

That evening Pushkin visited Mikhail Yakovlev, whose name-day it was. The only other guests were two other lycéens: Fedor Matyushkin, a naval officer, and Prince Dmitry Eristov, who had been a year below the others at school. They noticed that Pushkin was in a highly agitated state. After dinner, as they were drinking champagne, he suddenly pulled out the anonymous letter with the words, 'Look at this vile thing I've been sent'. Yakovlev, an expert on varieties of paper – he was the director of the press attached to the Second Department of the Imperial Chancery – examined it closely and pronounced it to be written on paper of foreign manufacture: because of the high import tax on such paper it must, he said, have come from some embassy. His view strengthened Pushkin's conviction that Heeckeren was the author.*[69]

On the next day, Monday the ninth, Zhukovsky met Heeckeren at about noon, and, after listening again to his proposals, agreed to continue as an intermediary. After they had been joined by d'Anthès, who had just come off duty, Zhukovsky proposed that the principals should meet to resolve the affair. Heeckeren greeted the suggestion with enthusiasm, and immediately drew up, in the form of a letter to Zhukovsky, a kind of protocol of their discussion. After establishing that so far d'Anthès had acted irreproachably, the letter continued:

> As you know, Sir, everything up to now has taken place through the mediation of third parties. My son has received a challenge, his first duty was to accept it, but he himself should at least be told why he has been challenged. A meeting between the two parties themselves therefore seems to me appropriate, obligatory, in the presence of a person who, like you yourself, Sir, could intervene between them with all the authority of complete impartiality, and could appreciate the real basis of the suscepti-bilities which have brought about this affair. At the stage that has been reached, after each party has been able to fulfil these duties of a gentleman of honour, I would like to believe that your mediation will be able to disabuse easily M. de Pushkin

---

* Doubt is thrown upon Yakovlev's expertise by Gagarin's admission that the letter was written on notepaper similar to his. 'As far as I remember,' he added, 'I bought it in the English shop, and probably half of Petersburg bought its notepaper there' (*RA*, 1865, 1246).

and bring together two people who have proved that they owe each other a mutual esteem.[70]

Zhukovsky retired to Wielhorski's with this disingenuous letter, which claimed that d'Anthès had no idea as to the cause of the challenge. Here he drafted a reply, agreeing to a meeting and stipulating that one side should definitively commit itself to a marriage proposal and the other to a withdrawal of the challenge. This, he hoped, might become the protocol of his discussion with Pushkin. Armed with both missives, he set off to see him. As might have been expected, he met with a furious reception. Pushkin upbraided him for being taken in by Heeckeren, and acting in his interests, rather than in those of his friend. He categorically refused to meet d'Anthès and Heeckeren: to do so would be to admit that he was in the wrong, rather than they. He still did not believe that they were serious in their marriage proposal. In fact, he believed so little in it that he had not yet mentioned it either to Natalya or to Ekaterina. On that same day Ekaterina had opened a letter to her brother with the words 'I doubt whether today's letter will be very gay, dear Dmitry, as I am not only not in a gay mood, but on the contrary am depressed to death [...] I am glad to know, dear friend, that you are as before content with your lot, God grant that it should be for ever, and for me, in those griefs which heaven has seen fit to send down upon me, it is a real consolation to know that you at least are happy; as for me, my happiness is already irrevocably lost, I am too well convinced that it and I will never meet on this suffering earth, and the only favour which I ask of God is to put an end to a life so useless, to say the least, as mine. Happiness for all my family and death for myself – that is all I want, that is for which I constantly entreat the Almighty.'[71] The melancholy might be partially assumed: it alternates with businesslike instructions for paying an English corsetière in Moscow who has furnished the sisters with stays. Nevertheless, it is clear that she has not received news which would transform her life.

Zhukovsky eventually left for Wielhorski's, whence he sent a note to Heeckeren and one to Pushkin. 'I cannot yet bring myself to consider our affair done for,' he wrote. 'I have not yet given the elder Heeckeren any answer; I told him in my note that I didn't find you at home and that, not having seen you, I could give no reply. So there is still the possibility of stopping everything. Tell me what I should reply. Your answer will end everything irrevocably. But for God's sake think better of it. Give me the happiness of saving you from an insane crime, and your wife from complete disgrace. I await your reply. I am now at Wielhorski's, where I dine.'[72]

On receiving this note Pushkin came round to see him. He had, for some reason, got it into his head that Zhukovsky had bruited the affair abroad, and that it would hence come to the notice of the authorities. In Wielhorski's presence he began a stormy complaint, but was cut short by Zhukovsky, who, equally anxious to avoid publicity, saw that this might not be best achieved by shouting about the affair in the presence of a third party. Later that evening Zhukovsky was one of the empress's supper guests in the Anichkov Palace; returning in the small hours, he wrote to Pushkin:

> I am bound to give you some explanations. Yesterday I was not sufficiently composed to do so. Yesterday you, I remember, said something about gendarmes, as though you feared that the government would interfere in your affair. On this count you can be completely at ease. No outsiders know anything, and if the ladies (that is lady Zagryazhskaya alone) keep quiet, the secret will remain unbroken. I must say however that your visit yesterday to Wielhorski opened his eyes; it was no use my pretending to him; he was one of those who received the anonymous letters; but one can rely on his friendship for you and his modesty.

He went on to explain d'Anthès's position: because of his extra duties he had had to leave matters to Heeckeren – 'his poor father, who was endeavouring to avoid a catastrophe, of which the expectation alone was driving him mad'. Heeckeren had turned to him, Zhukovsky:

> Not wishing to be the spectator of, nor actor in a tragedy, I offered my mediation, that is, I wished to offer it, by writing in reply to the father that letter, the rough draft of which I showed you, but which I have not sent and will not send. That is all. This morning I will tell the elder Heeckeren that I cannot take on myself any mediation, since from my conversations

with you yesterday I became convinced that mediation could serve no purpose, which is why I do not intend to subject anyone to the unpleasantness of a refusal. The elder Heeckeren will thus not know that my attempt with his *letter* did not succeed. That letter will be returned to him, and my official meeting with you yesterday can be considered as not having taken place.

I have written all this because I consider it a sacred duty to testify before you that the younger Heeckeren was a complete stranger to all that his father did, that he is as ready to fight you, as you him, and that he also fears lest the secret be somehow broken. And one must be as just to the father. He is in despair, but this is what he said to me: 'I am condemned to the guillotine; I make a plea for pardon, if I fail, I must mount the scaffold: and I will mount, for I love my son's honour as much as his life.' With this testimony my role, played wretchedly and unsuccessfully, ends. Farewell.[73]

Early on the morning of Tuesday the tenth d'Anthès called on Zhukovsky before going on guard duty. Zhukovsky returned Heeckeren's letter, together with a note explaining why he was withdrawing as a mediator.

At this point Zhukovsky, though extremely apprehensive of what might occur, would have given up, exhausted by Pushkin's recalcitrance. But on Wednesday Ekaterina Ivanovna summoned him to the Winter Palace. Heeckeren had played his trump card. D'Anthès had, he revealed, seduced Ekaterina. Heeckeren had not mentioned this earlier, not wishing to sully either his son's honour, or Ekaterina's virtue. Surely Pushkin, now that it was a question of redeeming his sister-in-law's honour, could not refuse to withdraw the challenge?* In addition, Aleksandra

---

* It must be admitted that this is a hypothesis for which there is no direct evidence. But on 14 November Zhukovsky wrote to Pushkin: 'Supposing that all the circumstances communicated to me by the elder Heeckeren were true (to doubt which I had neither cause nor necessity), I said that I considered him as a father justified and indeed obliged to avert a catastrophe by disclosing the matter *as it is*; that this disclosure would be at the same time reparation for that which had been done to your honour in society' (XVI, 186). Other than the loss of Ekaterina's virginity, it is difficult to imagine 'a matter', which, if disclosed, would simultaneously avert the duel and do as much harm to d'Anthès's honour as the anonymous letter had to Pushkin's. Whether Heeckeren was telling the truth is another question, equally unsusceptible of proof.

had reported that Pushkin had moderated his views: if Heeckeren could provide a written, cast-iron guarantee that the marriage would take place, he might withdraw the challenge. Hurrying back down the Nevsky to the Dutch embassy, Zhukovsky put this proposition to Heeckeren. The baron agreed, on condition that Pushkin produced a letter embodying his part of the bargain. Zhukovsky, now buoyant with new optimism, called once more on Pushkin, who, though obstinate to the last, finally yielded to the entreaties of Natalya and Zhukovsky. He drafted a rough note:

> Baron Heeckeren has done me the honour of accepting on behalf of his son Baron G. Heeckeren a challenge to a duel. Having learnt *by chance? by public rumour?* that M. G. Heeckeren has decided to ask for the hand in marriage of my sister-in-law, Mlle C. Goncharov, I beg Baron Heeckeren to be so kind as to consider my challenge as not having taken place.
>
> For having conducted himself towards my wife in a manner which it did not suit me to accept (in the case of M. Heeckeren demanding a reason for the challenge).[74]

On Thursday evening Heeckeren was with Ekaterina Ivanovna, concerting a plan. It was agreed that she would see Pushkin the next day. On Friday morning – the thirteenth – Heeckeren wrote to her:

> After eight days of anguish I was so happy and so at ease yesterday evening that I forgot, Mademoiselle, to advise you strongly to say in the conversation you will have today that the plan that concerns you for Catherine and my son has existed for a long time, that I had opposed it for motives known to you, but that when you invited me to call on you to discuss the dispute which had arisen, I had declared to you that I no longer wished to withhold my consent on condition, however, that the matter should be kept secret until after the Duel, since from the time of Pushkin's challenge the fact that my son's honour had been compromised made it imperative for me to keep silent. That is what is essential for no one can wish the dishonour of my Georges, moreover it would be wished for in vain for no one could succeed in obtaining it. For pity's sake,

Mademoiselle, send me a note immediately after your conversation, my terrors have returned and I am in a state difficult to describe.

You know too that I have not authorized you to speak with Pushkin, but that you are doing it of your own initiative to save your family.[75]

Heeckeren's anxiety that the attachment between d'Anthès and Ekaterina should be represented as a long-standing one stems, of course, from the fact that, if the engagement did not predate the challenge, it could be seen for what it really was: an excuse to avoid an encounter. With Ekaterina Ivanovna, as cynical and as worldly-wise as himself, he did not have to wrap up matters. The naive and trusting Zhukovsky, however, had to be gulled. He had received, he wrote to Pushkin, 'from father Heeckeren material proof that the matter which is now under discussion was begun long before your challenge'.[76] This 'material proof' was, presumably, Heeckeren's disclosure of Ekaterina's seduction.

On Friday afternoon Pushkin called, as arranged, on Ekaterina Ivanovna and listened, hiding his disbelief, to her repetition of Heeckeren's promises. He would, he said, withdraw his challenge, and would meet with Heeckeren the next day to formalize the agreement. Though he kept his anger in check during this conversation, it boiled over when he met Zhukovsky afterwards. It was all a hoax, he fulminated, cooked up by d'Anthès to keep his skin whole. In the evening he visited the Karamzins and, finding them sympathetic listeners, spilt the whole story to them. Zhukovsky, who came round to their apartment after his departure, was horrified by this indiscretion. 'You are acting very incautiously, unmagnanimously, and even unjustly towards me,' he wrote early on Saturday morning. 'Why have you told Ekaterina Andreevna and Sofya Nikolaevna about everything? What do you want? To make impossible that which now should end in the best possible fashion for you?' Nor could he give credence to Pushkin's assertions of the previous evening. Everything had been done by Heeckeren; d'Anthès had had no hand in the attempt to avert the duel. Zhukovsky was convinced that he had behaved honourably. 'I have told the Karamzins this,' he continued, 'firmly forbidding them to speak about what they heard from you, and assuring them that you will inevitably have to fight if the secret becomes known now or even later.' He begged Pushkin, for his sake, also to remain silent: 'I became involved in this matter unwillingly and do not wish to attract censure because of it; do not wish anyone to have the right to say that I broke a trust confided in me.'[77]

That afternoon Zhukovsky visited the Moika Embankment apartment; possibly as a precaution to make sure that Pushkin did not back out of the meeting with Heeckeren at the last moment. He did not. When the two met at Ekaterina Ivanovna's Heeckeren formally announced the engagement of his son to Ekaterina Goncharova; Pushkin formally withdrew his challenge, handing a note to that effect – a more polished version of the rough draft quoted above – to Heeckeren. The necessity to preserve a calm demeanour in face of the man responsible, not only for – as he believed – the gross insult of the anonymous letter, but also for the obscene attempts on Natalya's virtue, demanded a superhuman effort of the will. Afterwards, as he had done the previous evening, he had to find some way of releasing his emotions. This time he turned to Vera Vyazemskaya, pouring the whole story into her sympathetic ear. But this time, carried away by rage at the memory of Heeckeren's smiling countenance, he went further. 'I know the author of the anonymous letters,' he told her, 'and in eight days you will hear of a vengeance unique of its kind; it will be full, complete; it will hurl the man into the gutter: Raevsky's lofty deeds are child's play compared to what I propose to do.'[78] He is referring to the scandal caused by Aleksandr Raevsky in Odessa in 1826: with a cane in his hand, he stopped Countess Vorontsova's coach and 'addressed impertinences to her', ending with the appeal 'Look after our children', or 'my daughter'.[79]

The following day, Sunday 15 November, the first court ball of the season took place at the Anichkov Palace. Natalya, who had been invited without Pushkin, still in mourning for his mother, had been hesitant about going, and had consulted Zhukovsky. 'Didn't Pushkin read you my letter?' he replied. 'I think I wrote clearly to him about today's ball, why he was not invited, and why it was absolutely essential that you should go.'[80] Only her presence, Zhukovsky was implying, could still the rumours about her marriage that were beginning to circulate in society. Some hint of them had come to the emperor's ears, who took her aside during the evening. 'I spoke to her about the gossip to which her beauty exposed her in society,' he told Korff some years later. 'I advised her to be as cautious as possible and to guard her reputation, not only for her own sake, but also for her husband's happiness, given his well-known jealousy.'[81]

Zhukovsky had also been at the ball. On his way home, in the early hours of Monday morning, he called on Vera Vyazemskaya, who told him of Pushkin's threat to take vengeance on Heeckeren. This, coming on top of the indiscretions at the Karamzins, was too much for Zhukovsky. 'All this is very fine especially after the promise which you gave Heeckeren in the presence of your auntie (who told me of it), that the whole of what had happened should remain a secret.' And what would be thought of him, Zhukovsky, if, after he had promised all parties absolute secrecy, Pushkin then blurted everything out? 'Of course, I told the princess nothing of what has happened,' he wrote. 'I will tell you too nothing: do as you wish. But I am taking my piece out of your game, your part in which cruelly displeases me. And if Heeckeren now takes it into his head to ask my advice, that what am I in all honesty to tell him: watch out? That's what I'll do.' He concluded with a fable: a shepherd, protecting his favourite sheep against a wolf, asks a friend to lure the beast out of the forest by imitating a pig. The friend refuses, on the grounds that he will be thought of as a pig ever after.[82]

Meanwhile the other end of the agreement had begun to unravel. D'Anthès belatedly realized that his courage might be impugned were the proposal of marriage to be linked with the retraction of the challenge. Pushkin had no sooner read Zhukovsky's letter on Monday morning than Viscount d'Archiac, an attaché at the French embassy, was announced. He bore with him a stiff letter from d'Anthès.

> Sir,
> Baron de Heeckeren has just told me that he has been authorized by M. [Zhukovsky] to let me know that all the reasons on account of which you challenged me have ceased, and that in consequence I could consider this act on your part as not having taken place.
>> When you challenged me without telling me why, I accepted without hesitation, for honour made it my duty; today when you affirm that you no longer have grounds for wishing an encounter, before being able to release you from your word, I

wish to know why you have changed your mind, not having myself charged anyone to give you the explanations which I reserved for myself to impart to you. You will be the first to agree that before we withdraw explanations must be given by both parties in such a manner that enables us to esteem each other mutually henceforth.[83]

Handing this over, d'Archiac added that the fortnight's grace would end on the eighteenth; his principal would be at Pushkin's service at any time thereafter. His second, Pushkin replied, would call at the French embassy on the morrow.

The letter enraged Pushkin, sharpening his already ferocious appetite for a duel. It was unbearable beyond belief that d'Anthès, whose every action over the past months had reeked of dishonour, should now prate of his honour; unbearable, too, that he should imply that, according to the duelling code, he was in the right and Pushkin in the wrong. That afternoon Pushkin and Natalya were at Ekaterina Karamzina's birthday party – 'a large gathering, as always, and of necessity chaotic from the bringing together of so many heterogeneous individuals'.[84] At dinner Sollogub found himself sitting next to Pushkin. 'Come and see me tomorrow,' he said. 'I want you to call on d'Archiac to arrange the conditions for a duel.' Sollogub, who earlier, when discussing the anonymous letter, had offered to act as Pushkin's second if necessary, was astonished, but agreed.*[85]

In the evening the Ficquelmonts gave a rout: '400 people standing, moving and jostling one another in the doorways, all the ladies in black dresses, a uniformity which however I find attractive, and a crowd of foreigners, Frenchmen above all with beards of every form; this fashion is really very ugly and destroys, I think, any individuality of physiognomy,' commented Sofya Karamzina.[86] The women wore black because on 3 November Nicholas had ordered twenty-four days of mourning for the former French king, Charles X, who had died of cholera nine days earlier in Goritz, Austria. Ekaterina, however, joyfully anticipating her engagement, had obtained permission from the empress to wear white.

---

* In his memoirs, written ten years later, Sollogub makes the request more melodramatic. Asking him to agree the conditions with d'Archiac, Pushkin added: 'The bloodier the better. Do not agree to any explanations' (Sollogub, 363).

'Amidst the deep mourning for Charles X one white dress alone was to be seen, and that chaste bridal attire seems a fraud!' Countess Bobrinskaya wrote to her husband ten days later: a remark which suggests that rumours as to the relationship between d'Anthès and Ekaterina were already circulating in society.[87]

Pushkin, unaccompanied by Natalya, arrived late, and ran into d'Archiac on the stairs. 'You French are a very pleasant people,' he said. 'You all know Latin, but when you fight, you put yourselves thirty paces apart and aim at the mark. For us Russians the more aimless a duel, the fiercer it should be.'[88] He found Ekaterina talking to d'Anthès and brought her away, addressing 'a few more than rude words' to the Frenchman.[89] After they had gone Sollogub took d'Anthès aside. 'What kind of man are you?' he asked. 'What a question,' d'Anthès replied, and began to spout nonsense. Sollogub cut him short, repeating the question. 'A man of honour, my dear fellow, and I will prove it soon.' Sollogub spoke of Natalya. 'My dear fellow, she's nothing but airs and graces,' said d'Anthès.[90]

The next morning – Tuesday 17 November – the weather was atrocious, with snow and a high wind. Instead of calling on d'Archiac, as Pushkin had requested, Sollogub, violating the strict rule of the code duello, that only seconds should communicate with each other, went to see d'Anthès at the Dutch embassy. His motive is clear. Despite Pushkin's eagerness to fight, Sollogub, as his friend, wanted at all costs to avoid a duel. Had he gone to see d'Archiac, whom he did not know, he could only have agreed its conditions. From d'Anthès, a fellow-member of the Karamzin circle, he hoped to learn its cause, and how a rencontre might best be avoided. The previous evening d'Anthès, as one of the principals, had quite properly refused to discuss the matter, referring Sollogub to d'Archiac. Now, worn down by Sollogub's persistence, he said: 'Don't you understand that I am marrying Catherine. Pushkin has withdrawn his challenge, but I don't want it to look as though I'm getting married to avoid a duel. Moreover, I don't want a woman's name to be mentioned in all this. For a whole year the old man's prevented me from getting married.'[91]

From d'Anthès Sollogub went round to Pushkin. He was in a terrible passion. 'D'Anthès is a wretch,' he said. 'Yesterday I called him a blackguard.' Sollogub was to go straight to d'Archiac and agree conditions.

'As my second I am bound to tell you the cause of the duel,' Pushkin went on. 'They say in society that d'Anthès is courting my wife. Some say she likes him, others that she doesn't. No matter – I don't want their names to be linked.' 'D'Anthès,' said Sollogub, 'doesn't want women's names to be mentioned in the affair.' 'What!' cried Pushkin. 'Then what's this all about?' The thought that d'Anthès was again usurping the moral high ground – having, Pushkin believed, slandered Natalya in the anonymous letter, he was now posing as a chivalrous defender of women's honour – coupled with the news that Sollogub had already seen the Frenchman that morning, infuriated him beyond measure. If Sollogub did not want to be his second he would find another, he shouted, ranting on in this strain for some time.[92]

Sollogub now drove to the French embassy and saw d'Archiac, whom he found to be a very good sort of fellow, as anxious as he to avoid a rencontre. He showed Sollogub Pushkin's original challenge and withdrawal, and confessed that he hadn't slept a wink all night for thinking of the affair. Sollogub, remembering the state in which he had left Pushkin, said that they should treat him like a sick man, and not stick at trifles. They agreed to call together on d'Anthès at three in the afternoon. Here, after a protracted discussion, Sollogub, with d'Archiac's assistance, drew up a letter to Pushkin:

I have, as you wished, been to call on M. d'Archiac to arrange time and place. We have agreed on Saturday, in view of the fact that on Friday it is impossible for me to be free, in the direction of Pargolovo, early in the morning, at a distance of 10 paces. M. d'Archiac has added to me confidentially that Baron Heeckeren [d'Anthès] had taken a firm decision to announce his marriage plans, but that, being checked by the scruple that in doing so he might appear to wish to avoid a duel, in all conscience can only do this after everything is settled between you, and you have witnessed verbally before me or M. d'Archiac that you do not attribute his marriage to considerations unworthy of a man of good heart.

Not being authorized to promise on your part a step of which I wholeheartedly approve, I beg you in the name of your family to assent to this settlement, which will conciliate all parties. It goes without saying that M. d'Archiac and I stand guarantor for M. Heeckeren.[93]

D'Anthès wished to read the letter, but the seconds did not allow him to do so. Sollogub gave it to his coachman, telling him to deliver it to the apartment he had been to on the Moika. But that morning he had been to two apartments on the Moika: his father's and Pushkin's. The coachman took the letter to the wrong address, and it did not reach Pushkin until nearly two hours later.

He, meanwhile, annoyed not to have yet heard from Sollogub about the duel conditions, had called on Klementy Rosset, hoping to find in him a less pacific second. Rosset refused the request because 'the first task of seconds was to reconcile the opponents, and he could not do that as he could not stand d'Anthès and would be glad if Pushkin would rid Petersburg society of him; in addition, he did not write French well enough to carry on a correspondence which, in these cases, had to be done with extreme circumspection'.[94] He would be happy, however, to act as Pushkin's second on the ground. Pleased with these fire-eating sentiments, Pushkin carried him back to the Moika for dinner. Sollogub's letter was waiting. Having read it, he wrote:

I do not hesitate to write what I can declare verbally. I challenged M. G. Heeckeren to a duel, and he accepted without asking any explanation. It is I who begs MM the witnesses of this affair to be so kind as to regard this challenge as not having taken place, having learnt from popular report that M. Georges Heeckeren has decided to declare his plans of marriage with Mlle Goncharova, after the duel. I have no reason to attribute his resolution to considerations unworthy of a man of good heart.

I beg you, Count, to make of this letter whatever use you deem fit.[95]

'That will do,' said d'Archiac, reading this reply in the Dutch embassy at about six in the evening. Refusing to let d'Anthès see the note, he congratulated him on his engagement.[96] 'Tell M. Pushkin I thank him,' d'Anthès replied. Taking d'Archiac with him, Sollogub drove back to the Moika. Pushkin, looking rather pale, came out of the dining-room to greet them. D'Archiac thanked him on d'Anthès's behalf. 'For my part I thought I could promise that you would salute your brother-in-law in public,' added Sollogub. 'Not for all the world,' replied Pushkin. 'There will be nothing in common between the two families – however, I am only too pleased to say that in this affair M. G. Heeckeren has conducted himself like a man of honour.'[97] Bowing his guests out, he returned to the dinner table. 'I congratulate you on your engagement,' he said to Ekaterina. 'D'Anthès has asked for your hand.' She threw down her napkin and ran to her room, followed by Natalya. 'What a fellow!' Pushkin said to Rosset.[98]

That evening Heeckeren and d'Anthès paid a formal visit to Ekaterina Ivanovna at the Winter Palace. The following day she wrote to Zhukovsky:

> Thank God everything seems to be at an end. The bridegroom and his honourable father visited me with a proposal. Happily a quarter of an hour earlier the eldest Goncharov had arrived from Moscow and he gave them the parental blessing, and so no one will be any the wiser. Today the bridegroom will make a formal request for permission to marry and tomorrow the bride will approach the empress.
>
> Now allow me from the bottom of my heart to express my thanks to you and beg forgiveness for all the torments you suffered during all this stormy time, I would come to you myself to thank you but I really do not have the strength.[99]

After dinner Ekaterina had sufficiently recovered from her emotion to accompany Pushkin and Natalya to the regular Tuesday ball at the Saltykovs. Here she met d'Anthès – Pushkin cut him, as he had threatened – and their engagement was formally announced. Pushkin refused to believe that anything would come of it. 'He's got a weak chest,' he said to Sollogub. 'Before you know it, he'll be off abroad.' And he offered to bet his works against Sollogub's walking-stick that the marriage would not take place.[100]

The announcement of the engagement caused a sensation in society, provoking a flood of gossip. 'It would be never-ending, if I were to tell you all the *on dits*,' Sofya Karamzina wrote to her brother.[101] Amazement was universal. 'It is unbelievable, this marriage I mean,' Ekaterina Karamzina remarked. 'But all is possible in a world where so much is unbelievable.'[102] Andrey Karamzin, on receiving the news, was equally astonished. 'I cannot get over this marriage Sofya tells me about! And when I think about it, [. . .] I wonder whether I'm not dreaming, or at least whether d'Anthès wasn't in a dream when he made his move.' 'The story of d'Anthès, Pushkin and Co. is not only a story in the style of Balzac, but also one in the genre of *Histoire des Treize*,' he wrote.[103] 'It is some kind of mystery of love, of heroic self-sacrifice, it is Jules Janin, it is Balzac, it is Victor Hugo. It is the literature of our day. It is exalted and ludicrous,' rhapsodized the enthralled Sofya Bobrinskaya.[104]

Most perplexing of all was the question as to why d'Anthès had chosen to propose to Ekaterina. 'Is it devotion or sacrifice?' the empress wondered to her friend Countess Tiesenhausen.[105] That it was devotion, the result of a long-standing attachment to Ekaterina – the explanation put about by Heeckeren – was believed by no one: d'Anthès's pursuit of Natalya had been far too well-known. Heeckeren was forced to fall back to another position. His new version was the empress's alternative: d'Anthès had sacrificed himself to save Natalya's honour. In his letter to Nesselrode of March 1837 he writes, with a barefaced unscrupulousness which is almost endearing, of 'the high sense of morality which induced my son to put his future in chains in order to save the reputation of a woman he loved'.[106] This explanation was accepted in the circle of Heeckeren's allies, gradually gaining an accretion of circumstantial detail. Count Alfred de Falloux du Coudray, who as a twenty-six-year-old visited St Petersburg in 1836 with a letter of introduction to the Nesselrodes and became good friends with d'Anthès, d'Archiac and Aleksandr Trubetskoy, tells in his memoirs of meeting Countess Nesselrode in a Parisian salon the following year. From her, 'an unimpeachable source', he learnt the true story: one morning Pushkin called on d'Anthès. With him he had a bundle of passionate letters in the Frenchman's hand. Lying heroically, d'Anthès said that Natalya was merely a go-between: the letters were for Ekaterina, whom he desired to marry. 'This conversation created a very delicate position, and, if the marriage had not taken place, Mme Pushkina could have been seriously compromised.'[107]

Of the four principals in the affair, d'Anthès, at the outset, conducted himself exactly as a man should who has after a year's waiting finally gained the hand of the woman he loves. Though three months later he

was 'telling everyone who would listen that he had married to save his
sister-in-law's honour from insulting calumny, but that now he considers it his duty to devote himself to the unhappy victim who had
become his wife',[108] now he was almost daily sending her tender little
notes. Could she arrange, when they met at Ekaterina Ivanovna's on
the nineteenth, that they should be alone? 'I have so many things to
say to you, I want to talk to you about our happy future, and all that
excludes witnesses. Let me believe that you are very happy, for I am so
happy this morning. I could not speak to you, however my heart is full
of good and tender feelings for you, for I love you, my dear Catherine,
and want to tell you this again with that sincerity which is the heart of
my character and which you will always find in me.'[109] She sends him
a note, asking for his portrait. 'When a request is made so well, so tenderly,
it is always sure to be granted,' he replies; 'but, my dear friend, I have less
eloquence than you; the only portrait there is of me belongs to the baron
and stands on his table. I asked him for it, this is his literal reply: "Tell
Catherine that I have given her the original and am keeping the copy; later
perhaps . . ."'[110] And, after she thanks him for the present he has sent her
on her name-day, 25 November, he writes: 'The only response I will make
to your letter is to tell you that you are a great child to thank me thus; that
which will give you pleasure is the aim of my life, and if I have succeeded
I am only too happy.'[111] He displayed his feelings for her ostentatiously
in public – 'it was thought that yesterday evening we behaved towards
one another in an embarrassing manner, improper for young ladies' –
and, after she had visited the apartment on the Nevsky when he had
again been ill, wrote: 'My dear Catherine, you saw this morning that I
treat you almost as a *wife*, since I received you without ceremony in
the most disadvantageous of négligés.'[112]

Ekaterina's emotions were uncomplicated. 'From happiness Catherine doesn't touch the ground and says that she doesn't yet dare to
convince herself that she isn't dreaming at all,' Sofya Karamzina wrote.[113]
She threw herself into preparations for the wedding – first arranged for
7 January, then postponed to the tenth – and for married life. Dmitry,
having unwisely promised d'Anthès 5,000 roubles a year,* had returned

* The allowance was paid irregularly, and never in full: d'Anthès's and Ekaterina's letters
to Dmitry are full of complaints as to this. See, e.g. Obodovskaya and Dementev (1999),
325–30.

to Moscow soon after the engagement had been announced. He was bombarded with letters full of commissions. He was, Ekaterina wrote, to take 800 roubles out of the 4,000 he owed Ekaterina Ivanovna, 'to buy me a fur coat of blue fox; order it to be bought or taken on credit in Moscow, furs there are cheaper and better than here. [. . .] But, most important, do it quickly, for they don't work over the holidays, and my wedding is to take place on 7 January, it must without fail be ready for that day.' D'Anthès and she had both written to her mother, informing her of the engagement; in her letter she had enclosed a picture of d'Anthès. 'Does Mama find Georges's portrait handsome?' she asked.[114]

The newly-weds were to live in the Dutch embassy. 'My brothers, and particularly Vladimir (who is very susceptible to luxury),' Sofya wrote at the end of December, 'were dazzled by the elegance of the apartments, the richness of the silver, and the quite particular care with which Catherine's rooms had been arranged; d'Anthès speaks of her and to her only with affection and apparent satisfaction, and, what is more, father Heeckeren cherishes and makes a fuss of her.'[115] By this time Pushkin, too, had found himself affected by the forthcoming marriage. In a letter to his father he managed to keep his feelings largely concealed: Sergey Lvovich's discretion was not to be trusted, and Pushkin did not wish Petersburg gossip, inevitably exaggerated, to spread through Moscow. 'We are having a wedding,' he wrote. 'My sister-in-law Catherine is marrying Baron Heeckeren, the nephew and adopted son of the ambassador of the King of Holland.* He is a very handsome fine fellow, much in fashion, rich and 4 years younger than his intended. Preparations for the trousseau are occupying and much amusing my wife and her sisters, but are driving me mad. For my house has the appearance of a dress and lingerie shop.'[116]

D'Anthès's volte-face had astounded Natalya no less than society. Whereas reason told her that she should be thankful to be free of the harassment which had plagued her over the past months, irrationally she could not suppress some pique at the thought that the man who had threatened to kill himself for love of her was, a bare fortnight later, her sister's affianced suitor. At the same time this new alignment

---

* Pushkin has been taken in by Heeckeren's lie about the relationship, presumably communicated to him by Zhukovsky. The canard seems to have been generally accepted in Pushkin's circle.

threatened to alienate her from Ekaterina: a prospect which, since she was close to both her sisters, was distressing to her. She cherished the hope that with time some rapprochement between the two sides might take place; and, in order not to cause a definitive rupture, had to behave in a way which could appear equivocal. If Pushkin were not there she could treat d'Anthès, to some degree, as she had in the past; if he were there, however, she must ignore the other for fear of exacerbating her husband's anger. Sofya Karamzina noticed this contradiction – 'for her part she [Natalya] behaves in rather unorthodox fashion: in her husband's presence she affects not to salute and not to look at d'Anthès, and when he is not there, she recommences her old coquetry of lowered eyes, embarrassed and nervous conversation'[117] – but, not knowing the whole story, misinterpreted it, believing Natalya still to be attracted to her admirer.

Pushkin remained true to his promise that there would be no relations between the two families. In the first days after the engagement Natalya had tried to persuade him to change his mind and receive d'Anthès, so that the latter could call upon Ekaterina, but without success. Ekaterina herself soon put an end to these efforts. 'This morning I saw the lady in question,' d'Anthès wrote to her on 21 November, 'and, as always, my beloved, obeyed your supreme commands; I formally declared that I would be extremely obliged to her if she would deign to abandon this negotiation, which anyway is completely useless, and if Monsieur has not the wit to see that he alone is playing the role of a fool in this affair, then she was naturally wasting her time in trying to explain this to him.'[118] Over the next weeks Pushkin's anger showed no signs of subsiding: it was like a sore which will not heal, from being incessantly picked at. His behaviour at times seemed ridiculous not only to d'Anthès, but even to his friends, and certainly did not serve to quieten rumour. Towards the end of the year Sofya Karamzina, keeping her brother Andrey abreast of the situation, wrote: 'Pushkin continues to behave in the most stupid and absurd fashion; he has the look of a tiger-cat, and grinds his teeth whenever he speaks of that subject, a thing he does very willingly, always enchanted to find a new listener. You should have seen the eagerness with which he recounted all the obscure, half-imaginary details of this mysterious story to my sister Catherine, just as if he were narrating to her a drama or a novelette which had completely nothing to do with him. Up to now he persists in declaring that he will never allow his wife to attend the marriage, nor ever to receive her married sister. Yesterday I read a sermon to Natalie to the effect that she should make him put aside this absurd determination which will again set all the tongues of the town wagging.'[119]

Four days after the Saltykov ball, on Saturday 21 November, Sollogub chanced to call on Pushkin. The latter, taking his guest into the study, locked the door. 'You were more d'Anthès's second than mine,' he said. 'However, I should read you this letter to the old man. I've done with the young one – now it's the old one's turn.'[120] The letter began with the claim that, by the end of the recent imbroglio, he had forced d'Anthès to play 'such a pitiable and grotesque role' that Natalya, 'astonished at such servility, could not refrain from laughing, and that any emotion which she had perhaps come to feel for this great and sublime passion, evaporated into the calmest and most merited disgust'. He then turned to Heeckeren: 'You, the representative of a crowned head, have been paternally the pimp for your bastard, or the one so-called; all the behaviour of this young man has been directed by you.' His first glance at the anonymous letters put him on the track of the author; three days' search had made him sure it was Heeckeren. 'Perhaps you wish to know,' he continued, 'what has up to now prevented me from dishonouring you in the eyes of our court and yours.' He would not feel sufficiently avenged neither by a duel, nor by d'Anthès's marriage, nor by this letter, a copy of which he was keeping for his 'private use'. 'I want you yourself,' the letter concluded, 'to take the trouble to discover reasons which would be sufficient for me to undertake not to spit in your face and for me to destroy the last traces of this miserable affair.'[121] As Pushkin read, his passion increased. 'His lips trembled, his eyes became suffused with blood.'[122] Appalled by the letter, Sollogub recollected that the Odoevskys received on Saturday evenings. He hastened round to their apartment in Moshkov Lane, but a stone's throw away from the Pushkins. Here, luckily, he found Zhukovsky and warned him of this latest freak. Zhukovsky left immediately and managed to persuade Pushkin to abandon his intention.

Pushkin had in fact written not one letter, but two. The second, addressed to Benckendorff, was a far calmer, almost dispassionate account of the affair.

> I am entitled and believe myself obliged to inform Your Excellency of what has just taken place in my family. On the morning of 4 November I received three copies of an anonymous letter, outrageous to my honour and that of my wife. From the appearance of the paper, from the style of the letter, from the manner in which it was composed, I recognized immediately that it was by a foreigner, a man of high society, a diplomat. I began investigations. I learnt that on the same day seven or eight people had received a copy of the same letter, sealed and addressed to my direction within a double envelope. The majority of those who had received them, suspecting an infamy, did not send them to me.
>
> People were, in general, indignant at such a cowardly and gratuitous insult. But, whilst repeating that my wife's conduct was irreproachable, they said that the pretext for this infamy was the assiduous court paid to her by M. d'Anthès. On this occasion it did not suit me to see the name of my wife coupled with the name of anyone whatsoever. I had M. d'Anthès informed of this. Baron Heeckeren called on me and accepted a challenge for M. d'Anthès, asking me for a delay of 15 days.
>
> As it happens, during the interval M. d'Anthès fell in love with my sister-in-law, Mlle Goncharova, and asked for her hand in marriage. Being informed of this by public rumour, I caused the request to be made to M. d'Archiac (the second of M. d'Anthès) that my challenge should be regarded as not having taken place. Meanwhile I assured myself that the anonymous letter was from M. Heeckeren, of which I believe it my duty to warn the government and society.
>
> Being the only judge and guardian of my honour, and in consequence demanding neither justice nor vengeance, I cannot and will not deliver to anyone the proofs of what I assert.[123]

'In eight days you will hear of a vengeance unique of its kind,' Pushkin had said to Vera Vyazemskaya a week earlier. The letter to Heeckeren was the first step towards this. When he wrote that he would be satisfied not by a duel, or by d'Anthès's marriage, or by the letter itself, and invited Heeckeren to deduce what would satisfy him, he was not posing a difficult problem: he would be satisfied only by all three. The marriage, Pushkin thought (he had not taken into account Heeckeren's skill in circulating rumours), would make d'Anthès, the man who had proposed to the sister of the woman he loved because he was too cowardly to fight, a pariah in society. When he had written that he was keeping a copy of the letter for 'his private use', this implied, as Heeckeren would readily comprehend, that it would be circulated throughout Petersburg society, destroying the minister's reputation no less conclusively than that of his adopted son. Finally, the letter itself was so abusive both in tone and content that it could not fail to provoke a challenge. The letter to Benckendorff was not part of this scheme; indeed, it was not intended to be sent. It is hardly likely that Pushkin would, in writing to the head of the gendarmerie, confess to the criminal offence of issuing a challenge to a duel; nor would he have wished to call the attention of the authorities to his actions: a mere ten days earlier the thought that they might have been informed had induced in him something akin to paranoia. The letter was, rather, for use after the duel: to be explanatory of his actions, should he fall. After Zhukovsky's visit he put both letters away. They might be of use in the future.

Despite the passion with which Pushkin read his invective, it is difficult not to suspect that, at this moment, he was not wholly committed to forcing the issue with Heeckeren. Had he been, he would not – no part of the duelling code compelled him to do so – have read Sollogub the letter, knowing that the latter's first impulse would be to attempt to avert an encounter. Nor would he have yielded so meekly to Zhukovsky. This uncharacteristic behaviour is, perhaps, partly explained by the fact that at their meeting Zhukovsky warned him that he could no longer refrain from informing the tsar.

On the next day, Sunday, Zhukovsky saw Nicholas. He told the emperor about the events of the past weeks, confining himself to those of which he had personal knowledge. He mentioned the anonymous letter – this was no secret: by this time rumour of it had already reached Moscow, where it came to Turgenev's ears – but did not speak of Pushkin's conviction that Heeckeren was its author. Nicholas already knew of d'Anthès's pursuit of Natalya, and, obviously, of his engagement to Ekaterina, but Pushkin's challenge and the reason for its withdrawal were new to him. Zhukovsky concluded by warning the emperor that Pushkin was in the mood to reopen the issue.

That evening Nicholas repeated the news to the empress; the next day – Monday 23 November – she wrote to Countess Bobrinskaya, 'Since yesterday d'Anthès's marriage has become clear to me, but it is a secret.'[124] Almost at the same time as she was composing this note, Pushkin was being ushered into the emperor's study at the Anichkov Palace: it was soon after three, and Nicholas had just returned from a sleigh-ride round the city. At this audience Nicholas extracted from Pushkin a promise never, no matter how provoked, to engage again on a duel. If problems of this kind were to recur, he should turn to him, Nicholas, for help. Finally the emperor assured him that neither he, nor society, believed for a moment that Natalya's reputation was anything other than spotless.*

The incident now seemed finally to have been laid to rest; life reverted to that ceaseless social whirl that was St Petersburg in the winter. November the twenty-fourth was St Catherine's Day: the party at the Karamzins to celebrate Ekaterina Andreevna's name-day began at noon, and continued till well past midnight. Sofya, who calculated she poured 138 cups of tea in that time, thought there should be dancing in the evening, 'for it is cruel to do nothing when there are too many people to converse and not enough to stand shoulder to shoulder, as at a rout'.[125] But there was a sad lack of gentlemen, who were all at the Saltykovs' weekly ball. Pushkin and Natalya looked in to congratulate Ekaterina Andreevna, but stayed only a short time: it was also the name-day both of Natalya's sister and, more importantly, of her aunt.

Three days later, on Friday 27 November, the Bolshoy Theatre opened its season with the première of Glinka's new opera, *Ivan Susanin* (retitled, at Nicholas's behest, *A Life for the Tsar*), attended by 'the court, the diplomatic corps and all the state dignitaries'.[126] Sofya Karamzina shared a box in the upper circle with Mrs Shevich, Benckendorff's sister.

---

* After Pushkin's death Nicholas repeated his conviction of Natalya's absolute innocence in letters to his brother Michael and sister Marie, the wife of Karl Friedrich of Saxe-Weimar. See Suasso, 320, 322. There is no record of this conversation, but I find Stella Abramovich's analysis of the evidence and suggestions as to the topics discussed convincing (Abramovich, 1994a, 133–41).

Turgenev, who had arrived from Moscow two days earlier, taken a room at Demouth's, and put in an appearance at the Karamzins' evening tea – 'which he animated by his charming wit, so full of mots and piquant anecdotes on all the remarkable individuals of the human race'[127] – found it impossible to acquire a ticket, and gratefully accepted Heeckeren's amiable offer of a place in his box in the dress-circle.

On the twenty-ninth Pushkin and Natalya attended a dinner and ball at the Anichkov; Aleksandr Karamzin danced the mazurka with Natalya. On the thirtieth they were at an evening party given by the Vyazemskys; among the other guests was Emiliya Musina-Pushkina: 'How the other Pushkina pales beside her,' Turgenev commented in his diary.[128] But he was a prejudiced observer. 'Countess Emiliya Musina-Pushkina is remarkably handsome, and Turgenev has already been embroidering various sentimental patterns for her with his tender-passionate-penetrating glances,' remarked Vyazemsky.[129] On 1 December Pushkin, accompanied by Natalya and her sisters, was at the theatre with Turgenev. As they left, they met Danzas, who congratulated Ekaterina on her engagement. 'My sister-in-law doesn't know now what her nationality will be: Russian, French or Dutch,' joked Pushkin.[130]

Early in the evening on 4 December, Pushkin, on his way to the Mikhailovsky Palace, called on Grech, whose apartment was in the Kosikovsky mansion on the Nevsky. He found the family celebrating the name-day of Grech's wife, Varvara Danilovna, and stayed long enough to drink a glass of champagne and listen to Grech's son, Nikolay, declaim a speech from *Boris Godunov*. Impressed by the performance, he joked that the boy might become a second Garrick or Talma. 'These poets always have such baroque ideas,' Varvara Danilovna remarked acidly.[131] At the palace he joined Zhukovsky, Baron Krüdener, the Prince of Oldenburg and Countess Chicherina, the lady-in-waiting on duty, in the apartments of the Grand Duchess Elena – the former Charlotte of Württemberg. She was one of his admirers. 'I have twice invited Pushkin, whose conversation seems to me very entertaining,' she wrote to her husband, Grand Duke Michael.[132] He copied his poem on Barclay de Tolly, 'The Commander', into her album, and a week later was at the palace again, this time one of a much larger gathering.

On Sunday 6 December, he and Natalya attended the service and reception in the Winter Palace to mark the emperor's name-day. 'The singing in the church was entrancing!' Turgenev wrote to Aleksandr Bulgakov. 'I didn't know whether to listen or to gaze at Pushkina and her like. Her like! Are there many of them? The clever poet's wife eclipsed the others also with her attire; with diamonds and emeralds like the wife of a magnificent lord. She was asked whether she had many diamonds. "For the evening I have another dress, embroidered with different stones," she answered.'[133] The jewels were presumably paste. She was also wearing an imitation *povoinik* – a peasant headdress – in blue velvet, bought the previous day for 25 roubles from Zoé Malpart's boutique on Bolshaya Morskaya Street. Between October and January she ran up a bill of 471 roubles on hats at this establishment.

Money, as ever, was a problem, and one which became particularly acute at the beginning of each month. On 1 December two bills given to Prince Obolensky fell due: Pushkin could not pay the 8,000 roubles he owed, and was forced to negotiate an extension until March. Nor could he pay the next quarter's rent on the apartment, while most tradesmen were fobbed off with payments on account. At the beginning of January the situation was even worse. Many bills were left completely unpaid, including that of the livery-stable which supplied the carriage horses, the bakery, the dairy and the apothecary. Natalya's carefully kept household accounts showed clearly where the money was going, but seemed unable to hinder its departure. And the money-lenders were beginning to fight shy of Pushkin. Though he had raised 10,000 roubles from Vasily Yurev in September, at the end of December Natalya had to use her own name to secure a loan of 3,900 roubles. Pressed by his creditors – on 6 January the English Club reminded him that he owed 534.20 roubles – on 8 January Pushkin in desperation turned to Fedor Skobeltsyn for a loan of 3,000 roubles. The latter was a fifty-year-old Tambov squire, who, professing to be a great amateur of literature, though never known to read a book, had some years earlier attached himself to the Vyazemskys.* He replied with a note to Vyazemsky to which he attached Pushkin's begging letter: he could not comply

---

* Vyazemsky's son, Pavel, surprised at his father's acceptance of this character, asked Pushkin about him. Pushkin replied that he was 'a historical personage, being that very Skobeltsyn who by order of Emperor Paul Petrovich was transferred out of the guards "for having a face which induced melancholy"'. Skobeltsyn had a birthmark 'as big as a hen's egg' on his right cheek (*PVVS*, II, 188).

with the request, as he was himself in extremely straitened circumstances.

Some income was generated by new editions of Pushkin's works. On the suggestion of Vasily Polyakov – the manager of Glazunov's bookshop in the Gostiny Dvor, the shopping arcade on the Nevsky – a *Eugene Onegin* in miniature format was produced. This charming little – 11 cm. × 7 cm. – book, with its blue and white lithographed cover, the title set on a pattern of lace, was published at the end of 1836: on New Year's Day Pushkin gave a copy to Lyudmila Shishkina, the daughter of his favourite money-lender, Aleksey Shishkin. Glazunov printed 5,000 copies, and paid Pushkin 10,500 roubles. In December Pushkin was conducting negotiations with the book-seller Adolphe Pluchard – publisher of *Pluchard's Encyclopaedic Lexicon*, and owner of the press which had printed the *Tales of Belkin* – for the publication of a one-volume edition of his poems. On 22 December Pluchard paid him an advance of 1,500 roubles, but the project went no further. A third attempt to raise the wind produced no money, but gave rise to a bibliographical curiosity. In 1834 Pushkin had published, also with Glazunov, a second edition of the *Tales of Belkin*, which included in addition *The Queen of Spades* and two chapters of *The Blackamoor of Peter the Great*. The edition had sold badly, and a large stock remained in the warehouse. Another of Glazunov's employees, Lev Zhebelev, suggested in January that Pushkin should issue a two-volume edition of his prose, entitled *Novels and Stories*. The first volume would consist of his new historical novel, *The Captain's Daughter*. The second would be the 1834 book, given a new title page. Pushkin agreed, providing that Zhebelev bore the printing costs, for which he would be reimbursed out of the sales income. Publication was, however, delayed; the collection would have come out in May 1837, but by this time Pushkin's trustees were already contemplating the posthumous complete edition of his work and, not wishing for competition, bought up and destroyed the book: only one copy is known to exist.

At this time Pushkin saw much of Turgenev, who was living at Demouth's Hotel, a few minutes away along the Moika. They discussed the *Contemporary*, and articles Turgenev might write for it; Pushkin read his latest works, and spoke of his plans for the future. On 15 December Turgenev remained until past midnight. 'I spent the whole evening in intelligent and interesting conversation and did not go to the Shcherbatovs' ball,' he wrote in a letter to his brother. The previous day had been the anniversary of the Decembrist revolt: they had spoken of that, and of their friends in Siberia. Pushkin was planning, Turgenev wrote, to produce a critical edition of *The Tale of Igor's Campaign*, 'and show the mistakes in the views of Shishkov and other translators and commentators; but for that he would have to wait for Shishkov's death, so as not to kill him prematurely by criticism and others by laughter'.[134]

Pushkin's main preoccupation, however, was still his history of Peter the Great, which had not yet progressed beyond note form. He had begun work on it in 1834, after completing *Pugachev*. 'I am approaching Peter with fear and trembling,' he had then written to Pogodin.[135] But it was not until the very end of that year that he had begun to devote himself to it in earnest. 'From January I have been very occupied with Peter,' he had noted in his diary in February 1835.[136] And the greater part of the material he had collected – notes, synopses, transcriptions – was amassed during this year. He was able to do very little in 1836, though from Moscow he wrote to Natalya: 'I was in the Archives and will have to bury myself in them for another 6 months; what will you do then?'[137] 'Pushkin is with us here,' Chaadaev wrote to Turgenev. 'He is very taken up with his Peter the Great. His book will come just at the right moment, when the whole business of Peter the Great is destroyed: it will be an epitaph.'[138] Since then, however, work on the history had been overlaid by other concerns. But it still remained in the forefront of his mind. He brought it up in a conversation with Korff in October, and a few days later received a note from him. Fifteen years earlier, Korff wrote, he had had 'the idea of compiling a complete bibliographical catalogue of all books etc. published at any time about Russia, not just in the historical, but *generally in all* respects and in all languages: a compiler's work, but one which at the time afforded me indescribable pleasure'.[139] He was now enclosing that part of his unfinished bibliography which dealt with Peter in the hope that it might be of assistance. Pushkin replied the following day. 'What you sent me yesterday is in every respect valuable to me, and will remain a memorial for me. I really regret that governmental service has deprived us of a historian. I cannot hope to replace you. Reading this nomenclature, I became frightened and ashamed: the greater part of the works cited are unknown to me. I will make every effort to obtain them. What a field modern Russian history is! and when you think that it is as yet completely untilled, and that besides us Russians, no one can even undertake it! But history is long, life is short, and most of all human nature is lazy (Russian nature especially).'[140] There was a certain false modesty here. Pushkin did not think that Korff was a better historian than he; he was acquainted with those titles on the list that were of use: the majority, however, were valueless to the historian.

On 17 December Pushkin and Natalya attended a ball given by Major-General Meyendorff, commander of the Horse Guards, in the regimental barracks on Konnogvardeisky Boulevard. Among the guests was Dmitry Keller, a lycéen of the fourth intake, now a civil servant at the War Ministry. He had been commissioned by the tsar to translate the diary of General Patrick Gordon, who had been for many years in Russian service, becoming an intimate of Peter the Great.* Learning of this from the Meyendorffs, Pushkin demanded to be introduced, and eagerly plied Keller with questions about the manuscript. He was astonished to learn that it consisted of six large quarto volumes, saying, 'The emperor told me about this manuscript as a rarity, but I did not know that it was so extensive.'[141] He invited Keller to call on him; which the latter did early in January. 'He spoke much with me about the history of Peter the Great,' Keller recorded in his diary. 'When asked whether we would soon have the pleasure of reading his work on Peter, Aleksandr Sergeevich replied: "Up to now I have not yet written anything, I have busied myself solely with the collection of material: I want to form an idea about the whole work, then I will write the history in a year or year and a half."' He added, in French: 'It is killing work ... if I'd known in advance, I would not have taken it on.'[142]

On 22 December the fourth issue of the *Contemporary* appeared: it contained Pushkin's novel of the Pugachev rebellion, *The Captain's Daughter*. He had wanted to publish it as a separate work, but Kraevsky and Vrasky, the head of the printing-house which produced the journal,

---

* His carefully kept diary, in which he set down the occurrences of the day – telling of his doings, the people he had met and talked with, his debts and expenses, the money he had lent, his purchases of wine and beer, his difficulties about his pay – is invaluable to the student of the political as well as of the economical history of Russia' (Eugene Schuyler, *Peter the Great*. London, 1884, I, 257).

had insisted on its inclusion in the *Contemporary*, in the hope of bolstering the latter's flagging circulation. The novel had been completed at the end of October. On 1 November Pushkin read it to the Vyazemskys: 'It is full of interest, movement and simplicity,' Vyazemsky told Turgenev.[143]

On his way to Orenburg to serve in the army, the seventeen-year-old Petr Grinev is caught in a blizzard, but is guided to an inn by a chance-met peasant, to whom, in gratitude, he gives a hareskin jacket. He is posted to the fort at Belogorsk, where he falls in love with the commandant's daughter, Masha Mironova, and is wounded in a duel with a jealous fellow-officer, Shvabrin. When, after the outbreak of the rebellion, the fort is taken by Pugachev, Masha hides, her parents are put to death, Shvabrin joins the rebels, while Grinev is freed by Pugachev, in whom, to his surprise, he recognizes the recipient of the hareskin jacket. Later, when he attempts to rescue Masha from Shvabrin, he is captured again, but, together with her, is again released by Pugachev. After the suppression of the revolt, Shvabrin, now a prisoner, accuses Grinev of complicity with the rebels; he is sentenced to Siberia, but is saved by Masha, who travels to Tsarskoe Selo and makes a personal appeal to the empress.

In October 1833 Denis Davydov, writing to the Yazykov brothers about 'the mystery of Pushkin's appearance' in the Kazan and Orenburg provinces, had conjectured that he was planning 'a novel in which Pugachev will figure', and added 'perhaps we will see something close to Walter Scott'.[144] Certainly *The Captain's Daughter* owes much to Scott: narrative method, plot devices, characters – Belinsky calls Grinev's servant Savelich 'this Russian Caleb': a reference to Caleb Balderstone, the old butler of Ravenswood in *The Bride of Lammermoor*[145] – and situations are all heavily influenced by Scott. It is closest of all to *Rob Roy*: both novels are told in the first person, and there are remarkable similarities between the two intrigues.[146] But devotees of the other novelist might have felt they had been given short weight: by comparison to Scott's narrative amplitude, Pushkin's tale is little more than a short story. He has, however, managed to avoid plotting himself into a corner – which caused the abandonment of both *The Blackamoor of Peter the Great* and *Dubrovsky* – by keeping the intrigue as linear and as simple as those of the narrative poems. Written with terse economy, the tale bursts into life when Pugachev appears; as Belinsky notes, Grinev and Masha are pale and insubstantial characters, while Shvabrin's villainy is underexploited. *The Captain's Daughter* shows Pushkin to be a genial prosaist, unsurpassed in the creation of miniature scenes; it also shows that he is not, by nature, a novelist. 'Though I be a madman,' Chaadaev wrote to Turgenev, 'I hope that Pushkin will accept my genuine congratulations on this charming creation, his natural child, which a few days ago gave me a moment's respite from the melancholy which oppresses me.'[147]

With the approach of Christmas and the New Year the social round became, if possible, even more hectic. 'We have frosts – and balls!' Turgenev wrote to Bulgakov.[148] It was a relief to Pushkin that during this period d'Anthès was nowhere to be seen. The latter's chest complaint had returned, in more severe form, and he had been laid up since 13 December. On 22 December Princess Baryatinskaya – Mariya's mother – gave a ball at which the emperor and empress, the tsarevich and Prince Charles of Prussia – the empress's younger brother – were present, as were the Pushkins and Turgenev, who thought the occasion 'charmingly-magnificent', distinguished by 'brilliant toilettes, a crowd of beauties'.[149] The following day there was a ball at the Noble Assembly; on Christmas Eve the Musin-Pushkins gave a lunch at Demouth's Hotel: Zhukovsky, Wielhorski, Turgenev and Pushkin were among the guests: '. . . the lunch turned into a Lucullan feast,' wrote Turgenev, 'and I, lost in conversation with my fellow-topers, was dragged off by the poet Pushkin to his three-beautied family.'[150] Pushkin gave him a copy of the latest *Contemporary*, and Turgenev read himself to sleep that night with *The Captain's Daughter*. On Christmas Day Pushkin and Natalya went to the morning service in the Winter Palace; there was a ball at Prince Shcherbatov's in the evening, but they preferred to spend it quietly with the Karamzins. The following evening, however, they attended the grand masquerade and supper at the Winter Palace: nearly a thousand guests were present. As always the ball opened with a polonaise; that morning d'Anthès, still ill, had written to his fiancée: 'First of all, dear Catherine, I shall begin by executing a commission on behalf of the baron, who charges me to engage you for the first polonaise, and in addition asks me to beg you to place yourself close to the Court, so that he can find you.'[151]

On Monday the twenty-eighth d'Anthès finally rose from his sick-bed, and in the evening appeared at the Meshcherskys, 'all thin, pale and interesting,' wrote Sofya Karamzina. 'The next day he was back again, this time with his betrothed, and what is worse, with Pushkin: the histrionic displays of hate and poetic fury began again; black as night and with a brow as threatening as that of an enraged Jupiter, Pushkin only broke his farouche and embarrassing silence with a few brief, ironic and staccato words and an occasional demonic laugh: oh, it was highly amusing, I can assure you.'[152] The scene was repeated three days later, at the large party given by the Vyazemskys to see in the New Year, when Natalya Stroganova told Princess Vera that Pushkin's 'look was so terrifying, that, had she been his wife, she would not have dared go home with him'.[153] But this was a misapprehension: Pushkin's ire was directed solely at d'Anthès; at this time he was no less tender to Natalya than before, as Zhukovsky's terse and elliptic notes attest: 'In the aunt's presence, affection to his wife; in the presence of Aleksandra and others who could have reported brusqueness. At home gaiety and great accord.'[154]

The weather was appalling – snow and a high wind – on the morning of 6 January; nevertheless Pushkin and Natalya were at the Winter Palace at ten to celebrate Epiphany; after the service they took part in the procession to the Neva; were present at the Blessing of the Waters, the aspersion of the standards and colours, greeted by a cannon salute; and at the ensuing festivities in the Portrait Gallery. Turgenev watched, but could not take part in the ceremony, as his new uniform trousers had not been delivered. Later that day all three were at the Ficquelmonts. 'A veritably Parisian evening!' Turgenev exclaimed in his diary. 'A small circle formed consisting of Barante, Pushkin, Vyazemsky, the Prussian minister and your very humble servant,' he told Bulgakov. 'We *chatted*, a thing which is quite rare at the present time. The conversation was varied, brilliant, and extremely interesting, for Barante recounted to us some piquant things about Talleyrand and his memoirs the first part of which he had read; Vyazemsky played his part by producing mots worthy of the originality of his wit. Pushkin told us anecdotes, charac-terizing Peter I and Catherine II, and for a moment I too was the equal of these coryphaei of the Petersburg salons.'[155] Barante offered to translate *The Captain's Daughter* into French, and they were then joined by the Marquis of Londonderry, who, having failed to obtain the embassy at St Petersburg, was consoling himself by travelling in Russia as a private individual.

Three days later, on Saturday the ninth, Pushkin and Turgenev spent most of the day together. In the morning Turgenev called on Pushkin, who read him a curious little humorous sketch he had recently written, 'The Last of the Relatives of Joan of Arc'. This purported to be an article from the London *Morning Chronicle*, containing two letters found among the papers of the recently deceased Jean Dulys, the last descendant of Joan of Arc. The first, addressed by his father to Voltaire, protested against the portrayal of Joan in *La Pucelle*, and challenged its author to a duel. Voltaire, in his reply, excused himself on the ground of his age and ill-health, and denied authorship of the work. The article reproached the French for their treatment of Joan's descendants, and Voltaire for his treatment of Joan: 'Once in his life he chanced to be a genuine poet, and how did he use his inspiration! With satanic breath he blows upon the sparks smouldering in the ashes of the martyr's pyre, and like a drunken savage dances around his toy bonfire.'* When *La Pucelle* appeared, 'all enthusiastically greeted a work in which scorn for everything considered sacred to men and to citizens was taken to the last degree of cynicism.' And had Dulys's challenge been known, it would have aroused inextinguishable laughter in philosophical drawing-room and in ancient hall alike. 'Miserable age! Miserable nation!' the article concluded.[156] It is difficult not to see a reflection of recent events in this anecdote: Voltaire, cravenly avoiding a duel and denying authorship, is playing Heeckeren's role, and Dulys, defending a relative's honour, Pushkin's. But it is not as simple as this: Voltaire had been one of Pushkin's heroes since his schooldays, and *La Pucelle* was one of his favourite works, while Dulys is a crackbrained simpleton, who confuses fact and fiction.

After the reading the two went round to Turgenev's room at Demouth's, to study what Turgenev referred to as his 'French' or 'Parisian' papers. He had brought with him, he later wrote, 'rich and important acquisitions which I had discovered in the Parisian archives; especially in the Archive of the Ministry of Foreign Affairs, where I

---

* A reference to Voltaire's remark on *Hamlet* in his *Dissertation sur la tragédie ancienne et moderne*: 'One might believe that this work is the fruit of a drunken Savage's imagination.'

copied almost everything referring to Russia from the original documents, beginning with our first relations with France before Peter I –
up to the first two years of Elizabeth inclusively'.[157] Pushkin remained
with Turgenev until four, when he returned home for dinner. In the
early evening Turgenev called again, bringing with him material for the
Contemporary, including extracts from his journal describing travels in
Scotland and a visit to Weimar: some of this appeared in the first
posthumous issue of the journal. From here Turgenev, indefatigable in
his sociability, proceeded to visit his friends the Bravuras, and ended
the evening at the Ficquelmonts, who were giving 'a simple little rout,
about a hundred people'.[158]

In November d'Anthès had applied for permission to marry to his
regimental commander, and Ekaterina to the empress; Heeckeren,
through Nesselrode, had petitioned that the children of the marriage
should be brought up in the Catholic faith; more recently Wiegel, in
his capacity as director of the Department of Foreign Creeds, had given
Ekaterina permission to marry a Catholic. On 3 January the regimental
orders of the day excused d'Anthès from duties until the eighteenth, by
reason of his marriage. On the ninth Ekaterina's brothers, Dmitry and
Sergey, arrived from Moscow. 'I very much wish that the whole of my
family should gather together on this day, then I am assured in advance
of good wishes,' she had written.[159] She had, however, expressed no wish
to see her parents. A few days earlier Natalya had received a letter from
Benckendorff. 'His Majesty the Emperor,' he wrote, 'wishing to do
something which would be agreeable to your husband and yourself,
charges me to place in your hands the enclosed sum on the occasion
of Mlle your sister's marriage, being persuaded that it will give you
pleasure to present her with this wedding-present.'[160] The enclosed sum
was a thousand roubles.

The wedding took place on Sunday 10 January. There were two
ceremonies: one in St Isaac's Cathedral – not the present St Isaac's
which, begun in 1819, was not completed until 1858, but the church
within the Admiralty complex – and one in St Catherine's, the Roman
Catholic church on the Nevsky. The witnesses were Count Stroganov,
Ekaterina's first cousin once removed, her brother Ivan, d'Archiac, two
of d'Anthès's fellow-officers, Captain Bethancourt and Idaliya's husband
Colonel Poletika, and Heeckeren. In both churches the entries in the

registers were incorrect: both repeated the canard that d'Anthès was Heeckeren's adopted son. In addition, at St Isaac's, d'Anthès, who was twenty-four, put himself down as twenty-five, while Ekaterina, who was twenty-seven, put herself down as twenty-six; at St Catherine's d'Anthès gave his correct age, but Ekaterina took another year off.[161] 'I helped with the toilette of Mlle Goncharov,' Sofya Karamzina wrote to her brother, 'but her evil aunt Zagryazhskaya made me a scene when the ladies declared that I was coming with them to the church; for good motives, apparently, fearing inquisitiveness, she poured out on me all the bile which a week of indiscreet inquiries had given her [...] You must admit that, besides being disagreeable, I had to find this very disappointing. No observations to make, nothing to tell you about the physiognomies of the actors in this mysterious drama during the final denouement scene.'[162] Pushkin stayed at home, but Natalya was present for the two ceremonies. However, she left immediately afterwards, not staying for the supper. This was a protracted occasion: Aleksandr and Vladimir Karamzin did not get home until after midnight.

Over the next few days the newly-weds undertook the traditional round of calls on friends and relatives, visiting, among others, the Karamzins and the Vyazemskys. Aleksandr Karamzin lunched with them on the Monday, and was 'much pleased with their elegant interior'; on Tuesday it was Sofya's turn: her response was more gushing: 'Nothing could be more pretty, more comfortable, more deliciously elegant than their rooms, nothing could appear more serene and joyful than the countenances of all three, since the father is a completely inherent part of the drama and the menage: it would demand a superhuman dissimulation for all this to be feigned and moreover then the game would become the whole of life!'[163] Aleksandra, Ekaterina's sister, paints a somewhat different picture. 'Katya has gained, I think,' she wrote a week later, 'as far as decorum is concerned, she feels more at home in the house than at first: more tranquil, but, I think, at times rather sad. She is too clever to show this and too proud too; so she tries to mislead me, but my gaze is too penetrating to not notice this.'[164]

Early in the morning of Thursday the fourteenth the Goncharov brothers left for Moscow, without taking their farewells and without even informing anyone they were leaving. 'Upon my word, has anything like this ever been known before?' Ekaterina wrote indignantly. 'To deceive one's elder sister so unceremoniously; to tell her you are not leaving, but a few hours later – it's "whip them along, coachman!" and the gentlemen are galloping at top speed along the high-road.' Their aunt, Ekaterina Ivanovna, had been furious with rage, Aleksandra told them. 'She called on us completely beside herself, almost screaming about the disgrace; Tasha with great difficulty managed to calm her, she wouldn't listen to anything, saying that it was unforgivable. These are her exact words: "*What! two boys are living for four days in the town and can't spare a moment to call on their aunt.*" I heard this from my room, since between ourselves I must tell you that when I can avoid her I do so as often as possible. I don't remember the end of the conversation, all that I know is that you really caught it.'[165]

Ekaterina Ivanovna's indignation was not only due to the discourtesy shown to her; but also to that shown to Count Stroganov, who that day gave a dinner to celebrate the marriage. Pushkin was invited, but not told the purpose of the occasion: it was hoped that at it he and d'Anthès might become reconciled. Despite the excellence of the wines, commented on by Aleksandr Karamzin, this did not occur: when Pushkin was approached by Heeckeren after dinner, he said curtly that he did not wish to renew relations with d'Anthès. 'So finishes this novel à la Balzac, much to the annoyance of St Petersburg's male and female scandalmongers,' commented Karamzin afterwards.[166] Heeckeren, conscious that the rift between the two households would, on the contrary, stimulate rumour, continued his efforts to bring them together. He got the newly-married couple to call at the Moika apartment; they were not received. He made d'Anthès write to Pushkin, expressing the hope that the past might be forgotten and that they might become reconciled. Pushkin did not bother to answer. He made d'Anthès write again. Pushkin took the letter, unopened, to Ekaterina Ivanovna, intending to ask her to return it to d'Anthès, but, meeting Heeckeren, attempted to give it to him. Heeckeren refused it, on the grounds it was not addressed to him. Furious, Pushkin threw it in his face, saying, 'You shall take it, you scoundrel!'[167] With all hope of reconciliation gone, d'Anthès, remembering the ignoble role he had played a few weeks earlier, lost no opportunity to put about his version of events: his noble act of self-sacrifice for Natalya's sake; and, to make this version appear plausible, began once again to pay ostentatious attention to her.

From the Stroganov dinner most of the guests had gone on to a ball given by Barante, the French ambassador. According to Turgenev, who stayed until almost four in the morning, it was 'brilliant and magnificent from the toilettes and beauty of the sex'.[168] 'Madame Heeckeren had a happy look which made her seem ten years younger and gave her the appearance of a nun who had just taken the veil or a deluded newly-wed,' Vyazemsky told Emiliya Musina-Pushkina: 'I cannot conceal from you that her husband also danced much, much enjoyed himself, and no shadow of nuptial melancholy lay on his features, so handsome and *expressive*.'[169] D'Anthès also danced and flirted with Natalya, drinking her health at supper. Noticing this, Pushkin went up to Ekaterina, who was for a moment alone, and suggested to her that she should drink *his* health. Not taking the point, and thus shocked at this *outré* proposal, she refused, refusing again when he repeated the suggestion.

The following evening the Vyazemskys gave a 'children's ball' for their daughter Nadezhda, whose fifteenth birthday it was. 'Everyone enjoyed themselves – the children, their mothers and even the governesses, since I flirted with them,' wrote Turgenev.[170] Pushkin alone conveyed a far from happy impression. While d'Anthès danced attendance on Natalya, he sat gazing at Ekaterina with an air of gloomy menace. The next day, perhaps to cheer himself up, he ordered a 25-rouble *pâté de foie gras* from Feuillette's restaurant – 'Strasbourg's imperishable pie' (*Eugene Onegin*, I, xvi) had always been one of his favourite dishes. That it was not for a dinner party is suggested by the fact that no increase was made in the usual weekly order of wine – four sauternes and four claret – from Raoult.

On Sunday, a week after the wedding, Pushkin was surprised and pleased to be visited by Miss Khilevskaya, the governess at Trigorskoe. She brought with her a pot of home-made gooseberry conserve and a note from Praskovya Aleksandrovna. He learnt with delight that Zizi Vrevskaya had also come to St Petersburg, and was staying with her brother-in-law and his wife, the Serdobins. He made a note of the address – 8th Line, Vasilevsky Island – on the back of Praskovya's note, and called there the next day. He and Zizi talked about the disposal of Mikhailovskoe, which both her husband and her brother-in-law were interested in acquiring. He called again on Friday, and arranged to take her to the Hermitage on the following Monday – 25 January.

Zizi Vrevskaya

Earlier that week he had been to the literary soirée Pletnev regularly held on Wednesdays. He found Nikitenko there, and, still annoyed by the censorship of *Angelo*, avoided speaking to him. 'He has become a great aristocrat,' Nikitenko wrote in his diary that night. 'What a pity that he values himself so little as a man and a poet, and seeks entrance to one closed circle of society, when he could have complete sway over the whole of society. He wants most of all to be a lord, but with us a lord is of course the man with the largest income. How that affected tone, that refined haughtiness of manner, which tomorrow could be irretrievably brought low by disgrace, do not suit him. But besides his talent he is undoubtedly an intelligent man. For example, today he said much that was sensible, and, moreover, shrewd about the Russian language. He also confessed that at the moment it was impossible to write the history of Peter, that is it would not be allowed to be published. It is clear that he has read much on Peter.'[171] Pushkin was cheerful throughout the evening, promising, on leaving, to return the following week. Probably on the same day, learning that Korff, who lived a few doors away on the Moika Embankment, was ill, he had called round, bringing with him for the invalid 'various antiquarian and very interesting books on Russia': which, after Pushkin's death, Turgenev and Zhukovsky had some difficulty in retrieving.[172]

Turgenev, having been abroad for the previous two years, had, of course, known nothing of recent events when he had arrived in St Petersburg; learning something from Zhukovsky, in a letter to his brother at the end of November he had remarked: 'Pushkin is worried because of a family matter.'[173] Susceptible as he was to feminine beauty, he found it hard to join the critical chorus of voices – chiefly feminine – that condemned Natalya's behaviour and saw it as largely responsible for the situation. 'The evening at Princess Meshcherskaya's. About Pushkin; all attacked him on account of his wife, I defended. Compliments from Sofya Nikolaevna [Karamzina] on my courtesy,' he noted in his diary on 19 December;[174] and two days later wrote to Ekaterina Sverbeeva in Moscow: 'Pushkin is my neighbour, he is full of ideas, and we get along together very well in our interminable prattlings; others find him changed, preoccupied and no longer supplying his part to the conversation, which used to be so attractive; but I am not of that number, and we have difficulty in finishing a subject by not finishing it, that is, by never exhausting it; his wife is everywhere beautiful, at a ball or a home in her huge black wrap. Her sister's betrothed is very ill, he does not call on the Pushkins. We will talk of all this by your fireside.'[175] On 18 January he attended a rout given by Baron Lützerode, the ambassador of the Kingdom of Saxony, which turned into an impromptu ball in honour of the newly-weds. 'Natalya Pushkina and I talked for a long time, she from the bottom of her heart,' he recorded, and the next day wrote: 'At Prince Vyazemsky's: about the Pushkins, Goncharova, d'Anthès-Heeckeren.'[176]

On Thursday 21 January he breakfasted with d'Archiac, who read him the letter to d'Anthès of 17 November in which Pushkin had withdrawn his challenge. He then called at the apartment on the Moika and had another long conversation with Pushkin: they spoke of Chateaubriand – Pushkin was writing an article on the French author's translation of Milton's *Paradise Lost* – of Goethe and Turgenev's visit to Weimar, of the spread of civilization: Vyazemsky had passed on to Pushkin a letter Turgenev had sent him in September. 'How my Europeanism rejoiced, seeing in Simbirsk a steamer, sailing from Nizhny to Saratov and Astrakhan,' he had written. 'What that it was full of Tatars and Kirgizes! Walter Scott's fatherland is a benefactor to the mother country of Karamzin and Derzhavin. Tatarism cannot long resist this Scottish coal smoke; its eyes will be stung by it, and they will see more clearly.'[177]

That day they were both at a dinner given by Senator Lubyanovsky, who had the apartment above the Pushkins. Vyazemsky had been expected too, but had gone by mistake to the Rostopchins, where he had sat down at table and told his surprised host that Turgenev would be arriving shortly. He missed a number of interesting and curious anecdotes about personalities of Catherine II's reign, told by Lubyanovsky, and an excellent Tokay, which sent Turgenev to sleep after dinner so that he arrived late at the Ficquelmonts' ball. This was a large occasion, with more than five hundred guests, including Prince Charles of Prussia and the Londonderrys. The marchioness's jewels had stunned even St Petersburg society, not noted for its lack of ostentation. That evening she was, as Princess Durnovo observed, wearing 'all her emeralds and many diamonds'. 'Krüdener is really very beautiful, such fine skin, delicate features; Mme Pushkina had smooth hair, plaited very low, just like a beautiful cameo,' she added.[178]

Pushkin had already begun to prepare the next number of the *Contemporary*: he had secured some material from Turgenev, and, anxious also to include literary works, had determined to introduce Russian readers to an English poet he much admired, Barry Cornwall (pseudonym of Bryan Waller Proctor). His acquaintance with the work of this minor author – even then little known, and now completely forgotten – can be traced back to an encounter at the beginning of 1830 with an English officer, James Alexander, a captain in the 16th Lancers.[179] Alexander, who was travelling through Russia to the war in the Ottoman domains, met Pushkin in St Petersburg. They had a common acquaintance: George Willock, whom Pushkin had met in Pyatigorsk in 1820. Alexander was an amateur of poetry: his travel writings are stuffed with quotations; among his comments on Russian life he notes that Zhukovsky has produced an 'admirable' translation of Gray's *Elegy* and that 'Pouskin has been equally successful with Lord Byron's vigorous strains, and many of his original pieces have a satirical vein pervading them'.[180] In 1826 he had been aide-de-camp to Colonel Kinneir, the East India Company's envoy in Teheran. The legation's medical officer was John McNeill – later minister plenipotentiary to the shah – who had married, in 1823, Eliza Wilson, the sister of the Scottish critic and poet John Wilson – the 'Christopher North' of *Blackwood's Magazine*. Alexander knew her well, indeed had met her again recently on the steamer from Kronstadt to St Petersburg. To be acquainted with a poet's sister stimulates interest in the poet, and Alexander became an admirer of Wilson, 'one of the master spirits of our age'.[181] He now told Pushkin about the poet, gave him, or persuaded him to acquire, *The Poetical Works of Milman, Bowles, Wilson and Barry Cornwall*, published in Paris in 1829; and discussed with him Wilson's play, *The City of the Plague*, included in the anthology, one scene of which Pushkin translated that autumn in Boldino, and published as *A Feast in the Time of Plague* in 1832.

They may have spoken of Cornwall; or possibly Pushkin, leafing through the book, came across his poems and was taken with them. Also while in Boldino he proceeded to translate, or adapt, three of the other's trifles – 'Serenade', 'An Invocation', and 'Here's a health to thee, Mary' – and in 1835 made a start on one of Cornwall's *Dramatic Scenes*, the work for which the latter was best known, translating part of Frederigo's opening monologue from *The Falcon*.*[182] It was *The Falcon*, together with some other scenes, that he wished to publish in the *Contemporary*. Now, however, he could not afford the time to do the translation himself. Pletnev suggested that he employ Aleksandra Ishimova, who had translated Fenimore Cooper's *Red Rover*, and had just brought out the first part of her *History of Russia in Tales for Children*, which was to be very favourably received. On the day after the Ficquelmont ball, therefore, while out for his afternoon walk, Pushkin called at her apartment on Furshtatskaya Street, between the Summer and the Tauric Gardens, but did not find her in. He later wrote, offering her the commission, and received an enthusiastic acceptance.

The following day, 21 January, he attended, as he often did, the Saturday morning classical concert at Engelhardt House, where he was seen by Ivan Turgenev, the future novelist. 'He stood by the door, leaning against the jamb, and, with arms crossed over his broad chest, looked around with a dissatisfied air. I remember his small, swarthy face, his African lips, the bared strong white teeth, the drooping sidewhiskers, the dark, bile-shot eyes beneath a high, almost browless forehead – and the curly hair ... He cast a fleeting glance at me; the unceremonious attention with which I gazed at him must have produced an unpleasant impression; as if in annoyance he hunched a shoulder – he seemed generally to be out of sorts – and moved aside.'[183] In the afternoon Pletnev accompanied him on his customary walk. 'He was then in some kind of highly religious mood,' Pletnev recollected in 1842. 'He spoke to me about the ways of *Providence*, esteemed most of all in man the quality of good will to all, saw this quality in me, envied my life and extracted a promise that I would write my memoirs.'[184]

That evening there was a ball at the Vorontsov-Dashkovs. 'The most brilliant, the most fashionable, the most attractive house in St Petersburg at that time was the house of Count Ivan Vorontsov-Dashkov, thanks to the charm of his young wife, the delightful Countess Aleksandra

---

* 'Proctor's scenes, though graceful and poetical, are very obvious productions of the nineteenth century, and seldom transcend the forcible feeble in their attempts to exhibit vehement passion' (*Dictionary of National Biography*).

Kirilovna,' Sollogub writes in his memoirs. 'Each winter the Vorontsov-Dashkovs gave a ball, which the court favoured with its presence. The cream of St Petersburg society was invited to this ball, which always comprised, as it were, an event in the fashionable life of the capital.'[185] Pushkin and Natalya, d'Anthès and Ekaterina were among the guests.

In the course of the evening the emperor had a short conversation with Pushkin, during which he must have touched on the rumours circulating about Natalya, for Pushkin found himself constrained to express his thanks for Nicholas's solicitude in offering her advice on her conduct – as he had done at the Anichkov Palace in November. But gratitude was the last thing on his mind. Then he had been furious that the emperor should have usurped a right which he felt to be his alone; now this rage returned, in darker, more dangerous form, exacerbated by the conviction that his marital problems were the sole topic of conversation in St Petersburg. 'It is not enough,' he had said to Sofya Karamzina recently, 'that you, that my friends, that society here should be as convinced as I am of the innocence and chastity of my wife: my reputation and my honour must also be intact in every corner of Russia where my name is known.'[186] And when the emperor, in answer to his thanks, exclaimed, 'But could you have expected aught else from me?' Pushkin could not restrain himself. 'Not only could, Sire, but, to speak frankly, I suspected you too of paying court to my wife.'[187]

Natalya

Pushkin's mood was made even blacker by d'Anthès's outrageous behaviour. He followed Natalya around the ball, danced several times with her, partnering her in a quadrille; and, going in after her to supper with his wife, said loudly to Ekaterina, in Pushkin's hearing, 'Come, my lawful one.'[188] The sisters employed the same chiropodist, enabling him to bring out a laboured – no doubt the product of much thought beforehand – tasteless and suggestive witticism. '*Le pédicure prétend*,' he said to Natalya, '*que votre cor est plus beau que celui de ma femme*.'* Had Pushkin heard this, it must have produced an immediate

---

* A pun: *cor*, 'corn', and *corps*, 'body', are phonetically identical: 'The chiropodist says that your corn/body is more beautiful than that of my wife.'

blow. Natalya, conscious of the possible consequences, did not report it to him until after the ball.[189]

During the evening Pushkin had discussed the Pugachev uprising with General Karl Toll, who had served under Michelsohn, the commander chiefly responsible for putting down the revolt. The following morning he sent the general a copy of *Pugachev*. In the afternoon two young men, Lukyan Yakubovich and Ivan Sakharov, called on him. 'Pushkin was sitting on a chair,' Sakharov later recollected. 'On the floor lay a bearskin; on it sat Pushkin's wife, with her head on his lap.'[190] He was much calmer now. Natalya had unburdened her heart to him and he had resolved to act; he would do so on the morrow. That evening they were at a large rout at the Meshcherskys. With his host, Prince Petr Meshchersky, he retired to the study, where Arkady Rosset found them playing chess. 'You've come from the drawing-room,' Pushkin said to him. 'Is he already there, by my wife?' Rosset mumbled that he had seen d'Anthès. Pushkin looked at him closely, and when he blushed, roared with laughter.[191]

The next morning – Monday, 25 January – Pushkin took out again the letters he had written to Heeckeren and Benckendorff on 21 November. The one to Benckendorff could stand; putting it in an envelope, he laid it aside. The one to Heeckeren required some revision. He began to rewrite it, carefully preserving the particularly choice terms of abuse. The final version read:

Baron!
Allow me to sum up what has just taken place. Your son's behaviour had long been known to me and could not be a matter of indifference to me. I contented myself with the role of an observer, entitled to intervene when I judged it proper. An incident which at any other moment would have been very disagreeable, happily supervened to get me out of the difficulty: I received the anonymous letters. You know the rest: I made your son play such a pitiable role that my wife, astonished at such cowardice and servility, could not refrain from laughing, and any emotion which she had perhaps come to feel for this great and sublime passion evaporated into the calmest and most merited disgust.

I am obliged to admit, Baron, that your role has not been altogether seemly. You, the representative of a crowned head, have been paternally the pimp for your son. It appears that all his behaviour (clumsy enough, moreover) has been directed by you. It was probably you who dictated to him the sorry witticisms he has been mouthing and the twaddle he has taken upon himself to write. Like an obscene old woman, you would go and spy on my wife from every corner to speak to her of the love of your bastard, or the one so-called; and when, ill with the pox, he was confined to his home, you would say that he was dying of love for her; you would mumble: give me back my son.

You will be well aware, Baron, that after all this I cannot permit my family to have the least relation with yours. It was on this condition that I consented not to pursue this filthy affair and not to dishonour you in the eyes of our court and of yours, as I had the power and intention to do. I do not care for my wife to hear again your paternal exhortations. I cannot allow your son, after the despicable conduct he has shown, to dare to speak to my wife, still less to mouth to her these barrack-room calembours, and play devotion and unhappy passion whilst he is nothing but a coward and a scoundrel. I am thus obliged to address myself to you, to beg you to put an end to all these goings-on, if you wish to avoid a new scandal, from which I certainly shall not shrink.

I have the honour to be, Baron
You most humble and most obedient servant,
Aleksandr Pushkin.[192]

'Since the beginning of this affair, the only moment of respite I have had was after writing this letter,' he was to say two days later.[193] He sent it off by the town post: Heeckeren would receive it the following morning. Later that day he called on Zizi, to take her to the Hermitage, as they had arranged. In the evening he and Natalya were at the Vyazemskys, where once again they found d'Anthès and Ekaterina among the other guests. D'Anthès was particularly full of spirits that night. 'Look how gay he is,' Pushkin said to Princess Vyazemskaya. 'He doesn't know what is waiting for him at home.' He told her he had written to Heeckeren.[194] Alarmed, she informed Wielhorski; but he was leaving and had nothing to suggest. That evening Vyazemsky himself had been at a ball given by the Myatlevs in honour of Prince Charles of Prussia. He did not return home until early in the morning, when Vera told him of Pushkin's words. Vyazemsky had become rather tired of the whole affair: it savoured too much of a melodrama in which no one's behaviour was irreproachable. 'My uncle Vyazemsky says that he is covering his face and turning it away from the house of the Pushkins,' Sofya Karamzina remarked.[195] Like Wielhorski, Vyazemsky could not see what might be done. They would have to cease entertaining, Vera remarked. It was impossible to have Pushkin and d'Anthès in the same room together.

Early next morning – Tuesday 26 January – Pushkin called on Turgenev at Demouth's Hotel and looked through some of the material the latter had found in the French archives, and which had just been transcribed by a copyist. He was 'gay, full of life, without the slightest traces of pensiveness', joking and laughing.[196] Promising to return later, he left before midday. Heeckeren would have received the letter between ten and eleven, and might have responded without delay. But at home he found no cartel, merely a letter from General Toll, thanking him for *Pugachev*, and for the rehabilitation of Michelsohn's reputation. He replied immediately. 'I regret that I could not place in my book a few lines of your pen for the full justification of the meritorious warrior. However strong the prejudices of ignorance, however avidly calumny may be accepted, one word spoken by such a man as you destroys them forever. With one glance genius discloses the truth, and *truth is mightier than the king*, says Holy Writ.'*[197] In writing this he must have been thinking of his own situation: was he not surrounded by calumny, and was he not about to destroy it with the truth? But he still had had no word from Heeckeren. While waiting he scribbled a note to Turgenev to say that he would not be able to return: why did the other not visit him instead?

Later, in a letter to the Dutch Foreign Minister, Verstolk van Soelen, Heeckeren explained his delay in replying to Pushkin by maintaining that he did not receive the letter until he was leaving to dine with Count

* A reference to I Esdras 3.1–4.41.

Stroganov: an obvious lie, since the chronology of the following sequence
of events would then become wholly impossible. In fact, he had been
horrified by what he read, and for some time had hesitated as to a
course of action, hoping vainly to find a means of avoiding a duel. The
one possible stratagem had, however, already been used in November,
and he had finally to respond with a challenge. 'What could I do?' he
continues more veraciously. 'Myself challenge the author of this screed?
Firstly, the public character with which the King has deigned to invest
me forbade this; secondly, that would not end the matter. If the victor,
I would dishonour my son, since ill-will would whisper everywhere that
I had stood up because I had already once been obliged to settle an
affair of honour in which my son had lacked courage; if the victim, my
son would without fail avenge me and his wife would be without support.
However, I did not wish to be governed solely by my own opinion, and
I at once consulted my friend, Count Stroganov – his view being in
accordance with mine, I communicated the letter to my son, and a
cartel was addressed to M. Pushkin.'[198] In an almost identical letter to
Nesselrode written two days later he adds the detail that d'Anthès 'asked
me, as a proof of my affection, to give him the preference'.[199]

D'Archiac, who had once again agreed to be d'Anthès's second,
called on Pushkin later that afternoon and sent in his card, on which
he had written: 'I beg M. de Pushkin to do me the honour of letting
me know whether he can receive me; or if now he cannot, at what time
it will be possible.'[200] Pushkin saw him immediately. D'Archiac handed
him a letter from Heeckeren:

Sir
    Knowing neither your hand nor your signature, I turned to
Vicomte d'Archiac, who will deliver this to you, to certify that
the letter to which I am replying comes from you. Its content
is so far beyond the limits of what is acceptable that I refuse to
reply to all the details of this epistle. You appear to have forgotten, Sir, that it was you who retracted the challenge that you
had addressed to Baron Georges Heeckeren and which had been
accepted by him. The proof of that which I affirm here exists,
written by your hand, and has remained in the hands of the
seconds. It only remains for me to inform you that Vicomte

d'Archiac will call on you to arrange with you the place where you will meet with Baron Georges Heeckeren and that this rencontre will not admit of any delay.

Later I will know how, Sir, to make you appreciate the respect due to the Character with which I am invested and which cannot be affected by any action on your part.

A postscript ran: 'Read and approved by me. Baron Georges de Heeckeren.'[201] Pushkin waved the letter aside, but accepted the verbal challenge delivered by d'Archiac on d'Anthès's behalf. Soon after d'Archiac's departure Turgenev arrived. They talked again about the *Contemporary*, and Pushkin gave him a copy of the two-volume edition of his poems and stories, published by Smirdin in 1835, correcting a printing error on the cover of the second volume. Turgenev left about five: Princess Shakhovskaya was expecting him for dinner. Although the covers were already being laid in the dining-room, Pushkin left the house and had himself driven to the Serdobins on Vasilevsky Island. He remained there to dine. Zizi found him 'happy, free from those mental sufferings which had so terribly tortured him'.[202]

On returning to the Moika he found a note from d'Archiac: 'The undersigned informs M. de Pushkin that he will await at home until eleven this evening and thereafter at Countess Razumovsky's ball the person responsible for dealing with this affair which must be brought to a conclusion tomorrow.'[203] This called his attention to a problem he had so far completely ignored: the necessity of finding a second. Sollogub was no longer available; in early December he had been posted to Kharkov to join the staff of the new governor-general, Count Aleksandr Stroganov. In any case, Sollogub had been insufficiently bloody-minded. Pushkin wanted no one who would insist on reconciliation, or run to Zhukovsky with news of the duel. He was uneasily aware, too, that in writing to Heeckeren he had violated the promise he had given to the emperor; he wanted no one who had an inkling of that to learn of his intentions. Furthermore, since, whatever the outcome, the seconds would have been party to a criminal act, he wanted no one who could not view arrest with equanimity, or who was not, by virtue of his position, immune to it – in other words, a foreign diplomat, like d'Archiac.

Changing, and leaving Natalya at home, he left for the Razumovsky ball, where he arrived about midnight. He showed no signs of worry; he was 'calm, laughing, chatting, cracking jokes'.[204] He disarmed any suspicions Vyazemsky might have had by speaking to him about future issues of the *Contemporary*, and asking him to remind Prince Kozlovsky that he had promised to contribute an article on steam engines. This was a topical subject, for the first railway line in Russia, from Tsarskoe Selo to Pavlovsk, had been opened at the end of September, though, as the locomotive did not arrive until the following October, for the time being the carriages were being drawn by horses.* However, he had more important work to do. One of the diplomats who frequented Dolly Ficquelmont's salon was Arthur Magenis, counsellor at the English embassy, later ambassador in Lisbon and Vienna, 'a long-nosed Englishman, known as "the sick parrot"'.[205] Seeing him now among the guests, Pushkin drew him aside, told him that he had accepted d'Anthès's challenge to a duel, and asked him to act as his second. Magenis, who was by no means a close friend, and who, in addition, must have considered the effect participation in a duel might have on his career, hesitated, but said that he would speak to d'Archiac, who was also present. Satisfied that he had solved the problem, Pushkin left the ball and returned home. At about two in the morning he was knocked up by a messenger with a note from Magenis:

> I have just returned from Countess Razumovsky's where I sought you everywhere to tell you that I have just spoken to Mons-r d'Archiac. Not finding you, I supposed that you had left, and as a visit at this hour could awaken the suspicions of Madame your wife, I prefer to address these lines to you.
>
> I told Mons-r d'Archiac that you had spoken to me of your affair with Monsieur de Heeckeren, engaging me to act as your second – and that without taking on this role definitively I had promised to speak to him. He refused to discuss it with me unless I declared myself your second, which I did not do. The matter thus remained at that, and I promised him to inform you of what passed between us.

* Kozlovsky had already contributed two articles to the journal: his review of a French mathematical annual had appeared in the first issue, and an article on probability theory in the third; 'A Short Outline of the Theory of Steam Engines' would appear in the seventh.

However, I think I have understood that the affair cannot be settled peaceably, the hope of which might have tempted me to intervene; consequently I must beg you, Sir, not to request me to take on the role that you wished. I must confess myself flattered by the trust which you are kind enough to place in me, and I thank you once again. Nor do I believe that my refusal will cause you embarrassment.[206]

Pushkin rose early the next morning – Wednesday, 27 January; it was very sunny, with three degrees of frost. Meanwhile d'Archiac had become more and more impatient with this inexplicable failure to conform to the duelling code. At nine in the morning he wrote:

This morning I insist again on the request which I had the honour of making to you yesterday evening.

It is indispensable that I should be in touch with the second you have chosen; and that with the shortest possible delay. I shall be in my lodgings until midday. Before that time I hope to receive the person whom you will be kind enough to send to me.[207]

Annoyed by this ridiculous, pettifogging insistence on propriety, Pushkin replied immediately, sending his answer back with d'Archiac's messenger.

I have no desire whatsoever to let the idlers of Petersburg into the secrets of my family affairs; I therefore refuse all negotiations between seconds. I will bring mine only to the rendezvous. As it is M. Heeckeren who is challenging me and is offended, he can choose one for me, if that suits him; I accept in advance, even if it be only his flunkey. As to time and place I am wholly at his command. According to the customs of us Russians, that suffices. I beg you to believe, Vicomte, that this is my last word, and that I have nothing further to reply to anything that concerns this affair; and that I shall only budge to go to the meeting.[208]

If the previous year d'Anthès had described to Heeckeren his parting from Natalya in terms reminiscent of the renunciation scene of *Eugene Onegin*, Pushkin was now taking on the characteristics of Eugene himself, who turns up for his duel with Lensky an hour late and without a second, much to the astonishment of the latter's second, Zaretsky,

> In duels a classicist and pedant,
> He was emotionally attached to method,
> And to stretch one's man out
> Allowed – not anyhow,
> But by the strict rules of the art,
> According to all the traditions of olden days
> (Which we must praise in him).
>
> (VI, xxvi)

And Pushkin's readiness to accept d'Anthès's servant as his second echoes Eugene's frivolous suggestion that his valet, Monsieur Guillot, should fulfil the role.

Satisfied that he had put a stop to d'Archiac's importunities, Pushkin turned to more congenial matters. He worked all morning; lunched at eleven, and then walked gaily up and down his room, singing to himself. D'Archiac was not, however, to be deflected from 'the strict rules of the art' by Pushkin's bluster, nor by the assertion that things were done differently in Russia. He composed another stiff note:

> Having attacked the honour of Baron Georges de Heeckeren, you owe him redress. It is for you to produce your second. There can be no question of providing you with one.
>
> Ready on his part to betake himself to the ground Baron Georges de Heeckeren urges you to regularize your position. Any delay will be considered by him as a refusal of the satisfaction due to him and by noising this affair abroad could prevent it being brought to a conclusion.
>
> The meeting between the seconds, *indispensable before the encounter*, will become, if you persist in refusing it, one of Baron Georges de Heeckeren's conditions, and you told me yesterday and wrote today that you would accept them all.[209]

This letter, with its threat to call off the duel if Pushkin did not name a second, finally forced him to act. Young Nikolay Lubyanovsky, the senator's son, met him as he left the house. He appeared 'cheerful and jolly', and Nikolay saw him turn left, towards the Nevsky.[210] Here he hailed a sleigh, and had himself driven to the Rossets' apartment. Perhaps he had always intended to fall back on Klementy Rosset, if he could find no second among the diplomatic corps. Klementy had, after all, agreed to act in November, as long as he did not have to attempt a reconciliation. But the Rossets were not at home, and Pushkin ordered the coachman to drive on to Panteleimonskaya Street nearby, where his friend from the Lycée, Konstantin Danzas, lived. Like Rosset, Danzas was an unmarried military man – a lieutenant-colonel in the engineers – qualities which made him suitable for a second's role. But, unlike Rosset, he was not part of any of the sets, social or literary, which Pushkin frequented. Pushkin and he saw each other very rarely; usually only at the Lycée reunions. He had no knowledge of recent events, nor of the relations between Pushkin, d'Anthès and Heeckeren.

It was between one and two in the afternoon when, as the sleigh crossed the suspension bridge over the Fontanka at the bottom of the Summer Garden, Pushkin saw Danzas coming towards him along the street. Calling to him, he took him up, and asked him to be the witness of a conversation he was about to have with d'Archiac at the French embassy. Danzas, 'not foreseeing any serious consequences, least of all a duel', agreed.*[211] During the drive to the embassy Pushkin was calm, chatting to his friend on matters unrelated to the affair. At their meeting with d'Archiac he began by rehearsing the events of the past three months. He then read aloud his recent letter to Heeckeren, and concluded by saying, 'If the affair is not brought to a conclusion today, the first time I meet Heeckeren, father or son, I will spit in his face.'[212] Getting up, he turned to d'Archiac and said that he would leave his second to arrange the conditions of the duel. Sensing Danzas's astonishment, d'Archiac asked him if he consented to act as Pushkin's second. Honour, combined with long-standing friendship, could not allow Danzas to refuse.

When Pushkin arrived home, he found only his sister-in-law, Alek-

---

* Several commentators dispute the chance nature of this meeting, or deny that it ever took place, believing that Pushkin had already enlisted Danzas as his second, and that the charade was intended to minimize Danzas's involvement, should the duel result in a court-martial (see Abramovich (1994a), 229). The tone of Pushkin's letters to d'Archiac argues against this theory; it is also odd that Danzas, who gave a circumstantial account of the duel and his part in it to Ammosov in 1862, should not then have seized the opportunity to correct his earlier story.

sandra, there. The children were at the Meshcherskys, Natalya engaged on social calls. While waiting for Danzas to return, he wrote to Aleksandra Ishimova. He regretted that he would be unable to take up her invitation and call on her that afternoon. 'Meanwhile,' he continued, 'I have the honour of forwarding Barry Cornwall to you. You will find at the end of the volume some pieces marked with a pencil, translate them as you can – I assure you that you will translate them in the best possible way. Today I chanced to open your *History in Tales*, and involuntarily became engrossed. That's how one should write!'[213] Wrapping up the anthology together with his letter, he gave it to a servant to take to Ishimova's lodging in Furshtatskaya Street. The pieces he had marked were five of Cornwall's *Dramatic Scenes*: 'Ludovico Sforza', 'Love Cured by Kindness', 'The Way to Conquer', 'Amelia Wentworth', and 'The Falcon'. Ishimova's translations of them would appear later that year, in the eighth issue of the *Contemporary*.

At half past two Danzas and d'Archiac signed the protocol they had drawn up setting out the conditions for the duel. It read:

1. The two adversaries will be placed twenty paces apart, each five paces from the two barriers which will be ten paces apart.
2. Each armed with a pistol, at a given signal they may, while advancing on one another, but without ever passing the barrier, make use of their arms.
3. It is further agreed that once a shot has been fired, neither of the two adversaries will be allowed to change position, so that the one who has fired first shall in every case be exposed to the fire of his adversary at the same distance.
4. After the two parties have fired, if there is no result, the affair will begin again as before, the adversaries being placed at the same distance of twenty paces, and the same barriers and same conditions being maintained.
5. The seconds will be the intermediaries responsible for any communication between the adversaries on the ground.[214]

Seven types of pistol duel are recognized in Count Châteauvillard's canonical *Essay on the Duel*, published in Paris in 1836: d'Archiac perhaps was able to refer to a copy. Danzas and d'Archiac had chosen the third, termed *advancing*: the adversaries are placed thirty-five to forty paces apart; on the command they advance towards a barrier indicated by, for example, a white pocket handkerchief, which is ten paces in front of them; they may fire at any time after the command. They had, however, ignored one of Châteauvillard's cardinal rules: the adversaries should never be fewer than fifteen paces apart. If both Pushkin and d'Anthès were to advance to the barriers, there would be only ten paces between them.

Danzas appeared at the Moika apartment with the duel conditions just before three. Pushkin greeted him joyfully, took him into the study and locked the door. Without reading the document, he immediately agreed to everything; he was only concerned to know the time and place: five o'clock, by the commandant's villa beyond the Black River, Danzas told him. Now that he knew something about the circumstances that had led to the duel, he was curious as to why Pushkin was fighting the son, rather than the father, to whom the insulting letter had been addressed. Heeckeren's official position did not allow him to accept a challenge, Pushkin replied. They agreed to meet at four at Wolff and Béranger's café, on the corner of the Nevsky and the Moika Embankment. Natalya would return soon, and Pushkin wanted to avoid awkward questions as to why he was going out at this strange hour. He sent Danzas off to collect a pair of duelling pistols from Kurakin's 'emporium of martial objects' on the Nevsky. He had already paid for them, using the last of the 2,200 roubles he had obtained by pawning Aleksandra's table silver with Shishkin the previous weekend.

After Danzas had left, Pushkin washed himself from head to toe and put on clean linen. Taking the copy he had made of his letter to Heeckeren, he folded it and placed it in the inside pocket of his frock-coat. Later he would give it to Danzas, telling him to use it as he saw fit. He called a servant, was helped into the *bekesh*, the winter overcoat he had been wearing earlier that day, and went out. But the weather had got worse: the temperature was sinking, and there was a biting west wind. Disregarding superstition – to recross the threshold immediately after having left presages, according to Russian belief, ill-fortune – he turned back, and ordered his bearskin coat to be brought: the one he had acquired from Aleksey Vulf in the autumn of 1830. Meanwhile Danzas had taken a pair-horse sleigh and collected the pistols, made in Paris by Lepage – another echo of *Onegin*: Eugene kills Lensky with one of

'*Lepage*'s fell barrels' (VI, xxv). At Wolff and Béranger's he found Pushkin, drinking a glass of lemonade, or of water. The two mounted the
sleigh and drove off. It was about four o'clock.

On Dvortsovaya Embankment they passed Natalya, who was driving
in the opposite direction: she was going to the Meshcherskys to collect the
children. Short-sighted as she was, she did not recognize her husband. As
they swung left to cross the Neva Pushkin said jokingly, 'You're not taking
me to the fortress, are you?' This was the quickest way to the Black River,
Danzas replied.[215] They drove along the long and straight Kamennoostrovsky Prospect, passing a succession of acquaintances returning to town after
having spent the afternoon sledging down the artificial ice mountains on
the islands. Among these was Augustine Lützerode, the daughter of the
ambassador of the Kingdom of Saxony, who on seeing them cried out:
'You'll be late.' Pushkin bowed politely and waved to her. 'No, Mademoiselle Augustine, I shan't be.'[216] Two cornets of the Horse Guards,
Prince Vladimir Golitsyn and Aleksandr Golovin, passed them. 'Why
are you so late, everyone's leaving already,' shouted Golitsyn.[217]

They arrived at the commandant's villa at about half past four.
D'Anthès and d'Archiac drove up almost at the same time. The skies
were clear, but the wind had got up, and there were fifteen degrees of
frost. After conferring, the two seconds set out to look for a suitable
place for the encounter. They found one a few hundred yards away,
screened from the road by a tall thick hedge, which also acted as a
windbreak. The snow lay thick here; together they trampled down an
area twenty paces long and a few wide, and then summoned their
principals. When Danzas asked Pushkin whether he was satisfied with
the spot, he replied: 'It's all one to me, only try to be more quick about
it.'[218] Measuring out the distance, the seconds put their coats down to
mark the barriers, and began to load the pistols. For d'Anthès d'Archiac
had borrowed a pair made by Karl Ulbrich of Dresden from the son of
the French ambassador, Ernest de Barante, who on 18 February 1840
would use them in a duel with another Russian poet, Mikhail Lermontov.
Pouring about twenty grams of powder into the pistol barrels, they
followed this with a paper wad – made, on this occasion, from lottery
tickets. A lead ball was hammered down on top of the charge, and a
percussion cap placed on the nipple at the breech. 'Haven't you finished
yet?' Pushkin asked Danzas impatiently.[219]

The principals were placed twenty paces apart and given their pistols. Danzas gave the signal to begin by raising his hat. Pushkin reached the barrier first and had begun to take aim, when d'Anthès, still a pace from his barrier, fired. Pushkin fell on Danzas's coat: his blood would leave a stain on the lining. 'I think my thigh is broken,' he said. The seconds hurried towards him; d'Anthès made an involuntary movement forward, but was stopped by Pushkin. 'Wait!' he said, 'I feel strong enough to have my shot.' When he had gone down, his pistol had fallen in the snow. Danzas gave him the other. D'Anthès stood by the barrier, sideways on, with his right arm covering his chest. Raising himself on his left arm, Pushkin fired. D'Anthès fell. Asked by Pushkin where he was wounded, he replied, 'I think the ball's in my chest.' 'Bravo!' Pushkin cried, and threw his pistol aside.[220]

D'Anthès was mistaken. The bullet had, without touching the bone, gone through the flesh of his right arm just below the elbow, had then struck either a button on his tunic or his braces and been deflected, leaving only a severe contusion on his chest. Pushkin's wound was far more serious: the ball had hit him low in the right side, and, as was later discovered, passing through the abdominal cavity, had shattered the sacrum, remaining lodged in the bone.

The seconds called the coachmen and, together with them, pulled up a slight fence which prevented the sleighs from approaching the scene of the duel. Pushkin was carefully placed in his, which, at Danzas's order, proceeded at a walk and was accompanied by the seconds on foot. D'Anthès followed in the other. By the commandant's villa they found Heeckeren's carriage, sent by the minister in case of an emergency. D'Anthès and d'Archiac suggested that Pushkin should make use of it, as the ride would be smoother. Danzas agreed, and, without telling Pushkin to whom the carriage belonged, placed him in it and sat at his side. During the long drive back to the Moika Embankment Pushkin occasionally complained of severe pain. He reminded Danzas of a duel fought by two of their acquaintances, Rufin Dorokhov and Mikhail Shcherbachev, in September 1819. Shcherbachev had been shot in the stomach, and died two days later in agony. 'I fear I've been wounded like Shcherbachev,' he said.[221] He was worried, too, about the effect the news would have on Natalya.

At the door to the apartment Danzas was told that Natalya was not at home; ignoring this, and sending the servants to carry Pushkin in, he walked through the dining-room – where the table was already laid for dinner – and drawing-room into Natalya's boudoir. She was sitting here with Aleksandra, and was first astonished, then frightened by this sudden intrusion. He told her that Pushkin and d'Anthès had fought, and that her husband was slightly wounded. Rushing to the vestibule, she saw Pushkin being borne in by the servants, and collapsed. At that moment Pletnev arrived to take Pushkin to his Wednesday literary evening. While he revived Natalya, Pushkin had himself carried into his study, calling out that they were not to enter. He had himself undressed, put on clean linen again, and lay down on a bed which had been hastily made up on the divan. Only then did he allow Natalya in. 'Don't worry, it isn't your fault,' he told her repeatedly.[222]

Meanwhile Danzas had left in search of a doctor. Neither Arendt, the emperor's physician, nor Salomon, also a well-known St Petersburg doctor, was in. Leaving notes for both, he called on another doctor, Pearson. He too was out, but his wife advised Danzas to try the Foundling Hospital. This was also on the Moika Embankment, on the far side of the Nevsky Prospect. Danzas arrived there at quarter past six, and found Dr Scholz just leaving. After listening to Danzas he said that, as an obstetrician, he could be of little help, but that he would come to see Pushkin immediately, bringing another doctor with him. Danzas returned to the apartment; a little later Scholz arrived, bringing with him Dr Zadler, the chief physician of the Imperial Stables Hospital, who, by coincidence, had just been treating d'Anthès's injury. They examined Pushkin, and Zadler left to fetch the instruments necessary for probing the wound and extracting the ball.

'What do you think of my wound?' Pushkin asked Scholz, who was now alone with him. 'At the shot I felt a powerful blow in my side, and a burning stab of pain in the loins; I lost a lot of blood on the way – tell me frankly, how do you find the wound?' 'I have to tell you that it is dangerous,' Scholz replied. 'Fatal?' 'I consider myself bound to tell you that, – but let us hear what Arendt and Salomon, who have been sent for, have to say.' 'I thank you, you've been honest with me.' He wiped his forehead. 'I must put my house in order.' A little later he asked Scholz whether he was losing a lot of blood. Scholz examined the wound, and applied another compress. He asked Pushkin whether he would like to see his friends. 'Do you think I've got less than an hour?' Pushkin replied. Embarrassed, Scholz said this had not been the reason for the suggestion, but that Pletnev was here. Pushkin said he would like to see Zhukovsky and asked for water: he felt sick.[223] Scholz went out to execute the commissions, and was replaced by Danzas at the bedside. During the course of the evening Pushkin dictated to him a list of the debts he owed of which there was no record. Taking a ring from his finger, he gave it to him as a keepsake. He told Danzas he wished no one to attempt to avenge him.

Arendt and Salomon had now arrived, and Zadler had returned from the hospital. Arendt had a vast experience in dealing with bullet wounds: he had been a military surgeon throughout the Napoleonic wars, and in 1814 was the chief surgeon of the Russian army in France. He saw immediately that there was no possibility of extracting the ball and that the wound was bound to be fatal. To probe it with the instruments Zadler had brought would only make matters worse. He prescribed absolute quiet, cold compresses on the stomach, and cold drinks. Pushkin asked him for his candid opinion of the injury; he could tell him the truth: he needed to know in order to make certain arrangements. 'In that case,' Arendt replied, 'I have to tell you that your wound is very dangerous and that I have almost no hope as to your recovery.' He would have to inform the emperor of what had happened, he added. Pushkin asked him to convey a plea that he might be forgiven for having broken his promise not to quarrel with d'Anthès. He also asked for leniency to be shown towards Danzas, his second. The Pushkins' family doctor, Spassky, arrived as Arendt was about to leave. Saying that he would return at eleven, he gave Pushkin into the other's care. 'This is a filthy business,' he said to Danzas as he left. 'He's going to die.'[224]

Spassky found that Pushkin had no illusions as to his condition; he was anxious, too, that the truth should not be concealed from Natalya: the outcome would be all the more devastating, were she to have been buoyed up by false hopes. This attitude induced Spassky to suggest that he should receive the sacraments. Pushkin agreed immediately. A message was sent to the priest of the little Church of the Saviour not made with Hands, on Konyushennaya Square. While they were waiting Pushkin remembered that Grech's son Nikolay had died the previous day. 'If you see Grech,' he said to Spassky, 'give him my regards and express my heartfelt sympathy at his loss.'[225] On Father Petr's arrival Pushkin made his confession and took communion.

Of Pushkin's friends the Vyazemskys were the first to hear of the duel and its outcome. At about half past six their daughter, Mariya Valueva, received a note from Ekaterina d'Anthès: 'Our forebodings were justified. My husband has only just fought with Pushkin; thank God his wound is not at all dangerous, but Pushkin is wounded in the loins. Go and comfort Natalie.'[226] Mariya, who was heavily pregnant, was thrown into great agitation by the news. It was thought better that she should not go, and Princess Vera took her place. She found Natalya in the drawing-room with her sister and her aunt. Hearing from Arendt that Pushkin's wound was fatal, she sent a note to Vyazemsky, who arrived shortly afterwards. Zhukovsky did not learn what had happened until after ten, when, calling on the Vyazemskys, he found to his surprise that they were both at the Pushkins and was told by Valuev, who lived on the floor below, of the encounter. On his way to the Moika he stopped at the Mikhailovsky Palace and left a message for Wielhorski, who was attending a concert in the Grand Duchess Elena's apartments. Turgenev was at the Shcherbatovs' soirée. D'Anthès's fellow-officer, Grigory Skaryatin, came up and asked him how Pushkin was. In response to Turgenev's look of astonishment, Skaryatin told him of the duel. Pausing only to inform Ekaterina Karamzina, who also was unaware of what had happened, Turgenev hurried to the Meshcherskys: they had already heard the news. He drove to the Moika Embankment, where he found Zhukovsky and the Vyazemskys, and learnt that Pushkin was mortally wounded.

From now until the end Pushkin's closest friends would relay themselves in the apartment: one or more would be present at all times. They arranged for the front door to be blocked off with a chest that stood on the landing, in order that the dying man should not be disturbed by the constant passage of visitors through the vestibule. These now had to enter by the small door which led into the larder, through which food was brought up from the kitchen. On the street door Zhukovsky from time to time put up a bulletin on the state of Pushkin's health. The news of the duel spread rapidly through St Petersburg, and a crowd began to gather on the pavement outside the apartment. As time passed the press became so great that Danzas requested the Preobrazhensky

Guards to place sentries by the entrance, in order to let visitors come and go without hindrance.

Arendt, on leaving Pushkin, had gone to the Winter Palace, but, not finding Nicholas, had left a report for him. The emperor returned from the theatre just before eleven and was met, not only by Arendt's report, but also by Foreign Minister Nesselrode, the duty general, and the commanding officer of the Chevalier Guards, who had come to inform him of the duel. At about midnight a courier brought the emperor's orders to Arendt: he was to call immediately on Pushkin, was to read him the enclosed letter, written in pencil by Nicholas himself, and was to return to the Winter Palace without delay, bringing the letter with him, to report in person. 'I will not go to bed, but will wait,' the emperor's note ended.[227] No exact copy of his letter to Pushkin exists; Turgenev, writing to his cousin Aleksandra Nefedeva at eleven the following morning, gives the 'approximate' wording as: 'If God ordains that we are not to meet again in this world, then accept my forgiveness and my advice to die in a Christian manner and take communion, and do not worry about your wife and children. They will be my children and I will take them in my care.'[228] 'When Arendt read Pushkin the sovereign's letter,' Zhukovsky later wrote to Sergey Lvovich, 'instead of answering it he kissed it, and for a long time would not give it up; but Arendt could not leave it with him. Pushkin several times said: give me the letter, I want to die with it. The letter! where is the letter? Arendt calmed him with the promise to ask the sovereign's permission for this.'*[229] Nicholas's promise to see to the welfare of Natalya and the children had relieved one of Pushkin's chief fears. 'If I die, my wife will be on the streets and my children in misery,' he had written to his brother-in-law in 1833.[230]

Between three and four in the morning the pain intensified, and Spassky sent for Arendt, who came immediately – he lived close by, on Millionnaya Street. On examining Pushkin he found that his stomach had swollen, and, suspecting peritonitis, ordered an enema, the normal

---

* Nicholas had insisted on the return of the letter, since to leave it in a subject's hands would give it the force of an imperial rescript; as yet, however, he had not decided what he should do for Pushkin and his family. He did not, of course, know that Pushkin had already been shriven; indeed he later attributed this to the effect of his letter, saying to Zhukovsky, 'We brought him by force to a Christian death' (PIES, VI, 66).

procedure in such circumstances. 'This could only be achieved with difficulty: the patient could not lie on his side, and the sensitivity of the inflamed colon, due to the shattered sacrum – a circumstance then unknown – was the cause of severe pain and suffering after this enema.' The suffering was indeed excruciating. 'Pushkin's physiognomy changed. His gaze became wild, his eyes seemed ready to start from their sockets, a cold sweat covered his forehead, his hands went cold, and there was almost no pulse.'[231] Though hitherto he had only groaned in pain, this new agony forced a scream from him. Next door, in the bedroom, Princess Vera and Aleksandra were awoken by a 'wild, muffled, terrible cry', and clutched one another in horror. Another cry followed, and another. The last woke Natalya. 'Pushkin?' she asked. 'He is suffering terribly, terribly,' Vera replied, and Natalya – not for the first time since Vera had been there – succumbed to hysterics.[232]

The pain had sensibly diminished by seven, when Pushkin, fearing that he was on the brink of death, asked that Natalya should come to him. She, however, refused to abandon hope. 'Something tells me that he will live,' she told Turgenev.[233] Pushkin asked to see his children. They were brought in, half-asleep. He looked at them, then blessed each in turn, silently. His friends came in one by one to bid him farewell. 'Is Karamzina here?' he asked.[234] She was sent for immediately. 'He stretched out his hand to me,' she wrote to her son, 'I pressed it, he did the same, and then signed that I should go. Leaving, I made the sign of the cross over him from a distance, he stretched out his hand again and said faintly: "bless me again", then, pressing his hand again, I made the sign of the cross, putting my fingers to his forehead, and laid my hand against his cheek: he kissed it feebly and again waved me away.'[235]

Exhausted and irritated, physically and mentally, by the treatment he had undergone, he obstinately refused any medical assistance during the course of the morning. But at midday he was offered opium – it is incomprehensible why he should not have been given it the previous night to relieve his pain – which he took eagerly, and which greatly calmed him. And at about two Dahl, who had just heard the news, arrived and took over from Spassky: he would remain at Pushkin's bedside until the end. Under his care Pushkin became 'as docile and as obedient as a child'.[236]

He remained anxious about Danzas's fate: although he had asked Arendt to pass on to the emperor his plea for leniency towards his second, there had been no mention of him in Nicholas's note. He referred to the matter again on Arendt's next visit: 'I await the tsar's word, in order to die in peace,' he said. Hearing this, Zhukovsky determined himself to see Nicholas. What was he to say to the tsar on Pushkin's behalf, he asked. 'Tell him that it is a pity that I am dying,' Pushkin replied, 'I would have been wholly his.' Nicholas had, almost simultaneously, conceived a desire to hear the latest news on Pushkin's condition from Zhukovsky: when the latter emerged from the apartment he found a courier waiting to take him to the Winter Palace. During his conversation with Nicholas he mentioned Pushkin's anxiety about Danzas. 'I cannot change the process of the law,' Nicholas said, 'but I will do everything possible. Tell him from me that I congratulate him on fulfilling his Christian duty; he should not worry about his wife and children; they are mine.' He ended by telling Zhukovsky that, if Pushkin died, he was to seal his study, and later go through his papers.[237]

At about six in the evening Dahl noticed a change in Pushkin's condition. His pulse, throbbing, increased to 120; his temperature rose and his agitation increased. Following Arendt's instructions Dahl and Spassky placed twenty-five leeches on his stomach – or rather Pushkin did this himself: he disliked it when the doctors' attentions became too intimate. The pulse slowed, and became gentler, the fever subsided and the abdominal swelling went down. For a moment Dahl felt that there was still some hope, but this illusion was short-lived. For the greater part of that evening and night Pushkin lay holding Dahl's hand, being given alternate doses of laurel-water and of opium, occasionally sipping iced water from a glass, or putting a piece of ice to his forehead. 'What time is it?' he would ask Dahl, and, on the latter's reply, would exclaim, 'How long must I go on suffering like this! Make it quicker, please!'[238]

By midday on Thursday 29 January he was hardly conscious; his pulse was even slower, his hands and feet were becoming cold. At two in the afternoon, however, he opened his eyes and asked for stewed cloudberries, one of his favourite delicacies. They hurriedly sent round to Dmitriev's grocery on the Nevsky. When a plate was brought to him, he said, 'Call my wife, let her feed me.' Natalya knelt beside the bed and gave him first one, then another spoonful. She pressed her cheek to his; he stroked her head and said: 'Now, now, it's nothing, thank God, it's all right', and sent her away. Meeting Spassky as she went out, she said: 'Now you'll see, he'll live, he won't die.' At the same time Dahl said to Zhukovsky and Vyazemsky, 'He's going.' Pushkin reached out and took Dahl's hand. His eyes were closed. 'Lift me up,' he said, 'let's go, higher, higher – come on, let's go!' Then, coming to himself, said, 'I was just dreaming that you and I were climbing high up these books and shelves, and I grew dizzy.' A little later he took Dahl's hand again. 'Come on, please, let's go, and together.' Taking him under the arms, Dahl lifted him higher in the bed. Suddenly, as though awakening, he opened his eyes, his face brightened, and he said: 'Life is finished.' 'What is finished?' asked Dahl, who had not distinguished the words. 'Life is finished,' he said distinctly and positively. And then, 'It's difficult to breathe, I'm suffocating.' These were his last words. He died at a quarter to three.[239]

Vera Vyazemskaya went into the next room to tell Natalya, but found herself unable to speak. She could only nod when Natalya, again on the verge of hysterics, asked whether he was dead. Closing her eyes and screaming Pushkin's name, Natalya fell into convulsions. Then she rushed into the study, 'threw herself on her knees, and, now putting her face to the cold face of her husband, now to his breast, called him by the most tender of names, begged for his forgiveness, shook him to obtain an answer from him'.[240] Fearing for her sanity, his friends removed her forcibly from the bedside. The body was carried from the study and laid on a table in the vestibule. Following the emperor's instructions, Zhukovsky sealed both doors of the study with black sealing-wax – the only colour that was available in the house. He sent Pletnev to fetch Samuil Galberg, a professor of sculpture at the Academy of Arts, who took Pushkin's death-mask. Spassky and Dahl carried out a hurried autopsy.* When this was complete the

---

* Dahl's note on the autopsy reads: 'On opening the abdominal cavity all the intestines were found to be severely inflamed; in one place only about the size of a two-copeck piece the smaller intestine was affected with gangrene. At this spot, in all probability, the intestine was struck by the bullet. In the abdominal cavity was found not less than a pound of black, clotted blood, probably from the severed femoral vein. On the surface of the right side of the large pelvic bone were found a number of small fragments of bone, and, finally, the lower part of the sacrum was shattered. From the direction of the bullet it must be concluded that the deceased was standing half-turned to the side and that the direction of the shot was a little downwards. The bullet pierced the general integuments of the abdomen two inches away from the upper, forward end of the right hip or iliac bone

body was washed and dressed – not in his gentleman of the chamber's uniform coat, as protocol demanded, but, at Natalya's insistence, in his old black frock-coat. Nicholas, always a stickler for proprieties, was annoyed when he heard of this, saying he 'supposed Turgenev or Prince Vyazemsky was behind it'.[241] That evening Zhukovsky, the Vyazemskys and the other friends who had been present during Pushkin's last hours dined with Wielhorski; and Pushkin himself 'was invited from beyond the grave to this dinner': it was also the celebration of Zhukovsky's birthday.[242]

The following day a coffin lined with crimson velvet trimmed with gold braid was brought to the apartment. Arkady Rosset, who helped to lift the body into it, was surprised by the muscular development of Pushkin's calves, caused, he supposed, by much walking. A 'simple icon, without any frame, and so worn that no image could immediately be discerned on it', was put in Pushkin's hands, and the coffin itself placed on top of the table that stood in the vestibule.[243] Candles surrounded it; at the foot of the table stood one of a succession of lectors, reading aloud from the Psalter. While the body lay there, from Saturday morning to Sunday night, a constant stream of visitors – more than ten thousand, Zhukovsky told Sergey Lvovich* – passed through the little door into the pantry, then through the dining-room into the vestibule. Here they crossed themselves; many kissed Pushkin's hand. The heat of the apartment and of the many candles accelerated putrefaction. 'I saw Pushkin in his coffin, his features have not changed, only he is beginning to puff up, and blood is coming out of his mouth,' one visitor wrote.[244] A

(ossis iliaci dextri), then went, skating across the surface of the large pelvis, downwards and, meeting the resistance of the sacrum, shattered it and lodged somewhere in its vicinity. Time and circumstances did not allow a more detailed investigation to be conducted. As far as the cause of death is concerned it must be noted that the inflammation of the intestines had not yet reached its highest state: there were neither serous nor final effusions, nor increments, and still less was there general gangrene. Probably, as well as the inflammation of the intestines, there was also an inflammatory affection of the larger veins, beginning with the severed femoral; and finally, a severe affection of the extremities of the spinal cord (caudae equinae) due to the shattering of the sacrum' (Shchegolev (1999), 194–5).

* At not less than 250 visitors an hour, day and night, this is perhaps an over-estimate, though not as glaring a one as that of Baron Liebermann, the Prussian ambassador, who reported the figure of 50,000 to his government, or of the critic and journalist Yanuary Neverov, who told his friend, the historian Granovsky, that 32,000 had visited the apartment in a day (Veresaev (1936), II, 451, 437).

servant was stationed in the room to spray the body at intervals with eau de cologne. 'Smirdin says that since the day of his death he has already sold 40,000 roubles' worth of his books,' Turgenev wrote to his brother on 31 January.[245]

Natalya, prostrate with grief, was in no condition to cope with the arrangements for the funeral service. Her cousin, Count Stroganov, took on the responsibility, instructing his man of affairs to see to the matter. It was as well that he did so, and also covered the household expenses, for Natalya had less than seventy-five roubles at her disposal. The service was to take place at eleven a.m. on Monday 1 February at St Isaac's Cathedral, where d'Anthès and Ekaterina's marriage had been celebrated: it was also the Pushkins' parish church. Stroganov wished the occasion to be a striking one, in keeping with Pushkin's fame as a poet. He asked the Novgorod and St Petersburg metropolitan, Serafim, to conduct the service. Serafim refused on the grounds that a death in a duel was tantamount to suicide. Irritated by this refusal, which he regarded as illegal, Stroganov, on Vyazemsky's advice, turned to Count Protasov, the supreme procurator of the Holy Synod. Receiving no satisfaction, he had to content himself with the services of three archimandrites.

On Saturday 30 January Kraevsky had published a short necrologue, written by Odoevsky, in the literary supplement to the *Russian Invalid*. Surrounded by a heavy black border, this read:

> The sun of our poetry has set! Pushkin has died, died in the flower of his years, in the middle of his great career! ... We have not the strength to say more of this, but it is not necessary; every Russian heart knows the whole value of this irrevocable loss and every Russian heart will be lacerated. Pushkin! our poet! our joy, our national glory! Can it be that Pushkin is no longer with us! It is impossible to get used to this thought![246]

Uvarov was highly incensed by the tone of this piece; on his behalf Dondukov-Korsakov reprimanded Kraevsky, who also received a rebuke from Benckendorff. The minister 'is very occupied in curbing the loud wails caused by Pushkin's death', Nikitenko noted in his diary the following day. The St Petersburg censors were instructed not to pass anything on Pushkin, but to refer such articles either to Uvarov or to Dondukov-Korsakov; the chairman of the Moscow censorship committee was exhorted to make sure that the 'proper moderation and tone of decorum were observed'.[247] These actions were not the result of Uvarov's hatred for Pushkin; they reflected, rather, the general disquiet of the authorities at the revelation of Pushkin's immense and unsuspected popularity. Fearing paranoically that his funeral might be the occasion for popular disturbances, they took steps to prevent such an occurrence. A severe injunction was sent to the university, forbidding professors and students to leave their lectures and classes in order to attend the funeral. To make attendance more difficult, and to lessen the numbers who could attend, the venue was, without warning, switched from St Isaac's to the small Church of the Saviour not made with Hands on Konyushennaya Square. And, whereas the usual custom was to carry the coffin to the church in the morning, immediately before the service, it was now ordered that this should take place the previous midnight. To make sure that no disturbance accompanied the move gendarmes and police filled the apartment, and troops lined the streets between the Moika Embankment and Konyushennaya Square. 'At twelve, that is at midnight, gendarmes and police appeared: spies – ten in all, and there were hardly as many of us!' Turgenev noted in his diary. 'The public were no longer admitted. Between twelve and one we took the coffin to the Konyushennaya church, sang a requiem, and I returned quietly home.'*[248]

The following day Konyushennaya Square was crammed with carriages and crowds of people. Besides Pushkin's friends, the congregation in the church consisted chiefly of officialdom and diplomats. 'M. Pushkin's obsequies were celebrated in the most brilliant and at the same time in the most touching fashion,' Baron Lützerode reported to the Foreign Minister of Saxony. 'All the heads of the foreign missions were

* A report from the corps of gendarmes to Nicholas contained the following remarks: 'The gathering of visitors to the body was unusual; it was intended to hold a ceremonial funeral service, many proposed to follow the coffin to the place of burial itself in Pskov province; finally, rumours were heard that in Pskov itself the horses were to be unharnessed and the coffin dragged by people, the citizens of Pskov having been made ready for this. It would be difficult to decide whether all these honours related more to Pushkin the liberal than Pushkin the poet [. . .] Taking into consideration the views of many well-thinking people that a similar, as it were popular expression of grief at Pushkin's death would to some extent represent an indecent scene of triumph for the liberals, higher authority recognized it as its duty, by measures of secrecy, to eliminate all paying of respects' (quoted in Shubin, 114–15).

present, with the exception of the Earl of Durham and Prince Souzzo, ill, of Baron Heeckeren, not invited, and of M. Liebermann who refused, because he had been told that the said poet had been suspected of liberalism during his youth, in truth a stormy one, like that of many geniuses of his ilk.'[249] 'An immense crowd [. . .] rushed into the church as soon as the doors were opened after the service,' wrote Sofya Karamzina.[250] According to Turgenev, 'the veneration for the memory of the poet in the immense crowds of people, present at his funeral service in the Konyushennaya church, was so great, that the front of his frockcoat was reduced to ribbons, and he lay there almost in his jacket alone; his side-whiskers and hair were carefully trimmed by his female admirers'.[251] The coffin was borne out of the church on the shoulders of his friends: as they emerged Vyazemsky threw himself to the ground in front of them, and had to be persuaded to move. They made their way through the crowd to the entrance to the church crypt, where the body would remain until it was taken to the Svyatogorsky monastery and buried in the plot Pushkin had reserved for himself the previous April.

Natalya had, through Stroganov, asked the tsar whether, since she was too ill to accompany the coffin to Pskov, Danzas might be allowed to replace her. Danzas, Nicholas replied, had been allowed to remain at liberty until the funeral service; now, however, law must take its course. 'M. Turgenev, an old friend of the deceased, having no occupation at the moment, could perform this last service for M. Pushkin,' he added.[252] On the day after the funeral service Zhukovsky informed Turgenev of the emperor's decision. Turgenev, though annoyed at the unceremonious and somewhat dismissive manner in which he was being treated, accepted the commission. 'He is somewhat vexed with this and cannot hide it,' Sofya Karamzina wrote. 'Vyazemsky wanted to go, so I said to him: "Why should he not go with you?" "Go with me, for heaven's sake! He's not dead!"'[253]

For Turgenev that day and the next were taken up with a flurry of preparations: he sent Boris Fedorov, who came round with his verses on Zhukovsky's birthday, to gather information on Pskov; called on the postal director and was told he must take a postal courier with him; ordered a *kibitka*, a covered wagon: he would travel at his own expense on a special travel warrant; called on Count Stroganov, discussed with him travel warrants and the quality of the peasant horses available at relay stations, and was introduced to the gendarme captain Rakeev, who would accompany him. The coffin had been closed on Tuesday evening: Vyazemsky, in a melodramatic gesture, had thrown his glove into it. Turgenev called for it in the early hours of Thursday morning, 4 February, and set off post-haste for Pskov, with the gendarme captain galloping in front of his *kibitka*. With him was Nikita Kozlov, who had been Pushkin's servant since his childhood in Moscow. He sat on the cart next to the coffin, not moving, and neither eating nor drinking throughout the journey. Nikitenko's wife, returning from Mogilev, met the cavalcade at a post-station on the road. 'She saw a simple *telega*, covered with straw, under the straw was a coffin, wrapped in bast matting. Three gendarmes were bustling about in the post-yard, in an effort to change the post-horses as quickly as possible, so as to gallop on with the coffin. "What's all this?" my wife asked a peasant standing by. "God knows! It seems some Pushkin or other has been killed – and they're hurrying him along by post in bast and straw, as though he were, God forgive them, a dog." '[254]

At a post-station just before Pskov Turgenev caught up with Nikolay Yakhontov, the Pskov marshal of nobility, who – though he did not mention the fact as they drank tea together – bore a letter from Mordvinov, Benckendorff's deputy, to Aleksey Peshchurov, the governor of Pskov. 'Pushkin's body is being taken to Pskov province to be committed to the earth on his father's estate,' Mordvinov had written. 'I [. . .] have the honour to inform your excellency that it is the sovereign emperor's wish that you should prohibit any especial expression, any meeting, in a word, any ceremony, apart from those which according to our church ritual are usually performed on the burial of a nobleman. I do not consider it superfluous to mention that the funeral service has already taken place here.'[255] Turgenev hurried on, leaving Yakhontov behind, and, arriving in Pskov at nine in the evening – he had covered 285 versts in 19 hours – drove straight to the governor's. Peshchurov had guests; while Turgenev was renewing his acquaintance – they had known each other earlier in St Petersburg – Yakhontov arrived with Mordvinov's letter, 'which,' Turgenev writes, 'the governor began to read aloud, but when he got to the imperial order – about not allowing *meetings* – went quiet and showed it only to me, that is, the one person it should not have been shown to: you couldn't have a better scene in a comedy!'[256]

The same evening, he hurried on to Ostrov, and, leaving the coffin at a post-station, arrived at Trigorskoe the following afternoon. At his request Praskovya Osipova sent some of her serfs to dig the grave at the monastery. After dinner Turgenev went to inspect the work and, finding it was progressing slowly because of the frozen soil, ordered it to be completed in the morning. Meanwhile the coffin had arrived, and was placed in the church. He spent the night at Trigorskoe; the gendarme officer, wearied by long hours in the saddle, retired early, but Turgenev sat up late talking of Pushkin with Praskovya and her two daughters, Ekaterina and Mariya. The following morning – Saturday 6 February – at dawn he and the gendarme officer drove to the monastery. After a short service in the church Kozlov and some of the serfs took the coffin on their shoulders. As it was being lowered into the grave, Turgenev threw a handful of soil on the lid. He returned to Trigorskoe, and, after a visit with Mariya to Mikhailovskoe and breakfast with his hostess, set out for Pskov. In the cemetery of the Svyatogorsky monastery Pushkin and his mother now, as Aleksey Vulf remarked in his diary, 'lay together under one stone, far closer to one another after death than they had been in life'.[257]

EPILOGUE

Some are no more, others are far away,
As Sadi once said.

Eugene Onegin, VIII, li

O F THE OTHER PARTICIPANTS IN THE DUEL d'Archiac was immediately sent back to France with dispatches by Barante, the French ambassador, in order to avoid any possible diplomatic embarrassment. He left on 2 February, taking with him a letter from Turgenev to his brother Nikolay, and a little parcel from Ekaterina Karamzina to her son Andrey, containing a copy of the miniature edition of *Eugene Onegin*, which, she wrote, 'seemed to me very elegant and which at this moment might give you pleasure'.[1]

On 3 February a court-martial was convened at the Horse Guards to try d'Anthès and Danzas. Both were examined several times; the court also had at its disposal most of the documents concerning the duel, including Pushkin's letter to Heeckeren and his correspondence with d'Archiac. It handed down its verdict on 19 February. D'Anthès, for participation in a duel and for inflicting a fatal wound on Pushkin, was sentenced to death by hanging; 'the Accused Chamberlain Pushkin would have been subject to the same sentence, but since he is already deceased, his sentence is cancelled by reason of death.'[2] Though Danzas had spoken to d'Archiac about the possibility of reconciliation, he had not informed the authorities in good time of the duel, thus allowing it to take place and Pushkin to be killed. He too, therefore, was sentenced to hang. These draconic sentences were reviewed by the Auditor-General, whose decision was forwarded to the tsar on 17 March. D'Anthès was, 'for challenging Gentleman of the Chamber Pushkin to a duel and killing him in the same, having been stripped of his rank and of the Russian nobility he had acquired, to be inscribed as a private, his service posting to be determined by the Inspectorate'. Though Danzas should have been deprived of his rank for his actions, the Auditor-General, 'seeing from the dossier that he was without warning involved as a second, and, being from childhood a friend of Pushkin, did not have the strength to refuse to grant him the assistance requested; in addition taking into respect his long and zealous service and excellent behaviour, attested by his superiors, as well as his participation in campaigns and numerous actions, his wound, received at the storm of the fortress at Brailov, from a bullet which passed through his left shoulder shattering the bone and the decorations he has earned by bravery, considers it sufficient: to regard the time he, Danzas, spent under trial and arrest as punishment, in addition to keep him in custody in the fortress guardhouse for two months and subsequently return him to service as previously.' On 18 March Nicholas noted on the decision: 'So be it, but Private Heeckeren, not being a Russian subject, should be escorted to the frontier by a gendarme, his officer's commission having been confiscated.'[3] The decision was put into force the following day. By chance Turgenev saw d'Anthès's departure 'in a three-horse sleigh, wearing a cap embroidered with silk or gold thread, he was sitting there cheerfully, a gendarme was on the box, an officer in another sleigh'.[4]

Heeckeren and Ekaterina – now pregnant – were not long in following him. On 3 February in a letter to the Prince of Orange Heeckeren had written, 'I appeal to your opinion, Your Highness, to judge whether I can continue to reside by the Imperial Court after such an occurrence. In St Petersburg society I have at this moment partisans and detractors. As a private person I would remain, certain that good right would eventually win all to my cause; as a public person who has the honour to represent his Sovereign I cannot allow the least blame to attach to me.' He therefore asked to be recalled, and appointed to another embassy.[5] On 14 March (NS) Verstolk van Soelen, the Dutch foreign minister, gave him permission to leave St Petersburg as soon as the legation secretary, Gevers, had returned to Russia. Heeckeren prepared for his departure by selling off some of his possessions. 'As to the dear father,' Vyazemsky wrote to Countess Musina-Pushkina, 'he has turned shop-keeper, is selling all his furniture, and everyone is going to his house as though to an auction in an old warehouse. Someone took the chair on which he was sitting away from under him, telling him it had been sold.'[6]

Those whom Heeckeren referred to as his detractors consisted for the most part of Pushkin's friends and the general populace – 'the public is embittered against Heeckeren and it is feared that his windows will be broken,' Turgenev told his brother.[7] Society, on the other hand, tended to take his side, as Baron Lützerode had noted ironically in a dispatch to his government written immediately after Pushkin's death. 'In view of the lack of appreciation for his genius and his achievements in the first society it is not surprising that only a few were at his death bed, while the Dutch embassy was besieged by the beau monde, which shared the Heeckeren family's joy at the fortunate deliverance of the fashionable young man.'[8] But gradually society's attitude began to change. This was no doubt partly because the facts of the matter became more widely known. But it also soon became clear that the emperor had set his face against Heeckeren. In a letter to Grand Duke Michael of 3 February he wrote: 'This incident has given rise to a host of speculations, extraordinarily stupid for the most part, of which the censure of Heeckeren's behaviour is alone justified and deserved: he did indeed behave like a vile blackguard. He pimped for d'Anthès in Pushkin's absence, trying to persuade the wife to yield to d'Anthès, who he alleged was dying of love for her, and all this came out when, after Pushkin had first challenged d'Anthès to a duel, d'Anthès suddenly engaged himself to Mrs Pushkina's sister; then the wife revealed to her husband all the vileness of their behaviour, herself being completely innocent in everything [. . .] D'Anthès is under trial, as is Danzas; the law will take its course; and that blackguard Heeckeren will, it seems, leave here.'[9] An earlier incident had inclined Nicholas to think the worst of Heeckeren; he would be glad, for personal reasons, to see the back of him. William of Orange, the Crown Prince of the Netherlands, had married Nicholas's sister, Grand Duchess Anna. The previous May Heeckeren, in a dispatch to Verstolk van Soelen, had written that, at a private audience with Nicholas, 'His Majesty conversed with me for a long time about the domestic relations of His Royal Highness the Prince of Orange [. . .] His Majesty, having very naturally a lively affection for Their Royal Highnesses, expressed himself frankly on the unevenness of the Princess's character, and regretted that His Highness the Prince of Orange did not, as it appeared to him, make more concessions to this regrettable disposition and more effort to restore a pleasant harmony whose absence seemed to him a bad example for the august children of Their Royal Highnesses and far from reassuring for the future of the young Princes.'[10] William, understandably finding the remarks offensive, wrote to Nicholas, 'How is it, my good friend, that you could speak of my domestic arrangements with Heeckeren in his capacity as Minister or in any other capacity; he reported all that in an official despatch, which I read and it is painful for me to see that you blame me and think that I do not sufficiently defer to your sister's wishes.'[11] Excusing himself, Nicholas convinced his brother-in-law that much of the report was the product of Heeckeren's imagination; after learning of the latter's involvement in the duel, William wrote, 'It seems to me that in every respect he [Heeckeren] will not be a loss, and that we, you and I, were earlier remarkably mistaken about him. I hope above all that whoever replaces him will be more truthful and will not invent subjects in order to have something to fill his reports with as Heeckeren did.'[12] Gevers arrived in St Petersburg on 25 March; the following day Heeckeren solicited an audience to take his leave of the imperial family, but received, through Nesselrode, the reply that Nicholas, 'wishing to avoid explanations which could not be other than painful preferred not to see Monsieur de Heeckeren'.[13] At the same time the emperor pointedly sent him the traditional gift for ambassadors who would not be returning to St Petersburg: a diamond snuff-box, ornamented with his portrait. Other members of the diplomatic corps considered that, in the circumstances, he should not have accepted it; and, wrote the ambassador of Baden-Württemberg, 'on this occasion they did not blame him any less than on the many others when Monsieur de Heeckeren had not shown himself to be such as his colleagues would have wished'.[14] Of Heeckeren's leave-taking Count Simonetti, the Sardinian envoy, wrote, 'This envoy paid farewell visits neither to diplomats nor to other persons. He contented himself with having sent round after his departure visiting cards with the letters p.p.c.,* and he could not do otherwise, since his position had become embarrassing and demanded a prompt departure.'[15]

He and Ekaterina left on 1 April; Ekaterina had taken leave of her

* 'pour prendre congé', 'to take leave'.

sister six weeks earlier, on Natalya's departure for Polotnyany Zavod. 'Catherine then at last showed some little feeling for the calamity which she must also have some feeling for on her conscience; she wept,' Sofya Karamzina wrote, 'but up to then calm, gay, laughing, to all those who saw her she spoke of nothing but her happiness – what a stupid great lump!'[16] They met d'Anthès in Berlin, and a few weeks later travelled to Soultz. Here, in October, Ekaterina gave birth to a daughter, Mathilde Eugénie. Two more daughters followed, in 1839 and 1840; in September 1843 she had a son, but died of puerperal fever three weeks later. After her death d'Anthès took up politics, being elected to the National Assembly as the representative for Haut-Rhin in 1848, and re-elected to the Constituent Assembly in 1849. In 1850 he became one of Louis Napoleon's supporters, carried out a mission on his behalf to Vienna and Berlin in 1852, and was rewarded, when the president became emperor, by a senator's seat. Meanwhile Heeckeren, after being without a diplomatic post for five years, had, in 1842, become the Minister for the Netherlands in Vienna. He remained here until his retirement in 1875, when he came to live in Paris with d'Anthès. He died in 1884 at the age of ninety-three; d'Anthès survived him by eleven years, dying in Soultz in November 1895.

Immediately after Pushkin's death Zhukovsky had written to the emperor, soliciting his charity for Natalya and the children. In addition he suggested that Mikhailovskoe, which he erroneously believed to be the place of Pushkin's burial, the property of Sergey Lvovich, and to be mortgaged, should be freed from debt and entailed on the family;* and that a complete edition of Pushkin's works should be published, the income from which should also go to the family. Nicholas replied on 30 January with a hand-written note:

1. The debts to be paid.
2. The father's mortgaged estate to be freed from debt.

---

* Zhukovsky later corrected these mistakes: he did not, however, suggest that Boldino and Kistenevo, which did belong to Sergey Lvovich and were mortgaged to the hilt, should be redeemed. In July Lev wrote to his friend Yuzefovich from Pyatigorsk: 'You ask whether the freeing from debt extended to my father's estate. On the contrary, this is what happened: Zhukovsky learnt that my late mother's little village [...] was free from debt, imagined that it made up all our estate, and reported to the sovereign that my brother had no debts on this estate' (*PIM*, X, 345).

3. A pension to the widow and to the daughter until marriage.
4. The sons to be pages and 1,500 roubles for education to each until entry on service.
5. The works to be published at the expense of the state for the benefit of the widow and children.
6. An extraordinary payment of 10 thousand.*[17]

To contemporaries the settlement seemed extraordinarily generous – 'It is superb, but it is too much,' Durnovo noted in his diary[18] – though it compared in no way with the pension of 50,000 roubles which Karamzin's widow received, and which, after her death, would go to her children. When Karamzin had died Nicholas had issued a special imperial rescript, composed by Zhukovsky, which affirmed the national importance of the historiographer's work. Zhukovsky now wished Pushkin's achievement to be celebrated in the same manner. 'Allow me, Sire,' he wrote, 'also in the present instance to be the exegete of your monarchical will and to compose the document which will express it for a grateful country and for Europe.'[19] Nicholas refused. Ekaterina Karamzina wrote to her son: 'When Vasily Andreevich Zhukovsky asked the sovereign for the second time to be his secretary for Pushkin, as he had been for Karamzin, the emperor summoned Vasily Andreevich and said to him, "My dear fellow, listen, I will do everything that I can for Pushkin, but I will not write as I did for Karamzin; we forced Pushkin to die like a Christian, but Karamzin lived and died like an angel." What could be more judicious, more delicate, better thought and better felt than this sort of scale which he has placed between these two?'[20] 'What a crackbrain Zhukovsky is!' Nicholas said to Dashkov. 'He pesters me to appoint the same pension for Pushkin's family as for Karamzin's. He will not understand that Karamzin was a man who was almost a saint, but what was Pushkin's life like?'[21]

When Nicholas's decision became known, Zhukovsky composed a letter for Natalya to send to the emperor, thanking him for his generosity and asking that trustees should be appointed to administer the estate. 'I have not words to express that which I feel,' she wrote at his dictation.

* It will be seen that in his third point Nicholas has forgotten the nine-month-old Natalya. Natalya's pension was Pushkin's salary: 5,000 roubles a year; the daughters, like the sons, got 1,500 roubles a year each. The latter were enrolled in the Corps-des-Pages, which they entered in September 1847 and September 1849 respectively, graduating four years later.

'In my sombre destiny you have been for me a guardian angel, a visible messenger from God, who gives me the strength to support the present, who saves me from despair at the prospect of a future which I dare neither think of nor contemplate, and who dictates my duties for the rest of a life, broken almost at its beginning, but which may yet last for years. May God who has endowed you with a mercy worthy of Himself, shower you with rewards.' She asked that the trustees should be Count Stroganov, Mikhail Wielhorski, and Zhukovsky.[22] This was agreed, with the addition of Narkiz Tarasenko-Otreshkov, who in 1832 had briefly collaborated with Pushkin on his project to bring out a newspaper.

The first task of the trustees was to pay off Pushkin's debts. In January 1840, when the last bill had been paid, the total expended was 95,655 roubles. To this must be added the debt written off by the Treasury: 43,333.33 roubles. The sum total of Pushkin's obligations at the moment of his death was thus 138,988.33 roubles. He would have had absolutely no hope of paying off even a fraction of this, especially since the sum would have grown larger with each successive month. On the basis of the bills of January 1837 it has been calculated that his basic household expenses amounted to nearly two thousand roubles a month: though this figure includes the hire of horses, it does not include rent, clothes, books, Pushkin's subscription at the English Club, nor any capital outlay.[23] Nor does it take into account the continuing loss on the *Contemporary*. Had Pushkin not fallen in the duel, he would by the end of the year have been faced with an impossible financial situation.

When Zhukovsky sealed Pushkin's study three-quarters of an hour after his death, he imagined that he alone would perlustrate the poet's papers, and that he would do so in conformity with the principles he had put forward to the emperor, which, he believed, the latter had approved: 'to burn everything discreditable to Pushkin's memory, to return letters to their writers, to preserve compositions, to restore state papers to the proper quarter'.[24] He was therefore disconcerted, and indeed somewhat insulted, to learn that he would be assisted by one of Benckendorff's subordinates, General Dubelt, the chief of staff of the gendarme corps.* In

---

* Dubelt's son, Mikhail Leontevich, was the first husband of Pushkin's daughter Natalya; her second husband, married morganatically, was Nicholas William von Nassau. Their daughter, Sophia, married Nicholas I's grandson, Grand Duke Mikhail Mikhailovich; and this couple's daughter Nada married George Mountbatten, 2nd Marquess of Milford Haven.

addition, the principles had been varied: nothing would be destroyed, or returned, until it had been seen by Benckendorff. Zhukovsky had to accept these changes, which had been imposed by the emperor; he was, however, successful in opposing Benckendorff's suggestion that the inspection should take place in the offices of the Third Department. On 7 February the seals were removed from the study; all the written material – manuscripts, letters, notebooks – was packed into two chests which were then taken to Zhukovsky's rooms in Shepelevsky House.* Here Zhukovsky and Dubelt went through the material: a task which lasted until 27 February, when Zhukovsky took pleasure in announcing to the tsar: 'Pushkin's correspondence is completely innocent.'[25] At the same time he asked Benckendorff for permission to keep the manuscripts of Pushkin's work, as he would need them for the collected works and for future numbers of the *Contemporary*. 'You know better than I,' he wrote to Dmitriev, 'that what seems simple, to have leapt straight out of one's head on to the paper, is just that which costs the most labour. I see that now from Pushkin's manuscripts which have been delivered to me and which unfortunately I have to decipher [...] With what labour did he write his light, airy verses! There isn't a line without several crossings-out.' He went on to describe the plans of the trustees. 'We are now in the process of printing a complete collection of his published work. The unpublished will be printed separately. It will be a good edition, but simple, so as to be able to print more copies, sell it more cheaply and make a larger sum. I hope there will be no shortage of subscribers. Pushkin's memory must and always will be dear to his native land.'[26]

He had submitted a proposal for a seven-volume collected edition, which would include the unpublished work, to the tsar in February; on it Nicholas had written: 'Agreed, but with the condition that everything

---

* Not quite all: Tarasenko-Otreshkov managed to acquire Pushkin's rough notebook for 1820–22 and two sheets with notes of expenses, while Ivan Panaev, when going though Pushkin's library with Kraevsky, found Magenis's note declining to act as Pushkin's second on the floor under the table. The library itself was packed in crates – though not before a number of books had been stolen – and led a nomadic existence: at one time stored in the cellars of the Horse Guards' barracks, it then moved from estate to estate, until, in 1900, it came to St Petersburg, the crates were unpacked, and the books catalogued by B.L. Modzalevsky (the catalogue is in *PIES*, IX–X; on the fate of the mss and the library see Tsyavlovsky, 276–356).

indecent that I read in *Boris Godunov* should be omitted, and with the strictest possible selection of what is as yet not known.'[27] In the end the edition consisted of eight volumes, and only of published works; it came out in instalments in 1838. Zhukovsky co-opted Odoevsky and Pletnev to assist him in the editorial work, but the bulk of this, together with the proof-correction, fell on Pletnev alone. It proved too much for him: the edition was carelessly prepared; misprints and mistakes are rife. Thirteen thousand sets, of which 3,000 were on vellum, were printed. The ordinary edition cost twenty-five roubles; that on vellum forty. The price was in line with those obtaining at the time: the 1835 eight-volume edition of Zhukovsky cost thirty-five roubles. The sets were sold on subscription; most went through the book-sellers, but the trustees themselves also enlisted subscribers: Stroganov 1,061, Wielhorski 113, and Tarasenko-Otreshkov 10. For sales in the provinces the trustees utilized the machinery of the Ministry of the Interior. In May Bludov, the minister, sent a circular to all governors and provincial marshals of nobility, requesting them 'to take part in the distribution of vouchers for Pushkin's complete works to all amateurs of literature, all lovers of enlightenment'.[28] But this resulted in not more than 1,600 subscriptions. In all, some 7,000 sets were sold, producing just over 263,000 roubles. Expenses amounted to approximately 113,500 roubles, but against this must be set a grant from the emperor of 50,000 roubles. The edition produced, therefore, almost 200,000 roubles for the trustees. Three supplementary volumes, containing the unpublished work, appeared in 1841; these were brought out by a consortium of book-sellers, to whom the trustees, not wishing again to act as editors, sold the rights for 37,000 roubles; at the same time they sold, to the same consortium, the 5,000 unsold copies of the eight-volume edition for 50,000 roubles. Of this total of 287,000 roubles the trustees gave 50,000 to Natalya: which she banked and, considering it to be the children's money, spent it solely on them, taking only the interest for other expenses. The remainder was held by the trustees, enabling them to acquire for the children Mikhailovskoe and, apparently, the little estate of Nikulino, near Polotnyany Zavod, which Pushkin had thought of buying in 1834.

In the first days after Pushkin's death Natalya, overcome with grief, was physically and psychologically prostrate. Devout as she was, she found spiritual consolation in daily conversations with a priest recommended to her by Zhukovsky, Father Bazhanov, who, Vyazemsky wrote, 'is very touched by the state of her soul and also convinced of her chastity'.[29] Arendt, who also saw her every day, prescribed complete rest and quiet; she had indeed already decided to leave St Petersburg and go to Polotnyany Zavod. 'She is leaving in a week for her brother's estate at Kaluga, where she intends to stay for two years,' Sofya told Andrey. '"My husband," – she said, – "ordered me to wear mourning for two years" (what delicacy of feeling! he always wanted to save her from the censure of society!) "and I believe that I will best execute his wishes if I pass those two years quite alone in the country. My sister will come with me and that will be a great consolation."'[30] She left late at night on 15 February, accompanied by Aleksandra and her aunt Ekaterina Ivanovna, and escorted by her brother Dmitry, who had come up to St Petersburg for that purpose. Among those who saw her off were Turgenev and Sofya Karamzina, who found her demeanour less woebegone than was appropriate: 'She was not sufficiently sad, she was too busy with the packing, she did not have a sufficiently sorrowful air when bidding farewell to Zhukovsky, Danzas and Dahl, those three tutelary angels who sat round her husband's death-bed and who contributed so greatly to easing his last moments, she was happy to leave, which is natural, but it would also have been so to show heartbreaking emotion, but there was nothing at all, and even less sadness than usual! No, that woman will not be at all inconsolable.'[31]

In Moscow they stayed only long enough to change horses; Natalya's failure to call on Sergey Lvovich was much censured by Pushkin's friends. She did, however, send him a message through her brother Sergey: 'She was desolated to pass through Moscow and not see [him], but she had to obey her doctor's orders: he had insisted that she should leave St Petersburg, live quietly in seclusion, and avoid everything which could cause the least agitation.'[32] Once in Polotnyany Zavod she, Aleksandra and the children settled into the Red House, a separate annexe in the grounds of the estate, where she – and for a short time Pushkin – had lived in 1834. Zhukovsky came to stay with her that summer, as did Sergey Lvovich, who, according to Zizi Vrevskaya, 'found that her sister was more griefstricken by the loss'. But Zizi, like many of Pushkin's female friends, was inclined to place part of the blame for what had happened on Natalya, and hence was always pleased to pass on anything which showed her in an unfavourable light; earlier that year she had written to her brother: '[Natalya] has asked mamma's permission to come to pay her last respects to *poor Push* – as she calls him. What about that?'[33] In the autumn Ekaterina, who had not heard from either of her sisters, wrote to Dmitry from Soultz. 'You ask me what they are doing and how they are,' he replied. 'They lead a very sedentary life and spend their time as they can; naturally after the life they were used to in St Petersburg, Natalie, fêted as she was, cannot find much attraction in the monotonous life at the Zavod and is rather sad than gay, often indisposed, which obliges her quite often to stay in for whole weeks without coming to dinner with us [. . .] You ask me why she doesn't write to you: well, I don't know; but I don't imagine there are any reasons other than the fear of compromising her dignity or rather her reputation in society by corresponding with you, and I think that it will be a long time before she does.'[34]

Ekaterina Ivanovna was eager that Natalya should return to St Petersburg as soon as possible: it would be ridiculous for her to waste two of the best years of her life in a provincial backwater. She promised that, if the sisters returned, she would secure an appointment as maid-of-honour for Aleksandra; whereupon the latter added her urgings to those of their aunt. In the end Natalya, perhaps thinking too of her sons' education, succumbed. At the beginning of November 1838 she and Aleksandra returned to St Petersburg, and in January Aleksandra received her maid-of-honour's monogram. 'They live on the Aptekarsky,' Pletnev wrote to Grot after visiting them, 'but in completely monastic fashion. They go nowhere and do not drive out.'[35] This was somewhat exaggerated, though it was true that Natalya was no longer part of fashionable society, nor did she see much of former friends such as the Karamzins. But she did make new acquaintances, chief among whom were the Maistres and the Friesenhofs.

In 1813 Sofya Ivanovna Zagryazhskaya, Ekaterina Ivanovna's sister, and hence also Natalya's aunt, had married Xavier de Maistre, a close friend of the Pushkins. He and his wife had gone abroad in 1825, accompanied by Sofya Ivanovna's ward, Natalya Ivanova (the illegitimate daughter of Sofya's brother, Aleksandr Zagryazhsky). She had later married an Austrian diplomat, Gustav Friesenhof. When Friesenhof was posted to Russia in 1839, the Maistres accompanied him and his wife to St Petersburg. Natalya and Aleksandra saw much of these new relations over the next two years – Friesenhof was summoned back to Vienna in 1841 – though the intercourse had its problems, as the two aunts were often at loggerheads.

In 1841 and 1842 Natalya took the children to Mikhailovskoe for the summer; she was now living closer to the centre, by the Konyushenny Bridge over the Moika, not far from the apartment in which Pushkin had died. She had taken up smoking – 'the other of the above-mentioned sisters deigned to take a puff of her cigarito,' Vyazemsky wrote playfully[36] – and, still beautiful and still hardly thirty, had acquired a number of suitors: the diplomat Nikolay Stolypin; Prince Aleksandr Golitsyn, a Guards officer and friend of the Karamzin brothers; and, most serious of all, Count Griffeo, the secretary at the embassy of the Kingdom of Naples and the Two Sicilies. Vyazemsky, who had appointed himself her cicisbeo on her return to St Petersburg and sent her love letters with embarrassing assiduity, was horrorstruck at the thought she might leave. He warned her against marrying Griffeo, painting their future in the blackest possible colours. 'I always told you to beware of foreigners,' he wrote. 'Even with independent means such a union will always pose serious problems. Sooner or later you will be forced to leave your homeland and abandon your children, who will have to remain in Russia ... And without independent means the problems will be even more serious. By marrying a foreigner you will, in all probability, lose the pension you receive, and your future will be subject to even more serious uncertainties.'[37] Vyazemsky's prediction as to the children's future struck home: since Pushkin's death, they had become the centre of Natalya's existence. Nothing more was heard of Count Griffeo.

She did not need to be informed that her finances might be uncertain in the future: they were bad enough at the present. Her pension and those of the children – 11,000 roubles in all – together with her allowance from her brother Dmitry were insufficient for life in the capital, while Aleksandra, whose only income was her allowance, was no better off. But Dmitry, trying to run a business which was encumbered with a crushing amount of debt, inevitably found it impossible to pay the allowances on time and in full. Money matters are a constant refrain in their letters to him, which are full of chiding, occasionally angry, reminders as to the sums he owes them. Aleksandra, desperately needing money to make up a court dress – Ekaterina Ivanovna had given her a length of velvet worth 500 roubles – wrote: 'In the end I will be forced to go in the costume of Eve. I'm ashamed of my linen in front of the laundress who jeers at it. That's what I've come to.'[38] Things were slightly eased in October 1841 when the trustees, responding to a petition from Natalya, gave her an extra 4,000 roubles a year. The following August Ekaterina Ivanovna died, and Sofya Ivanovna, following her sister's wishes, gave Natalya her personal possessions, her furniture and her silver. She did not, however, pass on an estate with five hundred serfs which Ekaterina Ivanovna had also wished to give to her niece.

By the end of 1843 Dmitry had had to suspend payment of the allowances altogether. The Goncharov business was on the point of collapse: its debts amounted to over half a million roubles more than the value of the estate itself. In February 1844, through Natalya, he submitted a petition to the tsar, outlining the position and pointing out, that if the business did collapse, the workers – together with their wives and children numbering some three thousand – would 'be deprived of any subsistence, and as a result social order might be disturbed'. Nicholas passed this on to the acting Minister of Finance, Vronchenko (Cancrin was severely ill at the time), minuting, 'At our next meeting be so good as to inform me what can be done for this family.' Vronchenko reported that the petition did not contain enough information to allow a definite appraisal of the situation, but that a loan – given that the debts so greatly exceeded the value of the property – would not be feasible. On this report Nicholas minuted: 'Discuss with Mrs Pushkin. 18 February 1844.' After seeing Natalya and Dmitry, Vronchenko submitted a secret report to the tsar:

> By imperial order the deputy Minister of Finance spoke to Mrs Pushkina and her brother Goncharov in reference to the note, known to Your Imperial Highness, on the debts encumbering the Goncharov estates. He submitted another note, which together with this will be presented to Your Imperial Highness.
>
> As far as Mrs Pushkina is concerned, from her explanations it transpires that she and her sister Miss Goncharova have each lost 5,000 roubles of annual income, which they received from

the estate, and which has gone on the satisfaction of debts. Mrs Pushkina, having to support her sister, and receiving instead of the former 15,000 roubles only those 5,000 roubles, paid to her by the state treasury, has herself been constrained to enter into debts amounting to 25,000 roubles.

Throwing herself on monarchical charity, she begs in the accompanying note that a new boon be given her by the grant of 25,000 roubles to pay her own debts and by an increase in her pension since despite all her moderation she does not find it possible to support herself and her sister on 5,000 roubles.

On this report is minuted: 'The Sovereign Emperor has deigned to give an imperial order to give Mrs Pushkina twenty-five thousand roubles, drawing this sum for the use known to His Majesty from the state treasury, and, concerning the replacement of a rise in her pension by other means, has deigned to express personally to her the particular imperial will.'[39]

What Nicholas meant by 'other means' of relieving her financial difficulty soon became clear. Natalya had recently met a former St Petersburg acquaintance, Petr Lanskoy, an officer in the Chevalier Guards, who was reputed to have been Idaliya Poletika's lover. He was now promoted major-general, on 9 May given command of the Horse Guards, and on 16 July married Natalya. A fortnight before the marriage Korff made a malicious note in his diary:

Marie Louise defiled the couch of Napoleon by her marriage with Neipperg. After seven years of viduity the widow Pushkin is marrying General Lanskoy ... Society again asks, 'What do you think of this marriage?', but in a very different sense: neither Pushkina nor Lanskoy have anything, and society is only marvelling at this union of hunger with thirst. Pushkina belongs to that group of privileged young women, whom the emperor occasionally favours with his visits. Six weeks ago he was with her again, and whether it was in consequence of this visit or just by chance, it was after this that Lanskoy was appointed commander of the Horse Guards, which at least temporarily provides for their existence, since, besides quarters, fuel, a carriage and so on, the regiment, everyone says, gives a yearly

income of somewhere up to thirty thousand [. . .] Lanskoy was
previously an imperial aide-de-camp in the Chevalier Guards
and has only recently been promoted general. Slanderous
rumour affirms that he used to be in a very close liaison with
the wife of Poletika, another colonel in the Chevalier Guards.
Now they are saying that he has abandoned *politics* and turned
to *poetry*.[40]

Other than this succession of circumstances, there is no proof to support
Korff's insinuation that Natalya had been one of Nicholas's mistresses,
who had been paid off by marriage to Lanskoy. It is, however, abundantly
clear that Nicholas did play a large part in bringing the marriage about.
Wanting to see it through to its end, he even suggested that he should
be one of the bride's sponsors at the wedding. Natalya avoided this by
saying that she wanted a very simple ceremony. She could not, however,
avoid the diamond necklace he sent as a wedding present, nor prevent
him from standing as godfather to Aleksandra, her first child by Lanskoy.

Natalya seems to have been attracted to men older than herself.
Lanskoy, like Pushkin, was thirteen years her senior. 'Your feeling for
me,' she wrote to him, 'is one which corresponds to our years; while
preserving a shade of love, it is not, however, passion, and just for this
reason the feeling is longer-lasting.'[41] But they were deeply attached to
one another, and Natalya was particularly grateful that he was such an
affectionate stepfather to her children. They, too, were fond of him, as
they were fond of their three half-sisters: the spoilt and wilful Aleksandra,
Sofya and Elizaveta. Only Natalya's sister, Aleksandra, was hostile to the
new situation: slowly declining into an embittered spinsterhood, she
was resentfully jealous of the fact that Lanskoy had usurped her place
by Natalya's side. However, in 1850 the Friesenhofs returned to Russia.
Shortly thereafter Natalya Ivanovna died. And in 1852 Gustav married
Aleksandra, and took her back with him to the castle he owned at
Brodzany, at the head of the Nitra valley, just south of present-day
Partizanske in Slovakia. Here, with their daughter Natalya, born in 1854,
they lived for the rest of their lives: Gustav died in 1889, Aleksandra in
1891.

Sergey Lvovich, Natalya's father-in-law, in his seventies was obese,
toothless, bald, deaf and terribly out of breath, but deterred by none of

these failings from dangling after young women. He died on 29 July 1848, having proposed – unsuccessfully – a few days earlier to Anna Kern's daughter, the thirty-year-old Ekaterina Ermolaevna. Pushkin's brother, Lev, had had to leave the army in 1842; he turned for assistance to Natalya, who, through Vyazemsky, obtained a post for him with the custom-house in Odessa. Here he married Elizaveta, the daughter of Aleksandr Zagryazhsky, who had been governor of Simbirsk when Pushkin had visited the town in 1833. In 1851 he fell ill with dropsy, went abroad to take a cure, but, returning to Odessa and continuing to drink, died there in July 1852.

Since Natalya's return to St Petersburg her health had not been good. She had been seriously ill in 1843, and had spent the summer in Reval, as sea-bathing had been prescribed by her doctors. In 1851 she was ill again, suffering, among other things, from nervous exhaustion. Together with Aleksandra and her daughters, she travelled to Europe, visited Berlin, Bonn and took the waters at Bad Godesberg. By 1861 she was suffering from consumption; long coughing fits at night prevented her sleeping. Her doctors agreed that she should spend a long time abroad. In May 1862 Lanskoy took a year's leave and left for Europe with Natalya and their daughters. After visiting various spas in Germany, they spent the summer with the Friesenhofs in Brodzany, the autumn in Geneva and the winter in Nice. Natalya's health improved noticeably, and she was advised to spend another winter in a warm climate. She insisted, however, on returning to Russia. The summer passed without incident, but with the onset of autumn she fell ill again, and died on 26 November 1863. She is buried in the Alexander Nevsky Monastery in St Petersburg, under the same stone as Lanskoy, who followed her to the grave on 6 May 1877.

LIST OF ABBREVIATIONS

NOTES

PROLOGUE

1 Apollon Grigorev, *Sochineniya.* St Petersburg, 1876, 238.
2 *Golos,* 11 June 1880; quoted in Levitt, 85. In writing of this, and of later Pushkin celebrations, I have relied largely on this work.
3 I.S. Turgenev, *Polnoe sobranie sochineniy i pisem.* Moscow-Leningrad, 1960–8, XV, 67, 69, 71, 76.
4 F.M. Dostoevsky, *Polnoe sobranie sochineniy.* Leningrad, 1972–, XXVI, 136, 145, 146, 148, 149.
5 Ibid., 460–1.
6 Quoted in Levitt, 123.
7 *Pravda,* 10 February 1937.
8 *Izvestiya,* 4 February 1937.
9 http://www.cbr.ru/eng/bank-notes_coins/memorable_coins/99–4.pdf.

CHAPTER 1

1 See Nina Volovich, 'Gde rodilsya Pushkin?' and Sergey Romanyuk, 'Dokumenty utverzhdayut', in *Kuranty: istoriko-kraevedchesky almanakh,* 1983, 140–5, 145–50.
2 *RA,* 1897, I, 233.
3 Teletova, 123.
4 Ibid., 129.
5 *Rod i predki Pushkina,* 118.
6 XII, 304.
7 To P.A. Osipova, 11 August 1825; XIII, 205.
8 Printed in Teletova, 171–3.
9 Teletova, 13–14; see also Lavrenteva, 424.
10 Veresaev (1937), I, 14.
11 XI, 141.
12 'Puteshestvie iz Moskvy v Peterburg', XI, 245–6.

13 Ashukin (1998), 19, 20.
14 Ibid., 10.
15 *VPK,* 23, 17.
16 'Ezersky', V, 100.
17 XII, 308.
18 *PVVS,* I, 31.
19 Annenkov (1855), 8.
20 *PVVS,* I, 33.
21 Volovich, 27.
22 *PVVS,* I, 34.
23 *Letopis,* I, 21.

CHAPTER 2

1 Christopher Marsden, *Palmyra of the North: the First Days of St Petersburg.* London, 1942, 237–8.
2 Georges Loukomski, *Charles Cameron (1714–1812).* London, 1943, 61.
3 Marsden, 256.
4 Rudenskaya, Rudenskaya (1980), 7–8.
5 *Letopis,* I, 22.
6 To P.A. Vyazemsky, 14 and 15 August 1825; XIII, 210.
7 *Poety 1790–1810-kh godov.* Leningrad, 1971, 652.
8 Ibid., 865.
9 *Letopis,* I, 24.
10 Ibid.
11 'Moy pervy drug, moy drug bestsenny!'. III, 39.
12 *Letopis,* I, 25.
13 Kunin (1987), I, 143, 147.
14 Pushchin, 37.
15 Ibid., 41.
16 'Zautra s svechkoy groshevoyu . . .', I, 177.
17 XII, 308; Pushchin, 43.
18 Tynyanov, 241.
19 Pushchin, 52.
20 Veresaev (1937), I, 47.

21 Pushchin, 51.
22 II, 972.
23 Rukoyu Pushkina, 720.
24 Letopis, I, 38–9.
25 Kunin (1987), I, 152, 153; Letopis, I, 60.
26 Grot, 224.
27 Veresaev (1937), I, 67.
28 A.A. Delvig, Polnoe sobranie sochineniy. Leningrad, 1959, 110.
29 Rudenskaya, Rudenskaya (1976), 62.
30 Ibid., 112.
31 Grot, 80–1.
32 Kunin (1984), I, 315.
33 Napoléon, recueil par ordre chronologique de ses lettres [. . .] formant une histoire de son règne. Paris, 1853–7, II, 541.
34 Tynyanov, 238.
35 Lettres inédites de Napoléon Ier à Marie-Louise. Paris, 1935, 70.
36 Letopis, I, 37, 39.
37 To I.I. Martynov, 28 November 1815; XIII, I.
38 'Na vozvrashchenie gosudarya imperatora iz Parizha v 1815 godu', I, 147.
39 XI, 157.
40 'Nadpis na stene bolnitsy', I, 261.
41 'I ostaneshsya s voprosom . . .', I, 282.
42 'Na Babolovsky dvorets', I, 292.
43 Letopis, I, 70.
44 'Vospominaniya v Tsarskom Sele', I, 83.
45 XII, 158.
46 S.T. Aksakov, Sobranie sochineniy. Moscow, 1955, II, 318.
47 Letopis, I, 67–8.
48 Ibid., 82.
49 LN, 58, 33. The epistle to Zhukovsky has not survived.
50 To P.A. Vyazemsky, 27 March 1816; XIII, 2–3.
51 From V.L. Pushkin, 17 April 1816; XIII, 4.
52 Letopis, I, 89.
53 'Ot vsenoshchnoy vechor idya domoy . . .', I, 283.
54 PVVS, I, 58n.
55 'K molodoy aktrise', I, 131.
56 'Krasavitse, kotoraya nyukhala tabak', I, 45.
57 XII, 297.
58 'Elegiya', I, 208.
59 PIM, XIV, 193.

60 Pushchin, 51.
61 'Kzh. V.M. Volkonskoy', I, 191. I accept L. Kamenskaya's sensible emendation, in the last line, of garce for grâce (PIM, XIV, 193).
62 Chereisky, 405–6.
63 'K molodoy vdove', I, 241–2.
64 'Poslanie Lide', I, 226.
65 Vigel, 317.
66 'K Galichu', I, 122.
67 PVVS, I, 58.
68 [K Saburovu], II, 350.
69 Letopis, I, 109.

CHAPTER 3

1 'Yurevu', II, 139.
2 PVVS, I, 195–6.
3 Letopis, I, 112.
4 Zhuikova, 48.
5 PVVS, I, 195.
6 N.V. Gogol, 'Portret', Sobranie khudozhestvennykh proizvedeniy. 2nd edition. Moscow, 1960, III, 148.
7 PVVS, I, 103.
8 Pushkinsky Peterburg, 60.
9 LN, 58, 34.
10 'Est v Rossii gorod Luga . . .', II, 35.
11 'Otryvki iz puteshestviya Onegina', VI, 200.
12 'Derevnya', II, 89.
13 XII, 304.
14 Pavlishchev, 22.
15 'Prostite, vernye dubravy! . . .', II, 36.
16 Vigel, 340–1.
17 Ibid., 278.
18 Arzamas, I, 346.
19 To P.A. Vyazemsky, 27 March 1816; XIII, 3.
20 To V.L. Pushkin, 28 (?) December 1816; XIII, 4.
21 'K Zhukovskomu' I, 197, 464.
22 To P.A. Vyazemsky, 13 July 1825; XIII, 188.
23 Tomashevsky, I, 143–4.
24 'Volnost. Oda', II, 45–8. There is some controversy about the dating of this poem, but the arguments in Tomashevsky (I, 144–52) and in the article by V.V. Pugachev, 'Predystoriya soyuza blagodenstviya i Push-kinsk[...] da "Volnost" [PIM, IV,

94–6) in favour of December 1817, rather than 1819, seem decisive.
25 Vigel, 414.
26 Modzalevsky (1999), 481.
27 Tomashevsky, I, 162.
28 *Letopis*, I, 491.
29 II, 1030–2.
30 'Derevnya', II, 89–91.
31 [Na Arakcheeva], II, 126.
32 *PIM*, II, 383.
33 'Skazki', II, 69.
34 'Ty i ya', II, 130.
35 [Na Sturdzu], II, 554.
36 *Letopis*, I, 122.
37 Mazour, 17.
38 XII, 303.
39 Pushchin, 56–7, 60.
40 Yakushkin, 42–3.
41 *Letopis*, I, 175.
42 Pushchin, 57.
43 [K portretu Chedaeva], II, 134.
44 Gershenzon (1989), 114.
45 Vigel, 423.
46 Kunin (1984), I, 484.
47 V.V. Zenkovsky, *Istoriya russkoy filosofii*. Paris, 1948, I, 160.
48 Vigel, 424.
49 Modzalevsky (1999), 480.
50 'Chedaevu', II, 188.
51 'K Chedaevu', II, 72.
52 Andrzej Walicki, *The Slavophile Controversy*. Oxford, 1975, 84.
53 Yakushkin, 41.

CHAPTER 4

1 VI, 638.
2 Veresaev (1937), I, 166: cf. II, 77.
3 Pushchin, 58.
4 K.N. Batyushkov, *Sochineniya*. Moscow, 1989, II, 538.
5 Vigel, 380.
6 'Orlovu', II, 85.
7 'Orlov s Istominoy v postele', II, 37.
8 *Rukoyu Pushkina*, 726.
9 'Kogda sozhmesh ty snova ruku . . .', II, 57.
10 *OA*, I, 117.
11 *RA*, 1866, 1161–2.
12 'Za uzhinom obelsya ya . . .', II, 487.
13 *Letopis*, I, 160.
14 Gordin, A.M., Gordin, M.A., 69.

15 From I.I. Lazhechnikov, 19 December 1831; XIV, 250.
16 *Letopis*, I, 174.
17 Veresaev (1937), I, 96.
18 *PVVS*, I, 104.
19 *OA*, I, 174, 280, 253.
20 Vigel, 324.
21 *OA*, I, 150.
22 *RS*, I (1870), 259.
23 Lotman, 518.
24 *RS*, I (1870), 263.
25 Kern, 35–6.
26 *Letopis*, 163; Pushchin, 57.
27 *PVVS*, I, 180.
28 Vigel, 275.
29 Tomashevsky, I, 272.
30 *PVVS*, I, 182.
31 To P.A. Katenin, first half (not later than 14) September 1825; XIII, 225.
32 *Letopis*, I, 152.
33 To P.A. Vyazemsky, 14 October 1823; XIII, 70.
34 A.S. Griboedov, *Sochineniya*. Leningrad, 1945, 480.
35 [V albom Sosnitskoy], II, 124.
36 *RS*, 31 (1881), 609.
37 [Nimfodore Semenovoy], II, 128.
38 XI, 10–11.
39 XI, 529.
40 XI, 12, 11.
41 [Na Kolosovu], II, 110.
42 *Istorichesky vestnik*, 91 (1903), 1045.
43 To A.A. Bestuzhev, 29 June 1824; XIII, 101.
44 To N.V. Vsevolozhsky, end October 1824; XIII, 115.
45 [K Rodzyanke], II, 404.
46 [Mansurovu], II, 80.
47 To P.B. Mansurov, 27 October 1819; XIII, 11.
48 Annenkov (1998), 57n.
49 Tomashevsky, I, 197n.
50 Ibid., 195n.
51 Ibid., 196.
52 *RS*, 68 (1890), 505.
53 Tomashevsky, I, 209.
54 'Vsevolozhskomu', II, 102.
55 *Pisma*, I, 191.
56 [Iz pisma k Ya.N. Tolstomu], II, 264.
57 VI, 281.
58 See David Parlett, *The Oxford Guide to Card Games*. Oxford, 1990, 75–8; Nabokov, II, 258–61.

59 Modzalevsky (1999), 369, 363.
60 To P.A. Vyazemsky, 1 December 1826; XIII, 310.
61 *PVVS*, I, 110.
62 'N.N.', II, 83.
63 *Letopis*, I, 154.
64 *Letopis*, I, 130.
65 'Vyzdorovlenie', II, 58.
66 *OA*, I, 191.
67 XII, 305.
68 [Na Karamzina], XVII, 16. The attribution of this epigram to Pushkin has been questioned; in XVII it is included among *Dubia*. For a – to me conclusive – argument in favour of the attribution see B.V. Tomashevsky, 'Epigrammy Pushkina na Karamzina', *PIM*, I, 208–15.
69 From P.A. Vyazemsky, 12 June 1826; to P.A. Vyazemsky, 10 July 1826; XIII, 284, 285–6.
70 *Letopis*, I, 178.
71 To L.S. Pushkin, between 4 September and 6 October 1822; XIII, 50.
72 'Otryvki iz pisem, mysli i zamechaniya', XI, 52.
73 VIII, 55–6.
74 Veresaev (1937), I, 211.
75 *OA*, I, 462.
76 'Kn. Golitsynoy. Posylaya ey odu "Volnost"', II, 56.
77 *OA*, I, 119.
78 *PIM*, XI, 219–20.
79 *OA*, I, 350, 358–9.
80 M.L.-E. Vigée-LeBrun, *Souvenirs*. Paris, 1870, I, 325.
81 *OA*, I, 326, 338.
82 *OA*, I, 371; II, 11, 14.
83 II, 1061.

CHAPTER 5

1 *Letopis*, I, 135.
2 *VPK*, 1962, 31.
3 *OA*, I, 174.
4 'K Pushkinu', F.N. Glinka, *Izbrannye proizvedeniya*. Leningrad, 1957, 201.
5 *Letopis*, I, 174.
6 XI, 145.
7 *Peterburgskie vstrechi Pushkina*, 140.
8 IV, 5.
9 *Letopis*, I, 217.
10 Quoted in Tomashevsky, I, 144.

11 Ibid., 347–8.
12 Ibid., 349.
13 *Pushkin v priztiznenndoy kritike 1820–1827*, 80–1; Tomashevsky, I, 350.
14 Tomashevsky, I, 353.
15 *Fingal, an Ancient Epic Poem, in Six Books: Together with several other poems, composed by Ossian, the Son of Fingal*. Translated from the Galic Languages by James Macpherson. London, 1762, 127. Pushkin would have taken the line, not from the English edition, but from the French translation by Pierre Le Tourneur, *Ossian, fils de Fingal* (Paris, 1777: 2nd edition 1805).
16 Chereisky, 169.
17 Vigel, 175.
18 *OA*, I, 325.
19 *Letopis*, I, 163.
20 'Chedaevu', II, 188.
21 To Alexander I, between the beginning of July and 22 September 1825; XIII, 227.
22 *LN*, 16–18, 674.
23 See Nabokov, II, 432–4.
24 To A.A. Bestuzhev, 24 March 1825; XIII, 155.
25 See Zhuikova, 314.
26 'Chedaevu', II, 188.
27 S.L. Tolstoy, *Fedor Tolstoy Amerikanets*. Moscow, 1926, 53.
28 *LN*, 16–18, 674.
29 To P.A. Vyazemsky, 1 September 1822; XIII, 43–4.
30 Seton-Watson, 99–100.
31 Bazanov, 174.
32 Ibid., 173.
33 Ibid., 176–7.
34 Ibid., 177.
35 *PVVS*, I, 202–3.
36 Chereisky, 264; *Letopis*, I, 176.
37 Pushchin, 62.
38 *OA*, II, 35, 37.
39 *Letopis*, I, 184.
40 Vigel, 415.
41 *RS*, 53 (1887), 239–40.
42 Pushkin, who was very particular about recording the fatidic dates of his life, noted in Kishinev on 9 May 1821 that it was exactly a year since he had left St Petersburg (XII, 303). However, other evidence suggests that he

left earlier: see *Letopis*, I, 182, 492. But if the first stage of his journey was only to Tsarskoe Selo, and he spent the next day or two there with friends before leaving for the south, he was justified in dating his departure from Petersburg as the ninth.

CHAPTER 6

1 Pushchin, 61.
2 Kunin (1984), II, 68.
3 Veresaev (1937), I, 226.
4 To L.S. Pushkin, 24 September 1820; XIII, 17.
5 Yu.G. Oksman, 'K istorii vysylki Pushkina iz Peterburga', *Pamyati P.N. Sakulina. Sbornik statey*. Moscow, 1931, 165.
6 *RA*, 1879, III, 136.
7 *RA*, 1891, I, 400.
8 *RA*, 1863, 865.
9 *Arkhiv Raevskikh*. St Petersburg, 1908, I, 518.
10 VIII, 447.
11 To L.S. Pushkin, 24 September 1820; XIII, 17–18.
12 *Arkhiv Raevskikh*, I, 523.
13 To L.S. Pushkin, 24 September 1820; XIII, 17.
14 *PVVS*, I, 206.
15 Bryusov, 33.
16 *LN*, 91, 582.
17 *RS*, 115 (1903), 320.
18 To L.S. Pushkin, 24 September 1820; XIII, 19.
19 Veresaev (1937), I, 229.
20 Vigel, 490.
21 *Prometey*, X, 18.
22 Vigel, 490, 491.
23 'Demon', II, 299.
24 To L.S. Pushkin, 24 September 1820; XIII, 18.
25 Bryusov, 34.
26 Laurence Oliphant, *The Russian Shores of the Black Sea in the Autumn of 1852*. Edinburgh and London, 1853, 193.
27 To L.S. Pushkin, 24 September 1820; XIII, 18.
28 VIII, 437.
29 To L.S. Pushkin, 24 September 1820; XIII, 18.
30 *Otryvki iz puteshestviya Onegina*, VI, 199–200.

31 *OA*, II, 168.
32 *Otryvki iz puteshestviya Onegina*, VI, 200.
33 To P.A. Vyazemsky, 13 and 15 September 1825; XIII, 226.
34 'Rdeet oblakov letuchaya gryada . . .', II, 157.
35 See Nabokov, II, 125.
36 Kunin (1987), I, 353.
37 Edward Daniel Clarke, *Travels in various countries of Europe, Asia and Africa*. London, 1810, I, 530.
38 To L.S. Pushkin, 24 September 1820; XIII, 19.
39 VIII, 437.
40 Ibid.
41 Ibid., 438.
42 'Chedaevu', II, 364.
43 VIII, 439.

CHAPTER 7

1 *RA*, 1866, 1124.
2 *RA*, 1891, I, 399.
3 *RA*, 1866, 1223–4.
4 XI, 22.
5 'Razzevavshis ot obedni . . .' II, 192.
6 *PVVS*, I, 230.
7 L. Maikov, *Istoriko-literaturnye ocherki*. St Petersburg, 1895, 116.
8 Shchegolev (1931), II, 286–7.
9 *PVVS*, I, 234.
10 'Alekseevu', II, 228.
11 *PVVS*, I, 231.
12 Yakushkin, 40.
13 *Letopis*, I, 225.
14 Ibid., 225–6.
15 To N.I. Gnedich, 4 December 1820; XIII, 20.
16 *RA*, 1866, 1485.
17 'A son amant Eglé sans résistance . . .', II, 205.
18 [Denisu Davydovu], II, 202.
19 *Letopis*, I, 497.
20 IV, 363.
21 'Ya perezhil svoi zhelanya . . .', II, 165.
22 *OA*, II, 257.
23 To L.S. Pushkin, 24 January 1822; XIII, 35.
24 To K.V. Nesselrode, 13 January 1823; XIII, 55.
25 *RS*, 53 (1887), 245.
26 'K Ovidiyu', II, 220.

27 *OA*, II, 257.

28 *RS*, 53 (1887), 244.

29 *Rukoyu Pushkina*, 754.

30 *PV*, 6, 286.

31 To L.S. Pushkin, 4 September 1822; XIII, 46.

32 *VPK*, 21, 18.

33 To V.L. Davydov (?), first half of March 1821; XIII, 23–4. The Academy edition tentatively names V.L. Davydov as the addressee of this draft letter, and of two other fragmentary letters on the Greek revolt (XIII, 104, 105). Some doubt has been cast on this attribution, though there is no conclusive argument for any other candidate. See Feinberg, 288–92; Ya. L. Levkovich, 'Tri pisma Pushkina o grecheskoy revolyutsii 1821 goda', *VPK*, 21, 16–24; T.I. Levicheva, 'K zametkam Pushkina o Grecheskoy revolyutsii', *VPK*, 23, 109–11; Ya.L. Levkovich, 'Replika na statyu T.I. Levichevoy «K zametkam Pushkina o Grecheskoy revolyutsii»', *VPK*, 27, 208–10.

34 XII, 302.

35 *Pushkin. Itogi i problemy izucheniya*. Moscow-Leningrad, 1966, 257.

36 *VPK*, 21, 22.

37 XII, 314.

38 To V.L. Davydov, June 1823, July 1824; XIII, 105.

39 *RA*, 1866, 1422.

40 Ibid.

41 Ibid., 1422–3.

42 Vigel, 486.

43 *RA*, 1866, 1246.

44 Vigel, 485.

45 Ibid., 486.

46 To P.A. Vyazemsky, 5 April 1823; XIII, 61.

47 'Grechanke', II, 262.

48 Leslie A. Marchand, *Byron. A Biography*. New York & London, 1957, III, 1243.

49 *RS*, 53 (1887), 242, 243–4.

50 'My dobrykh grazhdan pozabavim . . .', II, 488.

51 [V.L. Davydovu], II, 179.

52 'Khristos voskres', II, 186.

53 To A.I. Turgenev, 7 May 1821; XIII, 29.

54 *Gavriiliada*, IV, 120–36.

55 'Tsar Nikita i sorok ego docherey', II, 248–54.

56 Ernest J. Simmons, *Pushkin*. London, 1937, 146.

57 *Rukoyu Pushkina*, 396.

58 To A.P. Poltoratsky, January 1822; XIII, 352.

59 *PVVS*, I, 271.

60 *RA*, 1866, 1163.

61 *Zvenya*, IX, 52.

62 *RA*, 1866, 1168.

63 Euphrosine Dvoicenco, 'Puškin et les Balsch à Kišinev', *Revue des Études slaves*, XVIII (1938), 73–5.

64 *Zvenya*, IX, 99–100.

65 [V.L. Davydovu], II, 178.

66 *Letopis*, I, 261, 263.

67 'Napoleon', II, 213.

68 *RA*, 1866, 1429.

69 Trubetskoy, 101.

70 *RA*, 1866, 1272.

71 Ibid., 1281.

72 'Vospominaniya v Tsarskom Sele', I, 79.

73 *RA*, 1866, 1283.

74 'Segodnya ya po utru doma . . .', II, 286.

75 *Zvenya*, IX, 22.

76 *VPK*, 27, 23.

77 *Letopis*, I, 272.

78 *LN*, 60, i, 75.

79 *RA*, 1866, 1451.

80 Pushchin, 67. Raevsky had, of course, been in prison for just under three years, not four.

81 To N.I. Gnedich, 24 March 1821; XIII, 28.

82 To N.I. Grech, 21 September 1821; XIII, 32–3.

83 To L.S. Pushkin, 24 January 1822; XIII, 35–6.

84 To N.I. Gnedich, 29 April 1822; XIII, 37.

85 *Letopis*, I, 247.

86 Ibid., 283–4.

87 *OA*, II, 263.

88 *Letopis*, I, 293.

89 *RA*, 1866, 1177.

90 To N.I. Gnedich, 27 September 1822; XIII, 48.

91 Gessen, 40–1.

92 To P.A. Vyazemsky, 19 August 1823; XIII, 66.

93 *OA*, II, 274–5.
94 To L.S. Pushkin, 24 September 1820; XIII, 18.
95 Quoted in Tomashevsky, I, 408.
96 To L.S. Pushkin, October 1822; XIII, 51.
97 *Letopis*, I, 298.
98 Ibid., 299.
99 *Pushkin v prizhiznennoy kritike*, 141.
100 To P.A. Vyazemsky, 14 October 1823; XIII, 69.
101 IV, 367.
102 XI, 145.
103 To V.P. Gorchakov, October–November 1822; XIII, 52.
104 To P.A. Vyazemsky, 6 February 1823; XIII, 57–8.
105 To V.P. Gorchakov, October–November 1822; XIII, 52.
106 *Letopis*, I, 324.
107 To A.I. Turgenev, 1 December 1823; XIII, 80.
108 *OA*, II, 322, 327, 333–4.
109 To L.S. Pushkin, 25 August 1823; XIII, 67.

CHAPTER 8

1 Robert Lyall, *Travels in Russia, the Krimea, the Caucasus, and Georgia*. London, 1825, I, 182.
2 'Otryvki iz puteshestviya Onegina', VI, 204.
3 *RA*, 1897, II, 25.
4 Ibid., 26.
5 'Otryvki iz puteshestviya Onegina', VI, 202.
6 To A.A. Bestuzhev, 12 January 1824; XIII, 85.
7 Chereisky, 447.
8 'Otryvki iz puteshestviya Onegina', VI, 201.
9 *RA*, 1866, 1471.
10 *Prometey*, X, 16.
11 Vigel, 454.
12 Lyall, I, 183.
13 'Otryvki iz puteshestviya Onegina', VI, 204.
14 From F.F. Wiegel, 8 October 1823; XIII, 68.
15 To F.F. Wiegel, 22 October–4 November 1823; XIII, 72.
16 *Rukoyu Pushkina*, 186.

17 Vigel, 537.
18 Ibid., 538.
19 To K.A. Sobańska, 2 February 1830; XIV, 64.
20 *Russky vestnik*, 1856, June, 203.
21 *PIES*, XXXI–XXXII, 93n.
22 'Madam Riznich s rimskim nosom . . .', II, 471.
23 'Pod nebom golubym strany svoey rodnoy . . .', III, 20.
24 From V.I. Tumansky, 2 March 1827; XIII, 321.
25 *Letopis*, I, 355.
26 Zhuikova, 97.
27 To P.A. Vyazemsky, 4 November 1823; XIII, 382.
28 To P.A. Vyazemsky, 14 October 1823; XIII, 70.
29 Gordin (1996), 58.
30 *RA*, 1866, 1454.
31 Vigel, 473–4.
32 *Dnevnik*, 144.
33 Kunin (1987), I, 492.
34 To A.A. Bestuzhev, 12 January 1824; XIII, 84.
35 K.F. Ryleev, *Polnoe sobranie sochineniy*. Leningrad, 1971, 211.
36 Voltaire, *Collection complette des oeuvres*. [Geneva], 1757, VI, 185.
37 *RA*, 1866, 1459.
38 To L.S. Pushkin, 25 August 1823; XIII, 68. There has been much heated debate about the identity of the woman who inspired *The Fountain of Bakhchisaray* and is referred to in the omitted lines; she has often also been identified with a shadowy figure known as Pushkin's 'secret love' ('uta-ennaya lyubov', a quotation from a draft of the dedication to *Poltava*). He is supposed to have fallen in love with this woman in St Petersburg between 1817 and 1820, addressed a large number of poems to her over the following years, and remained in love with her, either until his marriage or his death. The main contributions to the debate have come from M.O. Gershenzon, whose candidate, in 'Severnaya lyubov A.S. Pushkina' (1908), is Mariya Golitsyna, née Suvorova, the general's granddaughter, a talented musician, whom Push-

kin met in society in St Petersburg and Odessa; from P.E. Shchegolev, whose article 'Iz razyskaniy v oblasti biografii i teksta Pushkina' (reprinted as 'Utaennaya lyubov A.S. Pushkina') dismisses Golitsyna and puts forward Mariya Raevskaya; and from Yu.N. Tynyanov, who, in 'Bezymennaya lyubov' (1939), suggests Elizaveta Karamzina: these three articles are reprinted in *Lyubovny byt*, II, 144–247. L.P. Grossman argues for Sofya Kiseleva, née Potocka, in 'U istokov "Bakhchisaraiskogo fontana"', *PIM*, III, 49–100. Finally R.V. Iezuitova, in '"Utaennaya lyubov" Pushkina', *Legendy i mify*, 216–40, sensibly suggests that Ekaterina Raevskaya is the woman referred to in *The Fountain of Bakhchisaray*, and that no 'secret love' existed: a view with which I concur.

39 To P.A. Vyazemsky, 4 November 1823; XIII, 73.

40 To P.A. Vyazemsky, 20 December 1823; XIII, 82.

41 To A.A. Bestuzhev, 12 January, 8 February 1824; XIII, 84, 88.

42 To A.A. Bestuzhev, 29 June 1824; XIII, 100–1.

43 To L.S. Pushkin, January (after 12)–beginning February 1824; XIII, 86.

44 Smirnov-Sokolsky, 80.

45 Gessen, 51.

46 Smirnov-Sokolsky, 81.

47 To I.N. Inzov (?), around 8 March 1824; XIII, 90.

48 To P.A. Vyazemsky, 8 March 1824; XIII, 88–9.

49 *OA*, III, 42.

50 *LN*, 58, 44.

51 To P.A. Vyazemsky, 14 October 1823; XIII, 70.

52 Thomas Moore, *Lalla Rookh, an Oriental Romance*. 13th edition; London, 1826, 130.

53 To P.A. Vyazemsky, 2 January 1822, end March–beginning April 1825; XIII, 34, 160.

54 XI, 145.

55 Ibid.

56 To L.S. Pushkin, 25 August 1823; XIII, 67.

57 To P.A. Vyazemsky, 8 March 1824; XIII, 88.

58 To P.A. Vyazemsky, 15 July 1824; XIII, 104.

59 To P.A. Vyazemsky, 8 or 10 October 1824; XIII, 111.

60 To L.S. Pushkin, 7 April 1825; XIII, 161.

61 To P.A. Vyazemsky, 24–25 June 1824; XIII, 99.

62 To A.I. Turgenev, 1 December 1823; XIII, 79. The final version has an extra line in the second stanza. See 'Svobody seyatel pustynny . . .', II, 302.

63 'Nedvizhny strazh dremal na tsarstvennom poroge . . .', II, 310.

64 To P.A. Vyazemsky, April–first half May (?) 1824; XIII, 92. Only a portion of this letter exists: that copied by the police and attached to Nesselrode's letter to Vorontsov of 11 July 1824. The addressee is therefore unknown. Bartenev asserts that it was addressed to 'the editor of *The Fountain of Bakhchisaray*' (*RA*, 1872, 2355n), i.e. Vyazemsky, the view adopted by the Academy edition. Tomashevsky suggests, more plausibly, that it was sent to Küchelbecker (*PSS*, X, 86). In his 'Imaginary Conversation with Alexander I' Pushkin refers to the letter, saying that it was written 'to a comrade [tovarishch]' (XI, 23): a term he would have been more likely to apply to his old school-fellow Küchelbecker than to Vyazemsky.

65 From P.A. Vyazemsky, end May (?) 1824; XIII, 94.

66 Annenkov (1998), 184.

67 Smirnova-Rosset, 176. For the portraits, see Zhuikova. The relationship between Pushkin and Elizaveta Vorontsova has been the subject of much dispute among scholars. Views range from that of T.G. Tsyavlovskaya ('Khrani menya, moy talisman . . .', *Prometey*, X, 12–84), who believes it to have been the most important and long-lasting affair of Pushkin's life, the inspiration of much of his verse, and puts forward the hypothesis that Pushkin was the

father of the Vorontsovs' second daughter, Sofya (born 3 April 1825), to that of G.P. Makogonenko (*Tvorchestvo A.S. Pushkina v 1830-e gody*. Leningrad, 1974, 53–76) who denies that anything more than a mere acquaintanceship existed. Both positions seem extreme.

68 Vigel, 456.
69 Sollogub, 438.
70 *Rukoyu Pushkina*, 300.
71 Kunin (1987), I, 493.
72 'Priyut lyubvi, on vechno poln . . .', II, 472.
73 Kunin (1987), I, 503.
74 Vigel, 493n.
75 'Polu-milord, polu-kupets . . .', II, 317.
76 From P.A. Vyazemsky, end May (?) 1824; XIII, 94.
77 *PIES*, XXXVII, 137.
78 *RS*, 4 (1871), 670, 673.
79 *PIES*, XXXVII, 137.
80 *Russkaya literatura*, 1978, 4, 106–7.
81 *LN*, 58, 42.
82 *RS*, 26 (1879), 292.
83 *PIES*, XVI, 68.
84 *Letopis*, I, 398.
85 James Webster, *Travels through the Crimea, Turkey, and Egypt; Performed during the Years 1825–1828*. London, 1830, I, 41.
86 *PV*, 2, 276.
87 Ibid., 282.
88 To A.I. Kaznacheev, 22 May 1824; XIII, 93–4.
89 *Rukoyu Pushkina*, 835.
90 *PV*, 6, 30.
91 *Letopis*, I, 402.
92 To P.A. Vyazemsky, 24–25 June 1824; XIII, 98.
93 Kunin (1987), I, 554.
94 To A.I. Kaznacheev, beginning (after 2) June 1824; XIII, 95.
95 To A.I. Turgenev, 14 July 1824; XIII, 103.
96 XI, 254–5.
97 VIII, 266.
98 To A.A. Bestuzhev, end May–beginning June 1825; XIII, 179.
99 From K.F. Ryleev, first half of June 1825; XIII, 183.
100 VIII, 42.
101 Vigel, 317.
102 *OA*, V, 2, 103.
103 *OA*, V, 2, 106–7, 109, 115, 122, 137.
104 *Rukoyu Pushkina*, 301.
105 *OA*, III, 48–9.
106 *OA*, V, 1, 11.
107 *OA*, V, 2, 112–13.
108 To P.A. Vyazemsky, 24–25 June 1824; XIII, 99.
109 *OA*, V, 2, 123.
110 *OA*, V, 1, 13–14.
111 *OA*, V, 2, 122, 125.
112 *OA*, V, 2, 134.
113 *RA*, 1897, II, 15.
114 Modzalevsky (1999), 144.
115 *OA*, III, 57.
116 *RS*, 26 (1879), 293–4.
117 *RS*, 136 (1908), 110, 111–12.
118 To L.S. Pushkin, January (after 12)–beginning February 1824; XIII, 86.
119 *Moskovsky Pushkinist*, II, 55–6.
120 *Letopis*, I, 427.
121 *OA*, V, 1, 40.

CHAPTER 9

1 Kern, 38.
2 *VPK*, 1969, 67.
3 *PVVS*, II, 137.
4 *Letopis*, I, 436.
5 *RS*, 136 (1908), 112–13.
6 From A.A. Delvig, 28 September 1824; XIII, 110.
7 *Letopis*, I, 435.
8 *Letopis*, II, 12.
9 To V.F. Vyazemskaya, end October 1824; XIII, 114.
10 To V.A. Zhukovsky, 31 October 1824; XIII, 116–17.
11 To B.A. Aderkas, end October 1824; XIII, 115–16.
12 From V.A. Zhukovsky, 12 (?) November 1824; XIII, 119–20.
13 To L.S. Pushkin, 1–10 November 1824; XIII, 118.
14 *PIES*, I, 79.
15 Modzalevsky (1925), 57.
16 *RA*, 1878, III, 395.
17 To L.S. Pushkin, around, but not later than 20 December 1824; XIII, 130–1.
18 *Lyubovny byt*, I, 215–16.
19 *RA*, 1872, 2360–1.
20 *Letopis*, II, 57.

21 To L.S. Pushkin, first half November 1824; XIII, 121.

22 'Zimny vecher', II, 439.

23 To V.F. Vyazemskaya, end October 1824; XIII, 114.

24 *Lyubovny byt*, I, 201.

25 To L.S. Pushkin, around, but not later than 20 December 1824; first half of November 1824; XIII, 130, 120.

26 To A.N. Vulf, 27 October 1828; XIV, 33.

27 *PVVS*, II, 181.

28 *Lyubovny byt*, I, 298, 310.

29 To A.G. Rodzyanko, 8 December 1824; XIII, 128–9.

30 From A.G. Rodzyanko and A.P. Kern, 10 May 1825; XIII, 170.

31 To P.A. Vyazemsky, 8 or 10 October 1824; XIII, 111.

32 From V.A. Zhukovsky, 15–20 April 1825; to V.A. Zhukovsky, 20–24 April 1825; XIII, 165, 167.

33 *Letopis*, I, 465.

34 *OA*, III, 99–100.

35 To A.A. Bestuzhev, end January 1825; to L.S. Pushkin, end January–first half February 1825; XIII, 137, 142.

36 XI, 153.

37 Pushchin, 65, 67.

38 Ibid., 67–8.

39 To P.A. Vyazemsky, end April–beginning May 1826; XIII, 274–5.

40 From P.A. Vyazemsky, 10 May 1826; to P.A. Vyazemsky, 27 May 1826; XIII, 276, 279.

41 *Lyubovny byt*, I, 435.

42 To L.S. Pushkin, 14 March 1825; XIII, 152.

43 To A.P. Kern, 28 August 1825; XIII, 214, 216.

44 To L.S. Pushkin, 22–23 April 1825; XIII, 163.

45 To P.A. Pletnev, around, but not later than 19 July 1825; XIII, 189.

46 Kern, 42–3.

47 'K ***', II, 406–7.

48 To A.P. Kern, 25 July, 13 and 14 August, 21 (?) August, 22 September 1825; XIII, 192, 207, 213, 229.

49 To A.P. Kern, 13 and 14 August, 21 (?) August, 22 September 1825; XIII, 208, 212, 229.

50 To A.N. Vulf, 10 October 1825; XIII, 237.

51 To P.A. Vyazemsky, first half November 1825; XIII, 243.

52 To A.P. Kern, 8 December 1825; XIII, 249–50.

53 To A.N. Vulf, 7 May 1826; XIII, 275.

54 To S.A. Sobolevsky, second half February 1828; XIV, 5.

55 To Anna N. Vulf, 21 July 1825; from Anna N. Vulf, end February–8 March 1826; XIII, 190, 267.

56 To L.S. Pushkin, September–October 1822; XIII, 50.

57 To P.A. Vyazemsky, 10 August 1825; XIII, 205.

58 'Khotya stishki na imeniny . . .', II, 446.

59 From Anna N. Vulf, end February–8 March 1826; XIII, 268.

60 From Anna N. Vulf, 20 April 1826; XIII, 273.

61 From V.A. Zhukovsky, 15–beginning 20's April 1825; to V.A. Zhukovsky, between 20 and 24 April 1825; XIII, 164, 166.

62 Tsyavlovsky, 141n; cf. *Sovetskie arkhivy*, 1977, 2, 84.

63 *Sovetskie arkhivy*, 1977, 2, 84.

64 Ibid., 85–6.

65 To V.A. Zhukovsky, beginning July 1825; XIII, 186–7.

66 From P.A. Pletnev, 5 August 1825; XIII, 202.

67 To I.F. Moyer, 29 July 1825; XIII, 195.

68 To O.S. Pushkina, 10–15 August 1825; XIII, 208–9.

69 To A.N. Vulf, end August 1825; XIII, 219.

70 From P.A. Vyazemsky, 28 August and 6 September 1825; to P.A. Vyazemsky, 13 and 15 September 1825; XIII, 220–2, 226–7.

71 To Alexander I, beginning July–September 1825; XIII, 228.

72 To A.P. Kern, 22 September 1825; XIII, 229.

73 To V.A. Zhukovsky, 6 October 1825; XIII, 236.

74 *Sovetskie arkhivy*, 1977, 2, 86.

75 To P.A. Pletnev, 4–6 December 1825; XIII, 249.

76 'Andrey Shene', II, 401.

77 To P.A. Katenin, 4 December 1825; XIII, 247.

78 Quoted in Mazour, 156.
79 *Lyubovny byt*, I, 223–4.
80 To P.A. Pletnev, second half (not later than 25) January 1826; XIII, 256.
81 *Letopis*, II, 119, 139, 115.
82 Modzalevsky (1925), 15, 19.
83 To P.A. Pletnev, 7 (?) March; to V.A. Zhukovsky, 7 March 1826; XIII, 266, 265–6.
84 From V.A. Zhukovsky, 12 April 1826; XIII, 271.
85 To P.A. Vyazemsky, around 7 November 1825; XIII, 239–40.
86 To P.A. Vyazemsky, 27 May 1826; XIII, 280.
87 To Nicholas I, 11 May–first half June 1826; XIII, 283–4; Modzalevsky (1929), 346.
88 *Yazykovsky arkhiv*. St Petersburg, 1913, I, 256–7.
89 To A.A. Delvig, 16 November 1823; XIII, 74.
90 To P.A. Vyazemsky, 9 November 1826; XIII, 305.
91 Mazour, 220.
92 Efros, 221; *Rukoyu Pushkina*, 159.
93 'K Vyazemskomu', III, 21.
94 *PIES*, XIII, 136.
95 To P.A. Vyazemsky, 4 November 1823; beginning April 1824; XIII, 73, 92.
96 To L.S. Pushkin, 13 June 1824; XIII, 98.
97 From P.A. Pletnev, 22 January 1825; XIII, 133.
98 *Pushkin v prizhiznennoy kritike*, 258, 262–3.
99 *Yazykovsky arkhiv*, I, 157–8.
100 From K.F. Ryleev and A.A. Bestuzhev, 12 February 1825; from A.A. Bestuzhev, 9 March 1825; to A.A. Bestuzhev, 24 March 1825; XIII, 141, 149, 155.
101 From P.A. Pletnev, 29 August 1825; XIII, 217.
102 To L.S. Pushkin, 28 July 1825; XIII, 194–5.
103 To P.A. Pletnev, 4–6 December 1825; XIII, 248.
104 To L.S. Pushkin, 27 March 1826; XIII, 157–8.
105 *Letopis*, II, 122.
106 *Pushkin v prizhiznennoy kritike*, 299.
107 Ibid., 314.

108 From P.A. Pletnev, 21 January 1826; XIII, 255.
109 From A.A. Delvig, beginning February 1826; XIII, 260.
110 From P.A. Pletnev, 6 February 1826; XIII, 261.
111 To P.A. Pletnev, 3 March 1826; XIII, 264–5.
112 *Graf Nulin*, V, 1.
113 XI, 188.
114 From A.Kh. Benckendorff, 22 August 1827; XIII, 336.
115 XI, 155–7.
116 *Literatura slavyanskikh narodov*, 4 (1959), 133.
117 *Krasny Arkhiv*, II (9), 205.
118 *Byloe*, 1918, 2 (30), 68, 72, 73.
119 Ibid., 75, 76.
120 *Letopis*, II, 165.

CHAPTER 10

1 'Nicholas I', *Encyclopedia Britannica CD* (Chicago, 1998).
2 *PVVS*, II, 59.
3 To P.A. Osipova, 16 September 1826; XIII, 296.
4 Eidelman (1987), 171.
5 *PVVS*, II, 61.
6 *RA*, 1865, 1249n.
7 *PIES*, XIX–XX, 74.
8 'Stansy', III, 40.
9 To N.M. Yazykov, 9 November 1826; XIII, 305.
10 *Wiener Slavistisches Jahrbuch*, VII (1959), 63n.
11 Bryusov, 21.
12 'Prorok', III, 30–1.
13 S.T. Aksakov, *Sobranie sochineniy*. Moscow, 1956, III, 59.
14 To P.A. Osipova, 16 September 1826; XIII, 296.
15 Veresaev (1936), I, 331.
16 *RA*, 1865, 1249–51.
17 Veresaev (1936), I, 336.
18 Ibid.
19 To V.F. Vyazemskaya, 3 November 1826; XIII, 301–2.
20 Chereisky, 338.
21 To N.A. Polevoy, 2 August 1825; XIII, 198.
22 To P.A. Pletnev, 26 March 1831; XIV, 158.

23 To P.A. Vyazemsky, 9 November 1826; XIII, 304–5.
24 *RA*, 1865, 1252.
25 To A.A. Delvig, 2 March 1827; XIII, 320.
26 Tsyavlovsky, 161.
27 Ibid., 159.
28 Ibid., 162.
29 Ibid.
30 *PIM*, I, 429.
31 *RA*, 1878, II, 50.
32 From A.Kh. Benckendorff, 30 September 1826; XIII, 298.
33 Modzalevsky (1925), 36.
34 From V.F. Vyazemskaya, 19 November 1826; XIII, 306.
35 To P.A. Vyazemsky, 9 November 1826; XIII, 304.
36 To V.P. Zubkov, 1–2 November 1826; XIII, 301.
37 To V.P. Zubkov, 1 December 1826; XIII, 311.
38 From A.Kh. Benckendorff, 22 November 1826; XIII, 307.
39 To M.P. Pogodin, 29 November 1826; XIII, 307.
40 To A.Kh. Benckendorff, 29 November 1826; XIII, 308.
41 *Lyubovny byt*, I, 269.
42 From A.Kh. Benckendorff, 23 December 1826; XIII, 315.
43 Lemke, 608.
44 From A.Kh. Benckendorff, 14 December 1826; XIII, 313.
45 To A.Kh. Benckendorff, 3 January 1827; XIII, 317.
46 To P.P. Kaverin, 18 February 1826; XIII, 319.
47 *PIES*, XIX–XX, 83.
48 Veresaev (1936), I, 338–9.
49 Kunin (1984), II, 129.
50 'Vo glubine Sibirskikh rud . . .'; 'Moy pervy drug, moy drug bestsenny . . .', III, 49, 39.
51 *PVVS*, I, 358.
52 Veresaev (1936), I, 322.
53 *Zvenya*, II, 180–1.
54 To P.A. Vyazemsky, 10 July 1826; XIII, 286.
55 'Andrey Shene', II, 398.
56 *Russkaya literatura*, 1963, 3, 86.
57 Shchegolev (1931), 107.
58 *Rukoyu Pushkina*, 744.
59 Shchegolev (1931), 112.
60 *Rukoyu Pushkina*, 745–6.
61 *RS*, 99 (1899), 323–4.
62 Shchegolev (1931), 123, 125.
63 Veresaev (1937), II, 18.
64 Chereisky, 456.
65 To V.D. Solomirsky, 15 April 1827; XIII, 327.
66 Tsyavlovsky, 377n.
67 'Kto znaet kray, gde nebo bleshchet . . .', III, 97.
68 Vigel, 70–1.
69 *PIES*, V, 121.
70 To A.Kh. Benckendorff, 24 April 1827; from A.Kh. Benckendorff, 3 May 1827; XIII, 328, 329.
71 To A.A. Delvig, 2 March 1827; XIII, 320.
72 To L.S. Pushkin, 18 May 1827; XIII, 329.
73 *Literaturny arkhiv*, I (1938), 226.
74 Modzalevsky (1999), 289.
75 Veresaev (1936), I, 384.
76 Ibid., 378.
77 Veresaev (1937), II, 119.
78 *Pisma k Khitrovo*, 172n.
79 From E.M. Khitrovo, 18, 20, 21 March 1830; XIV, 71.
80 To S.A. Sobolevsky, 15 July 1827; XIII, 332.
81 Gessen, 86.
82 To S.A. Sobolevsky, 15 July 1827; from P.A. Pletnev, 22 September 1827; XIII, 332, 344.
83 From P.A. Pletnev, 22 September 1827; XIII, 344.
84 *Pushkin v prizhiznennoy kritike*, 325, 327.
85 XI, 146.
86 *LN*, 58, 68.
87 To A.A. Delvig, 31 July 1827; XIII, 334.
88 *Lyubovny byt*, I, 268.
89 'Poet', III, 65.
90 XII, 307.
91 Modzalevsky (1999), 315.
92 *VPK*, 26, 178.
93 *LN*, 58, 76–7.
94 Veresaev (1936), I, 380, 387.
95 Veresaev (1937), I, 32.
96 *LN*, 58, 71n.
97 Olenina, 68, 66.
98 *Rukoyu Pushkina*, 314, 317.

99 *LN*, 58, 75, 78.

100 From P.A. Vyazemsky, 21 May 1828; XIV, 19.

101 'To Dawe Esqr', III, 101.

102 *A.S. Griboedov v vospominaniyakh sovremennikov.* Moscow, 1980, 92.

103 *LN*, 47–8, 237.

104 *LN*, 58, 75–6.

105 Veresaev (1937), II, 103.

106 E.A. Baratynsky, *Polnoe sobranie sochineniy.* Leningrad, 1957, 250–1.

107 VIII, 40.

108 *LN*, 58, 78.

109 'Portret', III, 112.

110 *OA*, III, 179.

111 Olenina, 70–1.

112 From P.A. Vyazemsky, 26 July 1828; XIV, 23.

113 To P.A. Vyazemsky, 1 September 1828; XIV, 26.

114 From P.A. Vyazemsky, 18 and 25 September 1828; XIV, 28.

115 To A.A. Delvig, mid-November 1828; XIV, 34.

116 Olenina, 67–8.

117 'Dar naprasny, dar sluchainy', III, 104.

118 'Druzyam', III, 89.

119 *Lyubovny byt*, II, 221n.

120 XIV, 15.

121 *RA*, 1884, III, 318, 321.

122 XIV, 12.

123 To A.Kh. Benckendorff, 21 April 1828; XIV, 11.

124 *RS*, 9 (1874), 394–9.

125 Alekseev (1972), 304.

126 Ibid., 286n.

127 Modzalevsky (1925), 16.

128 *Rukoyu Pushkina*, 749–50.

129 To P.A. Vyazemsky, 1 September 1828; XIV, 26–7.

130 Tomashevsky (1956), I, 431.

131 *PIM*, VIII, 285.

132 Tomashevsky (1956), I, 432.

133 *LN*, 58, 71n.

134 Ibid., 84.

135 Ibid., 88–9.

136 To P.A. Vyazemsky, 1 September 1828; XIV, 26.

137 Laurence Oliphant, *The Russian Shores of the Black Sea in the Autumn of 1852.* London, 1853, 5.

138 *Lyubovny byt*, I, 274.

139 *LN*, 58, 84.

140 To A.A. Delvig, mid-November 1828; XIV, 34.

141 To A.N. Vulf, 27 October 1828; XIV, 33.

142 V, 17. The identity of this poem's dedicatee has been a subject of controversy among Pushkin scholars: the problem is connected to the debate on the identity of the poet's 'secret love' (see Chapter 8, note 38). The main contenders are Mariya Raevskaya and Annette Olenina: the arguments in favour of the latter appear to me decisive. Two recent discussions of the controversy are Yu.M. Lotman, 'Posvyashchenie "Poltavy" (Adresat, tekst, funktsiya)', in Lotman, 253–65, and V.M. Esipov, ' "Skazhite mne, chey obraz nezhny..." (K probleme utaennoy lyubvi)', *Moskovsky pushkinist*, IV (1997), 86–118.

143 'Ya vas lyubil: lyubov eshche, byt mozhet...', III, 188.

144 VI, 630, 514.

145 Veresaev (1936), I, 414.

146 *LN*, 58, 86.

147 To L.S. Pushkin, 18 May 1827; XIII, 329.

148 Gershenzon (1989), 100.

149 'Vsevolozhskomu', II, 102.

150 'Tak stary khrych, tsygan Ilya...', III, 467.

151 *LN*, 58, 85.

CHAPTER 11

1 *Lyubovny byt*, I, 302, 303.

2 Smirnova-Rosset, 184.

3 Ibid., 589.

4 Ibid., 591.

5 Veresaev (1936), I, 430.

6 To N.N. Pushkina, about 5 May 1834; XV, 143.

7 Veresaev (1936), I, 431, 430.

8 Tynyanov, 193.

9 *LN*, 58, 88.

10 Veresaev (1936), I, 437.

11 Vigel, 549.

12 *LN*, 58, 90.

13 V, 56.

14 XI, 158.

15 *RA*, 1881, II, 498.

16 To N.I. Goncharova, 1 May 1829; XIV, 45.

17 *PIM*, XI, 19.

18 Ibid.

19 Ibid., 20.

20 Ibid., 21.

21 Ibid., 25.

22 Ibid.

23 Jean Bonamour, *A.S. Griboedov et la vie littéraire de son temps*. Paris, 1965, 407.

24 VIII, 460.

25 Tynyanov, 204.

26 Veresaev (1936), II, 17–18.

27 VIII, 468.

28 VIII, 481, 480.

29 Eidelman (1987), 171.

30 *Dela III Otdeleniya*, 91, 94.

31 To A.Kh. Benckendorff, 10 November 1829; XIV, 51.

32 Quoted in A.S. Pushkin, *Puteshestvie v Arzrum vo vremya pokhoda 1829 goda*. Paris, 1935, 70.

33 'Na kholmakh Gruzii lezhit nochnaya mgla . . .', III, 158.

34 *Severnaya pchela*, 22 March 1830.

35 VIII, 468–9, 473.

36 *Rukoyu Pushkina*, 677.

37 For a recent commentary on the Don Juan list see Ya.L. Levkovich, ' "Donzhuansky spisok" Pushkina', *Utaennaya lyubov Pushkina*, 34–50.

38 To N.I. Goncharova, 5 April 1830; XIV, 76.

39 'Zima. Chto delat nam v derevne? Ya vstrechayu . . .', III, 181.

40 To A.N. Vulf, 16 October 1829; XIV, 50; to A.P. Kern, 28 August 1825; XIII, 216.

41 *PIES*, I, 85.

42 *RA*, 1877, I, 513.

43 *Slavia*, XXVIII (1959), 4, 560.

44 Gordin, A.M., Gordin, M.A., 126.

45 To E.F. Tiesenhausen, 1 January 1830; XIV, 54.

46 *Slavia*, 561.

47 From D.F. Ficquelmont, 8 or 15 February 1830; XIV, 65. The letter is misdated, as the quotation from Dolly's diary makes clear.

48 *Slavia*, 561.

49 Thomas Raikes, *A Visit to St Petersburg, in the Winter of 1829–30*. London, 1838, 84–5.

50 Lemke, 496.

51 To S.D. Kiselev, 15 November 1829; XIV, 51.

52 'Poedem, ya gotov; kuda by vy druzya . . .', III, 191.

53 To A.Kh. Benckendorff, 7 January 1830; from A.Kh. Benckendorff, 17 January 1830; XIV, 56, 58.

54 *RA*, 1882, III, 124.

55 To P.A. Vyazemsky, end January 1830; XIV, 61.

56 '*Literaturnaya gazeta*' *A.S. Pushkina i A.A. Delviga 1830 goda (No 1–13)*. Moscow, 1988, 5.

57 *Severnaya pchela*, 11 January 1830.

58 To A.Kh. Benckendorff, 7 January 1830; from A.Kh. Benckendorff, 21 January 1830; XIV, 56, 59.

59 XI, 154, 396.

60 From F.V. Bulgarin, 18 February 1830; XIV, 67.

61 *Literaturnaya gazeta*, 9 August 1830.

62 Ibid., 7 March 1830.

63 *Severnaya pchela*, 11 March 1830.

64 *RA*, 1878, II, 49.

65 Lemke, 499–500.

66 To A.Kh. Benckendorff, 24 March 1830; from A.Kh. Benckendorff, 3 April 1830; XIV, 73, 75.

67 *PSS*, VII, 679.

68 XI, 129–30.

69 [Na Bulgarina], III, 215.

70 *OA*, III, 193.

71 *Severnaya pchela*, 7 August 1830.

72 'Moya rodoslovnaya', III, 261–3.

73 To A.Kh. Benckendorff, 24 November 1831; from A.Kh. Benckendorff, 10 December 1831; XIV, 242, 247.

74 To P.A. Vyazemsky, end January 1830; XIV, 62.

75 'Chto v imeni tebe moem? . . .', *LN*, 16–18, 877; the album version differs slightly from that which Pushkin included in the 1832 edition of his verse: cf. III, 210.

76 To K.A. Sobańska, 2 February 1830; XIV, 62–3.

77 *LN*, 16–18, 804.

78 From A.Kh. Benckendorff, 17 March 1830; XIV, 70.

79 Chereisky, 125.

80 To P.A. Vyazemsky, 14 March 1830; XIV, 68

81 To P.A. Vyazemsky, second half (not before 18) March 1830; XIV, 74.

82 *LN*, 16–18, 805.

83 *RA*, 1882, III, 161.

84 *Literaturny arkhiv*, I, 223–4.

85 XII, 159.

86 Vyacheslav Koshelov, *Konstantin Batyushkov. Stranstviya i strasti.* Moscow, 1987, 331.

87 *Zvenya*, III–IV, 180.

88 *OA*, III, 192.

89 To N.I. Goncharova, 5 April 1830; XIV, 75.

90 To N.O. and S.L. Pushkin, 6–11 April 1830; XIV, 77.

91 From S.L. and N.O. Pushkin, 16 April 1830; XIV, 79.

92 To V.F. Vyazemskaya, end (before 28) April 1830; XIV, 81.

93 From P.A. Vyazemsky, 26 April 1830; XIV, 80.

94 To A.Kh. Benckendorff, 16 April 1830; XIV, 77–8.

95 From A.Kh. Benckendorff, 28 April 1830; XIV, 81–2.

96 *RA*, 1901, III, 382.

97 To N.O. and S.L. Pushkin and O.S. Pavlishcheva, 3 May 1830; XIV, 88.

98 To A.Kh. Benckendorff, 7 May 1830; XIV, 90.

99 Modzalevsky (1925), 97.

100 *PIES*, XXXVII, 152.

101 To A.Kh. Benckendorff, 29 May 1830; XIV, 95.

102 To A.N. Goncharov, 9 September 1830; XIV, 111.

103 From I.P. Myatlev, first half March 1832; XV, 16.

104 Chereisky, 520.

105 *Mir Pushkina*, I, 77.

106 To N.N. Goncharova, about (not later than) 29 July 1830, 30 July 1830; XIV, 103, 104.

107 *Letopisi GLM*, I (1936), 560; *RA*, 1888, II, 311.

108 *Mir Pushkina*, I, 75.

109 *Slavia*, XXVIII (1959), 4, 563.

110 To N.N. Goncharova, 20 July 1830; XIV, 102.

111 To V.F. Vyazemskaya, 4 August 1830; XIV, 106.

112 Veresaev (1936), II, 66.

113 To P.A. Pletnev, 9 September 1830; XIV, 112.

114 Ashukin (1998), 252.

115 *Mir Pushkina*, I, 75.

116 To P.A. Pletnev, 31 August 1830; XIV, 110.

117 To V.F. Vyazemskaya; to N.N. Goncharova, end August 1830; XIV, 110, 109.

118 VIII, 138.

119 VIII, 53.

120 To P.A. Pletnev, 31 August, 9 September 1830; XIV, 110, 112.

121 'Elegiya', III, 228.

122 Kupriyanova, 36.

123 To P.A. Pletnev, 9 September 1830; XIV, 112.

124 XII, 309.

125 To P.A. Pletnev, 29 September 1830; XIV, 113.

126 Shchegolev (1928), 91.

127 To N.N. Goncharova, 26 November 1830; XIV, 126.

128 To P.A. Vyazemsky, 5 November 1830; XIV, 122.

129 'Geroy', III, 251–3.

130 Kupriyanova, 68–9.

131 To N.N. Goncharova, 2 December 1830; XIV, 130.

132 To P.A. Pletnev, around (not later than) 29 October 1830; XIV, 117–18.

133 To M.P. Pogodin, beginning November 1830; XIV, 121.

134 To N.N. Goncharova, around (not later than) 29 October 1830; XIV, 119.

135 To N.N. Goncharova, 18 November 1830; XIV, 125.

136 To N.N. Goncharova, 26 November, 2 December 1830; XIV, 127, 130.

137 To N.N. Goncharova, 2 December 1830; XIV, 130.

138 To N.S. Alekseev, 26 December 1830; XIV, 136.

139 *LN*, 58, 100.

140 To P.A. Pletnev, 9 December 1830; XIV, 133.

141 To E.M. Khitrovo, 11 December 1830; XIV, 134.

142 *LN*, 58, 100.

143 To P.A. Vyazemsky, end (not before 27–28) December 1830; 10–13 January 1831; XIV, 137, 142.

144 To P.A. Vyazemsky, 2 January 1831; XIV, 140.

145 To P.V. Nashchokin, December (after 5) 1830; XIV, 136.

146 To E.M. Khitrovo, 21 January 1831; XIV, 148.

147 From P.A. Vyazemsky, 14 January 1831; XIV, 144.

148 XI, 15.

149 *PIES*, XXVI–XXVII, 130.

150 To E.M. Khitrovo, 9 December 1830; XIV, 134.

151 *Pisma k Khitrovo*, 290.

152 *Pisma*, III, 131.

153 *Zvenya*, VI, 151; *Prometey*, X, 123.

154 To E.M. Khitrovo, 21 January 1831; XIV, 147–8.

155 *Pisma k Khitrovo*, 273.

156 To E.M. Khitrovo, around (not later than) 9 February 1830; XIV, 149–50.

157 XI, 482. The 'reader of French newspapers' of this rough draft of *Puteshestvie iz Moskvy v Peterburg [A Journey from Moscow to Petersburg]* would seem to be identical with the mysterious 'polonophil' of the fragment of verse 'Ty prosveshcheniem svoy razum osvetil . . .' ('You enlightened your mind with education . . .'; III, 444). See Lednicki (1954), 68–94; Gleb Struve, 'Who Was Pushkin's "Polonophil"?' *Slavonic and East European Review*, 29 (1950–51), 444–55; and Wacław Lednicki, 'Some doubts about the identity of Pushkin's polonophil', ibid., 30 (1951–2), 206–212. None of the three candidates put forward – Chaadaev and Vyazemsky by Lednicki, and Prince P.B. Kozlovsky by Struve – seems wholly satisfactory.

158 To P.A. Pletnev, around (not later than) 5 May 1830; XIV, 89.

159 To P.A. Pletnev, around (not later than) 29 October 1830; XIV, 118.

160 To P.A. Pletnev, 7 January 1831; XIV, 142.

161 From A.Kh. Benckendorff, 9 January 1831; to A.Kh. Benckendorff, 18 January 1831; XIV, 142, 146.

162 *Lyubovny byt*, I, 306, 304.

163 To P.A. Pletnev, 21, 31 January 1831; XIV, 147, 149.

164 Ovchinnikova, 102.

165 To P. Pletnev, about (not later than) 16 February 1831; XIV, 152.

166 To N.I. Krivtsov, 10 February 1831; XIV, 150–1.

167 Ovchinnikova, 123–4.

168 *PVVS*, II, 248–9.

169 Ibid., 29.

170 Ovchinnikova, 130.

171 To P.A. Vyazemsky, second half (not later than 24) May 1826; XIII, 279.

172 *Lyubovny byt*, I, 347–8.

CHAPTER 12

1 To P.A. Pletnev, 24 February 1831; XIV, 154–5.

2 III, 213. The manuscript of this poem has not survived. It appears to have been written on 19 January, the year suggested variously as 1830, 1831 or 1832. One copy bears the title 'To my wife'. See III, 1203–4 and *Letopisi GLM*, I (1936), 538–9. Unless it is purely an exercise in technique, with no autobiographical significance, it is difficult to see whom Pushkin can be comparing, other than Natalya and a past love such as Sobańska or Zakrevskaya. For a – purely linguistic – analysis of the poem see Roman Jakobson, 'Stikhi Pushkina o deve-statue, vakkhanke i smirennitse', *Alexander Puškin. A Symposium on the 175th Anniversary of His Birth*. New York, 1976, 3–26.

3 Ovchinnikova, 156–7.

4 *PIES*, I, 65.

5 Ovchinnikova, 167.

6 To L.S. Pushkin, 6 April 1831; XIV, 159.

7 To A.N. Goncharov, 25 April 1831; XIV, 163.

8 To P.A. Pletnev, 26 March 1831; XIV, 159.

9 To P.V. Nashchokin, 22 October 1831; XIV, 237.

10 To P.A. Pletnev, 26 March 1831; XIV, 158.

11 *PIES*, XV, 50.

12 To P.A. Pletnev, around (not later than) 14 April 1831; XIV, 162.

13 To N.I. Goncharova, 26 June 1831; XIV, 182.

14 *PIES*, XV, 67.

15 To E.M. Khitrovo, second half (18–25) May 1831; XIV, 166.

16 *Slavia*, XXVIII (1959), 4, 564.

17 To P.V. Nashchokin, 3 September 1831; XIV, 220.

18 To P.V. Nashchokin, 7 October 1831; XIV, 231.

19 To P.A. Osipova, 29 June 1831; XIV, 184.

20 XIV, 285.

21 From M.Ya. von Fock, 8 June 1831; XIV, 171.

22 From F.F. Wiegel, June–July 1831; XIV, 202.

23 To A.Kh. Benckendorff, around (not later than) 21 July 1831; XIV, 256.

24 *Dela III Otedeleniya*, 120.

25 To P.V. Nashchokin, 21 July 1831; to P.A. Pletnev, 22 July 1831; XIV, 196, 198.

26 To P.A. Vyazemsky, 3 September 1831; from P.A. Vyazemsky, 11 September 1831; XIV, 220, 223.

27 *PIES*, V, 50.

28 *PVVS*, II, 221–2.

29 *PIES*, V, 62.

30 To N.N. Pushkina, around (not later than) 30 September 1832; XV, 33–4.

31 *PIES*, V, 64.

32 To P.A. Osipova, 29 June 1831; XIV, 184.

33 XII, 200.

34 XII, 199.

35 *PIES*, XV, 76.

36 To P.A. Pletnev, around (not later than) 11 July 1831; XIV, 189.

37 *Letopisi GLM*, I (1936), 415.

38 *PIES*, XV, 89.

39 *Pisma V.A. Zhukovskago k Aleksandru Ivanovichu Turgenevu*. Moscow, 1895, 256.

40 Smirnova-Rosset, 511.

41 Ibid., 24.

42 From P.A. Vyazemsky, 24 August 1831; to P.A. Vyazemsky, 3 September 1831; XIV, 214, 221.

43 To P.A. Vyazemsky, 3 September 1831; XIV, 220.

44 N.V. Gogol, *Polnoe sobranie sochineniy*. Moscow, 1937–52, X, 214.

45 To P.A. Vyazemsky, 1 June 1831; XIV, 169.

46 To E.M. Khitrovo, middle (after 10) September 1831; XIV, 225.

47 'Pered grobnitseyu svyatoy . . .', III, 268.

48 To P.A. Vyazemsky, 1 June 1831; XIV, 169.

49 To P.V. Nashchokin, 21 July 1831; to P.A. Vyazemsky, 3 August 1831; XIV, 197, 205.

50 *Pisma k Khitrovo*, 284.

51 Smirnova-Rosset, 25.

52 XII, 201.

53 'Klevetnikam Rossii', III, 269.

54 From D.I. Khvostov, 24 October 1831; XIV, 237.

55 From P.Ya. Chaadaev, 18 September 1831; XIV, 228.

56 *Pisma k Khitrovo*, 293–5.

57 *RA*, 1893, II, 581.

58 *Pisma k Khitrovo*, 292.

59 Ibid., 296.

60 *RA*, 1879, II, 252.

61 Gordin, A.M., Gordin, M.A., 107.

62 *PIES*, XV, 101.

63 *Slavia*, XXVIII (1959), 4, 564.

64 *PIES*, XXI–XXII, 371.

65 Ibid., XV, 106.

66 *Slavia*, XXVIII (1959), 4, 565.

67 Sollogub, 277.

68 To N.N. Pushkina, 20 August 1833; XV, 72.

69 To N.N. Pushkina, 11 July 1834; XV, 178.

70 *PIES*, XXIII–XXIV, 117.

71 To P.A. Pletnev, 9 December 1830; XIV, 133.

72 To P.A. Pletnev, around (not later than) 15 August 1831; XIV, 209.

73 XI, 118.

74 *Povesti pokoinogo Ivana Petrovicha Belkina*, 252, 249, 267.

75 Veresaev (1936), II, 127–8.

76 To N.N. Pushkina, 8 December 1831; XIV, 245.

77 To N.N. Pushkina, 16 December 1831; XIV, 249.

78 *PVVS*, II, 191.

79 To N.N. Pushkina, 16 December 1831; XIV, 249.

80 Ibid.

81 Veresaev (1936), II, 127.

82 To M.O. Sudienko, 15 January 1832; XV, 4.

83 *Prometey*, X, 418.

84 To N.N. Pushkina, around (not later than) 16 December 1831; XIV, 248.

85 Veresaev (1936), II, 143.
86 To N.N. Pushkina, 8, 16 December 1831; XIV, 246, 249.
87 To P.V. Nashchokin, 8 and 10 January 1832; XV, 3.
88 *PIES*, XXXVIII–XXXIX, 226.
89 *RS*, 99 (1899), 8.
90 *1799–1837. Pushkin i ego vremya*, 333.
91 *Rukoyu Pushkina*, 845.
92 To A.Kh. Benckendorff, 24 February 1832; XV, 14.
93 Viktor Afanasev, *Zhukovsky*. Moscow, 1986, 272.
94 To I.V. Kireevsky, 4 February 1832; XV, 9.
95 Afanasev, *Zhukovsky*, 270.
96 *PVVS*, II, 192–3.
97 To V.F. Vyazemskaya, 4 June 1832; XV, 25.
98 To N.N. Pushkina, 25 September 1832; XV, 31.
99 From P.V. Nashchokin, end November 1833; XV, 97.
100 To N.N. Pushkina, around (not later than) 3 October 1832; XV, 34.
101 To N.N. Pushkina, 27 September, 3 October, 25 September 1832; XV, 32, 34, 31.
102 To N.N. Pushkina, 8 October, 11 October 1833, 20 and 22 April 1834; XV, 86, 87, 130.
103 Veresaev (1936), II, 143.
104 To P.V. Nashchokin, 2 December 1832; XV, 36.
105 Abramovich (1994b), 62.
106 Ibid., 77.
107 Ibid., 88.
108 *Mir Pushkina*, I, 139–40.
109 Veresaev (1936), II, 151–2, 150.
110 To P.V. Nashchokin, around (not later than) 25 February 1833; XV, 50–1.
111 *Slavia*, XXVIII (1959), 4, 566.
112 K ***, III, 288.
113 To N.N. Pushkina, 21 October 1833; XV, 87.
114 *LN*, 58, 113.
115 Veresaev (1936), II, 157.
116 *RA*, 1888, II, 309.
117 *VPK*, 1970, 7–8.
118 Obodovskaya, Dementev (1978), 119.
119 From L.S. Pushkin, 21 February 1833; XV, 19.

120 *Lyubovny byt*, I, 406.
121 To N.N. Pushkina, 6 November 1833; XV, 93.
122 Abramovich (1994b), 59–60.
123 To P.V. Naschokin, 2 December 1832; XV, 36.
124 Ovchinnikov, 52.
125 To A.N. Mordvinov, 30 July 1833; XV, 70.
126 *Mir Pushkina*, I, 164.
127 Obodovskaya, Dementev (1999), 162.
128 Abramovich (1994b), 185.
129 To N.N. Pushkina, 30 October 1833; XV, 89.
130 *Rukoyu Pushkina*, 550.
131 To N.N. Pushkina, 20 August 1833; XV, 71–2.
132 To N.N. Pushkina, 21 August 1833; XV, 72–3.
133 Obodovskaya, Dementev (1982), 66–7.
134 To N.N. Pushkina, 26 August 1833; XV, 73–4.
135 Ibid., 74.
136 To N.N. Pushkina, 2 September 1833; XV, 76, 77.
137 Ibid., 78.
138 Ibid., 76.
139 To N.N. Pushkina, 12 September 1833; XV, 79–80.
140 To N.N. Pushkina, 2 September 1833; XV, 76.
141 Obodovskaya, Dementev (1978), 120–1.
142 IX, 493.
143 Abramovich (1994b), 341.
144 Ibid., 347.
145 To A.A. Fuchs, 8 September 1833; XV, 79.
146 *RS*, 98 (1899), 262.
147 To N.N. Pushkina, 12 September 1833; XV, 80.
148 Abramovich (1994b), 358.
149 To N.N. Pushkina, 14 September 1833; XV, 80.
150 Abramovich (1994b), 365.
151 Smirnova-Rosset, 470.
152 To N.N. Pushkina, 19 September 1833; XV, 81–2.
153 *PVVS*, II, 260.
154 *PIES*, XXIII–XXIV, 78–9.
155 To N.N. Pushkina, 2 October 1833; XV, 83.
156 IX, 19.

157 To N.N. Pushkina, 2 October 1833; XV, 83.
158 Abramovich (1994b), 399.
159 To N.N. Pushkina, 19 September 1833; XV, 81.
160 To N.N. Pushkina, 2 October 1833; XV, 83.
161 To N.N. Pushkina, 30 October 1833; XV, 89.
162 *PKZh*, 154.
163 To N.N. Pushkina, 11 October 1833; XV, 87.
164 To N.N. Pushkina, 21 October 1833; XV, 88.
165 To N.N. Pushkina, 30 October 1833; XV, 89.
166 To N.N. Pushkina, 21 October 1833; XV, 87.
167 To N.N. Pushkina, 30 October 1833; XV, 88–9.
168 To N.N. Pushkina, 6 November 1833; XV, 93.
169 To N.N. Pushkina, 30 October, 6 November 1833; XV, 89, 93–4.
170 From V.F. Odoevsky, 28 September 1833; XV, 84.
171 To N.N. Pushkina, 21 October 1833; XV, 88; from S.A. Sobolevsky, 2 October 1833; XV, 85.
172 Abramovich (1994b), 440.
173 Bartenev, 47.
174 'Osen (Otryvok)', III, 321.
175 To P.V. Nashchokin, 21 July 1831; XIV, 196.
176 From P.V. Nashchokin, 17–18 November 1833; XV, 94.
177 From P.V. Nashchokin, after 3 May–June 1834; XV, 168–9.
178 Abramovich (1994b), 482.
179 To P.V. Nashchokin, 24 November 1833; XV, 96.

CHAPTER 13

1 XII, 316.
2 XII, 314.
3 XII, 315.
4 *Dnevnik*, 61.
5 Abramovich (1994b), 526.
6 *Mir Pushkina*, I, 189.
7 Ibid., 187.
8 Ibid., 224.
9 XII, 317, 326.

10 *OA*, III, 284.
11 XII, 316.
12 From N.V. Gogol, 23 December 1833; XV, 100.
13 Abramovich (1994b), 533.
14 To A.Kh. Benckendorff, 6 December 1833; XV, 98.
15 XII, 317.
16 V.G. Belinsky, *Sobranie sochineniy*. Moscow, 1976–82, I, 97.
17 *VPK*, 1967–68, 7.
18 *Dnevnik*, 73.
19 *Medny Vsadnik*, 9. Quotations from the poem are taken from this edition, edited by N.V. Izmailov, which is in several respects superior to that in V, 131–50.
20 Adam Mickiewicz, *Dzieła*. Warsaw, 1995, III, 307.
21 'On mezhdu nami zhil . . .', III, 331.
22 XI, 14.
23 For an historical analysis of the numerous attempts to interpret the poem, see Igor Panfilowitsch, *Aleksandr Puškins 'Mednyi vsadnik'. Deutungsgeschichte und Gehalt.* Munich, 1995.
24 *PVVS*, I, 54.
25 Ibid., II, 278.
26 *Lyubovny byt*, I, 410.
27 XII, 318.
28 Vigel, 271.
29 *Mir Pushkina*, I, 204n, 205, 210.
30 *OA*, III, 253; *Dnevnik*, 80.
31 XII, 319.
32 *PIES*, XXIX–XXX, 33.
33 XII, 319.
34 To N.V. Nashchokin, mid-March 1834; XV, 118.
35 To N.N. Pushkina, around 28 June 1834; XV, 167.
36 *PVVS*, II, 278.
37 XII, 319.
38 XII, 333.
39 XII, 334.
40 XII, 320.
41 *Dnevnik*, 92.
42 To P.V. Nashchokin, mid-March 1834; XV, 117.
43 XII, 320.
44 To P.V. Nashchokin, mid-March 1834; XV, 117.
45 To N.N. Pushkina, 20 or 22 April 1834; XV, 130.

46 XII, 320.

47 From V.A. Zhukovsky, 29 January 1834; XV, 107.

48 XII, 319, 320.

49 VI, 637.

50 XII, 324.

51 To N.N. Pushkina, 3 June 1834; XV, 155.

52 XII, 330.

53 From D.V. Davydov, 4 April 1834; XV, 123.

54 XII, 324.

55 VIII, 235.

56 To N.N. Pushkina, 2 October 1833; XV, 83.

57 For an admirably concise analytical history of readings of the story, see Neil Cornwell, *Pushkin's 'The Queen of Spades'*. Bristol, 1993.

58 F.M. Dostoevsky, *Polnoe sobranie sochineniy*. Leningrad, 1972, XXX, i, 192.

59 VIII, 249.

60 To N.N. Pushkina, 28 April 1834; XV, 134.

61 From N.I. Goncharova, 14 May 1834; XV, 147.

62 To N.N. Pushkina, 19 April, 20 and 22 April, around 5 May, 28 April, 30 June, around 26 July 1834; XV, 128, 130, 143, 134, 170, 183.

63 To N.N. Pushkina, 3 August 1834; XV, 184–5.

64 To N.N. Pushkina, 20 and 22 April, around 14 July, 3 August 1834; XV, 130, 180, 184.

65 To N.N. Pushkina, 11 July 1834; XV, 178.

66 *Mir Pushkina*, I, 224.

67 To N.N. Pushkina, 11 July 1834; XV, 178.

68 *PIES*, XIV, 17–18.

69 To N.N. Pushkina, 20 and 22 April 1834; XV, 129–30.

70 XII, 329.

71 To N.N. Pushkina, 18 May 1834; XV, 150. I have preferred the reading *publiku prinimat v n [. . .]* ('receive the public in your privy') (*Dnevnik*, 175) to *publiku prinimat v napersniki* ('to take the public as a confidant'), given here.

72 To N.N. Pushkina, 8 June 1834; XV, 157.

73 To N.N. Pushkina, 11 June 1834; XV, 159.

74 To N.N. Pushkina, around (not later than) 29 May 1834; XV, 154.

75 To N.N. Pushkina, 18 May 1834; XV, 150.

76 To N.N. Pushkina, around (not later than) 29 May 1834; XV, 153.

77 To N.N. Pushkina, around 28 June 1834; XV, 167–8.

78 To A.Kh. Benckendorff, 25 June 1834; XV, 165.

79 From V.A. Zhukovsky, 2 July 1834; XV, 171.

80 To A.Kh. Benckendorff, 3 July 1834; XV, 172.

81 From A.Kh. Benckendorff, 30 June 1834; XV, 171.

82 From V.A. Zhukovsky, 3 July 1834; XV, 172–3.

83 To V.A. Zhukovsky, 4 July 1834; XV, 173–4.

84 To A.Kh. Benckendorff, 4 July 1834; XV, 174.

85 From V.A. Zhukovsky, 6 July 1834; XV, 175.

86 To V.A. Zhukovsky, 6 July 1834; XV, 176.

87 *PPL*, 232.

88 XII, 331.

89 To N.N. Pushkina, 11 July, around 14 July 1834; XV, 178, 180.

90 *PIES*, XXI–XXII, 325.

91 To N.N. Pushkina, 11 June, 14 July 1834; XV, 158, 181.

92 Gastfreind, 41.

93 XII, 332.

94 *PVVS*, II, 193.

95 *PIES*, XIV, 21.

96 *PIES*, XV, 92.

97 *PIES*, XVII–XVIII, 191.

98 *Mir Pushkina*, I, 160.

99 *PIES*, XV, 131.

100 *Mir Pushkina*, I, 183.

101 To P.V. Nashchokin, 24 November 1833; XV, 96.

102 To P.V. Nashchokin, between 23 and 30 March 1834; *PPL*, 31. The letter referred to is presumably that from Penkovsky of 13 March, to which he had attached an order of the Lukoyanov district court demanding an overdue interest payment of 4,113

roubles 40 copecks. He assured
Sergey Lvovich that the debt would
be paid, and confirmed that this had
been done in his following letter of
26 March. See *Letopisi GLM*, I (1936),
144–7.

103 To I.M. Penkovsky, 13 April 1834; XV,
126.

104 The pages of this home-made
account book are reproduced in
Shchegolev (1928), between 120–1. See
also 215–24 and *Rukoyu Pushkina*,
364–74.

105 *Mir Pushkina*, I, 219.

106 From N.I. Pavlishchev, 26 April 1834;
XV, 132–3; for the restaurant bill see
LA, I (1938), 47–8.

107 From S.A. Sobolevsky, end April–not
later than 4 May 1834; XV, 139–40.

108 To N.I. Pavlishchev, 4 May 1834; XV,
142.

109 To P.A. Osipova, 29 June and 13 July
1834; XV, 179.

110 To N.N. Pushkina, 12 May, 5 May, 8
June, around 19 June, around 28 June
1834; XV, 146, 143, 157, 162, 168.

111 To N.N. Pushkina, 14 July 1834; XV,
181.

112 *PIES*, XVII–XVIII, 165.

113 From A.P. Pleshcheev, 3 October
1836; XVI, 163.

114 From I.M. Penkovsky, 7, 15, 28 May
1834; XV, 144–5, 148–9, 152–3.

115 To P.A. Osipova, 29 June and 13 July
1834; XV, 179.

116 From P.A. Osipova, 17, 24 June 1834;
XV, 161–2, 164.

117 From K. Reichman, 22 June 1834; XV,
163.

118 To N.N. Pushkina, 30 June 1834; XV,
170.

119 From I.M. Penkovsky, 12 June 1834;
XV, 159.

120 Shchegolev (1928), 231; to I.M. Penkovsky, 20 November 1834; XV, 212.

121 From the Boldino peasants, end
October–beginning November 1833;
XV, 92.

122 XI, 261.

123 To P.V. Nashchokin, 3 August 1831;
XIV, 204.

124 To I.M. Penkovsky, 10 November
1834; XV, 200–1.

125 *Mir Pushkina*, I, 262–3.

126 From N.I. Pavlishchev, 31 January
1835; XVI, 9–10.

127 To L.S. Pushkin, 23–24 April 1835;
XVI, 20.

128 To I.M. Penkovsky, 1 May 1835; XVI,
22–3.

129 To N.I. Pavlishchev, 2 May 1835; XVI,
23.

130 *Mir Pushkina*, I, 283.

131 Ibid., 290.

132 *PIES*, XXIII–XXIV, 210.

133 To N.I. Pavlishchev, 2 May 1835; XVI,
24.

134 To N.N. Pushkina, 15 and 17 September 1834; XV, 191–2.

CHAPTER 14

1 Obodovskaya, Dementev (1982), 120.

2 Obodovskaya, Dementev (1978), 197.

3 Ibid.

4 *Mir Pushkina*, I, 257.

5 Obodovskaya, Dementev (1978), 196.

6 Ibid., 215.

7 Obodovskaya, Dementev (1987), 141.

8 Obodovskaya, Dementev (1978),
201–2.

9 XII, 336.

10 *PVVS*, II, 194.

11 Ibid.

12 *Prometey*, X, 380–1.

13 Ibid., 381.

14 To A.Kh. Benckendorff, 23 November
1834; XV, 201.

15 *Mir Pushkina*, I, 264.

16 *PPL*, 262.

17 *PIES*, XIX–XX, 175.

18 To P.V. Nashchokin, 20 January 1835;
XVI, 6.

19 From M.L. Yakovlev, 5 September
1835; XVI, 46.

20 To I.I. Dmitriev, 26 April 1835; XVI,
21.

21 XII, 337.

22 *RA*, 1870, 1145, 1149–50.

23 From S.S. Uvarov, 8 October 1831; to
S.S. Uvarov, 21 October 1831; XIV,
232, 236.

24 *PVVS*, II, 251.

25 XII, 325.

26 Nikitenko, I, 140.

27 Ibid., 141–2.

28 *PIES*, XXIII–XXIV, 120.

29 XII, 337.

30 XII, 156.

31 To A.Kh. Benckendorff, around (not later than) 11 April 1835; *PPL*, 84. Cf. XVI, 29, where the letter is dated incorrectly as April–May 1835.

32 To I.I. Dmitriev, 26 April 1835; XVI, 22.

33 [Na Dondukova-Korsakova], III, 388.

34 To P.A. Pletnev, around (not later than) 11 October 1835; XVI, 55–6.

35 To A.Kh. Benckendorff, around (not later than) 23 October 1835; XVI, 57.

36 *OA*, III, 277.

37 'Na vyzdorovlenie Lukulla', III, 404–5.

38 Nikitenko, I, 179.

39 *Istorichesky vestnik*, 41 (1890), 337.

40 *LN*, 58, 120.

41 Shchegolev (1999), 231.

42 Nikitenko, I, 180.

43 *RS*, 31 (1881), 606.

44 To N.G. Repnin, 5 February 1836; XVI, 83.

45 From N.G. Repnin, 10 February 1836; XVI, 84.

46 To N.G. Repnin, 11 February 1836; XVI, 84.

47 *RS*, 28 (1880), 559.

48 From D.V. Davydov, 8 February 1836; XVI, 83.

49 To A. Jobard, 24 March 1836; XVI, 94.

50 From A. Jobard, 17 April 1836; XVI, 106.

51 *PVPK*, 96.

52 *PIES*, XXVI–XXVII, 253–4.

53 Chereisky, 499.

54 Obodovskaya, Dementev (1978), 228.

55 To A.Kh. Benckendorff, around (not later than) 11 April 1835; *PPL*, 84 (XVI, 29).

56 From V.F. Odoevsky, April–May 1835; XVI, 28.

57 To A.Kh. Benckendorff, around (not later than) 11 April 1835; *PPL*, 84 (XVI, 29).

58 To P.A. Pletnev, around (not later than) 11 October 1835; XVI, 56.

59 To A.Kh. Benckendorff, 31 December 1835; XVI, 69.

60 *PIES*, XXIII–XXIV, 211.

61 To P.V. Nashchokin, 10–20 January 1836; XVI, 73.

62 To N.I. Pavlishchev, 2 May 1835; XVI, 24.

63 *Mir Pushkina*, I, 286.

64 Gastfreind, 43.

65 *Mir Pushkina*, I, 278–9.

66 *PIES*, I, 144.

67 *Lyubovny byt*, I, 204.

68 *PIES*, XXI–XXII, 325.

69 *Mir Pushkina*, I, 280–1.

70 To N.I. Goncharova, 16 May 1835; XVI, 25.

71 Obodovskaya, Dementev (1978), 215.

72 To N.I. Goncharova, 14 July 1835; XVI, 39.

73 *Mir Pushkina*, I, 284.

74 *Mir Pushkina*, I, 287.

75 To A.Kh. Benckendorff, April–May 1835; XVI, 30.

76 To A.Kh. Benckendorff, 1 June 1835; XVI, 31–2.

77 *Mir Pushkina*, I, 282.

78 Ibid., 284.

79 *Dela III Otdeleniya*, 155.

80 To A.Kh. Benckendorff, 4 July 1835; XVI, 37.

81 *Dela III Otdeleniya*, 157.

82 To A.Kh. Benckendorff, 22 July 1835; XVI, 41.

83 *Dela III Otdeleniya*, 158.

84 To A.Kh. Benckendorff, 26 July 1835; XVI, 42–3.

85 *Dela III Otdeleniya*, 160.

86 *PIES*, XVII–XVIII, 162.

87 To N.N. Pushkina, 14 September 1835; XVI, 47.

88 To N.N. Pushkina, 25 September 1835; XVI, 51.

89 To A.I. Bekleshova, 14–18 September 1835; *PPL*, 107 (XVI, 48).

90 *PIES*, XIX–XX, 107.

91 To N.N. Pushkina, 21 September 1835; XVI, 48–9.

92 To N.N. Pushkina, 29 September 1835; XVI, 51.

93 Ibid., 52.

94 Ibid., 51.

95 To N.N. Pushkina, 2 October 1835; XVI, 52–3.

96 To N.N. Pushkina, 21, 25, 29 September, 2 October 1835; XVI, 48, 50, 51–2, 53.

97 *PIES*, XIX–XX, 106.
98 To P.A. Pletnev, around (not later than) 11 October 1835; XVI, 56.
99 To N.N. Pushkina, 25 September 1835; XVI, 50.
100 '. . . Vnov ya posetil . . .', III, 400.
101 *PIES*, XVII–XVIII, 184.
102 To P.A. Osipova, around (not later than) 26 October 1835; XVI, 57.
103 *PIES*, XVII–XVIII, 193.
104 To P.A. Osipova, around (not later than) 26 October 1835; XVI, 57–8.
105 *Mir Pushkina*, I, 251, 252.
106 *PIES*, XXI–XXII, 389.
107 *Mir Pushkina*, I, 264.
108 Ibid., 287.
109 To L.S. Pushkin, to N.I. Pavlishchev, 2 May 1835; XVI, 23, 24.
110 *PIES*, XVII–XVIII, 162.
111 *Mir Pushkina*, I, 268.
112 *PIES*, XVII–XVIII, 182.
113 *PIM*, X, 343.
114 *PIES*, XXIII–XXIV, 220–1.
115 To N.M. Yazykov, 14 April 1836; XVI, 104.
116 *PIES*, XXI–XXII, 335.
117 From I.M. Penkovsky, 28 April 1836; XVI, 108.
118 *Mir Pushkina*, II, 167.
119 To L.S. Pushkin, 2 June 1836; XVI, 123–4.
120 From L.S. Pushkin, beginning (after 2) July 1836; XVI, 134.
121 From N.I. Pavlishchev, 27 June 1836; XVI, 130–3.
122 From N.I. Pavlishchev, 11 July 1836; XVI, 136–9.
123 From L.S. Pushkin, 20 August 1836; XVI, 154.
124 XVI, 150.
125 From S.L. Pushkin, 7 August 1836; XVI, 148.
126 *PIES*, XIX–XX, 108.
127 From N.I. Pavlishchev, 21, 28 August 1836; XVI, 155–7, 157–8.
128 *PIES*, XIX–XX, 108–9.
129 From P.A. Osipova, 6 January 1837; XVI, 215.
130 To S.L. Pushkin, 20 October 1836; XVI, 173.
131 *PIES*, XII, 101.
132 To N.I. Pavlishchev, 5 January 1837; XVI, 214.
133 To P.A. Osipova, 24 December 1836; XVI, 205.
134 From P.A. Osipova, 6 January 1837; XVI, 214–15.
135 Veresaev (1937), II, 453.
136 *Slavia*, XXVIII (1959), 562.
137 *Correspondence of Princess Lieven and Earl Grey*. London, 1890, III, 22.
138 *PIES*, XXVI–XXVII, 262.
139 XII, 319.
140 Veresaev (1936), II, 292.
141 Vitale, Stark, 90, 103.
142 *PIES*, XII, 94.
143 Veresaev (1936), II, 308.
144 *Dnevnik*, 89.
145 *PIES*, XXVI–XXVII, 264.
146 Shchegolev (1999), 389.
147 Gastfreind, 62.
148 Suasso, 351.
149 *PVPK*, 309.
150 *PIM*, VIII, 256.
151 Veresaev (1936), II, 335.
152 *RA*, 1888, II, 312.
153 To N.N. Pushkina, around 5 May 1834; XV, 143.
154 J.G. Kohl, *Russia*. London, 1842, 179.
155 *RS*, 70 (1891), 670–1.
156 Obodovskaya, Dementev (1978), 230–1.
157 Vitale, Stark, 84.
158 Ibid., 112–13.
159 *RS*, 103 (1900), 383–4.
160 Vitale, Stark, 118.
161 Shchegolev (1999), 68.
162 *RA*, 1888, II, 309.
163 *RS*, 103 (1900), 388.
164 Vitale, Stark, 123.
165 Ibid., 128, 131, 140–1.
166 Ibid., 131.
167 *PIES*, XII, 94.
168 *PIES*, XXI–XXII, 336.
169 Modzalevsky (1999), 542–5.
170 *Sovremennik*, I, 303.
171 From S.S. Khlyustin, 4 February 1836; XVI, 79.
172 Modzalevsky (1999), 492.
173 *RA*, 1865, 1218.
174 *PIES*, XXIII–XXIV, 215.
175 *RA*, 1865, 1220.
176 To N.N. Pushkina, 6 May 1836; XIV, 112–13.
177 Nikitenko, I, 180, 182.

178 XVI, 94.
179 *RS*, 118 (1904), 570.
180 From P.A. Vyazemsky, 11 August 1836; XVI, 153.
181 To N.N. Pushkina, 11 May 1836; XVI, 115.
182 *LN*, 16–18, 717.
183 To N.N. Pushkina, 6 May 1836; XVI, 113.
184 To N.N. Pushkina, 14 and 16 May; to P.V. Nashchokin, 27 May 1836; XVI, 116, 121.
185 Belinsky, *Sobranie sochineniy*, I, 491.
186 Quoted in M.I. Gillelson, 'Pushkinsky "Sovremennik"', in *Sovremennik, Prilozhenie k faksimilnomu izdaniyu*. Moscow, 1987, 5.
187 Ibid., 8–9.
188 *OA*, III, 281.
189 Belinsky, *Sobranie sochineniy*, I, 491.
190 Abramovich (1991), 168.
191 *LN*, 58, 128.
192 To P.V. Nashchokin, 27 May 1836; XVI, 121.
193 *RA*, 1882, I, 246.
194 To N.N. Pushkina, 4 May 1836; XVI, 111.
195 *Neva*, 1965, 2, 193.
196 *PVVS*, II, 324.
197 To D.V. Davydov, 14 June 1836; *PPL*, 145. Cf. XVI, 121–2, where it is erroneously dated 24–30 May.
198 To D.V. Davydov, August 1836; XVI, 160.
199 From D.V. Davydov, 20 July 1836; XVI, 143.
200 To V.A. Durov, 17 and 27 March 1836; XVI, 99.
201 *Sovremennik*, II, 54.
202 To N.N. Pushkina, 11 May 1836; XVI, 114.
203 To N.A. Durova, about 10 June 1836; XVI, 125–6.
204 *PVVS*, II, 296–7.
205 From N.A. Durova, 7, 24 June 1836; XVI, 125, 129.
206 To N.A. Durova, around 25 June 1836; XVI, 130–1.
207 N.A. Durova, *Izbrannoe*. Moscow, 1984, 415.
208 *PVVS*, II, 298.
209 Obodovskaya, Dementev (1978), 133–4.

CHAPTER 15

1 To S.L. Pushkin, 20 October 1836; XVI, 173.
2 *Arkhiv Opeki Pushkina*, 125.
3 From P.V. Nashchokin, end December 1831; XIV, 250.
4 *Arkhiv Opeki Pushkina*, 97.
5 *PVVS*, II, 352.
6 *PVPK*, 232.
7 Ibid., 234–5.
8 Ibid., 236, 243.
9 Abramovich (1994a), 46–7.
10 Obodovskaya, Dementev (1978), 243.
11 Abramovich (1994a), 47.
12 Obodovskaya, Dementev (1978), 240.
13 *Duel Pushkina c Dantesom-Gekkerenom*, 61.
14 To L. Heeckeren, 17–21 November 1836; XVI, 190.
15 Abramovich (1994a), 47, 48.
16 *PVPK*, 266.
17 Ibid., 273.
18 Abramovich (1994a), 51–2.
19 Abramovich (1991), 349–50.
20 Ibid., 393.
21 Quoted in Lemke, 408.
22 *OA*, III, 337.
23 *PVPK*, 278.
24 P.Ya. Chaadaev, *Stati i pisma*. Moscow, 1989, 42.
25 To P.Ya. Chaadaev, 19 October 1836; XVI, 171–3.
26 From K.O. Rosset, around (not earlier than) 22 October 1836; XVI, 176.
27 XVI, 336.
28 *OA*, III, 349, 352.
29 From D.V. Davydov, 23 November 1836; XVI, 194. This account agrees closely with the report on Chaadaev's interrogation sent by General Perfilev, the commander of the Moscow district gendarmerie, to Benckendorff. See Lemke, 418.
30 '19 Oktyabrya', II, 424; 'Chem chashche prazdnuet litsey . . .', III, 277.
31 Chereisky, 513.
32 *PIES*, XIII, 58, 59.
33 To M.L. Yakovlev, 9–15 October 1836; XVI, 168.
34 *PIES*, XIII, 53.
35 *Rukopisi Pushkina*, 737–8.

36 'Byla pora: nash prazdnik molodoy . . .', III, 431.
37 Vitale, Stark, 153–7.
38 To L. Heeckeren, 17–21 November 1836; XVI, 190.
39 Smirnova-Rosset, 192.
40 To N.N. Pushkina, 30 October 1833; XV, 89.
41 RA, 1908, III, 295.
42 RA, 1888, II, 310.
43 XVI, 180.
44 Vigel, 309.
45 Shchegolev (1999), 415.
46 Ibid., 242.
47 Modzalevsky (1999), 494.
48 On the anonymous letter and its authorship see especially Shchegolev (1999), 403–86 and Abramovich (1994a), 65–79.
49 RA, 1882, I, 235.
50 Eidelman (2000), 318.
51 PIES, XXVI–XXVII, 186.
52 Moskovsky Pushkinist, I (1927), 56–7.
53 Sollogub, 358.
54 PVPK, 309.
55 Shchegolev (1999), 394.
56 Sollogub, 371.
57 Modzalevsky (1999), 494.
58 Shchegolev (1999), 72.
59 RA, 1865, 1243.
60 On Dolgorukov see Shchegolev (1999), 436–86, 572–3.
61 The account of Zhukovsky's actions over the next few days is based largely on his – extremely laconic – notes of his actions (PVVS, II, 421–2). These should be read in conjunction with the very helpful commentary by I. Borichevsky ('Zametki Zhukovskogo o gibeli Pushkina', PV, 3, 371–92), and the two articles by Ya.L. Levkovich: 'Zametki Zhukovskogo o gibeli Pushkina', VPK, 1972, 77–83; and 'V.A. Zhukovsky i posledny duel Pushkina', PIM, XIII, 146–56.
62 Shchegolev (1999), 243.
63 PVVS, II, 232.
64 To E.F. Cancrin, 6 November 1836; XVI, 182–3.
65 From E.F. Cancrin, 21 November 1836; XVI, 192.
66 Shchegolev (1999), 243.
67 PIES, XXVI–XXVII, 185–6.
68 Vitale, Stark, 162–3. Here the note is tentatively dated 6 November, but the content suggests to me a slightly later date: either 8, or possibly 10 November.
69 Veresaev (1936), II, 323.
70 PIES, XXVI–XXVII, 172.
71 Obodovskaya, Dementev (1978), 247–8.
72 From V.A. Zhukovsky, 9 November 1836; XVI, 183.
73 From V.A. Zhukovsky, 10 November 1836; XVI, 184–5.
74 To V.A. Sollogub, 17 November 1836; XVI, 232–3. While I agree with the Academy edition and PPL that this letter was adapted for the letter to Sollogub of 17 November (XVI, 188), it seems to me more likely, as Letopis (IV, 650) suggests, to have been written not on the 17th, but on the 11th or 12th.
75 PIES, XXVI–XXVII, 173.
76 From V.A. Zhukovsky, 11–12 November 1836; XVI, 185. I accept Abramovich's arguments for redating this letter to 14 November. See S.L. Abramovich, 'Perepiska Zhukovskogo s Pushkinym v noyabre 1836 g. (utochnenie datirovok)', Zhukovsky i russkaya kultura. Leningrad, 1987, 477–83.
77 Ibid., 185–6.
78 From V.A. Zhukovsky, 14–15 November 1836; XVI, 186. I agree with M. Yashin (Zvezda, 1963, 8, 180), who emends the date to 16 November.
79 Lyubovny byt, II, 88–9.
80 V.A. Zhukovsky, Sochineniya. Moscow, 1902, I, 510.
81 RS, 99 (1899), 311.
82 From V.A. Zhukovsky, 14–15 November 1836; XVI, 186–7.
83 From Georges d'Anthès-Heeckeren, 15–16 November 1836; XVI, 187.
84 PVPK, 281.
85 Modzalevsky (1999), 494.
86 PVPK, 282.
87 Prometey, X, 268.
88 Modzalevsky (1999), 495.
89 Sollogub, 363.
90 Modzalevsky (1999), 495.

91 Ibid.
92 Ibid.
93 From V.A. Sollogub, 17 November 1836; XVI, 188.
94 *RA*, 1882, I, 247.
95 To V.A. Sollogub, 17 November 1836; XVI, 188.
96 Sollogub, 368.
97 Modzalevsky (1999), 496.
98 *RA*, 1882, I, 247.
99 Shchegolev (1999), 289–90.
100 Sollogub, 369.
101 *PVPK*, 288.
102 Ibid., 281.
103 *Starina i novizna*, 17 (1914), 235, 270.
104 *Prometey*, X, 269.
105 *Pisma k Khitrovo*, 200.
106 *PIES*, XXVI–XXVII, 186.
107 Shchegolev (1999), 419.
108 *RS*, 103 (1900), 387.
109 Vitale, Stark, 179.
110 Ibid., 187.
111 Ibid., 188.
112 Ibid., 181, 189.
113 *PVPK*, 283.
114 Obodovskaya, Dementev (1978), 249, 251.
115 *PVPK*, 288.
116 To S.L. Pushkin, end December 1836; XVI, 213.
117 *PVPK*, 288.
118 Vitale, Stark, 181.
119 *PVPK*, 288.
120 Modzalevsky (1999), 496.
121 To L. Heeckeren, 17–21 November 1836; *PPL*, 162–3 (cf. XVI, 189–91). Two drafts of this letter exist: the first (*PPL*, 200–1; XVI, 262–4) was later torn into 16 pieces, of which 11 have survived; the second (*PPL*, 202–4; XVI, 264–5) into 32 pieces, of which 16 have survived. The fullest, and so far most satisfactory reconstruction is that of *PPL*, from which I quote. On the letter see *PPL*, 211; B.V. Kazansky, 'Pismo Pushkina Gekkerenu', *Zvenya*, VI, 5–92; and N.V. Izmailov, 'Istoriya teksta pisem Pushkina k Gekkerenu', *Letopisi GLM*, I (1936), 338–57.
122 Sollogub, 370.
123 To A.Kh. Benckendorff, 21 November 1836; XVI, 191–2. The translation embodies the corrections to the text

made in Eidelman (2000), 306–7, which precede an account of the fate of this letter (307–17).
124 *Zvezda*, 1963, 9, 168.
125 *PVPK*, 285.
126 Ibid.
127 Ibid.
128 Shchegolev (1999), 257.
129 *RA*, 1879, II, 242.
130 Ammosov, 13.
131 *RA*, 1872, 1789–90.
132 *LN*, 58, 135.
133 *Pisma Aleksandra Turgeneva Bulgakovym*, 197.
134 Shchegolev (1999), 260.
135 To M.P. Pogodin, around (not later than) 7 April 1834; XV, 124.
136 XII, 336.
137 To N.N. Pushkina, 14 and 16 May 1836; XVI, 116.
138 P. Ya. Chaadaev, *Stati i pisma*. Moscow, 1989, 247–8.
139 From M.A. Korff, 13 October 1836; XVI, 164.
140 To M.A. Korff, 14 October 1836; XVI, 168.
141 Abramovich (1991), 443.
142 *Letopis*, IV, 566–7.
143 *OA*, III, 347.
144 *RS*, 43 (1884), 143–4.
145 Belinsky, *Sobranie sochineniy*, VI, 490.
146 For a detailed analysis of Pushkin's debt to Scott see D.P. Yakubovich, ' "Kapitanskaya dochka" i romany Valter Skotta', *PV*, 4–5, 165–97.
147 Chaadaev, *Stati i pisma*, 253.
148 *Pisma Aleksandra Turgeneva Bulgakovym*, 199.
149 Ibid., 200.
150 Ibid., 201.
151 Vitale, Stark, 190.
152 *PVPK*, 288.
153 *RA*, 1888, II, 310.
154 *PV*, 3, 373–4. Zhukovsky's notes are more than usually elliptic at this point, and lend themselves to various interpretations. This seems the most sensible.
155 Shchegolev (1999), 266; *Pisma Aleksandra Turgeneva Bulgakovym*, 203.
156 'Posledny iz svoistvennikov Ioanny d'Ark'; XII, 155.
157 Feinberg, 161.

158 Abramovich (1991), 485.
159 Obodovskaya, Dementev (1978), 251.
160 Suasso, 260.
161 See Suasso, 261; *PV*, 2, 354.
162 *PVPK*, 291.
163 Ibid., 154, 291.
164 Obodovskaya, Dementev (1978), 255.
165 Ibid., 253, 256.
166 *PVPK*, 154.
167 Ammosov, 15.
168 *Pisma Aleksandra Turgeneva Bulgakovym*, 205.
169 Akhmatova, 129–30.
170 *Pisma Aleksandra Turgeneva Bulgakovym*, 205.
171 Nikitenko, I, 193.
172 *Moskovsky Pushkinist*, I (1927), 28.
173 Shchegolev (1999), 257n.
174 Ibid., 261.
175 *Moskovsky Pushkinist*, I (1927), 23–4.
176 Shchegolev (1999), 269.
177 *Literaturny arkhiv*, I, 85.
178 *PV*, 1, 237.
179 On this episode see L.M. Arinshtein, 'Angliisky puteshestvennik o vstreche s Pushkinym', *VPK*, 1976, 139–44.
180 J.E. Alexander, *Travels to the Seat of War in the East through Russia and Crimea in 1829*. London, 1829, II, 250.
181 Ibid., I, 33.
182 'Ya zdes, Inezilya ...', 'Zaklinanie', 'Pyu za zdravie Meri ...', 'O bednost! zatverdil ya nakonets ...', III, 239, 246, 259, 402.
183 I.S. Turgenev, *Polnoe sobranie sochineniy i pisem*. Moscow-Leningrad, 1960–68, XIV, 13.
184 *PVVS*, II, 290.
185 Sollogub, 288–9.
186 *RA*, 1879, II, 250.
187 *RS*, 99 (1899), 311.
188 *PV*, 1, 244; cf. *RA*, 1888, II, 310.
189 Sollogub, 372.
190 *PIES*, XIII, 33n.
191 *RA*, 1882, I, 247.
192 To L. Heeckeren, 26 January 1837; XVI, 221–2. Only a copy of this letter exists; though it is dated, both here and in *PPL*, 26 January, the arguments for dating it a day earlier are overwhelming. See Abramovich (1994a), 226–7.
193 *RA*, 1879, II, 248–9.

194 *PV*, 1, 244–5; cf. *Novy mir*, 1931, 12, 189.
195 *PVPK*, 297.
196 *PIES*, VI, 48.
197 To K.F. Tol, 26 January 1837; XVI, 224.
198 Suasso, 303.
199 *PIES*, XXVI–XXVII, 187.
200 From O. D'Archiac, 26 January 1837; XVI, 223; reproduced in Suasso, 273.
201 From L. Heeckeren, 26 January 1837; XVI, 223.
202 *PIES*, XII, 111.
203 From O. D'Archiac, 26 January 1837; XVI, 224.
204 *PVPK*, 298.
205 *RA*, 1882, I, 248.
206 From A. Magenis, 1.30 a.m., 27 January 1837; XVI, 224–5.
207 From O. D'Archiac, 9 a.m., 27 January 1837; XVI, 225.
208 To O. D'Archiac, between 9.30 and 10 a.m., 27 January 1837; XVI, 225–6.
209 From O. D'Archiac, 27 January 1837; XVI, 226.
210 Veresaev (1936), II, 388.
211 *Duel Pushkina s Dantesom-Gekkerenom*, 99.
212 Ammosov, 19.
213 To A.O. Ishimova, 27 January 1837; XVI, 226–7.
214 *PIES*, XXVI–XXVII, 176–7.
215 Ammosov, 22.
216 *LN*, 58, 138.
217 Ammosov, 23.
218 Ibid., 24.
219 Ibid.
220 Ibid., 24–5.
221 Ibid., 27.
222 *PIES*, VI, 50.
223 Shchegolev (1999), 186.
224 Ammosov, 29–30.
225 Shchegolev (1999), 188.
226 *Novy mir*, 1931, 12, 189.
227 *PVVS*, II, 428–9.
228 *PIES*, VI, 53; misdated as 29 January. Other versions of the tsar's note have the same content, but different phrasing: see Turgenev's diary, the first draft of Zhukovsky's letter to S.L. Pushkin (Shchegolev (1999), 271, 169), and Vyazemsky's letter to Bulgakov of 5 February 1837 (*RA*, 1879, II, 244).

229 Shchegolev (1999), 170.
230 *VPK*, 1970, 7.
231 Shchegolev, 195, 188.
232 *Novy mir*, 1931, 12, 190.
233 *PIES*, VI, 53.
234 Shchegolev (1999), 172.
235 *PVPK*, 166.
236 Shchegolev (1999), 192.
237 Ibid., 172–3.
238 Ibid., 191.
239 Ibid., 177, 193–4.
240 *Novy mir*, 1931, 12, 192.
241 *PIES*, VI, 92.
242 Shchegolev (1999), 182.
243 Veresaev (1936), II, 439.
244 Ibid., 440.
245 *PIES*, VI, 61.
246 Veresaev (1936), II, 442.
247 Nikitenko, I, 195, 498.
248 Shchegolev (1999), 273.
249 *PIES*, XXVI–XXVII, 235.
250 *PVPK*, 301.
251 Veresaev (1936), II, 447.
252 Ammosov, 67–8.
253 *PVPK*, 302.
254 Nikitenko, I, 197.
255 Shchegolev (1999), 275n.
256 Ibid.
257 *Lyubovny byt*, I, 416.

EPILOGUE

1 *PVPK*, 299.
2 *Duel Pushkina s Dantesom-Gekkerenom*, 107.
3 Ibid., 144, 152.
4 *Pisma Aleksandra Turgeneva Bulgakovym*, 215.

5 *PIES*, XXVI–XXVII, 195.
6 *RA*, 1900, I, 393.
7 *PIES*, VI, 62.
8 *PIES*, XXVI–XXVII, 234.
9 Suasso, 320–1.
10 Ibid., 142.
11 Ibid., 198.
12 Ibid., 351.
13 Ibid., 368.
14 *PIES*, XXVI–XXVII, 226.
15 Ibid., 217.
16 *PVPK*, 305.
17 Shchegolev (1999), 206.
18 *PIM*, VIII, 257.
19 Shchegolev (1999), 205.
20 *PVPK*, 300.
21 *RA*, 1888, II, 298.
22 *Arkhiv Opeki Pushkina*, 344.
23 Ibid., 3.
24 Shchegolev (1999), 215.
25 Ibid.
26 Tsyavlovsky, 310–11.
27 Shchegolev (1999), 208.
28 Smirnov-Sokolsky, 466.
29 *RA*, 1879, II, 254.
30 *PVPK*, 302.
31 Ibid., 305.
32 *Krasny arkhiv*, 33 (1929), 230.
33 *PIES*, XIX–XX, 110.
34 *PIES*, XXVI–XXVII, 274.
35 Veresaev (1936), II, 480.
36 Obodovskaya, Dementev (1999), 242–3.
37 Ibid., 128.
38 Ibid., 243.
39 *VPK*, 25 (1993), 173–4.
40 *Novy mir*, 1962, 2, 226.
41 Obodovskaya, Dementev (1999), 154.

ACKNOWLEDGEMENTS

No biographer of Pushkin cannot but be sensible of the huge debt owed to those nineteenth- and twentieth-century Russian scholars – P.V. Annenkov, P.I. Bartenev, B.L. Modzalevsky, P.E. Shchegolev, B.V. Tomashevsky, M.A. Tsyavlovsky and S.M. Bondi are a few names among many – whose devoted and painstaking researches have cast so much light on almost every aspect of the poet's life. If this biography rests on firm foundations, it is due solely to their work.

The idea of embarking on a biography of Pushkin was originally suggested to me by my agent, Gillon Aitken, himself a translator of Pushkin's prose. I am grateful to him for providing the initial impetus, and to my editors at HarperCollins, Michael Fishwick and Arabella Pike, for sustaining and encouraging it with their support and enthusiasm. Paul Foote read each chapter as it was written: his eye for detail and his cogent comments were invaluable in averting error. Bernard O'Donoghue performed the same service: his remarks on style and presentation were equally invaluable. I am infinitely grateful to both.

In addition I owe particular thanks to Gerry Stone for his elegant versions of Mickiewicz's verse; to Nina Taylor for guidance through the complex Potocki family tree; to John Gurney for advice on Persian affairs; and to David Howells and the staff of the Slavonic section of the Taylor Institution library for their generous assistance in bibliographic matters. Many other colleagues have – perhaps sometimes unwittingly – contributed much to this book: for their help on a variety of subjects I would like to thank Derek Button, Tony Cross, Peter Derow, Dr Michael Dunnill, John Flemming, Stephen Goss, Jeff Hackney, Hannes Heino, Stephen Heyworth, Christina Howells, Michael Kenworthy-Browne, Jörn Leonhard, the late James Lunt, David Mabberley, Ray Ockenden, James Porterfield, the late John Potter, Richard Sharpe, Candadi Sukumar, and Professor Serena Vitale.

Finally, I would like to acknowledge the immense debt of gratitude I owe to my wife Helen, who has been a constant source of help, sympathy, encouragement and support. This biography could be dedicated to no one but her.

Wadham College, Oxford.   T.J. BINYON
March, 2002.

BIBLIOGRAPHY

The edition of Pushkin on which I have relied in preparing this biography is the so-called 'large Academy' edition: A.S. Pushkin, *Polnoe sobranie sochineniy* (16 vols in 20 with supplementary volume of corrections and indexes; Leningrad: USSR Academy of Sciences, 1937–59). References to this edition are given simply by volume and page number alone. However, to assist readers who do not have this edition to hand, in the case of *Eugene Onegin* chapter and stanza number (both in roman) are given instead. At times I have also made use of the 'small Academy' edition in ten volumes, edited by B.V. Tomashevsky (2nd edition. Moscow, 1956–8). References to this edition appear as *PSS*, followed by volume and page number.

The following list, which comprises, of course, only a minuscule fraction of the works on Pushkin, is confined to those of which I made the most use in writing of him. In the notes these are referred to either by author or short title, with, if the work is one of several by the same author, the date of publication in parentheses.

Pushkin's works, letters, diaries etc.

Eugene Onegin. A novel in verse by Aleksandr Pushkin translated from the Russian, with a commentary, by Vladimir Nabokov. 4 vols. London, 1964.

Medny vsadnik. Edited by N.V. Izmailov. Leningrad, 1978.

Kapitanskaya dochka. Edited by Yu.G. Oksman. 2nd edition. Leningrad, 1984.

Boris Godunov. Edited by S.A. Fomichev with commentary by L.M. Lotman. St Petersburg, 1996.

Povesti pokoinogo Ivana Petrovicha Belkina. Edited by N.K. Gey, I.L. Popova. Moscow, 1999.

Pisma. Edited by B.L. and L.B. Modzalevsky. 3 vols. Moscow-Leningrad, 1926–35. [Referred to in the notes as *Pisma*.]

Pisma Pushkina k Elizavete Mikhailovne Khitrovo 1827–1832. Leningrad, 1927.

Pisma poslednikh let 1834–1837. Edited by N.V. Izmailov. Leningrad, 1969.

Perepiska A.S. Pushkina. 2 vols. Moscow, 1982.
Pisma k zhene. Edited by Ya.L. Levkovich. Leningrad, 1986.
The Letters of Alexander Pushkin. Translated, with Preface, Introduction, and Notes by J. Thomas Shaw. 3rd edition. Los Angeles, 1997.
Dnevniki. Avtobiograficheskaya proza. Edited by S.A. Fomichev. Moscow, 1989.
Dnevniki. Zapiski. Edited by Ya.L. Levkovich. St Petersburg, 1995.
Dnevnik A.S. Pushkina 1833–1835. Edited by S.A. Nikitin, with commentaries by B.L. Modzalevsky, V.F. Savodnik and M.N. Speransky. Moscow, 1997. [A reprint of the two editions of Pushkin's diary published in 1923, one with a commentary by Modzalevsky, the other with a commentary by Savodnik and Speransky. Referred to in the notes as *Dnevnik*.]

Works by other authors

Abramovich, Stella, *Pushkin. Posledny god. Khronika*. Moscow, 1991.
——, *Predystoriya posledney dueli Pushkina*. St Petersburg, 1994.
——, *Pushkin v 1833 godu. Khronika*. Moscow, 1994.
Akhmatova, Anna, *O Pushkine. Stati i zametki*. Leningrad, 1977.
Albom Elizavety Nikolaevny Ushakovoy. St Petersburg, 1999.
Aleksandr Sergeevich Pushkin. Ego zhizn i sochineniya. Sbornik istoriko-literaturnykh statey. 3rd edition. Moscow, 1912.
Alekseev, M.P., *Stikhotvorenie Pushkina 'Ya pamyatnik sebe vozdvig . . .'. Problemy ego izucheniya*. Leningrad, 1967.
——, *Pushkin. Sravnitelno-istoricheskie issledovaniya*. Leningrad, 1972.
——, *Pushkin i mirovaya literatura*. Leningrad, 1987.
Ammosov, A.N., *Poslednie dni zhizni i konchina Aleksandra Sergeevicha Pushkina*. St Petersburg, 1863.
Annenkov, P.V., *Materialy dlya biografii Aleksandra Sergeevicha Pushkina*. St Petersburg, 1855 [vol. I of Annenkov's edition of Pushkin's works].
——, *Pushkin v Aleksandrovskuyu epokhu*. Minsk, 1998.
Arinshtein, L.M., *Pushkin: neprichesannaya biografiya*. Moscow, 1998.
Arkhiv opeki Pushkina. Moscow, 1939.
Arzamas. Edited by V.E. Vatsuro and A.L. Ospovat. 2 vols. Moscow, 1994.
Arzamas i Arzamasskie protokoly. Leningrad, 1933.
Ashukin, N.S., *Pushkinskaya Moskva*. St Petersburg, 1998.
[Bartenev, P.I.], *Rasskazy o Pushkine, zapisannye so slov ego druzey P.I. Bartenevym v 1851–1860 godakh*. Leningrad, 1925.
Bazanov, V.G., *Volnoe obshchestvo lyubiteley rossiiskoy slovesnosti*. Petrozavodsk, 1949.
Belyaev, M.D., *Natalya Nikolaevna Pushkina v portretakh i otzyvakh sovremennikov*. St Petersburg, 1993.

Bondi, S., *Chernoviki Pushkina. Stati 1930–1970 gg.* Moscow, 1971.

Bozyrev, V.S., *Muzey-zapovednik A.S. Pushkina.* Leningrad, 1979.

Bryusov, V.Ya., *Moy Pushkin.* Moscow-Leningrad, 1929.

Chereisky, L.A., *Pushkin i ego okruzhenie.* 2nd edition. Leningrad, 1988.

Dela III Otdeleniya Sobstvennoy Ego Imperatorskago Velichestva Kantselyarii ob Aleksandre Sergeeviche Pushkine. St Petersburg, 1906.

Druzhnikov, Yury, *Dose begletsa. Po sledam neizvestnogo Pushkina.* Tenafly, N.J., 1993.

Duel Pushkina s Dantesom-Gekkerenom. Podlinnoe voenno-sudnoe delo 1837 g. St Petersburg, 1900.

Dvoichenko-Markova, E.M., *Pushkin v Moldavii i Valakhii.* Moscow, 1979.

Efros, A.M., *Risunki poeta.* Moscow-Leningrad, 1933.

Eidelman, N.Ya., *Pushkin: iz biografii i tvorchestva 1826–1837.* Moscow, 1987.

——, *Stati o Pushkine.* Moscow, 2000.

Feinberg, Ilya, *Nezavershennye raboty Pushkina.* 3rd edition. Moscow, 1962.

Gastfreind, N.A., *Pushkin. Dokumenty Gosudarstvennago i S.-Peterburgskago glavnago arkhivov Ministerstva inostrannykh del, otnosyashchiesya k sluzhbe ego 1831–1837 gg.* St Petersburg, 1900.

Gershenzon, M.O., *Griboedovskaya Moskva. P.Ya. Chaadaev. Ocherki proshlogo.* Moscow, 1989.

——, *Mudrost Pushkina.* Tomsk, 1997.

Gessen, Sergey, *Knigoizdatel Aleksandr Pushkin. Literaturnye dokhody Pushkina.* Leningrad, 1930.

Gillelson, M.I., *Molodoy Pushkin i arzamasskoe bratstvo.* Leningrad, 1974.

Gnammankou, Dieudonné, *Abraham Hanibal. L'aïeul noir de Pouchkine.* Paris, 1996.

Gordin, A.M., *Pushkinsky zapovednik.* Moscow, 1956.

——, *Pushkin v Mikhailovskom.* Leningrad, 1989.

——, Gordin, M.A., *Pushkinsky vek.* St Petersburg, 1995.

Gordin, Ya.A., *Dueli i duelyanty.* St Petersburg, 1996.

Grech, N.I., *Zapiski o moey zhizni.* Moscow-Leningrad, 1930.

Grossman, Leonid, *Tsekh pera.* Moscow, 1930.

Grot, K.Ya., *Pushkinsky litsey (1811–1817). Bumagi I-go kursa, sobrannye akademikom Ya.K. Grotom.* St Petersburg, 1911.

Kern, A.P., *Vospominaniya o Pushkine.* Moscow, 1987.

Kunin, V.V., *Druzya Pushkina.* 2 vols. Moscow, 1984.

——, *Zhizn Pushkina, rasskazannaya im samim i ego sovremennikami.* 2 vols. Moscow, 1987.

Kupriyanova, N.I., *K semu: Aleksandr Pushkin.* Gorky, 1982.

Lavrenteva, Elena, *Svetsky etiket pushkinskoy pory.* Moscow, 1999.

Lednicki, Wacław, *Russia, Poland and the West. Essays in Literary and Cultural History.* London, 1954.

——, *Pushkin's Bronze Horseman: the Story of a Masterpiece.* Berkeley and Los Angeles, 1955.

Legendy i mify o Pushkine. St Petersburg, 1995.

Lemke, M.K., *Nikolaevskie zhandarmy i literatura 1826–1855 gg. Po podlinnym delam Tretyago otdeleniya Sobst. E.I. Velichestva Kantselyarii.* 2nd edition. St Petersburg, 1909.

Letopis zhizni i tvorchestva Aleksandra Pushkina. Compiled by M.A. Tsyavlovsky and N.A. Tarkhova. 4 vols. Moscow, 1999.

Levitt, Marcus C., *Russian Literary Politics and the Pushkin Celebration of 1880.* Ithaca and London, 1989.

Lotman, Yu.M., *Pushkin.* St Petersburg, 1995.

Lyubovny byt pushkinskoy epokhi. 2 vols. Moscow, 1994.

Mazour, Anatole G., *The First Russian Revolution, 1825. The Decembrist Movement: its Origins, Development, and Significance.* Stanford, 1965.

Mir Pushkina. Familnye bumagi Pushkinykh-Gannibalov. 2 vols. Moscow, 1993–4.

Modzalevsky, B.L., *Anna Petrovna Kern.* Leningrad, 1924.

——, *Pushkin pod tainym nadzorom.* 3rd edition. Leningrad, 1925.

——, *Pushkin.* Leningrad, 1929.

——, *Pushkin i ego sovremenniki.* St Petersburg, 1999.

Myasoedova, Natalya, *O Griboedove i Pushkine.* St Petersburg, 1998.

Nikitenko, A.V., *Dnevnik.* 3 vols. Leningrad, 1955.

Obodovskaya, I., Dementev, M., *Vokrug Pushkina.* 2nd edition. Moscow, 1978.

——, *Pushkin v Yaropoltse.* Moscow, 1982.

——, *Natalya Nikolaevna Pushkina. Po epistolyarnym materialam.* 2nd edition. Moscow, 1987.

——, *Posle smerti Pushkina.* 2nd edition. Moscow, 1999.

Olenina, A.A., *Dnevnik. Vospominaniya.* St Petersburg, 1999.

Ostafevsky arkhiv knyazey Vyazemskikh. 5 vols. St Petersburg, 1899–1913.

Ovchinnikov, R.V., *Pushkin v rabote nad arkhivnymi dokumentami ('Istoriya Pugacheva').* Leningrad, 1969.

Ovchinnikova, S.T., *Pushkin v Moskve: letopis zhizni A.S. Pushkina s 5 dekabrya 1830 g. po 15 maya 1831 g.* Moscow, 1984.

Pavlishchev, Lev, *Iz semeinoy khroniki: vospominaniya ob A.S. Pushkine.* Moscow, 1890.

Peterburgskie vstrechi Pushkina. Leningrad, 1987.

Pisma Aleksandra Turgeneva Bulgakovym. Moscow, 1939.

Polyakov, A.S., *O smerti Pushkina (po novym dannym).* St Petersburg, 1922.

Pushchin, I.I., *Zapiski o Pushkine. Pisma.* Moscow, 1988.

Pushkin v pismakh Karamzinykh 1836–1837 godov. Moscow-Leningrad, 1960.

Pushkin v prizhiznennoy kritike 1820–1827. St Petersburg, 1996.

Pushkin v vospominaniyakh sovremennikov. 2 vols. 3rd edition. St Petersburg, 1998.

Pushkinsky Peterburg. Leningrad, 1949.

Putevoditel po Pushkinu. St Petersburg, 1997.

Rod i predki Pushkina. Moscow, 1995.

Rudenskaya, M., Rudenskaya, S., *Oni uchilis s Pushkinym.* Leningrad, 1976.

——, *Pushkinsky litsey. Ocherk-putevoditel.* Leningrad, 1980.

Rukoyu Pushkina. Nesobrannye i neopublikovannye teksty. Moscow-Leningrad, 1935.

Seton-Watson, Hugh, *The Russian Empire 1801–1917.* Oxford, 1967.

Shchegolev, P.E., *Pushkin i muzhiki. Po neizdannym materialam.* Moscow, 1928.

——, *Iz zhizni i tvorchestva Pushkina.* 3rd edition. Moscow-Leningrad, 1931.

——, *Duel i smert Pushkina.* 5th edition. St Petersburg, 1999.

Shik, A., *Odessky Pushkin.* Paris, 1938.

Shubin, B.M., *Istoriya odnoy bolezni.* Moscow, 1983.

Skrynnikov, R.V., *Duel Pushkina.* St Petersburg, 1999.

Smirnova-Rosset, A.O., *Dnevnik. Vospominaniya.* Moscow, 1989.

Smirnov-Sokolsky, N.P., *Rasskazy o prizhiznennykh izdaniyakh Pushkina.* Moscow, 1962.

Sollogub, V.A., *Vospominaniya.* Moscow-Leningrad, 1931.

Suasso, Frans, *Dichter, dame, diplomaat: het laatste jaar van Alexander Poesjkin.* Leiden, 1988.

Suslov, I.M., *Pamyatnik Pushkinu v Moskve.* Moscow, 1968.

Teletova, N.K., *Zabytye rodstvennye svyazi A.S. Pushkina.* Leningrad, 1981.

Tomashevsky, B.V., *Pushkin.* 2 vols. Moscow-Leningrad, 1956–61.

——, *Pushkin. Raboty raznykh let.* Moscow, 1990.

Trubetskoy, B.A., *Pushkin v Moldavii.* 5th edition. Kishinev, 1983.

Tsyavlovsky, M.A., *Stati o Pushkine.* Moscow, 1962.

Tynyanov, Yu.N., *Pushkin i ego sovremenniki.* Moscow, 1969.

Utaennaya lyubov Pushkina. St Petersburg, 1997.

Veresaev, V., *Pushkin v zhizni.* 2 vols. 6th edition. Moscow, 1936.

——, *Sputniki Pushkina.* 2 vols. Moscow, 1937.

Vickery, Walter N., *Pushkin: death of a poet.* Bloomington and London, 1968.

Vigel, F.F., *Zapiski.* Moscow, 2000.

Vitale, Serena, *Pushkin's Button.* London, 1999.

——, Stark, Vadim, *Chernaya rechka. Do i posle. K istorii dueli Pushkina. Pisma Dantesa.* St Petersburg, 2000.

Volovich, N.M., *Pushkinskie mesta Moskvy i Podmoskovya.* Moscow, 1979.

Yakushkin, I.D., *Zapiski, stati, pisma.* Moscow, 1951.

Zhuikova, R.G., *Portretnye risunki Pushkina.* St Petersburg, 1996.

1799–1837: Pushkin i ego vremya. Moscow, 1997.

INDEX

Throughout the index Pushkin's name has been abbreviated to P, and that of his wife to NNP. Works by Pushkin and others are indexed under their authors. Both the English and Russian titles of Pushkin's works are given, the former coming first if it appears in the text, the latter if not. The text and the notes at the foot of the text pages (excluding references) are included in the index, but not the notes at the end of the volume. *Passim* following two page numbers separated by a dash indicates that there are scattered references to this subject between the pages mentioned.

Printed by RR Donnelley at Glasgow, UK